The Law of Treaties

The Library of Essays in International Law
General Editor: Robert McCorquodale

Titles in the Series

The Law of Treaties

Edited by

Scott Davidson

University of Canterbury, New Zealand

ASHGATE
DARTMOUTH

Published by
Ashgate Publishing Limited
Wey Court East
Union Road
Farnham
Surrey, GU9 7PT
England

Ashgate Publishing Company
Suite 420
101 Cherry Street
Burlington
VT 05401-4405
USA

Ashgate website: http://www.ashgate.com

British Library Cataloguing in Publication Data
The law of treaties. – (The library of essays in
    international law)
    1. Treaties
    I. Davidson, J. S. (J Scott), 1954-
    341.3'7

Library of Congress Cataloging-in-Publication Data
The law of treaties / edited by J. Scott Davidson.
        p. cm.
    Includes bibliographical references.
        ISBN 978-0-7546-2385-4
        1. Treaties. 2. International law. I. Davidson, Scott, 1954-

KZ1301.L39 2004
341.3'7—dc22

2003063996

ISBN 978-0-7546-2385-4

Transfered to Digital Printing in 2010

Mixed Sources
Product group from well-managed
forests and other controlled sources
www.fsc.org Cert no. SA-COC-1565
© 1996 Forest Stewardship Council
FSC

Printed and bound in Great Britain by
MPG Books Group, UK

Contents

PART V   INVALIDITY, SUSPENSION AND TERMINATION OF TREATIES

Acknowledgements

The editor and publishers wish to thank the following for permission to use copyright material.

American Society of International Law for the essays: Richard D. Kearney and Robert E. Dalton (1970), 'The Treaty on Treaties', *American Journal of International Law*, **64**, pp. 495–561. Copyright © 1970 American Society of International Law; Myres S. McDougal (1967), 'The International Law Commission's Draft Articles upon Interpretation: Textuality *Redivivus*', *American Journal of International Law*, **61**, pp. 992–1000. Copyright © 1967 American Society of International Law; Sir Gerald Fitzmaurice (1971), '*Vae Victis* or Woe to the Negotiators! Your Treaty or Our "Interpretation" of It?', *American Journal of International Law*, **65**, pp. 358–73. Copyright © 1971 American Society of International Law; Herbert W. Briggs (1974), 'Unilateral Denunciation of Treaties: The Vienna Convention and the International Court of Justice', *American Journal of International Law*, **68**, pp. 51–68. Copyright © 1974 American Society of International Law.

Cambridge University Press for the essay: Christine Chinkin (1997), 'A Mirage in the Sand? Distinguishing Binding and Non-Binding Relations Between States', *Leiden Journal of International Law*, **10**, pp. 223–47.

Maine Law Review for the essay: Martin A. Rogoff (1980), 'The International Legal Obligations of Signatories to an Unratified Treaty', *Maine Law Review*, **32**, pp. 263–99.

Martinus Nijhoff Publishers for the essay: Jan Klabbers (1997), 'Some Problems Regarding the Object and Purpose of Treaties', *Finnish Yearbook of International Law*, **8**, pp. 138–60.

Oxford University Press for the essays: Kelvin Widdows (1979), 'What is an Agreement in International Law?', *British Year Book of International Law*, **50**, pp. 117–49. Copyright © 1979 Kelvin Widdows; D.N. Hutchinson (1993), 'The Significance of the Registration or Non-Registration of an International Agreement in Determining Whether or Not it is a Treaty', *Current Legal Problems*, pp. 257–90; Catherine Redgwell (1993), 'Universality or Integrity? Some Reflections on Reservations to General Multilateral Treaties', *British Year Book of International Law*, **64**, pp. 245–82. Copyright © 1993 Catherine Redgwell; Francis G. Jacobs (1969), 'Varieties of Approach to Treaty Interpretation: With Special Reference to the Draft Convention on the Law of Treaties before the Vienna Diplomatic Conference', *International and Comparative Law Quarterly*, **18**, pp. 318–46; Daniel Reichert-Facilides (1998), 'Down the Danube: The Vienna Convention on the Law of Treaties and the *Case Concerning the Gabcïkovo-Nagymaros Project*', *International and Comparative Law Quarterly*, **47**, pp. 837–54.

Philippine Law Journal for the essay: Merlin M. Magallona (1976), 'The Concept of <u>Jus Cogens</u> in the Vienna Convention on the Law of Treaties', *Philippine Law Journal*, **51**, pp. 521–42.

Texas International Law Journal for the essay: Christine Chinkin (1982), 'Nonperformance of International Agreements', *Texas International Law Journal*, **17**, pp. 387–432.

T.M.C. Asser Instituut for the essay: Maarten Bos (1980), 'Theory and Practice of Treaty Interpretation', *Netherlands International Law Review*, pp. 3–38, 135–70.

Series Preface

Open a newspaper, listen to the radio or watch television any day of the week and you will read or hear of some matter concerning international law. The range of matters include the extent to which issues of trade and human rights should be linked, concerns about refugees and labour conditions, negotiations of treaties and the settlement of disputes, and decisions by the United Nations Security Council concerning actions to ensure compliance with international law. International legal issues have impact on governments, corporations, organisations and people around the world and the process of globalisation has increased this impact. In the global legal environment, knowledge of international law is an indispensable tool for all scholars, legal practitioners, decision-makers and citizens of the 21st century.

The Library of Essays in International Law is designed to provide the essential elements for the development of this knowledge. Each volume contains essays of central importance in the development of international law in a subject area. The proliferation of legal and other specialist journals, the increase in international materials and the use of the internet, has meant that it is increasingly difficult for legal scholars to have access to all the relevant articles on international law and many valuable older articles are now unable to be obtained readily. These problems are addressed by this series, which makes available an extensive range of materials in a manner that is of immeasurable value for both teaching and research at all levels.

Each volume is written by a leading authority in the subject area who selects the articles and provides an informative introduction, which analyses the context of the articles and comments on their significance within the developments in that area. The volumes complement each other to give a clear view of the burgeoning area of international law. It is not an easy task to select, order and place in context essays from the enormous quantity of academic legal writing prublished in journals – in many languages – throughout the world. This task requires professional scholarly judgment and difficult choices. The editors in this series have done an excellent job, for which I thank and congratulate them. It has been a pleasure working with them.

ROBERT McCORQUODALE
General Series Editor
School of Law
University of Nottingham

Introduction

The centrality of treaties to the international legal system requires little emphasis. Not only is the treaty a source of law that the International Court of Justice (ICJ) is bound to apply under Article 38(1)(a) of its Statute when resolving international disputes, but it is also the medium through which the vast preponderance of international legal intercourse is now conducted. While municipal law analogies are often used to demonstrate the multifunctional character of treaties, given the nature of international society these analogies will seldom, if ever, be entirely congruent. Thus the treaty as 'constitution', 'legislation', 'deed of incorporation' or 'instrument of transfer' is likely to be inexact at best. Despite this criticism, the analogies signify the fact that the ubiquitous treaty remains the primary means of creating international legal obligations involving a broad range of subject matter. Indeed, McNair's observation that the treaty is 'the only and sadly overworked instrument with which international society is equipped for carrying out its multifarious transactions' remains essentially true today (McNair, 1961, pp. 739–40).

While the emergence of 'soft law' as a precursor to treaty relations in recent years might be said to have had an important influence on the development of international legal transactions, the fact remains that soft law is not hard law and it is only the treaty that can be regarded as the authoritative key to the actual or presumed intentions of the parties (Boyle, 1999, pp. 901–13). Furthermore, as Aust points out, many soft law instruments which it was envisaged would be transmuted into legally binding instruments have never progressed beyond their intermediate stage (Aust, 2000, p 44). Similarly, the unilateral declaration remains too restricted in its application to have any significant effect on international relations. For all its shortcomings and drawbacks the treaty still remains the most versatile and best understood means by which to regulate the conduct of states; it remains the 'cement that holds the world community together' (Kearney and Dalton, Chapter 1, p. 3).

Evolution and Apologia

As noted above, treaties fulfil a broad range of functions in international law and they cover a wide variety of subject matter. They range from the bilateral treaty (*traités contrats*), through which two states secure reciprocal rights and obligations, to multilateral treaties (*traités lois*), which are capable of acting as a substitute for legislation in the international system by establishing a comprehensive legal regime of uncertain duration for particular facets of international relations. There are also framework treaties or *traités cadres* that require consummation via the adoption of secondary rules or through interpretation by nominated institutions or bodies. Although treaties of one sort or another have been used in interstate commerce since classical times, it is only relatively recently that a law of treaties has developed. Sir Hersch Lauterpacht's *Oppenheim* suggested that:

> Even before a Law of Nations in a modern sense of the term was in existence, treaties used to be concluded between States. Although in those times treaties were neither based on, nor were themselves a cause of, International Law, they were nevertheless considered sacred and binding, on account of religious and moral sentiment. (Lauterpacht, 1955, pp. 877–78)

It is in these notions of religious and moral sentiment that the fundamental rule of the law of treaties – *pacta sunt servanda* – can be located: treaties are binding and must be observed in good faith.[1] During the modern period, which can be dated from the Peace of Westphalia 1648, the evolution of a coherent body of rules of what might be termed the law of treaties began to evolve. The rules concerning such matters as the competence of various persons to conclude treaties, the nature of the acts which bound states, the obligation to perform treaties and the factors that might vitiate them began to emerge. Despite this, it was not until the twentieth century that international lawyers began to turn their attention towards developing a comprehensive code that would set down the rules governing international society's most ubiquitous instrument. The first attempts at codification were those of the Harvard Law School,[2] but in 1949 the International Law Commission (ILC) included the law of treaties in its provisional list of topics that it considered ripe for codification. In 1951 the ILC completed a special report on reservations which had been prompted by the ICJ's advisory opinion in the *Reservations to the Genocide Convention Case*,[3] but it was not until 1969, after much work by some of the most eminent international lawyers of the time, that the Commission's draft articles were adopted at the Vienna Diplomatic Conference.[4] Thus was born the Vienna Convention on the Law of Treaties 1969.[5] Kearney and Dalton in their essay 'The Treaty on Treaties' (Chapter 1) provide a comprehensive, well-informed and perceptive narrative of the evolution of the Vienna Convention that is indispensable reading for anyone who wishes to understand why the instrument is framed as it is and what compromises were necessary to achieve the final draft (see also Rosenne, 1970; Sinclair, 1970, pp. 47–69).

While the Vienna Convention itself is less than perfect, its genius lies in the fact that it provides a code on the law of treaties, often in general language, which commands widespread, though not always universal, approval. Even at its adoption the Convention was beset by political controversy, with France in particular objecting to the provisions on *ius cogens* and the members of the then Soviet bloc protesting at the exclusion in proceedings of certain 'states' such as East Germany, China, North Korea and North Vietnam. Despite these initial controversies and other doctrinal differences masked by skilful drafting, the Vienna Convention stands as a significant contribution to the codification and progressive development of possibly the most important area of contemporary international law. It is for this reason that the essays collected in this volume are concerned primarily with this landmark instrument. Critics might complain that this is too narrow a perspective to take, especially since the Vienna Convention on the Law of Treaties 1969 deals only with written agreements between states that are governed by international law. It is true that treaties can be concluded in other forms and by other international persons – facts that are recognized by Article 3 of the Convention itself. Nevertheless, a glimpse at the United Nations Treaty Series – which may now be done on the Internet only by the payment of a fee (Alston, 2001, pp. 551–58) – will reveal not only the numerical superiority of interstate agreements, but how essential they are to the governance of international society in all its aspects. This is not to deny the intrinsic importance of agreements between other international persons, but simply to emphasize the dominance of the interstate species.

Although it had been the ILC's original intention to include rules concerning agreements between other international persons within the 1969 Convention, the Commission decided that this would result in delay and unnecessary complexity given the particularly distinctive features affecting such agreements that would need to be accommodated. As a result, further deliberations resulted in the adoption by the General Assembly of the United Nations in 1982 of the Vienna Convention on the Law of Treaties between International Organisations or between States and International Organisations. A brief examination of this agreement shows that many of the rules contained therein are simply those of the 1969 Convention applied *mutatis mutandis* or with modification to take account of the peculiarities of international organisations (Gaja, 1987, pp. 253–69). For better or worse, therefore, this anthology of essays is devoted almost exclusively to the 'big beast' in the forest of treaties: the Vienna Convention on the Law of Treaties 1969.

The Nature of Treaties

The essential nature of treaties has been a matter of some dispute. Sir Gerald Fitzmaurice has argued that treaties in themselves are not sources of law but merely sources of obligation whose binding force is derived from the 'antecedent general principle of law' expressed in the maxim *pacta sunt servanda* (Fitzmaurice, 1958, p. 153). Even the fact that Fitzmaurice described this fundamental rule as a 'general principle of law' rather than a rule of customary international law is, as Virally has pointed out, controversial (Virally, 1968, pp. 127–28). On the other hand, Parry has described the principle as tautologous meaning only that binding treaties are binding (Parry, 1968, p. 177). The underlying nature of treaties as a source of law or source of obligation is not, however, the subject of the inquiry here; it is something more pragmatic – what is a treaty?

Treaties have been deftly defined by Georg Schwarzenberger as 'consensual engagements under international law' (Schwarzenberger, 1976, p. 121). While this conveys the essence of a treaty, it does not deal with the rather more prosaic issues of nomenclature, the capacity to conclude treaties and the signification of consent to be bound. As far as nomenclature is concerned, even under customary international law it was recognized that it is substance, rather than form, that governs the status of any particular instrument. A name might be chosen to convey some symbolic quality about the significance of a treaty – the 'sanctity' and thus the fundamental importance of a human rights covenant, for example – but, in general, nomenclature is irrelevant for the purposes of international law. Capacity is simply shorthand for international personality, for it is only international persons of sufficient capacity who are entitled to conclude agreements governed by international law. Before the advisory opinion of the International Court of Justice in *Reparations for Injuries Suffered in the Service of the United Nations*,[6] capacity was generally thought to be enjoyed only by states but, since then, international institutions have enjoyed such capacity which their functions allow and which are permitted by states' recognition of that capacity.

Signification of consent to be bound straddles the boundary of municipal and international law in the law of treaties. While municipal constitutional law is concerned with the internal distribution of treaty-making power or the competence of particular individuals to represent the state, international law must deal with situations in which an individual who purports to represent his or her state has acted *ultra vires* – that is, beyond his or her powers. The normal rules of agency regarding confirmation by a principal of the act of an agent who exceeds his or her authority represents a direct analogy from municipal law.[7] On the other hand, where signification of consent to be bound has taken place in violation of some municipal law of fundamental importance, this might have the effect of vitiating a treaty, but only if the norm is truly fundamental and sufficiently well-known to other members of international society.

An earlier draft of the ILC defined a treaty as:

> Any international agreement in written form, whether embodied in a single instrument or in two or more related instruments and whatever its particular designation (treaty, convention, protocol, covenant, charter, statute, act, declaration, concordat, exchange of notes, agreed minute, memorandum of agreement, *modus vivendi* or any other appellation), concluded between two or more States or other subjects of international law.[8]

The definition that was finally adopted in Article 2(1)(a) of the Vienna Convention was limited to states at the expense of other subjects of international law and omitted the lengthy description of the various names of international instruments. It therefore defines a treaty for the purposes of the Convention as 'an international agreement concluded between States in written form and governed by international law, whether embodied in a single instrument or two or more instruments and whatever its particular designation'. This provision is supplemented by Article 3, which provides that the legal status of agreements between other international legal persons and agreements in other forms remain unaffected by the Convention.

This definition begs the question of what constitutes an 'agreement . . . governed by international law'. Following a review of judicial and arbitral decisions, state practice and the writings of commentators, Kelvin Widdows in his essay 'What is an Agreement in International Law?' (Chapter 2) comes to the conclusion that whether an agreement is a treaty rests entirely on the question of the intention of the parties. Certainly it might be expected that in order for an agreement to exist there must be, as Widdows points out, some *consensus ad idem* between the parties. It seems, however, that this need not necessarily be so. The *Eastern Greenland*,[9] *Nuclear Tests*[10] and *Burkina Faso/Mali Frontier Dispute*[11] cases suggest that unilateral statements made in *foro publico* by states with the intention of creating legal relations under international law should be binding upon them. While the *Eastern Greenland* case can be explained as an oral treaty because of an identifiable element of reciprocity in the promise made, this is not a sufficiently convincing explanation of the *Nuclear Tests* cases where no such element is apparent. What is evident, however, is that the issue of form 'is not a domain in which international law imposes any special or strict requirements'.[12]

Furthermore, Christine Chinkin's assessment of the *Qatar* v. *Bahrain Case*[13] (Chapter 3) suggests that the ICJ is prepared to infer that a legally binding agreement can exist objectively regardless of the subjective intentions of the parties. While this view might be restricted to the question of whether the ICJ itself is seised of jurisdiction in any particular matter, it might nonetheless herald a worrying trend for those international lawyers who take the view that a, if not the, fundamental aspect of the law of treaties is consent to be bound. As Chinkin also argues, such an approach by the ICJ might inhibit states from engaging in informal negotiations over disputes.

In more recent history, questions have arisen over agreements that explicitly state that they are not intended to be legally binding. If the intention is clearly evinced in the instrument in question that it should not create legal relations, then that would seem to be the end of the matter, but there may be cases where the issue of whether an agreement is to be governed by international law or some other legal regime lacks clarity. While registration of an instrument under Article 102 of the UN Charter might be some indication of the intention of the registering parties that the instrument that they have concluded should be legally binding, it is in reality no more than evidential. David Hutchinson makes this point in his essay, 'The Significance of the Registration or Non-Registration of an International Agreement in Determining Whether or Not it is a Treaty' (Chapter 4), following a thorough and valuable examination of UN practice in the field.

Signification of consent to be bound also raises a number of difficulties connected with the most common method of concluding treaties today. While, historically, the use of signature by those competent to bind the state was the most common method of signifying consent, with the rise of the multilateral convention and municipal constitutional controls over treaty-making power, the form of expressing consent to be bound by signature and ratification has gained ascendancy (Blix, 1953, pp. 352–80). This raises the question of what international legal obligations, if any, exist between the signing of a treaty and its ratification, if indeed it is ever ratified. The response of the ILC to this question was to provide a specific rule that places signatory states to a treaty that requires ratification under an obligation of good faith not to defeat its object and purpose.[14]

The identification of the object and purpose of the treaty might, however, not always be readily identifiable in the singular, for a treaty might have a multiplicity of objects and purposes. The terminology used in Article 18 is identical to that used in other provisions of the Vienna Convention, including those relating to the important areas of reservations and material breach. Given the importance of this formulation to some of the most crucial areas of treaty law it is surprising that, as a concept, it has not been analysed more extensively than it has. The essay by Jan Klabbers, 'Some Problems Regarding the Object and Purpose of Treaties'(Chapter 5), goes a significant way towards addressing the concept of 'object and purpose' in the various provisions of the Vienna Convention by 'outlining its contours'.

Yet another problem inherent in Article 18 is the nature of the good faith obligation itself. There is no doubt that good faith is a slippery concept in international law, but a state that has signed an agreement must be presumed to intend to avoid behaviour that would undermine the agreement. As Martin Rogoff observes in his essay on 'The International Legal Obligations of Signatories to an Unratified Treaty' (Chapter 6), what must be assessed here are the reasonable expectations of states that find themselves in this position. Since treaties are often the products of long and complex negotiations, they often represent a delicate balance which must not be disturbed by inappropriate action by states prior to ratification. Rogoff's location of the rule in the abuse of rights doctrine suggests that its violation results in state responsibility. It might also be noted that states that are party to the Vienna Convention will be in violation of the *pacta sunt servanda* principle should they act in violation of Article 18.

Treaty Integrity

Any discussion of the modern law of treaties would be incomplete without an assessment of the law relating to reservations. Although reservations to treaties were used in multilateral treaty relations before the ICJ delivered its landmark advisory opinion in *Reservations to the Genocide Convention*, the profound shift which the Court's opinion effected in the conduct of treaty relations was probably not foreseeable. The shift away from the rule that required all parties to a treaty to accept a reservation (the unanimity rule favoured by the League of Nations states) to the more flexible system utilized by the Pan-American Union, presaged a profound change in the way in which states approached multilateral treaties. While the ICJ's opinion in *Reservations to the Genocide Convention* could have been interpreted simply as referring to the circumstances of the Genocide Convention alone, this view did not survive for long. Although the ILC reported in 1951 that it considered the compatibility test in the ICJ's opinion to be too subjective and preferred instead the application of the unanimity rule, its views were soon overtaken by international practice. In 1952 the General Assembly of the United Nations instructed the Secretary-General to apply the ICJ's ruling in respect of treaties concluded under the auspices of the UN and for which he was depositary.[15] By the time the ILC came to consider the question of reservations in 1962, its opinion had changed and it now indicated that it favoured the compatibility test. The ICJ's opinion in *Reservations to the Genocide Convention* was therefore eventually codified and elaborated upon in Articles 19–21 of the Vienna Convention. The residual rule in Article 19 is that, if a treaty is silent regarding reservations, then a state is entitled to make a reservation that is not incompatible with the object and purpose of the treaty. This raises once again the same problems with the 'object and purpose' test as we have encountered above in signification of consent to be bound, but it is compounded by introducing a strong element of subjectivity by allowing states to determine for themselves whether or not they consider the compatibility test to be met.

The question that arises here is whether the Vienna Convention rules on reservations are suitable for their purpose – in other words, does their flexibility advance or hinder treaty relations between states? Opinion on this question has been starkly divided from the outset with Schwarzenberger arguing that the rules on reservations 'jeopardise certainty on a fundamental aspect of the law of treaties: the identity of the parties' (Schwarzenberger, 1976, p. 127). Taslim Elias, however, argued that the flexibility introduced by the Vienna Convention rules on reservations encourage much greater participation in multilateral treaties than would otherwise be the case if the unanimity rule still prevailed (Elias, 1974, p. 27). Brownlie takes something of a middle way by stating that 'the "compatibility" test is the least objectionable solution but is by no means an ideal regime, and many problems remain' (Brownlie, 1998, p. 615). Authors who have probed the operation of reservations in the law of treaties more recently seem to confirm Brownlie's view, although Don Greig, in an essay which unfortunately is too long to include in this collection, has argued that the pendulum has swung too far in favour of reserving states and that there should be an amendment of the Vienna Convention to promote greater clarity or a more equitable balancing of interests (Greig, 1995, p. 164, p. 170). Catherine Redgwell's essay, 'Universality or Integrity? Some Reflections on Reservations to General Multilateral Treaties' (Chapter 7), not only provides a thorough overview of the development of the law relating to reservations since the ICJ's advisory opinion in *Reservations to the Genocide Convention*, but also critically examines how the rules operate and how they might better function in the future.

Treaty Interpretation

Treaty interpretation has been an issue over which there has, and still remains, much difference of opinion and about which a great deal has been written. The major point of disagreement has been over the extent to which the text of a treaty can be regarded as an authoritative and exclusive index of the parties' intentions sufficient unto itself or whether the intentions of the parties is an autonomous basis of interpretation extrinsic to the formal text of the treaty. Whichever of these views is favoured, it seems that there is agreement on one matter at least: treaty interpretation is concerned with trying to divine the intentions of the parties to the agreement. The preponderance of authoritative opinion appears to favour the view that it is the discovery of the intentions of the parties as expressed in the text that is the true purpose of interpretation. This view is held not only by the ILC and the ICJ but also by Jennings' and Watts' *Oppenheim* which states that:

> The purpose of interpreting a treaty is to establish the meaning of the text which the parties must be taken to have intended it to bear in relation to the circumstances with reference to which the question of interpretation has arisen. (Jennings and Watts, 1992, p. 1267, para. 629)

Having established the purpose of interpretation there then arises the question of which modes of interpretation are most satisfactory to achieve this end. Again, this has been a matter of considerable dispute. Brownlie is of the opinion that 'rules' and 'principles' of interpretation should be approached with caution since, in his view:

> Many of the 'rules' and 'principles' offered are general, question-begging, and contradictory. As with statutory interpretation, a choice of a 'rule', for example of 'effectiveness' or 'restrictive interpretation', may in a given case involve a preliminary choice of meaning rather than a guide to interpretation. (Brownlie, 1998, p. 632)

Despite this, most commentators generally concede that there are three broad methods of interpreting a treaty: the objective, the subjective and teleological. The objective or textual approach gives precedence to the text of the treaty; the intentions of the parties are concerned with giving effect to the actual or presumed intentions of the parties; while the teleological school is calculated to ascertain the object and purpose of the treaty and to give effect to this (Fitzmaurice, 1951, pp. 1–28). The provisions of the Vienna Convention that deal with the main issues of interpretation – Articles 31 and 32 – give precedence to the textual or literal approach to interpretation, but do not entirely exclude other forms of interpretation. The listing of the ordinary terms of a treaty that are to be considered in their context and in the light of their object and purpose preserves possible recourse to the teleological approach. The use of supplementary materials to confirm the meaning of the text arrived at after the application of the methods used in Article 31, or to avoid a meaning that is ambiguous or manifestly absurd or unreasonable, is provided for in Article 32. It was the creation of an apparent hierarchy in the methods of interpretation that moved the US representative at the Vienna Diplomatic Conference, Myres McDougal to suggest the merging of both provisions to avoid priority being ascribed to Article 31. The ILC considered this to be unnecessary as the two articles would, in effect, operate in conjunction and not exclusively. This did not appease McDougal who subsequently criticized the ILC draft in his essay, 'The International Law Commission's Draft Articles upon Interpretation: Textuality *Redivivus*' (Chapter 8), in the following terms:

> It can scarcely be doubted . . . that the 'basic approach' of the Commission in generally arrogating to one particular set of signs – the text of a document – the rôle of serving as the exclusive index of the shared expectations of the parties to an agreement is an exercise in primitive and potentially destructive formalism. (p. 276)

In order to appreciate the full extent of McDougal's critique of the Vienna Convention provisions on treaty interpretation and his alternative approach, it is necessary to consult his, and his Yale Law School colleagues', work entitled *The Interpretation of Agreements and World Public Order* (McDougal, 1967). In essence its argument is that treaty interpretation is a process which in turn must draw on all the factors involved in the treaty-making process itself, including non-verbal signs. Furthermore, the function of treaty interpretation is not only to discover the shared intentions of the parties, but to provide an interpretation that is consistent with the goal of world public order, which is underpinned by the super-value of human dignity. Clearly, there is much more to the New Haven approach than this, but it does not seem to have gained much traction in practice and has been criticized for its inaccessibility as a theory as Sir Gerald Fitzmaurice's review essay of this book – '*Vae Victis* or Woe to the Negotiators! Your Treaty or Our "Interpretation" of It?' (Chapter 9) – amply demonstrates. Francis Jacobs also reviews the arguments put forward by McDougal at the Vienna Conference in his essay, 'Varieties of Approach to Treaty Interpretation: With Special Reference to the Draft Convention on the Law of Treaties before the Vienna Diplomatic Conference' (Chapter 10), which examines the more traditional approaches to treaty interpretation.

Given the importance of treaty interpretation to the proper functioning of the international legal system, a further essay is included in this volume that locates the function of interpretation within the wider field of legal methodology. Maarten Bos, in his essay 'Theory and Practice of Treaty Interpretation' (Chapter 11), rejects the notion advanced by Sur (1974) that unwritten international law is also a subject for interpretation, by restricting the use of his proposed rational methodology to written agreements. By placing the function of interpretation within the widest context, Bos claims that he is '[d]elivering it from the shackles isolating it as a merely technical activity, and recognizing it as part and parcel of the legal process' and thus exposing it 'to the decisive and beneficial influence of the normative concept of law for international relations' (p. 398).

Invalidity, Suspension and Termination of Treaties

Although some treaties provide for their termination by various predictable means, such as the effluxion of time or the completion of a specified task, the majority of treaties contain no such clause and are presumed to continue in force for an indefinite period of time. There are, however, a number of ways in which treaties might terminate because of some vitiating factor that was unforeseen by their drafters. It is significant, however, that despite the amount of time spent by the ILC and commentators on factors that might render a treaty invalid, the number of such occurrences in actual practice are extremely rare, given the number of treaty transactions in any given period. As the ILC itself admitted, there are few international precedents dealing with issues such as fraud, error, corruption or coercion of a state's representative and therefore, as T.O. Elias points out in his essay 'Problems Concerning the Validity of Treaties' (Chapter 12), Part V of the Vienna Convention must be regarded as constituting progressive development. Having said this, the ICJ has recognized in the *Fisheries Jurisdiction Case* and, more recently, in the *Danube Dam Case* that the provisions of the Vienna Convention relating to the doctrine of *rebus sic stantibus* now reflect customary international law. The doctrine has, however, been identified by the Court as exceptional and its limits are clearly narrow. The review of the

Court's decision in the *Danube Dam Case* by Daniel Reichert-Facilides in 'Down the Danube: The Vienna Convention on the Law of Treaties and the *Case Concerning the Gabcïkovo-Nagymaros Project*' (Chapter 13) not only offers a shrewd critique of the case itself, but also highlights some of the problems of a code drawn as widely as the Vienna Convention.

While there are a considerable number of provisions of some technical complexity in the Vienna Convention dealing with questions of invalidity, suspension and termination of treaties, the essays in this volume are concerned only with the invalidity of treaties and termination of treaties through breach. The reason for this is that these were matters – especially the question of invalidity on grounds of *ius cogens* – which led to acute differences of opinion among states and detained the ILC in its deliberations for a significant period of time. Given that the Vienna Diplomatic Conference was required to obtain a two-thirds majority of states voting for the various provisions in order for them to be accepted, it is not surprising that a great deal of work had to be done to achieve consensus. Not only does Elias' essay provide a detailed guide to the grounds of invalidity in the Vienna Convention on the Law of Treaties, it also gives an indication of some of the problems of the consequences of invalidity and dispute settlement in this area. Since the issue of *ius cogens* caused considerable controversy at the Vienna Diplomatic Conference and as the status and substantive content of the concept itself remains the subject of debate, Merlin Magallona's essay, 'The Concept of Jus Cogens in the Vienna Convention on the Law of Treaties' (Chapter 14) considers these issues. He reviews not only the emergence of the concept of a doctrine of international *ordre public*, but also deals critically with some of the practical issues raised by the inclusion of *ius cogens* within the framework of positive law.

In addition to the grounds on which treaties might be declared invalid and thus be terminated – limitation on competence to conclude a treaty by municipal constitutional law, restrictions on a state representative's authority to bind the state, error, fraud, corruption, coercion of a state's representative, coercion of a state by the threat or use of force and conflict with a peremptory norm of general international law (*ius cogens*) – treaties might also be terminated by material breach. Under Article 60 of the Vienna Convention, a material breach may occur when there is a repudiation of a treaty that is not sanctioned by the Convention or there is a violation of a provision essential to the accomplishment of the object and purpose of the treaty in question. It is now generally accepted that Article 60 represents customary international law, and Herbert Briggs' essay, 'Unilateral Denunciation of Treaties: The Vienna Convention and the International Court of Justice' (Chapter 15), gives a useful critical insight into unilateral denunciations and their status in international law prior to the entry into force of the Vienna Convention. Christine Chinkin, in 'Nonperformance of International Agreements' (Chapter 16), and using a highly analytical approach that is clearly influenced by the New Haven School, usefully highlights the fact that, although a material breach may terminate a treaty, the Vienna Convention fails to deal with those circumstances of minor breach. As she notes, '[t]he effects, and indeed the possibility, of trivial breaches must be deduced from sources outside the Convention' (p. 544). This essay is also useful in that it not only clearly articulates the possible policy concerns of statesmen and women in cases of breach, but also does valuable service by identifying the perpetually crucial role of interpretation in the process of recognizing a breach and its various consequences. Chinkin's essay can also usefully be read in conjunction with Don Greig's lengthy essay on reciprocity and proportionality in the law of treaties in which he argues that proportionality should figure in any assessment of an appropriate response in the termination or suspension of treaties for breach (Greig, 1994).

Conclusion

Although the law of treaties has long been an integral part of interstate relations neither customary international law nor the Vienna Convention on the Law of Treaties can be said to deal comprehensively with the manifold theoretical and doctrinal issues that still abound in this area of international law. Even a brief glimpse at the essays contained in this volume will disclose a wide variety of opinion on a broad range of issues concerning the conclusion, application and termination of treaties. It is perhaps testament to the general stability of treaty relations between states that there are so few instances of international litigation over questions of the validity or breach of treaties. In the area of treaty interpretation where the possibilities for disagreement are greater in number, it is significant that both states and arbitral tribunals are in accord over the rules to be applied. That these rules are manifest in Articles 31 and 32 of the Vienna Convention demonstrates that, despite the vigorous debate at Vienna and in the ensuing academic literature over the suitability of these provisions, there has emerged a more or less well-settled appreciation of the applicable norms. Thus, while the Vienna Convention does not resolve all issues relating to treaty law – particularly those regarding treaties between international persons other than states, the effects of war on treaties and succession to treaties – it nonetheless stands as a triumph of the drafters' art that, at least superficially, clarifies a number of technically fraught areas. Rather than seeing the Convention as an end in itself therefore, it is perhaps better to approach it as a foundation upon which the law of treaties can be more securely built.

Notes

1   See Article 26 of the Vienna Convention on the Law of Treaties.
2   See *Harvard Research in International Law: The Law of Treaties* (1935) 29 AJIL (3 Supp) 1077–96.
3   1951 ICJ Rep 15.
4   *UN Conference on the Law of Treaties, First and Second Session 1968 and 1969*, Official Records, UN Docs A/Conf.39/11 and Add 1.
5   1155 UNTS 331; (1969) 8 ILM 679.
6   1949 ICJ Rep 174.
7   See Article 8 Vienna Convention on the Law of Treaties 1969.
8   *Yearbook of the International Law Commission*, 162-ii, p. 161.
9   *Norway* v. *Denmark* (1933) PCIJ Ser A/B, no 53.
10 *Australia and New Zealand* v. *France* 1974 ICJ Rep 253.
11 1986 ICJ Rep 554.
12 *Nuclear Tests Cases* 1974 ICJ Rep 267–8.
13 1994 ICJ Rep 112; 1995 ICJ Rep 6.
14 Article 18 Vienna Convention on the Law of Treaties 1969.
15 General Assembly Resolution 598 (VI), Supp. 20 at 84, UN Doc. A/2119 (1952).

References

Alston, Philip (2001), 'Charging for Access to International Law Treaty Information: Time for the UN to Rethink a Perverse Initiative', *European Journal of International Law*, **12**, pp. 551–58.
Aust, Anthony (2000), *Modern Treaty Law*, Cambridge: Cambridge University Press.
Blix, Hans (1953), 'The Requirement of Ratification', *British Yearbook of International Law*, **31**, pp. 352–80.

Boyle, Alan (1999), 'Some Reflections on the Relationship of Treaties and Soft Law', *International and Comparative Law Quarterly*, **48**, pp. 901–13.

Brownlie, Ian (1998), *Principles of Public International Law* (5th edn), Oxford: Oxford University Press.

Elias, T.O. (1974), *The Modern Law of Treaties*, Dobbs Ferry: Oceana.

Fitzmaurice, Sir Gerald (1951), 'The Law and Procedure of the International Court of Justice: Treaty Interpretation and Certain other Treaty Points', *British Yearbook of International Law*, **28**, pp. 1–28.

Fitzmaurice, Sir Gerald (1958), 'Some Problems Regarding the Formal Sources of International Law', *Symbolae Verzijl*, The Hague: Nijhoff, p. 153.

Gaja, G. (1987), 'A "New" Vienna Convention on Treaties between States and International Organisations or between International Organisations: A Critical Commentary', *British Yearbook of International Law*, **58**, pp. 253–69.

Greig, D.W. (1994), 'Reciprocity, Proportionality, and the Law of Treaties', *Virginia Journal of International Law*, **11**, pp. 295–403.

Greig, D.W. (1995), 'Reservations: Equity as a Balancing Factor?', *Australian Yearbook of International Law*, **16**, pp. 21–172.

Jennings, Sir Robert and Watts, Sir Arthur (1992), *Oppenheim's International Law – Volume I: Peace: Parts 2 to 4*, London and New York: Longmans.

Lauterpacht, Sir Hersch (ed.) (1955), *Oppenheim's International Law, Volume I – Peace* (8th edn), London: Longman.

McDougal, Myres, Lasswell, S., Harold, D. and Miller, James C. (1967), *The Interpretation of Agreements and World Public Order*, New Haven, CT: Yale University Press.

McNair, Sir Arnold (1961), *The Law of Treaties*, Cambridge: Cambridge University Press.

Parry, Clive (1968), 'The Law of Treaties', in Max Sorensen, *Manual of Public International Law*, London: Macmillan, pp. 175–212.

Rosenne, Shabtai (1970), *The Law of Treaties: A Guide to the Legislative History of the Vienna Convention*, Dobbs Ferry: Oceana.

Schwarzenberger, Georg (1976), *A Manual of International Law* (6th edn), Milton: Professional Books.

Sinclair, Sir Ian (1970), 'Vienna Conference on the Law of Treaties', *International and Comparative Law Quarterly*, **19**, pp. 47–69.

Sur, Professor (1974), *L'interpretation en droit international public*, Paris: Librairie générale de droit et de jurisprudence.

Virally, Michel (1968), 'The Sources of International Law', in Max Sorensen, *Manual of Public International Law*, London: Macmillan, pp. 116–74.

Part I
Evolution

[1]

THE TREATY ON TREATIES

By RICHARD D. KEARNEY and ROBERT E. DALTON *

The Vienna Convention on the Law of Treaties,[1] the product of two lengthy sessions of the hundred-and-ten-nation conference held in 1968 and 1969 and of preparatory work extending over fifteen years by the International Law Commission, is the first essential element of infrastructure that has been worked out in the enormous task of codifying international law pursuant to Article 13 of the United Nations Charter. The previous codification treaties, the four conventions on the Law of the Sea, the Vienna Convention on Diplomatic Relations, the Vienna Convention on Consular Relations and the Convention on the Reduction of Statelessness, did not, despite their intrinsic importance, grapple with the fundamentals of constructing a world legal order.

The Diplomatic and Consular Conventions are essentially "in-house" efforts, concerned with blueprinting the mechanics of international relations. The Law of the Sea Conventions, while affecting issues of primary interest to the international community, are concerned with special regimes within a substantially self-contained area of international law.[2]

The Convention on the Law of Treaties sets forth the code of rules that will govern the indispensable element[3] in the conduct of foreign affairs, the mechanism without which international intercourse could not exist, much less function. It is possible to imagine a future in which the treaty will no longer be the standard device for dealing with any and all international problems—a future in which, for example, the use of regulations promulgated by international organizations in special fields of activity, such as the World Health Organization's sanitary regulations,[4] will become the accepted substitute for the lawmaking activity now effected through international agreement. But, in the present state of international development, this is crystal-gazing. For the foreseeable future, the treaty will remain the cement that holds the world community together.

---

* Office of the Legal Adviser, Department of State. The views expressed are the personal views of the authors and are not to be attributed to the Department of State.

[1] 63 A.J.I.L. 875 (1969); 8 Int. Legal Materials 679 (1969).

[2] The Territorial Sea and the Contiguous Zone, the High Seas, Fishing and Conservation of the Living Resources of the High Seas, and the Continental Shelf.

[3] McNair described the treaty as "the only and sadly overworked instrument with which international society is equipped for the purpose of carrying out its multifarious transactions." "The Functions and Differing Legal Character of Treaties," 11 Brit. Yr. Bk. Int. Law 101 (1930); reprinted in McNair, The Law of Treaties 739, 740 (1961).

[4] See, e.g., the smallpox vaccination certificate regulations of 1956, 11 U.S. Treaties 133; or the regulations on the health part of the aircraft general declaration of 1960, 12 ibid. 2950.

496   THE AMERICAN JOURNAL OF INTERNATIONAL LAW   [Vol. 64

BACKGROUND

Given the indispensability of the international agreement and an ancestry that has been traced back to Sumer,[5] it is reasonable to expect that, of all the areas of international law, the law of treaties would have become the most thoroughly developed and the most broadly accepted. However, as late as 1935, the introductory comment to the Harvard Draft Convention on the Law of Treaties remarked that "at the threshold of this subject, one encounters the fact that there is no clear and well-defined law of treaties." [6]

Thirteen years later an even more pessimistic analysis was expressed in the *Survey of International Law in Relation to the Work of Codification of the International Law Commission,* the study that was prepared by the United Nations Secretariat to assist the International Law Commission in deciding upon a long-range program of work. Despite efforts to bring order into the field of treaty law, such as the codification efforts under the League of Nations,[7] the International Commission of American Jurists, and the Harvard Research in International Law, the United Nations Survey found that there was scarcely a topic in the entire field that was "free from doubt and, in some cases, from confusion." [8]

This judgment pertained "not only to the question of the terminology applied to the conception of treaties, to the legal consequences of the distinction between treaties proper and [other] intergovernmental agreements, and to the designation of the parties to treaties"; there was "uncertainty as to the necessity of ratification with regard to treaties which have no provision for ratification; in the matter of the important subject of the relevance of the constitutional limitations upon the treaty-making power; and in respect of conferment of benefits upon third parties." [9] Possibly this lack of law in light of the elemental importance of the subject impelled the Commission in drawing up its order of codification priority at the first session in 1949 to give the law of treaties top billing.[10] At the same session the Commission elected the distinguished British jurist, James L. Brierly, Chichele Professor at Oxford, as the special rapporteur for the subject.[11]

In the Commission's task of codifying international law, the special rapporteur plays the most important individual rôle. He does the basic research, delimits the scope of a topic, provides the conceptual approach, and submits the original content and form of specific rules.[12] In the fifteen

[5] Korff, "An Introduction to the History of International Law," 18 A.J.I.L. 246, 249 (1924).

[6] Research in International Law Under the Auspices of the Faculty of the Harvard Law School, Law of Treaties, 29 A.J.I.L. Supp. 653 at 666 (1935).

[7] See, League of Nations Committee of Experts Report to the Council on Questionnaire No. 5 (1927).

[8] Survey of International Law in Relation to the Work of Codification of the International Law Commission, U.N. Doc. A/CN.4/I/Rev. 1, at 52 (1948).

[9] *Ibid.*

[10] 1949 I.L.C. Yearbook 58, U.N. Doc. A/CN.4/SR.7 (1949).

[11] *Ibid.* at 238, U.N. Doc. A/CN.4/SR.33 (1949).

[12] See 1952 I.L.C. Yearbook (I) 220–222, 224–227, U.N. Doc. A/CN.4/SER.A (1952).

years the Commission was concerned with the law of treaties, four out-standing British lawyers successively served as special rapporteurs. In 1952 Brierly was succeeded by Sir Hersch Lauterpacht, widely known for a number of magisterial works, including his editions of Oppenheim's *International Law*, who in turn was succeeded by Sir Gerald Fitzmaurice, Legal Adviser of the British Foreign Office. Upon the latter's election to the International Court of Justice, the Commission selected in 1961 Sir Humphrey Waldock, Chichele Professor of International Law at Oxford and quondam Chairman of the European Commission on Human Rights, to carry on the work.

Each of the rapporteurs approached the law of treaties not only with a different colligatory approach [13] but also from widely varying viewpoints on many of the individual issues.[14]

The threshold question—who can be a party to a treaty—is an interesting illustration of variations on a theme. Brierly advanced the broad principle that all states and international organizations have capacity to make treaties, coupled with the vague qualification that this capacity could be limited in respect of some states entering into certain treaties.[15]

Lauterpacht handled the question as a validity issue and held "an instrument is void as a treaty if concluded in disregard of the international limitations upon the capacity of the parties to conclude treaties."[16] This would appear to imply that some states do not have capacity to enter into a treaty even though the instrument concerned may not lack all aspects of legal enforceability.

Fitzmaurice laid down the prescription "a State has the capacity to participate in a given treaty (a) if its general treaty-making capacity is not limited so as to exclude participation in that treaty or class of treaty; (b) if it fulfils any special conditions of participation that may be laid down by the treaty itself." [17] The proposition is almost, but not quite, circular. Finally, Waldock, in his first report, laid down as the guiding principle that every independent state, whether unitary or federated or otherwise unified, has capacity to become a party to treaties and that other subjects of international law have this capacity if given them by treaty or by international custom. Waldock also laid down specific rules regarding the capacity of

Cf. Statute of the International Law Commission, Art. 16 (f), General Assembly Res. 174, General Assembly, 2nd Sess., Official Records, U.N. Doc. A/519 at 105 (1947).

[13] 1961 I.L.C. Yearbook (I) 256, U.N. Doc. A/CN.4/SER.A (1961).

[14] See, *e.g.*, Jenks, "Hersch Lauterpacht—The Scholar as Prophet," 36 Brit. Yr. Bk. Int. Law 88–89 (1960).

[15] Brierly, (First) Report on the Law of Treaties, 1950 I.L.C. Yearbook (II) 223, U.N. Doc. A/CN.4/23 (1950).

[16] Lauterpacht, (First) Report on the Law of Treaties, 1953 I.L.C. Yearbook (II) 92, U.N. Doc. A/CN.4/63 (1953).

[17] Fitzmaurice, (First) Report on the Law of Treaties, 1956 I.L.C. Yearbook (II) 109, U.N. Doc. A/CN.4/101 (1956).

498   THE AMERICAN JOURNAL OF INTERNATIONAL LAW   [Vol. 64

constituent States of a federal union, of dependent states and of international organizations to enter into treaties.[18]

Differences in approach and viewpoint regarding the law of treaties were much greater in the Commission itself, which is intended to represent ". . . the main forms of civilization and . . . the principal legal systems of the world."[19] Its twenty-five members, in fact, come from every corner of the world. The members who worked out the final draft articles on the law of treaties were drawn from states as remote from each other as Finland and Argentina, as diverse in size as Brazil and Togo, as different in culture as the United States and Afghanistan, as unlike in legal practice as the United Kingdom and Uruguay, as dissimilar in political philosophy as Austria and Iraq, as disparate in economic theory as Japan and Poland.[20]

That a Commission containing such diversities and dealing with a subject as difficult and as unsettled as the law of treaties was able to reach agreement on the seventy-five draft articles[21] which served as the working text for the Vienna Conference was a substantial achievement. The Commission's methodology was to lay down general rules regarding treaties in general language. The vast majority of the articles set forth two or three basic rules on a subject that could have called for an entire section of detailed regulation.

The capacity of states to make treaties again supplies an apt example. Waldock's 1962 draft article was a series of rules that dealt with the major aspects of the problem in sufficient detail to answer the most obvious questions regarding the treaty-making powers of a constituent unit of a federal state, the circumstances under which a dependent state may enter into treaties and the capacity of international organizations to make treaties.[22] The article as it appeared at the end of the 1962 session in the Report to the General Assembly is much shorter and leaves open a number of questions:

> 1. Capacity to conclude treaties under international law is possessed by States and by other subjects of international law.
> 2. In a federal State, the capacity of the member states of a federal union to conclude treaties depends on the federal constitution.
> 3. In the case of international organizations, capacity to conclude treaties depends on the constitution of the organization concerned.[23]

The changes from the Waldock article represent not merely a different drafting approach or even different legal concepts but also mirror political issues that lie below the surface of this innocent-appearing topic. Thus

---

[18] Waldock, First Report on the Law of Treaties, 1962 I.L.C. Yearbook (II) 35–36, U.N. Doc. A/CN.4/144 (1962).

[19] I.L.C. Stat., Art. 8.

[20] I.L.C. Report, U.N. General Assembly, 21st Sess., Official Records, Supp. 9, at 6, U.N. Doc. A/6309/Rev. 1 (1966).

[21] *Ibid.* at 10–100. Reprinted in 61 A.J.I.L. 263–285 (1967).

[22] Waldock, note 18 above.

[23] I.L.C. Report, U.N. General Assembly, 17th Sess., Official Records, Supp. 9 at 7, U.N. Doc. A/5209 (1962).

the disappearance of the independent-dependent state antinomy was triggered by Tunkin of the U.S.S.R., who urged the thesis that contemporary international law did not sanction dependent territories such as colonies and protectorates.[24]

Another interesting example of a predisposition to generality in drafting is the final version of the Commission's article on fraud, which provided that "a State which has been induced to conclude a treaty by the fraudulent conduct of another negotiating State may invoke the fraud as invalidating its consent to be bound by the treaty." That is all there was on the subject of fraud. Clearly, there could have been a good deal more.[25]

There are cogent reasons for a spare approach in drafting codification treaties. One is the fact that some legal systems have a decided preference when dealing with basics to do so in a terse and general manner. Another is that attempts to construct detailed rules easily become bogged down in the conflicting claims of national legal systems and definitions. Reverting again to the subject of fraud, Waldock in his first draft included a definition of fraud based on common law principles. But after discussions in the Commission on the civil law concept of *dol*, he concluded a narrower definition was advisable.[26] And even this narrow definition eventually disappeared.

Generality in drafting, however, is well suited to the cosmetic method of disguising differences by a thick coating of undefined terms. It is a device too easily available and too often used in tailoring international documents. Concern was displayed on this point in the comments made by governments on the Commission's draft articles both during their formulation and after the final draft was submitted to the General Assembly. This was especially marked with regard to Part V of the Commission's draft on the Invalidity, Suspension and Termination of Treaties.[27] Moreover, criticism of the vagueness of language used was sometimes based on completely opposed positions as to what the language was intended to convey. One of the Commission's proposals was that a "treaty is void if its conclusion has been procured by the threat or use of force in violation of the principles of the Charter of the United Nations."[28] The principle as such was almost universally endorsed in the governmental comments.[29] A number

---

[24] 1962 I.L.C. Yearbook (I) 59, U.N. Doc. A/CN.4/Ser.A/1962.

[25] The Index to the U.S. Code requires three and a half columns to list the Federal enactments on various aspects of fraud. 18 U.S.C. 1341 on Mail Fraud, for example, begins, "Whoever, having devised or intending to devise any scheme or artifice to defraud, or for obtaining money or property by means of false or fraudulent pretenses, representations or promises . . ." and continues in the same way for another seventeen lines of very small type.

[26] 1963 I.L.C. Yearbook (I) 37, U.N. Doc. A/CN.4/ Ser.A/1963.

[27] See II Analytical Compilation of Comments and Observations Made in 1966 and 1967 with Respect to the Final Draft Articles on the Law of Treaties [hereinafter cited as Analytical Compilation] 235–387 *passim*. U.N. Doc. A/CONF. 39/5 (1968).

[28] I.L.C. Report, note 20 above, at 16.

[29] II Analytical Compilation, note 27 above, at 269–287.

500   THE AMERICAN JOURNAL OF INTERNATIONAL LAW   [Vol. 64

of states complained that the wording was too limiting, along the lines of the Algerian comment:

> . . . rather than the words "the threat or use of force", [his delegation] would have preferred a categorical and imperative formula excluding any form of coercion. Other forms of pressure, such as economic forms, should be mentioned as covered by the idea of coercion.[80]

On the other hand, the United States commented regarding "threat or use of force":

> . . . If a definite meaning had been given this phrase in United Nations usage, this would have aided in supplying protection against possible use of the article for unwarranted attempts to evade treaty obligations. But it is common knowledge that there are very substantial differences as to what is a use of force in violation of the Charter of the United Nations. It has been erroneously urged from some quarters that adverse propaganda or economic measures against a State constitute a threat or use of force in violation of Charter principles. . . .[81]

These, and other doctrinal disputes glossed over in the Commission's articles, resulted in some solid in-fighting at the Vienna Conference.

Trouble spots of this character were not too frequent in the technical provisions that comprised the bulk of the Commission's draft articles. The eighteen articles in Part II on the Conclusion and Entry into Force of Treaties appeared to raise problems more of the best way of doing things rather than whether they should be done at all. In general, this is true of Part III on the Observance, Application and Interpretation of Treaties. Part IV on the Amendment and Modification of Treaties and Part VII on Depositaries, Notifications, Corrections and Registration also seemed to fit into this category. Nonetheless there were sufficient technical difficulties and doctrinal disputes facing the conference when it assembled in Vienna on March 26, 1968, to lead some states to question whether a convention could be adopted in two sessions.[82]

The method of work adopted by the conference heightened this concern. Rather than parceling the draft articles out to two or three committees for review, redrafting if necessary, and initial approval, the conference functioned as a committee of the whole for practically the entire 1968 session. Each article was taken up for study seriatim by this one body. The time pressures this procedure generated, coupled with the extended debates arising out of issues such as the validity of treaties, settlement of disputes, and the "all-states" question, to mention only the most troublesome, made the conference a real cliff hanger. Proposals for a more efficient organization of the conference had been rejected on the ground that a number of the smaller states would have been hard pressed to spare experts to man more than one committee.[83]

---

[80] *Ibid.* at 269.   [81] *Ibid.* at 286.

[82] *Cf.* U.N. General Assembly, 22nd Sess., Official Records, Sixth Committee (1967), 967th meeting (Mr. Darwin).

[83] *Ibid.* "It was very important to the smaller countries that there should be only one main committee, so that they could participate effectively in the revision of [the] draft. . . ." (Mr. Mwenda [Kenya]).

In preparing for both sessions of the conference the United States Government relied heavily upon the Study Group on the Law of Treaties established by the American Society of International Law in 1965. With Oliver Lissitzyn of Columbia as chairman, this group of eminent international lawyers joined with representatives of the Departments of Justice and State in reviewing the Commission's draft articles in depth.

Subsequently the study group joined forces with the Special Committee on Treaty Law of the Section of International and Comparative Law of the American Bar Association. The basic United States positions for the conference were hammered out in this body. Three public members of the study group, Professor Herbert W. Briggs of Cornell, a member of the International Law Commission during the period in which the seventy-five draft articles were adopted, Professor Myres S. McDougal of Yale, and Dean Joseph M. Sweeney of Tulane served as representatives on the delegation to the 1968 session. John R. Stevenson, a member of both the Society study group and the Bar Association's committee on treaties, served as deputy chairman of the United States Delegation to the 1969 session.

This concentrated examination of the Commission's draft articles resulted in a good many United States proposals for amendment. A reasonable number of these proposals, or variations thereof, were accepted by the conference despite substantial reluctance among many delegations, and particularly those from newly independent states, to make any changes in the International Law Commission's draft. This reluctance came from a deeply held conviction on the part of the newer states that the Commission's draft articles reflected a new international law that took account of the problems of developing countries and that amendments proposed by the older and richer countries might be intended to undermine this new international law.[84] It is, of course, a widely held article of belief among former colonies that, prior to the United Nations, international law was largely developed by imperialist states to justify and support the policies of imperialism. The remarks of the representative of Ghana in the Sixth Committee discussion of the Commission's draft articles are enlightening:

> The Commission could not have found a better justification for its work and all the countries that had just shaken off the colonialist yoke were delighted with its achievement, for they saw in it proof that international law was becoming a set of legal principles that applied to all countries and not simply to a few favoured States. In that connexion, he pointed out that most African countries had been colonized as a result of "gin-bottle" treaties concluded between African chiefs and the colonial Powers, which, whenever it suited them to do so, elevated those treaties to the status of solemn international agreements or reminded their luckless partners that the agreements which they had thus concluded had no standing in international law.[85]

[84] See I Analytical Compilation, note 29 above, at 40–41 (Tunisia); *cf. ibid.* at 39–40 (Thailand).
[85] I Analytical Compilation 24.

502   THE AMERICAN JOURNAL OF INTERNATIONAL LAW   [Vol. 64

The Communist states devoted themselves assiduously to nurturing and fostering this belief. The Byelorussian representative in the Sixth Committee discussions affords a typical example:

> The obstacles to successful codification of the topic lay, not in the fact that certain provisions were not ripe for codification, as the representative of the United Kingdom maintained, but in the efforts of certain States to preserve outmoded colonial privileges and treaties that were not in keeping with the spirit of the times or with developments in international law. Happily, the draft articles represented a complete break with the old colonial practice of concluding unequal treaties imposed by force. . . .[86]

The consequence of this viewpoint was a somewhat blind opposition to any change in the Commission's articles, not only in those that embodied innovative or controversial aspects but also in the great number of technical articles. Proposals for purely technical improvements were oftener than not greeted with dubiety. A fundamental fact of life at the conference was that forty-one delegations came from states that became independent after the outbreak of World War II. Any amendment that could not attract a reasonable degree of support from that group, and particularly the Asian-African section, was doomed.

INTRODUCTION (ARTICLES 1–5)

The very first United States proposal encountered a variation of this obstacle. The basic issue with respect to Article 1 was the scope of the convention. The draft article prepared by the Commission limited the scope of the convention to treaties concluded between states, thus excluding treaties to which international organizations are a party. In introducing an amendment to Article 1 to expand the coverage of the convention to treaties concluded by international organizations,[87] the United States representative suggested the establishment of a working group which would include observers of international organizations at the conference to consider the drafting. In making the proposal the United States had taken into account that a number of developing countries had urged such action in commenting on the draft articles. The debate in the committee of the whole established that a majority of the delegations, while not opposed to codifying the law with respect to treaties concluded between states and international organizations, feared that the time allotted for the conference was insufficient to permit dealing with the topic. Corridor discussion also revealed that a number of delegations suspected the purpose of the United States was to delay the conference with the aim of blocking a convention. This may have been fanned by a Soviet assertion that the proposal meant "the conference would be doomed to failure from the

[86] *Ibid.* at 14.
[87] U.N. Doc. A/CONF. 39/ C.1/L.15 (1968).

outset." [88] Accordingly, a compromise was worked out, the United States withdrew its amendment, and a proposal by Sweden that the conference recommend reference of the subject to the International Law Commission for study was unanimously adopted.

The conference, in accordance with the general practice followed with respect to codification conventions, adopted Article 2 on definitions only after agreement had been reached on the substantive articles. However, there are advantages in treating the articles in the order finally adopted.

The nine subparagraphs of paragraph 1 of Article 2 define the following twelve terms: "treaty," "ratification," "acceptance," "approval," "accession," "full powers," "reservation," "negotiating State," "contracting State," "party," "third State," and "international organization." Paragraph 2 stresses that "the provisions of paragraph 1 regarding the use of terms in the present Convention are without prejudice to the use of those terms or to the meanings which may be given to them in the internal law of any State."

The caveat in paragraph 2 should alert persons who may be accustomed to thinking of international agreements as of two kinds—treaties in the constitutional sense (*e.g.*, Article II, Section 2, Clause 2, of the United States Constitution) and other international agreements—that the convention uses "treaty" in a generic rather than a specialized sense. The drafters of the *Restatement of Foreign Relations Law of the United States* faced a similar definitional problem. They solved it in Section 115 (a) by using "international agreement" as the generic term.[39]

The Harvard Draft specifically excluded from the definition of a treaty an agreement effected by the exchange of notes.[40] The Commission took the view that the convention should apply to a "treaty" whatever its particular designation. In its 1962 draft the Commission emphasized the generality of its definition by including the parenthetic catalog "(treaty, convention, protocol, covenant, charter, statute, act, declaration, concordat, exchange of notes, agreed minute, memorandum of agreement, *modus vivendi* or any other appellation)" immediately following the word "designation."[41] It also tentatively adopted a definition of "treaty in simplified form."[42] At the second reading of the articles in 1965 the Commission decided to use the generic term "treaty" to cover all forms of

[88] United Nations Conference on the Law of Treaties, First Session, Vienna, March 26–May 24, 1968, Official Records, Summary Records of the plenary meetings and of the meetings of the Committee of the Whole 13, U.N. Doc. A/CONF 39/11 (hereinafter cited as Official Records, First Session).

[39] See Restatement (Second), Foreign Relations Law of the United States § 115, comment *a* (1965).

[40] Art. 1(b), 29 A. J. I. L. Supp. 657 (1935).

[41] I.L.C. Report, U.N. General Assembly, 17th Sess, Official Records, Supp. 9, at 4 U.N. Doc. A/5209 (1962).

[42] *Ibid.*

504   THE AMERICAN JOURNAL OF INTERNATIONAL LAW   [Vol. 64

international agreements in writing concluded between states.[43] Accordingly, the parenthetic catalog and the definition of "treaty in simplified form" do not appear in the text considered at Vienna.

The definition proposed by the Commission was:

> "Treaty" means an international agreement concluded between States in written form and governed by international law, whether embodied in a single instrument or in two or more related instruments and whatever its particular designation.[44]

Among other amendments, a proposal by Chile would have replaced the Commission's definition by the following text: " 'Treaty' means a written agreement between States, governed by international law, which produces legal effects."[45] A highly political amendment proposed by Ecuador would have altered the text to read:

> "Treaty" means an international agreement concluded between States in written form and governed by international law *which deals with a licit object, is freely consented to, and is based on justice and equity,* whether embodied in a single instrument or in two or more related instruments and whatever its particular designation.[46]

Malaysia and Mexico were concerned at the omission from the definition of the element that the agreement must "establish a relationship between the parties" governed by international law and proposed incorporating that concept in the definition.[47]

At the second session of the conference Switzerland introduced an amendment to modify further the words "international agreement" in the definition of treaty. The Swiss delegate stated that the addition of the words "providing for rights and obligations" would rectify an omission in the Commission's text, which failed to distinguish between agreements which established legal rights and obligations and those which established only political relationships.[48]

After having been debated in the committee of the whole, the amendments discussed above were referred to the drafting committee for con-

---

[43] In response to the comments of a number of governments, the Commission had reexamined the concept of a treaty in simplified form and concluded that it lacked the degree of precision necessary to provide a satisfactory criterion for distinguishing between different categories of treaties in formulating rules relating to full powers and expression of consent to be bound. It therefore decided to recast those articles in terms which did not "call for any precise distinction to be drawn between 'formal treaties' and 'treaties in simplified form' " and to delete the definition of the latter. I.L.C. Report, U.N. General Assembly, 20th Sess., Official Records, Supp. 9, at 5 (par. 23), U.N. Doc. A/6009 (1965); 60 A.J.I.L. 155 (1966).

[44] I.L.C. Report, note 20 above, at 10.   [45] U.N. Doc. A/CONF.39/C.1/L.22.

[46] U.N. Doc. A/CONF.39/C.1/L.25 (1968).

[47] U.N. Doc. A/CONF.39/C.1/L.33 and Add. 1 (1968).

[48] U.N. Doc. A/CONF.39/C.1/SR. 87, at 3–4 (1969). It should be noted that this and subsequent footnotes cite the provisional records of the second session of the Conference, since the final records were not available at the time of preparation of this article.

sideration.[49] The latter reported that it had rejected all amendments to add to the text proposed by the Commission a reference to the legal effect of treaties as "superfluous in a definition, whose scope, as expressly stated at the beginning of the article, was limited to the 'purposes of the present Convention.'" In addition, the committee considered that the element with which the Swiss amendment dealt was already covered by the Commission's text. As for the Ecuadorean amendment, its insertion "would have been incompatible with the structure of Part V" of the convention. Indeed, the only amendment accepted by the drafting committee was one submitted by Spain to improve the French and Spanish texts.[50] The careful examination of the amendments to this subparagraph is characteristic of the skill and thoroughness with which the drafting committee, under the able chairmanship of Ambassador Yasseen of Iraq, carried out its important functions.

A different type of political opposition from that involved in Article 1 was encountered in connection with Article 5.[51] The Commission had proposed that the application of the convention to constituent instruments of an international organization or treaties adopted within an international organization should be subject to any relevant rules of the organization. The United States view was that the practical effect of this article was to exclude from the application of the convention a great number of important multilateral treaties. The Commission had not advanced any convincing reason for permitting an international organization to disregard the basic rules of treaty law in interpreting and applying its constituent instrument or a treaty adopted within the organization. The United States proposed to delete the article and to amend eight other articles to provide needed exceptions for international organizations.[52] Proposals to delete were also submitted by Congo (Brazzaville), the Philippines and Sweden. Zambia, Jamaica and Trinidad and Tobago proposed deleting the exception for treaties "adopted within an international organization." The Ukraine proposed replacing the words "shall be subject to any relevant rules" by "shall take into account the relevant rules." In addition, there were a number of proposals purportedly to clarify the language (France, Gabon, Peru and the United Kingdom) and a Ceylonese amendment to broaden the exception.

In the debates a goodly number of delegates expressed concern for the breadth of the exception contained in Article 5.[53] At the same time the observers for international organizations present at the conference were

[49] Report of the Committee of the Whole on its Work at the Second Session of the Conference, U.N. Doc. A/CONF.39/15, at 13, par. 24 (1969).

[50] U.N. Doc. A/CONF.39/C.1/SR.105, at 8–9 (1969).

[51] Unless otherwise indicated, all number references are to the Convention on the Law of Treaties rather than to the draft articles proposed by the Commission. A comparative table of the numbering of the two texts is contained in U.N. Doc. A/CONF.39/28 (1969), 8 Int. Legal Materials 714 (1969).

[52] U.N. Doc. A/CONF.39/C.1/L.21 (1968).

[53] Official Records, First Session 42–58 *passim.*

506   THE AMERICAN JOURNAL OF INTERNATIONAL LAW   [Vol. 64

urging on the floor and in the corridors the need for the exemption. C. Wilfred Jenks, the Principal Deputy Director General of the International Labor Organization, was especially eloquent on this need for a *lex specialis* for international organizations in general and the International Labor Organization in particular.[54] He was strongly supported by Sir Francis Vallat, chief of the British Delegation.[55] When the question was put to the vote all the proposals to delete were soundly beaten by 84 votes to 10.[56] The negatives included a number of states such as The Netherlands whose delegates had indicated support for the United States proposal in the discussions. The more limited proposals of Zambia, Jamaica and Trinidad and Tobago were withdrawn without explanation and the Ukrainian lesser modification was defeated by a lesser no-vote, 42 to 26. After this display of strength by the international organizations, the clarifying amendments were referred to the drafting committee. The committee reported out a proposal that included substantial clarification:

> The present Convention applies to any treaty which is the constituent instrument of an international organization and to any treaty adopted within an international organization without prejudice to any relevant rules of the organization.[57]

The article was adopted in this form by the committee of the whole and at the second session by the plenary. In its present form its character as *lex specialis* is less pronounced.

As was noted in reviewing the development in the Commission of rules on capacity to enter into treaties, an innocuous principle that appears desirable for technical reasons can contain political booby traps. The capacity article as finally reported out by the Commission[58] was truncated. Paragraph 1 stated simply that every state possessed capacity to conclude treaties. Paragraph 2 provided that States members of a federal union had treaty-making capacity if and to the extent provided in the federal constitution. The provision relating to the capacity of international organizations to make treaties had disappeared pursuant to the Commission's decision to confine its draft articles to treaties between states.

In the 1968 session of the conference there were a number of proposals to delete paragraph 1 on the basis it was so general as to be unnecessary. Abortive efforts were made to give it an appearance of meaningfulness by amendments requiring the state to be a subject of international law.[59] Eventually the paragraph was maintained unchanged in the text adopted at the 1969 session. (The underlying and explosive question of what states are entitled to become parties to treaties—the "all-states" issue—was

---

[54] *Ibid.* at 36–37.   [55] *Ibid.* at 44–45.

[56] I Draft Report of the Committee of the Whole on its Work at the First Session of the Conference 49, U.N. Doc. A/CONF.39/C.1/L.370/Rev.1 (1969).

[57] *Ibid.* at 50.   [58] I.L.C. Report, note 20 above, at 11.

[59] U.N. Docs. A/CONF.39/C.1/L.54/Rev. 1 (Finland), and A/CONF.39/C.1/L.80 (Congo [Brazzaville]) (1968).

raised by a new article[60] tabled by eleven states.) The second paragraph regarding federal states, however, occasioned a drawn-out fight. Canada was strongly opposed to it on several grounds and especially concerned that it might lead to the practice of interpretation by outside bodies of the constitutions of federal states. The Canadian Delegation emphasized that federal states having unwritten or partly written constitutions faced the greatest risk in this regard.[61]

The Soviet Union, however, came out in favor of the retention of the paragraph, pointing out that two of its constituent republics, the Ukrainian and the Byelorussian, were parties to many treaties.[62] France supported retention of the paragraph on the ground that the text reflected established practice.[63] It could have more fairly been said to support the French practice of negotiating and concluding agreements with the Canadian Province of Quebec.[64] The line as drawn was thus between Canada, which, because of the nature of its constitution, had grave concern regarding the paragraph, plus a group of other federal states that felt the paragraph was not worth the extensive revision required to make it tolerable and the Communist states that considered the paragraph contributed to the international prestige and status of Byelorussia and the Ukraine, plus France, which was pursuing an aspect of Gaullist foreign policy.

The amendments to delete were voted down by a relatively close margin, 45 to 38.[65] The article then went to the drafting committee where the second paragraph was somewhat polished up. When reported out, paragraph 2 was again voted upon and adopted by 46 votes to 39 and the article as a whole adopted by 54 votes to 17. This normally would have been the end of the story as far as the elimination of paragraph 2 was concerned. With very rare exceptions the articles adopted by simple majority in the committee of the whole were adopted by the required two-thirds majority in the plenary. Retention of paragraph 2 by the committee of the whole derived in substantial part from the reluctance to make changes in the Commission's draft on the part of the Asian-African group. The time lapse between the two sessions permitted reasoned arguments to be made in capitals on issues arising from the draft articles and reasoned consideration of those arguments. In the case of federal capacity it afforded Canada an opportunity to make the point that here was a rule whose deletion would not result in detriment to any state and whose reten-

---

[60] U.N. Doc. A/CONF.39/C.1/L.74 and Add. 1 and 2 (1968). The amendment proposed inserting the following new article . . . :

"*The right of participation in treaties*

"All States have the right to participate in general multilateral treaties in accordance with the principle of sovereign equality."

[61] Official Records, First Session, at 62; *cf.* U.N. Doc. A/CONF.39/SR.7, at 12 (1969).

[62] *Ibid.* at 64.   [63] *Ibid.* at 67.

[64] *E.g.*, Franco-Quebec Educational Entente of Feb. 27, 1965. See Fitzgerald, "Educational and Cultural Agreements and Ententes: France, Canada and Quebec—Birth of a New Treaty-Making Technique for Federal States?", 60 A.J.I.L. 529, 530–531 (1966).

[65] Official Records, First Session 69.

508   THE AMERICAN JOURNAL OF INTERNATIONAL LAW   [Vol. 64

tion would cause actual difficulties to Canada. The United States assisted Canada in making these arguments in capitals, particularly those where Canada did not have permanent representation. This intersessional work paid off at the eighth plenary meeting of the conference. Paragraph 2 was rejected by 66 votes to 28.[66]

CONCLUSION AND ENTRY INTO FORCE OF TREATIES (ARTICLES 6–25)

As previously noted, however, most of the problems in the earlier articles were technical ones. The rules proposed by the Commission and adopted by the conference in Articles 7 through 17 regarding full powers, the adoption and authentication of a treaty text and the manner of expression of consent to be bound embodied the generally accepted practice with respect to these essentials of the treaty-making process. The conference, however, disagreed with the decision of the Commission that a general rule on means of expressing consent to be bound should not be included in the draft articles and that no specific reference should be made to agreements in simplified form.

The Commission had been motivated by a desire to avoid disputes over whether the general rule should favor ratification or signature, and a wish to simplify the text.[67] The majority view at the conference was that the total absence of a general rule on consent to be bound left the position of agreements in simplified form uncertain. As the making of international agreements through exchanges of notes or similar instruments had become a standard international practice, there was substantial support for filling the gap. This was done by adopting a general rule, Article 11:

> The consent of a State to be bound by a treaty may be expressed by signature, exchange of instruments constituting a treaty, ratification, acceptance, approval or accession, or by any other means if so agreed.

During the discussions, the partisans of ratification on the one hand and of signature on the other urged the conference to include in Article 11 a residuary rule on the means of expressing consent to be bound which would apply to the parties unless they had agreed on some other method. A considerable majority of the delegates, however, appeared to agree with the Swedish delegate's remarks that "the length of the debate was in inverse proportion to the practical importance of the subject, for the problem under discussion in fact arose very seldom." [68] Article 11 thus leaves the issue open. Specific provision was then made for agreements in simplified form by a new Article 13:

> The consent of States to be bound by a treaty constituted by instruments exchanged between them is expressed by that exchange when:
> (a) the instruments provide that their exchange shall have that effect; or
> (b) it is otherwise established that those States were agreed that the exchange of instruments should have that effect.

[66] U.N. Doc. A/CONF.39/SR.8 at 16 (1969).
[67] I.L.C. Report, note 20 above, at 31.   [68] Official Records, First Session, at 88.

In Article 18, *Obligation not to defeat the object and purpose of a treaty prior to its entry into force,* the International Law Commission had proposed the following subparagraph: "A State is obliged to refrain from acts tending to frustrate the object of a proposed treaty when: (a) It has agreed to enter into negotiations for the conclusion of the treaty, while these negotiations are in progress." [69] Subparagraphs (b) and (c) proposed similar limitations for the periods between signature and ratification and after expressing consent to be bound and entry into force.

Sir Humphrey Waldock, in his capacity as expert consultant for the conference,[70] readily admitted subparagraph (a) did not constitute a rule of customary international law.[71] A number of delegations, including that of the United States, argued that rather than being a desirable innovation, the proposed rule might, if adopted, discourage states from entering into negotiations. Concern was also expressed as to the difficulty of determining the object of a treaty that is in process of negotiation. By a vote of 55 for, 33 against, with 11 abstentions, the subparagraph was deleted.[72]

The problem of reservations to treaties was the first major issue to be taken up by the conference. The articles adopted reflect the practice that has come to be followed since World War II. Before examining the details of the articles, a consideration of the history of the matter is needed.

The Harvard Draft accurately reflects the view generally accepted prior to World War II that, unless otherwise provided in the treaty itself, in order for a state to become party to a treaty with a reservation the unanimous consent of the other parties was required.[73] The first and second rapporteurs on the law of treaties, Brierly and Lauterpacht, proposed articles to this effect in 1950 [74] and in 1953. Lauterpacht, however, supplemented his article with four alternative texts which substantially retreated from the unanimity doctrine as possible statements of law for the future.[75] Support for the unanimity rule eroded rapidly after 1951, when the International Court of Justice handed down its Advisory Opinion on *Reservations to the Genocide Convention,* and as a result of successive resolutions of the General Assembly pushing for a more practical approach to the problem raised by multilateral treaties.

---

[69] I.L.C. Report, note 20 above, at 12.

[70] The functions of the expert consultant at a U.N. codification conference are nowhere defined. In his first intervention Sir Humphrey Waldock, having adverted to this point, said "that he regarded himself as the servant of the Conference in the same way that he had served the Commission in his capacity as Special Rapporteur on the law of treaties. He was anxious to help in formulating the best possible draft convention and should not be thought of as someone who was attending the Conference simply to defend the Commission's work." (Official Records, First Session, at 20). Sir Humphrey both answered questions on the draft articles and proposed amendments, and commented, as circumstances required, on issues raised in the debates.

[71] Official Records, First Session 104.   [72] *Ibid.* at 106.

[73] 29 A. J. I. L. Supp. 653, at 659–660 (1935), Arts. 14, 15 and 16.

[74] (First Report), note 15 above, at 223.

[75] (First Report), note 16 above, at 91–92, 124.

In its 1951 advisory opinion the International Court of Justice found that the unanimity principle had not been "transformed into a rule of law." [76] It went on to state that with respect to the Genocide Convention, if a reservation was compatible with the object and purpose of the convention, it should be permitted. The Court's opinion was but one factor in the Commission's decision to abandon the unanimity rule. Equally important were the evidence of an increasing predilection of states to formulate reservations to multilateral treaties and the pressures in the General Assembly to have the United Nations Secretariat employ a "flexible" system of reservations to multilateral treaties in its depositary practice.

The question of reservations to treaties was discussed in 1951 and 1952 at the Fifth and Sixth Sessions of the General Assembly and again at the Fourteenth Session in 1959. At the end of earlier debate the General Assembly adopted Resolution 598 (VI) [77] which requested the Secretary General as depositary of the Genocide Convention to conform with the opinion of the Court and, with respect to other future multilateral conventions of which he is depositary,

> (i) to continue to act as depositary in connexion with the deposit of documents containing reservations or objections, without passing upon the legal effect of such documents; and
> (ii) to communicate the text of such documents relating to reservations or objections to all States concerned, leaving it to each State to draw legal consequences from such communications.

The United States, which had urged abandonment of the unanimity doctrine in its submission in the Genocide Case, voted for the resolution. When the question of reservations to multilateral conventions was subsequently considered by the Assembly in 1959 in connection with the reservation of India to the Inter-Governmental Maritime Consultative Organization Convention, the General Assembly not only reaffirmed its 1952 directive to the Secretary General, cited above, but also extended it to cover all conventions concluded under the auspices of the United Nations prior to 1952 which did not contain contrary provisions. [78]

Taking as a point of departure that "what is essential to ensure both the effectiveness and the integrity of the treaty is that a sufficient number of States should become parties to it, accepting the great bulk of its provisions," [79] the Commission embarked upon an examination of state practice. It found that

> not infrequently a number of States have, to all appearances, only found it possible to participate in the treaty subject to one or more reservations. . . . [W]hen today the number of negotiating States may be upwards of one hundred States with very diverse cultural, eco-

---

[76] [1951] I.C.J. Rep. 15, 24.

[77] General Assembly Res. 598 (VI), Supp. 20 at 84, U.N. Doc. A/2119 (1952).

[78] General Assembly Res. 1452 B, U.N. General Assembly, 14th Sess., Official Records, Supp. 16, p. 56. See, generally, Schachter, "The Question of Treaty Reservations at the 1959 General Assembly," 54 A.J.I.L. 372 (1960).

[79] I.L.C. Report, note 20 above, at 38, par. 12 of the commentary.

nomic and political conditions, it seems necessary to assume that the power to make reservations without the risk of being totally excluded by the objection of one or even of a few States may be a factor in promoting a more general acceptance of multilateral treaties.[80]

The two basic provisions on reservations are Article 19 on formulation and Article 20 on acceptance of and objection to reservations. The former incorporates the rule in the Genocide Case; the latter the flexible approach endorsed by the General Assembly. The International Law Commission text on formulation of reservations read as follows:

> A State may, when signing, ratifying, accepting, approving or acceding to a treaty, formulate a reservation unless:
> (a) The reservation is prohibited by the treaty;
> (b) The treaty authorizes specified reservations which do not include the reservation in question; or
> (c) In cases where the treaty contains no provisions regarding reservations, the reservation is incompatible with the object and purpose of the treaty.[81]

It seemed to the United States that in the case of a treaty which authorizes specified reservations a categorical rule prohibiting all other reservations was inconsistent with the goal of encouraging general acceptance of multilateral treaties. Not infrequently a point on which a state wishes to reserve may be one which the negotiators did not consider but as to which they would have authorized reservation had a negotiating state raised the matter. ". . . [I]n many instances the essential purpose of including a provision [authorizing reservations to particular provisions] may . . . be to facilitate reservations with respect to certain provisions . . . but not to exclude reservations to other provisions." [82]

In addition to amendments to delete paragraph (b) proposed by the United States and Colombia and the Federal Republic of Germany, omnibus amendments by Spain and the U.S.S.R. to the reservations article envisioned its deletion. Yet after an extended discussion of the subject the committee of the whole by a vote of 23 for, 53 against, with 12 abstentions, rejected deletion of the paragraph.[83] An additional amendment proposed by Poland [84] to insert the word "only" between the words "authorized" and "specified" met the problem raised by the United States and was referred to the drafting committee. Indeed, in introducing this amendment the Polish representative echoed the United States view [85] that the Commission's text of paragraph (b) was "unduly rigid." A number of delegations agreed with this characterization of the Commission's text and, though unwilling to excise the paragraph, favored its being expressed along the more flexible lines suggested by the Polish amendment. There was, accordingly, general support for the drafting committee text which incorporated the Polish proposal in substantially the following terms: [A

---

[80] *Ibid.*   [81] *Ibid.* at 35.

[82] I Analytical Compilation 147; *cf.* Official Records, First Session 108.

[83] *Ibid.* at 135.   [84] U.N. Doc. A/CONF.39/C.1/L.136.

[85] Official Records, First Session 108.

512   THE AMERICAN JOURNAL OF INTERNATIONAL LAW   [Vol. 64

State may, when signing, ratifying, accepting, approving or acceding to a treaty, formulate a reservation unless:] "(b) the treaty provides that only specified reservations, which do not include the reservation in question, may be made. . . ."[86]

Paragraphs 1, 2 and 3 of Article 20 on *Acceptance of and objection to reservations* deal, respectively, with reservations expressly authorized by a treaty, reservations to certain treaties requiring acceptance by all the parties, and reservations to treaties which are constituent instruments of international organizations. Paragraph 4 deals with all other cases. It contains in subparagraphs (a), (b) and (c) "the three basic rules of the 'flexible' system which are to govern the position of the contracting States in regard to reservations to any multilateral treaties not covered by the preceding paragraphs."[87]

Switzerland and the United States introduced amendments[88] to incorporate in paragraph 4 of this article an express reference to the preceding article in order to clarify, in particular, the relationship between the substantive limitations on formulation and the procedural acts of accepting or objecting to a reservation. For example, under the proposed text, a state apparently could have accepted a reservation to a treaty that prohibits reservations, though the results of such action would have been highly problematical. These amendments were referred to the drafting committee, which declined to incorporate them in the provisional text adopted in 1968 or in the final text adopted in 1969. However, the inclusion in the introductory clause of paragraph 4 of the words "unless the treaty otherwise provides" to a considerable extent accomplishes the same objective.

Czechoslovakia introduced an amendment[89] to reverse the presumption in subparagraph (b) of paragraph 4 of the Commission's text that "an objection by another contracting State to a reservation precludes the entry into force of the treaty as between the objecting and reserving State unless a contrary intention is expressed by the objecting State." The same principle contained in the Czech amendment was included in broader amendments proposed by Syria and the U.S.S.R.[90] By a vote of 28 for, 48 against, with 8 abstentions, the committee of the whole rejected these amendments at the 1968 session.[91]

At the outset of the second session the Soviet Union circulated an "Explanatory Memorandum on the Question of Reservations to Multilateral Treaties."[92] The document asserted the traditional Soviet doctrine that "the formulation of a reservation is an act of State sovereignty and does not require acceptance by other States." The thrust of the memorandum, however, dealt with the presumption in subparagraph 4 (b) which was

---

[86] Art. 19 of the Convention. See Official Records, First Session 415 (1968), for drafting committee text.

[87] I.L.C. Report, note 20 above, at 39, par. 21 of commentary.

[88] U.N. Docs. A/CONF.39/C.1/L.97 and A/CONF.39/C.1/L.127 (1968).

[89] U.N. Doc. A/CONF.39/C.1/L.85 (1968).

[90] U.N. Docs. A/CONF.39/C.1/L.94 and A/CONF.39/C.1/L.115 (1968).

[91] Official Records, First Session 135.   [92] U.N. Doc. A/CONF.39/L.3 (1969).

characterized as "a departure from international practice" and "a patent step backward, a retrogression." The paper further asserted that the formulation adopted at the first session would "not only hamper any increase in the number of States bound to one another by future multilateral treaties, but [might] cast doubt on relations under treaties already in force." The paper concluded by re-proposing the substance of the Czech amendment.

In the relatively brief discussion of the U.S.S.R. proposal at the tenth plenary meeting on April 29, 1969, some states which had supported the International Law Commission text of paragraph 4 (b) at the first session, stated that, upon further reflection, they "considered the text approved by the committee of the whole" as "inadequate" and "would accordingly vote for the Soviet amendment." [93] Other states professed an equal willingness to accept either the International Law Commission text or the U.S.S.R. formulation.[94] In his summary statement preceding the vote, Sir Humphrey Waldock, the expert consultant, concluded on the following note:

> . . . as some delegates had pointed out, the problem was merely that of formulating a rule one way or the other. The essential aim was to have a stated rule as a guide to the conduct of States, and from the point of view of substance it was doubtful if there was any very great consideration in favour of stating the rule in one way rather than the other, provided it was perfectly clear. The International Law Commission had discussed various possible ways of formulating the rule; it had not considered that any great question of substance was at issue. The aim had been to find what was the normal intention to attribute to a State. It would appear that the views of members of the International Law Commission and of delegations had been evolving over the past seven or eight years. What was required now was to determine the general sense of the conference regarding the rule it would prefer to include in the convention.[95]

In the ensuing vote the plenary adopted the U.S.S.R. amendment by a vote of 49 for, 21 against, with 30 abstentions,[96] slightly more than the two-thirds majority required under the conference rules. Consequential changes were made in paragraph 3 of Article 21.[97]

Paragraph 5 of Article 20 provides: ". . . unless the treaty otherwise provides, a reservation is considered to have been accepted by a State if it shall have raised no objection to the reservation by the end of a period of twelve months after it was notified of the reservation or by the date on which it expressed its consent to be bound by the treaty, whichever is later." The Commission's commentary cites examples of similar provisions —though for shorter time periods—in existing multilateral conventions and the 1959 Recommendation of the Inter-American Council of Jurists endorsing a one-year rule.[98] The establishment of a cut-off date seems desirable

---

[93] U.N. Doc. A/CONF.39/SR.10 at 15 (Mexico) (1969).

[94] *Ibid.* at 21–22 (Jamaica); at 25 (U.K.).

[95] *Ibid.* 24.

[96] U.N. Doc. A/CONF.39/SR.10 at 25 (1969).

[97] See U.N. Doc. A/CONF.39/L.49 (1969).

[98] I.L.C. Report, note 20 above, at 40.

514   THE AMERICAN JOURNAL OF INTERNATIONAL LAW   [Vol. 64

in principle; many states have already developed procedures for early consideration of reservations to insure against timely failure to object.

In concluding his 1961 lectures on "Reservations to Treaties" at the Hague Academy of International Law, Professor William W. Bishop, Jr., noted that the traditional unanimity rule had been giving way to the flexible system ultimately proposed by the Commission. Although "the older requirement" was "simpler and easier to work with," it had "not satisfied the practical needs of the world's foreign offices." [99] The broad general agreement on the Commission's approach confirms the accuracy of Professor Bishop's observation and affords substantial evidence that the reservations articles fairly reflect contemporary international treaty practice.

Article 24 on *Entry into force* contains a sensible addition to the customary rules on that subject. It specifies that provisions which necessarily require action before the entry into force of the treaty itself, such as those relating to depositary functions, "apply from the time of the adoption of its text." [100]

In his first report in 1956 Sir Gerald Fitzmaurice included the following language in his proposed article on entry into force:

> . . . A treaty may, however, provide that it shall come into force provisionally on a certain date, or upon the happening of a certain event, such as the deposit of a specified number of ratifications. In such cases an obligation to execute the treaty on a provisional basis will arise, but, subject to any special agreement to the contrary, will come to an end if final entry into force is unreasonably delayed or clearly ceases to be probable. [101]

In view of his election to the Court and the pressure for work on other topics, the Commission took no action with respect to the Fitzmaurice proposal. In 1962 Sir Humphrey Waldock proposed a separate article along the lines suggested by Fitzmaurice. [102] The Commission adopted the article after a thorough discussion of state practice had established that the practice had become reasonably common [103] and was continuing to expand, particularly in the area of trade agreements.

At the second reading of the article in 1965, Messrs. Briggs, Lachs, Reuter and Verdross stated that it was not quite accurate to speak of provisional entry into force. [104] In their view states agreed to the provisional application of a treaty rather than to its provisional entry into force. Several members of the Commission also made the point that there was a gap in the article, since no provision was made for termination of provisional entry

---

[99] 103 Recueil des Cours de l'Académie de Droit International 337 (1961, II).

[100] Par. 4.

[101] Fitzmaurice, note 17 above, at 116, par. 1 of article on "Entry into force (Legal effects)."

[102] 1962 I.L.C. Yearbook (I) 259, U.N. Doc. A/CN.4/Ser. A/1962.

[103] Sir Humphrey Waldock subsequently stated: "The Commission as a whole appeared to be firmly of the opinion that it was dealing with a common phenomenon which had become an ordinary part of existing treaty practice." 1965 I.L.C. Yearbook (I) 112, 113, U.N. Doc. A/CN.4/Ser. A/1965.

[104] *Ibid.* at 106–108.

into force. Despite these doubts as to the formulation of the rule, an article along the lines proposed by the special rapporteur was adopted by a vote of 17–0.[105]

The issues raised in the Commission were re-examined at the first session of the conference in Vienna, where nine amendments to the article were introduced; three of these were adopted by the committee of the whole or incorporated in the final article by the drafting committee. A major improvement was acceptance of the view that the treaty did not enter into force provisionally but was applied provisionally. In the committee of the whole Mr. Charles I. Bevans stated that the United States favored deletion of the article on "provisional entry into force" which "merely affirmed a procedure which was possible in the absence of the article . . . [and which] . . . left unanswered the question how provisional force might be terminated." [106] He added that if, however, the article

> was to be retained, the United States delegation would wish to have it amended as follows: first, the words "be applied" should be substituted for "enter into force" in the introductory clause of paragraph 1, the words "shall be applied" for "shall enter into force" in paragraph 1, sub-paragraph (a), and "application" for "entry into force" in paragraph 2. Secondly, a paragraph on the termination of the provisional application of the treaty should be added along the following lines:
> "Provisional application of a treaty or part of a treaty may terminate as agreed by the States concerned or upon notification by one of those States to the other State or States that it does not intend to become definitively bound by the treaty." [107]

As the debate continued it became clear that most other delegations shared our concern as to the formulation of the rule but were not prepared to support deletion. Accordingly, the United States proposal for deletion was not pressed to the vote. Rather, the delegation supported the amendments of Yugoslavia [108] and Belgium [109] to effect the changes described in the United States statement. Both were adopted by a wide margin. The text of Article 25 recommended by the committee of the whole was adopted by a vote of 87–1–14 at the second session.[110]

Paragraph 1 of Article 25 in no way requires a state to agree to provisional application of a treaty. If, however, a state does agree to apply a treaty provisionally pending its entry into force, it may, unless it has agreed otherwise, terminate provisional application by notifying other states which are provisionally applying the treaty that it does not intend to become a party.

---

[105] *Ibid.* at 285. [106] Official Records, First Session 140.
[107] *Ibid.*
[108] U.N. Doc. A/CONF.39/C.1/L.185 (dealing with provisional application) (1968).
[109] U.N. Doc. A/CONF.39/C.1/L.194 (adding new paragraph on termination) (1968).
[110] U.N. Doc. A/CONF.39/SR.11, at 24 (1969).

516   THE AMERICAN JOURNAL OF INTERNATIONAL LAW   [Vol. 64

OBSERVANCE, APPLICATION AND INTERPRETATION OF TREATIES
(ARTICLES 26–38)

Part III of the convention deals with the Observance, Application, and Interpretation of Treaties. The defeat of an attempt to weaken the rule of *pacta sunt servanda* was the most significant action taken by the conference with respect to this part.

The foundation upon which the treaty structure is based is the principle that states must carry out their treaty obligations. The Commission's formulation of this principle was lapidary: "Every treaty in force is binding upon the parties to it and must be performed by them in good faith." Nonetheless, Bolivia, Czechoslovakia, Ecuador, Spain and Tanzania jointly proposed replacing the expression "Every treaty in force" by the words "Every valid treaty." [111] Congo (Brazzaville) proposed redrafting Article 26 to read as follows:

> 1. Treaties which have been regularly concluded and have entered into force are binding upon the parties and must be performed in good faith.
> 2. Good faith is presumed.[112]

Cuba proposed adding after the phrase "in force" the words "in conformity with the provisions of the present Convention." [113]

In the discussions, all of the proponents of amendments stressed their devotion to the principle of *pacta sunt servanda* and urged that the changes proposed were merely clarifications. With the exception of Congo (Brazzaville) and Tanzania, however, each of the states proposing an amendment is involved in a territorial dispute that concerns the continuing validity of treaty obligations.

In urging adoption of the International Law Commission text, Professor Briggs pointed out to the committee that the Commission had dealt with validity of treaties in Part V. He urged that "it would serve no purpose" to insert the word "valid" in Article 26. Indeed, "it might encourage States mistakenly to claim a right of non-performance before any invalidity had been established." As for the amendment submitted by the Congo, he stated that it "weakened the rule in article 26 by casting doubt *ab initio* on every treaty. . . ." [114]

A majority of delegations supported the International Law Commission text but were anxious to avoid forcing a vote. The sponsors of the amendments did not wish to have them voted down. Accordingly, the committee adopted the principle of the International Law Commission text and referred all amendments to the drafting committee,[115] a method which on some occasions was described by Chairman Elias as putting the amendments in the refrigerator. When the article was reported out in its original

---

[111] U.N. Doc. A/CONF.39/C.1/L.118 (1968).
[112] U.N. Doc. A/CONF.39/C.1/L.189 (1968).
[113] U.N. Doc. A/CONF.39/C.1/L.173 (1968).
[114] Official Records, First Session 151.   [115] *Ibid.* at 158.

form, it was approved without vote. In the twelfth plenary meeting it was adopted by 96 votes to none.[116]

A new article (27) on internal law and observance of treaties was proposed by Pakistan [117] and supported by a substantial group of states. It provides that a party may not invoke the provisions of its internal law as justification for its failure to perform a treaty. This is a restatement of a long-standing principle of customary international law. The Harvard Draft had provided:

> Unless otherwise provided in the treaty itself, a State cannot justify its failure to perform its obligations under a treaty because of any provisions or omissions in its municipal law, or because of any special features of its governmental organization or its constitutional system.[118]

Section 140 of the *Restatement of the Foreign Relations Law of the United States* provides:

> The duty of a state to give effect to the terms of an international agreement to which it is a party, as stated in § 138, is not affected by a provision of its domestic law that is in conflict with the agreement or by the absence of domestic law necessary for it to give effect to the terms of the agreement.[119]

The Commission had not included the principle in its draft articles because it considered the point to fall within the law of state responsibility rather than the law of treaties.[120] In explaining its vote in favor of Article 27 the U.S. Delegation observed:

> There is a hierarchy of differing legal rules in the internal legislation of most States. Constitutional provisions are very generally given primacy. Statutes, resolutions, and administrative provisions, all of which may be authoritative, may have different weights. Treaty provisions, when viewed as internal law, necessarily have to be fitted into that hierarchy.[121]

Article 30 grapples with the thorny problem of successive treaties relating to the same subject matter. Because it was necessary to deal with a variety of disparate situations, the article is somewhat long and complicated. In essence it provides that: (a) if a treaty says it is subject to another treaty, the other treaty governs on any issue of compatibility; (b) as between parties to one treaty who become parties to a second, the second governs on any point where it is incompatible with the first; (c) if some of the parties to the first treaty are not parties to the second treaty, and vice versa, the first governs between a party to both and a party only to the first; the second governs between a party to both and a party only to the second.

[116] U.N. Doc. A/CONF.39/SR.12, at 15 (1969).

[117] U.N. Doc. A/CONF.39/C.1/L.181 (1968).

[118] 29 A. J. I. L. Supp. 653, at 662 (1935), Art. 23, "Excuses for failure to perform."

[119] Restatement, note 39 above, at 430.

[120] Official Records, First Session 158 at par. 73 (Sir Humphrey Waldock).

[121] U.N. Doc. A/CONF.39/SR.13, at 3 (1969).

518   THE AMERICAN JOURNAL OF INTERNATIONAL LAW   [Vol. 64

In formulating these proposals the Commission had been troubled by how to deal with a second treaty which involved a breach of the first treaty. Lauterpacht had suggested that in such circumstances the second treaty should be considered void.[122] Fitzmaurice posited invalidity on narrower grounds[123]—prohibition in the first treaty of an inconsistent second treaty or a direct breach of the first treaty necessarily occasioned by the second treaty. These proposals were substantially akin to Article 22 of the Harvard Draft,[124] although that article speaks of frustration of the purpose of the first treaty.

Waldock abandoned the invalidity aspect, pointing out that the jurisprudence of the Permanent Court, particularly in the *Oscar Chinn* and *European Commission of the Danube* cases, had rejected inconsistency as a ground of invalidity.[125] He was also impelled by the practical difficulties of defining the circumstances that would support a claim of invalidity in cases of successive treaties. This viewpoint prevailed both in the Commission and in the conference, and the article was debated and adopted without doctrinal disputes.[126]

The net effect of Article 30 is to lay down a series of principles of interpretation to determine priorities among incompatible obligations. It leaves the consequences of assigning the priorities aside. As the commentary to the Commission's draft articles points out,

> The rules . . . determine the mutual rights and obligations of the . . . parties merely *as between themselves*. They do not relieve any party to a treaty of any international responsibilities it may incur by concluding or by applying a treaty the provisions of which are incompatible with its obligations towards another State under another treaty.[127]

Nevertheless, the convention does not relegate this problem of incompatibility completely to the realm of state responsibility. Paragraph 5 of the article, while specifically reserving the question of state responsibility, also reserves as to the application of Article 41, which relates to agreements to modify multilateral treaties between certain of the parties only.

The articles on interpretation demonstrate that a quite conservative (even old-fashioned) series of rules would be accepted by the conference if endorsed by the Commission. Articles 31 and 32 deal, respectively, with the general rule and supplementary means of interpretation. The Commission's formulation established a hierarchy of sources in which primacy was accorded to the text.[128]

---

[122] Lauterpacht, (First) Report on the Law of Treaties, note 16 above, at 156 (1953) (Art. 16, par. 1).

[123] Fitzmaurice, Third Report on the Law of Treaties, 1958 I.L.C. Yearbook (II) 27, U.N. Doc. A/CN.4/115 (1958) (Art. 18, par. 8).

[124] 29 A. J. I. L. Supp. 653, at 661–662 (1935).

[125] Waldock, Second Report on the Law of Treaties, 1963 I.L.C. Yearbook (II) 56–59, U.N. Doc. A/CN.4/156 and Add.1–3 (1963).

[126] Official Records, First Session 164–166.

[127] I.L.C. Report, note 20 above, at 48.   [128] *Ibid.* 49 (par. 2 of commentary).

Paragraph 1 of Article 31 requires that a treaty be "interpreted in good faith in accordance with the ordinary meaning to be given to the terms of the treaty in their context and the light of its object and purpose." Context is narrowly defined as comprising, "in addition to the text, including its preamble and annexes," related agreements made by all the parties and instruments made by less than all the parties but accepted by all as related to the treaty.[129] Paragraph 3 of Article 31, listing elements "extrinsic to the text" which shall be "taken into account" in interpretation, is limited to subsequent agreements between the parties, subsequent practice establishing agreement and relevant rules of international law.

Article 32 allows "supplementary means of interpretation" to be resorted to, "including preparatory work on the treaty and the circumstances of its conclusion, in order to confirm the meaning resulting from the application of article 31, or to determine the meaning when the interpretation according to article 31: (a) leaves the meaning ambiguous or obscure; or (b) leads to a result which is manifestly absurd or unreasonable."

A member of the Commission has observed that the method of presentation in both Articles 31 and 32 "is designed to stress the dominant position of the text itself in the interpretative process." [130]

In the Commission Messrs. Briggs,[131] El Erian,[132] Rosenne[133] and Tsuruoka[134] supported a proposal to combine the substance of Articles 31 and 32 into a single article. In addition, Mr. Bartoš[135] stated that he was inclined to favor the proposal, and Mr. Amado that he had no strong feelings either way. Among the governments which in their comments on the Commission's articles criticized treating the *travaux préparatoires* as a secondary means of interpretation were Hungary[136] and the United States.[137]

In light of the division in the Commission on the subject, the expressions of concern in governmental comments, and the traditional United States position in favor of according equal weight to *travaux*, the United States formally proposed an amendment, the principal objective of which was to eliminate the hierarchy between the sources of evidence for interpretation of treaties by combining the articles containing the general rule and the supplementary means of interpretation:

> A treaty shall be interpreted in good faith in order to determine the meaning to be given to its terms in the light of all relevant factors, including in particular:
>   (a) the context of the treaty;
>   (b) its objects and purposes;
>   (c) any agreement between the parties regarding the interpretation of the treaty;

---

[129] Par. 2.

[130] Rosenne, "Interpretation of Treaties in the Restatement and the International Law Commission's Draft Articles: A Comparison," 5 Col. J. Transnat'l. Law 205, 221 (1966).

[131] 1966 I.L.C. Yearbook (I, Pt. II) 187, 202, U.N. Doc. A/CN.4/Ser. A/1966.

[132] *Ibid.* at 204.   [133] *Ibid.* at 187, 205.

[134] *Ibid.* at 200.   [135] *Ibid.* at 202.

[136] Analytical Compilation, note 27 above, at 201–202.

[137] *Ibid.* at 203.

(d) any instrument made by one or more parties in connexion with the conclusion of the treaty and accepted by the other parties as an instrument related to the treaty;

(e) any subsequent practice in the application of the treaty which establishes the common understanding of the meaning of the terms as between the parties generally;

(f) the preparatory work of the treaty;

(g) the circumstances of its conclusion;

(h) any relevant rules of international law applicable in the relations between the parties;

(i) the special meaning to be given to a term if the parties intended such term to have a special meaning.

In introducing the amendment[138] Professor McDougal adverted to the practice of Ministries of Foreign Affairs in looking at the *travaux* when considering a problem of treaty interpretation and to the practice of international tribunals, as illustrated by the *Lotus* case, of looking at the preparatory work before reaching a decision on the interpretation of a treaty described as "sufficiently clear in itself." [139]

In the ensuing debate in the committee of the whole, the U.S. amendment received scant support. A principal source of arguments against it was the 1950 debates in the Institute of International Law which had adopted the textual approach. Fear was expressed that "too ready admission of the preparatory work" would afford an opportunity to a state which had "found a clear provision of a treaty inconvenient" to allege a different interpretation "because there was generally something in the preparatory work that could be found to support almost any intention." [140] Other arguments advanced included the assertion that recourse to *travaux* would favor wealthy states with large and well-indexed archives, fear that non-negotiating states would hesitate to accede to multilateral conventions, since they could hardly be aware of or wish to have their rights based on recourse to the *travaux,* and the characterization of the International Law Commission text as a "neutral and fair formulation of the generally recognized canons of treaty interpretation." Given the tenor of the debate, the rejection of the amendment was a foregone conclusion.

The adoption by the conference of two articles which the United States viewed as somewhat archaic and unduly rigid does not seriously weaken the value of the convention. It seems unlikely that Foreign Offices will cease to take into consideration the preparatory work and the circumstances of the conclusion of treaties when faced with problems of treaty interpretation, or that international tribunals will be less disposed to consult Article 32 sources in determining questions of treaty interpretation.[141]

---

[138] U.N. Doc. A/CONF.39/C.1/L.156 (1968).

[139] Official Records, First Session 167.

[140] *Ibid.* 170, Jiménez de Aréchaga (Uruguay) citing the remarks of Sir Eric Beckett in the Institute's debates.

[141] *Cf.* Gross, "Treaty Interpretation: The Proper Rôle of an International Tribunal," 1969 Proceedings, American Society of International Law 108, 117.

The reaction of the conference to a United States amendment[142] to Article 33, which deals with interpretation of plurilingual treaties, was more favorable. The amendment was referred to the drafting committee, which incorporated it in paragraph 4. The new rule provides that when a treaty has been authenticated in two or more languages, neither of which has been accorded priority, and a difference in meaning persists after recourse to the other articles on interpretation, "the meaning which best reconciles the texts, having regard to the object and purpose of the treaty, shall be adopted."

Articles 34 through 38 deal with treaties and third states. The first three of these derive from the principle *pacta tertiis nec nocent nec prosunt;* treaties neither impose any burdens nor confer any benefits upon third states.

Article 18 of the Harvard Draft formulated the rule somewhat more succinctly than the International Law Commission:

> (a) A treaty may not impose obligations upon a State which is not a party thereto.
> (b) If a treaty contains a stipulation which is expressly for the benefit of a State which is not a party or a signatory to the treaty, such State is entitled to claim the benefit of that stipulation so long as the stipulation remains in force between the parties to the treaty.[143]

The commentary explains why the Commission found it necessary to treat the topic in three articles. Members of the Commission were agreed that the *pacta tertiis* rule was well established in international law. All members shared the view that there are no exceptions to the rule as regards obligations, but there was a difference of opinion as to whether a treaty may of its own force confer rights upon a non-party. The Commission decided, therefore, to express the general principle in Article 34 and to deal separately in Articles 35 and 36[144] with treaties imposing obligations on third states and those granting rights to such states.[145]

The comments of governments on these three articles were generally laudatory. The new states, in particular, underlined the importance of the principles which they express.

Two significant attempts were made to change these articles at the first session of the conference. Venezuela proposed combining them into the first paragraph of a single article dealing with treaties and third states.[146] The Venezuelan amendment would have required "express consent" of third states both to treaties establishing obligations and to those conferring benefits. In light of the hostile reaction to this proposal, it was withdrawn.

Finland proposed deleting the second sentence of paragraph 1 of Article 36, which would have eliminated the presumption that a third state assented to a right provided for in a treaty "so long as the contrary [was] not in-

---

[142] U.N. Doc. A/CONF.39/C.1/L.197 (1968).

[143] 29 A. J. I. L. Supp. 653 at 661 (1935).

[144] The formulation of Art. 36 was calculated to avoid doctrinal arguments as to whether the institution of *stipulation pour autrui* is recognized in international law. I.L.C. Report, note 20 above, at 59.

[145] *Ibid.* at 57.

[146] U.N. Doc. A/CONF.39/C.1/L.305/Rev.1 (1968).

dicated."[147] The Finnish proposal was defeated by a vote of 25 for, 46 against, with 17 abstentions.

Article 37, which deals with the position of third states with respect to revocation or modification of .rights or obligations, was adopted without difficulty. It is interesting to compare the rule in Article 37 with that adopted by the American Law Institute in the *Restatement of Foreign Relations Law of the United States*.[148]

According to the International Law Commission's commentary, the purpose of the final article on treaties and third states was to include a "general reservation stating that nothing in [the preceding articles in that section] precludes treaty rules from becoming binding on non-parties as customary rules of international law."[149] The Commission emphasized that the provision "is purely and simply a reservation designed to negate any possible implication from articles [34] to [37] that the draft articles reject the legitimacy of the above-mentioned process."[150]

At the first session of the conference the delegations of Finland and Venezuela urged deletion of the article on the ground that the matter was beyond the scope of the law of treaties. By the substantial margin of 14 for, 63 against, with 18 abstentions, the amendments were rejected.[151] Amendments by Syria and Mexico to add at the end of the article the words "recognized as such" and "or as a general principle of law" were adopted; the former by a vote of 59 for, 15 against, with 17 abstentions; the latter by a vote of 38 for, 28 against, with 28 abstentions.[152] The resulting text,[153] which reads as follows, received careful scrutiny at the second session:

> Nothing in articles [34] to [37] precludes a rule set forth in a treaty from becoming binding upon a third State as a customary rule of international law, recognized as such, or as a general principle of law.

A number of delegates pointed out that the words "or as a general principle of law" created substantial difficulty and urged their deletion. In an unusual action, the plenary then reversed the committee of the whole and deleted the words added by the Mexican amendment by a vote of 50 to 27, with 19 abstentions. Immediately thereafter, it adopted the amended text by a substantial majority.[154]

---

[147] U.N. Doc. A/CONF.39/C.1/L.141 (1968).

[148] § 156. Consent of Parties

An international agreement may be modified, suspended, or terminated by the consent of the parties, except that when an international agreement confers a right, as indicated in § 139, upon a state not a party to the agreement, the consent of that state is required for the modification, suspension, or termination of the right, if either

(a) the agreement provides for acceptance of the right and it has been accepted, or

(b) there is no such provision but the state has changed its position in reliance upon the continuing existence of the right and its modification, suspension, or termination would be a substantial detriment to the state.

[149] I.L.C. Report, note 20 above, at 61.   [150] *Ibid.*

[151] Official Records, First Session 201.   [152] *Ibid.*

[153] *Ibid.* at 444.

[154] U.N. Doc. A/CONF.39/SR.15, at 17 (1969).

In view of the traditional Soviet view of international custom, few delegates can have been surprised when the Soviet representative proceeded to explain that "his delegation had voted for article 38 on the understanding that a rule set forth in a treaty could become binding on a third State as a customary rule [only] if the third State recognized that rule and accepted it as binding." [155]

A number of governments in their comments on the International Law Commission's articles on treaties and third states stated that the rule in Article 35 should not apply with respect to treaty provisions imposed upon an aggressor state in consequence of action taken with respect to such states in conformity with the Charter of the United Nations. A similar point was made with respect to the rule in Article 52 on coercion of a state by the threat or use of force. The point was noted in the Commission's commentary to each of those articles. To deal with these problems Sir Humphrey Waldock proposed a new article. Although some members of the Commission questioned the need for a general reservation to deal with treaties imposing an obligation on an aggressor state "in consequence of measures taken in conformity with the Charter of the United Nations with reference to that State's aggression," a majority of the Commission concluded that such a reservation would serve a useful purpose. Amendments[156] proposed by Japan and Thailand which would have deleted the word "aggressor" were defeated by lopsided majorities and the substance of the Commission's text adopted as Article 75.

AMENDMENT AND MODIFICATION OF TREATIES (ARTICLES 39–41)

Article 40 on the amendment of multilateral treaties provides needed clarification in an area of treaty law in which there had been a good deal of custom but relatively little formulation of customary international law. The Harvard Draft, for example, has no provisions regarding amendment, and the subject is not even mentioned in the Eighth Edition of Oppenheim's *International Law* (1955). As the Commission's commentary points out, "the development of international organization and the tremendous increase in multilateral treaty-making have made a considerable impact on the process of amending treaties." [157] A mere glance at the maze of supplementary protocols, declarations of rectification and implementing agreements spawned by the General Agreement on Tariffs and Trade is convincing proof.

Article 40 provides residuary rules that safeguard the rights of parties to a treaty to participate in the amending process by requiring notification to all parties of any proposed amendment and by specifying their right to participate in the decision to be taken on the proposal and in the negotiation and conclusion of any amendatory agreement. The right to become party to the new agreement is also extended to every state entitled to become a party to the treaty.

[155] *Ibid.; cf.* Official Records, First Session 201 (Mr. Khlestou).
[156] U.N. Docs. A/CONF.39/C.1/L.366 and A/CONF.39/C.1/L.367 (1968).
[157] I.L.C. Report, note 20 above, at 62.

Paragraphs 4 and 5 contain a much needed clarification of the relationships between the various parties to an original treaty and a series of amending agreements, particularly with regard to a state that becomes a party to an amended treaty. In that case, the state, unless it expresses a different intention, becomes both a party to the treaty as amended and a party to the unamended treaty vis-à-vis any party to the treaty not bound by the amendment.

The distinction between Article 40 on amendments and Article 41 on modification is based upon whether the proposal to change the treaty is directed to all the parties or only a part of them. The Commission's rationale for Article 41 was that it dealt not with the amendment of a treaty but with an *inter se* agreement "in which two or a small group of parties set out to modify the treaty between themselves alone without giving the other parties the option of participating in it. . . ." [158] The commentary indicates considerable dubiety in the Commission regarding such agreements: "An *inter se* agreement is more likely [than an amendment] to have an aim and effect incompatible with the object and purpose of the treaty. History furnishes a number of instances of *inter se* agreements which substantially changed the régime of the treaty and which overrode the objections of interested States. . . ." [159] Reflecting this view, Article 41 provides:

> 1. Two or more of the parties to a multilateral treaty may conclude an agreement to modify the treaty as between themselves alone if:
> (a) the possibility of such a modification is provided for by the treaty; or
> (b) the modification in question is not prohibited by the treaty and:
>
>> (i) does not affect the enjoyment by the other parties of their rights under the treaty or the performance of their obligations;
>> (ii) does not relate to a provision, derogation from which is incompatible with the effective execution of the object and purpose of the treaty as a whole.

Moreover, paragraph 2 lays down the procedural requirement that the parties contemplating such a modification agreement must notify the other parties to the treaty of their "intention" to conclude the agreement and what the "modification" is, unless the treaty itself dispenses with the requirement. This cautionary approach is a reasonable one, even though the vast majority of *inter se* agreements are unexceptionable. As Jiménez de Aréchaga, the distinguished Uruguayan jurist, pointed out in the committee of the whole, regional arrangements are an important example of *inter se* agreements:

> In technical conventions, such as those on air navigation or postal relations, the *inter se* procedure had become a necessity of everyday international life and to prohibit such agreements, or render them unnecessarily difficult, would give to a single party a right of veto in matters when there was a genuine need to keep abreast of developments.[160]

---

[158] *Ibid.* at 65.   [159] *Ibid.*
[160] Official Records, First Session 206.

The strict limitations on action listed in Article 41 do not apply if the action to amend is instituted under Article 40. Some concern was expressed in the committee of the whole that selection of the one or the other approach might be based upon an intent to avoid a particular procedural require-ment.[161] The likelihood appears small, however, and while there may be some overlapping of amendments and modifications, the basic distinction is fair and workable.

The only instance in which the conference completely deleted one of the Commission's draft articles was in connection with the articles on amend-ment and modification. The International Law Commission had proposed an article on modification of treaties by subsequent practice.[162] The text read as follows:

> A treaty may be modified by subsequent practice in the application of the treaty establishing the agreement of the parties to modify its provisions.

In its commentary on the article, the Commission relied for precedent upon the 1963 decision in the arbitration between France and the United States regarding the interpretation of the bilateral 1946 Air Transport Services Agreement.[163] The tribunal, in language quoted in the commentary, speaks of a modification by practice at the outset of its consideration of the effect of the parties' actions on Pan American's right to serve Tehran. In con-cluding its consideration of this aspect of the case, however, the tribunal, in affirming the right, said that the right was accorded "by virtue of an agree-ment that implicitly came into force at a later date" than the 1946 Agree-ment.[164] This would seem to lean toward an amendment rather than a modi-fication approach. It might be noted that in discussions in the Commission, support for the position was based upon the *Temple of Preah Vihear* case,[165] although the Court's decision does not go into any discussion of a modifica-tion-by-practice theory.

Substantial concern over the unpredictable effects of the article was expressed in the committee of the whole. The U.S. Delegation urged de-letion of the article. It voiced concern that relatively low-ranking officials might interpret a treaty erroneously and follow a course of conduct which, unknown to governments, could lead to modification of the treaty. Some of the African states also expressed concern. On a roll-call vote, 54 states voted for deletion of the article; only 15 voted for its retention.[166]

INVALIDITY, TERMINATION AND SUSPENSION OF THE OPERATION OF TREATIES (ARTICLES 42–72)

In dealing with Part V on the Invalidity, Termination and Suspension of the Operation of Treaties, the concern of former colonies that changes in the

---

[161] *Cf.* remarks of the French representative (de Bresson) *ibid.*
[162] I.L.C. Report, note 20 above, at 65.
[163] Digested in 58 A.J.I.L. 1016 (1964); *cf.* 3 Int. Legal Materials 668, 713 (1964).
[164] *Ibid.* at 716.
[165] 1966 I.L.C. Yearbook (I, Pt. II) 168, U.N. Doc. A/CN.4/Ser.A/1966.
[166] Official Records, First Session 207–215.

Commission's draft articles would adversely affect their interests was a formidable obstacle to improvements, particularly with respect to disputes-settlement procedures, which the United States considered were badly needed. Part V, in which the previously cited article on fraud is to be found, had occasioned the greatest difficulty in the Commission, contained the greatest number of unresolved difficulties, and had the greatest appeal to the newer states.

The expressed intention of the Commission with respect to these articles was exemplary. "As a safeguard for the stability of treaties," it wished to provide that "the validity and continuance in force of a treaty is the normal state of things which may be set aside only on the grounds and under the conditions provided for in the present articles." [167] The execution of the intention, however, required the Commission to produce a series of articles to deal with all the grounds on which a claim could legitimately be made that a treaty was invalid or subject to termination, denunciation, withdrawal or suspension. This required the Commission to include a variety of grounds for claiming invalidity which were essential for complete coverage but which had arisen rarely, if at all, in international law.

Nonetheless, Part V as proposed by the Commission contained a variety of safeguards to protect the stability of the treaty structure. Article 42 carries out the Commission's intention to subject all challenges of the continuing force of treaty obligations to the rules of the convention. The termination of a treaty, its denunciation or suspension, or the withdrawal of a party may take place only as a result of the application of the provisions of that treaty or of the convention. [168] Article 43 is a cautionary rule which makes clear that a state that sheds a treaty obligation does not escape any similar obligation to which it is subject under international law independently of the treaty.

Article 44 deals with separability of treaty provisions. Paragraph 3 requires separability with respect to certain grounds of invalidity, termination and suspension, such as error and impossibility, when the ground relates solely to particular clauses, and where criteria as to feasibility and equity are met. A United States amendment to add to those criteria the requirement that "continued performance of the remainder of the treaty would not be unjust" [169] was adopted. In fraud and corruption cases the complaining party is given an option, while in coercion and peremptory norm cases the treaty must be dealt with as a unit. Efforts to modify this limitation with respect to a peremptory norm that affected only a separable part of a treaty failed.

The rule in Article 45 is described in the Commission's commentary as one of "good faith and fair dealing." [170] The formulation proposed is derived in large part from two cases decided by the International Court of Justice, the *Arbitral Award made by the King of Spain* [171] and the *Temple*

[167] I.L.C. Report, note 20 above, at 66.
[168] Art. 42, par. 2.
[169] Official Records, First Session 389.
[170] I.L.C. Report, note 20 above, at 68.
[171] [1960] I.C.J. Rep. 213–214.

of Preah Vihear.[172] The requirements will afford substantial protection against ill-founded efforts to avoid meeting treaty obligations. A state is prohibited from claiming a treaty is invalid on grounds of lack of competence, restrictions on authority to consent, error, fraud or corruption, or from terminating or suspending the operation of a treaty on the ground of material breach or fundamental change of circumstances if, after becoming aware of the facts, it expressly agrees the treaty is valid or is to remain in effect or (and this would be the usual case) is considered to have acquiesced by reason of its conduct in the validity of the treaty or its maintenance in force or effect.[173] The United Kingdom representative made the point during debate in the committee of the whole that the article was concerned with acquiescence rather than estoppel. (Waldock in his second report had cast the rule in terms of preclusion or waiver.)[174] Consequently the principle of estoppel would apply, under customary law, "to any article of the convention except those on coercion and *jus cogens.*"[175]

In its commentary the Commission points out the need for a rule, in addition to those providing general protection against risk of abuse of the articles in Part V, for the case in which

> a State, after becoming aware of an essential error in the conclusion of the treaty, an excess of authority committed by its representative, a breach by the other party, etc., may continue with the treaty as if nothing had happened, and only raise the matter at a much later date when it desires for quite other reasons to put an end to its obligations under the treaty. The principle [in Article 45] places a limit upon the cases in which such claims can be asserted with any appearance of legitimacy.[176]

In order to provide further insurance against the risk of abuse, the United States joined with Guyana in proposing an amendment in the nature of a statute of limitations that would have barred a state from challenging the validity of a treaty after it had been in force for ten years.[177] The proposal was defeated 42 to 21, with 26 abstentions, by a combination of the votes of those states that wished to reopen or preserve old claims and the group that was opposed to changes in the Commission's text as a matter of principle. While the amendment would have been a worthwhile clarification, the principle it supports is embodied in the language of Article 45 as adopted, though with less precision.

Although the opposition of developing states to changes in the Commission's text led to the rejection of a series of amendments that the United States Delegation considered improvements, the same type of opposition led to the defeat of a series of amendments that would have impaired the value of the convention and threatened the stability of the treaty structure. An apt illustration was another amendment[178] to Article 45 sponsored by

---

[172] [1962] I.C.J. Rep. 23–32. [173] Art. 45.
[174] Waldock, note 125 above, at 39–40. [175] Official Records, First Session 398.
[176] I.L.C. Report, note 20 above, at 68–69.
[177] U.N. Doc. A/CONF.39/C.1/L.267 and Add.1 (1968).
[178] U.N. Doc. A/CONF.39/C.1/L.251 and Add. 1 to 3 (1968).

528   THE AMERICAN JOURNAL OF INTERNATIONAL LAW   [Vol. 64

Bolivia, Byelorussia, Colombia, Congo (Brazzaville), the Dominican Republic, Guatemala, the Soviet Union and Venezuela to gut the article by deleting the rule regarding acquiescence by reason of conduct. Each of the Latin American sponsors of the amendment is involved in a boundary dispute. Spain, which put forward a more sophisticated proposal for weakening the article,[179] also is concerned in a territorial dispute. The eight-Power amendment was defeated 47 to 20, with 27 abstentions; the Spanish proposal, 40 to 25, with 25 abstentions.[180]

The appearance of the Soviet Union as a sponsor of this amendment has curious aspects. With the assortment of actual or potential territorial disputes that face the Soviet Union, its interests would apparently have been served better by supporting proposals to strengthen the conclusive effect of treaty settlements rather than joining in efforts to weaken the stability of the treaty structure. Yet in a number of instances, such as the direct assault upon Article 45, the Soviet Delegation joined in supporting proposals that would have undermined the *pacta sunt servanda* principle [181] and almost without exception opposed proposals that would have strengthened it.

Section 2 of Part V (Articles 46 through 53) sets forth the grounds on which claims of treaty invalidity must be based. The United States comments on the draft articles submitted to the General Assembly in 1967 underlined its concern with the high level of abstraction characteristic of the invalidity articles.[182] The prior discussion of Article 49 on fraud illustrates the nature of this concern. The Commission had proposed an article that left wide open the question of what constitutes fraud. The Commission's commentary frankly admitted that the scope of the concept is not the same in all systems.[183] The "paucity of precedents" in international law "means that there is little guidance to be found either in practice or in the jurisprudence of international tribunals as to the scope to be given to the concept." [184] In these circumstances, the Commission decided not to attempt to define fraud.

The decision itself was not without precedent, as Article 31 of the Harvard Draft had not defined fraud. The comment remarks that there is ". . . a general agreement among jurists as to the essential characteristics of fraudulent conduct. It may be said that its distinguishing characteristic is that the act was done with a willful intent to deceive another." [185]

The United States, in the committee of the whole, proposed adding two elements of definition to the article: reasonable reliance upon the fraudulent conduct and the material importance of the conduct in inducing the consent of the other party.[186] The amendment was defeated. A proposal

---

[179] U.N. Doc. A/CONF.39/C.1/L.272 (1968).
[180] Official Records, First Session 401.
[181] See, *e.g.*, remarks by Mr. Talalaev, Official Records, First Session 152.
[182] II Analytical Compilation, note 27 above, at 242 (1968).
[183] I.L.C. Report, note 20 above, at 73.   [184] *Ibid.*
[185] 29 A. J. I. L. Supp. 653, 1145 (1935).
[186] U.N. Doc. A/CONF. 39/C.1/L.276 (1968).

by Chile and Malaysia to delete the article as unnecessary in view of the lack of precedent was defeated by the overwhelming vote of 74 to 8.[187]

Article 49 was considered in the committee of the whole in conjunction with Article 50, which permits a state to invalidate its consent to be bound by a treaty if the consent was procured by the direct or indirect corruption of its representative by another negotiating state. Chile, Japan and Mexico proposed deletion of the article principally on the ground that the provision was unnecessary because it would fall within the rule on fraud.[188] The proposal gained some support but was defeated 61 to 28. On the other hand, Venezuela and Congo (Brazzaville) introduced amendments [189] to these two articles that would have made treaties procured by fraud or corruption void *ab initio* rather than voidable at the option of the injured state. These were decisively defeated. This, again, illustrated the double-edged effect of the disposition to keep the articles of the Commission in their form as drafted.

The Commission had proposed an article regarding "error in a treaty" that was adopted by the conference without change as Article 48. This article does contain a number of limitations upon invoking error in a treaty as a ground for invalidating consent to be bound. The error must relate to a fact or situation assumed by the complaining state to exist at the time of the treaty's conclusion and forming an essential basis of its consent to be bound. The complaining state is debarred if its own acts contributed to the error or if circumstances were such as to put it on notice "of a possible error." Finally, errors in the wording of the text are specifically excluded from the scope of the article.[190]

The commentary to the Commission's draft recognizes that attempts to invalidate treaties on the ground of error "have not been frequent. Almost all the recorded instances concern geographical errors, and most of them concern errors in maps. . . ."[191] The commentary then points out that in the *Eastern Greenland* and the *Temple of Preah Vihear* cases there is some discussion of error but only as *dicta* and that in the *Readaptation of the Mavrommatis Jerusalem Concessions* case the holding was merely a negative one that if the error did not relate to a matter "constituting a *condition* of the agreement" it was not a basis for invalidation.[192]

The basic rule adopted by the Commission and the conference is essentially the same as that proposed in Article 29(a) of the Harvard Draft:

> A treaty entered into upon an assumption as to the existence of a state of facts, the assumed existence of which was envisaged by the parties as a determining factor moving them to undertake the obligations stipulated, may be declared by a competent international tribunal

---

[187] Official Records, First Session 265.

[188] *Ibid.* 256–257 (remarks of Mr. Suarez on behalf of the co-sponsors).

[189] U.N. Docs. A/CONF.39/C.1/L.259 and Add. 1, and A/CONF.39/C.1/L.261 and Add. 1 (1968).

[190] Art. 79 (p. 559 below) applies to an error of the latter character.

[191] I.L.C. Report, note 20 above, at 72.   [192] *Ibid.* at 73.

or authority not to be binding on the parties, when it is discovered that the state of facts did not exist at the time the treaty was entered into.[193]

There are, of course, two differences. The Harvard Draft requires a tribunal and is limited to mutual mistake. Leaving the first problem aside for the moment, the view expressed in the Harvard Draft that the error must be mutual was based on an analogy drawn from private contract principles. Williston, *Corpus Juris,* and the *Restatement of the Law of Contracts* were cited as authority.[194]

Waldock in his second report had distinguished between mutual and unilateral error.[195] In this he followed the example of Fitzmaurice who had also based his position on private law concepts, particularly as expounded by Cheshire and Fifoot.[196] In the Commission it became clear that while the differentiation proposed was accepted to a certain extent in common law systems, it was not recognized in other legal systems. As a result the distinction was dropped.[197]

The United States introduced a clarifying amendment to the error article which would have required the fact or situation assumed to exist to have been of material importance to the consent to be bound. A second aspect of the proposal was designed to preclude a state from invoking an error as invalidating its consent if that state's own conduct contributed to the error, by adding to paragraph 2 the phrase "or could have avoided it by the exercise of reasonable diligence." [198]

Although the committee of the whole followed its customary practice in rejecting the amendments, the discussions indicated that a number of states considered the points in the United States amendments were substantially implicit in the Commission's draft.[199]

Not every proposal for improvement of the invalidity articles was rejected. The first of the grounds for invalidity, the effect of a limitation of internal law upon competence to conclude treaties, had been proposed by the Commission as follows:

> A State may not invoke the fact that its consent to be bound by a treaty has been expressed in violation of a provision of its internal law regarding competence to conclude treaties as invalidating its consent unless that violation of its internal law was manifest.[200]

The Commission's text represents a compromise between the monist and dualist schools of thought regarding the nature of international law. If international and internal law are unitary, then violation of a domestic law restriction on capacity to make a treaty must, to a monist, invalidate the

[193] 29 A. J. I. L. Supp. 653, 1126 (1935).
[194] *Ibid.* at 1131.   [195] Waldock, note 125 above, at 48–50.
[196] Fitzmaurice, Third Report, note 123 above, at 37 (1958).
[197] 1963 I.L.C. Yearbook (I)43–45 (par. 60), U.N. Doc. A/CN.4/Ser.A/1963.
[198] U.N. Doc. A/CONF.39/C.1/L.275 (1968).
[199] Official Records, First Session 250–254.
[200] I.L.C. Report, note 20 above, at 69.

treaty. On the other hand, if the international legal order exists independently of the internal legal system, then an internal restraint can be effective only internally and cannot impair the validity of consent on the international level to a treaty.

Either view is too extreme for practical purposes and of only hypothetical value in a workaday world. The history of the article in the Commission reflects a rather uneasy movement of thought between the two extreme positions that culminated in a realistic compromise.[201] The process was aided by a number of analyses, principally that of Hans Blix, of the actual practice of states in applying internal rules regarding treaty-making capacity.[202] Blix reached the conclusion that very few internal legal requirements actually went so far as to determine what happens on an international level if those requirements are violated. He found that "(t)he bodies having apparent ability, in general, to secure the performance of treaty obligations are attributed plenary competence under international law to pledge the state."[203]

The Commission in its commentary concluded that its limitation of invalidity claims to cases of manifest violation of internal law was supported by the relatively small body of international adjudication that had dealt with the issue. The commentary then pointed out two additional factors of a practical character that demanded its inclusion:

> When a treaty has been made subject to ratification, acceptance or approval, the negotiating States would seem to have done all that can reasonably be demanded of them in the way of taking account of each other's constitutional requirements. It would scarcely be reasonable to expect each Government subsequently to follow the internal handling of the treaty by each of the other Governments, while any questioning on constitutional grounds of the internal handling of the treaty by another Government would certainly be regarded as an inadmissible interference in its affairs. . . .
>
> The second consideration is that the majority of the diplomatic incidents in which States have invoked their constitutional requirements as a ground of invalidity have been cases in which for quite other reasons they have desired to escape from their obligations under the treaty. . . .[204]

In the committee of the whole an amendment was put forward by Japan and Pakistan to delete the manifest violation limitation. This amendment, which embraced the extreme dualist position, was defeated.[205] Two other amendments which aided considerably in defining the effect of the article were adopted. A Peruvian proposal[206] requiring that the rule of internal law be of fundamental importance was accepted. The United Kingdom

---

[201] For an extended analysis of the genesis of the article see Kearney, "Internal Limitations on External Commitments—Article 46 of the Treaties Convention," 4 International Lawyer 1–21 (1969).

[202] Treaty-Making Power (1960).   [203] *Ibid.* at 393.

[204] I.L.C. Report, note 20 above, at 71 (pars. 8 and 9 of commentary).

[205] Official Records, First Session 246.

[206] U.N. Doc. A/CONF.39/C.1/L.228 (1968).

532   THE AMERICAN JOURNAL OF INTERNATIONAL LAW   [Vol. 64

proposed an amendment defining a manifest violation as one that would be
"objectively evident to any State dealing with the matter" in accordance
with normal practice "and in good faith." This also was accepted.[207]

At the plenary meeting at which the improved article was adopted without any negative votes, the United States Delegation emphasized that it
had supported the article on the basis that it deals solely with the conditions under which a state may invoke internal law on the international
plane to invalidate its consent to be bound and that it in no way impinges
on internal law regarding competence to conclude treaties.[208]

A minor clarifying change was made in Article 47, which deals with
failure of a representative of a state to comply with a specific restriction
upon his authority to express consent to a treaty. The Commission had
made a claim of invalidity dependent upon whether the restriction was
"brought to the knowledge of the other negotiating States" before the representative expressed consent. As a result of concern that knowledge might
be defined to include "constructive knowledge," the requirement was
changed to "unless the restriction was notified to the other negotiating
States. . . ."[209]

Article 51, which voids a treaty procured through coercion of a state's
representative, was adopted in the committee of the whole without change
or extended discussion. The United States and Australia proposed that the
injured state should have the option of determining whether the treaty
should be voided, but a majority agreed with the conclusion of the Commission that the use of force was of such gravity that consent obtained
thereby should be null and void.[210] At the eighteenth plenary meeting a
minor change was made so that the article would cover forms of indirect
coercion such as "threat against the next-of-kin of the representative." [211]

On the other hand, Article 52 on the *Coercion of a State by threat or use
of force* gave rise to a major confrontation. The principle in Article 52 that
treaties imposed by the threat or use of force are void was not challenged in
the extended discussions that continued through five meetings of the committee of the whole. The newer states, in general, took the rule for granted;
the older ones, in general, recognized the evolution described in paragraph 1
of the Commission's commentary:

> (1) The traditional doctrine prior to the Covenant of the League of
> Nations was that the validity of a treaty was not affected by the fact
> that it had been brought about by the threat or use of force. However,
> this doctrine was simply a reflection of the general attitude of inter-
> national law during that era towards the legality of the use of force for
> the settlement of international disputes. With the Covenant and the
> Pact of Paris there began to develop a strong body of opinion which
> held that such treaties should no longer be recognized as legally valid.
> The endorsement of the criminality of aggressive war in the Charters
> of the Allied Military Tribunals for the trial of the Axis war criminals,

---

[207] Official Records, First Session 246.
[208] U.N. Doc. A/CONF.39/SR.18, at 11 (1969).
[209] Official Records, First Session 249.   [210] *Ibid.* at 260–269 *passim.*
[211] U.N. Doc. A/CONF.39/SR.18, at 17 (1969).

the clear-cut prohibition of the threat or use of force in Article 2 (4) of the Charter of the United Nations, together with the practice of the United Nations itself, have reinforced and consolidated this development in the law. The Commission considers that these developments justify the conclusion that the invalidity of a treaty procured by the illegal threat or use of force is a principle which is *lex lata* in the international law of today.[212]

The initiative for amendment of Article 52 came from many of the states which for weeks had been arguing that the International Law Commission's text was sacrosanct. Afghanistan, Algeria, Bolivia, Congo (Brazzaville), Ecuador, Ghana, Guinea, India, Iran, Kenya, Kuwait, Mali, Pakistan, Sierra Leone, Syria, United Arab Republic, United Republic of Tanzania, Yugoslavia and Zambia proposed that the International Law Commission text, which provided that "a treaty is void if its conclusion has been procured by the threat or use of force in violation of the principles of the Charter of the United Nations," [213] be amended by defining force to include any "economic or political pressure." [214]

The nineteen-state amendment was vociferously supported and vehemently attacked in the committee debate. The Commission's commentary had made it clear that the notion of pressure was not included within the meaning of the draft article:

> . . . Some members of the Commission expressed the view that any other forms of pressure, such as a threat to strangle the economy of a country, ought to be stated in the article as falling within the concept of coercion. The Commission, however, decided to define coercion in terms of a "threat or use of force in violation of the principles of the Charter" and considered that the precise scope of the acts covered by this definition should be left to be determined in practice by interpretation of the relevant provisions of the Charter.[215]

The discussion in the Commission underscored this intention.[216]

The proponents of the amendment made it quite clear in the committee of the whole that their amendment was directed toward "economic needs." The representative of Tanzania described "the withdrawal of economic aid or of promises of aid [and] the recall of economic experts" as the type of conduct which should be prohibited.[217] The Algerian representative advanced the thesis:

> . . . the era of the colonial treaty was past or disappearing, but there was no overlooking the fact that some countries had resorted to new and more insidious methods, suited to the present state of international relations, in an attempt to maintain and perpetuate bonds of subjection. Economic pressure, which was a characteristic of neo-colonialism, was becoming increasingly common in relations between certain countries and the newly independent States.

[212] I.L.C. Report, note 20 above, at 75.   [213] *Ibid.*
[214] U.N. Doc. A/CONF.39/C.1/L.67/Rev.1/Corr.1 (1968).
[215] I.L.C. Report, note 20 above, at 75.
[216] See, *e.g.,* 1963 I.L.C. Yearbook (I) 211–213, U.N. Doc. A/CN.4/Ser.A/1963.
[217] Official Records, First Session 271.

> Political independence could not be an end in itself; it was even illusory if it was not backed by genuine economic independence. That was why some countries had chosen the political, economic and social system they regarded as best calculated to overcome under-development as quickly as possible. That choice provoked intense opposition from certain interests which saw their privileges threatened and then sought through economic pressure to abolish or at least restrict the right of peoples to self-determination. Such neo-colonialist practices, which affected more than two-thirds of the world's population and were retarding or nullifying all efforts to overcome under-development, should therefore be denounced with the utmost rigour.[218]

Statements of this character reinforced the already deep misgivings as to the effect of the amendment held by the states concerned with the stability of treaties.

The scope of the phrase "threat or use of force" in Article 2, paragraph 4, of the United Nations Charter, as is well known, has been for many years the source of acrimonious dispute. The legislative history of the San Francisco Conference is clear as to its original intent. The Chilean delegate made that point:

> ... The Brazilian delegation to the 1945 San Francisco Conference had proposed the inclusion of an express reference to the prohibition of economic pressure, and its proposal had been rejected. Consquently, any reference to the principles of the Charter in that respect must be a reference to the kind of force which all the Member States had agreed to prohibit, namely, physical or armed force.[219]

The discussions were complicated by the fact that the United Nations Special Committee on Principles of International Law concerning Friendly Relations and Cooperation Among States had been studying the "threat or use of force" issue since 1964, and action by the Conference could only cut across the deliberations of that body. The question was also raised whether the conference was attempting to amend the United Nations Charter.[220] The basic problem was well summed up by the Dutch representative:

> In itself, the rule stated in article [52] was perfectly clear and precise. He supported the principle underlying the article, namely, the principle that an aggressor State should not, in law, benefit from a treaty it had forced its victim to accept. Nevertheless, it must be borne in mind that there was a fundamental difference of opinion as to the meaning of the words "threat or use of force" in Article 2, paragraph 4, of the United Nations Charter. If those words could be interpreted as including all forms of pressure exerted by one State on another, and not just the threat or use of armed force, the scope of article [52] would be so wide as to make it a serious danger to the stability of treaty relations.[221]

The course of the debate had made it clear that if the amendment were put to the vote it would carry by quite a substantial majority. On the other hand, in private discussions it had been made quite clear to the proponents that adoption could wreck the conference because states concerned with the stability of treaties found the proposal intolerable.

---

[218] *Ibid.* at 276.
[220] *Ibid.* at 283.
[219] *Ibid.* at 285.
[221] *Ibid.* at 275.

To reduce tension, discussion of the article was adjourned and private negotiations resorted to. A compromise solution was reached after some days of cooling off. The amendment was withdrawn. In its place, a draft declaration condemning threat or use of pressure in any form by a state to coerce any other state to conclude a treaty was unanimously adopted by the committee.[222] Although at one point during the plenary it appeared that the compromise might be unraveling, it was adhered to by both sides. The declaration finally approved by the conference in 1969 is annexed to the Final Act.[223]

From this heated discussion the committee of the whole moved immediately to one of the most controversial articles produced by the Commission— Article 53 on treaties conflicting with a peremptory norm of international law or, as it is customarily described, the *Jus Cogens* Doctrine. The Commission's proposal was:

> A treaty is void if it conflicts with a peremptory norm of general international law from which no derogation is permitted and which can be modified only by a subsequent norm of general international law having the same character.[224]

Although the principle that there are fundamental requirements of international behavior that cannot be set aside by treaty is considered a fairly recent development, it has been incorporated into Section 116 of the *Restatement of the Foreign Relations Law of the United States* in the following terms:

> An international agreement may be made with respect to any matter except to the extent that the agreement conflicts with
> a) the rules of international law incorporating basic standards of international conduct. . . .[225]

Both the Commission's article and the *Restatement,* however, present the same difficulty: they leave open the question what is a peremptory norm of international law or what is a basic standard of international conduct.

The Commission did not attempt to define a peremptory norm or to provide even an illustrative list of the norms that it considered peremptory. In the commentary to this article, the Commission noted: "The formulation of the article is not free from difficulty, since there is no simple criterion by which to identify a general rule of international law as having the character of *jus cogens.*" [226] The Commission explained the formulation of the article as follows:

> The emergence of rules having the character of *jus cogens* is comparatively recent, while international law is in process of rapid development. The Commission considered the right course to be to provide in general terms that a treaty is void if it conflicts with a rule of *jus cogens* and to leave the full content of this rule to be worked out in State practice and in the jurisprudence of international tribunals. . . .[227]

---

[222] *Ibid.* at 328–329.
[224] I.L.C. Report, note 20 above, at 77.
[226] I.L.C. Report, note 20 above, at 76.

[223] U.N. Doc. A/CONF.39/26.
[225] Restatement, note 39 above, § 116.
[227] *Ibid.*

536   THE AMERICAN JOURNAL OF INTERNATIONAL LAW   [Vol. 64

In his second report Waldock had proposed three categories of *jus cogens:* (a) the use or threat of force in contravention of the principles of the United Nations Charter; (b) international crimes so characterized by international law; (c) acts or omissions whose suppression is required by international law.[228] The discussion in the Commission indicated such varying viewpoints on what constituted *jus cogens*[229] that the categories were dropped. A comment regarding the resulting draft is pertinent: "Mr. Bartoš explained that the drafting committee had been compelled to refrain from giving any definition of *jus cogens* whatever, because two-thirds of the Commission had been opposed to each formula proposed." [230]

The position in the conference reflected the position in the Commission. There was no substantial attack made upon the concept of *jus cogens.* Indeed, it would be very difficult to make a sustainable case that two states are free to make a treaty in which they agree to attack and carve up a third state or to sell some of their residents to each other as slaves.[231] But as Minagawa points out,[232] "examples such as the treaty permitting piracy or re-establishing slavery appear to concern merely 'une pure hypothèse d'école'." The real problem was how to define the test for recognizing a rule of *jus cogens.*

The United States proposed a two-part amendment.[233] The first part— that the article applied only to a treaty which "at the time of its conclusion" violated a peremptory norm—was intended to make clear that a rule of *jus cogens* did not void a treaty retroactively. The second part was designed to incorporate in the article a test by which to determine whether a rule of general international law was *jus cogens*—recognition "in common by the national and regional legal systems of the world" as a peremptory norm "from which no derogation is permitted." A less stringent requirement that the peremptory character of the norm "be recognized by the international community" was proposed by Finland, Greece and Spain.[234]

The debates, which extended through six meetings, revealed considerable opposition to the United States amendment on the ground it was too restrictive and would block the "evolution of *jus cogens.*" The positions taken were, however, less doctrinaire and emotional than the positions taken regarding Article 52. A good number of the Afro-Asian states recognized that a gap existed in the Commission's text.[235] The Ukrainian representative waved the red shirt of colonial treaties in connection with the proposals

---

[228] Waldock, note 125 above, at 52.

[229] 1963 I.L.C. Yearbook (I) 73–78, U.N. Doc. A/CN.4/Ser.A/1963.

[230] *Ibid.* at 214.

[231] There are the attacks by Schwarzenberger (43 Texas Law Review 455; 18 Current Legal Problems 191), to which convincing rebuttals were made by, among others, Verdross (60 A. J. I. L. 55 (1966)) and Schwelb (61 A. J. I. L. 946 (1967)).

[232] Minagawa, *"Jus Cogens in Public International Law,"* 6 Hitotsubashi Journal of Law and Politics 16, at 17 (1968).

[233] U.N. Doc. A/CONF.39/C.1/L.302 (1968).

[234] U.N. Doc. A/CONF.39/C.1/L.306 (1968).

[235] See, *e.g.,* Official Records, First Session 314 (Ethiopia), 319 (Ceylon), 322 (Zambia), 325–326 (Malaysia).

to clarify the article,[236] but this did not touch off any similar denunciations by ex-colonies. The bulk of the criticism was directed to importing the concept of internal law into the *jus cogens* principle.[237]

The Austrian jurist, Hanspeter Neuhold, gives in his analysis of the 1968 session a lively account of the conclusion of debate:

> After five meetings had been devoted to discussing the various problems of jus cogens, the scene was set for the final showdown at a night meeting on 7 May which lasted almost till midnight. It was fought with all the weapons which the arsenal of the rules of procedure offered the delegates. Thus, the representative of the USA introduced a motion to defer the vote on article [53] and to refer all amendments to the Drafting Committee with a view to working out a more acceptable text. This proposal was endorsed by the United Kingdom and France. Conversely, the Ghanaian delegate, who was supported by the representatives of India and the USSR, moved to take a vote immediately, since the various delegations had made their positions sufficiently clear. Motions to adjourn the debate and to close the discussion were defeated. Other motions requesting a division of the original United States proposal caused considerable confusion. At last, a roll call was taken on the motion submitted by the USA to defer voting on article [53] and the amendments thereto, which failed to obtain the necessary majority by the narrowest margin possible: 42 votes were cast in favour, the same number against, with 7 abstentions! Ironically enough, if a request by Ghana for priority of her motion to vote at once had been adopted and the votes cast in the same way, the United States motion would have prevailed indirectly . . . The first part of the substantive amendment introduced by the USA which specified the non-retroactive character of article [53]—which had been stressed by the ILC in its commentary—was adopted, whereas reference to recognition of jus cogens by the national and regional legal systems of the world was rejected. The somewhat similar amendment co-sponsored by Finland, Greece and Spain requesting [sic] recognition by the international community of a peremptory norm was, on the contrary, referred to the Drafting Committee. . . .[238]

A dispute then arose as to the meaning of that vote and whether the principle of *jus cogens* had been adopted. The chairman settled the matter by ruling that the *jus cogens* principle had been adopted and that the drafting committee was to see if the text could be made clearer.[239] In the drafting committee, Dean Sweeney performed superbly in helping frame, against substantial opposition, an addition to Article 53 that achieved the objective of the United States. A peremptory norm was defined as "a norm accepted and recognized by the international community of States as a whole. . . ." [240] At the eightieth meeting, the chairman of the drafting committee, in introducing the revised text, stated that the phrase "as a whole" had been included to avoid any implication that an individual state had a right of

---

[236] *Ibid.* 322.

[237] See, *e.g.*, Official Records, First Session 323 (Philippines), 298 (Nigeria).

[238] Neuhold, "The 1968 Session of the United Nations Conference on the Law of Treaties," 19 Österreichische Zeitschrift für öffentliches Recht 59, at 86 (1969).

[239] Official Records, First Session 334.   [240] *Ibid.* at 471.

veto. The Ghanaian delegate, on the basis that the phrase might be interpreted otherwise, asked for a separate vote on those three words. The phrase was approved 57 votes to 3 with 27 abstentions.[241] No change was made in 1969.

Article 64 is a corollary of Article 53 which provides that if a new peremptory norm of general international law emerges, any existing treaty which is in conflict with that norm becomes void and terminates. There was little discussion of this article at the conference because it is so clearly implicit in the principle of *jus cogens*. The necessity for it as a separate article springs from the fact that different legal consequences attend a treaty that is entered into in violation of an existing rule of *jus cogens* (which is considered as void *ab initio*) and the annulment of an existing treaty by the emergence of a new rule. The differing effects are spelled out in Article 71. In a case falling under Article 53 the parties must:

> (a) eliminate as far as possible the consequences of any act performed in reliance on any provision which conflicts with the peremptory norm of general international law; and
> (b) bring their mutual relations into conformity with the peremptory norm of general international law.[242]

In an Article 64 case, however, "the termination of the treaty:

> (a) releases the parties from any obligation further to perform the treaty;
> (b) does not affect any right, obligation or legal situation of the parties created through the execution of the treaty prior to its termination; provided that those rights, obligations or situations may thereafter be maintained only to the extent that their maintenance is not in itself in conflict with the new peremptory norm of general international law." [243]

Section 3 of Part V is entitled Termination and Suspension of the Operation of Treaties. Articles 54, 55, 57, and 58 are unexceptional, specifying that various aspects of termination and suspension must be dealt with in conformity with the treaty or with the consent of all the parties, or, if by agreement between certain of the parties, subject to the same limitations expressed in Article 41 on agreements to modify.

Paragraph 1 (b) of Article 56 permitting denunciation of or withdrawal from a treaty which includes no provision on the subject if such right "may be implied by the nature of the treaty" was added at the first session of the conference. The United States was concerned that the provision might facilitate unilateral denunciation without regard to procedures for disputes-settlement, since Article 65 did not mention denunciation. The delegation raised the problem in the drafting committee at the second session and established a clear legislative history, including statements by the chairman of the drafting committee,[244] the expert consultant, and the

---

[241] *Ibid.* at 472. [242] Art. 71, par. 1.
[243] Art. 71, par. 2.
[244] U.N. Doc. A/CONF.39/SR. 25, at 2 (1969).

sponsor of the amendment that the procedure of Section 4 of Part V applied to notices of denunciation grounded upon Article 56.

Article 59 restates two long-established rules for deciding whether the termination or suspension of a treaty is effected by a later treaty—the intent of the parties and the compatibility of the two treaties.

The International Law Commission proposed the following article on breach:

> *Termination or suspension of the operation of a treaty as a consequence of its breach*
> 1. A material breach of a bilateral treaty by one of the parties entitles the other to invoke the breach as a ground for terminating the treaty or suspending its operation in whole or in part.
> 2. A material breach of a multilateral treaty by one of the parties entitles:
> (a) The other parties by unanimous agreement to suspend the operation of the treaty or to terminate it either:
> (i) in the relations between themselves and the defaulting State, or
> (ii) as between all the parties;
> (b) A party specially affected by the breach to invoke it as a ground for suspending the operation of the treaty in whole or in part in the relations between itself and the defaulting State;
> (c) Any other party to suspend the operation of the treaty with respect to itself if the treaty is of such a character that a material breach of its provisions by one party radically changes the position of every party with respect to the further performance of its obligations under the treaty.
> 3. A material breach of a treaty, for the purposes of the present article, consists in:
> (a) A repudiation of the treaty not sanctioned by the present articles; or
> (b) The violation of a provision essential to the accomplishment of the object or purpose of the treaty.
> 4. The foregoing paragraphs are without prejudice to any provision in the treaty applicable in the event of a breach.[245]

The point made in the Commission's commentary that "the great majority of jurists recognize that a violation of a treaty by one party may give rise to a right in the other party to abrogate the treaty or to suspend the performance of its own obligations under the treaty"[246] was borne out in the discussions at Vienna. No delegation denied the principle,[247] although several expressed the view that a less strict approach to the article was required. The conference rejected all initiatives to weaken the rather conservative formulation adopted by the Commission.

[245] I.L.C. Report, note 20 above, at 82. [246] *Ibid.*

[247] The commentary to the corresponding article in the Harvard Draft summarizes the traditional international law doctrine regarding breach and demonstrates that the principle has been recognized in United States courts since late in the eighteenth century. 29 A. J. I. L. Supp. 653, 1078 (1935), Comment on Art. 27. For a recent treatment of the subject, see Bhek Pati Sinha, Unilateral Denunciation of Treaty Because of Prior Violations of Obligations by Other Party (1966).

540   THE AMERICAN JOURNAL OF INTERNATIONAL LAW   [Vol. 64

In the debate on the article the U.S. representative noted that the text and commentary served the cause of the stability of treaty relations by providing that a material breach could be invoked by a party to terminate a treaty or suspend its operation but did not produce that effect in itself. However, the article did not clearly indicate when a party invoking breach could suspend the operation of the treaty in whole and when in part. He thought it would be helpful to introduce into the article itself an element of proportionality.[248]   Accordingly, he proposed adding at the end of paragraph one the following language: "as may be appropriate considering the nature and extent of the breach and the extent to which the treaty obligations have been performed."[249]   He also suggested a similar formulation be added at the end of subparagraph (b) of paragraph 2.[250]

The tenor of the debate in the committee of the whole made it clear that no amendment would be possible in the article in 1968.   In light of this attitude the United States Delegation responded positively to the United Kingdom suggestion that the delegation withdraw its amendments to the breach article on the understanding that the principle of proportionality embodied therein would be considered in connection with the separability article, on which a vote had not then been taken.   In the separability context, although attracting substantial support, the principle failed to obtain a majority when put to the vote.   This left before the house amendments by Finland, Spain and Venezuela.   The Finnish amendment might have clarified the text, but adoption of either the Spanish or Venezuelan amendment would have militated against the stability of treaties.   At the conclusion of the debate the committee decisively rejected all three.

An amendment to subparagraphs 2(a) and (c) was introduced by the United Kingdom at the 1969 session and, in most respects, adopted by the plenary.   The article as amended permits separability in cases in which it entitles one or more parties to a multilateral treaty to suspend or to invoke the material breach as a ground for suspending the operation of the treaty. The Conference also adopted a Swiss proposal which appears as paragraph 5 of Article 60:

> 5. Paragraphs 1 to 3 do not apply to provisions relating to the protection of the human person contained in treaties of a humanitarian character, in particular to provisions prohibiting any form of reprisals against persons protected by such treaties.

With regard to most treaties, the rules in paragraphs 1 and 2 of the amended article should suffice to insure that a state will not suffer from unjustified repudiation by another party of its treaty obligations.   The Commission recognized, however, that some treaties may include special provisions on breach.   In such cases, Article 60 would not preclude the parties from applying those special provisions.   Paragraph 4, which reserves

---

[248] Official Records, First Session 354.

[249] U.N. Doc. A/CONF.39/C.1/L.325 (1968).

[250] *Ibid.   Cf.* Restatement, note 39 above, § 158 (1) (c), (1965).

the rights of the parties in such cases, parallels language in §158 (1) of the *Restatement.*[251]

In formulating its article on *Supervening impossibility of performance* the International Law Commission was principally concerned with laying down a rule to govern termination or suspension in cases such as "the submergence of an island, the drying up of a river or the destruction of a dam or hydro-electric installation indispensable for the execution of a treaty." [252] The Commission decided not to include in the article a provision that a party cannot take advantage of a supervening impossibility resulting from its own wrongful act.[253] The conference adopted the substance of the Commission's text but reversed its decision as to the additional provision. The Commission's rule is incorporated in paragraph 1 of Article 61; the well-founded exception, in paragraph 2:

> 1. A party may invoke the impossibility of performing a treaty as a ground for terminating or withdrawing from it if the impossibility results from the permanent disappearance or destruction of an object indispensable for the execution of the treaty. If the impossibility is temporary, it may be invoked only as a ground for suspending the operation of the treaty.
> 2. Impossibility of performance may not be invoked by a party as a ground for terminating, withdrawing from or suspending the operation of a treaty if the impossibility is the result of a breach by that party either of an obligation under the treaty or of any other international obligation owed to any other party to the treaty.

In the debate on paragraph 1, Professor Briggs stated that while the United States did not propose to submit a formal amendment, he wished to draw the attention of the committee to a possible inconsistency in the draft: "Although the first sentence referred to an impossibility of performance resulting from permanent disappearance or destruction, the second sentence appeared to imply that the so-called permanent disappearance or destruction might be only temporary." [254] He suggested eliminating that implication by making it clear that if the object could be replaced suspension rather than termination was the only course of action permissible under that article.

The drafting committee did not adopt the drafting change suggested by Professor Briggs, but it did in large measure resolve the problem. In recommending the text of the article to the committee of the whole the chairman stated that "the drafting committee wished to emphasize that the destruction or disappearance of an object of a treaty did not constitute a permanent impossibility of performance if the object could be replaced." [255]

---

[251] *Ibid.*, note 39 above.

[252] I.L.C. Report, note 20 above, at 84 (1966).

[253] 1966 I.L.C. Yearbook (I, Pt. I) 129–130, U.N. Doc. A/CN.4/Ser.A/1966; *cf. ibid.* 67–75.

[254] Official Records, First Session 362–363.

[255] *Ibid.* at 479.

542   THE AMERICAN JOURNAL OF INTERNATIONAL LAW   [Vol. 64

In introducing the text of paragraph 2, the Netherlands Delegation explained it was "derived from the general principle of law that a party could not take advantage of its own wrong. Article [62] expressly stated that exception, and there was no reason to proceed differently in article [61]. . . ."[256] The debate on the amendment followed a pattern surprisingly different from that on most of the invalidity articles. Although not all delegations endorsed the Netherlands amendment—France, Poland, and Trinidad and Tobago were mildly opposed and Bulgaria characterized it as introducing "a purely subjective factor"[257]—representatives of the Democratic Republic of the Congo, Malaysia, Singapore, the United States and the U.S.S.R. supported the proposal. No delegate urged that the committee uphold the Commission's decision. When put to the vote, the amendment was adopted by a 3-to-1 margin.[258]

Article 62 incorporates a carefully phrased version of the doctrine of *rebus sic stantibus*. The principles expressed in Article 62 may be regarded as largely reflecting existing international law rather than as formulating a new norm. As the commentary states: "Almost all modern jurists, however reluctantly, recognize the existence in international law of the principle with which this article is concerned and which is commonly spoken of as the doctrine of *rebus sic stantibus*."[259] In United States practice the major precedent is the suspension of the International Load Line Convention in 1941.[260]

Professor Lissitzyn has reviewed relevant state practice which either escaped the attention of prior scholars or occurred too late to be incorporated in earlier studies.[261] Lissitzyn points out that parties did not regard their obligations as terminable at will when circumstances had changed; they generally claimed the right to suspend performance. In none of the cases cited is there any indication that the suspending state contemplated review of its claim by an international tribunal in order that suspension of its obligations might be "justified definitively," as the Harvard Draft would have required.

---

[256] *Ibid.* at 362.   [257] *Ibid.* at 363.

[258] *Ibid.* at 365.

[259] I.L.C. Report, note 20 above, at 85 (1966). *Cf.* Art. 28 of the Harvard Draft which provided that a state might be relieved from further performance under "a treaty entered into with reference to the existence of a state of facts the continued existence of which was envisaged by the parties as a determining factor moving them to undertake the obligations stipulated . . . when that state of facts has been essentially changed." 29 A. J. I. L. Supp. 662–663 (1935).

[260] In his opinion supporting the suspension the Acting Attorney General stated:
". . . the implicit assumption of normal peacetime international trade, which is at the foundation of the Load Line Convention, no longer exists.

"Under these circumstances there is no doubt in my mind that the convention has ceased to be binding upon the United States. It is a well-established principle of international law, *rebus sic stantibus*, that a treaty ceases to be binding when the basic conditions upon which it was founded have essentially changed. . . ." 40 Op. Att'y Gen. 119, 121 (1941).

[261] "Treaties and Changed Circumstances (Rebus Sic Stantibus)," 61 A. J. I. L. 895, 902–911 (1967).

The International Law Commission proposed the following text:

> 1. A fundamental change of circumstances which has occurred with regard to those existing at the time of the conclusion of a treaty, and which was not foreseen by the parties, may not be invoked as a ground for terminating or withdrawing from the treaty unless:
> (a) The existence of those circumstances constituted an essential basis of the consent of the parties to be bound by the treaty; and
> (b) The effect of the change is radically to transform the scope of obligations still to be performed under the treaty.
> 2. A fundamental change of circumstances may not be invoked:
> (a) As a ground for terminating or withdrawing from a treaty establishing a boundary;
> (b) If the fundamental change is the result of a breach by the party invoking it either of the treaty or of a different international obligation owed to the other parties to the treaty.[262]

An important feature of the Commission's text (which had not been incorporated in Article 28 of the Harvard Draft) was subparagraph 2 (a) which precluded invocation of the article as a ground for terminating or withdrawing from a treaty establishing a boundary. The United States, which supported this substantial improvement in the formulation of the principle, proposed that subparagraph 2 (a) be broadened to read as follows: "(a) As a ground for terminating or withdrawing from a treaty drawing a boundary or otherwise establishing territorial status."[263] The purpose of the U.S. amendment was to extend the subparagraph to cover "several important groups of treaties, which, while not establishing boundaries, established territorial status or settled territorial disputes."[264] Although there was some support for the U.S. amendment, the committee of the whole rejected the proposal.

In the course of the debate on this article representatives from several African and Latin American states called for deletion of subparagraph 2 (a). Mr. Tabibi (Afghanistan), for example, argued:

> . . . The exceptions stated in paragraph 2 greatly weakened the doctrine by excepting boundary treaties from the general rule, in the name of the stability of treaties but to the detriment of the interests of nations and individuals. He agreed with the Swiss representative that certain treaties establishing a legal régime should not be capable of being voided, but it was wrong to claim that boundary treaties and treaties establishing territorial status, of which the United States representative had spoken, should be excepted from the application of the rule. . . . [Paragraph 2 (a) was] incompatible with the principle of peaceful relations among States, since undue rigidity was a source of disputes. A boundary line was not a geometric line, but determined the fate of millions of human beings. . . . A treaty imposed during the colonial era for colonial or military reasons should not be exempted from the rule. Paragraph 2 (a) should therefore be deleted.[265]

[262] I.L.C. Report, note 20 above, at 18.　　[263] A/CONF. 39/C.1/L.335 (1968).

[264] Official Records, First Session 367.　　[265] *Ibid.* at 373.

On the other hand, a number of African states took the floor to endorse the Commission's text. Typical of these remarks were those of Mr. Mutuale of the Democratic Republic of the Congo:

> . . . his delegation approved of the principle expressed in [the] article. . . . As formulated by the International Law Commission, that principle was based on justice and equity. It was also a useful principle which helped to promote the stability of treaty relations, prevented their violent rupture and provided a remedy for the desperate plight of a State which found itself unable to meet burdensome obligations because the circumstances which had induced it to accept those obligations had ceased to exist, without such an eventuality having been contemplated in the treaty. The principle should however be watered down because its application by States entailed certain risks; it should therefore be made subject to conditions such as the International Law Commission had very wisely provided.[266]

Similar views were expressed by other Africans, by India and Pakistan, by the U.S.S.R. and the Eastern European countries, and, subject to adoption of a satisfactory procedure for settlement of disputes, by a number of Western Europeans. By the end of the discussion it was clear that partisans of the Tabibi view had been severely isolated; they did not press their proposal for deletion of paragraph 2 (a) to the vote.

During the debate on the article the Canadian representative referred to Professor Lissitzyn's suggestion in this JOURNAL that in some cases of changed circumstances suspension rather than termination of the treaty obligation might be appropriate,[267] and proposed an amendment to this effect. A similar proposal was made by Finland. By a vote of 31 for, 26 against, with 28 abstentions, the principle of the amendment was adopted.[268]

A comparison of the International Law Commission's draft article and the text of Article 62 shows very little difference except for the addition of a new paragraph 3 on suspension, which is derived from the Canadian and Finnish amendments, and the replacement in paragraph 1 (b) of the word "scope," which Professor Lissitzyn had characterized as "puzzling,"[269] by "extent."

Given the delicacy of the article and the doctrinal dispute as to whether or not the principle represented an implied term in treaties—a matter which received little attention in the debates—its adoption nearly unchanged in the form proposed is a tribute to the skill with which the International Law Commission had balanced a rule which afforded "a safety-valve in the law of treaties"[270] yet provided protection of the security of treaties by "adequate safeguards . . . against its arbitrary application."[271]

[266] *Ibid.* at 377.
[268] Official Records, First Session 382.
[270] I.L.C. Report, note 20 above, at 86 (par. 6 of commentary).
[271] *Ibid.* (par. 5 of commentary).

[267] 61 A. J. I. L. 916 (1967).
[269] 61 A. J. I. L. 917 (1967).

SETTLEMENT OF DISPUTES

During the debates on the articles on invalidity, suspension and termination, one of the major concerns expressed was the absence in the Commission's draft of any adequate provisions for dealing with an assertion of the invalidity of a treaty or a claim of a right to unilateral termination or suspension. In the explanations of vote that followed adoption of Article 53 on *jus cogens*, for example, Belgium, Canada, Chile, the Federal Republic of Germany, France, Italy, Portugal, Sweden, the United Kingdom and the United States stated that their final positions regarding the article depended upon adoption of a system for impartial settlement of disputes. [272]

The Commission had proposed a procedure for dealing with claims of a state to be released from a treaty obligation under one of the grounds contained in Part V. The state would be required to notify the other parties to the treaty of its claim, of the grounds therefor and of the action to be taken regarding the treaty. If no objection to the proposed action were made within three months, it could then be carried out. If objection were made, then a solution was to be sought through the means indicated in Article 33 of the United Nations Charter.[273]

Article 33 of the Charter merely lays down a catchall rule that disputes should be settled by peaceful means of the parties' own choice. The Commission's procedure left undecided the crucial issue whether a party claiming, for example, the right to withdraw from a treaty could go ahead and withdraw if either it did not agree with the other parties on a peaceful means for settling the dispute or if the peaceful means selected failed to result in a settlement.

This elemental gap in the draft articles had been the subject of considerable adverse comment prior to the conference. In the debate on the Commission's draft articles in the Sixth Committee of the General Assembly in 1967, the United States representative observed that a major weakness of the draft articles was that they

> pointed out a good many ways to begin arguments over the validity . . . of a treaty. But they do not contain any sure methods of settling such arguments. . . . The [procedural] safeguard proposed did not afford real protection. . . .
> Failure to provide for ready recourse to some mandatory means for the impartial settlement of disputes would mean a Convention on the Law of Treaties which would be incomplete, one-sided, and susceptible to misuse.[274]

Improvement of the flawed provisions of the draft article for the settlement of disputes over the continuance in force of a treaty became the major issue of the conference. The states fighting for the stability of the treaty structure were agreed that unless some form of impartial disputes-settlement procedure was incorporated into the Convention on the Law of

---

[272] Official Records, First Session 472–473.
[273] I.L.C. Report, note 20 above, at 89.
[274] 59 Department of State Bulletin 721–722 (1967).

Treaties, the possibility of abuse through claims of unilateral termination on specious or non-existent grounds could negate the great contribution that the convention over-all offered for the development of international law.

The obstacles to incorporation of an adequate disputes-settlement procedure were formidable. Precedent was against the attempt. In previous codification conferences,[275] efforts to include provisions for the settlement of disputes by establishing mandatory jurisdiction in the International Court of Justice had been defeated. The defeats were engineered in each case by procedural maneuvers which resulted in substituting optional protocols that provided for I.C.J. jurisdiction on application of a party to a dispute arising out of the convention concerned. There was, however, no requirement that a party to the convention had also to be a party to the protocol. The inadequacy of the protocols as a substitute for compulsory requirements in the conventions themselves is demonstrated by the fact that in no case have as many as half of the parties to a convention ratified the relevant protocol.[276]

A second obstacle was the fervid and long-standing opposition of the Soviet Union and its associates to any form of impartial decision-making for the settlement of international disputes.[277] This opposition stems in large measure from the basic tenet of the Marxist-Leninist ideology that courts exist to further state policies and not to judge them. To have a tribunal outside the system scrutinizing state action doubled the unacceptability. The Communist bloc was reinforced by a heterogeneous group of states whose opposition to mandatory disputes-settlement derived from a variety of reasons. The Arab states were almost solidly opposed, as were India, Indonesia, Kenya, and Tanzania, to give a few prominent examples. All of the states mentioned and the Communist bloc made strenuous efforts in the first session of the conference to block any improvement in the draft article. As their relations and influence with other Asian and African states were extensive, these active opponents were able

---

[275] Those on the Law of the Sea, on Diplomatic Relations, and on Consular Relations.

[276] *E.g.*, as of Jan. 1, 1970, there were 91 parties to the Diplomatic Relations Convention and 38 to the Consular Relations Convention. The Optional Protocols to those Conventions concerning the Compulsory Settlement of Disputes had, respectively, 38 and 15 parties.

[277] "The Soviet Union has neither accepted the 'Optional Clause' of the Statute of the International Court of Justice nor (generally) the articles of multilateral conventions providing for compulsory jurisdiction of the Court with respect to disputes arising under those conventions. A Soviet commentator on the Law of the Sea Conference held in 1958 has discussed the provisions for settlement of disputes under the fisheries convention in the following terms: 'The provisions of the Convention on the settlement of disputes between states on the question of fishing are unsatisfactory as they establish a procedure under which disputes may be decided on the request of any one of the interested parties in a special arbitration commission composed of five members. Such a procedure is compulsory arbitration and is a serious departure from the principle of the sovereign equality of states. Naturally, the delegation of the Soviet Union and many other delegations took a position vigorously against compulsory arbitration. . . .' " Larson, Jenks and others, Sovereignty Within the Law 291 (1965), citing Molodstov, Codification and Further Development of the International Law of the Sea.

to persuade a large number of delegations to oppose the compulsory settlement of disputes.

A third major obstacle was the 1966 decision of the International Court of Justice in the Second Phase of the *South West Africa Cases* (*Liberia and Ethiopia* v. *South Africa.*)[278] Almost every African state, like many others around the world, deeply resented the holding that the Court was unable to decide whether South African imposition of *apartheid* in South West Africa violated the terms of the League of Nations Mandate, under which South Africa administered the territory. The conclusion that former Member States of the League, including the plaintiffs Liberia and Ethiopia, had no legal right or interest in the matter intensified antagonism to the Court because of the legitimate expectations based on the 1962 decision on Preliminary Objections[279] which logically entailed the conclusion that the Court possessed the authority to determine whether or not South Africa had lived up to its mandate responsibilities. The effect of the decision especially among the newly-independent African states was to undermine confidence in the Court as an impartial dispute-settling mechanism. The adamant opposition of these states to seeking an advisory opinion from the Court on the question whether *apartheid* violates the Mandate before voting through the resolution terminating the Mandate[280] underscores this alienation.

The World Court was the logical choice for determining such issues as the existence of a rule of *jus cogens* or whether a state was induced to conclude a treaty by fraud. The United States comments in 1965 on the subject stated that "the rule of law . . . argues most strongly for compulsory reference to the Court."[281] But it was quite clear that the intervening South West Africa decision reduced to near zero the chance of obtaining an eventual two-thirds majority for judicial settlement by the Court of disputes arising out of Part V.

The fourth major obstacle to attaining an effective disputes-settlement procedure was disarray among the states that favored incorporation of such provisions. Some states, such as Japan, Switzerland and Turkey, considered adjudication by the International Court the *sine qua non* for acceptance of Part V and determined to push for the Court despite the prohibitive odds. Others, such as Sweden, Tunisia and Peru, were prepared to accept arbitration in a variety of forms. Still others supported a compulsory conciliation process with major emphasis on fact-finding.

Given the general fluidity of the situation, the United States Delegation at the 1968 session of the conference concentrated in the conference hall and in the corridors of the Hofburg on convincing as many delegates as possible that an optional protocol approach should be rejected and, without specifying any particular mode of settlement, that there must be an effective disputes-settlement procedure for Part V.

---

[278] [1966] I.C.J. Rep. 6.   [279] [1962] I.C.J. Rep. 319.

[280] General Assembly Res. 2145, General Assembly, 21st Sess., Official Records, Supp. 16 at 2, U.N. Doc. A/6316 (1966).

[281] I.L.C. Report, note 20 above, at 180 (1965 comment on Art. 51).

548 THE AMERICAN JOURNAL OF INTERNATIONAL LAW [Vol. 64

As the committee of the whole, under the able chairmanship of Attorney General Elias of Nigeria, worked its way through the first sixty articles, support began to coalesce around a Dutch-Swedish draft on disputes-settlement. A two-step procedure was suggested, requiring first a somewhat institutionalized form of conciliation, and, if that failed, then access to a simple system of arbitration. This proposal was merged with one supported by a number of the francophone African states, which resulted in a less formal series of conciliation provisions.[282] The revised amendment was co-sponsored by the Central African Republic, Colombia, Dahomey, Denmark, Finland, Gabon, Ivory Coast, Lebanon, Madagascar, The Netherlands, Peru, Sweden and Tunisia. As the debate proceeded it became clear that, of the proposals for disputes-settlement, the thirteen-state amendment would receive the widest support.[283]

The United States also put in a proposed amendment to develop a number of technical points not covered in the thirteen-state amendment. The main elements of the United States proposal included establishment of a commission on treaty disputes charged with effecting settlement through conciliation and empowered to order provisional measures to preserve the rights of parties, a special rule governing performance in breach cases, and reference of disputes not resolved through conciliation to arbitration at the request of any disputant unless the parties agreed to submit the dispute to the International Court of Justice.[284]

A Swiss proposal[285] was simple but unacceptable to the bulk of the African and Asian states. A key provision was an irrebuttable presumption of abandonment of a claim of invalidity unless the invoking party promptly brought the matter before the International Court of Justice or an arbitral tribunal.

A Japanese proposal[286] had two elements. Disputes concerning *jus cogens* (*i.e.*, those in which a party claimed a treaty was void because it violated a peremptory norm of international law) would be decided by the Court on the application of either party. Other claims that a treaty no longer applied would ultimately be referred to arbitration unless the parties agreed to go to the Court. The first part of the Japanese proposal elicited scattered support.

Finally, a Uruguayan amendment[287] sought to establish the applicability of the United Nations Charter provisions for disputes-settlement so that treaty disputes might be considered by the Security Council.

In the eight meetings at which the committee of the whole discussed the article in 1968, no clear trend emerged. The U.S.S.R. and the Eastern Europeans opposed all proposals to improve procedures for settlement of disputes. Influential African and Asian delegations joined in this oppo-

[282] U.N. Doc. A/CONF.39/C.1/L.352/Rev.1 and Corr.1 (English only) (1968).

[283] Official Records, First Session 402–441 *passim*.

[284] U.N. Doc. A/CONF.39/C.1/L.355 (1968).

[285] U.N. Doc. A/CONF.39/C.1/L.347 (1968).

[286] U.N. Doc. A/CONF.39/C.1/L.339 (1968).

[287] U.N. Doc. A/CONF.39/C.1/L.343 (1968).

sition. On the other hand, a majority of the Latin American group, most Western Europeans, members of the Old Commonwealth, and some African and Asian states favored improvement. Of the 53 delegations that spoke in the committee, 30 favored improvement, 22 were opposed, and 1 was undecided.[288] Neither side knew accurately how the 50 silent states would vote. The United States Delegation estimated that there was a majority against disputes-settlement. Opponents of improved procedures, such as the Ukrainian Soviet Socialist Republic Delegation, seemed to believe that they would be able to defeat any disputes-settlement proposal.[289] On May 16 debate was adjourned to permit the holding of "informal consultations."[290]

One aspect of the consultations was that disputes-settlement had, as a result of Soviet maneuvering, become entangled with the "all-states" issue. The "all-states" proposals related to two matters. The substantive issue involved the right to participate in multilateral treaties. The International Law Commission's articles reflected the traditional rule that states are free to choose their treaty partners. As the conference progressed, the Communist bloc supplemented its proposal set out at footnote 60 above by a series of related amendments similarly designed to achieve recognition for entities such as the German Democratic Republic by permitting them to become parties to general multilateral treaties. Dealing with this problem was complicated when France introduced a series of amendments[291] to establish special rules for restricted multilateral treaties. The Commission had found it impossible to define either of these concepts.[292]

There was no logical relationship between the disputes-settlement issue and the "all-states" proposals, but a nexus was established largely through the co-operation of three or four influential Asian and African delegates who pushed the position among their colleagues that nothing should be done regarding disputes-settlement unless something was done for the Soviet Union on "all-states." However, nose counts had established that if the "all-states" amendments were put to a vote, they would be defeated and that the thirteen-state disputes-settlement proposal was likely to be defeated. As a result of the general uncertainty, both sets of proposals as well as the French amendments on restricted multilateral treaties were put over until the 1969 session.[293]

Following the close of the first session of the conference the United States sought to rally support for inclusion of a settlement-of-disputes provision at the second session. It chose the thirteen-state proposal as the most likely basis for an agreed amendment. It initiated approaches in a number of capitals for support. In addition, certain United States embassies undertook to encourage countries that had not participated in the

[288] Official Records, First Session 402–415, 418–425, 429–441.
[289] Official Records, First Session 411. [290] *Ibid.* 441.
[291] To Arts. 9, 20, 30, 40, 41, 58, 69, and 70.
[292] I.L.C. Report, note 20 above, at 22–23, par. 8 of commentary (1966); *ibid.* at 38, par. 14 of commentary.
[293] Official Records, First Session 474, 476.

first session but which seemed likely to support an effective procedure for settlement of disputes to attend the second session. Yeoman service was also rendered by Professor McDougal, who attended the meeting of the Asian-African Legal Consultative Committee in Karachi in January, 1969, as an observer for the American Society of International Law.

When the committee of the whole resumed its labors in Vienna on April 9, 1969, the principal items of business were the two postponed problems. The disputes-settlement issue was taken up first. One result of intersessional missionary work was a revision of the thirteen-state proposal to embody a number of the features of the U.S. amendment. The revision [294] acquired six additional co-sponsors: Austria, Bolivia, Costa Rica, Malta, Mauritius and Uganda. After eight sessions of debate, it had become clear that there was a majority in favor of the amendment. On April 22, following the rejection of a motion by Ghana to adjourn the debate for forty-eight hours, sought by opponents in an effort to regroup their forces, various amendments were put to the vote. The Swiss and Japanese amendments were defeated but the nineteen-state proposal was adopted by 54 votes in favor, 34 against, with 14 abstentions.[295] A last-ditch move by India, Indonesia, Tanzania and Yugoslavia to convert the amendment into a kind of optional protocol was turned back 47 to 37, with 19 abstentions.[296]

Immediately thereafter a totally new proposal was taken up. There had been a good deal of off-the-record concern expressed during the 1968 session regarding amendments whose major purpose seemed to be improvement of the position of one or another party to a treaty dispute. Practically all such proposals had been voted down, but these efforts had forced many delegates to appreciate that existing treaties could be adversely affected by the application of principles that were not clear or not recognized at the time those treaties were concluded.

The Commission's proposal on non-retroactivity of treaties had been adopted by the committee of the whole without change. It provided that a treaty did not bind a party with respect to a fact or act which had taken place or a situation which had ceased to exist prior to the date of the treaty's entry into force for that party.[297] Its precise effect upon the relationships between existing treaties and the far-ranging effects of the proposed convention would have been difficult to calculate.

As the second session moved on, a growing sentiment was apparent for making the application of the convention strictly prospective. A number of amendments were floated in the corridors and several introduced. Support solidified behind a proposal co-sponsored by Brazil, Chile, Kenya, Iran, Sweden, Tunisia and Venezuela:

> Without prejudice to the application of any rules set forth in the present Convention to which treaties would be subject, in accordance

---

[294] U.N. Doc. A/CONF.39/C.1/L.352/Rev. 3 and Add. 1 and 2 and Corr. 1 (English only) (1969).

[295] U.N. Doc. A/CONF.39/C.1/SR.99 at 8 (1969).

[296] *Ibid.* at 7.   [297] Art. 28 of the convention.

with international law, independently of the Convention, the Convention will apply only to treaties which are concluded by States after the entry into force of the present Convention with regard to such States.[298] This amendment was discussed in connection with consideration of the final clauses on April 23 and 24. There was general support for the proposal, and it was adopted by 71 votes to 5, with 29 abstentions.[299]

The "all-states" issue had been again debated at the opening of the committee proceedings. The French had withdrawn their amendments on restricted multilateral treaties, and this sharpened the focus of the discussions. Voting, however, was postponed until April 25. On that date all outstanding amendments relating to the "all-states" question were defeated by substantial majorities.[300]

The committee of the whole having completed its labors, the battleground shifted to the plenary. As the nineteen-state proposal on disputes-settlement had not attained the support of two thirds of the conference in the committee of the whole, strenuous efforts were made to improve the voting position in the plenary. Eight additional votes were secured, bringing the total of affirmative votes up to 62. However, the opponents of compulsory settlement were able to net 3 additional negative votes which prevented the adoption of the proposal.[301]

In view of the unequivocal statements by a substantial number of states that they would not become parties to a convention on the law of treaties that did not contain adequate procedures for the settlement of disputes arising under the invalidity articles, it appeared that the conference would fail. In an almost continuous series of meetings the leaders of the conference endeavored to find a solution to the impasse. On a number of occasions it appeared that satisfactory compromise arrangements had been worked out, but they failed to gain enough support to ensure the necessary two-thirds majority.

Renewed efforts to incorporate an "all-states" substantive article in the convention were again rejected.[302] A second aspect of the "all-states" issue had arisen, this one involving the Final Clauses. Ghana and India had taken the initiative in sponsoring a formula for the articles on signature and accession which would have permitted unrecognized regimes in split states to become parties to the convention.[303] After lengthy contention in the committee of the whole this proposal was rejected.[304] A proposal by Brazil and the United Kingdom that embodied the traditional "Vienna formula" [305]

[298] U.N. Doc. A/CONF.39/C.1/L.403 (1969).

[299] U.N. Doc. A/CONF.39/C.1/SR.104, at 11 (1969).

[300] U.N. Docs. A/CONF.39/C.1/SR.104, at 13, 14; A/CONF.39/C.1/SR.105, at 5 (1969).

[301] U.N. Doc. A/CONF.39/SR.27, at 8 (1969).

[302] U.N. Doc. A/CONF.39/SR.34, at 8–9 (1969).

[303] U.N. Doc. A/CONF.39/C.1/L.394 (1969).

[304] U.N. Doc. A/CONF.39/C.1/SR.104, at 13–14 (1969).

[305] "This Convention shall be open for signature [for accession] by all States Members of the United Nations or of any of the specialized agencies or of the International Atomic Energy Agency or parties to the Statute of the International Court of Justice, and by any other State invited by the General Assembly of the United Nations to become a party to the Convention. . . ."

was adopted. These decisions were reaffirmed by the plenary. Their substance is reflected in Articles 81, 82 and 83, which deal, respectively, with signature, ratification and accession.

Although in most respects the final clauses of the convention follow those of prior codification conventions, there is a difference worth noting in the article on entry into force. The conventions of 1958 on the Law of the Sea required twenty-two instruments of ratification or accession prior to entry into force. This precedent was followed in the Vienna Conventions on Diplomatic Relations in 1961 and on Consular Relations in 1963. There was a general consensus that the number should be increased for the Treaties Convention.

The committee of the whole, faced with choosing between amendments proposing 35, 45, and 60 ratifications, left the figure blank in the final clauses it adopted and charged the plenary with resolution of the problem. In summing up the debate the expert consultant expressed the view that the figure of thirty-five "would serve the purpose of recognizing the existence of an enlarged community, would not unduly delay the bringing into force of the Convention, and would not endanger some of the benefits of the . . . work done on the Convention at the . . . Conference." [306] In the plenary, a seven-nation proposal containing the number thirty-five was adopted without objection.

In the closing days of the conference there were meetings going on at all hours among the leaders of the various political and geographical groups. A variety of compromises for settling the two major points of contention were floated, but none attracted sufficient support. The most popular was a proposal that coupled a declaration on the "all-states" issue with a disputes-settlement formula that provided arbitration for a few articles in Part V and conciliation for the remaining articles.

On the final full day of the second session a caucus of Asian and African delegations met to discuss the problem. A group of those delegations, led by Nigeria, succeeded in putting together a compromise proposal which included a new article entitled *Procedures for judicial settlement, arbitration and conciliation,* and a non-binding declaration on the right to accede to the convention, which in effect relegated the matter to the General Assembly. The sponsors, Ghana, Ivory Coast, Kenya, Kuwait, Lebanon, Morocco, Nigeria, Sudan, Tunisia and Tanzania, declined to permit division of their proposal and insisted that it be put to the vote without delay. By a vote of 61 for, 20 against, with 26 abstentions, the proposal carried.[307]

---

[306] U.N. Doc. A/CONF.39/C.1/SR.103, at 27 (1969). Forty-seven countries, including the United States, had signed the convention as of April 30, 1970, the closing date for signature specified in Art. 81. One country, Nigeria, had ratified the convention. The convention remains open for accession by any state belonging to any of the categories mentioned in footnote 305. No "undue delay" in entry into force of the convention is anticipated.

[307] U.N. Doc. A/CONF.39/SR.34, at 27 (1969).

The new article, Article 66, combines elements of the Japanese and nineteen-Power amendments. It authorizes any party to a dispute arising under the *jus cogens* articles to submit the dispute to the International Court of Justice for adjudication whenever the procedures in Article 33 of the Charter have not led to the solution of the dispute within twelve months and unless the parties have agreed instead to submit it to arbitration. A party to a dispute concerning "the application or the interpretation of any of the other articles in Part V" [308] can initiate the conciliation procedures provided in the annex to the convention by submitting a request to the Secretary General of the United Nations.

The annex envisages the establishment of a list of qualified jurists to serve as conciliators. When the Secretary General receives the request he brings the dispute before a conciliation commission comprised as follows:

> The State or States constituting one of the parties to the dispute shall appoint:
> (a) one conciliator of the nationality of that State or of one of those States, who may or may not be chosen from the list referred to in paragraph 1; and
> (b) one conciliator not of the nationality of that State or of any of those States, who shall be chosen from the list. [309]

The fifth member, who serves as chairman, is selected from the list by the other four members. The Secretary General makes any appointment that is not made within prescribed time periods.

Paragraphs 5 and 6 of the annex provide:

> 5. The Commission shall hear the parties, examine the claims and objections, and make proposals to the parties with a view to reaching an amicable settlement of the dispute.
> 6. The Commission shall report within twelve months of its constitution. Its report shall be deposited with the Secretary-General and transmitted to the parties to the dispute. The report of the Commission, including any conclusions stated therein regarding the facts or questions of law, shall not be binding upon the parties and it shall have no other character than that of recommendations submitted for the consideration of the parties in order to facilitate an amicable settlement of the dispute.

Paragraph 7 of the annex provides that the expenses of the commission will be borne by the United Nations. The conference requested the General Assembly to note and approve that provision at its Twenty-Fourth Session. The General Assembly did so on December 8, 1969. [310]

The annex reflects to a degree the stresses and strains inside the group that put forward the compromise proposal. The emphasis in paragraph 6 of the annex that the report of a conciliation commission is not binding on the parties and is solely of a recommendatory character may have been influenced not only by the struggle within the conference but also

---

[308] Art. 66 (b).   [309] Annex, par. 2.

[310] General Assembly Res. 2534 (XXIV). For discussion on the item in the Assembly, see Doc. A/PV.1825, at 56–68 (1969).

by the cultural antipathy to formal adjudication that is a feature of a number of Asian and African societies.[811] These same factors may also have a bearing on the elliptical fashion in which the authority of a commission to present conclusions of fact and law in its report to the Secretary General is set forth.

Neither the nineteen-state proposal nor the earlier thirteen-state proposal for a conciliation-arbitration procedure contained a provision expressly authorizing a conciliation commission to make findings of fact and of law. On the other hand, the 1968 proposal by the United States on settlement of disputes required that the report of the conciliation commission "deal fully with the factual and legal elements of the dispute" if a friendly solution could not be effected.[812]

This United States proposal was discussed in connection with the transformation of the thirteen-state 1968 amendment into the nineteen-state 1969 proposal. There was a consensus among the co-sponsors that it was not desirable to give the conciliation process too many of the aspects of a legal proceeding. Because conciliation, if unavailing, could be followed by arbitration, a duplication of procedures was to be avoided.

In the private discussions that preceded the final compromise proposal, the United States and the other states concerned with adequate disputes-settlement provisions made it clear that a conciliation procedure that was limited to a "good offices" proposal would not be acceptable. A form of disputes-settlement that would determine the legality of any assertion to terminate a treaty obligation was a *sine qua non*. To achieve this, a provision empowering the conciliation commission to decide controverted issues of law and fact was essential. The somewhat convoluted language of the second sentence of paragraph 6 of the annex represents the acceptance of that position.

The adjudicatory aspects of the conciliation procedure are also underlined in another change made in the text of the annex to the nineteen-state amendment. The first sentence in paragraph 3 provided: "The commission thus constituted shall establish the facts and make proposals to the parties with a view to reaching an amicable settlement of the dispute." [813] In the annex to the convention, that clause has been changed to provide that "the commission shall hear the parties, examine the claims and objections and make proposals to the parties. . . ." [814] The changes again resulted from insistence that if there was to be no arbitration then conciliation must embody the essentials of proceedings of a judicial character. The original requirement of "establishing the facts" has been broadened to examining "the claims and objections," with the necessary consequence that the legal aspects be taken under consideration. The requirement that the commission hear

---

[811] See R. David and J. E. C. Brierley, Major Legal Systems in the World Today 442, 463 (1968).

[812] U.N. Doc. A/CONF.39/C.1/L.355, Art. 5, par. 2 of the Annex (1969).

[813] U.N. Doc. A/CONF.39/C.1/SR.105, at 16 (1969).

[814] Par. 5.

the parties was added to make clear that the commission was not to function as a go-between but as a tribunal.

In one respect the uncertainties of the International Law Commission's original article remain: There is no provision that prescribes what can or cannot be done after a conciliation commission has made its report. If the commission should find in favor of the state urging the invalidity of a treaty as a ground for release from a treaty commitment, that state, even though the findings are purely recommendatory, would have a reasonable legal basis for taking the measure proposed in the notification it had made under Article 65. The commission's findings would also support defense against any charge of breach against that state for then proceeding to take the measure proposed, provided such measure was consistent with Article 69 on the consequences of the invalidity of a treaty.

If a conciliation commission should find, on the other hand, that a claim, say, of a right to terminate on the ground of fundamental change of circumstances had *not* been made out, would there be any legal barrier to the claimant state's carrying out the actions authorized under Article 70 as the consequence of the termination of a treaty? A characterization of the commission's findings as either non-binding or recommendatory is not an answer to this problem, because the anterior question—the effect of a unilateral assertion that a treaty is terminated—remains open. The reasonable and sensible position in these circumstances is that the overriding principle of *pacta sunt servanda* applies and that, under Article 26, the claimant state, to be acting in good faith, must continue to perform its obligations.

The concluding section of Part V contains four articles dealing with the consequences of the invalidity, termination, or suspension of a treaty. Articles 69 and 70 treat, respectively, the legal effect of a treaty established as invalid under the convention and the legal consequences of termination of a valid treaty. Article 71[315] deals with the consequences of a treaty conflicting with a peremptory norm of general international law. Article 72 governs the legal consequences of suspension of the operation of a treaty. Although a substantial improvement was made in Article 69 and a clarification introduced in Article 72, the general framework proposed by the Commission for this section was endorsed by the conference.

The basic principle in Article 69 was phrased: "The provisions of a void treaty have no legal force." That formulation failed to make clear that the detailed rules that followed on the consequences of the invalidity of a treaty applied only to treaties which had been established as invalid under the convention. Australia, France, and the United States introduced amendments to express this point.[316] After consideration of the text proposed by the drafting committee and further discussion in the committee of the whole, paragraph 1·of Article 69 was changed to read: "A treaty the invalidity of

[315] P. 535 above.
[316] U.N. Docs. A/CONF.39/C.1/L.297 (Australia), A/CONF.39/C.1/L.363 (France), A/CONF.39/C.1/L.360 (United States) (1968).

556   THE AMERICAN JOURNAL OF INTERNATIONAL LAW   [Vol. 64

which is established under the present Convention is void. The provisions of a void treaty have no legal force." [317] Paragraph 2 provides:

> 2. If acts have nevertheless been performed in reliance on such a treaty:
> (a) each party may require any other party to establish as far as possible in their mutual relations the position that would have existed if the acts had not been performed;
> (b) acts performed in good faith before the invalidity was invoked are not rendered unlawful by reason only of the invalidity of the treaty.

However, when a treaty has been found invalid under an article relating to fraud, corruption, or coercion, paragraph 2 does not apply "with respect to the party to which the fraud, the act of corruption or the coercion is imputable." [318] The United States took the position that the rules in paragraph 2 (a) and the exception with respect to fraud, corruption, and coercion in paragraph 3, though reasonable in theory, would not always prove satisfactory in practice. Its proposal to delete those rules was also grounded on the theory that the sanctions impinged on the subject of state responsibility, a topic excluded from the scope of the convention by Article 73.[319] The expert consultant, Sir Humphrey Waldock, stated in his summary that the United States and Switzerland "had objected, not without some justification, that the provisions adopted [by the Commission] might prove too strict. It was for the Conference to decide whether or not the usefulness of those provisions made up for the shortcomings that had been pointed out." [320] The conference decided by a substantial majority to retain paragraphs 2 and 3 in the form proposed by the Commission.[321]

Article 70 defines the legal consequences of the termination of a treaty under its provisions or in accordance with the convention. The gist of the reasonable rule in this article, which closely paraphrases Article 33 (d) of the Harvard Draft,[322] is that such termination, while releasing the parties from the obligation of further performance, "does not affect any right, obligation or legal situation of the parties created through the execution of the treaty prior to its termination." [323]

Article 72 on the consequences of the suspension of the operation of a treaty is designed to emphasize that, while suspension relieves the parties between which the operation of a treaty is suspended from performance of their mutual obligations, the "legal nexus between the parties established by the treaty remains intact." [324] The Commission's commentary also explains that paragraph 2 carries further the point as to the continuing legal nexus by specifying the obligation of the parties to do nothing to prevent resumption of the operation of the treaty "as soon as the ground or cause of suspension ceases." [325]

The Mexican Delegation introduced an amendment to Article 72, somewhat akin to the language in Article 18, which would have added an obliga-

---

[317] Official Records, First Session 493.   [318] Par. 3.
[319] Official Records, First Session 446.   [320] *Ibid.* at 447.
[321] *Ibid.* The final text was slightly revised by the drafting committee.
[322] 29 A. J. I. L. Supp. 664 (1935).   [323] Art. 70, par. 1.
[324] I.L.C. Report, note 20 above, at 94.   [325] *Ibid.*

tion to refrain during the period of the suspension from acts which would "frustrate the object of the treaty." [326] In its report on the article, the drafting committee proposed deletion of the expression "to render . . . impossible," which had been suggested by the Commission, and substitution of the words "to obstruct." This improvement, which not only resolved the point raised by the Mexican amendment but also avoided possible confusion with Article 61 on supervening impossibility of performance, was adopted without objection. [327]

MISCELLANEOUS PROVISIONS (ARTICLES 73–75)

Part VI of the convention as proposed by the Commission contained two articles: *Cases of State succession and State responsibility* and *Case of an aggressor State.* The latter is treated above as an exception to Article 35, *Treaties providing for obligations for third States.*

The conference made two changes in Part VI. To the catalog of questions of state succession and state responsibility excluded from the applicability of the convention by Article 73, the conference added treaty questions arising from the outbreak of hostilities. The Commission had recognized that

> the state of facts resulting from an outbreak of hostilities may have the practical effect of preventing the application of the treaty in the circumstances prevailing . . . [and] that questions may arise as to the legal consequences of an outbreak of hostilities with respect to obligations arising from treaties. But it considered that in the international law of today the outbreak of hostilities between States must be considered as an entirely abnormal condition, and that the rules governing its legal consequences should not be regarded as forming part of the general rules of international law applicable in the normal relations between States. . . . [328]

Accordingly it did not mention hostilities in the draft articles.

Hungary and Poland introduced an amendment[329] to add a reference to "outbreak of hostilities between States" at the end of the article proposed by the Commission; Switzerland introduced a similar proposal. After a surprisingly brief discussion, in which only one delegation[330] supported the omission of the reference to hostilities, the principle contained in the two amendments was adopted by a vote of 72 in favor, 5 opposed, with 14 abstentions. [331]

The conference also added a new Article 74 to Part VI, which provides that severance or absence of diplomatic or consular relations between states does not prevent the conclusion of treaties between those states. The article grew out of an amendment by Chile to Article 63, which provides that in principle "the severance of diplomatic or consular relations between parties to a treaty does not affect the legal relations established between them by the treaty. . . ." A substantial majority of the conference supported the new

[326] U.N. Doc. A/CONF.39/C.1/L.357 (1968).
[327] Official Records, First Session 484.   [328] I.L.C. Report, note 20 above, at 95.
[329] U.N. Doc. A/CONF.39/C.1/L.279 (1968).
[330] Uruguay.   [331] Official Records, First Session 453.

558   THE AMERICAN JOURNAL OF INTERNATIONAL LAW   [Vol. 64

article, perhaps persuaded by its sponsor that "although it might be considered unnecessary to state such a self-evident fact . . . the absence of such a provision might lead to the assumption that States could not conclude treaties among themselves if diplomatic relations had been severed." [332] The rule in the article is in accordance with modern treaty practice.

DEPOSITARIES, NOTIFICATIONS, CORRECTIONS AND REGISTRATION
(ARTICLES 76–80)

In his searching article, "The Depositary of International Treaties," in this JOURNAL, Ambassador Rosenne pointed to the fact that, despite its unusual character, the institution of depositary had received little attention from scholars.[333] Only in 1966, with the adoption by the Commission of the draft articles on the law of treaties, did it emerge as "a completely independent institution of contemporary international law, with an independent rôle and independent rights and duties in the general context of the modern law of treaties, and not merely as a kind of adjunct to the states themselves concerned in the treaty, regardless of whether the depositary is one of those states or not." [334]

In this highly technical field, which was considered during the closing days of the first session of the conference, it would have been quite understandable had the exhausted delegates somewhat perfunctorily adopted the text proposed by the Commission. Nevertheless, the conference gave most careful attention to the Commission's proposals and clarified them in a number of respects.

The Commission's text of the article on depositaries of treaties dealt with the identity of the depositary, the method of its designation, and the international character of its functions:

> 1. The depositary of a treaty, which may be a State or an international organization, shall be designated by the negotiating States in the treaty or in some other manner.
> 2. The functions of a depositary of a treaty are international in character and the depositary is under an obligation to act impartially in their performance.[335]

Mr. Castrén opened the debate by proposing to amend the first paragraph to cover agreements such as the Test Ban and Outer Space Treaties for which there were multiple depositaries.[336] Although Sir Humphrey Waldock had earlier expressed doubt "whether the precedent of a trinity of depositaries" [337] required a similar amendment to the definition of depositary proposed in his first report (but subsequently abandoned), the Finnish amendment substituting "one or more states" for "a state" was adopted by a substantial majority.[338] A second amendment proposed by Mexico to

---

[332] *Ibid.* at 383.   [333] 61 A.J.I.L. 923, 925–926 (1967).
[334] *Ibid.* at 926.   [335] I.L.C. Report, note 20 above, at 96.
[336] Official Records, First Session 457.

[337] Waldock, Fourth Report on the Law of Treaties, 1965 I.L.C. Yearbook (II) 15, U.N. Doc A/CN.4/177 and Add. 1 and 2 (1965).

[338] Official Records, First Session 468.

clarify the paragraph by specifying that the chief administrative officer of an international organization might be designated as depositary was also adopted.[339]

The principle of paragraph 2 underscoring the international character of the depositary's function and its duty to act impartially was welcomed by the committee of the whole. In addition, it adopted two proposals affirming the rule on impartiality in certain special circumstances, which the Commission believed were included within its formulation.[340]

The United States, as the depositary of more international treaties than any other country, played an active rôle in the discussion of the depositary articles. The first part of the United States amendment to Article 77 on *Functions of depositaries* was intended to "make it clear that any functions not specified either in the treaty or in [the article under consideration] could appropriately be performed by the depositary by agreement of the States concerned, without the treaty actually having to be amended." [341] In introducing the United States amendment Mr. Bevans stated that

> its purpose was to bring the article into conformity with customary depositary practice. A treaty normally specified at least some of the functions to be performed by the depositary. Certain other functions were understood to exist as a result of practice. From time to time, however, certain functions needed to be performed which had not been anticipated and had therefore not been specified in the treaty. Such functions were usually related to the customary depositary functions and could be performed more efficiently and conveniently by the depositary than by any other agent. In such cases, the States concerned agreed to entrust the new functions to the depositary.[342]

Another paragraph of the U.S. amendment proposed that registration of the treaty with the Secretariat of the United Nations should be included as a depositary function. This change would not only fix clearly the responsibility for the performance of this important function but also insure that accurate data would be provided since in the nature of things the depositary could be expected to have complete and authoritative information regarding the treaty.

Ten amendments to Article 77 were adopted by the committee of the whole.[343] Their combined effect was to produce in paragraph 1 a more comprehensive catalog of depositary functions than had originally been envisioned by the Commission.

As indicated in the discussion of Article 48,[344] vitiating error "as to a fact or situation which was assumed by that State to exist at the time when the treaty was concluded and formed an essential basis of its consent to be bound by a treaty" has seldom arisen in international practice. Errors "re-

---

[339] *Ibid.*
[340] Official Records, First Session 467, par. 55, remarks of Sir Humphrey Waldock.
[341] *Ibid.* at 459.   [342] *Ibid.*
[343] Official Records, First Session 468. Five of the proposals adopted were sponsored by the United States.
[344] P. 529 above.

560   THE AMERICAN JOURNAL OF INTERNATIONAL LAW   [Vol. 64

lating only to the wording of the text of a treaty" are not infrequent.[345] Article 79 contains simple and sensible rules for the prompt correction of such errors in texts and in certified copies of treaties.[346]

In its comments on Article 80 on *Registration and publication of treaties*[347] the Organization of American States suggested that the article would be improved if it were to contain a provision authorizing the depositary of a treaty to transmit it to the United Nations Secretariat for registration and publication. The United States and Uruguay introduced an amendment along those lines at the eightieth meeting of the committee of the whole.[348] In speaking to the amendment Mr. Bevans said:

> [T]he United Nations Secretariat was in favour of the registration of treaties by depositaries, but in some instances certain technical difficulties stood in the way of such a procedure. For example, many treaties for which the Organization of American States (OAS) was depositary did not contain any provision regarding their registration, and in order for them to be registered with the United Nations, the OAS had first to obtain the agreement of all parties. Similarly, when States Members of the United Nations were depositaries for treaties containing no provision on registration, they were unable to register them unless every party agreed. The joint amendment was designed to overcome those technical difficulties.[349]

When several delegations questioned whether the amendment would be compatible with Article 102 of the United Nations Charter, the expert consultant expressed the view that it would simplify the registration of certain types of multilateral treaties. The amendment was then put to the vote and adopted without opposition.[350]

The adoption by the conference of sound rules governing depositaries, notifications, corrections, and registration should bring uniformity and clarity to an area of international law which hitherto has not been governed by any generally accepted body of rules.

CONCLUSION

This codification of provisions on depositary practice is a final demonstration of the great value of the convention in providing solutions for a host of technical problems in the negotiation, adoption and execution of treaties.

[345] See, *e.g.*, Procès-verbal of rectification of the International Convention on Load Lines, 1966, of Jan. 30, 1969, 20 U.S. Treaties 17; T.I.A.S., No. 6629. A second *procès-verbal* of rectification of that convention was signed on May 5, 1969, T.I.A.S., No. 6720.

[346] In discussing the relationship between Arts. 48 and 79 the Commission noted that an error or inconsistency in the text of a treaty "may be due to a typographical mistake or to a misdescription or misstatement due to a misunderstanding and the correction may affect the substantive meaning of the text as authenticated. If there is a dispute as to whether or not the alleged error or inconsistency is in fact such, the question is not one simply of correction of the text but becomes a problem of mistake which falls under article [48]. The present article only concerns cases where there is no dispute as to the existence of the error or inconsistency." I.L.C. Report, note 20 above, at 99.

[347] U.N. Doc. A/CONF. 39/7, at 40, 43–44 (1968).

[348] U.N. Doc. A/CONF.39/C.1/L.376 (1968).

[349] Official Records, First Session 470 (1968).

[350] *Ibid.* at 471.

Had the solution of those technical problems been the only achievement of the treaties conference, the years of study and toil would have been well justified. But, as the foregoing discussion hopefully has demonstrated, much more was achieved.

One substantial achievement is the provision of a mechanism to adjust the conflicting demands between the forces of stability and change. By codifying the doctrines of *jus cogens* and *rebus sic stantibus* the convention provides a framework for dealing with change in an orderly fashion. By reasserting the principle of *pacta sunt servanda* it strengthens the customary law rule which has always been the keystone of the treaty structure.

The limitation of grounds for challenging treaty obligations to those contained in the convention is, in the context of the convention as finally agreed, a buttress to the stability of treaties, as are the articles on separability and loss of a right to challenge the continued applicability of a treaty because of agreement or implied acquiescence in its continued effectiveness. Further, the fact that under Article 4 the convention applies only to future treaties eliminates very many of the fears about possible abuses. Treaties that are entered into in contemplation of the application of the convention can be negotiated or drafted to guard against possible misapplication of its provisions.

A major achievement was the provision for reference of disputes concerning *jus cogens* to the International Court of Justice. This reflects a willingness on the part of many states that had voiced disappointment with the Court in 1966 to recognize its signal appropriateness as a forum for resolution of disputes relating to *jus cogens*—the one principle that presents the most basic issue in the development of a world rule of law.

In addition, the procedures for dealing with disputes are not only an essential element in maintaining the stability of treaty relationships but are the first such procedures to be included in a general codification treaty. Even though the report of the conciliation commission is not "binding," the determination that a party is either justified or not justified in claiming release from a treaty obligation will constitute a powerful deterrent to unwarranted action on either side of a dispute. The provision for meeting the expenses of the commission is a desirable innovation and a worthwhile investment, since the concern of many newly independent and small states with the cost of third-party settlement procedures has been a very real obstacle to their general acceptability.

The treaty on treaties does not approach perfection. The international legislative process remains much too primitive a mechanism to produce an approach to perfection. This convention is, however, in an unspectacular and earthbound way, a giant step for mankind toward a world in which the rule of law will be not a dream but a reality.

Part II
The Nature of Treaties

[2]

WHAT IS AN AGREEMENT IN INTERNATIONAL LAW?*

By KELVIN WIDDOWS†

THE quest for a precise definition or description of the terms 'treaty' and 'international agreement' has drawn scholars over the years into a labyrinth of tautology.

The terms, to begin with, have many senses of meaning. A 'treaty' in its narrowest sense is often thought of as a particularly formal instrument recording and constituting an international agreement. But the term is elastic and employed just as often to describe any binding international agreement. Hence the name 'Treaty Department' in most Foreign Offices today.[1] Indeed, much of the doctrinal argument in the International Law Commission, when it began to deal with the law of treaties, arose out of misunderstandings and confusion over the scope of the Commission's mandate: if it were to deal with 'treaties', argued some, should it not confine itself to those more formal instruments of agreement requiring ratification? Later in the Commission's dealings, the Special Rapporteurs made it clear that the draft articles were intended to cover all forms of binding international agreement excepting those not recorded in writing.[2]

Accordingly, there are dangers in reading the 'definition' section of the codes on treaty law as anything more than self-limiting provisions concerning the scope of the rules that follow.[3] The present Article, however, is concerned with the term

* © Kelvin Widdows, 1980.
† Formerly Tapp Student, Gonville and Caius College, Cambridge.

[1] Judge Jessup in his separate opinion in the *South West Africa* case (*First Phase*), *I.C.J. Reports*, 1962, p. 402, went as far as to claim: 'The notion that there is a clear and ordinary meaning of the word "treaty" is a mirage.' For some indication of the problems involved, Myers in *American Journal of International Law*, 51 (1957), p. 574, provides a lucid account of what a treaty is not.

[2] It is arguable that the disputes in the early days of the Commission's consideration of the question were as much an expression of concern after the Second World War that the treaty-making procedure be subject to as much of the 'democratic process' as possible: hence the attempted link between treaty as a concept of obligation and the ratification process.

The Reports of the Special Rapporteurs of the International Law Commission will be referred to by name and a number indicating the particular report, e.g., Waldock III: Sir Humphrey Waldock's Third Report; Lauterpacht I: Sir Hersch Lauterpacht's First Report, and so on. For convenience the United Nations reference numbers for the relevant reports are given below:

Brierly I, A/CN. 4/24, *Yearbook of the International Law Commission*, 1950, vol. 2, p. 222; Brierly II, A/CN. 4/43, ibid., 1951, vol. 2, p. 70; Lauterpacht I, A/CN. 4/63, ibid., 1953, vol. 2, p. 90; Lauterpacht II, A/CN. 4/87, ibid., 1954, vol. 2, p. 123; Fitzmaurice I, A/CN. 4/101, ibid., 1956, vol. 2, p. 104; Fitzmaurice II, A/CN. 4/107, ibid., 1957, vol. 2, p. 16; Fitzmaurice IV, A/CN. 4/120, ibid., 1959, vol. 2, p. 37; Waldock I, A/CN. 4/144, ibid., 1962, vol. 2, p. 27; Waldock II, A/CN. 4/156, ibid., 1963, vol. 2, p. 36; Waldock IV, A/CN. 4/177, ibid., 1965, vol. 2, p. 3; Waldock V, A/CN. 4/183, ibid., 1966, vol. 2, p. 1; Waldock VI, A/CN. 4/186, ibid., 1966, vol. 2, p. 51.

[3] e.g. Field, 'Outline of an International Code', *American Journal of International Law*, 29 (1935), Supplement, p. 1207; Bluntschli, *Le Droit international codifié* (5th French edn., 1895);

118   WHAT IS AN AGREEMENT

'treaty' in its broadest sense. It is an enquiry into the elements comprising a binding international agreement.

The terminological problem, which is not critical for present purposes, is whether a treaty is the consensus ad idem itself or the instrument recording the terms of the agreement. Judge Basdevant,[1] for example, has, as is well-known, asserted that a 'treaty' is not an agreement but an instrument. If the term 'treaty' is used in its narrow sense (as he uses it) this may indeed be correct; for, considering that most definitions of treaty, in the narrow sense, require a formal instrument as a constituent element, Basdevant is going no farther than stressing one element of his definition. And for the rest, it must surely depend on whether or not a written record is required for an agreement to be binding in international law.[2]

Either way,[3] this Article is concerned with the creation of obligation; the question whether the obligation arises through consensus or through an instrument recording that consensus is not one that causes any debate in practice. There appears, for example, to be only one reported case, and that of minor character, of rectification of an international agreement.[4]

Is it necessary to define 'treaty' or 'international agreement'? Perhaps there is no need to attempt to define with the precision of a philologist, but it is necessary to ascertain the elements that lead to bindingness: the requirements giving rise to obligation in this form. It is no doubt true, as Professor Jennings has written,[5] that definitions of a general character, and not related to a particular context, have not often been made in practice, because 'it is hardly possible to discover any discriminating characteristic of "treaty" which would command general assent'. But clearly, as Professor Jennings asserts, some sort of working hypothesis is necessary.

It should be stated at the outset that it is not the purpose of this Article to discuss the question of capacity to conclude international agreements or treaties.

Fiore, *International Law Codified* (Borchard trans., 1918); Liszt, *Le Droit international* (Gidel trans., 1913); Harvard Research Draft on the Law of Treaties, *American Journal of International Law*, 29 (1935), Supplement, p. 666; Havana Convention on the Law of Treaties adopted by the Sixth International Conference of American States (in force for seven States), *American Journal of International Law*, 29 (1935), Supplement, p. 1205; American Law Institute, *Restatement of Foreign Relations Law* (2nd edn., 1965); American Institute of International Law Draft on Treaties, *American Journal of International Law*, 20 (1926), Supplement, p. 348.

[1] *Recueil des cours*, 15 (1926–V), p. 539. See also Genet, *Traité de diplomatie et de droit diplomatique*, vol. 3 (1932), p. 377; and, for an account of the I.L.C.'s attitude, Rosenne, *Transnational Law in a Changing Society* (1972), p. 205. The Harvard Research Draft, loc. cit. (previous note), at p. 686, took the same approach but it was concerned only with 'formal' instruments. Fitzmaurice I (commentary to Article 14, p. 119) took the view that if the text was not itself the agreement it was nevertheless indispensable and usually the sole evidence of what the agreement was. Brierly I (p. 228) thought the real nature of a treaty to be a legal act or transaction rather than a document.

[2] The majority of commentators appear to claim that writing is not necessary though the instances of practice cited in the books are few and ancient. It is here assumed that writing is not necessary to constitute a binding agreement. It does not seem to be a problem for Foreign Offices.

[3] Sir Gerald Fitzmaurice's sensible approach seems to treat it as an amalgam of consensus and instrument.

[4] Below, pp. 148–9.   [5] Jennings, *Recueil des cours*, 121 (1967–II), p. 529.

The term 'international entities' will be employed to cover parties to agreements, and is meant to comprehend entities having capacity under international law to conclude treaties.[1]

What, then, is meant by 'international agreement' or 'treaty'? Clearly there is first the element of agreement: consensus ad idem.[2] Most bilateral agreements are drawn up during negotiations and reflect the joint wishes of the parties. In the case of an exchange of notes the proposition is put, or offer made, by one party and subscribed to or accepted by the other in reply. Most multilateral agreements are negotiated in long and usually technical sessions of conference, and the text finally arrived at is said to reflect the agreement of all the States parties. In one sense it might be illusory to speak of agreement in such cases, in so far as agreement might be no more than resigned acceptance of a compromise text. But the text is nonetheless accepted, agreed to and subscribed.

To agree can, however, be to disagree, to agree on broad guidelines, to agree 'in honour', to agree to consider, to agree to endeavour to do something, to agree to do one's best and so on.[3] What sort of agreement is it that leads to binding obligation in international law?

The books take a number of different stands. Many of the older ones proclaimed that the agreement must be moral, that the obligations undertaken must be equal and just, for both parties, and so on.[4] That these requirements were necessary appears never to have been accepted in practice, and so far as any of them may be considered potent these days, their force would lie in the realm of the *jus cogens* rule, a rule which renders an infringing treaty void. In such cases, it

---

[1] We shall not discuss agreements between States and non-international entities to which, for some reason, international law applies.

[2] In fact agreement free of defects such as error, coercion, etc.

[3] Scelle, in his book *Théorie juridique de la révision des traités* (1936), makes the point that not all agreements are agreements in law. In a municipal system, for example, two judges might agree on a judgment they are delivering but the result is not an 'agreement' in law. Judges Spender and Fitzmaurice in their joint dissent in the *South West Africa* cases (*First Phase*), *I.C.J. Reports*, 1962, p. 464, make the same point, stressing characterization of the agreement: did the parties bind themselves through the agreement or in some other way? This is perhaps a little far-fetched. The examples of Scelle do not involve rights and duties between the parties, a notion inherent in the concept of contract or treaty even when not explicitly stated, as in the American *Restatement* (§ 115). What is important is that the agreement be settled and final and not simply one stage of protracted negotiations: see the remarks of Lord Sumner in *The Blonde*, [1922] 1 A.C. 313, 321.

[4] Otelelechano, *De la valeur obligatoire des traités internationaux* (1916), discusses this point in some detail, giving a multitude of references. The writer concludes that there was by 1916 no State practice in support of injecting adjectival requirements such as 'moral' or 'humane' into the concept of international agreement. The debates in the International Law Commission and at the Vienna Conference on the alleged necessity for treaties to be 'equal' (not adopted by the Conference except as a Declaration on the Prohibition of Military, Political or Economic Coercion, in the form of a solemn condemnation forming portion of the Final Act of the Convention) reflect a similar preoccupation, though based on political considerations. State practice gives little comfort to the proponents of such a doctrine. There are many examples of one-sided bargains, most of which could scarcely be labelled immoral: aid agreements alone need be mentioned. And it is worth recalling that when the classical writers treated of 'equality', they did so in the context of classification rather than validity (e.g. Vattel, book II, ch. 12). Hall (*International Law* (8th edn., 1924), p. 416) claimed that these alleged requirements were of such pernicious looseness that an unscrupulous State would never be in want for plausible excuses for repudiation.

may be argued, an agreement comes into existence under the rules here being considered but is instantaneously avoided by a rule of a different kind.

Coming to the core of the problem, the nature of the agreement that leads to binding obligation, some of the writers[1] speak of the need for intention by the parties to create rights and/or obligations between them in international law or to annul or modify ones already existing. Others[2] add to these the alternative requirement of an agreement with intent to establish relations, or to produce effects, in international law ('between the parties' must always be implied in these formulations); and yet others[3] speak of intention to create an obligation or, as an alternative, the actual creation of an obligation, or indeed omit, as did the International Law Commission in its final draft,[4] reference to intention altogether.

Professor Jennings,[5] after acknowledging the need for a working definition, adopts the one cautiously drafted by Lord McNair:

. . . a written agreement by which two or more States or international organizations create or intend to create a relation between themselves operating within the sphere of international law.[6]

No assistance, it would appear, can be obtained from the use of the terms 'treaty and international agreement' in Article 102 of the United Nations Charter. The words there seem to have no specific or technical meaning, it having been agreed at San Francisco that no attempt at definition should be made. The United Nations Monthly Statement preface sets out the position taken by the Secretariat in this way:

. . . since the terms 'treaty' and 'international agreement' have not been defined either in the Charter or in the Regulations, the Secretariat, under the Charter and the Regulations, follows the principle that it acts in accordance with the position of the Member State submitting an instrument for registration that so far as that party is concerned the instrument is a treaty or an international agreement within the meaning of Article 102. Registration of an instrument submitted by a member State, therefore, does not imply a judgement by the Secretariat on the nature of the instrument, the status of a party or any similar question. It is the understanding of the Secretariat that its action does not confer on the instrument the status of a treaty or an international agreement if it does not already have that status . . .[7]

---

[1] For a general survey of definitions, see Foulke, *Treatise on International Law* (1920), vol. 1, pp. 405 et seq. Examples of writers employing the definition in question are: Fiore, op. cit. (above, p. 117 n. 3), s. 744; Kraus, *Recueil des cours*, 50 (1934–IV), p. 322; Cosentini, *Code internationale de la paix* (1937), s. 814; Despagnet, *Cours de droit international public* (1910), p. 676; Vellas, *Droit international public* (1967), p. 98.

[2] For example: L'Huillier, *Eléments de droit international public* (1950), p. 171; Rousseau, *Droit international public*, vol. 1 (1970), p. 63.

[3] For example: Anzilotti, *Cours de droit international* (Gidel trans., 1929), p. 333; Oppenheim, *International Law*, vol. 1 (Lauterpacht, 8th edn., 1955), p. 877; Sen, *A Diplomat's Handbook of International Law and Practice* (1965), pp. 439 et seq.

[4] See Doc. A/CONF. 39/11/Add. 2, pp. 7 et seq.

[5] Loc. cit. (above, p. 118 n. 5), at p. 530.

[6] McNair, *The Law of Treaties* (1961), p. 4. The Harvard Research Draft and American *Restatement* adopt similar definitions.

[7] On the scope and history of Article 102 see Rosenne, 'United Nations Treaty Practice', *Recueil des cours*, 86 (1954–II), p. 281, and Brandon, *American Journal of International Law*, 47 (1953), p. 49.

While the question of accurate definition, of tracking down the essential requirements, does not appear to tax the minds of Foreign Office legal advisers nor to appear often in the centre-stage of international controversy, some conclusions can be drawn in terms of reason alone: most importantly, that a definition framed in terms of the parties' intention is to be preferred. For if the parties wish to make a non-binding agreement they are free so to do by making that intention plain: from the intention flows the force of bindingness. Whatever be the constitutive nature of the principle *pacta sunt servanda*, its coming into operation is a function of State volition.

It is all very well to say, as did members of the International Law Commission,[1] that to employ the term 'treaty' to denote 'an agreement under international law' implies, through incorporation of the phrase 'under international law', that the parties intend to bind themselves; but this is tautologous. In the end all that is said is that an international agreement is an agreement governed by international law.

A definition couched in terms of the parties' intentions must be favoured. Whether that intention should relate to the creation of rights and/or obligations (and it must be enquired whether a reference to rights is necessary at all: if an obligation is intended, a correlative right is implicit in it) or to establishment of a relationship or production of effects in law is not easy to say.

It is axiomatic that a binding agreement gives rise to an obligation on the part of at least one of the parties. It is the intention to pledge oneself to some act or omission that gives rise to the application of the principle *pacta sunt servanda*. If no 'obligation' is intended there can be no question of 'being bound'. These are general principles of law, as Sir Hersch Lauterpacht pointed out in his separate opinion in the *Norwegian Loans* case.[2]

Whether the words 'establish a relationship' or 'produce effects' adequately capture the essence of obliging, or putting oneself under a disability, is debatable. The proponents of such formulations seldom divulge what they mean by 're-lationship'.[3] Unless they mean a relationship constituted by binding obligations *inter se*, the term appears unduly vague and might cover, for example, a joint communiqué where two Foreign Ministers speak in political terms of their aspirations for future relations, an instrument not normally considered a treaty.

The essence of these definitions is agreement considered by the parties to be binding on them, an undertaking whose terms they must carry out. Another way to express the same idea, and this formulation draws attention to the real question that must be asked, is, are the parties (or is one of them) making serious promises or undertakings: undertakings that are intended to be acted upon and relied upon?

Yet however a definition be framed, whether in terms of intention or of the actual creation of an obligation or relationship, that gash in the side of the international system, the absence of a system of compulsory settlement of disputes, disgorges monstrous complications even at this stage. For without such a system how does one demonstrate intention to create a 'binding' rather

[1] Below, pp. 132–4.　　[2] *I.C.J. Reports*, 1957, p. 9 at p. 49.　　[3] See Lauterpacht I, p. 100.

than a 'hope to fulfil' type of promise? Can it be assumed that a State is 'undertaking' when there is likely to be no impartial judicial settlement of any dispute arising out of the transaction and certainly no enforcement agency?

It was this dilemma that led Professor Fawcett to make his acute observations in this *Year Book* in 1953.[1] While conceding that he was writing largely *de lege ferenda*, Professor Fawcett stressed the need for greater care over form in international agreements so that the juridical character of an agreement may be more readily ascertainable. More ambitiously, he built up his own theory that there is no presumption that States, in concluding an agreement, intend to create legal relations at all and that this intention must be clearly manifested before legal character is attached to the agreement. He is using the term 'legal' in the sense of 'binding' undertaking.

Professor Fawcett touches upon the English Law of Contract and particularly the leading case on intention to create legal relations, *Rose and Frank* v. *Crompion*,[2] which appears to hold that parties to an agreement can make it binding 'in honour' only but that they must do so precisely and clearly. Further, the decision suggests that if the agreement is in the normal form of a contract there will be a presumption that the parties intended to create legal relations. These principles exist, Professor Fawcett shows, in all the major legal systems but they are not, in his view, equally applicable to the international system for two reasons:

(a) States and governments differ greatly from individuals in the type of business they transact by means of agreements: it is mainly of an administrative and technical nature resembling inter-departmental co-operation agreements, not in private law the subject of legal obligations.

Two criticisms can be made of this view. First, administrative and technical agreements form only one class (admittedly a large class) of international agreements. Secondly, the reason inter-departmental agreements are not usually enforced in municipal courts is not because they are treated as inherently different from ordinary contracts but rather because the parties are the same person-in-law, the State.

(b) The requirement of the consent of States for judicial settlement of international disputes raises the contrary presumption[3] because there can be no general assumption of intention to create a legal obligation if there is no compulsory dispute settlement procedure.

---

[1] This *Year Book*, 30 (1953), p. 381.

[2] *Rose and Frank* v. *Crompton Bros.*, [1923] 2 K.B. 261 (in the Court of Appeal). This case is referred to by Dr. Münch in his article in *Zeitschrift für ausländisches öffentliches Recht und Völkerrecht*, 30 (1969), p. 1. His conclusion is that the case, and all those of its kind, shows only that the opinion of the parties regarding the effect and force of their agreement is insignificant. The true position seems to be the reverse: in business dealings the English courts will assume intention to create legal relations; in social affairs they will assume the opposite. But either presumption may be defeated by a clear indication of the intention of the parties: see Bankes L.J. at p. 282. See also Treitel, *The Law of Contract* (4th edn., 1975), pp. 97 et seq.

[3] A similar controversy rages in Anglo-American labour law. In the labour law context the normally efficient enforcement-settlement system has collapsed because one of the parties to the dispute has, in the *de facto* sense, more power than the system itself.

This second argument can be dismissed with the theoretical response that it confuses substantive legal norms with access to a particular remedy. (And if one is speaking in practical terms, as Fawcett appears to be, surely it is enforcement that is important, not access to legal machinery for dispute-settlement. There is no adequate enforcement procedure over any category of agreement under international law.)

Even after dealing with this view, however, the dilemma remains: what are the criteria of a legal agreement? We can only return here to the formulation raised earlier: if the parties agree and one or both of them is or are obliged to act in a certain way, in other words if the promise or promises is or are serious and intended to be acted upon, a legal, rather than political, relationship is established. Clearly this view implies that the principle *pacta sunt servanda* is accepted as a legal directive whether or not the *pactum* in question is the subject of an agreed dispute settlement procedure.

Thus the severity of Professor Fawcett's system is rejected but the legitimacy of its intellectual bases acknowledged. The system will later be tested against some tentative conclusions from the relevant State practice.

Having stated his theory, Professor Fawcett continues by setting out a number of cases in which intention to create legal relations will, in his opinion, be manifested:

(i) where there is provision in the agreement for compulsory judicial settlement of disputes;

(ii) where both parties have accepted in advance the jurisdiction of the International Court of Justice and that acceptance covers disputes concerning the application or interpretation of the agreement in question;[1]

(iii) where the subject-matter of the agreement demonstrates an intention on the part of those concluding it that it be governed by international law. As examples of this third category Professor Fawcett cites constitutions of international organizations, conventions touching rights and obligations under private law and those operating under a framework of accepted rules of international law, such as consular conventions.

The precise ambit of class (iii) is unclear. In one sense all international agreements intended to create binding obligations operate under a framework of accepted rules of international law, the rules of treaty law, but this is obviously not what Professor Fawcett has in mind. His illustrations tend to suggest that the agreements he is discussing are those of specific and particular obligation, customs, navigation, consular, diplomatic and so on, but the only inherent difference between these agreements and those such as scientific and cultural co-operation conventions is that one set of obligations is likely to be more

---

[1] There is just the tiniest support for Professor Fawcett in a curious passage by Denmark in the Pleadings for the *Eastern Greenland* case (*P.C.I.J. Documents*, vol. 62, p. 112), where the following is found (to be read bearing in mind that one allegation was that Norway had breached the terms of certain agreements with Denmark): 'Étant donné qu'il existe entre les deux pays des traités d'arbitrage et autres qui les obligent à faire résoudre par voie judiciaire tous différends qui pourraient s'élever entre eux . . . la déclaration Norvégienne . . . constitue un acte illicite.'

specifically delimited. This latter set of agreements will be investigated below at greater length and it will be suggested that, despite broad drafting, discernible obligations are often undertaken. Why, then, should a cultural convention differ juridically from a consular convention?

Professor Fawcett rejects a fourth possible test, registration under Article 102 of the United Nations Charter, for the reasons (a) that neither Article 102 of the Charter nor the Regulations made under it define 'treaty' or 'international agreement' and do not therefore require there to be evidenced an intention to create legal relations and (b) that registration is not a mandatory requirement of being 'a treaty or international agreement' but is rather a condition precedent of agreements being considered by United Nations organs.

To conclude, Professor Fawcett analyses those agreements which contain provisions appearing to negative any intent to create legal obligations—provisions which in one way or another leave it to the parties or one of them to determine the extent of the obligation they have assumed. Terms such as 'subject to the law in force' (a formula sought by the Soviet Union to be inserted into the Human Rights Conventions), or 'to assist by such action as it deems necessary' (Article 1, North Atlantic Treaty), can, he claims, in most cases amount to no more than a declaration of policy or goodwill 'for an obligation cannot be properly called a legal obligation unless its existence and extent are determinable judicially'.

It has already been suggested that a promise, or exchange of promises, cannot be considered binding if no obligation is thereby undertaken. If the promise is so hedged with reservations and self-judging riders that it cannot be truly said to be a promise at all, there is no substance to pour into the agreement form, and it must be assumed that no obligation was intended. It might be going too far to speak of this requirement, as some do, as a 'general principle of law', basing it on the premiss common to all legal systems,[1] that obligations undertaken must be capable of judicial ascertainment. In a system where compulsory jurisdiction is not established, it is clearly more accurate to talk in terms of evidence of intention of the parties. But whether Professor Fawcett's examples are really of this non-legal character is debatable. The clause 'subject to the law in force' cuts down the size of the obligation that might otherwise have arisen but cannot be said to annihilate it completely. There is something left, something ascertainable by both parties, a discernible realm of obligation.

Another difficulty with Professor Fawcett's approach is that in concentrating unduly on the provision of *ante hoc* submission of disputes to a tribunal, it ignores the fact that the parties to an agreement can, at any time, agree to submit a dispute to the Court or an arbitral tribunal. If both parties trust each other's seriousness they will not have excluded the possibility of *post hoc* submission.

There appears to be no distinction made in the practice of States between those treaties subject to a system of compulsory dispute settlement and those not so subject. And, in connection with Fawcett's second class of binding agreements, is it really suggested that Foreign Offices link their treaty-making with acceptance

[1] Below, p. 130.

of the Optional Clause of the Statute of the International Court of Justice? Certainly, Foreign Office treaty lists do not reflect these distinctions.

In a survey of 'treaties and international agreements' registered with the Secretary-General of the United Nations in the five years between 1967 and 1971 (Volumes 588–799 of the *United Nations Treaty Series*)[1] some 2,400 bilateral and plurilateral instruments (plurilateral in the sense of more than one entity on one side but undertaking jointly as a single group, e.g. Benelux) were studied. Out of this figure only approximately 450 (fewer than 20 per cent) contained dispute settlement clauses of the type envisaged by Professor Fawcett.[2] This figure can be broken down thus:[3]

Type of Instrument	Percentage Containing Dispute Settlement Clause
Treaty	5
Convention	7·5
Agreement	33
Exchange of notes/letters	1·5
Others	0

The most interesting aspect of this part of the survey is that, in the case of agreements and exchanges of notes, the subject-matter of both of which was wide-ranging and intrinsically alike, they were treated so differently in the matter of inclusion of dispute-settlement clauses. This, however, is most sensibly explained by the fact that 'Agreement' is the form of instrument used by the International Bank for Reconstruction and Development and by the International Development Association for loan and guarantee transactions with States, as well as the form recommended by the International Civil Aviation Organization for civil aviation agreements between member States. These number probably over 30 per cent of all 'agreements' registered. All (or nearly all) of them contain a compulsory dispute settlement clause.

[1] A few volumes (six) were not at the time available, but the remaining ones are considered representative of registration practice in the period. Sometimes a bundle of instruments would be registered at the same time and given a single number in the series. In such cases, usually involving a major convention or agreement followed by a protocol or exchange of notes, spelling out, interpreting or even amending certain provisions of the master agreement, we have included in the survey only the master agreement. The subsidiary instruments concern the same transaction and are usually expressed to be an integral part of the master agreement, it being the master agreement which contains provisions on termination, dispute settlement and so on.

[2] While Professor Fawcett has argued that registration is not indicative of intention 'to create legal relations', this is a view with which we disagree for reasons given later in the Article. But even assuming he is correct, if any conclusions at all are to be drawn from State practice, they can only be based on the *United Nations Treaty Series* (of registered treaties and international agreements) as the only comprehensive collection available. It must be assumed that even if Professor Fawcett is correct, nearly all of these instruments are intended to be binding.

[3] In the case of multilateral instruments, the conclusions were as follows: Treaties 0; Conventions 20%; Agreements 33%. The percentages here are higher, presumably because most of these instruments are concluded within international organizations where the organization itself may have a policy on compromissory clauses. The Secretariat of the organization might even have drafted the instrument.

With this in mind, the low percentages in all forms of instrument do not suggest that States believe that inclusion of a compulsory dispute settlement clause is of significance in ascertaining the legal status of the instrument.[1] It can, of course, be argued that many of the instruments not containing such a clause will be covered by declarations under Article 36 (2) of the I.C.J. Statute, but recalling the fact that fewer than one third of U.N. members have filed declarations, the vast cavities of reservations hollowed out of them and the necessity for both parties to a dispute to have lodged declarations in terms covering the particular dispute in question, it seems unlikely that the figures would be much improved.

Apart from the I.B.R.D., I.D.A. and I.C.A.O. instruments mentioned above, there were no specific subjects on which a dispute settlement clause was relatively more often to be found.

The most obvious conclusion from the survey was that in about 99 per cent of the instruments containing a dispute settlement clause, at least one of the parties was a Western country (West European, North American, Australasian), most often the U.S.A., France, the Netherlands and Denmark. This indicates, it is submitted, that the use of such a clause is more related to one of the parties' views on the compulsory settlement of disputes in international law generally.[2]

*   *   *

Some of these tentative conclusions on the nature of 'international agreement' will now be supported by the Reports of the Special Rapporteurs on Treaties in the International Law Commission. The Commission's involvement in studying the law of treaties lasted some sixteen years and it is perhaps most sensible to look at the Reports seriatim.

The first Special Rapporteur (Professor Brierly) defined 'treaty', for the purposes of the draft articles, as 'an agreement recorded in writing . . . which establishes a relationship under international law'. Paragraph 19 of his commentary makes it clear that by 'establishment of a relationship' the Special Rapporteur meant creation of rights and obligations, but no criteria or tests are suggested.

The Special Rapporteur accuses the Harvard Research Draft on Treaties of excessive ambit in including instruments which merely seek to establish a relationship under international law, stating that if no rights or obligations are established there can be no legal act. But according to the Commentary of the Harvard Research Draft, what was being attempted was to find a term which included within it both rights and obligations at the same time.[3] However, in so far as there is a suggestion in the Harvard Commentary to Article 1 that there may be 'treaties' not giving rise to rights or obligations, one could agree with Professor Brierly. It should be noted that when intention to create an obligation

---

[1] See p. 125 n. 2, above.

[2] Of the present parties to the optional clause of the I.C.J. Statute, nearly half are Western European Union members and about one-fifth Latin American.

[3] Loc. cit. (above, p. 117 n. 3). If an obligation is intended, a concurrent right will *ipso facto* be intended. As long as there is agreement, there need not be obligations on both sides. There is certainly no doctrine of consideration or *causa*.

is spoken of it is not necessarily a provision to act immediately. The obligation to act or not to act may relate to the future as in the case, for example, of an undertaking 'to allow free passage when demanded' or, as in the case of many law-making treaties, it might be a continuing obligation (for example, to respect another State's claim in a particular matter).

Discussion in the Commission about this draft Article was frustrated by an outbreak of confusion over the place of municipal law concepts of 'treaty',[1] and a cloud of ambiguity was thrown over the scope of the articles by Professor Scelle and others who refused to acknowledge, for example, that an exchange of notes constituted a 'treaty' (presumably in the narrow sense, but the fact that the debate took this course is some indication of the terminological confusion inherent in these terms).

Professor Brierly was succeeded in 1952 by Professor (later Sir Hersch) Lauterpacht who made it clear at the very outset that his draft articles were to apply to all forms of international agreement.

Draft Article 1 provided that:

Treaties are agreements . . . intended to create legal rights and obligations of the parties

and Article 2:

Agreements constitute treaties regardless of their form and regardless of whether they are expressed in one or more instruments.[2]

In his Commentary,[3] the Special Rapporteur stressed that his main purpose was to exclude from his definition instruments in the nature of statements of policy, the test for distinguishing between the two types of instrument being one of intention. Capacity to carry out that intention was a relevant consideration within the test: for if the act promised was incapable of being rendered, this would suggest a lack of intention to bind.

As an example of a non-binding agreement the Special Rapporteur cited the Communiqué of the Moscow Conference of 26 December 1945.[4] This lack of bindingness in law Lauterpacht derived from a statement in the Communiqué that the discussions 'took place on an informal and exploratory basis'. Nonetheless

[1] *Yearbook of the International Law Commission*, 1951, vol. 1, pp. 13 et seq.
[2] Lauterpacht I, pp. 93 et seq.
[3] Ibid., pp. 93 et seq., and see Lauterpacht II, pp. 123 et seq.
[4] *United Nations Treaty Series*, vol. 20, p. 272. Another example he gives is that of an exchange of notes reported in the *Department of State Bulletin* of 7 September 1940 (vol. 3, p. 195). On 4 June 1940 the Prime Minister of the United Kingdom issued a statement to the effect that should the British Isles become untenable for British ships of war, the British fleet would in no event be surrendered but would be sent overseas for defence of other parts of the Empire. On 29 August 1940 the following enquiry was received by the British Ambassador to the U.S.A.: 'The Government of the U.S.A. would respectfully enquire whether the foregoing statement represents the settled policy of the British Government.' An affirmative answer was given. It is difficult to conceive of such an exchange as constituting a binding agreement. It is surely no more than an enquiry from one Government to another about future policy in war-time: a contingent matter. The British reply does in fact refer to hypothetical contingencies. In any case the obligation, if one existed, would seem to be more in the nature of a unilateral undertaking by Great Britain, the U.S.A. being an enquirer rather than party to an agreement.

the Communiqué does speak of 'agreement' and uses words of obligation in some clauses:

> . . . have agreed to meet regularly;
> . . . have agreed to the following procedures with respect to the preparation of the Peace Treaties;
> . . . have agreed to establish a Far East Commission and a Council of Japan.

Other clauses were less likely to have been intended to be binding: ' . . . the three Foreign Secretaries exchanged views on China and were agreed on the need for a unified China . . . they reaffirmed their adherence to a policy of non-interference in internal affairs . . .'. Such formulations as these give some indications of the problems involved in ascertaining the intention of the parties.

Lauterpacht's Commentary notes with impeccable logic[1] that the fact that the obligation provided for in the instrument can be fulfilled by a somewhat nominal act of the parties does not detract from its character as a treaty (e.g., an obligation to consult). It is for the parties to limit the extent of the obligations flowing between them. Similarly, an undertaking to negotiate implies a legal obligation so to do although it usually leaves a wide measure of discretion to the State bound by it.[2] A legal duty must also, he writes, be deemed to exist in those marginal cases in which, by virtue of the instrument in question, a State reserves for itself the right to determine both the existence and extent of the obligation undertaken by it[3] as, for instance, in the case of some declarations of acceptance of Article 36 (2) of the Statute of the I.C.J. in which the declaring States have reserved for themselves the right to determine whether a matter falls within their domestic jurisdiction. Such a determination must take place in accordance with the implied obligation to act in good faith.[4]

Professor Lauterpacht was obviously concerned lest his formulation result in uncertainty, for in his second Report he submitted for consideration the question whether it might be desirable to add to draft Article I the following words:

> In the absence of evidence to the contrary an instrument finally accepted by both parties in the customary form of an international undertaking and registered with the United Nations in accordance with Article 102 of the United Nations Charter shall be deemed to be an instrument creating rights and obligations.[5]

The Special Rapporteur repeated his observation that the fact that the scope of the obligation is elastic is not a decisive factor for denying that there is in existence a legal duty to be fulfilled in good faith: the same considerations must apply as would to agreements allowing both parties to suspend, temporarily

---

[1] At p. 124.   [2] E.g., the *Tacna-Arica* decision. See Lauterpacht I, p. 97, n. 11.

[3] This, the Special Rapporteur writes, is also the position with agreements such as the North Atlantic Treaty of 4 April 1949 in which each party agrees to assist others by such action as it deems necessary in cases of attack against them. Such a provision does not exclude the final impartial determination of the legitimacy of the action then taken. Cf. Fawcett, loc. cit. (above, p. 122 n. 1), pp. 391 et seq., and see below, p. 139.

[4] Cf. Judge Lauterpacht's separate opinions in the *Norwegian Loans* and *Interhandel* cases, below.

[5] Lauterpacht II, p. 123. Registration, he says, should not be considered decisive but weight should be attached to it.

or fully, the agreement on immediate notice. Lauterpacht II contains many examples of broadly drafted clauses in treaties, all considered by the Special Rapporteur to contain some element of binding obligation.

In a reply to Fawcett, Lauterpacht states quite firmly that there is no warrant for the suggestion that instruments do not, on account of either the large measure of discretion inherent in their application or of their purely administrative character, exhibit the essential characteristics of an international treaty. As to the importance of a dispute settlement clause, Sir Hersch rests content with the observation that there was no reason why requirements in the law of treaties should be higher than in any other branches of the law.[1]

Sir Hersch Lauterpacht became a Judge of the International Court of Justice before his draft articles were considered by the Commission. His place was taken in 1955 by Sir Gerald Fitzmaurice.

Soon after taking his place in the International Court of Justice, Judge Lauterpacht's views on elasticity in obligation were put to the test in two cases. Both involved the efficacy of reservations to declarations made under Article 36 (2) of the Court's Statute.

In the first, the *Norwegian Loans* case,[2] France took action against Norway. Norway claimed the right to take advantage of a French reservation excluding 'matters which are essentially within the national jurisdiction as understood by the Government of the French Republic'. While the majority of the Court understood Norway to be relying on the self-judging nature of the reservation (although Norway for the most part argued that under international law, the matter was one of domestic jurisdiction),[3] the validity of the reservation or the declaration as a whole was not questioned by either party. This is an odd matter in itself, for if such a declaration is invalid as containing no obligation, the Court would have no jurisdiction. The Court is under a duty to ascertain that it does indeed have jurisdiction in cases brought before it.[4]

Some of the separate opinions, however, raised the question. Judge Guerrero[5] thought that the French declaration conformed neither to the spirit of the Statute nor to paragraphs 2 and 6 of Article 36 and that the reservation was thus void; it ceased to be compulsory jurisdiction if France rather than the Court held the power to determine. It was also in conflict with Article 36 because there was no real obligation to submit the matter to the Court's jurisdiction.

Judge Read, on the other hand,[6] considered that, properly construed, the French declaration meant that the Respondent State must establish that there was a genuine understanding, i.e. that the circumstances were such that it would be reasonably possible to reach the understanding that the dispute was essentially national, whether the circumstances were such being a matter for decision not by

---

[1] Ibid., p. 126. [2] *I.C.J. Reports*, 1957, p. 9.

[3] In fact Judges Basdevant and Read based their decisions on the assumption that Norway had not in fact wished to press this argument (at pp. 71 and 79 respectively).

[4] Judge Lauterpacht raised this point at p. 61. It could be argued that, in so far as the point was not argued by the parties, this could be considered a waiver by Norway, giving rise to implied consent, *pro tanto*, to jurisdiction.

[5] Pp. 67 et seq. [6] Pp. 94 et seq.

national government but by the Court.[1] One is tempted to agree with this viewpoint, for 'understood' has indeed a core of objective meaning, far more so than the word 'claimed', for example.

Judge Lauterpacht in a very long separate opinion[2] maintained with vigour that the Court had acted in disregard of both its Statute and Article 92 of the United Nations Charter, which lays down that the Court shall function in accordance with the provisions of its Statute.

Judge Lauterpacht had two grounds for his views. The first is that, as the Court cannot act other than in accordance with its Statute, an acceptance of jurisdiction in these terms was a clear contradiction of the Statute and therefore invalid. States were free, he said, to make reservations but the question whether 'the little that is left' was or was not subject to the jurisdiction of the Court must be determined by the Court itself.

This argument, concerned with interpretation of the Court's Statute, does not appear convincing. One finds force in the counter-argument that the Court is still free in such a case to determine its jurisdiction: however wide the words employed, they must still be interpreted.

The second ground[3] is that the automatic reservation was invalid because it lacked the essential conditions of validity necessary in a legal obligation. In reality the French Republic had undertaken no obligation and there is a 'general principle of law' that an undertaking in which one party reserves for itself the right to determine the extent or the very existence of the obligation is not a legal undertaking. 'It is irrelevant', Judge Lauterpacht added, 'that having regard to public opinion, an enlightened State is not likely to invoke any such reservation capriciously, unjustifiably or in bad faith. These are expectations which may or may not materialise.'

While the result achieved by this approach is agreeable it would, for reasons given earlier, be preferable to base such a finding on the implication that an undertaking so hedged with self-judging reservations is not intended to be serious or binding, rather than on a general legal principle more appropriate to a compulsory municipal system.

Judge Lauterpacht next dealt shortly with the view that, in such cases, the State must be considered to be under an obligation to act in good faith and, to that extent, there is in existence a valid legal obligation. In so doing he reversed the position he took in the International Law Commission, admitting that after further study he could not support that view. If no room is left for an impartial finding whether the duty to act in accordance with 'good faith' has been fulfilled, then the requirement to act in 'good faith' has no meaning.

With respect, this is tautologous: if the 'good faith' requirement is incorporated into the obligation, then there is indeed something to grasp. Judge Lauterpacht seems to be saying that France has excluded the Court's power of jurisdic-

---

[1] He supports his view by the plain terms rule of interpretation. Recent cases in English Administrative Law clearly demonstrate the Courts' ability to find objective meaning in words like these.

[2] *I.C.J. Reports*, 1957, pp. 34 et seq.

[3] Ibid., pp. 48 et seq.

tional determination therefore there can be no investigation of *fides*. It can be replied that if France were under an obligation to make a determination in good faith (it is assumed that to act in good faith is not inconsistent with the actual words used), there must be room for the Court to investigate and reject extremely capricious and extravagant action.[1]

Judge Lauterpacht concluded that the reservation was invalid and, being an essential part of the French Government's consent to be bound, not separable. The whole Declaration was invalid.

In the second case, *Interhandel*,[2] the majority did not need to consider Swiss arguments based on the American Connally Clause. Judge Lauterpacht[3] in another strong separate opinion, however, repeated the views he had expressed in *Norwegian Loans*. This time he traced the history of the formulation of the United States' reservation and found no ground for the suggestion that its plain meaning could be limited by concepts of reasonableness or good faith. It was simply not so intended.[4]

Judge Spender[5] agreed with Judge Lauterpacht for the same reasons and added, somewhat gratuitously, that Judge Read would not, on the particular formulation now before the Court, have been able to imply an obligation that the determination must be 'reasonable'. Nor was there room, from the plain terms of the reservation, to add a duty to act in good faith.

The President, Judge Klaestad,[6] agreed but felt the offending reservation could be severed because the declarant party doubtless wished to be in a postion to sue other States: this was the clear purpose of the declaration. The reservation was a subsidiary matter.[7]

The next stage of the I.L.C. process was Fitzmaurice I in a different form from that of any other Rapporteur: a draft code, impeccably logical, containing copious commentary and opening with the following two Articles:

(1) The present code relates to treaties and other international agreements in the nature of treaties embodied in a single instrument and to international agreements embodied in other forms . . . provided always that they are in writing.

The present code does not as such apply to international agreements not in written form the validity of which is not, however, on that account to be regarded as prejudiced.

(2) For the purposes of the application of the present code, a treaty is an international

---

[1] Judge Lauterpacht says that an enquiry into 'good faith' would end up becoming an enquiry into the merits, not possible at the jurisdictional stage. This need not be so: a better analogy is that with an application to the Court for provisional measures of protection where a prima facie case on the merits may have to be made out. In any case, an enquiry into the decision by a State to 'understand' a dispute as involving national jurisdiction need not necessarily touch upon the legal merits of the dispute at all.

[2] *I.C.J. Reports*, 1959, p. 6.

[3] Ibid., pp. 95 et seq.

[4] All these views will be further considered later.

[5] *I.C.J. Reports*, 1959, pp. 55 et seq.

[6] Ibid., pp. 75 et seq. Judge Armand-Ugon agreed with this view, pp. 91 et seq.

[7] It seems difficult to summon up a good argument in favour of severance. The reservation was certainly intended to percolate throughout the declaration. It was not really a reservation at all, more an integral part of the declaration.

agreement embodied in a single formal instrument intended to create rights and obligations or to establish relationships governed by international law.[1]

Thus the Special Rapporteur has defined 'treaty' narrowly but not limited his
draft articles to such instruments.[2]

So far as concerns a test for discerning a treaty obligation, Sir Gerald has, in
Article 2 (1), added to the Lauterpacht formula the earlier Brierly I criterion of
'intention to establish a relationship' because 'it seems difficult to refuse the
designation of treaty to an instrument such as, for instance, a Treaty of Peace
and Amity or of Alliance even if it only establishes a bare relationship and leaves
the consequences to rest on the basis of an implication as to the rights and
obligations involved'.[3]

One senses that Sir Hersch Lauterpacht's reply would have been, and rightly,
that if such an implication must be made, then there are indeed rights and
obligations intended to be created. Moreover, if treaties of peace are not intended
to give rise to rights and obligations, nothing is.

Sir Gerald did not adopt Lauterpacht's proposal concerning the effect of
registration. First, in regard to the fact of registration with the U.N.,[4] he thought
that because Article 102 provided that only a 'treaty or international agreement'
was registrable, such instruments must have this character before the obligation
to register would arise. (Is this not an argument for, rather than against, the
Lauterpacht formulation?) Secondly, such a test or presumption would be
dangerous in a system where registration is by one party only in most cases.[5]

From our point of view the most interesting debate within the Commission
took place over the passage 'intended to create rights and obligations or to
establish relationships governed by international law.'

Professor Ago[6] wondered whether it might not be better to find a more general
formulation. Were agreements intended to establish rules rather than to create
directly rights and obligations covered by it? And agreements dealing with
interpretation of an earlier treaty or settlement of a particular dispute? And Mr.
Alfaro[6] added to this list agreements amending, regulating or terminating rights.

Sir Gerald agreed that all these instruments must be subject to the draft
articles. He had, rightly it is submitted,[7] assumed they were. His main concern

---

[1] In order to avoid the problem faced by Professor Brierly in the early Commission debates
(confusion between international and municipal concepts), the Special Rapporteur provided in
draft Article 2 (4) that the fact that an instrument is or is not, as the case may be, regarded as a
treaty for the purpose of the present code does not in any way affect its status in relation to the
constitutional requirements of particular States.

[2] There was some concern in the Commission in 1959 (*Yearbook of the International Law
Commission*, vol. 1, pp. 4 et seq.) concerning the way in which the Special Rapporteur had treated
upon all forms of international agreement. The extreme doctrinaire views prevalent at the discussion on Brierly I seem, however, to have been dissipated. At the 485th Meeting (loc. cit.,
p. 26) the Special Rapporteur re-entitled his definition section: 'Definition of International
Agreement' to make his position even clearer.   [3] Fitzmaurice I, p. 117.

[4] See p. 128 above.   [5] These arguments will be considered later.

[6] *Yearbook of the International Law Commission*, 1959, vol. 1, p. 34.

[7] Above. If the agreement is intended to establish rules, the rules must create obligations.
Even the great law-making conventions begin as obligations and rights (rules) for the parties.

had been to except agreements subject to some legal system other than the international one. He suggested that a more general formula, if such were required, might be, 'the provisions of which are intended to be governed by international law'. Or, as another alternative, he suggested insertion of the words '. . . or to produce effects' after the word relationship in the final draft. The articles were referred to the Drafting Committee and, as Sir Gerald was elevated to the bench soon afterwards, time stood still until Sir Humphrey Waldock produced his first Report in 1962.

Article II of Sir Humphrey Waldock's first Report contains the following provisions on use of terms:[1]

(a) 'International Agreement' means an agreement intended to be governed by international law;

(b) 'Treaty' means any international agreement in any written form whether embodied in a single instrument or in two or more related instruments and whatever its particular designation.

The Special Rapporteur has, then,[2] in contradistinction to Sir Gerald, widened the term 'treaty' so as to include, for example, an exchange of notes. He is dealing with the law of treaties. Sir Gerald dealt with the law of international agreements. The scope of both drafts, however, is essentially the same.

Sir Humphrey's criterion, 'intention to be governed by international law', beneficially salvages the intention test but otherwise is a wide formulation leaving as much hidden as it reveals.

The Commission debated Waldock I during its 1962 session.[3] Following suggestions that description of the terms 'treaty' and 'international agreement' might sensibly be combined, the Special Rapporteur produced a new simple text reading:

Treaty means any international agreement in any written form whether embodied in a single instrument or in two or more related instruments and whatever its particular designation . . . which is intended to be governed by international law.[4]

Mr Tsuruoka[4] asked why the words 'intended to be . . .' were necessary. Mr. Gros replied, correctly it would seem, that whatever wording was adopted in the Commission, the intention of the parties would always have to be sought in

Similarly, an agreement interpreting an earlier agreement contains an obligation: the parties are no longer free to interpret the earlier agreement in any other way. Agreements for the settlement of disputes oblige the parties to settle the dispute in the manner agreed. Mr Alfaro's examples of agreements regulating, amending or terminating can be treated likewise. Any agreement intended to alter a previous obligation must contain within itself an obligation of like force.

[1] Sir Humphrey was often at pains to point out that he was not dealing with absolute definitions but the use of terms for the purpose of his draft articles.

[2] The Special Rapporteur states that the term treaty in the narrow sense probably constitutes a particular type of international instrument consisting of a single formal instrument and commonly subject to ratification but that the law of treaties applies to many other forms of agreement. In justifying his use of the term treaty in the wider sense, he refers to Article 36 (2) of the Statute of the I.C.J. where the term is used generally. He follows Sir Gerald in providing that the use of terms in the draft articles is without prejudice to their meanings in municipal constitutional law.

[3] *Yearbook of the International Law Commission*, 1962, vol. 1, pp. 46 et seq.

[4] Ibid., p. 51.

order to ascertain whether any given agreement was meant to be governed by international law. Professor Ago, however, wished to see the reference to intention deleted, claiming that it implied that the parties were free to decide whether a treaty would or would not be governed by international law.

It is, of course, the view of this writer[1] that a reference to intention is desirable. Professor Ago's contention can be met with the reply that even if there is a class of agreements which cannot be subjected to any legal system other than the international one, it still remains to be shown that the parties intended to create a legal obligation, a binding undertaking. And the number of agreements which can be submitted to no other legal system than the international one must be small indeed.[2] Mr. Yasseen,[3] in the same debate, thought it inconceivable that an agreement concerning territorial seas should not be subject to international law, whatever the will of the parties. This must be true only to the extent that to alter or to transfer rights in international law, an international legal agreement is necessary; but it is not inconceivable that State A might wish to grant, under its own municipal law, some rights to State B over its territorial sea resources.

In short, it is difficult to contemplate that there is a large class of agreements which can be submitted only to international law and, even more important, it is denied that the existence of such a class would prove in any way that the parties' liberty to agree, without binding themselves, is dependent on something other than their own intention.

The Special Rapporteur, however, agreed, a little too readily, to delete the 'intention' formula 'if misunderstandings might be caused by it'.[4] The Drafting Committee formally extinguished it.

This, then, leaves the definition, or use of terms provisions, in a tautologous and unhelpful state. Despite Mr. Amado's pointing out[5] that there was now no real working definition (it had been reduced to the proposition that 'an international agreement is an agreement governed by international law'), the revised article was adopted by the Commission.

Sir Humphrey's fourth Report[6] consisted of remarks and amendments made in the light of comments by Governments. Both Australia and Austria felt deep concern over the scope of the term 'treaty'. Australia foresaw a danger that the revised article might include within its ambit informal understandings not intended to give rise to legal rights or obligations. The intention test would, it was thought, have provided greater protection. Austria and the United Kingdom made similar suggestions and Luxembourg noted the tautologous nature of the draft scope article.

In reply, Sir Humphrey traced the history of the formulation as it now appeared, stressing his opinion that the term 'governed by international law'

---

[1] Above, p. 121.

[2] If any. The example given by Professor Ago is a treaty of cession. This might constitute the only example.

[3] *Yearbook of the International Law Commission*, 1962, vol. 1, p. 52.

[4] Ibid., p. 53. Sir Humphrey expressed some feelings of regret at the deletion during the Second Session at Vienna, below, p. 135 n. 7.

[5] Ibid., p. 169.   [6] At pp. 10, 11 and 12.

conveyed within it the requirement of intent. At its 810th meeting, on 24 June 1965,[1] the Commission adopted the revised article:

I (a). 'Treaty' means an[2] agreement in written form governed by international law whether embodied in a single instrument or two or more related instruments and whatever its particular designation.

In the Sixth Committee of the United Nations General Assembly in 1962, and 1966, and again in 1967, and in the later replies and views of Governments the wish by many to return to a formula involving 'intention' was strongly expressed, as was a wish by some to return to a 'definition' containing an express reference to the creation of obligations.[3]

Following resolution 2166 (XXI) of the General Assembly, an international conference on the law of treaties was held in Vienna in 1968 and 1969. The procedure adopted by the Conference involved formation into a Committee of the Whole which proceeded mainly by way of article by article discussion of the draft and of amendments submitted. After consideration, and a vote if necessary on principle, articles were referred to the Drafting Committee, returning to the Committee and finally to Plenary for adoption.[4]

On Article 2, the renumbered scope article, a number of delegations tabled amendments[5] in favour of reinsertion of a clause along the lines of 'producing legal effects' or 'creating rights and obligations' or 'establishing a relationship', all of these more explicit than 'governed by international law', but not necessarily adding significantly to the definition. Malaysia and Australia[6] spoke in favour of an intention test[7] but by and large the argument was unproductive. Further consideration was postponed to the Second Session where Switzerland tabled a further amendment adding the words 'providing for rights and obligations' after the words 'international agreement'[8] for the reason that the draft article was silent on agreements such as declarations not intended to have legal effect.[9]

The Soviet representative[10] savagely attacked the Swiss proposal claiming that by limiting the notion of a treaty to agreements which provided for rights and obligations, it would exclude important legal agreements such as the Atlantic

---

[1] *Yearbook of the International Law Commission*, 1965, vol. 1, p. 244.

[2] The Drafting Committee's formulation of 'any' was changed to 'an' on the suggestion of Mr. Briggs in order to attenuate, to some extent, the worries of Australia and Austria.

[3] In the 1962 debate in the Sixth Committee (*General Assembly Official Records*) Colombia (714th meeting) raised the question of circularity in the use of terms, as did Ceylon in 1966 (908th meeting), and Chile (912th meeting) and, in 1967, Tunisia (981st meeting) strongly desired a return to the creation of rights and obligations test.

[4] See Report of the Committee of the Whole, *U.N. Conference on the Law of Treaties, Official Records*, A/CONF. 39/11/Add. 2, p. 101.

[5] Chile, Malaysia, Mexico (A/CONF. 39/11/Add. 2, p. 111), New Zealand (A/CONF. 39/11, p. 29) and the U.K. (A/CONF. 39/11, p. 10).

[6] Ibid., pp. 28 and 29.

[7] Sir Humphrey Waldock (ibid., p. 34), when it was decided to postpone consideration of draft Article 2, spoke regretfully at deletion of the intention test.

[8] A/CONF. 39/11/C.384/Corr. 1.

[9] A/CONF. 39/11/Add. 1, p. 225. Examples given by Switzerland were the Three Power Declaration on Moroccan Affairs made at Madrid in 1907, the Atlantic Charter, the 1943 Declaration on Despoliation and the 'Gentleman's Agreement' on U.N. Security Council seats.

[10] A/CONF./39/11/Add. 1, p. 226.

136   WHAT IS AN AGREEMENT

Charter (mentioned by Switzerland as an example of an agreement not having legal effect), the Potsdam and Yalta Agreements, all of which not only provided for rights and obligations (if they did, there should be no Soviet qualms about the Swiss proposal) but also laid down very important rules of international law. Chile[1] supported Switzerland in seeking to distinguish an international agreement from an agreement merely recording identical views and general aspirations: States should not have to hesitate to express in writing their long-term political goals for fear they might be bound by such instruments. The United Kingdom, too,[2] supported Switzerland and thought the U.S.S.R. to be adopting too broad a view; there had always been a distinction between international agreements so-called, intended to create rights and obligations, and declarations simply setting out policy objectives. In any case, the United Kingdom representative added, the Soviet representative's view was not shared by the Academy of Sciences of the U.S.S.R.[3]

The amendments were referred to the Drafting Committee which, in oracular fashion, pronounced them superfluous,[4] claiming that the expression '... governed by international law' comprised the element of intention to create legal obligation. After reconsideration by the Committee of the Whole, the draft article was formally adopted by the Conference.

In view of the chequered history of Article 2 and the myriad of assurances that whatever formulation was adopted an examination of the intention of the parties would be necessary to ascertain both that they had intended to be bound and that they had intended to be bound under the international rather than another legal system, it would be pedantic to continue to criticize the formulation adopted at Vienna and those maintained by the text-writers.[5] They may be guilty of tautology but whatever form of words they adopt, the freedom of the parties to evade 'bindingness', or to submit their agreement to a particular legal system out of all those available has to be recognized.

*   *   *

[1] Ibid., p. 227.   [2] Ibid., pp. 227–8.
[3] A reference to the Academy's text on International Law which takes the orthodox approach to the definition of treaty (ed. Kozhevnikov).   [4] A/CONF. 39/11/Add. 1, pp. 345–6.
[5] One serious contribution to the work in this field, however, remains to be mentioned. It is that by Dr. Münch, in an article in the *Zeitschrift für ausländisches öffentliches Recht und Völkerrecht*, 30 (1969), p. 1, when the author takes to task the International Law Commission for not paying more explicit attention to the requirement of 'intention to create legal relations'. Dr. Münch's survey of writing in the field indicates that virtually all writers admit the existence of non-binding agreements. He gives a number of illustrations of non-binding agreements, including a 1907 Exchange of Notes (called a Declaration of Policy) between France and Spain concerning the status quo in the Mediterranean and Northern Atlantic which was expressly stated not to be a 'treaty'. Other of his illustrations are certain of the Allied declarations concluded towards the end of the Second World War. He also mentions the recommendatory expressions and *voeux* that often find a place in the Final Acts of Conferences. The point of Dr. Münch that the 'definition' adopted by the I.L.C. is a long way from perfect is accepted. His anxiety that 'intention to bind' may no longer be considered a requirement for an instrument to be classed as a treaty or international agreement is not, however, compelling. It has been noted that within the Commission, the condition of intent was agreed to be implicit in the term 'governed by international law'. And, as Dr. Münch admits, virtually no writer has claimed otherwise. It was perhaps for the reason that this element was in no real danger of being overlooked in practice that the Commission was not unduly exercised by the controversy.

Ascertainment of intention is, however, no easy matter.[1] The terms used in agreements are often treacherously unclear and there may have in fact been no common intention. The parties may not have considered the question of the force of an instrument and cloaked it in ambiguous language. The decision-maker must, in such cases, reach the most reasonable decision he can on the facts. Of course, if it is clear that the parties have not agreed that the agreement was binding it cannot be considered binding.

The language used must be the fundamental gauge to the parties' intention. Words of obligation, 'will', 'must' and so on normally suggest a serious under-taking. But some of the problems that might arise have already been seen in recording the views of Lauterpacht I. When one looks at some of the broad provisions in that class of agreements so little respected by Professor Fawcett, cultural, educational, scientific and technical co-operation agreements, one sees the difficulties. The following provisions may illustrate the point:

(a) Argentina–Nicaragua Cultural Agreement,[2] 1964; the Parties agree:

. . . to accord each other all possible facilities for the mutual dissemination of culture;

. . . to encourage exchanges of teachers, technicians . . .;

. . . to consider how recognition can be made for each other's degrees and diplomas;

. . . to encourage co-operation between institutions;

. . . to appoint two Commissions to ensure execution of the agreement.

(b) France–Portugal Cultural, Scientific and Technical Co-operation Agreement,[3] 1970; the Parties:

. . . shall organize exchanges of teachers;

. . . undertake to seek ways and means of granting recognition for each other's qualifications;

. . . should facilitate contacts between specialist French and Portuguese institutes and bodies;

. . . shall establish a mixed commission to determine the procedures for applying the agreement;

. . . shall allow, on conditions laid down in their domestic regulation, duty-free import of educational, scientific, cultural and technical materials.

---

[1] The problem involved in ascertaining the parties' common intention was nicely put by Judge Dillard in the *I.C.A.O.* case, *I.C.J. Reports*, 1972, p. 107: ' . . . Multilateral treaties establishing functioning institutions frequently contain articles that represent ideals and aspirations which, being hortatory, are not considered to be legally binding except by those who seek to apply them to the other fellow. On the other hand there are other articles which are generally recognised as imposing definite legal obligations. The point at which the former merge into the latter con-stitutes one of the most delicate and difficult problems of law and especially so in the international arena where generally accepted criteria for determining the meaning of language in the light of aroused expectations are more difficult to ascertain and apply than in domestic jurisdictions.'

See *American Journal of International Law*, 70 (1976), p. 242, for an account of the measures taken at Helsinki in order to make it clear on the face of the instrument that the principles adopted in the 1973 Declaration on East–West Relations were not intended to be binding.

[2] *United Nations Treaty Series*, vol. 671, p. 172.   [3] *Ibid.*, vol. 793, p. 233.

(c) Netherlands–Hungary Cultural Agreement,[1] 1968; the Parties, being desirous of promoting co-operation, agree:

  . . . to further exchanges of professional teachers;
  . . . to provide scholarships;
  . . . to provide co-operation between institutions;
  . . . to encourage exchange visits;
  . . . to establish and further develop lectureships or courses on the language and culture of the other;
  . . . to have translations made of works of the literature of each other;
  . . . to establish a mixed commission.

(d) Denmark–Hungary Agreement on Economic, Industrial and Technical Co-operation,[2] 1969; the Parties shall:

  . . . endeavour to promote co-operation on projects of common interest;
  . . . endeavour to promote exchange of specialists (Sending State to pay all expenses incidental to travel);
  . . . establish a mixed commission.

(e) United States–Spain Friendship and Co-operation Agreement,[3] 1970; the Parties agree:

  . . . to continue close co-operation;
  . . . to expand exchanges in cultural fields;
  . . . the U.S.A. agrees, subject to U.S. legislation to assist Spain in research and training.

(It contains also a number of very specific provisions on defence co-operation.)

Some other, less representative, examples are given in the footnotes.[4]

Many social conventions, while containing specific and detailed terms of obligation, contain also rather elastic provisions, such as the Australia–Yugoslavia Convention[5] of 1970, Article 7 of which reads: 'The Australian Government, in the light of the first-hand investigation by an Australian Tripartite Mission on training of skilled workers in Yugoslavia, shall continue to use its good offices to advance recognition and acceptance of Yugoslav qualifications in Australia.'

To what extent Australia will continue to use its good offices is obviously dependent upon the conclusions and recommendations of the Tripartite Mission. But some obligation exists: to continue using its good offices to the extent called for by the Mission's report.

Undertakings such as some of those described above, couched in terms of 'encourage', 'promote', 'subject to domestic regulations', often supplemented by an 'as far as possible' are, of course, deliberately wide and vague. The agreements

---

[1] Ibid., vol. 724, p. 253.
[2] Ibid., vol. 733, p. 149.   [3] Ibid., vol. 756, p. 141.
[4] For example, the U.S.A.–Republic of China Agreement for Scientific and Scholarly Co-operation 1969 (ibid., vol. 714, p. 139) contains the general obligation 'to increase contacts' and provides that each Government shall bear its own costs and designate an executive agency to supervise the 'contacts'. The Israel–Nicaragua Technical Co-operation Agreement 1966 (ibid., vol. 770, p. 77) records agreement to establish, at the request of either party, technical co-operation projects, each one to be dealt with later in a special agreement. This must be considered as *pactum de contrahendo*.
[5] Ibid., vol. 742, p. 300.

IN INTERNATIONAL LAW?

containing such clauses are creatures of policy; they often establish frameworks for relations between the States parties. A Cultural Co-operation Convention can be as much an indication of an attempt by the States parties either to prove that a state of 'good relations' exists or, even more, to attempt to improve relations,[1] as a joint communiqué of two Foreign Ministers. This, however, is not to say that such instruments are to be considered deprived of legal force: to be dismissed as of peripheral and ephemeral importance, Foreign Office toys.

States may use any form of agreement they wish and make it clear that they are speaking in terms of aspirations[2] and hopes rather than binding undertakings. But if they do not and instead use the form of agreement together with the language of obligation, they must be assumed to have intended something more. Obligations to 'encourage' and 'promote', broad as they might be, are not meaningless. It is possible to ascertain the meaning of such a term and on the facts as they are presented in any dispute conclude whether or not the undertaking has been carried out. Moreover, in many of these cases the provision for the establishment of mixed commissions to supervise implementation of the agreement must suggest that the parties are not operating wholly on a plane of aspiration. Questions such as whether or not the subject-matter involved justifies employment of the treaty vehicle must be left for the parties alone to decide.

It might, of course, be rather difficult for State A to find evidence that State B has not 'promoted' teacher exchanges, but this is not a reflection going to obligation; rather, it goes to evidence of breach. It can also be argued that it is more than difficult to envisage circumstances under which a State would take legal action against another alleging breach of such an undertaking. Only on very rare occasions could the compensation demanded amount to much more than a declaration of unlawful breach. But again, these are reflections of evidence and remedy rather than intention and obligation.

It is here, too, that Fawcett's suggested tests of intention to create legal relations suffer from practical flaws. Agreements such as those cited above occasionally contain a compulsory dispute settlement clause, but does this change the nature of the obligation? No—it would be just as curious to contemplate the dispute settlement clause's ever being used. This is the major reason why such clauses do not often appear in this class of agreement.

It is perhaps because questions of remedy and evidence are too often confused with those of intention and obligation that odd notions of what is, and what is not, a treaty arise. The difficult problems of enforcement are best left in that realm and not pushed ahead and injected into the very notion of

---

[1] It is interesting to note how often the first agreements between States which have recently established relations between each other are of this type. When many Western States decided in the 'sixties or 'seventies to improve the state of their relations with the Soviet Union or the People's Republic of China, a cultural agreement was often a vehicle for the fulfilment of the policy. Holder and Brennan, *The International Legal System* (1972), p. 711, make the valid point that one of the major uses of the treaty is as a policy instrument.

[2] None of what is written is intended to suggest that non-binding agreements do not fulfil a purpose. They are immensely important as policy instruments.

treaty.[1] Why should a transaction not be treated at its highest level of legal potential?

In connection with the painstaking task of ascertaining the intention of the parties at the time of concluding an agreement, a number of tests or guides have suggested themselves to writers. Most of these, however, ultimately return to the language employed. The principal suggestion for a test is whether or not the obligation is susceptible of judicial interpretation and application.[2] This, it is sometimes said, is something more than a test of intention. Some of the separate opinions in the *Norwegian Loans* and *Interhandel* cases[3] suggested, as has been noted earlier, that if the obligation undertaken is incapable of third-party interpretation, if it is so wide that there is no discernible core of obligation or if the sphere of its application is left solely in the discretion of one party without there arising a duty to act in good faith, these circumstances would not only negative an alleged intention to be making a serious undertaking, but also could not give rise to an act in the law. It has likewise earlier been suggested that, in the international system, it is more in keeping with the nature of things to base such a conclusion on intention rather than to link it with a general principle of law of municipal systems based on compulsory enforcement procedures.

Moreover, one finds attractive the rather liberal approach adopted by Judge Read in the *Norwegian Loans* case and advocated in Lauterpacht I of, wherever possible, subjecting formulations framed in discretionary terms to the overriding duty under international law to act in good faith, thus salvaging some element of discernible obligation out of a pottage of subjectivity.

Dr. Münch, in his conclusions in this field,[4] suggests a test which at least leads us to something a little less flighty than the language used. He makes the observation that the degree of commitment necessary to make an agreement binding must be lacking if one party is promising a result the achievment of which is not in the power of the parties to the treaty alone (similar to the Lauterpacht 'capability' test). Thus in the Potsdam Declaration the signatories pledge themselves to support the Soviet claim to North-East Prussia which, says Dr. Münch, on the basis that the formal agreement of Germany would be necessary for implementation of the plan, suggests that there is no intention to reach a binding agreement. Whatever the merits of this general thesis, his example is not convincing. The other parties are not, one would have thought, agreeing to cede German territory to the Soviet Union; they are agreeing to support a claim by the Soviet Union to such territory.

---

[1] The same situation can be found in all legal systems. The existence of a right even when linked with the availability of a remedy does not mean that the right will be enforced. In day-to-day transactions of an ordinary kind, it will seldom be worth our while to seek to enforce our strict legal rights.

[2] O'Connell, *International Law* (1971), vol. 1, pp. 195 et seq. Reuter seems to take a very liberal and not unambiguous view of this requirement. He criticizes, at p. 44 of his *Introduction au droit de traités*, the view that precise obligations must be intended to result before an instrument can be considered a treaty or international agreement, saying that international responsibility is engaged 'même si les règles ne posent qu'une obligation mal définie'.

[3] Above, pp. 129–31.

[4] Loc. cit. (above, p. 136 n. 5). Münch also employs a basic test of precision in drafting.

The general principle would, however, seem to be something of an aid in seeking the intention of the parties. If they appear to be agreeing on matters over which they do not themselves have exclusive control, it is likely that they are expressing a hope or desire or stating an intention rather than binding themselves to a set course of action.[1] But care must be taken that the parties are not intending to promise each other to attempt to take certain action, to do everything in their power. In many cases, it is submitted, this is exactly what the parties will have in mind.

Another view put forward by Dr. Münch is that agreements concerning future action consisting of unspecified measures, the expediency of which would normally be determined later on, would usually not be intended to be binding. He cites as examples those clauses in the Potsdam Declaration dealing with future occupation policy in Germany. While it could be agreed that certain contingency plans between allies concerning war policy may not be intended to bind, in the case of Potsdam the parties were concerned with settling their relations with a defeated Germany, an altogether different matter.

Dr. Münch's final suggested category of 'non-binding' agreements comprises what he calls 'gentlemen's agreements' which, however, he fails to define. He here gives as his examples the 1946 United Nations agreement on election to the Security Council and the 1966 Luxembourg compromise on voting in the Council of the European Communities. The exact status of such instruments,[2] however, remains unclear: they are at times and by some commentators considered binding, at other times and by other commentators not. Moreover, their provisions must be reconciled with those of the instruments they supplement or even amend. Their terms are nowhere carefully enunciated and, while it does seem in practice that violations are tolerated (the most outraged reaction being a demand for re-negotiation), this does not necessarily mean that they are not binding. Such agreements as these within international institutions are a trifle bizarre and it might be inaccurate to speak of them as gentleman's agreements[3]

[1] O'Connell, op. cit. (above, p. 140 n. 2), p. 202, is another supporter of this view.

[2] Certain 'agreements' by the members of the United Nations concerning seat allocation between the various regional groups in organs of limited and rotating membership have in fact been the subject of controversy. L. C. Green, in *Current Legal Problems*, 13 (1960), p. 255, discusses the agreement on seating in the Security Council. The different views of States (ranging from India's: a binding agreement which cannot be violated, to that of the U.S.A.: a temporary agreement which has lapsed) suggest that the status of the agreement has never been settled. For many years it could not be operated on the East European seat.

The 1971 and 1976 elections to the International Law Commission showed similar confusion about a 'gentleman's agreement' of 1956 concerning allocation of seats. The Latin Americans, while calling the agreement 'binding' and seeking its revision, spoke of many violations. See *American Journal of International Law*, 66 (1972), p. 356. These and later elections in the I.L.C. are dealt with most helpfully by E. Lauterpacht in *Internationales Recht und Wirtschaftsordnung*; *Festschrift für Mann* (1977). Lauterpacht's conclusion is that these 'gentleman's agreements' are not considered binding practices. He is hard put to find the criterion which separates a binding practice from a non-binding practice but assumes it must be intention.

[3] Münch criticizes the view of Bittner that, while States might not be bound by a 'gentleman's agreement', Governments or the officials who signed it might be. There is simply no authority for the view that Governments or officials are responsible, but not States, in these circumstances. The closest illustration of this we have found in recent practice is an Exchange of Letters between the Netherlands and Indonesia (*United Nations Treaty Series*, vol. 799, p. 14) where one

as that term is usually employed to describe arrangements that are not intended
to be legally binding, where the parties have set out intentionally not to bind
themselves. This was probably not the case in the Luxembourg compromise.

Can any other worthwhile guidelines be grasped as further aids towards
ascertaining intention? Form and procedure used by the parties will, it is
submitted, often be of value in such an enquiry. The more usual forms of binding
agreement—treaty, convention, agreement and exchange of notes—must
(particularly the first two) raise a presumption that binding force is intended.[1]
Other forms such as protocol and arrangement are probably ambiguous, while
joint statements, communiqués and so forth might give rise to a counter-presumption.
'Declaration' is a particularly ambiguous title: there is a whole class of
instruments often entitled 'declaration' where obligations are directed outwards
to a third party or indeed the world in general and are not intended to flow
between the parties. These would seem to lack the essential characteristic of
creation of rights *inter se* necessary to the 'agreement' form of obligation.

But one must be wary of reading too little into the more exotic appellations.
Considerations of domestic constitutional provisions often lead States away from
the terms 'treaty' or 'convention'.

The preamble, too, may give some clue to the purpose to be fulfilled by the
instrument. Whilst most often it will be drafted in hortatory style, it might on
occasion give expression to the results desired by the parties.[2]

Kaplan and Katzenbach[3] suggest also the 'relationship of the parties, the
seriousness of detrimental action in reliance and the subject matter' as tests.
These are vague considerations and perhaps unhelpful in the abstract, but they
lead us towards the goal we are in fact seeking: positive evidence of a serious
undertaking intended to be kept.[4] In the case of subject-matter, for example, it
is difficult to conceive of the parties to an agreement of cession not intending to
bind themselves. Similarly in view of the reliance that would be placed upon it,

---

functionary wrote to his counterpart: 'I would greatly appreciate it if you could exercise your
good offices to ensure that this request is favourably considered by the . . . authorities entrusted
with implementation . . . .'

[1] Kaplan and Katzenbach, *Political Foundation of International Law* (1964), pp. 236 et seq.
See also the American *Restatement*, commentary on § 115, and Hungdah Chiu, *The Capacity of
International Organizations to conclude Treaties* (1966), p. 209.

Lauterpacht II, p. 125, reports that 'although the parties may have intended a treaty to mean
little, no assumption is possible that they intended it to mean nothing and that the instrument
concluded in the form of a treaty—with the concomitant solemnity, formality, publicity and
constitutional and other safeguards—is not a treaty'. This formulation may be too narrow. Any of
the forms in use by custom to record binding international agreements must raise some presumption,
a view in accordance with the actual article drafted by Lauterpacht.

[2] Kiss, *Répertoire de la pratique française en matière de droit international public*, vol. 1 (1962),
§§ 130 et seq.

[3] Op. cit. (above, n. 1).

[4] Corbin on *Contracts* (1963), §15, makes a similar point in a municipal context: ' . . . expression of intention is not always a promise to act in that way. There must be an invitation to
reliance.' This is close to Judge Nervo's remark in the *North Sea Continental Shelf* cases, *I.C.J.
Reports*, 1969, p. 95, that: ' . . . the fact that the Federal Republic informed the two Kingdoms
that it was preparing to ratify the Convention cannot be considered as a legal and binding promise
to do so.'

IN INTERNATIONAL LAW?   143

an agreement on wheat-aid in time of drought could only with cynicism be considered as intended to raise no more than a hope on the part of the recipient State.

For subsidiary indications, a joint statement of the views of the parties at the time of conclusion of the agreement would be of probative value. For example, in the case of the 1943 Inter-Allied Declaration of Despoliation there was a Note attached setting out the views of the signatories on what they hoped to achieve by the Declaration. While not as unambiguous as it might have been, it is of some assistance in such an enquiry.[1] The precise value of later views of the parties is hard to gauge. An expression of joint views of all the parties must carry weight and, as the parties to a treaty can always agree to suspend or terminate it, they should by the same token be able to alter by agreement its binding character.

The views of one party at the time of conclusion of the instrument will be of some assistance, subject to all other considerations being equal, but one party's statements made at a later stage should be disregarded, unless no more cogent evidence were available, as self-serving.[2] One must be a little wary when whole instruments are dismissed out of hand by one party as statements of intention, notwithstanding the inclusion of articles containing words of clear and specific obligation.

Registration under Article 102 of the U.N. Charter by one party alone may be considered in much the same way as a statement of bindingness by one party shortly after conclusion of the instrument. But there are here other factors at play and it was as a means of providing some light in the darkness of borderline cases that Sir Hersch Lauterpacht in his Second Report inserted a provision raising a presumption of legal obligation in favour of registered instruments. Sir Gerald Fitzmaurice did not share the view that any such presumption should arise.[3] Nor, apparently, did Sir Humphrey Waldock.

The principal argument against reading an implication of this nature into registration flows from the nature of the act: in nearly all cases it is unilateral. But Hungdah Chiu provided the rebuttal to this argument: it is equally open to the other party to protest in cases where, in its view, the instrument is not a treaty or international agreement.[4]

[1] Misc. No. 1 (1943) (Cmnd. 6418). See *International and Comparative Law Quarterly*, 5 (1956), p. 84, and *American Journal of International Law*, 51 (1957), p. 802.

[2] The same criticism could be made of U.K. and U.S.A. statements concerning the effect of the Allied War agreements, Yalta, Potsdam, etc. In the *Aegean Sea Continental Shelf* case, the Greek interpretation of the May 1975 communiqué was communicated in a Note Verbale to the Turkish Government. The Turkish reply simply expressed disagreement with the Greek interpretation (Greek memorial on jurisdiction).

[3] Above. Despite this, the dissenting opinion of Judges Spender and Fitzmaurice (and Judge van Wyk) in the *South West Africa* cases (*First Phase*), I.C.J. *Reports*, 1962, p. 494, suggest that non-registration raises an inference that the parties do not consider the instrument is a treaty or agreement.

[4] Hungdah Chiu, op. cit. (above, p. 142 n. 1), p. 707. We saw no such 'protests' published in the *United Nations Treaty Series* during the period 1964–71. An illustration of the type of dispute possible in this field occurred over an agreement on title to certain old Dutch shipwrecks off the Australian coast. In return for the Dutch title, Australia promised the Netherlands a share in the treasure recovered. Australia all along treated the instrument as an international agreement and wished it to be registered with the U.N. For the Netherlands it was a contract,

The argument that the terms employed in Article 102 are more elastic and flexible than the term 'international agreement' in general law can be met with the reply that, however wide may be the terms in Article 102, they must include the more restricted class of binding treaties and international agreements with which we are concerned.

Article 102, of course, does not make registration compulsory but in so far as the most direct access to relief will often be provided under the auspices of one or other of the organs of the United Nations, it is in the interests of the parties to register. It scarcely need be added that the International Court of Justice is an organ of the U.N.: registration is essential for a judicial remedy.

One is, then, led to the conclusion that it is likely that binding agreements will be registered under Article 102. But so too will other instruments. In such a case, the presumption may perhaps best be treated from the other direction: an unregistered agreement will be presumed, prima facie, not to be binding.[1]

Publication in a State's own treaty series would be of much the same force as a unilateral statement.[2]

The American Law Institute Restatement on Foreign Relations Law[3] treats insertion of a compulsory judicial–arbitral dispute settlement clause as an indication of an intention to bind. It does indeed suggest that the parties are serious. It may even raise a presumption but it is doubtful whether it can be considered as conclusive proof of bindingness. The parties might simply wish it to be open to a tribunal to interpret a 'non-binding' agreement.

These guidelines then, together, assist one in reaching a conclusion on the force of clauses in international instruments. Individually, however, the most any of them can do is raise a presumption.

*   *   *

Having thus reached some conclusions on the elements of a treaty and the nature of intention to bind and be bound, the second task is to distinguish from the class of treaty those agreements which most worried the International Law Commission—those which the parties intend to submit to a particular municipal legal system, or at least some system other than international law.[4]

No problems arise, of course, when the parties to a transaction make it clear

---

presumably under Dutch law, whether or not registered. The agreement was not in fact registered.

[1] Mann is critical of Lauterpacht's presumption in his article 'Reflections on a Commercial Law of Nations', this *Year Book*, 33 (1957), p. 20, at pp. 30–1. He could probably agree with the reverse formulation adopted in our text. It is, to some extent, the view of Judges Spender and Fitzmaurice (above, p. 143 n. 3).

[2] See Myers, loc. cit. (above, p. 117 n. 1), p. 584, on U.S.A. practice.   [3] Above, p. 117 n. 3.

[4] The Harvard Research Draft, loc. cit. (above, p. 117 n. 3), Commentary on Article 1, reported that some early writers claimed that such agreements were not entered into by States in their capacity as States and should not be considered as treaties (e.g. Liszt). Others claimed that they were all treaties and all subject to international law. Anzilotti and Gidel maintained that the parties were free to choose which law would govern the agreement. The Harvard suggestion is that if it is recorded in a formal instrument (the only type of agreement in the scope of the Harvard Draft) under which the obligation is apparently one of international law, then international law will govern it.

on the face of the instrument that they are agreeing under international law. But this is rarely the case. More often the agreement is silent on the point. Most 'loan agreements' and 'guarantee agreements' contain no express choice of law clause.[1] The vast network of United States' commodities agreements[2] is silent on the point, though they are registered under Article 102 of the Charter.

One can do no more than return to the guidelines and presumptions, or those that are relevant, listed earlier, for ascertaining the intention of the parties. The subject-matter of the agreement will, of course, be of immense importance.[3] It is scarcely likely that a cultural co-operation convention, for example, will be intended to be concluded under a private law system. Then, as a general premiss, it must be assumed, in the absence of any clear indication to the contrary, that if the parties choose the form of international agreement (treaty, convention and so on, and even agreement, rather than contract) they are agreeing under international law.[4]

It will, of course, be in the field of loans, sales and other commercial transactions that this question will most often arise. Certainly, as Dr. Mann has so lucidly shown,[5] international law is quite capable of governing such a transaction, the device of the implied term not being a monopoly of private law. But so too are municipal systems able to deal with commercial transactions between international entities.

The fact that many of these commercial transactions in the form of international agreements contain dispute settlement clauses referring disputes to international tribunals, and that most are registered under Article 102,[6] must suggest that they are being submitted to international law even it if be the case that international tribunals are able to apply municipal law.[7]

Occasionally an inter-State agreement will expressly declare that it is to be governed by a municipal legal system. But such provisions are not often to be seen in the *United Nations Treaty Series*. And is it not possible to contemplate an agreement constituting a 'treaty' in international law and a 'contract' under a

[1] See any of the I.B.R.D. or I.D.A. agreements listed in a recent volume of the *United Nations Treaty Series*.

[2] See, for example, U.S.A.–Tunisia, *United Nations Treaty Series*, vol. 692, p. 155. For an agreement on loan of vessels see that between U.S.A.–Japan, ibid., vol. 707, p. 207.

[3] An example from Swiss practice suggests itself: Guggenheim's *Répertoire Suisse*, vol. I, pp. 1–2, where an agreement between two railway administrations was considered to be a contract under private law because it did not concern matters of direct interest to States. This consideration is also present in the reasoning of the Court in the *Anglo-Iranian Oil Co.* case.

[4] The I.A.E.A. occasionally calls its supply agreements 'contracts'. But they are no different from those which it calls 'agreements'. They speak of entry into force and so on. There is nothing to suggest that they are not concluded under international law.

[5] 'Reflections on a Commercial Law of Nations', this *Year Book*, 33 (1957), p. 20. It must, however, be borne in mind that if the assistance of a municipal system of law is required to carry out a transaction, for example, if property is to be secured, the transaction will have to be subject to that system. The most an international tribunal could do would be to direct the parties to carry out the obligation: to take the necessary steps in municipal law. See Sommers, Broches and Delaume, *Law and Contemporary Problems*, 21 (1956), p. 463 at p. 479.

[6] For example, loan agreements with the I.B.R.D. and I.D.A.

[7] The I.C.J. can apply municipal law according to the decision in the *Serbian Loans* case (*P.C.I.J.*, Series A, No. 20 (1929)), assuming that to be correctly decided. A decision by an international tribunal may, of course, be of no effect in municipal law.

private law system at the same time? If, in these cases, there is no express choice of law clause such a situation should cause no offence so long as both systems refuse to allow a litigant a double remedy.[1] Under the 'general principles of law' source, the *non bis in idem* rule is said to be incorporated into international law.[2] There might be certain differences of treatment of validity, termination and so on, but the same problems arise in conflict law and can be solved at the dispute settlement stage. If there is a formal defect in the instrument in either jurisdiction, it should not prohibit a party from seeking the aid of the other jurisdiction.

There is one complicating factor. In certain agreements, while there is no choice of law clause, there is either substantial reference to the terminology of a particular legal system or incorporation of a partial choice of law clause. Examples of the former are often to be found. Some agreements for the sale of agricultural commodities, for example, refer to 'bills of lading'.[3] Examples of the latter are less easy to come upon, but a series of United States' investment guarantee agreements[4] provide that 'the Agreement shall be interpreted in accordance with the rules of Public International Law'. But they also contain a clause that 'the Guaranteeing Government shall accept no greater rights than those of the transferring investor under the laws of the Host Government'. They contain an international dispute settlement clause covering disputes which, in the opinion of either of the parties, involve a question of international law. Jurisdiction of the United States' Courts is excluded. In such cases (unless the clause cannot be read in such a fashion)[5] it is bound to be most felicitous to avoid labyrinthine conflicts problems and treat the whole agreement as subject to international law with an incorporation of some private law provisions.

Reference to private law terminology can be interpreted in the same way as any other technical expression. And references to the substantive rules of

---

[1] See, for example, a similar rule in the English Law of Conflicts: Graveson, *Conflict of Laws* (7th edn., 1974), pp. 597 et seq.

[2] Bin Cheng, *General Principles of Law* (1953), Chapter 14 on the *non bis in idem* rule. The defendant State will often be able to claim sovereign immunity. Mann, in 'The Law Governing State Contracts', this *Year Book*, 21 (1944), p. 22, mentions some English cases which adopted the principle that transactions between States governed by other laws than those administered by municipal courts are not cognisable in English Courts. The tendency there is to link the doctrine of sovereign immunity with choice of law. We would prefer to consider choice of law purely in terms of intention and not according to whether or not the State is acting *in imperii* or *in commercio*.

[3] For example, that between U.S.A.–Tunisia, *United Nations Treaty Series*, vol. 692, p. 155.

[4] For example, that between U.S.A.–Zambia, ibid., vol. 616, p. 267. Some Danish loan agreements used to contain a clause reading: 'Except where this Agreement expressly provides otherwise all rights and obligations will be governed by Danish law.' The agreements contained international dispute settlement clauses, e.g. Denmark–Morocco, ibid., vol. 657, p. 195.

[5] The body of law referred to in the American investment guarantee clauses can be incorporated into the terms of the agreement. Even the Danish formula, which could be read as a choice of law clause, can equally be read as simply incorporating substantive Danish law provisions on loans into the agreement, while allowing it to remain an agreement subject to international law. In other words, while international law will regulate validity, termination and so on, the parties have saved the international judge from having to devise implied terms by giving him a Danish set. It matters nothing that the Danish courts might read it as a Danish contract.

another system can without pain be incorporated into the terms[1] of obligation (with which international law is not generally, excluding rare outbursts of *jus cogens*, concerned). In this connection Dr. Mann, in his article 'The Proper Law of Contracts concluded by International Persons',[2] argues that while the distinction between 'incorporation' and 'choice of law' is a real one, the distinction between the formula 'to be construed in accordance with English law' and the clause 'shall be governed by English law' is merely verbal, citing the Privy Council in the *Vita Foods* case.[3] The point is important in this context because a number of inter-State agreements contain such a term as 'the provisions of this Agreement shall be interpreted in accordance with the laws of the State of New York'.[4] Dr. Mann finds the *Vita Foods* view unanswerable and would call the type of clause cited above an express choice of law. Others have taken the view that such a clause refers only to the provisions of New York law concerning interpretation.[5] Surely the direction of such a clause must depend on the intention of the parties and the context of the clause. To begin with, the *Vita Foods* analysis can be countered: the terms 'mortgage' or 'bill of lading' can be construed or interpreted according to the English law of interpretation without subjecting the transaction in question to the full force of the English law of commercial security or shipping. It is this that one assumes to be in the minds of parties when they use the term 'interpretation'. If they wish expressly to choose a legal system, why do they not employ the term 'govern'?[6]

[1] The debate in the I.L.C. at the 638th and 655th meetings (*Yearbook of the International Law Commission*, 1962, vol. 1) is again relevant. Mr Amado (at p. 169), it will be recalled, raised this point in connection with deletion of the intention test from the draft articles on use of terms. Mr. Amado seemed to have in mind just this problem: an international law treaty incorporating municipal law terms. No helpful views were expressed but Professor Ago (at p. 172) suggested that it was a question of whether or not the parties had intended to contract under the municipal system.

The Commission in 1959 had been 'clear that it ought to confine the notion of an international "agreement" for the purposes of the law of treaties to one the whole formation and execution of which (as well as the obligation to execute) is governed by international law' (Waldock I, p. 32). It is not clear how far this goes: where terminology is derived from a municipal system or where portions of a municipal system have been incorporated into the agreement, the 'formation and execution' is still governed by international law: the parties are merely using a form of shorthand in drafting the terms of the agreement. Lauterpacht I, p. 100 (Note 4), treated all such instruments as being governed by international law in the last resort: if the parties stipulate that an instrument shall be governed by private law it is international law which gives force to this direction.

[2] This *Year Book*, 35 (1959), p. 34 at pp. 38 et seq. See his municipal law references on 'incorporation' and 'choice of law'.

[3] [1939] A.C. 277. Lord Wright put it this way at p. 298: ' . . . the conclusion of a contract by English law involves the application to its terms of the relevant English Statutes, whatever they may be, and the rules and implications of the English common law for its construction, including the rules of conflict of laws. In this sense the construing of the contract has the effect that the contract is to be governed by English law.'

[4] For example, the early I.B.R.D. loan agreements. See Sommers, Broches and Delaume, loc. cit. (above, p. 145 n. 5), and also Broches, *Recueil des cours*, 98 (1959-III), pp. 341 and 356; Delaume, *Legal Aspects of International Lending* (1967), p. 84; Sereni, *Recueil des cours*, 96 (1959-I), p. 206. Mann, 'The Proper Law of Contracts', this *Year Book*, 35 (1959), p. 34, takes the view that such a clause involves an express choice of law. Delaume takes into account the relevant regulations of the I.B.R.D.

[5] Sommers, Broches and Delaume, loc. cit. (above, p. 145 n. 5).

[6] For a different view on some aspects of this, Delaume, op. cit. (above, n. 4), p. 78.

It was a reflection of these complicating factors which led the Special Rapporteur (Mr. Reuter) of the International Law Commission's study on Treaties concluded between International Organizations and between States and International Organizations[1] to adopt, in his 'scope' section, the following terminology:

... treaty ... means an international agreement ... governed principally by general[2] international law ... ,

although his Commentary[3] suggests that the addition of neither 'principally' nor 'general' was considered essential. From his study of such agreements, he concludes that there are in practice no real problems: there is always a general legal regime which applies principally and it is this regime which determines what sort of an instrument it is.

This seems a somewhat confusing explanation. Mr. Reuter appears to take characterization of the instrument out of the hands of the parties and into some sort of prima facie relevant legal system. The test suggested earlier seems more attractive: if the parties can be said to intend to agree to create obligations in international law, it will be a treaty, even if it incorporates aspects of municipal law, and even, it may be added, if some of the incorporated provisions concern validity, since most rules of the law of treaties can be varied by the parties to the treaty in question.[4]

A nice practical illustration of these problems has recently come to hand.[5] It concerns an Agreement between the U.S.A. and the Federal Republic of Germany. The Agreement, which was registered under Article 102,[6] provided that paintings from East Germany found in the U.S.A. after the Second World War would be transferred to the Federal Republic to be held on the same trust as a certain East German Museum had held them before the war. In an action in the Federal German courts a woman, who was able to show that the museum had held one of the paintings on trust for her, succeeded in obtaining title to the painting. The Court reasoned that the term 'trust' must be interpreted in the American sense of the term and found that the museum had in fact held the painting on the plaintiff's behalf in such a sense.

---

[1] *Yearbook of the International Law Commission*, 1974, vol. 2, pp. 135 et seq.

[2] 'General' was added to cover cases where the international organization concerned had evolved a complete legal system of its own. One would have thought that in such a case a term would be added to the agreement, incorporating by reference such a code or set of rules. Indeed the I.B.R.D. does something similar now, incorporating conditions into its agreements. The word 'general' was deleted after debate (*Yearbook of the International Law Commission*, 1974, vol. 1, pp. 124 et seq.).

[3] Loc. cit. (above, n. 1), pp. 139 et seq. Mr. Ushakov (at p. 135) could not conceive of an agreement being anything less than completely subject to international law or, alternatively, completely within a municipal system. Mr. Yasseen (at p. 146) thought that the distinction need not be spelt out: the tenets of interpretation would solve most problems. Mr. Sette Càmara (at p. 150) agreed: any problems of choice of law or 'double choice' could be settled by choice of dispute settlement machinery or by interpretation.

[4] See, for example, the remarks of the Swedish representative at the First Session of the Conference (A/CONF. 39/11, p. 45).

[5] See Mann, 'Another Agreement between States under National Law', *American Journal of International Law*, 68 (1974), p. 490.

[6] *United Nations Treaty Series*, vol. 681, p. 57.

IN INTERNATIONAL LAW? 149

Dr. Mann suggests that the Court applied American law to the agreement without even considering the relevance of public international law or German law. He criticizes this, claiming there was no reason to apply American law and, in any case, which American law was it: federal law or the law of a particular State?

An alternative explanation is that the Court was not intending to transform the agreement into a private law contract but was merely interpreting the terms employed.[1] Dr. Mann rejects this approach because the plaintiff, as a private person, should have no right in the courts to base a claim on an international treaty. In this case, however, the plaintiff could be said to be relying on her prior title. The F.R.G., as defendant, might be said to be relying on the treaty but the plaintiff is not necessarily so doing. Moreover, if one assumes, as does Dr. Mann, that the Court is treating the instrument as a contract under 'American law', one is left in the same corner; the plaintiff was not a party to that contract. Also, the Court 'rectified' the instrument by amending a date patently inserted in error. The Court did this without any investigation of 'American law' on that subject.[2]

* * *

It is the intention of this Article to clarify some of the ideas behind use of the terms 'treaty' and 'international agreement' and come to some conclusions in the nature of a working hypothesis. It seems at the end to relate to nothing less esoteric than the parties' intent. But some helpful guidelines have, it is hoped, been discerned.

[1] Since the term was 'trust', a term of Anglo-American law, there was more reason to suppose American rather than German law would be appropriate. Mann is, of course, correct to criticize the use of the term 'American law'.

[2] If we treat the instrument as an international agreement, this seems to be the first reported instance of rectification.

[3]

A Mirage in the Sand? Distinguishing Binding and Non-Binding Relations Between States

Christine Chinkin[*]

Keywords: dispute settlement; International Court of Justice; international agreements.

Abstract: The article discusses the two decisions (thus far) of the International Court of Justice in the case concerning *Maritime Delimitation and Territorial Questions between Qatar and Bahrain*, especially its consideration of when an internationally binding agreement has come into existence. The Court's willingness to infer a legally binding agreement, regardless of the intentions of at least one of the parties, appears to displace the primacy of consent it has emphasized in its earlier jurisprudence. The decision seems to hold states bound by informal commitments, an approach that might inhibit open negotiations between states and undermine genuine attempts to pre-empt disputes or to comply with the obligation of peaceful settlement of disputes.

1.   INTRODUCTION

Readers of the judgments and opinions of the International Court of Justice have become accustomed to the extraordinary range of issues relating to international legal process that are drawn together, often in seemingly random fashion. They are also used to the innovative approaches to substance and procedure sometimes chosen by the Court to the claims of states that obscure or evade the issues raised in the application before it.[1] Even

---

[*]   Professor of International Law, London School of Economics. The author thanks Sir Ian Sinclair and Anthony Aust for their assistance, including a preview of the text of the latter's forthcoming book on treaty law.

[1].   Perhaps the most famous example is the holding in the Nuclear Tests cases (Australia *v.* France; New Zealand *v.* France), Judgment, 1974 ICJ Rep. 253 and 457, respectively, that there was no longer a dispute between the parties and thus no object to continuation of the proceedings; *see* the discussion in M. Koskenniemi, From Apology to Utopia 307-311 (1988).

considered against these standards, however, the decision in the case concerning *Maritime Delimitation and Territorial Questions* between Qatar and Bahrain (*Qatar* v. *Bahrain*) may be regarded as 'novel and disquieting'.[2]

The jurisdiction and admissibility phase of the *Qatar* v. *Bahrain* case combined issues of the relationship between negotiations for the resolution of an international dispute and seising the Court with that dispute, determining how states indicate their consent (or unwillingness) to be bound by the outcome of negotiations, the use of *travaux préparatoires* in treaty interpretation, and the role of the Court in overseeing and affirming the legal consequences of the entire process. While all these elements were inextricably fused, this article will concentrate upon the Court's consideration of when an internationally binding agreement has come into existence.

In its first judgment, the Court stated that it did not "find it necessary to consider what might have been the intentions of the Foreign Minister of Bahrain, or for that matter, those of the Foreign Minister of Qatar" in determining whether signed minutes of a meeting created rights and obligations binding upon the two states.[3] In its countenance of the conclusion of a legally binding agreement regardless of the intentions of at least one of the parties, this statement appears to displace the primacy of consent. The decision has accordingly been hailed as 'monumental' in that it opens the way to holding states bound by commitments however informally given.[4] On the other hand such an approach might cause misgivings in that it could make states reluctant to agree to even the most imprecise and unofficial formulations, for example in diplomatic exchanges, for fear of their subsequently being held to have incurred legal rights and obligations. This could impede the regular flow of communications between states and inhibit negotiations, unless unequivocal wording disavowing intent was incorporated at all stages.[5] This in turn might undermine genuine attempts

---

2.   Maritime Delimitation and Territorial Questions Between Qatar and Bahrain (Qatar *v.* Bahrain), Jurisdiction and Admissibility, Judgment of 1 July 1994, 1994 ICJ Rep. 112; Judgment of 15 February 1995, 1995 ICJ Rep. 6. The adjectives are those of Vice President Schwebel, 1994 ICJ Rep. 112, at 130 (Judge Schwebel, Separate Opinion).

3.   Qatar *v.* Bahrain, Judgment of 1 July 1994, *supra* note 2, at para. 27.

4.   J. Klabbers, The Concept of Treaty in International Law (1996).

5.   Aust refers to the "slightly tiresome, if harmless - even quaint - British obsession" of adhering strictly to unequivocal form and wording for binding agreements. This would surely increase if states are to be bound by the most informal of arrangements; A. Aust, *The Theory and Practice of Informal International Instruments*, 35 ICLQ 787 (1986). McNeill explains how the US Office of General Counsel, Department of Defense, instructed its officials to avoid all language that might denote non-binding arrangements to avoid misun-

to pre-empt disputes or to comply with the obligation of peaceful settlement of disputes.[6] The advantages of simplicity, informality, speed, and flexibility motivate states to eschew formal treaty-making processes in finalising their understandings.[7] Nevertheless the objectives of stability and certainty in international dealings make it desirable for decision and policy makers to be able to determine with some confidence when states have indeed entered into legal relations. However the surrounding circumstances of parties' interactions vary greatly, as do the objects and purpose of negotiations and the form in which any outcome is expressed. The interpretation of each is open to objective and subjective evaluation with the inevitability of future disputes as to true intent. The question is whether the ruling in *Qatar* v. *Bahrain* has undermined certainty in differentiating between binding and non-binding agreements.

The article examines the *Qatar* v. *Bahrain* case in this light. It first considers the context in which the statement cited above was made and then assesses the Court's earlier jurisprudence on the importance of the intentions of the parties in determining whether agreement with legal effect has been reached. It concludes that such certainty was never more than a mirage in that the Court has oscillated between giving explicit primacy to the intentions of the parties or to the text and surrounding circumstances. Neither can be decisive and focus upon one or the other distorts the reality of the parties' dispute.

2.   *QATAR* V. *BAHRAIN* (JURISDICTION AND ADMISSIBILITY)

The case arose out of a long-term territorial and boundary dispute between the two Arab states and mediation attempts by the King of Saudi Arabia to steer the parties towards an acceptable resolution of their differences. In May 1983 the parties agreed five Principles for the Framework for Reaching a Settlement that had first been proposed in 1978. For some years there was little progress in putting these into effect until in 1987 the King exchanged identical, but separate, letters with each party that included the

---

derstanding; J. McNeill, *International Agreements: Recent US-UK Practice Concerning the Memorandum of Understanding*, 88 AJIL 821 (1994).

6.   United Nations Charter, Arts. 2(3), 33.

7.   Aust, *supra* note 5.

following provision:

> [a]ll the disputed matters shall be referred to the International Court of Justice, at The Hague, for a final ruling binding upon both parties, who shall have to execute its terms.[8]

On 21 December 1987 Saudi Arabia announced the parties' agreement expressed in these letters that the matter would be 'submitted for arbitration'. The establishment of a Tripartite Committee comprising the parties and Saudi Arabia was also agreed

> for the purpose of approaching the International Court of Justice and satisfying the necessary requirements to have the dispute submitted to the Court in accordance with its regulations and instructions so that a final ruling, binding upon both parties, be issued.[9]

The Committee met on a number of separate occasions in 1988 but a joint submission to the Court was not agreed. At the December 1990 Gulf Co-operation Council Summit Meeting, where the primary concern was the Iraqi occupation of Kuwait, Qatar raised this continuing failure. After further negotiations at the Council Meeting, Minutes were prepared in Arabic and signed by the Foreign Ministers of Qatar, Bahrain and Saudi Arabia.

The Minutes (known as the Doha Minutes) reaffirmed previous commitments between the parties and recorded agreement to recommence mediation by the King of Saudi Arabia until the month of Shawwal, 1411 H (May 1991, in five months time). If at the expiry of this time there was still no agreement, the case could then be submitted to the Court in accordance with the so-called 'Bahraini formula'. The Bahraini formula stated:

> [t]he Parties request the Court to decide any matter of territorial right or other title or interest which may be a matter of difference between them; and to draw a single maritime boundary between their respective maritime areas of seabed, subsoil and superjacent waters.[10]

The formula had first been proposed in October 1988 by Bahrain for the phrasing of a joint submission to the Court. Qatar had initially rejected it and its willingness to accept it at the Doha Summit facilitated acceptance of the Minutes.[11]

---

8. Qatar *v.* Bahrain, Judgment of 1 July 1994, *supra* note 2, at para. 17.
9. *Id.* The appropriate translation from the original Arabic was disputed by the parties.
10. *Id.*, at para. 18.
11. The Court commended the Bahraini formula as being carefully constructed to avoid any

After the required lapse of time, Qatar filed a unilateral application to the Court on 8 July 1991 asserting that the combined effect of the 1987 exchange of letters (the 1987 Agreement) and the Doha Minutes was to give the Court jurisdiction under Article 36(1) of its Statute. It defined the subject of the disputes as sovereignty over the Hawar Islands, sovereign rights over the shoals of Dibal and Qit'at and Jaradah and delimitation of the maritime boundary between Qatar and Bahrain. The application omitted Bahrain's claim to Zubarah on the mainland of Qatar which had been understood to be encompassed by the Bahraini formula.[12] In a letter dated 14 July 1991 Bahrain claimed that Article 38(5) of the Rules of the Court excluded Qatar's application from being entered upon the list and requested the Court to act accordingly. The case was however entered on the General List and in a subsequent letter Bahrain rejected the Court's jurisdiction based upon Qatar's unilateral application. The President of the Court brought together representatives of Qatar and Bahrain in two meetings at his chambers where it was agreed that jurisdiction and admissibility should be dealt with before the merits of the dispute.[13]

The key as to whether Qatar's unilateral submission of the dispute accorded the Court jurisdiction under Article 36(1) of the Statute of the International Court of Justice was the legal nature of the 1987 Agreement and the Doha Minutes and their correct interpretation. Neither party contested that the 1987 exchanges of letters between each one of them and the King of Saudi Arabia constituted an international agreement creating rights and obligations for the parties, including referral of all disputed matters to the Court.[14] There was however no agreement as to the terms of any such submission, as evidenced by the establishment of the Tripartite Committee

---

express reference to the sensitive areas in dispute while sufficiently clearly comprehending the entire dispute; Qatar *v.* Bahrain, Judgment of 15 February 1995, *supra* note 2, at para. 31.

12. E. Lauterpacht, *'Partial' Judgments and the Inherent Jurisdiction of the International Court of Justice*, in V. Lowe & M. Fitzmaurice (Eds.), Fifty Years of the International Court of Justice 468 (1996).

13. The President's Order of 11 October 1991 reflected this understanding.

14. As was pointed out by Judge Oda, the form of the 1987 Agreement was unusual. No letters were exchanged between the parties but between Saudi Arabia and Qatar and Saudi Arabia and Bahrain. For this reason Judge Oda denied their legal effect: Qatar *v.* Bahrain, Judgment of 15 February 1995, *supra* note 2, at 44-45 (Judge Oda, Dissenting Opinion). However, this arrangement is not so unusual where an outcome has been facilitated by a third party mediator substituting for direct negotiations between the parties. E.g., the Algerian Declarations of 19 January 1981 were not directly between the parties, although they clearly constituted legal rights and obligations.

to work towards achieving this.

In contrast, Bahrain did dispute Qatar's assertion of the legally binding nature of the Doha Minutes and their intended meaning. Bahrain contended that the Minutes recorded the continuing negotiation attempts and comprised only a political understanding that there would be eventual joint recourse to the Court. The Minutes did not constitute legal consent to a unilateral application by Qatar. Indeed, Bahrain argued, it would be contrary to Article 37 of its 1973 Constitution for an international agreement to be entered into in this informal way without reference to the Amir and Council of Ministers. It supported its arguments by reference to the subsequent behaviour of both parties that it claimed supported their common understanding that there was no legal consequence to be drawn from the Minutes. Qatar (like Bahrain) had not complied with its constitutional requirements for treaty making and had not applied to register the document under United Nations Charter Article 102 until six months after the meeting,[15] that is only just prior to its application to the Court.[16] Bahrain's immediate protest against Qatar's application to have the Minutes registered was also registered. In addition, Qatar had not filed the Minutes with the Secretariat of the League of Arab States as required by Article 17 of the Pact of the League.

In addition to the dispute as to the legal effect of the Doha Minutes, there was disagreement as to their interpretation. Qatar contended that the Minutes provided for unilateral seisin by either party while Bahrain insisted they required joint seisin by special agreement. The focus of this difference of opinion was the English meaning of the Arabic word *Al-tarafan* which was used to indicate 'the parties'. Qatar translated the crucial section of the Minutes as "[a]fter the end of this period, *the parties* may submit the matter to the International Court of Justice in accordance with the Bahraini formula [...]", while Bahrain claimed that the proper translation was "*the two parties* may at the end of this period submit the matter to the International Court of Justice in accordance with the Bahraini formula [...]" (emphasis added).

In its first judgment in July 1994 the Court found that, while the 1987

---

15. United Nations Charter, Art. 102(1) states: "Every treaty and every international agreement entered into by any Member of the United Nations after the present Charter comes into force shall as soon as possible be registered with the Secretariat and published by it."
16. Qatar applied for registration in June 1991 and filed its application on 8 July 1991.

Agreement and the Doha Minutes constituted internationally binding agreements creating rights and obligations upon the parties, the dispute as submitted by Qatar was not the whole dispute between the parties as envisaged by those agreements. It did not determine the jurisdictional question but instead gave the parties until 30 November 1994 "jointly or separately to take action to this end", that is to do precisely what they had failed to achieve over many years, agree the terms of a joint submission to the Court.

Not surprisingly there was no success and on 30 November 1994 Qatar addressed to the Court "[a]n Act to comply with [...] the judgment of the Court dated 1-7-1994." Qatar claimed that this application submitted the whole of the dispute in accordance with the Bahraini formula and included Zubarah and areas for pearl fishing and fishing for swimming fish. Bahrain again contested jurisdiction, arguing that a second individual act by Qatar, even though it inserted Bahrain's claims with respect to Zubarah, could not cure the original defective jurisdiction. In its decision of 15 February 1995 the Court decided by a majority of 10 to 5 that it had jurisdiction upon the dispute submitted to it between Qatar and Bahrain.[17]

3. A LEGALLY BINDING AGREEMENT?

3.1. The indeterminacy of form

It is axiomatic that neither the form nor the nomenclature of an instrument is determinative of its legal status.[18] As has been pointed out by the ICJ,[19] the International Law Commission,[20] commentators,[21] and docu-

---

17. Qatar *v.* Bahrain, *supra* note 2. Vice-President Schwebel, Judges Oda, Shahabuddeen, Koroma, and Judge *ad hoc* Valticos dissented.

18. Judge Jessup described how terminology has always bedevilled the law of treaties, for example in 1925 a Sub-committee of the League of Nations Committee on the Codification of International Law referred to "the prevailing anarchy as regards terminology in the law of treaties." South West Africa cases (Ethiopia *v.* South Africa; Liberia *v.* South Africa), Preliminary Objections, Judgment, 1962 ICJ Rep. 319, at 402 (Judge Jessup, Separate Opinion).

19. *See, e.g.,* Temple of Preah Vihear (Cambodia *v.* Thailand) (Preliminary Objections), Judgment of 26 May 1961, 1961 ICJ Rep. 17, at 32; Nuclear Tests case (Australia *v.* France), *supra* note 1, at para. 45.

20. Report of the International Law Commission on the work of its eighteenth session, 1966-2 YILC 172.

21. *See, e.g.,* R. Jennings & A. Watts, Oppenheim's International Law, Vol. I, 1200 (1992);

mentation of state practice[22] there are many different terms employed to indicate a binding legal agreement and such agreements may be concluded in a variety of forms.[23] The Vienna Convention on the Law of Treaties is limited by its terms to:

> [a]n international agreement concluded between States in written form and governed by international law, whether embodied in a single instrument or in two or more related instruments and whatever its particular designation; [...].[24]

However, since the Convention states that this is without prejudice to the legal force of agreements not falling within this definition,[25] the threshold question remains that of distinguishing between instruments with legal force and those of only political and moral effect.[26] Aust describes the distinction in the following terms:

> [t]he fundamental distinction between an informal instrument and a treaty is that, although the former puts on record the mutual understandings of the States concerned as to how each will act in relation to the other, or others, the parties have no intention that the instrument should itself create a legal relationship and be binding upon them.[27]

3.2.   The intention of the parties: drafting history and language

The insignificance of the form chosen by parties to record their undertakings has meant that decision-makers have had to turn to other factors to determine their legal significance, most notably the intentions of the parties.[28] The Vienna Convention criterion of governance by interna-

---

I. Brownlie, *Principles of Public International Law* 606 (1990). Brownlie gives the example of minutes of a conference as a potentially binding agreement.

22. *E.g.*, the United States State Department International Agreement Regulations, 27 April 1981 (5) states that departures from the customary form "will not preclude the agreement from being a customary agreement." Cited by Aust, *supra* note 5, at 799.

23. R. Baxter, *International Law in "Her Infinite Variety"*, 29 ICLQ 549 (1980).

24. Vienna Convention on the Law of Treaties, 23 May 1969, 1155 UNTS 331 (1980), Art. 2(1)(a).

25. *Id.*, Art. 3.

26. O. Schachter, *The Twilight Existence of Non-Binding International Agreements*, 71 AJIL 296 (1977).

27. Aust, *supra* note 5, at 794.

28. The editors of Oppenheim, e.g., suggest that the 'decisive factor' is the intention of the parties: Jennings & Watts, *supra* note 21, at 1202. State officials repeatedly emphasise the crucial nature of the intention of the parties; *see e.g.*, Aust, *supra* note 5; M.J. Nash (Leich),

tional law subsumes the intention of the parties to enter into legally binding relations.[29]

There is no requirement as to how that intention must be evidenced
and it can be expressed in different ways and in diverse arenas. In the words
of former Judge Jessup:

> [i]nternational law, not being a formalistic system, holds states legally bound
> by their undertakings in a variety of circumstances and does not need either
> to insist or to deny that the beneficiaries are 'parties' to the undertakings.[30]

An intention to be bound has generally been deduced from the language
employed in the agreement, the circumstances of its conclusion and occasionally the subsequent actions of the parties.[31] The ICJ and its predecessor, the PCIJ, have considered these factors on a number of occasions. In
the *South West Africa* cases South Africa raised as a preliminary objection
that the Mandate had never been a 'treaty in force' conferring rights and
obligations upon South Africa within the terms of Article 37 of the Statute
of the International Court of Justice, either in its entirety or with respect
to Article 7.[32] It based this argument on the confirmation of the Mandate
as a Declaration of the Council of the League of Nations. The Court
rejected this objection holding that the formal status of the Mandate as a

---

International Instruments Not Constituting Agreements, 88 AJIL 515 (1994); McNeill, *supra*
note 5.

29. E.g., the Fourth Special Rapporteur of the International Law Commission asserted that in
so far as an intention to create legal relations is required under international law "the
element of intention is embraced in the phrase 'governed by international law'." H. Waldock, Special Rapporteur, 1965 YILC II, at 12. Munch considered that this phrase excluded
political declarations and municipal contracts. Attention focussed on the latter and the
former became obscured because of their difficulty; F. Munch, *Comment on the 1968 Draft
Convention on the Law of Treaties: Non-binding Agreements*, 29 ZaöRV 1 (1969).

30. South West Africa cases, *supra* note 18, at 411 (Judge Jessup, Separate Opinion).

31. The differing views as to whether there is a presumption that an agreement is binding is a
less extreme form of the debate as to whether all informal commitments have legal effect:
J. Klabbers, The Concept of Treaty in International Law (1996). Fawcett argued against
such a presumption: J. Fawcett, *The Legal Character of International Agreements*, 30 BYIL
381 (1953). Mullerson prefers the presumption that every agreement duly signed by states
has a legally binding intent unless the opposite intention is clearly manifested: R. Mullerson, *Sources of International Law: New Tendencies in Soviet Thinking*, 83 AJIL 511 (1989).

32. Article 7 of the Mandate provided for the submission of disputes as to the interpretation
or application of the Mandate to the International Court of Justice. Article 37 states:
"[w]henever a treaty or convention in force provides for reference to a tribunal to have
been instituted by the League of Nations, or to the Permanent Court of International
Justice, the matter shall, as between the parties to the present Statute, be referred to the
International Court of Justice."

Council Declaration was of no legal significance and the Mandate "in fact and in law, is an international agreement having the character of a treaty or convention."[33]

Judge Jessup expressed the fundamental question as "whether a State has given a promise or undertaking from which flow international rights and duties."[34] The question emphasises the subjective will of the parties, but in reality states rarely make their intentions explicit.[35] Accordingly they must be deduced from the surrounding circumstances in an *ex post facto* objective evaluation. In the *South West Africa* cases the majority derived the intentions of all the parties from the drafting history and imperative language of the Mandate agreement. The negotiating history and the Mandate Preamble verified that its conferral had been agreed by the Allied and Associated Powers and accepted by His Britannic Majesty for and on behalf of the Union of South Africa in May 1919. The initial agreement was presented to the Council in December 1920, amended and confirmed by it. This arrangement was intended and understood by all concerned to constitute a legally binding agreement. This conclusion was bolstered by the requirement that the Mandate instrument be deposited in the archives of the League of Nations and forwarded to all states parties to the Treaty of Peace with Germany. For the majority, the effect of these different factors was to uphold the conclusion that the parties had intended to create a legally binding instrument, and had succeeded in so doing.[36]

Judges Spender and Fitzmaurice however drew the opposite conclusion from these same surrounding facts. They noted that all Mandates except one, that over Iraq, were concluded by Declarations of the Council of the League. The Iraq Mandate alone was in treaty form between Great Britain and Iraq. This choice of different form was deliberate and could not be ignored. Preference was generally given to a quasi-legislative act of the Council of the League over mutually adopted rights and obligations by the parties. The condition that the Mandate could only be modified with the consent of the Council (as opposed to confirmation by the Council) was also inconsistent with an autonomous agreement between the parties.

---

33. South West Africa cases, *supra* note 18, at 330.
34. South West Africa cases, *supra* note 18 (Judge Jessup, Separate Opinion).
35. It has been commented that parties only make it explicit in the text or through preparatory statements when an agreement is not to be considered binding; *see, e.g.*, Munch, *supra* note 29; Jennings & Watts, *supra* note 21, at 1202.
36. South West Africa cases, *supra* note 18.

Indeed at its December 1920 meeting the Council had exercised this power and amended the earlier text, further proof to the dissenting judges that an agreement had not been concluded.[37]

The background to the negotiations and prior diplomatic exchanges were also crucial in determining the parties' intentions in the *Aegean Sea Continental Shelf* case.[38] The Court had to decide whether Greece and Turkey had agreed to accept the Court's jurisdiction over their dispute. Greece claimed that the Court's jurisdiction had been accepted by an unsigned, uninitialed joint communiqué between the Prime Ministers of the respective states issued at Brussels on 31 May 1975. The communiqué stated:

> [i]n the course of their meeting the two Prime Ministers had an opportunity to give consideration to the problem which led to the existing situation as regards relations between their countries.
>
> They decided [*ont décidé*] that those problems should be resolved [*doivent être résolus*] peacefully by means of negotiations and as regards the continental shelf of the Aegean Sea by the International Court at the Hague. They defined the general lines on the basis of which the forthcoming meetings of the representatives of the two Governments would take place.
>
> In that connection they decided to bring forward the date of the meeting of experts concerning the question of the continental shelf of the Aegean Sea and that of the experts on the question of air space.

The Court again held that form is not determinative and that international law does not preclude a joint communiqué from constituting a binding agreement to refer a case to arbitration, or to adjudication. In deciding whether the particular instrument does in fact have that character the Court must have regard to its nature and above all 'to its actual terms and to the particular circumstances in which it was drawn up'. Accordingly it examined the communiqué in its entirety with special attention given to the language used and the context of the May 1975 meeting. This required examination of the many diplomatic exchanges that had previously occurred. The Court found that Turkey had been consistent in demanding that referral to the Court be through a joint submission after the conclusion of a special agreement that clarified the issues to be resolved by the Court. Turkey had agreed to 'contemplate a joint submission to the Court'

---

37. South West Africa cases, *supra* note 18 (Judges Spender and Fitzmaurice, Separate Opinion).

38. Aegean Sea Continental Shelf case (Greece *v.* Turkey) (Jurisdiction), Judgment, 1978 ICJ Rep. 3, at para. 97.

but the joint communiqué was insufficient to found jurisdictional consent. Vierdag concludes that the careful analysis of the true intentions of the parties "represents another example of the Court's endeavour to avoid imposing upon States obligations that are not firmly rooted in customary law or that do not unequivocally correspond to a state's intention to be bound."[39]

Except for being unsigned, the joint communiqué resembles the 1987 Agreement in the *Qatar* v. *Bahrain* case. The Court did not dismiss the former as being without any legal effect but only as insufficient to support a unilateral application of the dispute to the Court. Similarly, the 1987 Agreement could not have been the basis of a unilateral application. In both cases a commitment was made to continue negotiations towards conferring jurisdiction on the Court. In *Qatar* v. *Bahrain* too the question was whether that had been achieved. The 1987 Agreement was supplemented by the establishment of the Tripartite Committee, but there was disagreement as to the function of this Committee. Bahrain alleged its sole purpose was to produce an agreed joint submission and that consequently a unilateral application was never anticipated. The Court noted that much of the work of the Committee had indeed been directed towards this end, but that did not mean this was the only approach sanctioned by the 1987 Agreement. The Court explained the Committee's task as being to assist the parties in fulfilling the commitment to have recourse to the Court.

Unlike the joint communiqué, the 1987 agreement was supplemented by further agreed exchanges as recorded in the Doha Minutes. These essentially acknowledged that since the Tripartite Committee had failed in its purpose, the good offices of the King of Saudi Arabia were again to be attempted for a final five months during which there could be no recourse to the Court. After that time the parties could apply to the Court and the Minutes addressed the circumstances in which the Court would be validly seised.

It was in its July 1994 judgment that the Court asserted that it need not consider the intentions of the parties in signing the Doha Minutes. Their legal effect was to be found in the text as signed and the surrounding circumstances rather than in evidence as to the intentions of the parties. The Court restated its *dicta* in the *Aegean Sea* case that it "[...] must have regard

---

39.   *Cf.* E. Vierdag, *The International Court of Justice and the Law of Treaties*, in Lowe & Fitzmaurice (Eds.), *supra* note 12, at 153.

above all to its actual terms and to the particular circumstances in which it was drawn up."[40] In an extremely brief passage the Court held that the Foreign Minister of Bahrain could not subsequently argue that he intended only to subscribe to a statement of political undertaking contrary to the wording of the text. The signed Minutes did not merely record the discussions at Doha but summarised areas of agreement and disagreement and reaffirmed commitments already undertaken by the parties. Even if such a limited intention as that expressed by the Foreign Minister of Bahrain existed, it could not prevail over the actual terms of the instrument in question.

In the February 1995 judgment this conclusion was reiterated. In determining precisely what had been agreed by the parties, the Court looked to the object and purpose of the 1990 negotiations. These were said by the Court to be the advancement of the dispute settlement process by setting a specified time limit upon attempts at mediated resolution of the substantive differences and then by giving practical effect to the commitment to have recourse to the Court that had been made in 1987. This was done by settling the controversial question of the definition of disputed matters through Qatar's acceptance of the Bahraini formula and reaffirming earlier commitments.[41] These encompassed point one of the 1987 Agreement, to have recourse to the Court, but not point three, re-establishment of the Tripartitite Committee that had not reconvened since December 1988. In these circumstances a further agreement that was confined to opening up the possibility of a joint submission would not have furthered the dispute resolution process as this was precisely what the parties had conspicuously failed to accomplish over many years of assisted negotiations. As the majority put it: "It could not have been the purpose of the Minutes to delay the resolution of the dispute or to make it more difficult."[42]

Bahrain did not only refute the legal nature of the Doha Minutes, but also challenged their meaning with respect to seising the Court of the dispute. In determining whether they provided for unilateral seisin the Court emphasised the need to examine the wording of the Minutes and the surrounding circumstances - precisely the same criteria as those specified for

---

40. Aegean Sea Continental Shelf case, *supra* note 38, at para. 96, cited in Territorial Dispute (Libyan Arab Jamahiriya/Chad), Judgment, 1994 ICJ Rep. 6, at paras. 22-23.

41. Qatar *v.* Bahrain, Judgment of 15 February 1995, *supra* note 2, at para. 35.

42. *Id.*, at para. 36.

deciding their legal nature. Article 32 of the Vienna Convention allows recourse to the *travaux* as a supplementary (and subjective) means of interpreting a text where the meaning is ambiguous or obscure.[43] This was patently the case in *Qatar* v. *Bahrain* and indeed in any case where there is a good faith disagreement as to interpretation. Nevertheless, the Court largely discounted the usefulness of the *travaux préparatoires* because of their 'fragmentary nature'. They could not provide conclusive supplementary evidence of either the circumstances, nor the meaning to be attached to the text.[44] The Court rejected the relevance of the parties' motives in signing the Minutes:

> [w]hatever may have been the motives of each of the Parties, the Court can only confine itself to the actual terms of the Minutes as the expression of their common intention, and to the interpretation of them which it has already given.[45]

The Court adopted a 'reasonable man' approach in its assessment of the purpose of the Doha discussions in the interlocking questions of their legally binding outcome and meaning.[46] A reasonable person might well have assumed with the Court that the Minutes were to move the dispute resolution process along, but the behaviour of parties in dispute does not always conform to rational expectations. Indeed, subjectively it may be perfectly reasonable to negotiate with the intention of stalling the process. The Court acknowledged that the central focus of the Doha summit was not the territorial dispute between Qatar and Bahrain but the invasion of Kuwait. It even accepted that this background might explain why there was not a more explicit text, but refused to draw any further conclusions. It is at least possible that less care was given by the parties to the Minutes in order to revert to the main agenda item. Unlike its careful consideration of

---

43. Vienna Convention on the Law of Treaties, Arts. 31 and 32 presuppose the existence of a treaty. There is no provision in the Convention with respect to interpretation for the purposes of deciding whether a treaty has been concluded. The structure of the Court's judgment in Qatar v. Bahrain emphasises the wording and surrounding circumstances for both.

44. Dismissal of the *travaux préparatoires* as a supplementary means of interpretation discounted the parties' intentions although the meaning of the words were not clear. Qatar v. Bahrain, Judgment of 15 February 1995, *supra* note 2, at 27 (Vice-President Schwebel, Dissenting Opinion).

45. *Id.*, at para. 41.

46. *Cf.* Koskenniemi, *supra* note 1, at 306: "[t]herefore it is necessary to look, not at what other States subjectively experienced but how a "reasonable man" acting in good faith, would have understood the declaration."

how Turkey evinced its intentions with respect to agreeing the joint communiqué and contents, it paid scant regard to the Bahrain pleadings in which the negotiations were analysed and Bahraini intentions explained. *Travaux préparatoires* provide subjective and contemporaneous evidence of both words and circumstances but were only sparingly referred to. The dilemma is that emphasis upon parties' intentions allows any party to reinterpret those intentions, but emphasis upon the surrounding circumstances enables those intentions to be discounted even while the decision maker purports to determine them through interpretation of the words used.

3.3.   Subsequent behaviour

In the *Aegean Sea* case the Court expressly rejected the form of the joint communiqué as determinative of its legal status. However in a passage that was not referred to in *Qatar* v. *Bahrain* it asserted that it was for the two governments to consider the implications of the joint communiqué and the impact, if any, on their attempts to resolve the dispute.[47] This raises the relevance of the parties' subsequent behaviour. Judge Lachs rejected the dicta of the majority in words that are echoed in *Qatar* v. *Bahrain*:

> [o]n the contrary, insofar as the Communiqué is an international instrument, the question of its precise legal implications cannot be regarded as lying within the direction of either of the governments concerned.[48]

The statement by the majority in the *Aegean Sea* case assumed the parties to be willing to consider jointly the implications of the communiqué,[49] but such cooperation might not be possible. In *Qatar* v. *Bahrain* the two states drew differing conclusions as to the implications and effects of the Doha Minutes. The Court rejected any subsequent statements as to those intentions as relevant to the legal characterisation of the Minutes. It must be correct that the parties cannot effectively deny the consequences of what can be objectively determined to constitute a legal instrument, although subjective intentions are germane to the determination of the existence of a

---

47.   Aegean Sea Continental Shelf case, *supra* note 38, at para. 108.
48.   *Id.*, at 50 (Judge Lachs, Dissenting Opinion).
49.   In the Heathrow Airport User Charges case the arbitral award found that a Memorandum of Understanding between the US and UK was not a source of independent legal rights and duties but that it had value as consensual subsequent practice by the parties. The award is described in 88 AJIL 738 (1994).

binding legal agreement. Subsequent contrary actions might be alternatively construed as objective evidence of those original intentions, or as
attempts to change and conceal those intentions. Indeed inconsistent behaviour might amount to breach of the agreement, even if committed immediately after its conclusion.[50] Domestic courts are also wary of parties who
attempt to renege on their obligations by denying that they entered into a
binding agreement. Similarly, failure to comply with domestic constitutional requirements for valid treaty making can only exceptionally detract
from the legal nature of the instrument under international law.[51] However, Bahrain did not refer to Article 46 of the Vienna Convention in an
attempt to invalidate its consent to be bound, but as an objective indication
of what it claimed to be its true intentions with respect to the Minutes.

The ICJ has taken account of subsequent behaviour as evidence of the
parties' intentions at the time of entering into the agreement rather than as
construing that behaviour as completing or denying the existence of a legal
instrument. In the *South West Africa* cases, for example, the majority were
mindful of the actions, statements and practice of parties and other members of the international community in reliance upon the existence of the
Mandate. However there is no doubt that the Mandate instruments were of
a very special nature. Together they created an institutional regime that
could only be effective if all involved recognised its legal basis. As Judge
Bustamante stressed, the history and sociology of the Mandate concept
cannot be ignored. He considered that the actual agreement could not be
separated from the overall Mandate system since 'the former takes its inspi-
ration from the latter'.[52] It must also be remembered that in the *South
West Africa* cases the Court was examining the origins of the Mandate after
some 40 years of operation and its replication in the Trusteeship System. In
the context of decolonisation and international condemnation of the apartheid regime in South West Africa, it was inconceivable that the Court
would find in 1962 that the entire edifice had no legal foundations. The
Mandate had imposed responsibilities on all Members of the League, including South Africa, and all had acted upon the assumption of its legality.
As the Court has spelled out, without the Mandate South Africa had no
entitlement to South West Africa at all.[53] Similarly in 1970 when the

---

50. Vienna Convention on the Law of Treaties, *supra* note 24, Art. 60.
51. *Id.*, Art. 46.
52. South West Africa cases, *supra* note 18, at 351 (Judge Bustamante, Separate Opinion).
53. In 1950, the Court had opined that "[t]he authority which the Union Government exer-

Court was considering the termination of the Mandate, it accepted without question the conclusion reached in 1962 that the Mandate agreement had treaty status.[54] This enabled the Court to apply the Vienna Convention on the Law of Treaties provisions with respect to termination, leaving the way legally open for assertion of UN authority there. These factors differentiate an institutional agreement entered into in pursuance of the 'sacred trust of civilisation' from a bilateral agreement for the resolution of territorial disputes.[55] It cannot therefore be assumed that the Court would apply similar reasoning in the second situation.

One particular type of subsequent behaviour that was in issue in both *South West Africa* and *Qatar* v. *Bahrain* is failure to complete procedural formalities, for example registration under Article 102 of the United Nations Charter or its forerunner, Article 18 of the League Covenant. Article 18 stipulated that no treaty was binding until so registered. Despite the clear wording of Article 18 the majority of the Court in the *South West Africa* cases held failure to register the Mandate agreement to be irrelevant to its binding character. The Court surmised the purpose of registration to be to inhibit secret agreements. The requirements within the Mandate for its deposit within the League archives and distribution to other Member States provided alternative mechanisms for ensuring publicity and failure to register was therefore irrelevant. Indeed, these formalities provided support for the conclusion that a legally binding instrument had been concluded.[56] Unlike UN Charter Article 103, the League Covenant contained no priority clause, but nevertheless this pragmatic conclusion ignored the strict requirements of the Covenant.

In contrast to Article 18 of the Covenant, the United Nations Charter Article 102 makes no judgment as to the binding nature of unregistered

---

cises over the Territory is based on the Mandate. If the Mandate lapsed, as the Union Government contends, the latter's authority would equally have lapsed." Advisory Opinion Concerning the International Status of South West Africa, 1950 ICJ Rep. 133. In 1962, Judge Mbanefo explicitly asserted that estoppel precluded South Africa from raising the non-legal effect of the Mandate in face of its own conduct over the past forty years; South West Africa cases, *supra* note 18, at 440 (Judge Mbanefo, Separate Opinion).

54. Legal Consequences for States of the Continued Presence of South Africa in Namibia (South West Africa) Notwithstanding Security Council Resolution 276 (1970), Advisory Opinion of 21 June, 1971 ICJ Rep. 16, at para. 94.

55. Covenant of the League of Nations, 1919, Art. 22.

56. Thus while form is not determinative, increased formality may be further evidence of the parties' intention to be bound.

treaties but instead stipulates that:

> (2) No party to any such treaty or international agreement which has not
> been registered in accordance with paragraph 1 of this Article may invoke
> that treaty or agreement before any organ of the United Nations.

While the binding nature of the treaty is not therefore challenged by non-registration *per se*, failure to do so might constitute evidence as to whether the parties perceived an agreement as a treaty.[57] Neither Bahrain nor Qatar registered the 1987 Agreement although both parties conceded its binding nature. Even when it registered the 1990 Minutes Qatar made no reference to the earlier documents. Despite not being registered the 1987 Agreement was invoked before the Court, as indeed were the oral undertakings in the *Nuclear Tests* cases. Bahrain adduced the failure by Qatar to register the 1990 Minutes until shortly before its application to the Court as evidence of Qatar's real belief that this was not a binding agreement, until it sought reliance upon it. The Court dismissed this argument saying it could draw no conclusions from actions with respect to registration, including its timing. To have decided otherwise would have been to impute bad faith to Qatar, or at least a change of opinion, but the consequence is that compliance or otherwise with Article 102 is irrelevant in determining the legal nature of an instrument.[58]

For its part, Bahrain did not simply not register either the 1987 Agreement or the Doha Minutes but immediately protested Qatar's registration of the Minutes. Failure to protest may be regarded as objective evidence of acquiescence, or lead to a state being estopped from later denying that it intended to be bound.[59] Koskenniemi has described the relationship between acquiescence and estoppel as equivocal, although he considers that

---

57. This point is highlighted by the difference between these two statements: "Non registration [...] does not have any consequence for the actual validity of the agreement, which remains binding upon the parties." Qatar *v.* Bahrain, Judgment of 1 July 1994, *supra* note 2, at para. 29. "Non-registration is good evidence that [...] neither the Council nor any Member of the League [...] thought that it was." South West Africa cases, *supra* note 18, at 494 (Judge Spender and Judge Fitzmaurice, Joint Dissenting Opinions).

58. This is consistent with the approach of the Secretariat which makes no judgment as to whether documents submitted for registration have the legal character of an international agreement. *See further* H. Han, *The U.N. Secretary-General's Treaty Depositary Function: Legal Implications*, 14 Brooklyn Journal of International Law 549, at 567 (1988).

59. Anglo-Norwegian Fisheries (United Kingdom *v.* Norway), Judgment, 1951 ICJ Rep. 116; Delimitation of the Maritime Boundary in the Gulf of Maine Area (Canada *v.* United States of America), Judgment, 1984 ICJ Rep. 246.

estoppel seems more related to justice in that it prevents a state from blowing 'hot and cold'.[60] In *Military and Paramilitary Activities in and Against Nicaragua* the Court allowed subsequent behaviour to substitute for the formal requirements of acceptance of the jurisdiction of the PCIJ (and after 1946 the ICJ).[61] Nicaragua's long failure to ratify its acceptance of the Statute of the PCIJ was discounted in favour of acquiescence for over forty years by all concerned (including the United States, respondents to the disputed application) and continued official records noting the anomaly. Presumably, if the United States had at some point protested the listing of Nicaragua as having a valid Declaration, it would not have been bound by Nicaragua's assertion of jurisdiction. Despite its failure to do so, it remains difficult to see how "passivity and inaction on the part of officials and States can transform a Nicaraguan will into a Nicaraguan deed".[62]

Conversely, Bahrain's protests against formal registration of the 1990 Minutes by Qatar were not deemed pertinent as evidence of its intentions with respect to their status. Positive acts by a party were accorded less weight in *Qatar v. Bahrain* than omission to act by everyone else in the *Nicaragua* case. The difference is that the US was viewed as acquiescent in Nicaragua's failure to complete procedural formalities while, once the Minutes are accepted as a binding agreement, Bahrain's protests were directed at Qatar's compliance with the legal obligation of registration. It can be argued that Bahrain was not 'blowing hot and cold' but consistently challenging Qatari actions that characterised the Minutes as a legally binding agreement. What is missing from the Court's decision are clear criteria for distinguishing subsequent actions that are relevant as evidence of the parties' original intentions from those that constitute effective protest, situations where silence is deemed tacit consent, or actions that are incapable of altering an already determined legal status. It might be noted that in *South West Africa*, *Nicaragua*, and *Qatar v. Bahrain* the outcome of all these uncertainties and inconsistencies was to uphold the jurisdiction of the Court.

---

60. Koskenniemi, *supra* note 1, at 312-320.
61. Military and Paramilitary Activities in and Against Nicaragua (Nicaragua *v.* United States of America) (Jurisdiction and Admissibility), Judgment, 1984 ICJ Rep. 392.
62. R. Higgins, *Fundamentals of International Law, in* N. Jasentuliyana (Ed.), Perspectives on International Law: Dedicated to Manfred Lachs 3 (1995).

3.4.   Unilateral agreements

In oral argument in the *Aegean Sea* case it was argued on behalf of Greece
that failure to accept the intentions of the parties as set out in the joint
communiqué would cause the Court's jurisprudence with respect to unilateral statements to crumble.[63] In these cases the Court has formally at least
paid great heed to the declarant's intentions.[64] For example, in the *Temple*
case the Court stated that the "sole relevant question is whether the language employed in any given declaration does reveal a clear intention".[65]
However, as with bilateral or multilateral agreements, such intentions can
only be surmised through objective analysis of the surrounding circumstances and the words used. In the *Nuclear Tests* cases, for example, the
Court held that the requisite intention is to be ascertained by the 'interpretation of the act', a concept that is broader than interpretation of the statement.[66] In determining the legal effect of the statements of the French
President the Court accordingly had regard to their substance and to the
circumstances in which they were made. The public nature of the undertakings by the French President to the international community as a whole
(*erga omnes*) meant that all other states, including the applicant states,
Australia and New Zealand, were entitled to act in reliance upon them. Yet
since they wanted a determination of the substantive issues, neither of these
states had relied, nor wished to rely, upon the French statements. At the
same time it is arguable whether the French President intended to incur
binding obligations.[67] The result was a fiction that was constructed from

---

63.   Aegean Sea Continental Shelf case, Pleadings, Oral Arguments and Documents, at 345.
64.   Legal Status of Eastern Greenland (Norway *v.* Denmark), 1933 PCIJ (Ser. A/B) No. 53;
      Nuclear Tests cases, *supra* note 1, at 457; Military and Paramilitary Activities in and
      Against Nicaragua (Nicaragua *v.* United States of America), Merits, Judgment, 1986 ICJ
      Rep. 14; Frontier Dispute case (Burkino Faso *v.* Mali), Judgment, 1986 ICJ Rep. 554.
65.   Temple of Preah Vihear, *supra* note 19, at 32. The statement was made in the context of a
      declaration made under the Statute of the International Court of Justice, Article 36(2).
      Such declarations have been described as unilateral acts giving rise to bilateral engagements;
      Military and Paramilitary Activities in and Against Nicaragua, *supra* note 61, at para. 60.
      Since a number of the cases discussed concern the question of consent to the jurisdiction of
      the Court these *dicta* are especially pertinent.
66.   Nuclear Test cases, *supra* note 1.
67.   "Many commentators have stressed the extreme unlikeliness that France would really have
      inteded (sic) to assume an obligation - not least because it had itself in another connexion
      denied that unilateral statements of this kind would be binding.": Koskenniemi, *supra* note
      1, at 307.

subjective intent, assumed reliance and good faith.[68] In the *Frontier Dispute* case the Chamber again combined subjective intention with objective assessment of the circumstances. "Thus it all depends upon the intention of the State in question, and [...] it is for the Court 'to form its own view of the meaning and scope intended by the author of a unilateral declaration which may create a legal obligation'."[69] In doing this the decision maker must take account of "all the factual circumstances in which the act occurred."[70] This formulation is not in fact so far different from the Court's stance in *Qatar* v. *Bahrain* in the context of a bilateral agreement. There the Court asserted its dependence upon the language and circumstances of the agreement of the Minutes that encompassed what it construed as the intention of the parties at that time. In both situations, however, it is the constructed will of the parties, rather than their real will, that is decisive. In the *Frontier Dispute* case the Chamber based its conclusion that the President of Mali had no intention to be bound by statements made in an interview on the fact that the parties had not manifested their intentions through negotiation of "a formal agreement on the basis of reciprocity."[71] This accentuates what the circumstances might have been (a decision of the Mediation Commission of the Organisation of African Unity) rather than those actually surrounding the interview. This again illustrates the fluidity of the Court in determining when an intention to be bound exists.

It can be problematic whether an action is correctly characterised as unilateral or bilateral. In *South West Africa*, Judge Jessup itemised instances where the Permanent Court had held an agreement to exist that included a unilateral manifesto issued by a domestic organ of Sardinia, a Lithuanain statute and the participation of two states in the adoption of a resolution of the League Council. All these combined unilateral actions with some bilateral elements.[72] The Chamber stated in the *Frontier Dispute* case that for a unilateral statement to be held binding there is no requirement that it be

---

68. *Id.*, at 308.
69. Frontier Dispute case, *supra* note 64, para. 39.
70. *Id.*, at para. 40.
71. In Military and Paramilitary Activities in and Against Nicaragua, *supra* note 64, at para. 261, the Court denied that there was anything in a communication from the Junta of National Reconstruction to the Organisation of American States from which it could infer a legal status.
72. South West Africa cases, *supra* note 18, at 403 (Judge Jessup, Separate Opinion).

made during the course of international negotiations, nor is it necessary for it to be directed towards another party. It considered it had a duty to "show even greater caution when it is a question of a unilateral declaration not directed to any particular recipient."[73] By definition, the lack of any negotiation process does not arise in the context of bilateral (or multilateral) agreements. However, negotiation strategy envisages the presentation by all parties of without prejudice offers, the weighing of compromises and consideration of offers and counter-offers. Those involved will have different intentions at various stages of the process, for example a desire to maintain its momentum, to make a political gesture, to stall for time, or to reject the latest offer. It cannot be assumed that any statement issued, or even agreed, accurately reflects the true intentions of the parties, nor that the purpose of the negotiations has been achieved. The Court should exercise similar caution in determining the intentions of parties involved in negotiations as was expressed with respect to unilateral statements outside of such processes.

4.   CONCLUSIONS

In the context of unilateral statements, Koskenniemi has identified three understandings upon which the Court may choose to rest its decision: declarant will, reliance, and non-subjective justice. He explains that none of these choices can be consistently applied and "the problem-solver must have recourse to a strategy of evasion."[74] In determining whether an agreement exists, the Court has emphasised the subjective intention of the parties but has simultaneously accepted that a legally binding agreement can objectively exist, as determined from the surrounding circumstances and the text of the instrument. "The difficulty here is that statements or contexts do not demonstrate their objective nature automatically" and construction inevitably denies the subjectivity of at least one of the parties, in the form of the "Court knowing better".[75] Reliance upon subsequent statements by the parties as to their earlier intentions reverts to subjectivity, but allows for subsequent reappraisal and changed expressions of what

---

73. Frontier Dispute case, *supra* note 64, at para. 39.
74. Koskenniemi, *supra* note 1, at 300.
75. *Id.*, at 304.

may or may not have been earlier intentions. This outcome the Court rejected in *Qatar* v. *Bahrain*.

Thus the Court's options are in reality limited. Objective evaluation of the surrounding circumstances does not conceal the Court's subjectivities in their interpretation. Similarly in other cases, apparent emphasis upon subjective intent has not concealed construction of that intent through reliance upon external evidence. The Court may seek its solution in what Koskenniemi has termed 'non-subjective justice' based upon policy considerations of good faith, legitimate expectations and reasonableness.[76] These are not easily applied in the context of submission to the jurisdiction of the Court where consensuality is paramount.[77] The facts in *Qatar* v. *Bahrain* lead to two divergent, but reasonable, conclusions. In the words of Judge ad hoc Valticos "ultimately there was indeed an agreement to come to the Court"[78] while Lauterpacht sees the decision as "a further step along the path of the gradual erosion of specific consent as the basis of the Court's jurisdiction."[79] Nor is it easy to be confident about which approach is 'just' and upholds more effectively international community objectives. If the Court too readily concludes from the surrounding circumstances that there has been consent, it is likely to inhibit states from considering even in general terms the desirability of the Court as a dispute resolution forum. Parties to a dispute might be prepared to consider a joint submission, which has advantages for both. They can set out the parameters of dispute, reduce the potential for lengthy proceedings on jurisdiction and admissibility, minimise the likelihood of third party intervention, and move the focus directly to the substance of the disputed matters. Neither party gains the advantages of defining the dispute that is gained through unilateral application. Fear of without prejudice statements or exploratory proposals being construed as constituting consent could impede attempts at negotiating a joint submission to the Court. Further, compliance with the Court's judgment is less likely where genuine consent to its jurisdiction is lacking and its legitimacy to hear the dispute accordingly undermined.

---

76. The Court especially emphasized good faith and trust in international relations in the Nuclear Tests cases, *supra* note 1, at para. 46. *Cf.* Jennings & Watts, *supra* note 21, at 1202.

77. It is noticeable that in many of these cases, South West Africa, Aegean Sea, Nicaragua and Qatar v. Bahrain itself, the issue of the legal status of an instrument has arisen in the context of determining whether the parties have consented to the Court's exercise of jurisdiction within the terms of Article 36.

78. Qatar *v.* Bahrain, Judgment of 1 July 1994, *supra* note 2.

79. Lauterpacht, *supra* note 12, at 467.

Non-compliance inevitably weakens the Court's authority however much the state in question considers it justified. On the other hand, if the Court declines jurisdiction unless the state's subjective will to participate is manifest, it may become marginalised and be perceived as having abdicated any role in encouraging states to have recourse to it.[80] Seen in this light, the decision of the Court to allow the parties one final attempt at defining their dispute is a commendable instance of directive case management, although it conformed to the expectations of neither party. Once it had failed however, the continued assertion of Bahraini consent is a striking denial of subjective will.

Qatar v. *Bahrain* is not only relevant to the construal of consent to the Court's jurisdiction, but to other informal binding agreements. In that the Court was perhaps more transparent in relying upon objective criteria to the exclusion of subjective assertions than it has been previously, Vierdag considers that the decision will have a decisive impact upon what he terms the prevalent practice of drawing up all kinds of informal arrangements between states, governments, ministries, and state agencies. He argues that at present the possible legal significance of these arrangements is commonly ignored or left ambiguous.[81] Nevertheless, the considerable advantages of informality means that states will continue to conduct their international relations in this way. In some cases misunderstandings can arise through different expectations as to legal effect. In others ambiguity may be deliberate in order to facilitate some appearance of agreement. It is only subsequently when divergent interpretations threaten the stability of the arrangement that clarity is sought.[82] Construction of the 'real' intention of the parties is then fictitious and ignores the reality of the dispute. States may be able to resolve those differences, for example through renegotiation and clarification.[83] If third party assistance is sought, inevitably the current intentions of at least one of the parties are discounted. Drawing the

---

80. This point was made by P. Kooijmans in his Commentary, Increasing the Use and Appeal of the Court, at The Hague in April 1996.

81. Vierdag, *supra* note 39, at 166.

82. In the Heathrow Airport User Charges case (*supra* note 49), UK contentions that the Memorandum of Understanding was no more than a 'gentleman's agreement' with no legal effect caused US consternation with respect to other Memoranda of Understanding on defense issues. This led to substantial delays in the negotiation of defense programs between the two states, and between the US and other states that were thought likely to adopt the UK approach: see McNeill, *supra* note 5.

83. As was done through the so-called Chapeau Agreement between the US and UK to resolve the difference of opinion with respect to Memoranda of Understanding. *See id.*

line between binding and non-binding agreements has always been problematic and has not been simplified by the International Court of Justice in *Qatar* v. *Bahrain*. Apparent reliance upon intention and consent to be bound merely obscures the many nuances of states' actions over time, while external facts and circumstances explicitly preferred in this case can be manipulated to produce different results. The finding that the Minutes constituted a binding legal agreement may well be appropriate in light of the specific reaffirmation of earlier agreements, but the *dicta* serve only to blur still further the grey twilight zone between binding and non-binding international agreements.

[4]

THE SIGNIFICANCE OF THE REGISTRATION OR NON-REGISTRATION OF AN INTERNATIONAL AGREEMENT IN DETERMINING WHETHER OR NOT IT IS A TREATY

*D. N. Hutchinson**

In order to determine the juridical nature of an agreement which has been concluded between two or more actors each of which is a subject of international law—whether that agreement is a treaty,[1] whether it is a contract which is binding solely under a system of national law or whether it is a so-called "gentlemen's agreement" which is not binding under any system of law at all—it is necessary to examine, among other things, the manner in which the actors which concluded the agreement—and any actor which may have later subscribed to it—have treated that agreement subsequently to the date of its conclusion.[2] Indeed, the suggestion has been made that the manner in which an agreement is treated subsequently to its conclusion is often likely to be the best indicator of its legal nature.[3]

One factor which is frequently said to be of relevance in this connexion is whether or not the agreement concerned has been

---

* Lecturer in Laws, University College London.
[1] For the definition of "treaty" in international law, see: Barberis, *Annuaire Français de Droit International*, 30 (1984), p. 239 at pp. 248–260; and Reuter, P., *Introduction aux Droit des Traités* (2nd. ed.; 1985), pp. 33–37.
[2] See, for example: Virally, *Annuaire de l'Institut de Droit International*, 60-I (1983), p. 166 at para. 171 (though note paras. 140–141); Aust, *International and Comparative Law Quarterly*, 35 (1986), p. 787 at pp. 802–803; and Remiro Brotons, A., *Derecho Internacional Público, vol. II: Derecho de los Tratados* (1987), p. 34.
[3] Virally, loc. cit. above (preceding note), at paras. 176 and 177.

registered with the Secretariat of the United Nations.[4] However, there is much confusion in the doctrine as to the degree of significance, if any, which may be attached to the fact that an agreement has or has not been so registered. Certainly, it is nowhere suggested that the registration of an agreement serves, in and by itself, to make an agreement into a treaty, if that was not otherwise its true legal nature. Similarly, the fact that an agreement has not been registered is nowhere said to dictate the conclusion that it is not a treaty. However, beyond this point, there is disagreement, ranging from, on the one hand, the point of view that the registration or non-registration of an agreement can throw no light whatsoever on its juridical nature[5] to the suggestion, on the other hand, that the registration of an agreement should give rise to a presumption that it is a treaty, at least if that agreement bears a form which is usually reserved in practice for treaties.[6]

The purpose of the present study is to establish the significance, if any, which may be attached to the fact that an agreement between two or more entities each of which is a subject of international law[7] has or has not been registered with the Secretariat of the United Nations[8] in determining whether or not that agreement is a treaty.[9]

---

[4] See, for example: Schachter, *American Journal of International Law*, 71 (1977), p. 296 at p. 298; Busuttil, *International and Comparative Law Quarterly*, 31 (1982), p. 474 at p. 485; and Jennings, Sir R., and Watts, Sir A. (eds.), *Oppenheim's International Law*, vol. I pts. 2–4 (9th. ed.; 1992), p. 1202.

[5] Mann, *British Year Book of International Law*, 33 (1957), p. 20 at p. 31.

[6] Lauterpacht, *Yearbook of the International Law Commission*, vol. II (1954), p. 123 para. 2.

[7] It is, therefore, not the purpose of the present study to examine the light which the fact that an agreement has been registered may throw on the legal status under international law of an actor which has participated in the conclusion of that agreement—though see nn. 35 and 49, below.

[8] The system operated by the Secretariat of the United Nations is not the only one which currently exists for registering agreements concluded between two or more subjects of international law. However, in view of its general scope and importance, the present study is confined to that system—though some reference will be made to the system which was operated by the League of Nations under Article 18 of its Covenant.

[9] The act of a party to an agreement in effecting its registration might possibly have significance for other reasons, too. Assuming the agreement in question to be a treaty, that act may serve to have the effect of making imputable to that party an act relating to the treaty which would not otherwise have been attributed to it: cf. the case described in nn. 65 and 69, below. It may operate to preclude that party from invoking a ground for invalidating its consent to be bound by the treaty which it otherwise might have been able to rely upon: cf. the cases described in nn. 71 and 72, below. Assuming that the instrument which is registered is a unilateral act, its registration by an entity other than that which issued it may serve to constitute acceptance by that entity of an undertaking which is given in the instrument by the

International Agreements 259

To this end, it will be assumed that the opinions which the actors which concluded an agreement may subsequently hold regarding the juridical nature of that agreement—and, likewise, the attitudes which they may evince on that issue—are relevant to a determination of whether or not that agreement is a treaty.

I. Registration with the Secretariat of the United Nations

A State which is a Member of the United Nations is under an obligation, by virtue of Article 102 (1) of the Charter,[10] to register with the Secretariat any "treaty" or "international agreement" into which it may enter.[11] The General Assembly, in adopting regulations to give effect to Article 102,[12] has purposefully avoided formulating a definition of the terms "treaty" and "international agreement",

entity which issued it: Tabory, *International and Comparative Law Quarterly*, 32 (1983), p. 981 at p. 993. Assuming that the instrument in question is one among several agreed texts, the fact that it is transmitted for registration together with those other texts may serve as evidence that the party transmitting it is of the opinion that that instrument forms part of the treaty which is constituted by those texts: Rosenne, *Recueil des Cours*, 86 (1954), p. 277 at pp. 302–303; and Tabory, loc. cit. above, esp. at pp. 987, 991–992, 994 and 995–997. The failure of a party to an agreement to register an instrument may also be significant in these connexions, as may the failure of the other parties to an agreement to respond to the act of one of their number in registering it. The possible significance in these contexts of registration, non-registration and failure to protest registration will not be examined here, though.

[10] Article 102 (1) does not state explicitly on whom the obligation to register falls. It simply states that the treaties and international agreements into which Members of the United Nations may enter must be registered: Broches and Boskey, *Nederlands Tijdschrift voor International Recht*, 4 (1957), p. 159 and p. 277 at p. 161. However, Article 102 (1) has always been understood in practice to impose an obligation to effect the registration of an agreement solely upon States which are Members of the Organization (loc. cit.), and, more particularly, solely upon those States Members of the Organization which have entered into that agreement: see, for example, the third preambular paragraph of General Assembly Resolution 254 B (III).

[11] States which are party to the Convention on the Law of Treaties, done at Vienna on 23 May 1969 (*United Nations Treaty Series*, vol. 1155, p. 331), are also under an obligation, by virtue of Article 80 (1) of that convention, to register the treaties into which they might enter. However, this obligation does not extend to "international agreements" in so far as that expression in Article 102 of the Charter encompasses undertakings which are not treaties (see text at n. 15, below, and n. 15 itself); nor does it extend to treaties concluded between a State, on the one hand, and one or more subjects of international law which are not States, on the other (Articles 1, 2 (1) (*a*) and 3 (*c*) of the Convention). Moreover, it applies only to those treaties which States party to the Convention may conclude with each other subsequently to the entry into force of the Convention between them (Article 4).

[12] Regulations to give effect to Article 102 of the Charter of the United Nations, adopted by General Assembly Resolution 97 (I) and amended by General Assembly Resolutions 364 B (IV), 482 (V) and 33/141 A.

260   *D. N. Hutchinson*

preferring to leave their meaning to be clarified through practice.[13]
They clearly embrace treaties of all types.[14] However, it has long

[13] *Repertory of United Nations Practice*, vol. V (1955), p. 292 para. 20 and p. 294
paras. 25 and 29.

[14] Thus, attempts by some States to limit the scope of Article 102 (1) by suggesting
particular types or categories of treaties which should be excluded from its ambit have
been firmly resisted: ibid., p. 293 paras. 22 and 23 and pp. 295–296 para. 31 (i). Note
also ibid., p. 294 para. 27.
    Common sense has, nevertheless, been said to suggest that some types of treaty
must fall outside the scope of Article 102 (1): Broches and Boskey, loc. cit. above (n.
10), at pp. 172–176, 191–192, 292 n. 1 and 299. Similar arguments were made in
relation to Article 18 of the Covenant of the League of Nations: ibid., pp. 170–172;
McNair, Lord, *The Law of Treaties* (1961), p. 181; Hudson, *American Journal of
International Law*, 19 (1925), p. 273 at pp. 280–285; and, most notably, the report of
the committee of jurists which was appointed by the Council of the League of Nations
on 21 February 1921 to study the scope of Article 18 of the Covenant (Doc. C. 256.
1921. V.), at p. 5. The practice which both States Members of the United Nations and
the Secretariat of the Organization have followed in applying Article 102 (1) indicates
that they understand that provision to embrace most, if not all, of those categories of
treaty which it was suggested either did or should fall beyond the reach of Article 18
of the Covenant: Broches and Boskey, loc. cit. above (n. 10), at pp. 176, 189–190 and
298; and Schachter, *British Year Book of International Law*, 25 (1948), p. 91 at p. 131.
Nonetheless, *pace* Schachter (ibid., at pp. 131–132), the practice of the United Nations'
Secretariat does contain some indications that it interprets Article 102 (1) in such a
way as to place some types of treaty beyond its ambit. See: *Repertory of United
Nations Practice, Supplement No. 3*, vol. IV (1973), p. 196 para. 13 (cf. also p. 192 at
notes (*a*) and (*b*) and n. 11 of the general survey of practice relating to Article 2 of
the regulations to give effect to Article 102 of the Charter); and ibid., *Supplement No.
5*, vol. V (1986), p. 164 para. 5.
    Whether or not certain types of treaty do, indeed, fall outside the scope of Article
102 (1) is an issue which need not be considered here, though. Whatever the answer
to that question might be, it remains the case that the great majority of treaties, at
the very least, come within its ambit. Moreover, and more importantly for present
purposes, it is clear that Article 102 (1) does not extend beyond treaties to encompass
agreements which are not binding in international law: see the text following this
note. That being so, it is possible to attach to the act of registration the significance
described in the text at nn. 33 and 43, below. Furthermore, given the difficulties which
confront any attempt to draw inferences as to the opinions of the parties to an
agreement regarding its juridical nature from their failure to effect its registration (see
text at nn. 73–87, below), the answer to this question is likely to be of little practical
interest in determining the significance which may be attached to the non-registration
of an agreement in assessing its legal status—though see n. 86, below.
    It should be added that a distinction has been made between treaties—according to
their degree of practical or political importance and the degree of publicity which they
would otherwise receive—for the purpose of determining the manner in which to
effect their publication. See, in particular, Paragraphs (2)-(4) of Article 12 of the
regulations to give effect to Article 102 of the Charter, as amended by General
Assembly Resolution 33/141 A. See also Tabory, *American Journal of International
Law*, 76 (1982), p. 350 at pp. 355–357. It should be emphasised that this distinction
between different types of treaties is made solely for the purpose of determining how
to publish them—in particular, in order to determine whether they should be published
in extenso in the *United Nations Treaty Series*. It, therefore, does not affect in any

International Agreements 261

been established that they also encompass certain forms of under-takings which, in themselves, do not constitute treaties, a prominent example being declarations by States that they accept the jurisdiction of the International Court of Justice under Article 36 (2) of the Court's Statute.[15] Nevertheless, those non-treaty undertakings which fall within the purview of Article 102 (1) are all ones which, like treaties, directly give rise to juridical effects in international law. Consequently, Article 102 (1) does not encompass contracts which are binding solely under systems of national law,[16] nor does it embrace agreements which are not binding under any system of law at all—so-called "gentlemen's agreements".[17]

way the range of agreements whose registration is required by Article 102 (1) of the Charter (or which is eligible for filing and recording under Article 10 of the regulations to give effect to Article 102 of the Charter): ibid., p. 358.

[15] *Repertory of United Nations Practice*, vol. V (1955), p. 293 para. 24; ibid., *Supplement No. 2*, vol. III (1963), p. 506 para. 4; and ibid., *Supplement No. 3*, vol. IV (1973), p. 196 para. 11. That these declarations are not, in themselves, treaties was made clear by the International Court in the case concerning *Military and Paramilitary Activities in and against Nicaragua (Jurisdiction of the Court and Admissibility of the Claim)*, *I.C.J. Reports 1984*, p. 392 at paras. 59 and 63.

For further examples of undertakings which are not treaties, but have been considered to fall within the purview of Article 102 (1), see: *Repertory of United Nations Practice*, vol. V (1955), p. 293 para. 24, p. 299 para. 47 and p. 300 para. 49; ibid., *Supplement No. 2*, vol. III (1963), p. 506 at para. 4 and at paras. 5–8; and ibid., *Supplement No. 3*, vol. IV (1973), p. 196 at para. 11. Cf. also *United Nations Juridical Yearbook*, 1978, pp. 198–199, esp. at para. 6. For general discussion of the scope of Article 102 (1), in so far as it encompasses undertakings other than treaties, see: *Repertory of United Nations Practice*, vol. V (1955), p. 293 n. 43 and p. 294 para. 26; and Brandon, *American Journal of International Law*, 47 (1953), p. 49 at pp. 53–55.

The appearance in Article 102 (1) of the expression "international agreement" in addition to the term "treaty" may be justified not only on the ground that it extends the scope of Article 102 (1) to embrace certain important forms of international undertaking which are not treaties, but also on the ground that it avoids any impression which might have been occasioned by the word "treaty" had it appeared alone and unsupplemented that Article 102 is limited in scope to only that particular group of treaties which are accorded the appellation "treaty" in the domestic law of certain States—for example, the U.S.A. Cf., for example, the remark of El Khoury, quoted in Brandon, loc. cit. above, at p. 60 n. 43. Moreover, at and around the time of the drafting of the Charter, there was a widely held reluctance not only to describe exchanges of notes as "treaties", but even to regard the law of treaties as applicable to them: ibid., pp. 60–61. Similarly, there was reticence about describing as "treaties" agreements between States and international organizations: ibid., p. 63. The expression "international agreement" avoids any impression which might otherwise have been created by the term "treaty", had it stood alone, that Article 102 (1) does not encompass such agreements.

[16] *Repertory of United Nations Practice*, vol. V (1955), p. 293 para. 22.

[17] *Repertory of United Nations Practice*, vol. V (1955), p. 295 para. 31 (e). *Pace* Fawcett, *British Year Book of International Law*, 30 (1953), p. 381 at pp. 389–390 and 393–395.

262   *D. N. Hutchinson*

Therefore, a State which is a Member of the United Nations has
no obligation under Article 102 (1) of the Charter to register an
agreement into which it has entered if that agreement is a contract
or if it is a "gentlemen's agreement".[18] Indeed, not only is it not
bound to register such an agreement, but, strictly speaking, it is not
even free to do so.[19] The system of registration instituted by and
pursuant to Article 102 (1) is solely for "treaties" and "international
agreements". That being so, only "treaties" and "international agreements" are eligible for registration.[20] However, that does not mean

[18] Aust, loc. cit. above (n. 2), at p. 790. As Aust points out, it is to avoid registration
and the publicity which ensues from consequent publication in the United Nations
Treaty Series that States often resort to the use of agreements which are not binding
in international law: ibid., pp. 792–793.

[19] See the statement of the UK which is quoted in Repertory of United Nations
Practice, Supplement No. 1, vol. II (1958), at p. 402 para. 18. The Secretariat has
accordingly taken the view that the answer to the question whether an agreement is a
treaty or an international agreement in the sense of Article 102 (1) of the Charter is
determinative of the answer to the question whether or not it may be registered with
the Secretariat: Repertory of United Nations Practice, vol. V (1955), p. 294 para. 29.
    That a State is not free to register agreements which fall outside the scope of Article
102 (1) does not mean that it is under a duty not to register a particular agreement
which is beyond the ambit of that provision, such that it commits an international
wrong should it register it. There is certainly no evidence that either States or the
United Nations consider that a State which sends such an agreement for registration
commits a breach of international law.
    However, it does not follow that States are free to register such agreements. Article
102 (1) does not either state or imply there to be any freedom to register agreements
which fall outside the scope of the duty to register which that provision lays down.
That being so, the United Nations is empowered by Article 102 to establish a system
of registration solely for those agreements which fall within the scope of the duty laid
down in Paragraph (1) of that article. (Admittedly, the General Assembly has gone
beyond the terms of the Charter by establishing a system whereby agreements which
need not be registered may voluntarily be sent to the Secretariat for a form of official
logging: Bogdan, Revue de Droit International et de Sciences Diplomatiques et Politiques,
55 (1977), p. 114 at pp. 119 and 120. However, such agreements are subject to a
system which is completely distinct from registration, registration being reserved solely
for those agreements which fall within the purview of Article 102 (1).) Since States
Members of the United Nations have a general duty to act in good faith so as not to
cause the Organization or its organs to act beyond their legal powers (see the joint
dissenting opinion of Judges Basdevant, Winiarski, McNair and Read in Conditions
of Admission of a State to Membership in the United Nations (Article 4 of the Charter),
I.C.J. Reports 1948, p. 57 at paras. 3, 20, 21 and 25), Members have a general, though
diffuse, duty not to subvert the system of registration by systematically transmitting
for registration agreements which are not subject to that process.

[20] Consequently, States have considered that to insert in an agreement a statement to
the effect that it is not eligible for registration is to make clear that it is not a treaty. See:
the third paragraph of the concluding recitals of the Final Act of the Conference on
Security and Co-operation in Europe, done at Helsinki on 1 August 1975 (Bloed, A.,
From Helsinki to Vienna: Basic Documents of the Helsinki Process (1990), p. 43); and
Russell, American Journal of International Law, 70 (1976), p. 242 at p. 247.

that a contract or "gentlemen's agreement" may not end up being registered.

In certain cases, it is the Secretariat of the United Nations itself which initiates the process of registration. Thus, Article 4 (1) of the regulations which were adopted by the General Assembly to give effect to Article 102 of the Charter directs the Secretariat to register *ex officio* certain categories of those agreements which fall within the scope of Article 102 (1) of the Charter.[21] Consequently, in those cases in which an agreement, if it were a treaty, would be one which it were the responsibility of the Secretariat itself to register under Article 4 (1) of the registration regulations, the Secretariat, in order to determine whether it is a case for the exercise of that responsibility, will inevitably have to make an independent assessment of whether or not that agreement is a treaty.[22] If the Secretariat concludes that the agreement is not a treaty, it will not itself proceed to register it.[23]

However, in the majority of cases, it will be an entity other than the Secretariat—typically a State[24] and most typically a State party

---

[21] See Article 4 (1) of the regulations to give effect to Article 102 of the Charter, as amended by General Assembly Resolution 364 (IV).

[22] *Repertory of United Nations Practice, Supplement No. 1*, vol. II (1958), p. 400 para. 12 at para. 5 of the passage quoted from the *Statement of Treaties and International Agreements Registered or Filed and Recorded with the Secretariat during November 1955*.

[23] See, for example, the case discussed in the *Repertory of United Nations Practice*, vol. V (1955), at pp. 295–296 para. 31 (g), including n. 48.

Such an agreement may, nevertheless, end up being registered by some entity other than the Secretariat. Cf. the case described in the *Repertory of United Nations Practice, Supplement No. 5*, vol. V (1986), p. 162 in note (*a*), especially at n. 5, of the general survey of practice relating to Article 2 of the regulations to give effect to Article 102 of the Charter.

[24] Article 1 (3) of the regulations to give effect to Article 102 of the Charter provides that "any party" to an agreement may effect its registration, if that agreement falls within the scope of Article 102 (1). Consequently, a subject of international law other than a State may register an agreement, if it is party thereto: *Repertory of United Nations Practice*, vol. V (1955), p. 302 para. 57.

Moreover, on occasions, agreements which fall within the scope of Article 102 (1) may be registered by an entity other than a State, even though that entity is not a party to the agreement concerned. Thus, a Specialized Agency may register agreements in the cases listed in Article 4 (2) of the regulations to give effect to Article 102 of the Charter. (The expression "Specialized Agency" as it used in the regulations is understood to include the International Atomic Energy Agency: ibid., *Supplement No. 4*, vol. II (1982), p. 364 n. 11.) Even though it is not expressly envisaged by the regulations, the registration of an agreement may also be effected by an international organization other than a Specialized Agency if that organization is authorised by the parties to the agreement to accomplish that act (*Repertory of United Nations Practice*, vol. V (1955), p. 304 para. 70) or if it is the depositary of the agreement (*United Nations Juridical Yearbook*, 1974, pp. 193–194).

to the agreement concerned[25]—which will take the steps which are needed to initiate the process of registration.[26] In law, registration of the agreement is then effected by the State which transmitted it for registration, and not by the Secretariat.[27] That being so, the Secretariat adheres to the principle that, while, in cases of doubt, it may initiate consultations with a State in order to clarify whether the agreement which it has transmitted for registration is a "treaty" or "international agreement",[28] it should, nonetheless, act in accordance with the position which the transmitting State takes regarding the nature of the agreement.[29] Therefore, if that State affirms that the agreement which it has transmitted for registration is a "treaty" or "international agreement" in the sense of Article 102 (1),[30] the Secretariat will carry out the administrative steps which are needed to effect its registration,

---

[25] Article 1 (3) of the regulations to give effect to Article 102 of the Charter. A State which is not party to an agreement may, nevertheless, register it either if that State is expressly authorised by the agreement to do so or if it is the depositary of the agreement: *United Nations Juridical Yearbook*, 1974, pp. 192–193.

[26] Of the 8989 agreements which were registered between 1 January 1970 and 31 December 1978, 581 were registered by the Secretariat acting *ex officio* in accordance with its responsibility under Article 4 (1) of the regulations. Of the remaining 8408, 2046 were registered by Specialized Agencies, 80 by other international organizations and 6282 by States: *Repertory of United Nations Practice, Supplement No. 5*, vol. V (1986), p. 162 para. 3.

[27] See: para. 7 (a) of the Report of the Sixth Committee to the General Assembly at the General Assembly's first session (A/266); Note (a) of the Commentary of Sub-Committee 1 of the Sixth Committee of the General Assembly on Article 6 of the draft regulations to give effect to Article 102 of the Charter (A/C.6/125); *Repertory of United Nations Practice*, vol. V (1955), p. 303 para. 68; and ibid., *Supplement No. 4*, vol. II (1982), p. 364 para. 8.

[28] *Repertory of United Nations Practice*, vol. V (1955), pp. 294–295 para. 29; and ibid., *Supplement No. 1*, vol. II (1958), p. 400 at para. 12. This is presumably what occurred in the case described in ibid., *Supplement No. 5*, vol. V (1986), at p. 164 para. 6.

[29] *Repertory of United Nations Practice, Supplement No. 1*, vol. II (1958), p. 400 para. 12. See also the Note by the Secretariat which has prefaced every volume of the *United Nations Treaty Series* since volume 212. The Secretariat's position has received the explicit approval of several States as a correct interpretation of its function under Article 102 of the Charter: ibid., p. 401 para. 15, p. 402 para. 18 and p. 403 para. 23.

[30] The Secretariat does not require a State which transmits an agreement to the Secretariat for registration to provide any evidence that the States which concluded that agreement were of the understanding either that it should be registered or that it was eligible for registration: *United Nations Juridical Yearbook*, 1967, pp. 332–334 at para. 8. The reason for this is simple. It is not necessary that such an understanding be reached between the States concluding an agreement for that agreement to be a treaty. Since Article 102 (1) requires the registration of all treaties and international agreements without exception, the existence of such an understanding cannot, therefore, be a necessary pre-condition to the registration of an agreement: ibid.

regardless of what the true character of that agreement might be.[31] It will, accordingly, only be in those exceptional cases in which, if an agreement is a treaty, it is the responsibility of the Secretariat itself to effect its registration that the Secretariat will be able to exercise any independent control in order to prevent the registration of agreements which are not treaties.[32]

(A) The significance of registration

It follows from what has been said that, if a State transmits an agreement to the Secretariat for registration, it is acting as if that agreement is a treaty, since only treaties are eligible for registration[33]— assuming, of course, that, were it binding in international law, the agreement would not constitute one of those instruments which are not treaties, but which, nevertheless, fall within the ambit of Article 102 (1) by virtue of the words "international agreement".[34] Its act of transmitting the agreement for registration, therefore, will serve as evidence that it considers the agreement in question to be a treaty.[35]

[31] See, for example, *Repertory of United Nations Practice, Supplement No. 2*, vol. III (1963), p. 506 paras. 5 and 6.

[32] Even in those cases, an agreement which is not a treaty may, nevertheless, end up being registered: see n. 23, above.

[33] It was to avoid any of the participating States creating such an impression that a number of States participating in the Conference on Security and Co-operation in Europe took steps to prevent the Helsinki Final Act being registered: Russell, loc. cit. above (n. 20), at pp. 247–248; and see n. 49, below. It is doubtful that the steps taken would have prevented the Final Act from being registered, had a participating State endeavoured to have this done. Nevertheless, they served to clarify in advance of any registration of the States in question regarding the Final Act's juridical nature: see, once more, n. 49, below.

[34] See text at n. 15, above.

[35] Bogdan, loc. cit. above (n. 19), at p. 121. (Bogdan describes the act of transmission as if it were typically accomplished by all the parties to an agreement and so serves to evidence that they are all of the opinion that the agreement is a treaty. On this point, see the text following this note.)

Thus, Syria contended before the Security Council that the fact that the Netherlands had registered an agreement which it had concluded with Indonesia evidenced that the Netherlands was of the opinion that the agreement was a treaty and, consequently, served as evidence of the fact that the Netherlands was of the opinion that Indonesia was a subject of international law: Broches and Boskey, loc. cit. above (n. 10), at p. 166 n. 2.

In so far as the opinion which one of the parties to an agreement may hold regarding its juridical nature may serve as a piece of evidence as to whether or not that agreement is a treaty, it is, therefore, impossible to agree with the statement of the UK that registration of an agreement is no evidence of its legal status: *Repertory of United Nations Practice, Supplement No. 1*, vol. II (1958), p. 402 para. 18. Admittedly, the opinion of just one party on this issue will, in and of itself, not be of much weight.

However, it is not necessarily the case that the agreement is in fact
a treaty. Registration is typically a unilateral act, effected by one
party to the agreement acting alone and without express authorisation
from its partners.[36] That being so, the most that the act of registration
itself can usually do is to afford evidence that one of the parties
considers the agreement to be a treaty[37]—and it is certainly not the
case that one party to an agreement may unilaterally determine its
proper juridical characterisation.[38] The fact that the Secretariat has
taken the administrative steps which were needed to effect registration
of the agreement adds nothing. Registration cannot by itself convert
an agreement into a treaty if that is otherwise not its true juridical
nature.[39] Moreover, since the Secretariat, in discharging its responsibilities under Article 102 of the Charter, acts in accordance with the

However, it remains a piece of evidence and may serve, together with other pieces of
evidence, to assist in determining the agreement's juridical nature.

[36] Registration may be, and usually is, effected by just one of the parties to an
agreement: see Articles 1 (3) and 4 (1) (*a*) of the regulations to give effect to Article
102 of the Charter. However, it is possible that two or more States may jointly register
an agreement: *Repertory of United Nations Practice*, vol. V (1955), p. 303 para. 66. In
law, the parties to an agreement are considered to have jointly effected its registration
if it was transmitted for registration by a State or organization which was expressly
authorised by them to take that step (ibid., p. 304 para. 70; and ibid., *Supplement No.
4*, vol. II (1982), p. 364 para. 9) or which was implicitly so authorised by being
designated the depositary of that agreement (ibid., p. 364 n. 14).

[37] Aust, loc. cit. above (n. 2), at p. 803. Fitzmaurice seems also to have been of this
opinion; for he acknowledged that registration of an agreement may be "some
evidence" that it is a treaty, while at the same time pointing out that registration is
typically a unilateral act: *Yearbook of the International Law Commission*, vol. II (1956),
p. 118 para. 10. Cf. Widdows, *British Year Book of International Law*, 50 (1979), p.
117 at p. 143. Cf. also Tabory, loc. cit. above (n. 9), at pp. 990 and 992.

As Fitzmaurice points out (loc. cit.), it is, for this reason, impossible to accept the
suggestion, advanced by Lauterpacht (loc. cit. above (n. 6)), that the fact that an
agreement has been registered should give rise to a presumption that it is a treaty.

[38] However, if the entity which registered the agreement was expressly authorised
by the parties to take this step, then there will be cogent evidence that it is the opinion
of all of the parties that the agreement is a treaty. Nevertheless, in such a case, it will
not be the act of registration itself, but the giving of the authority to perform that
act, which will evidence that they are of that opinion. The act of registration itself
will remain evidence solely of the opinion of the registering party. If the authority to
register was expressly conferred by the agreement itself, then the clause which gave
that authority will itself be a factor which indicates that the agreement in question is
a treaty (cf. the case discussed in the *Repertory of United Nations Practice, Supplement
No. 2*, vol. III (1963), at p. 506 paras. 5 and 7). If the authority of the entity which
registered the agreement to accomplish that act arose by virtue of its having been
designated the depositary of the agreement (see nn. 24 and 25, above), then that
designation will itself be a factor which indicates the agreement to be a treaty.

[39] *Repertory of United Nations Practice, Supplement No. 1*, vol. II (1958), p. 400
para. 12. See also: the Note by the Secretariat which has prefaced every volume of the

position which the State transmitting an agreement takes regarding the eligibility of that agreement for registration, the fact that the Secretariat has carried out the administrative steps which were needed to effect the registration of the agreement does not imply any judgment on its part as to whether or not that agreement is a treaty.[40] It is only in those exceptional cases in which it is the Secretariat itself which has registered an agreement that the registration of an agreement will carry the implication that the Secretariat considers it a treaty.[41]

Nevertheless, this by no means exhausts the significance which registration may have; for, while the fact that an agreement has been registered may in itself usually serve to evidence solely the opinion which one party to that agreement harbours regarding its juridical nature, it may be the case that the opinions of the other parties on that issue may be inferred from their reaction, or from their failure to react, to its registration.

A party to an agreement which transmits it to the Secretariat for registration treats that agreement in a manner appropriate to a treaty.[42] Yet for that agreement to be a treaty might well be contrary to the interests of the other party or parties.[43] It might deprive them of the flexibility in liberating themselves from the agreement which is made desirable by the changeable nature of the circumstances in

United Nations Treaty Series since volume 212; and Jacqué, in Cot, J.-P., and Pellet, A. (eds.), *La Charte des Nations Unies* (1985), p. 1355 at p. 1358.

However, that registration by itself does not convert an agreement which is not a treaty into one that is does not mean that other factors, together with registration, may not have this effect. See text at nn. 64–70, below, and n. 68, below.

[40] *Repertory of United Nations Practice, Supplement No. 1*, vol. II (1958), p. 400 para. 12. See also the Note by the Secretariat which has prefaced every volume of the *United Nations Treaty Series* since volume 212.

Pace the UK (loc. cit. above (n. 35)), it does not follow that the registration of an agreement is no evidence of its legal nature; for, as has already been observed, it can be inferred from the fact that an agreement has been registered that the State which transmitted it to the Secretariat for registration was of the opinion that it is a treaty: see text at nn. 33–35, above.

[41] Bogdan, loc. cit. above (n. 19), p. 121. The Secretariat has itself taken the position that its act of registering an agreement *ex officio* indicates it to be of the opinion that that agreement is a treaty: *United Nations Juridical Yearbook*, 1970, pp. 183–185 at para. 5.

[42] See text at nn. 33–34, above.

[43] In those cases in which an agreement is registered either by the Secretariat itself under Article 4 (1) (*b*) or (*c*) of the regulations to give effect to Article 102 of the Charter or by a Specialized Agency under Article 4 (2) of the regulations or by a State or international organization which is not party to the agreement but which is its depositary, what is said below applies to all of the parties to the agreement.

view of which the agreement was concluded.[44] The potential which
it might create for them to incur responsibility in international law
for failing to comply with the stipulations of the agreement might
have been something which they needed to avoid, given the uncertain
constellation of political factors making for compliance by their
respective national administrations.[45] The consequent requirement
under their respective constitutional laws that the agreement be
submitted to their legislatures for approval might, in view of the
preponderance of political forces therein, give rise to the possibility
that the agreement might never be implemented at all.[46] And so on.[47]
In such circumstances, it would only be natural to expect the other
party or parties to protest the agreement being treated as a treaty—
or at least to put their views on record—if they did not consider it
one.[48] On occasions, States have, indeed, taken just such a step when
faced with the registration of an agreement.[49] Admittedly, there may

[44] Virally, loc. cit. above (n. 2), at paras. 165–167.

[45] Ibid., para. 110.

[46] Ibid., para. 161. Cf. the Procedure for the Establishment of a Firm and Lasting
Peace in Central America, done at Guatemala City on 7 August 1987 (the "Esquipulas
II Agreement"): A/42/521, S/19085; on which agreement see Caminos and Lavalle,
American Journal of International Law, 83 (1989), p. 395 at n. 17.

[47] For other advantages which States may derive from concluding agreements which
are not binding in international law, see: Virally, loc. cit. above (n. 2), at paras. 110
and 160–164; and Aust, loc. cit. above (n. 2), at pp. 789–790 and 791–793.

[48] Certainly, the fact that the Secretariat has carried out the administrative steps
needed to effect the registration of an agreement which has been transmitted to it for
that purpose implies no judgment on its part that that agreement is a treaty: see text
at n. 40, above. That being so, Jacqué contends there is no reason to expect parties
to an agreement which consider it not to be a treaty to protest its registration, since
the fact that an agreement has been registered does not involve the advancement of
the proposition that it is a treaty: loc. cit. above (n. 39), at p. 1363. However, this is
not so; for, whenever an agreement is registered, the proposition that that agreement
is a treaty is necessarily advanced by some international actor. If it was the Secretariat
which registered the agreement, acting *ex officio*, then it is implicit in the fact that it
performed that act that the Secretariat considers the agreement to be a treaty: see text
at n. 41, above. If the agreement was registered by some other entity, then the
proposition that that agreement is a treaty was advanced by that entity implicitly in
its transmitting the agreement to the Secretariat for registration: see text at n. 42,
above.

[49] See, for example: *Repertory of United Nations Practice, Supplement No. 1*, vol. II
(1958), p. 401 paras. 15 and 17, p. 402 paras. 19 and 20 and pp. 402–403 para. 21;
ibid., *Supplement No. 2*, vol. III (1963), p. 506 para. 8; and Fawcett, J.E.S., *The British
Commonwealth in International Law* (1963), pp. 154–156. Note also the case discussed
in n. 71, below.
Admittedly, the majority of these cases are ones in which the protest was directed
at the proposition that one of the parties to a bilateral agreement was a subject of
international law, it being contended that, since one of the parties did not enjoy that
status, it was impossible for the agreement concerned to be a treaty and so be subject

be cases where it would not be reasonable to expect such a thing to occur. While they may not consider the agreement to be a treaty, the other parties might be happy for it to come to be treated as one, since that might better advance their interests than would be the case were it simply a "gentlemen's agreement" or a contract.[50] Their failure to protest its registration might, therefore, merely reflect their willingness to improve their positions by going along with the agreement's being characterised as binding in international law. However, given that the characterisation of an agreement as a treaty depends largely upon the extent to which its possessing such a nature comports with the interests of those entities which concluded it,[51] it

to registration under Article 102 (1) of the Charter. Indeed, with the exceptions of the case discussed by Fawcett and that discussed in n. 71, below, these protests were made by States which were not even party to the agreement concerned. None are cases of a State which does not contend that the parties to the instrument concerned are not subjects of international law with capacity to conclude a treaty on a matter of the type in hand and which does not allege that there are any necessary impediments to the instrument concerned directly creating juridical effects in international law, but which alleges simply that the instrument in question did not in fact create such effects. None, therefore, involves a protest of the type discussed in the text.

Nevertheless, these cases indicate that States—including even States not party to an agreement—consider it necessary either to protest the registration of an agreement or else to make clear their views regarding its nature in order to avoid the possibility that their juridical positions may end up being altered as a result, at least in part, of their failure to respond to the juridical propositions which are implicitly advanced by the State registering an agreement when it transmits it to the Secretariat for registration. Indeed, on at least one occasion, States have apparently assumed that, were an agreement to be registered, failure on their part to have their views on record that that agreement was not a treaty might be taken as assent by them to the proposition that that agreement was a treaty. Thus, even though no State had yet registered that instrument—and no State subsequently has —, several of the States participating in the Conference on Security and Co-operation in Europe took the precaution of drafting a letter for transmission by Finland to the Secretary-General of the United Nations which "dr[e]w [his] attention" to the fact that the Final Act of the Helsinki Conference "is not eligible, in whole or in part, for registration": *Digest of United States Practice in International Law* (1975), p. 326.

[50] They may have tried and failed, when concluding the agreement, to persuade the party which has had it registered to make it binding in international law; their interests may have changed—for example, while the administrations which were responsible for concluding the agreement were not confident of gaining parliamentary approval for it, the new administrations might be; and so on.

[51] It is frequently said that whether or not an agreement is a treaty is dependent, largely, if not entirely, upon whether or not the States which concluded that agreement shared, at the time of its conclusion, a common intention that it be directly productive of juridical effects between them in international law. See, for example: Aust, loc. cit. above (n. 2), at p. 794; Jennings and Watts, op. cit. above (n. 4), at pp. 1201–1202; Remiro Brotons, op. cit. above (n. 2), at p. 32; Schachter, loc. cit. above (n. 4), at p. 296; Virally, loc. cit. above (n. 2), at paras. 169 and 170; Widdows, loc. cit. above (n. 37), at pp. 122–124; and 22 Code of Federal Regulations Part 181.2(a). However, while

is likely that such cases will be exceptional. That being so, and despite the contention of certain States to the contrary,[52] it will generally be the case that the failure of the other parties to an agreement to protest its registration by one of their number will serve as evidence that they share the opinion of the registering State that that agreement is a treaty.[53] However, whether such an inference may be made and, if so, what its cogency will be must ultimately depend upon the circumstances which prevail at the time that the other parties learn of the agreement's registration.

Moreover, even in those cases in which it is possible to draw some inference regarding the other parties' views on the nature of an agreement from their failure to protest the act of one of their number in registering it, the cogency of that inference will generally not be great. In the early years of the United Nations, the Secretariat, once it had carried out the registration of an agreement which had been transmitted to it for that purpose,[54] issued all the "signatories and parties" thereto with a certificate of registration.[55] However, this

it may be admitted that an agreement's status as a treaty is subject, to some extent, to the conscious control of those who conclude it, grave doubt must, nevertheless, be felt regarding the correctness of this proposition: Münch, *Zeitschrift für ausländisches öffentliches Recht und Völkerrecht*, 29 (1969), p. 1 at pp. 3, 7 and 11. It is not necessary to resolve this controversy here, though. If and in so far as an agreement's status as a treaty is dependent upon the intentions of those who concluded it, the extent to which its having the status of a treaty would correspond to their interests, as they stood at the time of its conclusion, is certainly a consideration which may legitimately be taken into account in inferring what their intentions most probably were regarding its juridical nature: see, in particular, Virally, loc. cit. above (n. 2), at paras. 50–52.

[52] See the statements of the USA (*Repertory of United Nations Practice, Supplement No. 1*, vol. II (1958), p. 401 paras. 15 and 16.) and the Philippines (ibid., p. 403 para. 23). It is notable that, in spite of its position of principle, the USA (ibid., p. 401 para. 15) took the opportunity to put on record its views regarding the status of those particular agreements whose registration had served to pose the general question of whether the registration of an agreement has any significance in determining its juridical nature.

[53] Remiro Brotons, op. cit. above (n. 2), at p. 34; and Hungdah Chiu, *The Capacity of International Organizations to Conclude Treaties, and the Special Legal Aspects of the Treaties so Concluded* (1966), p. 207. Cf. also Widdows, loc. cit. above (n. 37), at p. 144, though note p. 145; and cf. Tabory, loc. cit. above (n. 9), at p. 991.

It should be added that the argument outlined in the text applies equally to States which are not Members of the United Nations—though see n. 63, below.

[54] No certificates of registration have ever been issued in respect of those agreements which are registered by the Secretariat itself, acting *ex officio*: *Repertory of United Nations Practice*, vol. V (1955), p. 288 at note (c) of the general survey of practice relating to Article 7 of the regulations to give effect to Article 102 of the Charter.

[55] Article 7 of the regulations to give effect to Article 102 of the Charter, as originally adopted by Resolution 97 (I).

International Agreements 271

practice was soon discontinued and a certificate was sent, as a matter of course, to the registering party alone, other "parties" being issued with one only upon request.[56] Every month, the Secretariat sends to all States Members of the United Nations a statement of the agreements which have been registered with it during the preceding month;[57] and every agreement which is registered with the Secretariat eventually[58] appears in the *United Nations Treaty Series*[59]—a publication which, once more, is sent to every Member of the United Nations.[60] However, neither of these publications is apt to draw the attention of the other parties to an agreement specifically to the registration of that particular agreement, if one of their number decides to register it.[61] Nor is their attention specifically drawn to its

[56] Article 7 of the regulations to give effect to Article 102 of the Charter, as amended by Paragraph 3 of Resolution 482 (V). A State may make a standing request to be issued with certificates of registration pertaining to treaties to which it is party: *Repertory of United Nations Practice*, vol. V (1955), p. 288 at note (b) of the general survey of practice relating to Article 7 of the regulations to give effect to Article 102 of the Charter. By 31 December 1954, only four States had made such a request, though: loc., cit., at n. 35.

[57] Articles 13 and 14 of the regulations to give effect to Article 102 of the Charter. The Statement of Treaties and International Agreements Registered or Filed and Recorded with the Secretariat during [Month and Year] is published as document number ST/LEG/SER.A/ . . .

Towards the end of the 1970s, a delay of over two years built up in the publication of the monthly Statement: Tabory, loc. cit. above (n. 14), at p. 352, including n. 10. However, delay in publication of the monthly Statement has now been entirely eliminated.

[58] The time-lag between registration of an agreement and its publication in the *United Nations Treaty Series* is currently something like seven years. Since registration of an agreement may be effected only once it has entered into force (Article 1 (2) of the regulations), the publication of an agreement may occur even longer after its conclusion.

[59] However, since the late 1970s, not every treaty has been reproduced therein *in extenso*: see the last paragraph of n. 14, above.

[60] Articles 12 (1) and 14 of the regulations to give effect to Article 102 of the Charter.

[61] However, the General Assembly has taken the view that an indication by the Secretariat in the monthly Statement of those treaties which it does not intend to publish *in extenso* in the *United Nations Treaty Series*, together with the publication in the latter of basic information relating to such treaties and the institution of a system under which the Secretariat will issue to States and international organizations a copy of the text of such an agreement on request, discharges the Secretariat's duty under Article 102 (1) of the Charter to publish those treaties which are registered with it: Tabory, loc. cit. above (n. 14), at pp. 355–357. More significantly for present purposes, the General Assembly appears to have shared with the Secretariat the opinion that an indication by the Secretariat in the monthly Statement that it does not intend to publish an agreement *in extenso* in the *United Nations Treaty Series* is sufficient to put States on notice of that proposed step and so enable them to exercise control of the discretion to take such action which is vested in the Secretariat by

registration by any other means. In particular, it is apparently not
the practice of States which transmit an agreement to the Secretariat
for registration to inform the other parties to the agreement that they
have taken this step.[62] It is quite likely, therefore, that, in the normal
course of events, over-worked national bureaucracies will not be
sufficiently put on notice of the registration of an agreement for it to
be possible to draw from their silence any strong and reliable
inferences as to their opinions on whether or not that agreement is
eligible for registration.[63]

It might be thought that, in some cases at least, the failure of the
other parties to an agreement to protest the act of one of their
number in effecting its registration might possibly have a more
determinative effect on the juridical characterisation of that agreement. In the jurisdictional phase of the *Nicaragua* case, the International Court of Justice held that Nicaragua's failure to protest its
being listed in various publications of the Court and of the United
Nations' Secretariat as having made a valid and binding declaration
accepting the jurisdiction of the Court under Article 36 (2) of the
Court's Statute not only served to evidence that it held the same
opinion as did the Court regarding the effect of Article 36 (5) of the
Statute of the Court, so corroborating the Court's interpretation of
that provision,[64] but it also served to signify Nicaragua's consent to
its being a party to the "Optional Clause" system, regardless of
whether or not Article 36 (5) would otherwise have had the effect of
making it one.[65] That being so, it might be thought that the failure

Article 12 (2) of the regulations to give effect to Article 102 of the Charter, as amended
by Resolution 33/141 A: ibid., at p. 357.

[62] Information supplied by the Treaty Section of the U.K. Foreign and Commonwealth office.

[63] This is particularly so in the case of those parties to an agreement which do not
receive the two publications described in the text at nn. 57 and 59, above. However,
very few subjects of international law fall into this category. Although the regulations
to give effect to Article 102 of the Charter do not provide for this, the monthly
Statement and the *United Nations Treaty Series* are sent, as a matter of course, both
to the Specialized Agencies of the United Nations and to those other international
organizations, those States not Members of the United Nations and those international
actors which enjoy observer status with the United Nations: Suy, *Recueil des Cours*,
160 (1978), p. 75 at pp. 120–122.

[64] Loc. cit. above (n. 15), at paras. 36–42.

[65] Ibid., at paras. 42–47.

The opinion of the Legal Counsel of the United Nations relating to the date of
entry into force of the Convention on the Agency for Cultural and Technical Co-
operation, done at The Hague on 20 March 1970, is also of interest in this connexion:
United Nations Juridical Yearbook, 1978, pp. 196–197. The depositaries of that treaty

of the other parties to an agreement to respond to the act of one of their number in registering it with the Secretariat and to the consequent publication of that agreement in the *United Nations Treaty Series*[66] may be taken to signify their consent to the agreement's being considered a treaty, and so to their being bound by it in international law, whether or not they were so bound prior to its registration. Since the party which transmitted the agreement to the Secretariat for registration might be taken thereby also to have signified its consent to this, a special custom might be said to have arisen between the parties to the agreement requiring them to treat it as a treaty,[67] even if it was not so previously.[68]

communicated to certain States, among others, a note declaring it to have entered into force on 30 August 1970. In so doing, they counted those States as having validly and effectively established their consent to be bound by that treaty. In fact, those States had not done so; for the acts by which their representatives apparently established the consent of those States to be bound by the Convention were not imputable to those States in international law. Nevertheless, the Legal Counsel was of the opinion that the failure of those States to protest the assertion in the depositaries' note—implicit in the statement that the Convention had entered into force on 30 August 1970—that they had already validly established their consent to be bound by the treaty served to alter the juridical situation of those States, from not having consented to be bound by that treaty to being considered to have already done so, in accordance with the rule of customary law embodied in Article 8 of the Vienna Convention on the Law of Treaties 1969: see p. 197. In other words, their failure to protest the attribution to them of their representatives' acts served to make those acts imputable to them.

[66] Admittedly, the *United Nations Treaty Series* carries a general disclaimer regarding the legal character *vel non* of the agreements which are published in it: see the Note by the Secretariat which has prefaced every volume in the series since volume 212. However, so does the *Yearbook of the International Court of Justice*, which was one of the publications relied upon by the Court in the *Nicaragua* case: see the Preface to the *Yearbook* and the introductory comments to the section which is now entitled "Declarations Recognizing as Compulsory the Jurisdiction of the Court".

[67] Cf. the *Fisheries* case, *I.C.J. Reports 1951*, p. 116 at pp. 138–139.

[68] It may, indeed, happen that the conduct of the parties to an agreement might cause its juridical nature to change through time, from not being legally binding at all in international law to being a treaty which is so binding: Virally, loc. cit. above (n. 2), at paras. 41 and 46; and Barberis, loc. cit. above (n. 1), at p. 259.

Cf. the Opinion of the Inter-American Court of Human Rights in the *Interpretation of the American Declaration of the Rights and Duties of Man within the Framework of Article 64 of the American Convention on Human Rights: International Legal Materials*, 29 (1990), p. 379. The Court there held that, although the American Declaration of the Rights and Duties of Man, at the time of its adoption, simply had the status of a statement of recommended good practice (see the observations of certain States which are cited in paras. 11, 12, 15, 17 and 18), it has, since that time, come to be viewed by States Members of the Organization of American States as containing a statement of certain legal obligations which are binding upon them under that organization's Charter: paras. 37–45, esp. at para. 37. It has, therefore, come to have the status of an exposition of certain legal duties which States Members of that organization have bound themselves to interpret that treaty as imposing upon them: paras. 43 and 45. It

However, it is doubtful in the extreme that the failure of a State to protest the registration of an agreement, when it has been put on notice thereof by the agreement's appearing once in the monthly list of agreements which have been registered with the Secretariat and once, many years later, in the *United Nations Treaty Series*, can be compared with Nicaragua's failure to protest the "extremely numerous" and explicit "attestations" of its legal position which were contained "over a period of nearly 40 years" in the *Yearbook of the International Court of Justice*, the annual report of the International Court to the U.N. General Assembly and the annual collection of *Signatures, Ratifications, Acceptances, Accessions, etc., concerning the Multilateral Conventions and Agreements in respect of which the Secretary-General acts as Depositary*.[69] Nevertheless, it does not follow that the judgment of the International Court in the *Nicaragua* case is completely without relevance in the present context; for a State's failure to protest the registration and publication of an agreement might well serve, together with other actions or omissions on its part, to signify its consent to the proposition that that agreement is a treaty and so bind that State to treat it as one, even if that agreement's original status was not that of a treaty.[70] It should

should be emphasised that the Declaration did not thereby become a treaty: paras. 35 and 47. Its status was, rather, that of evidence of the content of the customary rule which had come into existence between the Members of the Organization of American States as to how to interpret the Charter of that organization. (For the possibility that rules of this type might emerge, see Article 31 (3) (b) of the Vienna Convention on the Law of Treaties 1969.)

[69] Loc. cit. above (n. 15), at para. 38. Nicaragua was also faced with the "attestations" of a number of States: para. 40.

The case described in n. 65, above, may be distinguished on several grounds. The letter from the depositaries of the treaty concerned specifically drew the attention of the States in question to that treaty. Moreover, by stating that the Convention had entered into force on the date specified, that letter quite clearly, albeit implicitly, put the States in question on notice that the proposition was being advanced that they had already validly established their consent to be bound by that treaty. Furthermore, those States had failed to take steps to ensure that their representatives made it clear to the other States which concluded the Convention, either prior to, at the time that or immediately subsequent to the time that they executed the acts which appeared to establish the consent of the States concerned to be bound by that treaty, that those acts were not in fact imputable as such to the States in whose names they acted. This failure had led the other States concerned and the depositaries to believe that those States had in fact consented to be bound by the Convention: *Untied Nations Juridical Yearbook*, 1978, pp. 196–197 at p. 197. That being so, there was good reason to treat those States as actually having consented to be bound by the Convention, if it were possible to do so, and, therefore, to require very little for them to be deemed to have signified their acceptance of the proposition implicitly advanced by the depositaries.

[70] See n. 68, above.

perhaps also be added that failure by a State to protest the registration and publication of an agreement which is undoubtedly a treaty might well serve, together with other factors, to alter the juridical position of that State in some other fashion, as by making that treaty binding upon that State, in spite of the fact that it otherwise would not have been so,[71] or by causing it to lose a right which it otherwise might have had to invalidate its consent to be bound by that agreement.[72]

The registration of an agreement will, therefore, generally serve as some evidence that that agreement is a treaty. This will certainly be so if its registration meets with no protest from the other party or parties. It would be so, though, even if all of the other parties were to protest that the agreement was not a treaty and so was not eligible for registration; for it would, nevertheless, remain true that the registration of that agreement would serve to evidence the opinion of the party which was responsible for that act that the agreement was a treaty. However, evidence that it is a treaty is the most that the registration of an agreement can provide. In particular, neither the act of registration itself, nor that act combined with the failure of any party to protest its being done, may, without more, convert

---

[71] Cf. the case described in nn. 65 and 69, above.

It was to avoid any possibility that such a thing might be held to have occurred that Pakistan, upon registering a certified statement of the termination of an agreement between India and Pakistan which had been previously registered by India, made clear that it reserved its position as to whether that agreement had ever been binding upon it: *United Nations Treaty Series*, vol. 85, p. 356 n. 2.

[72] Cf. the sixth preambular paragraph and Paragraph 2 of Security Council Resolution 687 (1991). The Security Council, in treating the Agreed Minutes between the State of Kuwait and the Republic of Iraq Regarding Restoration of Friendly Relations, Recognition and Related Matters, done at Baghdad on 4 October 1963, as binding upon Iraq, pointed to the fact that that agreement had been registered—by Kuwait (*United Nations Treaty Series*, vol. 485, p. 321)—with the Secretariat and had subsequently been published in the *United Nations Treaty Series*. It might simply have done this the better to identify that agreement. However, it is difficult to resist the impression that the Security Council attached some importance to these facts as sustaining its affirmation that the Agreed Minutes were binding upon Iraq. If it did, it was probably on the basis that Iraq's failure to respond to the registration of the Agreed Minutes and to their subsequent publication in the *United Nations Treaty Series*, together with its participation in their execution (Mendelson and Hulton, *Annuaire Français de Droit International*, 36 (1990), p. 195 at p. 220), served, in accordance with the rule of customary law embodied in Article 45 (*b*) of the Vienna Convention on the Law of Treaties 1969, to preclude it from invoking any of the grounds for invalidating its consent to be bound by that agreement upon which it might otherwise have been able to rely. Indeed, the U.S.A. made just such an argument before the Security Council: S/PV.2981, pp. 84–86. Cf. also: China, ibid., p. 96; India, ibid., p. 78; and the UK, ibid., p. 113.

into a treaty an agreement which does not otherwise possess that juridical character.

THE SIGNIFICANCE OF NON-REGISTRATION

In contrast, the fact that an agreement has not been registered with the Secretariat is—except in a number of cases—no evidence that that agreement is not a treaty.

Certainly, for a Member of the United Nations to fail to ensure that a treaty to which it is party is registered is for it to breach its obligation under Article 102 (1) of the Charter.[73] That being so, the maxim *omnia praesumuntur rite et solemniter esse 'acta* may be invoked and the argument made that failure to register an agreement which, if it were a treaty, the parties would be duty-bound to register must afford at least some indication that they are of the opinion that that agreement is not a treaty; for, otherwise, the parties—or at least those among them which are Members of the United Nations[74]— would be in breach of their obligations under the Charter.[75] However, just because the parties to an agreement have failed to act in a manner which is appropriate for a treaty does not mean that there is no treaty,[76] nor that they are of the opinion that there is none:

---

[73] And, possibly, its obligation under Article 80 (1) of the Vienna Convention on the Law of Treaties 1969, too. See n. 11, above.

[74] And those which, though they are not Members of the United Nations, are party to the Vienna Convention on the Law of Treaties 1969 and are, therefore, subject to the obligation which is set forth in Article 80 (1) of that convention: see n. 11, above. In the case of such a party, the argument described in the text would only have any application if the agreement which has not been registered would, were it a treaty, fall within the ambit of the Vienna Convention: ibid.
It should be added that a party to an agreement which itself is not a Member of the United Nations may register that agreement if it has been entered into with at least one State which is a Member of the Organization: see text at n. 80, below. Article 80 (1) of the Vienna Convention of 1969 imposes on the parties thereto which are not Members of the United Nations an obligation to exercise this right.

[75] See the Separate Opinion of Judge *ad hoc* Van Wyk in the *South West Africa* cases, *I.C.J. Reports*, 1966, p. 6 at pp. 113–114. Cf. also the Joint Dissenting Opinion of Judges Spender and Fitzmaurice in the *South West Africa Cases, Preliminary Objections, I.C.J. Reports*, 1962, p. 319 at p. 494, which makes the same argument in relation to Article 18 of the Covenant of the League of Nations.

[76] The consequence of failure to comply with the duty to register a treaty is simply, as Article 102 (2) lays down, that it cannot be invoked before the organs of the United Nations: *Arbitral Award of 31 July 1989 (Guinea-Bissau v. Senegal), International Law Reports*, vol. 83, p. 1 at para. 58. Therefore, failure to register an agreement can hardly preclude that agreement from having been or from continuing to be a treaty: Aust, loc. cit. above (n. 2), at p. 803; and the Joint Dissenting Opinion of Judges Spender and

they may just have failed to act as they should have done. There is a whole host of reasons why none of the parties to a treaty may have complied with its duty and effected the treaty's registration, most particularly, a lack of bureaucratic time and resources.[77] It is probably for reasons such as this that many agreements which are undoubtedly treaties have in fact gone unregistered.[78]

Once more, for a Member of the United Nations to fail to ensure that an agreement to which it is party is registered is not only for it to breach its obligation under Article 102 (1) of the Charter, but also for it to run the consequent risk that, should it at some time in the future need to "invoke" that agreement for some purpose before an organ of the United Nations, it will be precluded from so doing by Article 102 (2) of the Charter.[79] Indeed, if the registration of an agreement is required by Article 102 (1), Article 102 (2) will probably serve to prevent even a party thereto which is not a Member of the

Fitzmaurice in the *South West Africa Cases*, loc. cit. above (preceding note).

[77] For other possible reasons, see: Lillich *American Journal of International Law*, 65 (1971), p. 771 at p. 772; and Broches and Boskey, loc. cit. above (n. 10), at pp. 184–185 and 299; and note the statement of the UK in the General Assembly's Sixth Committee which is quoted by Broches and Boskey, loc. cit. above (n. 10), at p. 174.

[78] Lillich found that, of the 126 agreements which had been concluded between 1945 and 1971 settling international claims with the payment of a lump-sum, only 56 had been registered with the Secretariat of the United Nations: loc. cit. above (preceding note) at p. 771. The experience of the Secretariat is that "hundreds" of treaties go unregistered: *United Nations Juridical Yearbook*, 1979, pp. 195–197 esp. at para. 7; and *Repertory of United Nations Practice, Supplement No. 5*, vol. V (1986), p. 164 para. 10.

Reuter cites studies to the effect that approximately 25% of treaties are not registered with the Secretariat of the United Nations: op. cit. above (n. 1), at p. 52. It is not clear whether this figure is a percentage of all treaties or of all those which are eligible either for registration or for filing and recording or of all those whose registration is required by Article 102 (1) of the Charter. It is also not clear how far this percentage has changed through time—though this certainly has occurred (see below). Nevertheless, this figure, if correct, certainly tends to indicate that a significant proportion of those agreements which fall within the ambit of Article 102 (1) is not registered.

The problem of non-registration was particularly acute in the years immediately following the end of the Second World War. In November 1948, the General Assembly noted that "relatively few" treaties had been registered and less than half the number of States Members of the United Nations had registered any treaties at all: see the second preambular paragraph of Resolution 254 B (III). By 1951, not one of the agreements which the International Bank for Reconstruction and Development had concluded with States Members of the United Nations had been registered with the Secretariat: Broches and Boskey, loc. cit. above (n. 10), at p. 190.

[79] For the meaning of "invoke", see: Bogdan, loc. cit. above (n. 19), at pp. 124–127; Brandon, *British Year Book of International Law*, 29 (1952), p. 186 at pp. 198–199; and Broches and Boskey, loc. cit. above (n. 10), at pp. 179–181 and 284 (and note p. 163 n. 1). See also n. 83, below.

United Nations from invoking it before the organs of the Organization, if it has not been registered.[80] Parties to a treaty whose registration is required by Article 102 (1) of the Charter, therefore, have a practical interest in ensuring that it is registered with the Secretariat. That being so, the argument may be made that, if an agreement is not registered, it may be inferred that the parties are probably of the opinion that it is not a treaty; for, if they considered that it were one, it is unlikely that they would have let it go unregistered.[81]

However, this argument is unconvincing. On the one hand, in so far as it assumes that, conscious of the possibility that they may at some time need to rely on at least some of their agreements before organs of the United Nations, bureaucracies may institute an administrative policy of registering with the Secretariat all of the treaties they might conclude, this argument adds little to the previous one, other than to broaden its scope *ratione personae*. On the other hand, in so far as it assumes that, upon or subsequently to the entry into force of an agreement,[82] the parties thereto typically enter into a calculation of how likely it is that they may, at some time in the future, need to rely upon that particular agreement for some purpose before some organ of the United Nations, the argument not only rests upon an improbable supposition, but it is also quite unpersuasive; for, in the vast majority of cases, it is most unlikely that any of the parties, were it to turn its attention to the matter, would make the

---

[80] *Repertory of United Nations Practice*, vol. V (1955), p. 299 para. 43, *in fine*; paragraph 2 of the International Law Commission's Commentary on Article 75 of the Draft Articles on the Law of Treaties which were adopted by the Commission at its eighteenth session, *Yearbook of the International Law Commission*, vol. II (1966), p. 177 at p. 274; Bogdan, loc. cit. above (n. 19), at p. 112; Brandon, loc. cit. above (preceding note), at pp. 202–203; Broches and Boskey, loc. cit. above (n. 10), at pp. 161–162; and Higgins, R., *The Development of International Law through the Political Organs of the United Nations* (1963), pp. 331–332.

For this reason, it was decided to permit agreements to be registered by parties which are not Members of the United Nations: *Repertory of United Nations Practice*, vol. V (1955), pp. 298–299 paras. 43 and 44. However, since they are not party to the Charter, such parties are not subject to any obligation to effect registration by virtue of Article 102 (1)—though see n. 74, above, and n. 93, below.

[81] Widdows, loc. cit. above (n. 37), at p. 144. Cf. also Broches and Boskey, loc. cit. above (n. 10), at p. 187.

[82] An agreement may only be registered once it has entered into force: Article 1 (2) of the regulations to give effect to Article 102 of the Charter. For this purpose, an agreement is considered to have entered into force if, by agreement, it is being applied provisionally between two or more parties: *Repertory of United Nations Practice*, vol. V (1955), p. 296 paras. 32 and 33.

assessment that there was any prospect that it might be faced with the need to invoke the agreement in such a forum for any reason whatsoever. The argument, therefore, can only have any application in that small proportion of cases in which, by the time that the question of the juridical character of an agreement falls to be considered, a party to that agreement has already been faced with the immediate prospect that it might wish to invoke it before some organ of the United Nations. Even then, though, it is doubtful that it can justify drawing from the failure of that party to register the agreement any reliable inferences as to what its opinion is regarding the agreement's juridical character; for the very premise upon which the argument proceeds is weak. Both the political organs of the United Nations[83] and its principal judicial organ, the International Court of Justice,[84] have shown little or no inclination to ascertain whether or not an agreement has been registered with the Secretariat before permitting it to be invoked in proceedings before them. As a result, they have permitted reliance to be placed on unregistered treaties on a number of occasions.[85] This being so, it might be

[83] Higgins, op. cit. above (n. 80), at p. 335.

The Secretariat, however, routinely checks agreements which are transmitted to it for registration in order to ascertain whether they refer to other agreements, and, if so, whether those other agreements have themselves been registered: Tabory, loc. cit. above (n. 9), at pp. 981–982. If it discovers that such an agreement, although apparently subject to registration in accordance with Article 102 (1) of the Charter, has not in fact been registered, then, if that agreement appears still to be in force, but knowledge of it is not necessary for application of the agreement which has been transmitted for registration, the Secretariat will suggest to the transmitting party, if it is a party thereto, that it effects its registration: *United Nations Juridical Yearbook*, 1979, pp. 195–197, at para. 6 and at para. 10 (conclusion (2) (i)). If knowledge of the unregistered agreement is in fact needed in order to apply the agreement which has been transmitted for registration, then the Secretariat will take the steps described in the last paragraph of n. 85, below.

[84] Bogdan, loc. cit. above (n. 19), at p. 126; Brandon, loc. cit. above (n. 79), at p. 201 n. 1; Broches and Boskey, loc. cit. above (n. 10), at p. 300; and Higgins, op. cit. above (n. 80), at p. 334; though see Tabory, loc. cit. above (n. 9), at p. 1002.

[85] Broches and Boskey, loc. cit. above (n. 10), at pp. 277–288; Higgins, op. cit. above (n. 80), at p. 335; and *United Nations Juridical Yearbook*, 1979, pp. 195–197 at para. 9.

The Permanent Court did likewise in the case of treaties which had not been registered with the Secretariat of the League of Nations and which should, therefore, have been held not to be "binding" by virtue of Article 18 of the Covenant: Bogdan, loc. cit. above (n. 19), at p. 116; and McNair, op. cit. above (n. 14), at pp. 183–184.

It is worthy of note that the *Repertory of United Nations Practice* does not contain a separate section relating to Article 102 (2) in its analytical summary of practice, the reason being that, in the period up to 31 December 1954, "no practice ha[d] developed in respect of its application": vol. V (1955), p. 280 para. 6. No separate section relating to Article 102 (2) has appeared in any of the five *Supplements* to the *Repertory* which

doubted whether parties to a treaty attach the practical significance to its registration which the argument presupposes that they do.[86]

It is, therefore, difficult to accept that any reliable inference regarding the views of the States party to an agreement as to its juridical nature may legitimately be drawn from their failure to effect its registration.[87] It is likely to be otherwise only in those cases in which an agreement is of such importance that, if it were a treaty, it

have appeared to date and which together cover the period from 1 January 1955 to 31 December 1978.

Certainly, none of the political organs of the United Nations which are composed of States has ever made a formal decision to preclude a party to an agreement which should have been registered with the Secretariat, but was not, from invoking that agreement before it. Nevertheless, on at least one occasion, certain of the States members of such an organ have referred to Article 102 (2) of the Charter in order to establish that an argument made before that body was barred by the failure of the State advancing that argument to register an agreement on which that argument was based: Davidson, S., *Grenada: a Study in Politics and the Limits of International Law* (1987), p. 144.

The Secretariat, on the other hand, has frequently declined to register an agreement transmitted to it for registration for the reason that that agreement referred to another agreement knowledge of which was necessary for the application of the agreement transmitted for registration, but which itself, though apparently subject to registration in accordance with Article 102 (1) of the Charter, had not in fact been registered: *United Nations Juridical Yearbook*, 1979, pp. 195–197, esp. at paras. 6 and 7. It has proceeded to register such an agreement only once the agreement to which it refers has itself been transmitted for registration (*Repertory of United Nations Practice, Supplement No. 5*, vol. V (1986), p. 164 para. 10) or once the party which has transmitted the agreement for registration has informed it that, in its opinion, the agreement to which it refers is not in fact eligible for registration: *United Nations Juridical Yearbook*, 1979, pp. 195–197 at para. 6 and at para. 10 (conclusions (2) (i) and (ii)). The Secretariat's reason for adopting this course of action is possibly that to permit a party to register an agreement which refers to an unregistered agreement would be to permit it to invoke that, latter, agreement before the Secretariat, an organ of the United Nations, contrary to Article 102 (2) of the Charter: ibid., para. 3. Alternatively, for the Secretariat to proceed to carry out the administrative steps needed to effect the registration of such an agreement would make it an accessory to a violation of Article 102 (1): ibid., para. 8.

[86] Furthermore, if it is the case that there are certain categories of treaties which, because of their nature or their lack of importance, fall outside the scope of Article 102 (1) (see n. 14, above), then it will be more difficult still to rely upon the fact that an agreement has not been registered as a ground for inferring that the parties thereto consider it not to be a treaty, if that agreement is of such a nature that, even if it were a treaty, it would, nevertheless, belong to one of those categories which fall outside the ambit of Article 102 (1). The failure of the parties to such an agreement to effect its registration might then be just as well explained on the ground that that agreement need not—indeed, since it falls outside the scope of Article 102 (1), may not—be registered, as it may on the basis that it is not a treaty.

[87] *Pace* Widdows, loc. cit. above (n. 37), at p. 144.

would be unlikely that even the most heavily overworked bureaucracy would overlook the task of registering it.[88]

To these cases should be added those in which, were the agreement a treaty, the Secretariat itself would have the responsibility of effecting its registration.[89] Although it will generally be difficult to infer from their failure to transmit the agreement to the Secretariat for registration that the States parties are of the opinion that the agreement is not a treaty, the inference may certainly be drawn that the Secretariat at least is of that opinion, if it fails to effect its registration; for it is most unlikely that the task of registering an agreement which it is its responsibility to register would escape the notice of the Secretariat.[90] Indeed, it may not even be necessary to resort to inference; for the reasoning behind the decision of the Secretariat not to take steps itself to register certain agreements is reported from time to time in the *Repertory of United Nations Practice* and its *Supplements*.[91]

For much the same reasons, there should also be added those cases in which, were the agreement a treaty, it would be open to a Specialized Agency to effect its registration.[92] In certain cases, Specialized Agencies have a legal duty to transmit treaties to the Sec-

---

[88] This seems to have been the thrust of the argument of Judge *ad hoc* Van Wyk in the *South West Africa Cases, Judgment,* regarding the alleged agreement between the United Nations and South Africa that the United Nations should assume the supervisory functions in relation to the Mandate for South West Africa which had previously been exercised by the League of Nations: see n. 75, above. A similar point was made by Judges Spender and Fitzmaurice in the *South West Africa Cases, Preliminary Objections*, regarding the Mandate itself: loc. cit.

Another possible case where failure to register an agreement may evidence the parties' opinion that it is not a treaty is where the number of parties is such that, were the agreement a treaty, it would be improbable that all of them might have neglected its registration.

[89] See text at n. 21, above.

[90] Cf. the argument of Judges Spender and Fitzmaurice in their Joint Dissenting Opinion in the *South West Africa Cases, Preliminary Objections,* that, had the Mandate for South West Africa been a treaty, the need for its registration under Article 18 of the Covenant could hardly have escaped the notice of the League's Secretary-General: loc. cit. above (n. 75).

[91] See, for example: *Repertory of United Nations Practice*, vol. V (1955), pp. 295–296 para. 31 (a) and (g), including n. 48; ibid., *Supplement No. 3*, vol. IV (1973), p. 196 para. 13; and ibid., *Supplement No. 5*, vol. V (1986), p. 164 para. 5.

[92] For these cases, see n. 24, above. (The expression "Specialized Agencies" should here be understood to include the International Atomic Energy Agency: loc. cit.)

There may also be added—again, for much the same reasons—those cases in which registration may be effected by an international organization other than a Specialized Agency. For these cases, see, once more, n. 24, above.

282   *D. N. Hutchinson*

retariat for registration.[93] If an agreement is of such a nature that, were it a treaty, it would attract such a duty, then the opinion of the Specialized Agency concerned that that agreement is not a treaty may certainly be inferred from its failure to effect its registration; for it is unlikely that a Specialized Agency would overlook the task of registering such an agreement. In other cases, though, while a Specialized Agency is free to register a treaty, it has no legal responsibility to do so.[94] Nonetheless, it is, once more, unlikely that a Specialized Agency will fail to take steps to register such an agreement, if it is a treaty. The discharge of such tasks as the registration of treaties is an important part of the work of such

[93] At least one Specialized Agency has concluded a treaty with the United Nations in which it has assumed a legal duty to transmit to the Secretariat for registration those treaties which it is open to it to register in accordance with Article 4 (2) of the regulations to give effect to Article 102 of the Charter: see Paragraph 2 of the Memorandum of Agreement concerning the Procedure to be Followed for the Deposit and Registration with the United Nations of International Labour Conventions and Certain other Instruments Adopted by the International Labour Conference, done at Lake Success on 17 February 1949 (*United Nations Treaty Series*, vol. 26, p. 323).

The constituent treaties of several Specialized Agencies impose a duty on the administrative organs of those organizations to transmit certain categories of agreement to the United Nations' Secretariat for registration. See, for example: Article XIV (7) of the Constitution of the Food and Agriculture Organization of the United Nations; and Article 20 of the Constitution of the International Labour Organisation. See also Article 22 B. of the Statute of the International Atomic Energy Agency. (Such cases are contemplated by Article 4 (2) (*a*) of the regulations to give effect to Article 102 of the Charter.) At least one Specialized Agency, although it has no such provision in its constituent treaty, has adopted internal rules imposing such a duty on its secretary-general: see Article 8 of the rules adopted by the Council of the International Civil Aviation Organization for registration with ICAO of aeronautical agreements and arrangements (ICAO Doc. 6685-C/767).

Should the Convention on the Law of Treaties between States and International Organizations or between International Organizations done at Vienna on 21 March 1986 (A/Conf. 129/15), enter into force, then Article 81 (1) of that convention will impose on those Specialized Agencies which may become party thereto an obligation to register those agreements which they might subsequently conclude with States party to the Convention which are Members of the United Nations.

[94] Although a Specialized Agency may have no legal duty, either under a treaty or by virtue of its internal rules, to transmit to the Secretariat for registration all or some of the categories of treaty whose registration it is open to it to effect, it may, nevertheless, have given the Secretariat an informal undertaking to register those treaties with it or have concluded with it other administrative arrangements to this end. The *Repertory of United Nations Practice* reports the existence of an informal arrangement of this kind between the Secretariats of the United Nations and the International Civil Aviation Organization: vol. V (1955), p. 301 n. 67. Note also in this connexion Article XXI of the Agreement concerning the Relationship between the United Nations and the International Atomic Energy Agency, done at Vienna on 23 October 1957 and at New York on 14 November 1957 (*United Nations Treaty Series*, vol. 281, p. 369).

bodies.[95] Moreover, unlike the majority of States, Specialized Agencies are equipped with legal officers whose very task it is to see to such matters. They are also able to—and do—call on the United Nations' Office of Legal Affairs for assistance in this regard.[96]

For the sake of completeness, it should be pointed out that no significance can be attached to the failure of any of the parties to an agreement to protest its non-registration. Until such time as a treaty is registered, every party thereto is duty-bound to take the steps which are needed to effect its registration.[97] Consequently, if a treaty is not registered, every party is in breach of its obligation under Article 102 (1) of the Charter. That being so, it is hardly to be expected that any of them would protest the wrongdoing of any of its partners; for that would only be to attract attention to its own wrongdoing. There would also be little practical point in one party to an agreement protesting the failure of the others to register an agreement, since it would be within its power to remedy the situation itself by the simple act of transmitting the agreement to the Secretariat for registration.

The fact that an agreement which, were it a treaty, would be subject to registration has not in fact been registered with the Secretariat will, therefore, typically not serve in any way as evidence that that agreement does not have the status of a treaty. The most that can usually be said about non-registration of an agreement is that it is compatible with that agreement's not being a treaty; but nothing more.

---

[95] See the account by Broches and Boskey of the careful examination which the International Bank for Reconstruction and Development gave to the question whether it should register all, some or any of the agreements concluded by the Bank: loc. cit. above (n. 10), at pp. 187–192.

[96] See, for example: *Repertory of United Nations Practice, Supplement No. 5*, vol. V (1986), p. 165 para. 14; and Broches and Boskey, loc. cit. above (n. 10), at pp. 187, 188 n. 2, 189, 190 and 191 nn. 1 and 3.

Broches and Boskey also point out that certain international organizations, such as the International Bank for Reconstruction and Development, may have a much more direct interest in registering treaties to which they are party than States typically do: loc. cit. above (n. 10), at p. 187.

[97] Article 3 (1) of the regulations to give effect to Article 102 of the Charter. This is so, even if the agreement designates an authority which is to be responsible for effecting its registration: *United Nations Juridical Yearbook*, 1978, pp. 196–197 at p. 196.

284   *D. N. Hutchinson*

II. Filing and Recording with the Secretariat of the United Nations

Article 102 (1) of the Charter requires that a treaty or international agreement be registered with the Secretariat only if it has been entered into by one or more Members of the United Nations subsequently to 24 October 1945—the date on which the Charter entered into force.[98] Treaties which were entered into by one or more Members of the Organization prior to that date, therefore, need not—indeed, may not[99]—be registered with the Secretariat.[100] Moreover, Article 102 (1) does not either require or permit the registration of a treaty if none of the entities which have entered into it is a Member of the United Nations. Nevertheless, the preceding discussion may still be of some assistance in determining the juridical character of such an agreement.

Alongside, but distinct from, registration, the General Assembly of the United Nations has instituted a system of "filing and recording" for at least certain of those treaties which fall outside the scope of Article 102 (1) of the Charter.[101] This system has been made applicable to, amongst others: treaties entered into by Members of the United Nations prior to the entry into force of the Charter, provided that those treaties have not already been published in the *League of Nations Treaty Series*;[102] treaties entered into by two or more States none of which are Members of the United Nations, whether they were concluded prior or subsequently to the entry into force of the Charter (provided, once more, that they do not appear in the *League*

---

[98] In addition to Article 102 (1) of the Charter, see Article 1 (1) of the regulations to give effect to Article 102 of the Charter. Such an agreement is subject to registration even if it was entered into by a State at a time when that State was not yet a Member of the United Nations: *Repertory of United Nations Practice, Supplement No. 5*, vol. V (1986), p. 164 para., 7.

[99] There is no freedom to register agreements whose registration is not required by Article 102 (1): see text at nn. 18–20, above, and n. 19.

[100] The words "entered into" as they appear in Article 102 (1) have been understood to mean "signed or otherwise authenticated": *Repertory of United Nations Practice*, vol. V (1955), p. 304 n. 80.

[101] An agreement is not eligible for filing and recording if it falls within the scope of Article 102 (1) and, therefore, must be registered: *Repertory of United Nations Practice*, vol. V (1955), pp. 306–307 para. 78. Thus, Article 10 of the regulations to give effect to Article 102 (1) of the Charter prefaces its direction to the Secretariat to file and record certain categories of agreements with the proviso "other than those subject to registration". The Secretariat has consequently declined to file and record agreements whose registration was required by Article 102 (1) of the Charter: Broches and Boskey, loc. cit. above (n. 10), at pp. 188–189.

[102] Article 10 (*b*) of the regulations to give effect to Article 102 of the Charter. See also the first limb of Paragraph 2 of General Assembly Resolution 23 (I).

of Nations Treaty Series);[103] treaties concluded between the United Nations and a Specialized Agency or between two Specialized Agencies;[104] and treaties concluded between the United Nations or a Specialized Agency, on the one hand, and a State which is not a Member of the United Nations, on the other.[105] However, in contrast with registration, the filing and recording of treaties is optional only, their being no legal duty incumbent on the parties to an agreement to ensure that it is done.[106]

Should a party to an agreement which, were it a treaty, would be eligible for such treatment choose to take the step of having it filed and recorded,[107] the same inferences might be drawn as to that party's opinions regarding the juridical nature of that agreement as might be drawn in the event of an agreement's registration. Like registration,

[103] Article 10 (*c*) of the regulations to give effect to Article 102 of the Charter. See also Paragraph 3 of General Assembly Resolution 23 (I).

[104] Article 10 (*a*) of the regulations to give effect to Article 102 of the Charter.

[105] Article 10 (*a*) and (*c*) of the regulations to give effect to Article 102 of the Charter.

[106] See *Repertory of United Nations Practice*, vol. V (1955), p. 305 para. 75 and p. 306 para. 77. Thus, in Part Two of the regulations to give effect to Article 102 of the Charter, which relates to filing and recording, there is no provision parallel to Article 1 (1) in Part One, which provision restates the obligation to register agreements falling within the scope of Article 102 (1) of the Charter.

However, Article 80 (1) of the Vienna Convention on the Law of Treaties 1969 imposes on parties to that convention an obligation not only to register the treaties which are concluded between them, but also to file and record them in cases in which they are permitted to do this by the regulations to give effect to Article 102 of the Charter. This obligation, though, is extremely limited in its potential scope, being confined to treaties concluded between States two or more of which are party to the Vienna Convention and none of which are Members of the United Nations.

Moreover, Article 10 of the regulations to give effect to Article 102 of the Charter imposes on the Secretariat a duty itself to file and record those treaties eligible for filing and recording to which the Untied Nations is party: see n. 115, below.

Furthermore, should the Vienna Convention on the Law of Treaties between States and International Organizations or between International Organizations 1986 enter into force, then Article 81 (1) of that convention will impose on those organizations which may become party to it an obligation to file and record those agreements which they might subsequently conclude with other organizations (or States not Members of the United Nations) which are also party to the Convention.

[107] Any party to an agreement which is eligible for filing and recording may have it filed and recorded. Admittedly, there is no express provision to this effect in Part Two of the regulations to give effect to Article 102 of the Charter—which part relates to filing and recording. However, Article 1 (3) of the regulations—which provides that any party to an agreement which falls within the scope of Article 102 (1) of the Charter may effect its registration—has been applied in practice, *mutatis mutandis*, to agreements which are eligible for filing and recording: *Repertory of United Nations Practice*, vol. V (1955), p. 291 at note (b) of the general survey of practice relating to Article 10 of the regulations.

the system of filing and recording applies solely to agreements which are directly productive of juridical effects in international law.[108] That being so, a party which transmits an agreement to the Secretariat for filing and recording acts in a manner which indicates it to be of the opinion that that agreement is a treaty.[109] However, the fact that the Secretariat carries out the administrative steps needed to effect the filing and recording of the agreement does not imply any judgment on its part as to whether or not that agreement is a treaty; for, as in the case of registration, the Secretariat acts in accordance with the position which the party transmitting an agreement takes regarding its eligibility for filing and recording.[110] It is only otherwise in those cases in which it is the Secretariat itself which takes the steps needed to initiate the process of filing and recording.[111]

[108] Like Article 1 of the regulations to give effect to Article 102 of the Charter, which relates to registration, Article 10 of the regulations refers to the filing and recording of "treaties and international agreements". It may safely be presumed that those terms bear the same sense in Article 10 as they do in Article 1 of the regulations and in Article 102 (1) of the Charter: Broches and Boskey, loc. cit. above (n. 10), at p. 168. Indeed, in cases in which, were the agreement concerned a treaty, it would be the responsibility of the Secretariat itself to effect its filing and recording (see text at n. 113, below), the Secretariat has declined to take such a step if it did not consider the agreement in question to be a "treaty" or "international agreement" in the sense of Article 1: *Repertory of United Nations Practice, Supplement No. 5*, vol. V (1986), p. 164 para. 11 and p. 165 para. 12. Cf. text at nn. 21–23, above.

[109] Cf. text at nn. 33–35, above.

[110] The Secretariat has not made any clear and unequivocal statement to this effect. In particular, the Note by the Secretariat which has prefaced every volume of the *United Nations Treaty Series* since volume 212 (see nn. 29 and 40, above) refers solely to registration, and not to filing and recording. Nevertheless, the proposition which is advanced in that note—that the fact that the Secretariat has taken the administrative steps which are needed to effect the registration of an agreement which has been transmitted to it for that purpose implies no judgment on its part as to whether that agreement is a treaty—appears to be applicable equally to filing and recording.

As has already been observed, that proposition is but a corollary of the principle that a treaty which is transmitted to the Secretariat for registration is registered by the party transmitting it, and not by the Secretariat: see text at nn. 24–31, above. It is this principle which underlies Article 1 of the regulations to give effect to Article 102 of the Charter: *Repertory of United Nations Practice*, vol. V (1955), p. 287 at note (a) of the general survey of practice relating to Article 6 of the regulations. Since Paragraphs (2) and (3) of that article have been made applicable, *mutatis mutandis*, to the filing and recording of agreements (see n. 107, above), it is presumably, therefore, also a principle of filing and recording that those agreements which are transmitted to the Secretariat for filing and recording are filed and recorded by the parties which transmit them, and not by the Secretariat. If so, the proposition follows that the Secretariat acts in accordance with the position which the transmitting party takes regarding an agreement's eligibility for filing and recording.

[111] See n. 113, below.

Of the 168 agreements which were filed and recorded during the period from 1

International Agreements   287

Once more, since only treaties are eligible for filing and recording, and since the same publicity is given to the filing and recording of an agreement as is given to one's registration,[112] the same inferences can be drawn from the failure of the parties to protest the filing and recording of an agreement by one of their number as may be drawn in the event of an agreement's being registered.

Moreover, just as in the case of failure to register an agreement, and for much the same reasons, no inferences regarding the parties' opinions of the juridical nature of an agreement can legitimately be drawn from their failure to effect its filing and recording. Indeed, the arguments which may be made for making such an inference in the case of failure to register an agreement which, were it a treaty, would fall within the ambit of Article 102 (1) cannot even apply in the case of failure to file and record an agreement; for not only is there no duty to file and record treaties which are eligible for filing and recording,[113] but failure to file and record such an agreement also does not attract any disadvantageous consequence of the type stipulated in Article 102 (2) of the Charter, the consequence stipulated in that provision applying solely in the case of failure to register an agreement whose registration is required by Article 102 (1).[114]

Nevertheless, in certain cases at least, the fact that an agreement has not been filed and recorded with the Secretariat may serve as some evidence that it is not a treaty. Thus, there are certain treaties whose filing and recording it is the responsibility of the Secretariat itself to effect.[115] If an agreement is of such a type that, were it a

January 1970 to 31 December 1978, 37 were filed and recorded by the Secretariat on its own initiative. Of the remaining 131, 74 were filed and recorded by the Specialized Agencies or the IAEA, 39 by other international organizations and 18 by States: *Repertory of United Nations Practice, Supplement No. 5*, vol. V (1986), p. 162 at para. 3.

[112] Agreements which have been filed and recorded with the Secretariat are published in the *United Nations Treaty Series* in the same way as those which have been registered, except that they appear in a separate section: see n. 60, above. They are also listed in the monthly Statement which is issued by the Secretariat of the agreements which have been registered or filed and recorded with it during the preceding month: see text at n. 57, above.

[113] Though see n. 106, above. Even if and in so far as such a duty may arise, the same problems would confront an argument founded on the existence of that duty as face an argument which is premised on the obligation to register: see text at nn. 76–78, above.

[114] Aust, loc. cit. above (n. 2), at p. 790.

[115] Namely, those treaties to which the United Nations is party and which are not subject to registration: Article 10 (*a*) of the regulations to give effect to Article 102 of the Charter.

It may perhaps be thought that the Secretariat is under a duty to initiate the filing and recording of every agreement which is eligible for such treatment; for the *chapeau* of Article 10 of the regulations to give effect to Article 102 of the Charter stipulates that the Secretariat "shall" file and record all of the categories of agreements described in that article—the three paragraphs of which, together with its *chapeau*, define those agreements which are eligible for filing and recording. However, paragraphs (*b*) and (*c*) of Article 10 describe the agreements to which they refer as having been "transmitted" to the Secretariat. The mandate in the *chapeau*, therefore, does not apply in the absence of their transmission and so cannot enjoin the Secretariat itself to initiate their filing and recording. Rather, that mandate simply directs the Secretariat to carry out the administrative steps which are needed to effect the filing and recording of agreements which have been transmitted to it for that purpose. In respect of agreements of the types described in paragraphs (*b*) and (*c*) at least, the injunction in the *chapeau*, consequently, plays a role corresponding to that which, in the case of registration, is played by Article 1 (4) of the regulations, which provision directs the Secretariat to "record . . . in a Register established for that purpose" agreements which are transmitted to it for registration in accordance with Paragraphs (1)-(3) of that article. Furthermore, although paragraph (*a*) does not describe the agreements to which it refers as having been "transmitted" to the Secretariat, there is, nevertheless, good reason to suppose that, in so far as it relates to agreements which may be entered into by one or more of the Specialized Agencies, the injunction in the *chapeau* does not apply in such a way as to require the Secretariat to initiate their filing and recording, either, the direction to the Secretariat that it file and record such agreements simply requiring it to carry out the administrative steps needed to effect their filing and recording once they have been transmitted to it by some party thereto: see n. 119, below.

In contrast, in the case of those agreements falling within the scope of paragraph (*a*) to which the United Nations is party, there is no reason to imply any reference to their prior transmission to the Secretariat, since such agreements will typically be in the possession of the Secretariat in its capacity as the Organization's administrative organ. The direction issued to the Secretariat in the *chapeau* of Article 10 to file and record such agreements, therefore, serves to enjoin the Secretariat itself to initiate their filing and recording, as well as, that having been done, to carry out the administrative steps needed to complete the process.

Admittedly, this is not the only possible reading of Article 10. The injunction in the *chapeau* may be understood in all cases to refer solely to the administrative steps needed to effect the filing and recording of an agreement. In the case of those agreements to which the United Nations is party, the Organization, as a party thereto, would, like any party to an agreement which is eligible for such treatment, remain free to decide whether or not to effect its filing and recording; and the Secretariat, acting on behalf of the Organization, would similarly be at liberty to decide whether or not to take such a step, in the absence of any internal rule of the Organization requiring it to do so. The duty laid down in the *chapeau* to carry out the administrative steps needed to effect the filing and recording of such an agreement would, accordingly, only fall on the Secretariat once, acting *qua* administrative organ of the Organization, it decided to transmit an agreement to the Secretariat *qua* registering and filing and recording agency. That the Secretariat is not subject to any duty to file and record agreements to which the United Nations is party may, indeed, be indicated by Article 11 of the regulations. While that article makes certain of the provisions which apply to the registration of treaties applicable also, *mutatis mutandis*, to filing and recording, it does not include amongst them Article 4 (1), which imposes on the Secretariat the responsibility itself to register certain agreements, including those to which the United Nations is party. Furthermore, although certain other provisions of the regulations

treaty, it would attract this responsibility, it may certainly be inferred from the failure of the Secretariat to file and record it that the Secretariat at least is of the opinion that that agreement is not a treaty; for it is unlikely that the Secretariat would overlook the discharge of its responsibilities, were it to consider that agreement to be a treaty.[116] Indeed, it may not even be necessary to resort to inferences; for the reasoning behind the decisions of the Secretariat not to file and record certain agreements is reported, from time to time, in the *Repertory of United Nations Practice* and its Supplements.[117]

relating to registration have in practice been applied to filing and recording, these have not been said to include Article 4 (1): *Repertory of United Nations Practice*, vol. V (1955), p. 291 at note (b) of the general survey of practice relating to Article 11 of the regulations.

Nevertheless, that the *chapeau* of Article 10 should be read to impose on the Secretariat a responsibility itself to initiate the filing and recording of agreements to which the United Nations is party is suggested by at least certain of those considerations of policy which justify its subjection to the duty laid down in Article 4 (1) of the regulations. Indeed, the need for such a duty is more pressing still in respect of those agreements which are eligible for filing and recording, since the other party or parties to such an agreement will not be under any duty themselves to ensure that it is filed and recorded: see text at n. 106, above.

The practice of the Secretariat throws little light on the matter. The tables in the *Repertory* and its *Supplements* which show the numbers of agreements which have been registered and filed and recorded by various categories of international actors have placed registration by the Secretariat and filing and recording by that body on a par, both being described as effected *"[e]x officio"*. Since this expression is employed in Article 4 (1) of the regulations, which imposes on the Secretariat a duty to register certain treaties, its use to describe filing and recording might possibly be thought to suggest that the Secretariat considers itself to be subject to a duty to file and record certain treaties, too. However, no entry for *"ex officio"* filing and recording appears in the table which was published in the most recent *Supplement* to the *Repertory*. A new entry for filing and recording "[b]y the Secretariat" was inserted in its place. The category of "[s]ubmitting party" which is alluded to by the words *"[e]x officio"*, consequently, refers solely to registration by the Secretariat, and not to filing and recording by it: *Supplement No. 5*, vol. V (1986), p. 162 para. 3. This change in terminology and presentation might, in turn, be thought to indicate that the Secretariat has taken steps to avoid giving any impression that, when it comes to filing and recording, it is subject to a duty of the type laid down in Article 4 (1) of the regulations. However, there is another possible explanation for this change. Article 10 of the regulations does not employ the expression *"ex officio"*. Moreover, Article 4 (1) of the regulations, which does employ that expression, is not made applicable by Article 11 to the process of filing and recording. That being so, such terminology is, strictly speaking, inapposite to describe filing and recording which is effected by the Secretariat. Whether filing and recording "[b]y the Secretariat" is effected voluntarily or in discharge of a legal duty remains unclear, therefore.

[116] Cf. text at nn. 89–90, above.

[117] See, for example, *Supplement No. 5*, vol. V (1986), p. 164 para. 11 and p. 165 para. 12.

Moreover, the opinion of a Specialized Agency that an agreement to which it is party is not a treaty may legitimately be inferred from its failure to transmit it to the Secretariat for filing and recording, if it is the case that that agreement would have been eligible for filing and recording, were it a treaty.[118] Certainly, a Specialized Agency has no duty to transmit to the Secretariat for filing and recording treaties to which it is party.[119] Nevertheless, for reasons which have already been discussed,[120] it is unlikely that it will fail to take steps to file and record a treaty whose filing and recording it is free to effect.

---

[118] For much the same reasons, the opinion of an international organization other than a Specialized Agency that an agreement to which it is party is not a treaty may legitimately be inferred from its failure to transmit that agreement to the Secretariat for filing and recording.

[119] Though note the last paragraph of n. 106, above.

Rather oddly, Article 10 (*a*) of the regulations to give effect to Article 102 of the Charter is so worded as to give the impression that the Secretariat itself has the responsibility to file and record such agreements: see n. 115, above. However, this is most unlikely to be so; for agreements to which a Specialized Agency is party will not automatically be in the possession of the Secretariat, unless the United Nations is also a party thereto. Paragraph (*a*) must, therefore, presuppose that such agreements will be transmitted to the Secretariat by the Specialized Agency concerned. The duty which the *chapeau* of Article 10 imposes on the Secretariat to file and record those agreements is, accordingly, but one of carrying out the administrative steps needed to complete that process.

[120] See text at nn. 94–96, above.

[5]

SOME PROBLEMS REGARDING THE OBJECT
AND PURPOSE OF TREATIES.

by

Jan Klabbers[*]

1. INTRODUCTION

The codified law of treaties contains many references to the object and purpose of treaties. Thus, signatory and ratifying states are obliged not to defeat a treaty's object and purpose pending ratification or entry into force[1]. Treaties must be interpreted in light of their object and purpose[2], and reservations to a treaty are, in the absence of any specific provisions, only permissible to the extent that they are not incompatible with a treaty's object and purpose[3]. Modification of a multilateral treaty among certain of its parties is permissible if it "does not relate to a provision, derogation from which is incompatible with the effective execution of the object and purpose of the treaty as a whole"[4], whereas suspension of the operation of a treaty among only some of its parties may also not be incompatible with the treaty's object and purpose[5]. Finally, a material breach of a treaty is, amongs other things, a breach that consists in "the violation of a provision essential to the accomplishment of the object or purpose of the treaty".[6]

The notion of object and purpose of a treaty is also referred to in the Vienna Convention on the Succession of States in Respect of Treaties.[7] E.g., under Article 15, treaties of the successor state will be deemed to apply to any newly acquired territory unless this application would be incompatible with the treaty's object and purpose, while under Article 17, Newly Independent States may succeed to multilateral treaties unless succession would conflict with the treaty's object and purpose. In addition, as was to be expected, the notion of object and purpose returns in the 1986 Vienna Convention on the Law of Treaties with

---

[*] Associate Professor of International Law, University of Helsinki. The author wishes to express his gratitude to Professor E.W. Vierdag for his helpful comments on an earlier draft of this paper.

[1] Article 18 of the Vienna Convention on the Law of Treaties (hereinafter: the Vienna Convention). Reprinted in *American Journal of International Law (AJIL)* (1969) p. 875 et seq.

[2] Article 31 Vienna Convention; see also Article 33(4) concerning multilingual treaties.

[3] Article 19(c) Vienna Convention. See also Article 20(2).

[4] Article 41(1)(b)(ii) Vienna Convention.

[5] Article 58 Vienna Convention.

[6] Article 60(3)(b) Vienna Convention.

[7] In *International Legal Materials (ILM)* (1978) p. 1488 et seq.

or between International Organizations.[8]

Given the fact that the notion of object and purpose figures so prominently in the codified law of treaties, several interesting questions present themselves. Some of these were already noted by Judges *Guerrero, McNair, Read* and *Hsu Mo* in their joint dissenting opinion to the *Reservations to the Genocide Convention* advisory opinion, handed down by the International Court of Justice in 1951.[9] To their minds, establishing the compatibility of a reservation with a treaty's object and purpose was a test which would be "so difficult to apply", for:

> "What is the object and purpose of the Genocide Convention? To repress genocide? Of course: but is it more than that? Does it comprise any or all of the enforcement articles of the Convention? That is the heart of the matter."[10]

While identifying a treaty's object and purpose may well be "the heart of the matter", before approaching the identification of a given treaty's object and purpose several preliminary questions of a more or less methodological nature must be asked and answered. Are object and purpose notions which can be viewed in isolation, or are they to be studied and interpreted as one single notion? Does the term "object and purpose ", with respect to a given treaty, always mean the same thing? Does the object and purpose of a treaty include the object and purpose of individual treaty provisions or parts of a treaty, or is it limited to the treaty as a whole? How should treaties consisting of various interrelated documents be regarded? To be sure, these questions are not merely academic as will be illustrated below, they underlie each and every claim made in regard to any given treaty's object and purpose, albeit usually only implicitly.

2. AN INDETERMINATE NOTION

Throughout history, notions akin to the concept of object and purpose of a treaty have always been present in international legal doctrine. *Grotius* wrote long passages about conjectures as to the meaning of treaties, such conjectures being derived, e.g., from the treaty's subject-matter and effect, as well as its "reason".[11] *Emeric de Vattel*, not otherwise known for his fondness of non-positive notions, cautiously advocated interpretation of treaties in light of their spirit or, again, their "reason".[12] *Christian Wolff* spoke freely of the

---

[8] In *ILM* (1986) p. 543 et seq.

[9] *Reservations to the Convention on the prevention and punishment of the Crime of Genocide,* Advisory Opinion, *ICJ Reports* 1951, p. 15.

[10] *Id.,* p. 44.

[11] Hugo Grotius, *On the Law of War and Peace* (first published 1625) [Kelsey transl.], book II (1925) pp. 411-413.

[12] Emeric De Vattel, *The Law of Nations* (first published 1758) [Chitty transl.], pp. 255-257.

"purpose" of treaties.[13]

It would seem, however, that the modern notion[14] of object and purpose was used first by the International Court of Justice in its Advisory Opinion on *Reservations to the Genocide Convention*, albeit not with complete consistency. The Court appears to have used terms such as "purpose and *raison d'être*", "purpose", "objects", "*raison d'être*", "purposes", "the very object", and "object and purpose" interchangeably[15], although, in the *dispositif* only the phrase "object and purpose" is used, in answer to two of the three questions submitted to the Court.[16]

In the literature, the possible meaning of the notion of object and purpose has received little systematic attention.[17] The notion of object and purpose has, however, frequently been applied by learned writers, but in ways that do not necessarily shed much light on its meaning and only highlights its indeterminate character. For instance, the object and purpose of the 1982 Law of the Sea Convention[18] has been held, for purposes of determining the scope of the interim obligation as laid down in Article 18 of the Vienna Convention on the Law of Treaties, to consist of the establishment of an effective or comprehensive legal regime with participation of the greatest possible number of interested states; as the 1994 implementation agreement on Part XI[19] contributes to ensuring entry into force of the 1982 Convention and facilitates widespread participation, it could be categorized as being compatible with, perhaps even conducive to, the object and purpose of the 1982 Convention.[20]

On the other hand, attempts in the early 1980s to depart from the regime for deep

---

[13] Christian Wolff, *Jus gentium methodo scientifica pertractatum* (1934) first published 1764, [*Drake* transl.], e.g. pp. 197-198.

[14] Compare Shabtai Rosenne, *Breach of Treaty* (1985) p. 20.

[15] *Reservations* case (note 9), e.g., pp. 21-24.

[16] *Id.*, p. 29.

[17] Despite the fact that, as one commentator put it with a keen eye for understatement, the term object and purpose "has a certain vagueness about it ...". Frank Horn, *Reservations and Interpretative Declarations to Multilateral Treaties* (1988) p. 115. See also D.N. Hutchinson, "Solidarity and Breaches of Multilateral Treaties", *British Year Book of International Law (BYIL)* (1988) p. 151 et seq., at p. 196, footnote 177.

[18] In *ILM* (1982) p. 1261 et seq.

[19] Agreement Relating to the implementation of Part XI of the United Nations Convention on the Law of the Sea, 10 December 1982. In *ILM* (1994) p. 1309. For an interesting discussion on the legal nature of the implementation agreement, see Wybo P. Heere, ed., *Contemporary International Law Issues: Conflicts and Convergence. 1995 Joint Conference, American Society of International Law & Nederlandse Vereniging voor Internationaal Recht* (1996) pp. 313-318.

[20] See Jonathan I. Charney, "Entry into force of the 1982 Convention on the Law of the Sea", *Virginia Journal of International Law (VaJIL)* (1995) p. 381 et seq., at pp. 398-399.

seabed mining pending ratification or entry into force[21] gave rise to quite different appraisals of its object and purpose. As one author concluded, "at the very least the Convention has the object of exploiting as quickly as possible and especially for the benefit of poorer countries, resources which belong to mankind as a whole and not to any individual state or group of states."[22] Interestingly, this different conclusion was (at least in part) the result of the adoption of a shift in perspective: the compatibility of deep seabed mining activities and plans was set off against the object and purpose, not of the Law of the Sea Convention as a whole, but of the Convention's Part XI.

As the examples above indicate, the notion of object and purpose of a treaty is seemingly rather flexible, allowing publicists to employ it in various ways, dependent mainly on the point they wish to make.[23] However, it may be wondered whether this is inevitably so: does the notion of object and purpose defy abstract delimitation, or is it possible to delineate it in some form? The present paper represents a modest attempt at illuminating some general aspects of the notion of object and purpose in the codified law of treaties, while accepting that its very open-texturedness allows for some flexibility in international relations and international law. As an abstract category which is supposed to fit a whole variety of circumstances, the notion of object and purpose cannot have a single fixed meaning: its precise meaning in any given context must be determined on a case by case basis, depending on the treaty concerned and the circumstance in which the notion is invoked.

Nevertheless, trying to delimit the scope of "object and purpose" is all the more interesting once it is realized that, apart from the well-known provisions on *jus cogens*[24], the notion of object and purpose is one of the few references, however indeterminate or elusive, to substantive law contained in the law of treaties. As *Riphagen* once put it, the

---

[21] This problem was felt by at least some of the states involved, such as the Netherlands. Others, including the US, had not signed the Convention, so no obligation deriving from article 18 Vienna Convention or its customary counterpart could possibly rest upon those states.

[22] Paul V. McDade, "The Interim Obligation Between Signature and Ratification of a Treaty: Issues Raised by the Recent Actions of Signatories to the Law of the Sea Convention with respect to the Mining of the Deep Seabed, *Netherlands International Law Review* (1985) p. 5 et seq., p. 30. Similarly, Said Mahmoudi, *The law of deep sea-bed mining* (1987) p. 51. Incidentally, applying this test may well lead to the conclusion that the 1994 agreement itself defeats object and purpose of the Law of the Sea Convention, in violation of the interim obligation. To retort that it really is a modification between a number of signatories or ratifying states is not necessarily helpful, as modification of a treaty also will have to be tested against object and purpose. An interesting jurisprudential question is, however, whether a treaty which is not yet in force can nevertheless be modified.

[23] Its flexible nature was explicitly recognized by the International Law Commission when presenting its draft articles on state succession in respect of treaties to the General Assembly: the object and purpose test with respect to a uniting of states "should provide a reasonable, flexible and practical rule" which could "cover all possible situations and all kinds of treaties." *Yearbook of the International Law Commission (YILC)* (1972) vol. II, p. 230 et seq., at p. 292.

[24] Especially articles 53 and 64 of the Vienna Convention. On *jus cogens* generally, see Lauri Hannikainen, *Peremptory Norms (jus cogens) in International Law* (1988).

notion of object and purpose of a treaty "suggests the existence of a normative element beyond the rules laid down in a treaty".[25] Much the same attitude was displayed by the International Court of Justice in the *Nicaragua* case, holding in effect that the object and purpose of a treaty in force can be defeated independently from, and in addition to, a breach of its actual terms.[26]

For reasons of time and space, I shall look primarily at the 1969 Vienna Convention on the Law of Treaties, to the detriment of its 1986 counterpart as well as the 1978 Vienna Convention on the Succession of States in Respect of Treaties. Nevertheless, most of the following is of a rather general nature. While the specifics may be limited to the 1969 Convention, the suggestions made below may possibly be of wider application.

In trying to analyze the scope of the notion of object and purpose, I will deliberately refrain from analyzing state practice in any detail. As the above example of the Law of the Sea Convention already illustrates, in practice the notion of object and purpose often means whatever states say it means.

To this example, several other examples of the indeterminacy of the notion of object and purpose can be added. When it comes to establishing a material breach of treaty, which, under Article 60 of the Vienna Convention, is a breach of a provision essential for the accomplishment of the treaty's object and purpose, states generally adopt conceptions of the treaty's object and purpose as they see fit. Thus, with regard to South Africa's breach of the Mandate over South West Africa, the United States claimed that South Africa's refusal to recognize the authority of the United Nations, its systematic rejection of the recommendations of the General Assembly and the Security Council, and its application of apartheid policies, all constituted material breaches.[27] If so, it must mean that either the Mandate had three distinct objects and purposes (establishing UN supervision, establishing UN authority, and pursuance of human rights standards) or one object and purpose of such a general nature as to subsume various acts contrary to it as material breaches.

In addition, other governments held that South Africa had lost its status as mandatory partly as a result of violating other instruments such as the United Nations Charter and the Universal Declaration of Human Rights, which appears to imply that a treaty's object and

---

[25] Willem Riphagen, "State Responsibility: New Theories of Obligations in Interstate Relations", in R.St.J. MacDonald & D.M. Johnston, eds., *The Structure and Process of International Law* (1983) p. 581 et seq., at p. 601.

[26] *Case Concerning Military and Paramilitary Activities in and Against Nicaragua (Nicaragua v. United States of America)*, Merits, Judgment, *ICJ Reports* 1986, p. 14, et seq., at pp. 135-142, paras. 270-282. But see the vigorous dissenting opinions of Judge *Oda* (esp. p. 250) and Judge *Sir Robert Jennings* (pp. 540-542).

[27] Written statement by the Government of the United States of America, *Legal Consequences for States of the Continued Presence of South Africa in Namibia (South West Africa) Notwithstanding Security Council Resolution 276 (1970)*, Pleadings, Oral arguments, Documents, ICJ 1971, vol. I, p. 843 et seq., at pp. 863-864.

purpose is not limited to the treaty itself but can also be derived from extraneous sources.[28]

In the *Air Services Agreement* case, the US argued that the losses suffered by one of its aircraft carriers demonstrated that France had materially breached the treaty under consideration by suspending flights.[29] This would appear to come close to holding that the object and purpose of the Air Services agreement was, simply, to provide air services.[30] Yet elsewhere, the US argued that the "fundamental objective" was to provide cheap air travel.[31] Again, the notion of object and purpose turns out to be employed in substantiation of various distinct arguments.[32]

Recently, in its advisory opinion on *Legality of the Threat or Use of Nuclear Weapons*[33], the International Court of Justice also saw itself confronted with an 'object and purpose' type of problem when it had to assess differing claims as to the import of several treaties providing for limitation or elimination of nuclear weapons. According to some states, this bore witness to "the emergence of a rule of complete legal prohibition of all uses of nuclear weapons"[34], whereas for others, the very existence of such treaties presupposed that in some circumstances, the use of nuclear weapons could be lawful.[35] Again, different states reach different conclusions about the object and purpose of international instruments, and in part those different conclusions follow from different conceptions of 'object and purpose'.

In other contexts too, there appears to be little certainty as to the object and purpose of a given treaty. Thus, with respect to the Convention on the Rights of the Child, Iran reserved the right not to apply any provisions or articles which are incompatible with Islamic law and Iranian domestic law in effect. Several governments objected to the

---

[28] *Compare* the Written Statement of the Government of Finland, in *id.*, p. 370 et seq., at pp. 370-372.

[29] *Case Concerning the Air Service Agreement of 27 March 1946 between the United States of America and France*, 18 *United Nations Reports of International Arbitral Awards*, vol. 18, p. 417 et seq., at p. 428.

[30] Which comes dangerously close to *Judge Lachs'* ironic quip that a treaty's object and purpose is little else but *pacta sunt servanda*. See Manfred Lachs, "The Development and General Trends of International Law in our Time", 169 *Recueil des Cours (RdC)* (1980/IV) p. 3 et seq., at p. 190.

[31] *Air Services Agreement* case (note 29) pp. 424-425.

[32] It may be added that in the *Rainbow Warrior* arbitration between New Zealand and France (award of 30 April 1990), *International Law Reports* (ILR), vol. 82, p. 499, the tribunal designated all France's breaches (to the extent that wrongfulness was not precluded) as "material", without, however, specifying the concerned treaty's object and purpose nor indicating explicitly whether France's breaches related to provisions essential for the accomplishment of that treaty's object and purpose.

[33] *Advisory Opinion on the Legality of the Threat or Use of Nuclear Weapons*, Advisory Opinion of 8 July 1996, *ILM* (1996), vol. 35, p. 814.

[34] *Id.*, para. 60.

[35] *Id.*, para. 61.

Iranian reservation, considering it to be incompatible with object and purpose of the Convention. Denmark, e.g., claimed that the incompatibility was the result of the reservation's "unlimited scope and undefined character"[36]. Finland also objected, partly on the same ground, but in Finland's view the incompatibility also followed from Iran's attempt to accord its national legislation priority[37], which reveals a conception of the Convention's object and purpose which differs from the one entertained by Denmark.[38] Indeed, one can only sympathize with the statement of *F.D. Berman*, the United Kingdom's representative to the Sixth Committee of the United Nations General Assembly, proposing that the International Law Commission work on "an examination of the criteria by which the compatibility of a reservation with the object and purpose of a treaty is to be judged ..."[39]

If state practice reveals that object and purpose means whatever states say it means, then it may be doubted whether it is wise, productive, or even possible, to draw general conclusions from the practice of states. Therefore, instead, I will approach the matter from another angle, trying to analyze the notion of object and purpose by "thinking things through", to paraphrase *Hedley Bull*[40], where appropriate and possible with the help of case law and the invaluable reports of the International Law Commission's rapporteurs on the law of treaties.

3. A CONCEPTUAL PAIR?

As noted, in its opinion on *Reservations to the Genocide Convention*, the Court's *dispositif* referred only to the Convention's "object and purpose". While this seems to indicate that the Court's intention was to develop and use the notion of "object and purpose" as a comprehensive catch-all phrase, capable of subsuming the goal of a convention without postulating a distinction between that convention's object and its purpose, it has been contended both before tribunals and in scholarly works that nonetheless such a distinction is appropriate. E.g., in her study of good faith in international law, *Elizabeth Zoller* posits that "object" relates to a treaty's immediate goal, whereas "purpose" refers to

---

[36] Compare Laurids Mikaelsen, "State Practice 1995/Denmark", *Nordic Journal of International Law (NJIL)* (1996) p. 257 et seq., at pp. 261-262.

[37] Compare Päivi Kaukoranta, "State Practice 1995/Finland", *NJIL* (1996) p. 267 et seq., at pp. 273-274.

[38] On problems relating to object and purpose in the context of human rights treaties, see generally Liesbeth Lijnzaad, *Reservations to UN-Human Rights Treaties: ratify or ruin?* (1995).

[39] Quoted in *BYIL* (1993) p. 634. Compare also *Pellet*, arguing that it would be advisable if the International Law Commission were "to undertake a study of the very notion of "object and purpose of a treaty"." Alain Pellet, *First Report on the Law and Practice Relating to Reservations to Treaties*, UN Doc. A/CN.4/470 of 30 May 1995, para. 109.

[40] Hedley Bull, *The Anarchical Society: a Study of Order in World Politics* (1977) p. x.

something more distant ("plus lointain").[41]

As a matter of abstract logic, *Zoller*'s argument carries considerable force. It is not at all eccentric to distinguish between a treaty's immediate object and its more distant purpose; it could well be argued that the object of a treaty such as the Chemical Weapons Convention[42] is to eliminate the use and production of chemical weapons, whereas its ultimate purpose is the protection of human life or the promotion of human welfare or human dignity.

Furthermore, the thesis that "object and purpose" is to be seen as a comprehensive term encounters at least one problem in terms of the Vienna Convention on the Law of Treaties. Whereas Articles 18, 19, 20, 31, 33, 41 and 58 consistently refer to a treaty's "object *and* purpose"[43], Article 60 speaks of "object *or* purpose", thus clearly suggesting, when contrasted with the repeated references to "object *and* purpose", a distinction between the two elements.

However, the distinction between a treaty's object and its purpose is hardly borne out by international practice and doctrine. To start with the latter, numerous authors, including the most distinguished, appear to conceive of object and purpose as a single comprehensive phrase[44], although possibly allowing for treaties to possess various `object and purposes'.[45]

In the *Guinea - Guinea-Bissau Maritime Delimitation* case[46], decided in 1985, one of the arguments invoked by Guinea-Bissau was that with respect to the interpretation of the 1886 Franco-Portuguese Convention under consideration, a distinction had to be made between that Convention's object and its purpose. The purpose of that Convention, so Guinea-Bissau argued, was delimitation, while its object "was the possessions of the two States".[47]

At first sight, the Tribunal appeared to agree with Guinea-Bissau's characterization, finding that the object of the Convention was "the colonial possessions of France and

---

[41] Elizabeth Zoller, *La bonne foi en droit international public* (1977) p. 74.

[42] In *ILM* (1993) p. 800.

[43] As do the pertinent articles of the 1978 Convention (note 7).

[44] Compare Shabtai Rosenne (note 14); E.W. Vierdag, "Some Remarks about Special Features of Human Rights Treaties", *Netherlands Yearbook of International Law (NYIL)* (1994) p. 119; T.O. Elias, *The Modern Law of Treaties* (1974); Paul Reuter, *Introduction to the Law of Treaties*, 2d. ed., 1989) [Mico and Haggenmacher transl.]; Lord McNair, *The Law of Treaties* (1961).

[45] Thus, e.g., Sir Ian Sinclair, *The Vienna Convention on the Law of Treaties*, (2d. ed., 1984) p. 130. Similarly, Mark E. Villiger, *Customary International Law and Treaties* (1985) p. 321. Also D.W. Greig, "Reciprocity, proportionality, and the law of treaties", *VaJIL* (1994) p. 295, although the possibility of there being various object and purposes is the reason why Greig is critical of the notion to begin with.

[46] Award of 14 February 1985, in *ILR*, vol. 77, p. 636.

[47] *Id.*, p. 665, para. 55.

Portugal in West Africa", whereas its "main purpose" was the distribution of territories.[48] It would seem, however, that in talking about the Convention's object, both Guinea-Bissau and the Tribunal referred specifically to some physical manifestation, as opposed to some normative aim or goal. In other words: reference was made to the subject-matter of the Convention, as opposed to what the Convention endeavoured to achieve. This contention finds support in the Tribunal's determination of what it called the "true object" of the Convention: preparing delimitation.[49] Indeed, elsewhere in the award this is generally referred to as the Convention's "object and purpose".[50] There may, thus, be a distinction between a treaty's physical object and its purpose, but it is not a distinction which gives any ground for regarding the notions of "object" and "purpose" as distinct. If anything, it rather appears that the word "object" has a dual meaning, but clearly the physical meaning is not contained in the notion of "object and purpose".

Unfortunately, most of the preparatory work of the Vienna Convention does not shed much light on the various issues related to the meaning of the notion of object and purpose, including the question whether the notion is comprehensive or whether it comprises two distinct elements. The International Law Commission's first special rapporteur on the law of treaties, *J.L. Brierly*, managed deftly to circumvent the problem; with respect to reservations, he merely referred to the "nature"[51] of certain types of treaties[52], while his version of the "interim obligation" held that states were, pending a treaty's entry into force, to "refrain from taking action which would render performance by any party of the obligations stipulated impossible or more difficult."[53]

Brierly's successor as special rapporteur, *Sir Hersch Lauterpacht*, was also sparing in his comments. Writing after the ICJ had rendered its opinion on *Reservations to the Genocide Convention*, he limited himself to stating that the faculty to append reservations to treaties can only be admitted "within the limits of propriety and good faith"[54], thus, purposefully (we may presume) avoiding any reference to "object and purpose".[55] Nevertheless, when it came to depicting the consequences of concluding a treaty in violation of

---

[48] *Id.*, para. 56.

[49] *Id.*, para. 56.

[50] *Id.*, p. 670, para. 71; p. 673, para. 79.

[51] The term "nature" has found a separate place in the Vienna Convention. Article 56, paragraph 1, acknowledges that there may be situations in which "a right of denunciation or withdrawal may be implied by the nature of the treaty".

[52] J.L. Brierly, "Report on the Law of Treaties", *YILC* (1950) vol. II, p. 222 et seq., at p. 223.

[53] J.L. Brierly, "Second Report on the Law of Treaties", *YILC* (1951) vol. II, p. 70 et seq., at p. 73.

[54] Hersch Lauterpacht, Report on the Law of Treaties, *YILC* (1953) vol. II, p. 90 et seq., at p. 126.

[55] It is no secret that *Lauterpacht* was far from convinced (as a matter *de lege lata*) by the Court's finding in the *Reservations to the Genocide Convention* opinion. See, e.g., Hersch Lauterpacht, "Second Report on the Law of Treaties", *YILC* (1954) vol. II, p. 123 et seq., at p. 131.

an earlier treaty, he felt compelled to refer to the earlier treaty's "original purpose"[56], which he later qualified to be limited to "an essential aspect of its original purpose".[57]

However, *Sir Gerald Fitzmaurice*, the ILC's third special rapporteur, did address our problem to some extent, although perhaps not in the most unambiguous of terms. In his first report, he referred several times to a treaty's "objects", thus suggesting, that a treaty can have more than one object[58] or, alternatively, suggesting that a treaty's normative object must be distinguished from its physical object.[59] However, while discussing the doctrine of *rebus sic stantibus, Sir Gerald* mostly, but not consistently, referred to a treaty's "objects and purposes", both in the plural, therewith strengthening the idea of a treaty possessing several objects and purposes, but not necessarily that object and purpose, or object and purposes, or objects and purposes, should not be regarded as single, comprehensive notions.[60]

Sir Humphrey Waldock's extensive reports provide little further clarification; *Sir Humphrey* appears to have used phrases such as "objects"[61], "object and purpose"[62], and "objects and purposes"[63] rather indiscriminately. The final report submitted by the International Law Commission to the General Assembly is not of much help either on this particular point, as it generally reiterates *Sir Humphrey*'s language.[64]

Be that as it may, the debates during the two sessions of the Vienna Conference on the Law of Treaties, in 1968 and 1969, clearly indicate that "object and purpose" is to be

---

[56] Lauterpacht, First Report (note 54), draft article 16(3). In his commentary, he repeatedly mentioned a treaty's "purpose" and once even made reference to a treaty's "true purpose". *Id.*, p.158.

[57] Lauterpacht, Second Report (note 55), p. 133, draft article 16(3).

[58] Sir Gerald Fitzmaurice, "Report on the Law of Treaties", *YILC* (1956) vol. II, p. 104, draft articles 30(I)(c) and 33(2), both dealing with the interim obligation.

[59] Sir Gerald Fitzmaurice, "Second Report on the Law of Treaties", *YILC* (1957) vol. II, p. 16 et seq., at p. 29, draft article 17 on the consequences of extinction (and related phenomena) of a treaty's physical object. *Compare* also the discussion above on the *Guinea - Guinea-Bissau Maritime Delimitation* case, text accompanying notes 46-50.

[60] Fitzmaurice, Second Report (note 59), p. 33, draft article 22(2)(iii), and especially the commentary, 61.

[61] Sir Humphrey Waldock, "First Report on the Law of Treaties", *YILC* (1962) vol. II, p. 27 et seq., at p. 46 and 53, draft articles 9(3)(b) and 12(3)(b), respectively, on the legal effects of signature and ratification pending entry into force.

[62] E.g., Waldock, *id.*, p. 60, draft article 17(2)(a) on reservations.

[63] E.g., Sir Humphrey Waldock, "Third Report on the Law of Treaties", *YILC* (1964) vol. II, p. 5, et seq., at p. 53 and 62, draft articles 72 (effective interpretation) and 75 (interpretation of treaties in several versions or texts). Also Sir Humphrey Waldock, "Fifth Report on the Law of Treaties", *YILC* (1966) vol. II, p. 1 et seq., at p. 37, discussing draft article 42 on breach.

[64] *YILC* (1966) vol. II, p. 177.

regarded as a single notion. The history of what is now Article 18 of the Vienna Convention is particularly pertinent. As drafted by the ILC, Article 15, as it then was, prescribed that states are "obliged to refrain from acts tending to frustrate the object of a proposed treaty". The Drafting Committee deemed it appropriate to change this reference to "object" alone into a reference to "object and purpose". According to the Chairman of the Drafting Committee, Mr *Yasseen*, this "change in no way affected the substance of the provision and did not widen the obligation imposed on States by Article 15." It was nothing but "a purely drafting change, made in the interests of clarity."[65]

Moreover, the reference in Article 60 to "object *or* purpose" appears to have slipped in inadvertently, or unnoticed. Neither the Conference nor the Drafting Committee paid any attention to this incongruity between the notions as used in Article 60 and as phrased elsewhere in the Convention.[66]

Additionally, if "object " and "purpose" are to be regarded as separate notions, they would mostly (with the possible, but not very plausible exception of breach) have to be applied in cumulative fashion.[67] Thus, pending a treaty's entry into force, states should neither defeat the treaty's object nor its purpose. Yet, if a treaty's purpose, being something more distant than its object, will usually be something akin to the protection of human life or the promotion of human welfare or human dignity, there is little point in adding "purpose" as a separate requirement, for most if not all treaties would share the same purpose.[68] And if that holds true, the separate reference to "purpose" would be rendered quite nugatory.[69]

In short, given the drafting history of "object and purpose", given also the circumstance that it is not normally applied in cumulative fashion and that, moreover, there would be little point in doing so, it stands to reason to hold that the notion is best understood as a comprehensive blanket term.

4. SAME MEANING?

A rather different question is whether a given treaty's object and purpose will always

---

[65] UN Doc. A/Conf.39/11, p. 361.

[66] *Id.*, pp. 352-360, p. 478.

[67] Given the sanctity of treaties, one would especially in the context of breach expect the stringency of cumulative criteria. Yet, with respect to breach, the unfortunate disjunctive "or" is used. Hence, a strict literal interpretation of the Vienna Convention would lead to the surprising result that precisely with respect to breach, the criteria are the most lenient.

[68] Indeed, it is exceedingly difficult to think of any treaty which does not in one way or another purport to promote human welfare. As Christian Wolff (note 13, 193) already acknowledged, "treaties are made for the sake of public advantage".

[69] To be sure, the suggestion that "object" and "purpose" are cumulative criteria has, as far as we are aware, never been made. It would, however, be the logical consequence of distinguishing between "object" and "purpose", given the specific terms of the Vienna Convention.

have the same substantive content, regardless of the precise circumstances at hand and the legal issue concerned. Put differently, once it is established, e.g., for purposes of assessing the compatibility of reservations with any given treaty, what that treaty's object and purpose is (or are[70]), will the same content of that treaty's object and purpose also be applied when it comes to interpreting that treaty, or when it comes to applying the treaty to some newly acquired territory?

The Vienna Convention's preparatory works do not address the issue. While at first sight it would appear logical to infuse the term with one and the same meaning within any given treaty, several considerations may militate against this.

First, there is the maxim of treaty interpretation according to which a treaty must not only be interpreted in the light of its object and purpose, but also "in accordance with the ordinary meaning to be given to the terms of the treaty in their context".[71] Arguably, the context may encompass the precise issue of the law of treaties concerned, thus opening up the possibility that the object and purpose with respect to modification will differ from the object and purpose in regard of the obligations arising from a treaty pending its ratification or entry into force, which may in turn not coincide exactly with the same treaty's object and purpose when it comes to determining whether a material breach has occurred.

Such a potentially varied meaning of object and purpose also follows from the consideration that whoever is to apply the treaty will start his or her analysis from a different perspective, dependent on the law of treaties question concerned. For instance, when it comes to assessing a treaty's object and purpose in order to establish whether any obligations arise from it pending ratification or entry into force, the point of departure of the process is and must be that *pacta non sunt servanda*. As the treaty has not yet entered into force, and possibly consent to be bound has not even been expressed[72], restrictions upon the freedom of states are not to be presumed, which in turn implies that the scope of the interim obligation must be narrowly delimited. Otherwise, the institutions of ratification and entry into force would become almost redundant: a broad interpretation of object and purpose with an eye to the interim obligation would effectively result in the entry into force of the treaty, or parts thereof, upon signature.[73]

By contrast, once the treaty has entered into force the analysis will start from different premises, for instance when it comes to interpreting some of its provisions, or in order to

---

[70] Here, the question as to whether a treaty has one object and purpose, or one object and one purpose, or several objects alongside several purposes, is of little relevance.

[71] Article 31 Vienna Convention.

[72] For this reason, *Sir Humphrey Waldock*'s fleeting suggestion that a violation of the interim obligation "may amount to a breach of the treaty" is not very persuasive. See Waldock, First Report (note 61), p. 47.

[73] J. Mervyn Jones, *Full Powers and Ratification* (1947) p. 81. Compare *Ambatielos* (Greece v. United Kingdom), Preliminary Objections, Judgment, *ICJ Reports* 1952, p. 28 et seq., p. 43, where the ICJ held that where a treaty provides for ratification, ratification is indispensable. It is not "a mere formal act, but an act of vital importance."

establish the permissibility of the treaty being modified between a limited number of its parties. Here, the point of departure will inevitably be that *pacta sunt servanda*; therefore, restrictions upon states' freedom of action may, indeed must, legitimately be presumed. And where the point of departure is different, the result may also (though need not necessarily) be different.

Another consideration pointing in the same direction relates to the origins of a treaty's object and purpose. They are, and can only be, the result of the parties' intentions.[74] Yet, the treaty's object and purpose may not be the only expression of those intentions; the parties may also have decided to express their intentions in additional ways, sometimes perhaps even by omitting things.[75] Those other expressions will, where relevant, nonetheless have to be taken into account. But, needless to say, they will vary according to the legal point at issue. Thus, when it comes to determining the scope of the interim obligation pending ratification or entry into force of a treaty, a forceful circumstance to take into account is often the absence of any provision to have the treaty applied provisionally, which will lead to a rather strict interpretation of the treaty's object and purpose for purposes of the interim obligation. A similarly strict interpretation may be warranted when the permissibility of reservations is concerned, in the absence of clauses explicitly providing for reservations.[76]

In other circumstances, however, object and purpose may well be interpreted more leniently, or rather, at the very least, the absence (or presence, for that matter) of any clauses on provisional application or reservations can have no bearing upon the treaty's object and purpose when it comes to, e.g., interpretation of the substantive terms of the treaty, or determining its object and purpose with a view to modification.

There are, in other words, good reasons to refrain from jumping to conclusions when it comes to applying the notion of object and purpose. The very fact that a treaty's object and purpose may have been delimited previously, e.g., when it comes to assessing the permissibility of reservations, need not necessarily lead to the result that in the context of interpretation, or modification, the same object and purpose must be upheld. At the very least, the different contexts must be taken into account.

---

[74] Sir Gerald Fitzmaurice, *The Law and Procedure of the International Court of Justice*, vol. II, (1986) pp. 813-814.

[75] In *Officier van Justitie v. Van den Hazel*, the Court of Justice of the European Communities admonished the EC's member states to take into account the intention behind an omission. Case 111/76, preliminary ruling of 18 May 1977, 1977 *European Court Reports* (ECR) 901.

[76] It has been argued, that at least with respect to reservations and breach, object and purpose ought to have the same meaning, for "[t]he conditions under which a State may relief itself of one obligation under a treaty, while remaining a party in all other respects, cannot be made less onerous in the case of that State's breach of the obligation than in the case of its making a reservation at the time of acceptance of the treaty obligations." Richard Plender, "The Role of Consent in the Termination of Treaties", *BYIL* (1986) p. 133 et seq., at p. 159.

5. OBJECT AND PURPOSE OF WHAT?

5.1 Single Instruments

In the literature, the suggestion has sometimes been made that when it comes to identifying a treaty's object and purpose, what matters is not just the object and purpose of the entire convention, but perhaps also the object and purpose of parts of a convention[77], and possibly even the object and purpose of each and every single provision.[78] Similar arguments have been made before courts: thus, in *S.E.B. v. State Secretary of Justice*, applicant argued before the Judicial Division of the Dutch Council of State that the breach of a provision of the Convention on the Rights of Children prior to its entry into force amounted to defeating the Convention's object and purpose in terms of Article 18 of the Vienna Convention[79], thereby equating a single provision with the Convention's object and purpose.

In the above-mentioned *Guinea - Guinea-Bissau Maritime Delimitation* case, the Tribunal made a fleeting suggestion seemingly in support of such contentions, analyzing the purposes of a handful of articles of the 1886 Franco-Portuguese Convention before it reached its conclusion on the "true object" of the "entire Convention".[80]

Nonetheless, the approach of singling out the object and purposes of various parts of a treaty is not always warranted. Of course, when interpreting a treaty provision, such singling out will usually be the case[81], but in the context of reservations, e.g., there is no place for such an approach, for it would amount to a finding that every proposed reservation would be incompatible with object and purpose of the provision or section of the treaty concerned.

Such singling out is also difficult to accept in other contexts, e.g., those relating to material breach or the interim obligation. It would quite simply follow that any breach is material, and that any breach committed pending ratification or entry into force would amount to a breach of the interim obligation.

Moreover, the plain language of the Vienna Convention itself does not support the singling out of parts of a treaty, let alone single provisions, when it comes to determining object and purpose. All provisions in the Vienna Convention where the notion of object and purpose is mentioned make reference to the treaty as such[82], and Article 41(1)(b)(ii)

---

[77] *Compare* the references in note 22.

[78] As suggested by Villiger (note 45), pp. 321-322.

[79] Decision of 9 July 1992, reported in *NYIL* (1994) p. 530. The Judicial Division did not accept the argument.

[80] *Guinea - Guinea-Bissau Maritime Delimitation* case (note 80), p. 665, para. 56.

[81] But *see* below, text accompanying note 85.

[82] Referring either to "a treaty" or "the treaty".

puts it in unambiguous terms, allowing a modification between certain parties provided such modification "does not relate to a provision, derogation from which is incompatible with the effective execution of the object and purpose *of the treaty as a whole*."

Additionally, allowing for parts or provisions to be singled out for purposes of compatibility with object and purpose would raise a host of other questions. If individual provisions can be singled out, does that stop at individual articles, or include paragraphs of articles, or perhaps even mere sentences included in articles? Who is to decide on such issues? And what to do if behaviour would be incompatible with object and purpose of a limited part of a Convention, but would be perfectly compatible with both object and purpose of the Convention as whole, as well as with the individual articles included in that specific part of the Convention? Moreover, it would open the door for allegations of breach where actually none took place. After all, sometimes provisions are cast in such vague terms that it would be next to impossible to actually breach them, whereas it would take fairly little to act contrary to their object and purpose.[83] As it may (or even must) be presumed that the vagueness of provisions reflects the precise intentions of the drafters of a text[84], using object and purpose to undermine those intentions cannot be expected to lead to very practicable results.

Indeed, it may be argued that even in the context of treaty interpretation, where it is often deemed necessary to give full effect to provisions (with obvious "object and purpose" overtones), there may nevertheless be a danger in not looking at the treaty in its entirety. As much as was indicated by the Permanent Court in the *Diversion of Water from the River Meuse* case, when it held that the 1863 Belgo-Dutch treaty under consideration

> "brought into existence a certain régime which results from all of its provisions in conjunction. It forms a complete whole, the different provisions of which cannot be dissociated from the others and considered apart by themselves."[85]

In summation, arguments advocating that one must look at acts defeating or incompatible with object and purpose of part of a treaty or individual provisions, are unwarranted. They find no support in the text of the Vienna Convention or in its preparatory works[86], and they would arguably render the notion of object and purpose even more unworkable

---

[83] Unless it could be posited that the notion of object and purpose embodies a qualitative element as well. Thus, under such a postulate, a softly phrased treaty on protection of the environment will have as its object and purpose not merely environmental protection, but environmental protection in a soft way. If this holds true, however, with such treaties the notion of object and purpose would soon lapse into nothingness.

[84] See generally Jan Klabbers, *The Concept of Treaty in International Law* (1996).

[85] *Diversion of Water from the River Meuse*, in *PCIJ* 1937, Ser. A, no. 70, p. 21. In a similar vein, the Tribunal deciding the 1978 *Air Service Agreement* case (note 29, p. 435) could not agree with the parties' interpretations based on provisions viewed in isolation, but found it necessary, instead, "to turn to the text of the Agreement as a whole."

[86] These are characterized by silence on this issue.

than it already is.

5.2 Complex Instruments

That still leaves a related question unanswered, though: what exactly constitutes the treaty as a whole in cases where treaties consist of various interrelated documents? The problem assumed some prominence in the *Air Service Agreement* case of 1978, where the US argued that the objective of the 1946 Air Service Agreement between France and the US was stated in its Annex.[87] It may most obviously arise in situations where, indeed, treaties contain annexes or protocols, but several situations must nevertheless be distinguished.

First, a treaty may provide that protocols or annexes form integral parts of the treaty itself[88]; here then, it appears most logical to consider them as part of the treaty as a whole, as indeed has been done with some consistency by, e.g., the Court of Justice of the European Communities.[89]

Second, there is the situation where protocols are later concluded in order to deal with issues left unaddressed in the original convention. Perhaps the most conspicuous example is the European Human Rights Convention which has been complemented by a number of protocols. In the European system, the protocols require separate expressions of consent to be bound; they are not, as such, integral parts of the Convention, although the protocols may specify that their provisions shall, in whole or in part, "be regarded as additional articles to the Convention".[90]

The problem here is not so much, for those states party to the Convention that have also expressed their consent to be bound to a Protocol, whether the terms of the Protocol must be seen in light of the Convention's object and purpose; there appears to be consensus on the desirability of such an approach.[91] The problem is rather whether it also works the other

---

[87] *Air services agreement* case (note 29), pp. 424-425. The Tribunal, without explicitly commenting on the argument, must have implicitly rejected it when noting that "it is obvious that the object and purpose of an air services agreement such as the present one is *the conduct of air transport services ...*". *Id.*, p. 432 (emphasis in original).

[88] Compare e.g. Article 239 of the EC Treaty, or Article 318 of the 1982 Law of the Sea Convention.

[89] See already, based on Article 84 of the European Coal and Steel Community Treaty, Joined cases 7 & 9/54, *Industries Sidérurgiques Luxembourgeoises v. High Authority*, 1954-56 *ECR* 175.

[90] Article 6(1), of Protocol No. 4, protecting certain additional rights. Reprinted in Ian Brownlie, ed., *Basic Documents in International Law*, 3d. ed. (1983) p. 344.

[91] For a recent illustration, *see, e.g.,* the Commission's report in the *Gradinger* case (d.d. 19 May 1994), reprinted in *Publ. EurCourtHR, Ser.* A, vol. 328, p. 69, holding that a proposed interpretation of article 4 of Protocol No. 7 would be "incompatible with the "practical and effective" guarantees the Convention is intended to provide ..." (pp. 77-78). Compare also P. van Dijk & G.J.H. van Hoof, *The Theory and Practice of the European Convention on Human Rights*, 2d. ed. (1990) 469, arguing that Article 2 of Protocol No. 1 must be viewed in the light of "the whole

way around: do the protocols provide any insight into object and purpose of the Convention system, and are they to be regarded as part of the Convention, if only for those purposes? Given the fact that not all protocols have attracted the consent of all states parties to the Convention, at least with regard to those "plurilateral"[92] protocols, non-parties might seriously object to what could amount to an extension of their obligations without their express consent.[93] On the other hand, the object and purpose of the Convention have in the past been rather generously interpreted by the supervisory organs to begin with, rendering it unlikely that the addition of concrete rights is by itself of such a nature as to be able (or perceived to be able) to alter object and purpose of the Convention.[94]

That is not to say that the same applies in other, seemingly similar situations. It could well be argued that the several side agreements concluded between a number of GATT's Contracting Parties are (or were, perhaps) not to be considered as parts of the GATT, for instance because of their separate dispute settlement procedures.[95] Thus, for purposes of the present discussion, these may have their own object and purpose, distinct from GATT's. Whether the same distinction can be made with regard to the agreements concluded as a result of the Uruguay Round is still open for debate: being presented as a package, with no opting out possibilities, one should probably look upon them as a single whole[96]; on the other hand, the fact that the Agreement on TRIPs has a separate provision on reservations may militate against this conclusion.[97]

Third, there is the situation, increasingly popular, of concluding framework conventions, to be complemented by later protocols which may themselves contain elaborate annexes. Perhaps the most well-known example is the régime relating to the protection of the ozone layer. Concluded in 1985, the Vienna Convention for the Protection of the

---

system of the Convention".

[92] The term is borrowed from the world trading regime, where essentially the same problem can be seen to operate. See also below, text accompanying notes 95-97.

[93] But for an impressive overview of obligations created for states without their consent, see Christian Tomuschat, "Obligations Arising for States Without or Against their Will," *Recueil des Cours* (1993/IV) vol. 241, p. 195.

[94] See also below, text accompanying notes 122-128.

[95] Compare John H. Jackson, *The World Trading System* (1989) pp. 55-56, noting that the side agreements of the Tokyo Round "are drafted as "stand-alone" treaties, each with signatory clauses, in most cases with institutional measures which include a committee of signatories with certain powers, and with a dispute settlement mechanism." Note that under Article II(3) WTO, their status is slightly ambivalent: they are part of the WTO Agreement, but only "for those members that have accepted them". The various agreements are reprinted in Joseph F. Dennin, gen. ed., *Law and Practice of the WTO* (looseleaf).

[96] See Article II(2) of the Agreement establishing the WTO. The unity is underlined by Articles XIV (on amendment) and XV (on withdrawal).

[97] See Article 72 of the TRIPs agreement.

Ozone Layer[98] explicitly envisages the introduction of protocols containing substantive terms, and most of its pertinent provisions appear to indicate that the Convention and its protocols are to be seen as a single unity.[99] Nevertheless, by mentioning that annexes to the Convention or "to any protocol shall form an integral part of this Convention or such protocol, as the case may be ...", Article 10(1) of the Convention suggests that the Convention is legally distinct from any of its protocols.

Fourth, we may distinguish situations where a treaty is accompanied by joint interpretative declarations, as was at issue in the *Ambatielos* case. It will be recalled that here, the Court found an Anglo-Greek declaration to form an integral part of a treaty concluded on the same day, mainly by virtue of the two instruments having been simultaneously submitted for ratification: neither the treaty itself, nor the declaration, contained a provision on their mutual relationship.[100] However, the same considerations need not always apply; it has been argued for instance that the declarations accompanying the adoption of the Single European Act were legally non-binding.[101]

Generally speaking, then, two conclusions can be drawn. It can firmly be stated that there is little ground for investigating the object and purpose of each and every single treaty provision or part of a treaty, in whatever context; even when it comes to treaty interpretation such a limited focus may not be without its dangers, as the Permanent Court admonished in the *Diversion of Water* case. When it comes to interrelated instruments a certain degree of caution is warranted; much will depend on the actual terms thereof.

6. HOW TO IDENTIFY OBJECT AND PURPOSE?

The heart of the matter is, as the joint dissenting opinion to the *Reservations to the Genocide Convention* case demonstrates, the identification of a particular treaty's object and purpose. In some cases, intuition and common sense may provide useful indicators. Thus, there can be little doubt that the European Convention for the Protection of Human Rights and Fundamental Freedoms[102] can roughly be summarized as having the protection of human rights as its object and purpose. Similarly, few will contest that the object and purpose of the Montreal Protocol on Substances that Deplete the Ozone Layer[103] will

---

[98] *ILM* (1987) p. 1529.

[99] Compare, e.g., its Article 16 (only states parties to the Convention can become parties to any protocol), article 17 (entry into force of convention and protocols) and Article 19 (withdrawal from convention and protocols). See also article 14 of the Montreal Protocol, reprinted in *ILM* (1987) p. 1541, which regulates relations with the Convention.

[100] *Ambatielos* case (note 73), pp. 43-44.

[101] See A.G. Toth, "The Legal Status of the Declarations Annexed to the Single European Act", *Common Market Law Review* (1986) p. 803.

[102] Reprinted in Brownlie (note 90), p. 320.

[103] Note 99.

consist of, in a nutshell, the eradication of substances which deplete the ozone layer.

Nevertheless, with a host of other treaties, a variety of problems may be presented. What, e.g., is generally the object and purpose of Friendship, Commerce and Navigation treaties?[104] What would have been object and purpose of the Treaty of Versailles? What do we regard as object and purpose of the Treaty on European Union? Such treaties may well have several, actually or potentially conflicting, objects and purposes. How does one go about finding them and, where necessary, determining which one is of overriding value?[105]

Studies on international legal method, unfortunately, are in habit of the leaving the matter unaddressed.[106] However, some guidance as to identifying a treaty's object and purpose can be derived from international case-law, and again it is the ICJ's opinion on *Reservations to the Genocide Convention* which may serve as a useful starting point.

The Court, in its classic opinion, appeared to derive the object and purpose of the Genocide Convention mainly from two sources: first, the preambular provisions, and second, the preceding work of the General Assembly as reflected in resolutions on the topic.[107] Interestingly, the Court did not rely on the Convention's *travaux préparatoires* properly speaking. Moreover, it is noteworthy that the Court explicitly held that the desire to secure universal participation did not itself constitute object and purpose of the Convention, but was rather implied by the Convention's object and purpose.[108]

Other courts have tended to follow similar methods, investigating especially the meaning of preambular provisions, possibly in conjunction with a treaty's title (if any), and where available accompanied by similar instruments concluded between the same or a similar group of parties on the same or a similar topic[109], and, in particular, paying regard

---

[104] In the *Nicaragua* case (note 26), the ICJ found that the Nicaragua-US FCN-Treaty had friendship as its overall object and purpose. One may wonder whether Judge *Anzilotti* would have agreed with such a conception, given his elaborate rendition of the object and purpose of the Belgo-Dutch treaty at issue in the *Diversion of Water* case (note 85, dissenting opinion, p. 51). For him, this treaty was not concluded with an eye to canals and irrigation, nor with navigation of the Meuse in mind, but rather, and most intricately, it had as its object and purpose the reconciliation of those two interests.

[105] It has also been suggested that where multilateral treaties create a bundle of bilateral relationships, these multilateral treaties may well be devoid of a unitary object and purpose. As mentioned in Martti Koskenniemi, "Breach of Treaty or Non-compliance? Reflections on the Enforcement of the Montreal Protocol", *Yearbook of International Environmental Law* (1992) p. 123 et seq., at p. 127, footnote 26, with further references.

[106] Compare Maarten Bos, *A Methodology of International Law* (1984).

[107] *Reservations* case (note 9), p. 23.

[108] *Id.*, p. 24. In this light, *Charney*'s conclusion with respect to object and purpose of the 1982 Law of the Sea Convention (note 20) becomes somewhat problematic.

[109] In the *Diversion of Water* case (note 85, p. 13), the PCIJ seemed to rely primarily on the preamble of an 1863 Belgo-Dutch Treaty in order to establish its "purpose". It did note, however, that there was a certain connection, albeit not juridical, between this Treaty and two other treaties

to the treaty's text.[110]

While generally speaking it makes perfect sense to refer to the text of a treaty in order to identify its object and purpose, it may very well also introduce problems similar to the ones noted above. If anything, undue reliance on the text alone may result in losing sight of the object and purpose of the treaty itself, and instead give rise to propositions relating to object and purpose of singular provisions or parts of provisions, thus resulting in a blunting of the analytical potential of the notion of object and purpose. With that in mind, the ICJ, in the *Nicaragua* case, felicitously invoked other factors as well, most notably the Preamble to the 1956 FCN treaty[111] and, moreover, issued something of a methodological warning:

> "In the view of the Court, an act cannot be said to be one calculated to deprive a treaty of its object and purpose, or to impede its due performance, if the possibility of that act has been foreseen in the treaty itself, and it has been expressly agreed that the treaty "shall not preclude" the act, so that it will not constitute a breach of the express terms of the treaty."[112]

While this statement is itself not without problems, as *Thirlway* indicates[113], nonetheless it does point to a limit concerning the admissibility of considering the text of a treaty for the sole purpose of determining its object and purpose.[114]

That said, the text of an agreement may of course play a vital role for purposes of identifying its object and purpose. If, as occurred in the *Guinea - Guinea-Bissau Maritime Delimitation*[115] case, most of the treaty's substantive provisions deal with a certain topic, one may well surmise that dealing with this topic constitutes object and purpose of the treaty concerned, or at least provides a forceful indication of object and purpose.

---

concluded the same day; but this interdependence "is found only in the fact that the concessions made by one or other of the Governments in one of the treaties would not have been made without the concessions made by the other Government in the other treaties."

[110] *Nicaragua* case (note 26), p. 137, para. 273.

[111] *Id.*, p. 138, para. 275.

[112] *Id.*, p. 136, para. 272.

[113] Hugh Thirlway, "The law and procedure of the International Court of Justice 1960-1989", part IV, *BYIL* (1992) p. 1 et seq., at p. 52.

[114] Hutchinson (note 17, pp. 193-196), considers that the *Nicaragua* case might be regarded as possible authority for the opinion that apart from the material breach referred to in Article 60 of the Vienna Convention, there is a category of breaches even more severe: those which "actually thwart, or seriously menace" accomplishment of a treaty's object and purpose, which would arguably go beyond the violation of a provision merely essential for the accomplishment of the treaty's object and purpose. He does qualify his statement, however, by pointing out that the *Namibia* case does not seem to support such a fine distinction.

[115] Note 46, p. 665, para. 56.

It is submitted, that recourse to the title[116] of a treaty may often offer a convenient shortcut in the process of identifying a treaty's object and purpose.[117] Especially where the preamble and the text of a treaty indicate several possible object and purposes, recourse to the treaty's title may be of some help. Thus, while one of the objectives of the Chemical Weapons Convention, as listed in its preamble, is the desire to "promote free trade in chemicals as well as international cooperation and exchange of scientific and technical information ... in order to enhance the economic and technological development of all States parties"[118], it can hardly be maintained that this particular objective should qualify as the object and purpose of a treaty bearing the title Convention on the Prohibition of the Development, Production, Stockpiling and Use of Chemical Weapons and on their Destruction.[119] Of course, the title of a treaty will only offer a presumption regarding the treaty's object and purpose, which will have to be substantiated by closer analysis of other factors, but it does not appear to be a presumption which will often be rebutted in practice. And where it will be rebutted, the treaty has been seriously misnamed.

Obviously, however, the utility of having recourse to a treaty's title is limited to those treaties that actually have a title indicating the subject matter of the instrument. Whereas this will usually hold true for the more solemn of instruments, things may well be different with respect to what Judge *Baxter* referred to as the "vast sub-structure of intergovernmental paper".[120] Where an agreement carries no title to speak of, there can be no reliance on a title.

Occasionally, courts have also relied on elements extraneous to the document under consideration for purposes of identifying object and purpose.[121] Thus in the *Golder* case[122], the European Court of Human Rights, while acknowledging in general the utility of a trea-

---

[116] By which we mean the full title of a treaty, not the designation of the type of instrument (e.g., convention, charter, protocol) involved. For such a conception, compare the American Law Institute, *Restatement of the Law (second): Foreign Relations Law of the United States* (1965) p. 451, paragraph 147(1)(b), plus the commentary.

[117] In their joint dissenting opinion to the *Case Concerning the Arbitral Award of 31 July 1989 (Guinea-Bissau v. Senegal)*, *ICJ Reports* 1991, p. 53 et seq., at p. 125, Judges *Aguilar Mawdsley* and *Ranjeva* pointed, amongst other things, to the title of a tribunal for purposes of identifying what that tribunal was supposed to have done.

[118] Note 42, ninth consideration.

[119] Compare Walter Krutzsch & Ralf Trapp, *A Commentary on the Chemical Weapons Convention* (1994) p. 225, holding that the Convention's object and purpose "comprises as the final goal a worldwide ban of chemical weapons, especially of their use, effectively verified by an international organization."

[120] Richard R. Baxter, "International Law in 'Her Infinite Variety'", *International and Comparative Law Quarterly* (1980) p. 549 et seq., at p. 556.

[121] Compare also the remarks made by the Finnish government in connection with the *Namibia* opinion (note 28).

[122] Judgment of 21 February 1975, *Publ. EurCourtHR*, Ser. A, no. 18.

ty's preamble in identifying its object and purpose[123], appeared to rely primarily on the Statute of the Council of Europe to determine the scope of Article 6, paragraph 1, of the Convention[124]. In addition, the Court also invoked such other considerations as the principle of good faith and its opinion that it would be "natural" to bear the Convention's preamble in mind, despite the fact that the preamble did not mention the "rule of law" which was to be at the heart of the Court's reasoning.[125] Moreover, the Court appeared to attach some importance to the circumstance that the Convention is a law-making treaty[126], which meant that, as the Court had earlier stated, it is "necessary to seek the interpretation that is most appropriate in order to realise the aim and achieve the object of the treaty, not that which would restrict to the greatest possible degree the obligations undertaken by the parties."[127]

Whether this is an entirely felicitous way of doing things remains open for debate, though. At its most extreme, it may result in introducing obligations through the back door of object and purpose, after those have been refused entry through the front door. As *Sir Gerald Fitzmaurice* argued in his dissenting opinion to the *Golder* judgment, where the drafters have rejected a certain obligation to rest upon the parties, it seems improper to derive such an obligation from the treaty's object and purpose.[128] Yet, invoking extraneous instruments to identify a treaty's object and purpose will almost inevitably lead to such a result: the larger the number of instruments and the wider their scope, the wider will also be the scope of the treaty's object and purpose.

7. CONCLUDING REMARKS

Given the prominent place occupied by the notion of object and purpose in the codified law of treaties, it is rather surprising that we know so little about it. The aim of the present paper was to address some of the more general issues relating to a treaty's object and purpose, in the hope of outlining its contours. The underlying premise was that in order to approach "the heart of the matter", as the joint dissenters to the *Reservations to the Genocide Convention* opinion put it, several preliminary questions must be answered: do object and purpose form a conceptual pair? Do the terms have the same meaning in different circumstances? And, what exactly is it that the object and purpose must be

---

[123] *Id.*, p. 16, para. 34.

[124] *Id.*, p. 17, para. 34.

[125] *Id.*, p. 16, para. 34. It has been suggested that it was precisely for this reason that the Court needed to look at extraneous factors. J.G. Merrills, *The Contribution of the European Court of Human Rights to the Development of International Law*, 2d. ed. (1993) p. 93.

[126] *Golder* case (note 122), p. 18, para. 36.

[127] It had said so in the *Wemhoff* case, judgment of 27 June 1968, *Publ. EurCourtHR*, Ser. A, no. 7.

[128] *Fitzmaurice*'s dissenting opinion to the *Golder* case (note 122), para. 45.

determined of?

While one of the possible attractions of international law is, generally speaking, its indeterminate (some would say flexible) nature[129], the turning point is reached where indeterminacy lapses into "anything goes". Where the notion of object and purpose can be utilized to support or substantiate even diametrically opposed claims, surely its usefulness as "a normative element beyond the rules laid down in a treaty"[130] proper leaves a thing or two to be desired.

That is not to say, as alluded to above, that the notion of object and purpose can ever be substantively delimited *in abstracto*. The meaning of object and purpose in any given situation depends to a large extent on the characteristics of that situation; it depends not only on the treaty itself which may be at issue, but also, as argued above, on the particular treaty-problem concerned. As such, object and purpose is and will remain indeed an utterly flexible notion, able to cater to various needs and different circumstances.

It is also clear that determining a treaty's object and purpose, in whatever situation, is essentially a subjective act over which no impartial or objective control exists. This has generally been acknowledged to be the case with respect to reservations: whether or not a reservation is deemed to be compatible with the treaty's object and purpose depends, in the final analysis, on whether or not it meets with the acceptance of the other treaty partners. The situation is much the same in other contexts, whether it concerns modification, the interim obligation, interpretation, succession, or breach. Given this essentially subjective nature, it is all the more imperative that the notion of object and purpose be handled with care. And even then, it is likely to remain "so difficult to apply".[131]

---

[129] See Ulrich Fastenrath, *Lücken im Völkerrecht* (1990) or, more accessible perhaps, Fastenrath's "Relative Normativity in International Law", *European Journal of International Law* (1993) p. 305. In a different context, compare Ian Ward, "Identity and Difference: the European Union and postmodernism", in Jo Shaw & Gillian More, eds., *New Legal Dynamics of European Union*, (1995) p. 15.

[130] See Riphagen (note 25).

[131] *Reservations* case (note 9), joint dissenting opinion of Judges *Guerrero, McNair, Read & Hsu Mo*, p. 44.

[6]

THE INTERNATIONAL LEGAL OBLIGATIONS OF SIGNATORIES TO AN UNRATIFIED TREATY

*Martin A. Rogoff**

I. Introduction

There are currently two major international agreements of the United States which have been signed by the parties and transmitted by the President to the Senate for its advice and consent: the Treaty with the Soviet Union on the Limitation of Strategic Offensive Arms, known as SALT II,[1] and the Agreement with Canada on East Coast Fishery Resources and the accompanying Treaty to Submit to Binding Dispute Settlement the Delimitation of the Maritime Boundary in the Gulf of Maine Area.[2] Both agreements were signed after lengthy and complex negotiations.[3] Both agreements are ex-

---

* Professor of Law, University of Maine School of Law. B.A., Cornell University, 1962; M.A., University of California (Berkeley), 1963; LL.B., Yale University, 1966.

1. The Treaty on the Limitation of Offensive Arms and Protocol Thereto (SALT II Treaty) was signed by Presidents Carter and Brezhnev in Vienna on June 18, 1979. The Treaty was transmitted by President Carter for the advice and consent of the Senate to ratification on June 22, 1979. The following related documents were also transmitted to the Senate:

    1. a series of Agreed Statements and Common Understandings concerning the obligations of the Parties under particular articles of the Treaty;

    2. a Memorandum of Understanding that will establish an agreed data base by categories of strategic offensive arms along with associated statements of current data;

    3. a Joint Statement of Principles and Basic Guidelines on the Limitation of Strategic Arms concerning the next phase of negotiation on this subject; and

    4. a Soviet statement on the Backfire bomber, together with a United States response.

For the text of the Treaty and related documents, see TREATY ON THE LIMITATION OF STRATEGIC OFFENSIVE ARMS AND PROTOCOL THERETO (SALT II TREATY), S. EXEC. DOC. No. Y. 96th Cong., 1st Sess. (1979).

2. The Agreement on East Coast Fishery Resources was signed by Secretary of State Cyrus Vance and Canadian Ambassador Peter Towe in Washington, D. C. on March 29, 1979. The Agreement was transmitted by President Carter for the advice and consent of the Senate to ratification on May 3, 1979. For the text of the Agreement and the accompanying Treaty to Submit to Binding Dispute Settlement the Delimitation of the Maritime Boundary in the Gulf of Maine Area, see MARITIME BOUNDARY SETTLEMENT TREATY WITH CANADA AND THE AGREEMENT ON EAST COAST FISHERY RESOURCES WITH CANADA, S. EXEC. DOC. No. U, V, 96th Cong., 1st Sess. (1979).

3. The process of negotiation which ultimately produced the SALT II Treaty began on November 17, 1968 in Helsinki. On May 26, 1972, two agreements, known collectively as SALT I were signed. These were the Treaty on the Limitation of Anti-Ballistic Missile Systems, May 26, 1972, United States-Union of Soviet Socialist Republics, 23 U.S.T. 3435, T.I.A.S. No. 7503 (1972), [hereinafter cited as ABM Treaty]

tremely detailed and represent a delicate balancing of the interests

---

and the Interim Agreement on Certain Measures with Respect to the Limitation of Strategic Offensive Arms, May 26, 1972, United States-Union of Soviet Socialist Republics, 23 U.S.T. 3462, T.I.A.S. No. 7504 (1972), [hereinafter cited as Interim Agreement]. The ABM Treaty was of unlimited duration, ABM Treaty, art. XV §1, whereas the Interim Agreement was for a duration of five years, Interim Agreement, art. VIII §2. Both agreements contain provisions for the continuation of active negotiations for limitations on strategic offensive arms. ABM Treaty, art. X; Interim Agreement, arts. VII and VIII §2. When it became clear that a SALT II agreement could not be concluded before the expiration of the Interim Agreement, Secretary of State Vance issued the following statement on September 23, 1977:

> In order to maintain the status quo while SALT II negotiations are being completed, the United States declares its intention not to take any action inconsistent with the Interim Agreement on Certain Measures with Respect to the Limitation of Strategic Offensive Arms which expires on October 3, 1977, and with the goals of these ongoing negotiations provided that the Soviet Union exercises similar restraint.

77 DEP'T STATE BULL. 642 (1977).

In response, the Soviet Union made a similar unilateral statement. For related documents, see U.S. DEP'T OF STATE, DIGEST OF U. S. PRACTICE IN INT'L LAW 425-33 (1977). For speculation on why the negotiating process has been so drawn out, see Doty, Carnesale, & Nacht, *The Race to Control Nuclear Arms*, 55 FOREIGN AFF. 119, 123-26 (1976). For detailed discussions of the SALT negotiations, see T. WOLFE, THE SALT EXPERIENCE (1979); SALT: THE MOSCOW AGREEMENTS AND BEYOND (M. Willrick & J. Rhinelander eds. 1974); SALT: IMPLICATIONS FOR ARMS CONTROL IN THE 1970's (W. Kintner & R. Pfaltzgraff, Jr. eds. 1973). For a study of the Soviet negotiating behavior during the SALT I negotiations, see SENIOR SPECIALISTS DIVISION, CONGRESSIONAL RESEARCH SERVICE, LIBRARY OF CONGRESS, SOVIET DIPLOMACY AND NEGOTIATING BEHAVIOR: EMERGING NEW CONTEXT FOR U. S. DIPLOMACY 443-510, 535-40 (1979). It is contemplated by the parties that the SALT negotiations will continue following the conclusion of the SALT II Treaty. SALT II Treaty, art. XIV. *See also* SALT II TREATY: JOINT STATEMENT ON PRINCIPLES AND BASIC GUIDELINES FOR SUBSEQUENT NEGOTIATIONS ON THE LIMITATION OF STRATEGIC ARMS, S. EXEC. DOC. No. Y, 96th Cong., 1st Sess. 70 (1979).

In 1970, the United States and Canada began negotiations to resolve the boundary on the continental shelf in the Gulf of Maine area. The enactment by the United States of the Fishery Conservation and Management Act of 1976, 16 U.S.C. §§ 1801-1882 (1976), whereby the United States asserted exclusive fishery management authority in a fishery conservation zone extending 200 miles from its baseline, and similar claims by Canada, 119 House of Commons Debates 14164-69 (June 4, 1976), led to further conflict. Since 1976, negotiations aimed at resolving the boundary and resource problems have been ongoing. On February 24, 1977, the United States and Canada signed an agreement containing a provisional arrangement for fishery exploitation in the disputed area. Reciprocal Fisheries Agreement between the Government of the United States of America and the Government of Canada, Feb. 24, 1977, 91 Stat. 283, T.I.A.S. No. 8648 (1977). Canada repudiated the agreement on June 2, 1978, and the United States suspended its obligations under the agreement immediately after the Canadian action. For discussions of the negotiations leading up to the 1979 agreements, see Pickering, *Address before the Oceans Policy Forum in Washington, D. C., on April 5, 1979*, 79 DEP'T STATE BULL. 7-9 (June 1979); Comment, *Boundary Delimitation in the Economic Zone: The Gulf of Maine Dispute*, 30 MAINE L. REV. 207, 234-38 (1979). *See also* Emanuelli, *Boundary and Resource Issues: Modes de règlement des différends entre le Canada et les États-Unis en matière de frontières et de ressources maritimes*, 1 CANADA-UNITED STATES L.J. 36, 51-52 (1978).

of the nations involved.[4] Already there have been considerable delays in the ratification of both agreements.[5] Perhaps neither agreement will be ratified.[6] The President, however, continues to insist

---

4. President Carter has described SALT II as "the most detailed, far-reaching, comprehensive treaty in the history of arms control. Its provisions are interwoven by the give-and-take of the long negotiating process. Neither side obtained everything it sought. But the package that did emerge is a carefully balanced whole . . . ." Address Delivered Before a Joint Session of Congress, 15 WEEKLY COMP. OF PRES. DOCS. 1089 (June 25, 1979). For a discussion of the compromises and reciprocal concessions that resulted in the final agreement, see T. WOLFE, *supra* note 3, at 226-35. Highlighting the complexity of the agreement are the lengthy and detailed accompanying Agreed Statements and Common Understandings which add further precision to the already detailed Articles of the Treaty. Secretary of State Vance has said that the Treaty and related documents were "meticulously negotiated over more than six years." Secretary's Letter of Submittal of June 21, 1979, 79 DEP'T STATE BULL. 4 (July 1979).

The East Coast Fishery Resources Agreement, in Annexes which are an integral part of the Agreement, establishes the terms of fishing access and entitlements to various fish stocks. The Agreement allocates, on a percentage basis, the "annual permissible commercial catch" for all commercially significant fish stocks in the area of the Gulf of Maine shared by both countries between American and Canadian fishermen. Agreement on East Coast Fishery Resources, *supra* note 2, art. 9.

5. The SALT II Treaty was transmitted by President Carter to the Senate on June 22, 1979. The Senate Committee on Foreign Relations has held hearings on the Treaty. *The SALT II Treaty: Hearings on S. Exec. Y Before the Senate Committee on Foreign Relations: Parts 1-6*, 96th Cong., 1st Sess. (1979). The East Coast Fishery Resources Agreement was transmitted by President Carter to the Senate on May 3, 1979. The Senate Committee on Foreign Relations has held hearings on the Agreement. *Maritime Boundary Settlement Treaty and East Coast Fishery Resources Agreement: Hearings on S. Exec. U, V Before the Senate Committee on Foreign Relations*, 96th Cong., 1st Sess. (1980). Neither agreement has been reported out of Committee.

6. On June 22, 1979, when President Carter transmitted the SALT II Treaty to the Senate for its advice and consent, political and popular opposition to the Treaty appeared substantial. President Carter undertook a massive effort to win support for the Treaty both within the Senate and in the country. Subsequent international developments, however, reduced the likelihood of favorable action by the Senate. On January 3, 1980, President Carter, in response to the crisis created by the Soviet invasion of Afghanistan, asked Senate Majority Leader Robert Byrd to delay consideration of the SALT II Treaty on the Senate floor. Letter to the Majority Leader of the Senate Requesting a Delay in Senate Consideration of the Treaty. January 3, 1980, 16 WEEKLY COMP. OF PRES. DOC. 12 (Jan. 7, 1980). *See also* President Carter's Address to the Nation, January 4, 1980, 16 WEEKLY COMP. OF PRES. DOC. 25, 26 (Jan. 14, 1980).

The East Coast Fishery Resources Agreement also had been characterized as "controversial." *See* Pickering, *supra* note 3, at 7. Senate Committee hearings on the Agreement indicated considerable opposition. *Maritime Boundary Settlement Treaty and East Coast Fishery Resources Agreement: Hearings on S. Exec. U, V Before the Senate Committee on Foreign Relations*, 96th Cong., 2d Sess. (1980). *See also* Lovell, *Fishing Treaty: Who Really Wants It?*, Maine Sunday Telegram, March 30, 1980, at 1.

For a complete collection of treaties which the United States has concluded but which have not entered into force, see I-V UNPERFECTED TREATIES OF THE UNITED STATES: 1776-1976 (C. Wicktor ed. 1980). For an interesting consideration of the role

that ratification of both agreements is in the national interest, and eventual favorable action on them is still possible.[7]

Most contemporary treaties provide that they will enter into force only upon ratification by the states that are to become parties to the agreement.[8] While at one time signature played a more important

---

of the Senate in the treaty-making process, see W. HOLT, TREATIES DEFEATED BY THE SENATE (1964). *See also* J. HAYDEN, THE SENATE AND TREATIES, 1789-1817 (1970).

7. In his letter to Senator Byrd, the President reaffirmed his commitment to eventual ratification of the Treaty. *See* Letter to Majority Leader, *supra* note 6, at 12. The President reiterated this position in his State of the Union Message three weeks later. *See* Address Delivered Before a Joint Session of Congress. January 23, 1980, 16 WEEKLY COMP. OF PRES. DOC. 194, 196 (Jan. 28, 1960); News Conference of March 14, 1980, 16 WEEKLY COMP. OF PRES. DOC. 484, 488-89 (March 17, 1980). *See also* Address and excerpts from question-and-answer session before the American Society of Newspaper Editors, April 10, 1980, 80 DEP'T STATE BULL. 3, 5 (May 1980).

Kenneth Curtis, U.S. Ambassador to Canada, has reaffirmed the support of the administration for the East Coast Fishery Resources Agreement. *Curtis airs fish treaty,* Portland Press Herald, May 29, 1980, at 21. Secretary of State Muskie is reported to be working actively for ratification of the treaty. *See* Membrino, *Meeting Fails to Get Compromise on Fishing Treaty,* Bangor Daily News, July 12-13, 1980, at 29.

It appears that renegotiation of certain particulars of both treaties may be necessary to meet Senate concerns before favorable Senate action is even possible. Burt, *There's a Greater Uncertainty Than the Outlook for SALT,* N.Y. Times, Aug. 24, 1980, § 4, at 4; *Fishing treaty: Mitchell 'no,' Bush not sure,* Portland Press Herald, Aug. 8, 1980, at 1. *See also* Blechman, *Do Negotiated Arms Limitations Have a Future?,* 59 FOREIGN AFF. 102 (1980).

8. *See, e.g.,* SALT II Treaty Article XIX §1: "This treaty shall be subject to ratification in accordance with the constitutional procedures of each Party. This treaty shall enter into force on the day of the exchange of instruments of ratification. . . ." East Coast Fishery Resources Agreement Article XXV §1: "This Agreement shall be subject to ratification in accordance with the domestic requirements of the Parties and shall enter into force on the date instruments of ratification of this Agreement . . . [and the accompanying Treaty to Submit to Binding Dispute Settlement of the Maritime Boundary in the Gulf of Maine Area] are exchanged." For descriptions of the ratification process in the Soviet Union, see Triska & Slusser, *Ratification of Treaties in Soviet Theory, Practice and Policy,* 34 BRIT. Y. B. INT'L L. 312 (1958), and in Canada, see J. G. CASTEL, INTERNATIONAL LAW 935-45 (3d ed. 1976). *See also* United Nations, Laws and Practices Concerning the Conclusion of Treaties, U. N. Doc. ST/LEG/Ser.B/3 (1952); Nascimento e Silva, *Le facteur temps et les traités,* 154 RECUEIL DES COURS 215, 223-41 (1977).

It is necessary to distinguish (1) the date on which the international obligation of a treaty is perfected so that the treaty becomes binding on the parties and enters into force; (2) the date as from which, having become binding, it operates; and (3) the date as from which the treaty speaks.

A. McNAIR, THE LAW OF TREATIES 191 (1961).

The date upon which a treaty enters into force is a matter for the parties to establish. "The critical date may be related to a particular event such as the exchange of ratifications, the deposit or notification of all or a certain number of ratifications, the passing of certain necessary legislation by the parties, [or] formal promulgation of the treaty . . . ." *Id.* At the time of entry into force the treaty becomes legally binding on the parties.

The entry into operation of a treaty is contingent upon its entry into force. The

role in the process whereby a state assumed treaty obligations, today the crucial event is ratification.[9] Signature may impose the obligation to comply with the procedural provisions of the agreement, such as those provisions relating to the submission of the agreement for ratification in accordance with the internal law of the signatories or those provisions relating to the exchange of ratifications or their deposit.[10] But it is now well settled that the signature imposes no legal duty on a signatory state to actually ratify a treaty. Ratification is discretionary with the signatory state and may be withheld for any reason.[11] Furthermore, unless the signatories provide other-

---

commencement of operation of a treaty may relate back to the date of signature or some other past date or event; it may be the same as the date of entry into force; or it may be dependent on some stipulated future date or event. *Id.* at 193-204.

The date as from which a treaty speaks is a question of interpretation, and the answer will depend on the circumstances of each case. McNair illustrates the problem with the following example:

> Let us suppose that a clause . . . requires one of the parties to transfer certain rights and interests owned by it or by its nationals to the other parties or to a commission on their behalf, does that mean rights and interests existing at the time of (*a*) signature, or (*b*) the entry into force, or (*c*) the entry into operation, of the treaty?

Id. at 204-05.

9. For the historical background of ratification, see J. JONES, FULL POWERS AND RATIFICATION 66-157 (1949). *See also* Blix, *The Requirement of Ratification,* 30 BRIT. Y. B. INT'L L. 352 (1953); K. HOLLOWAY, MODERN TRENDS IN TREATY LAW 40-64 (1967).

10. Article 24 § 4 of the Vienna Convention on the Law of Treaties provides:

> The provisions of a treaty regulating the authentication of its text, the establishment of the consent of States to be bound by the treaty, the manner or date of its entry into force, reservations, the functions of the depositary and other matters arising necessarily before the entry into force of the treaty apply from the time of the adoption of its text.

Vienna Convention on the Law of Treaties, U. N. Doc. A/CONF. 39/27, *reprinted in United Nations Conference on the Law of Treaties,* Documents of the Conference 287 (First and Second sessions; Vienna, 26 March - 24 May 1968 & 9 April - 22 May 1969), U. N. Doc. A/CONF. 39/11/Add. 2; *also reprinted in* 63 AM. J. INT'L L. 875 (1969) [hereinafter cited as Vienna Convention]. *See also* Nisot, *La force obligatoire des traités signés, non encore ratifiés,* 57 JOURNAL DU DROIT INT'L 878 (1930).

Mr. Sinclair, representative of the United Kingdom at the Vienna Conference, explained this provision as follows:

> It was generally accepted that when the text of a treaty was adopted, certain provisions had legal effects which were impliedly accepted by the countries concerned even if the treaty was not formally in force. The provisions were those dealing with the processes of ratification, accession, acceptance, approval, the functions of the depositary and reservations.

United Nations Conference on the Law of Treaties, Summary Records 139 (First Session: Vienna, 26 March - 24 May 1968), U. N. Doc. A/CONF. 39/11 [hereinafter cited as *United Nations Conference,* First Session].

11. "The stream of unratified treaties since 1920 has established beyond doubt that the contemporary rule of practice is that ratification is discretionary and that no reasons need be given for refusing to ratify a treaty." J. JONES, *supra* note 9, at 79 (footnote omitted).

wise, a treaty has no retroactive effect.[12] Thus, with the possible exception of obligations arising from its procedural provisions, a treaty has no obligatory force prior to its entry into force.[13] Once a treaty is

---

12. Article 28 of the Vienna Convention on the Law of Treaties provide:
    Unless a different intention appears from the treaty or is otherwise established, its provisions do not bind a party in relation to any act or fact which took place or any situation which ceased to exist before the date of the entry into force of the treaty with respect to that party.
Vienna Convention, *supra* note 10.
    Modern treaties typically enter into force on the date of exchange of instruments of ratification and not on the date of signature. At one time, however, the United States took the position that upon ratification of a treaty its provisions were deemed to have been in force from the date of signature even though ratification was necessary for the treaty to enter into force. The principal American case which established the now discredited doctrine of the retroactivity of treaty obligations was Hylton's Lessee v. Brown, 12 F. Cas. 1122 (C.C.D. Pa. 1804)(No. 6,980). In *Hylton's Lessee* the court stated that "ratification is nothing more than evidence of the authority under which the minister acted. . . ." *Id.* at 1128. The function of ratification was therefore simply to confirm the act of an agent by his principal. Professor Jones distinguishes this view of the function of ratification from the modern view as follows:
    In the eighteenth century, full powers gave authority to make a binding agreement, subject to a confirmation which was usually held to be obligatory. Today, full powers give authority merely to discuss, to negotiate, and to sign a project, which may or may not become an international treaty by the formal acceptance of it by the States concerned. Ratification is now regarded as *being* this formal acceptance. It means the ratification of the treaty itself, although formerly it meant the ratification of the act of an agent signing it. With such a theory of the nature of ratification, it is impossible to reconcile the doctrine of retroactivity, for the theoretical basis of agency upon which the doctrine rests can no longer be maintained.
Jones, *The Retroactive Effect of the Ratification of Treaties*, 29 Am. J. Int'l L. 51, 65 (1935). For a further discussion of the non-retroactivity of treaties, see the International Law Commission Commentary to Article 24 of the Draft Articles on the Law of Treaties, *United Nations Conference on the Law of Treaties*, Documents of Conference 31-33 (First and Second sessions; Vienna, 26 March - 24 May 1968 & 9 April - 22 May 1969), U.N. Doc. A/CONF. 39/11/Add. 2 [hereinafter cited as *United Nations Conference*, Documents]. *See also* Schrager v. Workmen's Accident Insurance Institute for Moravia and Silesia, 4 I.L.R. 396 (Sup. Ct. of Poland, 3d Div., 1927).
    13. Provisional application may also be regarded as an exception to the general rule. Article 25 of the Vienna Convention on the Law of Treaties provides for the provisional application of a treaty or part of a treaty.
    1. A treaty or a part of a treaty is applied provisionally pending its entry into force if:
        (a) the treaty itself so provides; or
        (b) the negotiating states have in some other manner so agreed.
    2. Unless the treaty otherwise provides or the negotiating States have otherwise agreed, the provisional application of a treaty or part of a treaty with respect to a State shall be terminated if that State notifies the other States between which the treaty is being applied provisionally of its intention not to become a party to the treaty.
Vienna Convention, *supra* note 10.
    Thus,
    Owing to the urgency of the matters dealt with in the treaty or for other

ratified and does enter into force, the principle *pacta sunt servanda* imposes the obligation on the parties to carry out the agreement in good faith.[14]

The fact that treaties do not typically create obligations prior to ratification poses potential problems. In situations where ratification is delayed, actions by the signatories during the period between signature and entry into force may upset the delicate balance struck by the signatories during the negotiating process. For example, Canada or the United States would certainly be acting contrary to the purpose and spirit of the *East Coast Fishery Resources Agreement* if either should engage in large-scale fishing of certain stocks that are subject to the management provisions of the Agreement because those stocks might be fished to extinction or severely reduced. Such action, however, would not violate the Agreement since the Agreement is not yet in force and therefore cannot be a source of binding legal obligations.[15]

Multilateral conventions provide particularly good examples of the problem. These treaties are often negotiated and concluded by large international conferences and usually provide that they will enter into force following the deposit of a certain number of instruments of ratification or accession.[16] Where a state has signed and

---

reasons the States concerned may specify in a treaty, which it is necessary for them to bring before their constitutional authorities for ratification or approval, that it shall come into force provisionally. Whether in these cases the treaty is to be considered as entering into force in virtue of the treaty or of a subsidiary agreement concluded between the States concerned in adopting the text may be a question. But there can be no doubt that such clauses have legal effect and bring the treaty into force on a provisional basis.

Commentary to Draft Article 22, *United Nations Conference*, Documents, *supra* note 12, at 30.

14. *See generally* Kunz, *The Meaning and the Range of the Norm* Pacta Sunt Servanda, 39 AM. J. INT'L L. 180 (1945). Article 26 of the Vienna Convention on the Law of Treaties provides: "Every treaty in force is binding upon the parties to it and must be performed by them in good faith." Vienna Convention, *supra* note 10.

15. See K. HOLLOWAY, *supra* note 9, at 60-61, for a discussion of the actions of the signatories contrary to the provisions of the Treaty of Sèvres which resulted in the destruction of the Treaty and "in the abandonment of thousands of defenceless people—Armenians and Greeks—to the fury of their persecutors, by engendering subsequent holocausts in which the few survivors of the 1915 Armenian massacres perished."

16. For example, Article 84 of the Vienna Convention on the Law of Treaties provides:

1. The present Convention shall enter into force on the thirtieth day following the date of deposit of the thirty-fifth instrument of ratification or accession.

2. For each State ratifying or acceding to the Convention after the deposit of the thirty-fifth instrument of ratification or accession, the Convention shall enter into force on the thirtieth day after deposit by such State of its instrument of ratification or accession.

perhaps ratified a treaty that has not entered into force because the
requisite number of states have not ratified the treaty, does the signatory state come under a legal obligation not to take any action
inconsistent with the treaty before its entry into force? This question has some importance in the context of the on-going United Nations Conference on the Law of the Sea.[17] The negotiators are attempting to resolve extremely important and timely problems, such
as the right of a coastal state to control fishing in extensive areas

Vienna Convention, *supra* note 10. For other examples see Article 11 of the Convention on the Continental Shelf, 499 U.N.T.S. 311, 15 U.S.T. 471, 475, and Article 13 of
the Convention for the Prevention and Punishment of the Crime of Genocide,
adopted December 9, 1948, 78 U.N.T.S. 277. *See also* UNITED NATIONS, HANDBOOK OF
FINAL CLAUSES, U.N. Doc. ST/LEG/6, at 21-38 (1957). *See* Alvarez, Representative of
Uraguay, *United Nations Conference,* Documents, *supra* note 12, at 102, who points
out that there may be different considerations concerning multilateral and bilateral
treaties with respect to obligations arising upon signature.

17.   The current basis for negotiations at the United Nations Conference on the
Law of the Sea is the Draft Convention on the Law of the Sea (Informal Text), U.N.
Doc. A/Conf.62/WP.10/Rev.3/Add.1 (Aug. 28, 1980). For a series of articles describ-
ing the progress of negotiations at the Conference on the Law of the Sea, see Oxman,
*The Third United Nations Conference on the Law of the Sea: The Eighth Session
(1979),* 74 AM. J. INT'L L. 1 (1980); Oxman, *The Third United Nations Conference on
the Law of the Sea: The Seventh Session (1978),* 73 AM. J. INT'L L. 1 (1979); Oxman,
*The Third United Nations Conference on the Law of the Sea: The 1977 New York
Session,* 72 AM. J. INT'L L. 57 (1978); Stevenson & Oxman, *The Third United Nations Conference on the Law of the Sea: The 1976 New York Sessions,* 71 AM. J.
INT'L L. 247 (1977); Stevenson & Oxman, *The Third United Nations Conference on
the Law of the Sea: The 1974 Caracas Session,* 69 AM. J. INT'L L. 1 (1975); Stevenson
& Oxman, *The Preparations for the Law of the Sea Conference,* 68 AM. J. INT'L L. 1
(1974).

The United States has enacted legislation dealing with fishery conservation and
management that may, in certain respects, conflict with future obligations under a
Law of the Sea convention, see Fishery Conservation and Management Act of 1976,
16 U.S.C. §§ 1801-1882 (1976); Jacobson & Cameron, *Potential Conflicts Between a
Future Law of the Sea Treaty and the Fishery Conservation and Management Act
of 1976,* 52 WASH. L. REV. 451 (1977). It should be noted, however, that the United
States has made some attempt to accommodate its law to potential obligations under
a Law of the Sea convention. *See* 16 U.S.C. § 1881 (1976). *See also* § 1801(c)(5) of
title 16, U.S.C., which declares it to be the policy of the United States "to support
and encourage continued active United States efforts to obtain an internationally acceptable treaty, at the Third United Nations Conference on the Law of the Sea,
which provides for effective conservation and management of fishery resources." *See
also* Ports and Waterways Safety Act §§ 101-201, 33 U.S.C. §§ 1221-1232 (1976).

The United States has recently enacted legislation concerning deep seabed mining.
Deep Seabed Hard Minerals Resources Act, Pub. L. No. 96-283, 49 U.S.L.W. 105
(Aug. 12, 1980). The Act declares in section 2(b)(1) that one of its purposes is "to
encourage the successful conclusion of a comprehensive Law of the Sea Treaty which
will give legal definition to the principle that the hard mineral resources of the deep
seabed are the common heritage of mankind and which will assure, among other
things, nondiscriminatory access to such resources for all nations." *See also* Rosenne,
Reflections on the Final Clauses in the New Law of the Sea Treaty, 18 VA. J. INT'L
L. 133 (1978).

adjacent to its coast and the establishment of a regime for the conservation and exploitation of deep ocean mineral resources. Once a Law of the Sea treaty is signed, but before it enters into force, what are the obligations of signatory states? Could the United States, for example, enact legislation to regulate fishing in a 200-mile zone and even beyond? Could the United States enact legislation to authorize or license its nationals to engage in the mining of the deep seabed?

International legal obligations may arise by virtue of general international law as well as by treaties.[18] There is growing agreement that general international law imposes on the signatories to an unratified treaty the obligation not to defeat the object and purpose[19] of that treaty prior to its entry into force.[20] Once viewed as a moral admonition,[21] this obligation has come increasingly to be regarded as legal in nature. The desirability of such a principle is of course evident. The long and complicated process of negotiation during which each state may have made numerous concessions should be protected, especially where a signed agreement is the result. Furthermore, during negotiations the states may have refrained from taking certain actions—heavy fishing of certain stocks or the development of new weapons systems for example—because negotiations were pending. This self-restraint in expectation of a binding agreement should be encouraged.

It is the thesis of this Article that general international law im-

---

18. Article 38 of the Statute of the International Court of Justice provides that, in addition to "international conventions," the Court shall apply "international custom, as evidence of a general practice accepted as law" and "the general principles of law recognized by civilized nations." U.N. Doc. OPI/84-16500 (1964). As subsidiary means for the determination of rules of law, the Court may apply "judicial decisions and the teachings of the most highly qualified publicists of the various nations." *Id.*

19. The obligation discussed in this Article will be characterized as an "obligation not to defeat the object and purpose of a treaty prior to its entry into force." Vienna Convention, *supra* note 10. This is the terminology in Article 18 of the Vienna Convention on the Law of Treaties, *id.*, and for the sake of consistency will be utilized throughout this Article.

20. Law of Treaties, [1953] 2 Y.B. INT'L L. COMM'N. 108-12, U.N. Doc. A/CN.4/Ser.A/1953/Add.1 (Lauterpacht, Special Rapporteur); Law of Treaties, [1962] 1 Y.B. INT'L L. COMM'N. 46-48, U.N. Doc. A/CN.4/Ser.A/1962 (Waldock, Special Rapporteur); Law of Treaties, [1965] 2 Y.B. INT'L L. COMM'N 43-45, U.N. Doc. A/CN.4/Ser.A/1965 (Waldock, Special Rapporteur); Law of Treaties, [1956] 2 Y.B. INT'L L. COMM'N 104, 113, U.N. Doc. A/CN.4/Ser.A/1956/Add.1 (Fitzmaurice, Special Rapporteur); K. HOLLOWAY, *supra* note 9, at 40-64; D. O'CONNELL, 1 INTERNATIONAL LAW 222-24 (2d ed. 1970); Vienna Convention, *supra* note 10; RESTATEMENT (REVISED) OF THE FOREIGN RELATIONS LAW OF THE UNITED STATES § 314 (Tent. Draft No. 1, 1980).

21. Documents of the third session, [1951] 2 Y.B. INT'L L. COMM'N 73, U.N. Doc. A/CN.4/Ser.A/1951/Add.1 (Brierly, Special Rapporteur); *Research in International Law*, 29 AM. J. INT'L L. 778-87 (Supp. 1935). Some recent writers still regard the obligation as moral in character. *See* H. KELSEN, PRINCIPLES OF INTERNATIONAL LAW 466-68 (2d rev. ed., R. Tucker ed. 1962); A. MCNAIR, THE LAW OF TREATIES 204 (1961).

poses on the signatories to a treaty the obligation not to defeat the
object and purpose of that treaty prior to its entry into force. Decisional law, state practice, and the Vienna Convention on the Law of
Treaties all support this proposition. The obligation has a firm theoretical basis in the general principle of abuse of rights. Finally, after
examining the existence and nature of the obligation, the Article
concludes with a discussion of the content of the obligation and attempts to discern its contours and extent.

II. The Obligation Not to Defeat the Object and Purpose of a Signed But Unratified Treaty

A. Decisional Law

The legal effect of signed but unratified treaties has been considered in a number of international court and arbitral decisions. While
some commentators regard this line of decisions as establishing a
legal obligation not to defeat the object or purpose of the treaty
prior to its entry into force,[22] others regard it as inconclusive at
best.[23] In those proceedings where the question has been considered,
the tribunal has typically either refused to impose the obligation or
has regarded it as not violated on the basis of the particular facts
involved in the case. In most of the cases where the tribunal does
deem the obligation to exist, the obligation does not actually provide
the rule for decision, but is stated either arguendo or as dicta. The
international decisions standing alone, then, are probably insufficient authority on which to rest the obligation. When considered in
the context of other legally relevant materials, however, these cases
do provide some support and do articulate theoretical justifications
for the imposition of the obligation.

Furthermore, virtually all the cases that have considered the question involve peace treaties, concluded upon the termination of hostilities. They are not treaties like SALT II or the East Coast Fishery
Resources Agreement that represent the conclusion of a long negotiating process where the negotiating states are bargaining on the basis of equality. Rather they are treaties that to a greater or lesser
degree are imposed by one party or parties upon another party or
parties.[24] Where true bargaining on the basis of equality takes place,

---

22. See note 20 *supra; see* B. Cheng, General Principles of Law as Applied by
International Courts and Tribunals 111-12 n.28 (1953).

23. See note 21 *supra.*

24. Schwarzenberger, *The Fundamental Principles of International Law,* 87
Recueil des Cours 191 (1955), draws the distinction between "treaties governed by
the law of power . . . which are imposed under irresistible pressure" and "the sphere
of the law of reciprocity . . . [where] treaties are freely concluded." *Id.* at 295. For
definitions of the "law of power" and "law of reciprocity," see G. Schwarzenberger,
A Manual of International Law 9-10 (6th ed. 1976). For a fuller discussion, see G.
Schwarzenberger, Power Politics 198-207 (3d ed. 1964).

there would appear to be more justification for creating rights and imposing obligations intended to increase the likelihood of the states involved achieving the purposes embodied in the signed agreement.

    1. The Legal Effect of Signature. Coming at the conclusion of long and complex negotiations, signature should have some legal effect.[25] This is especially true where the negotiators have been granted full powers[26] by the states which they represent and where,

---

    25. Governments have full freedom of action in confirming or rejecting a treaty which they have signed subject to the condition of subsequent confirmation—such condition being the normal rule in the absence of express or implied provisions to the contrary . . . . What, as a matter of good faith, they cannot do is to sign a treaty and subsequently conduct themselves as if they had no concern with it or as if their signature thereto were merely a clerical act of authentication. There is no warrant in international law for reducing to that level the meaning of the signature. Signature of an instrument—even when made subject to subsequent confirmation or ratification—is more than a method of authenticating a text. In many cases the text exists already, as is the case when an established text is approved by a conference and opened for signature, subject to ratification, within a prescribed period, or when accession to or acceptance of an already established text takes place throught [sic] signature subject to ratification. . . . There are compelling reasons why a signatory should not be permitted to treat his signature as a meaningless formality. In signing a treaty it exercises an important influence on some of the procedural clauses of the treaty . . . . Its signature is instrumental in determining such matters as the right of accession, the admissibility of reservations, the conditions of entry into force, and many others. In fact this consideration applies not only to the formal and procedural clauses of the treaty but to its substantive provisions as well. For these provisions may have been substantially—or decisively—influenced by the signatory State or States in question. The treaty is in many respects the result of a painfully achieved compromise to which some States agree, often with reluctance, in order to secure the participation of others. Often a State signs—or ratifies—a convention because the signature of another State or States is regarded by it, in case of doubt, as a sufficient inducement for its own signature. But if these other States are subsequently at liberty to treat their signature as implying no manner of obligation whatsoever, the concessions made by other signatories will have been made in vain seeing that the consideration which they could legitimetely [sic] expect will not be forthcoming . . . . All these considerations prompt the conclusion that signature, although not implying an obligation of ratification, implies the duty to take some action showing a deliberate acknowledgement of the principle that eventual ratification is the natural outcome and purpose of the signature.

Law of Treaties, [1953] 2 Y.B. INT'L L. COMM'N 90, 109-10, U.N. Doc. A/CN.4/Ser.A/1953/Add.1 (Lauterpacht, Special Rapporteur).

    26. Paragraph 1(c) of Article 2 of the Vienna Convention on the Law of Treaties defines full powers:

    (c) "full powers" means a document emanating from the competent authority of a State designating a person or persons to represent the State for negotiating, adopting or authenticating the text of a treaty, for expressing the consent of the State to be bound by a treaty, or for accomplishing any other act with respect to a treaty . . . .

Article 7 provides:

as is often the case, the executive of the states and perhaps those
other organs which must be involved in the ratification process
under internal law keep apprised of and involved in the negotiating
process.[27] The legal effect of signature has been considered in a

---

1. A person is considered as representing a State for the purpose of adopting or authenticating the text of a treaty or for the purpose of expressing
the consent of the State to be bound by a treaty if:

    (a) he produces appropriate full powers;

    . . .

2. In virtue of their functions and without having to produce full powers,
the following are considered as representing their State:

    (a) Heads of State, Heads of Government and Ministers for Foreign
Affairs, for the purpose of performing all acts relating to the conclusion of a
treaty . . . .

Vienna Convention, *supra* note 10, at 289-90. *See generally* J. JONES, *supra* note 9, at
1-65; 14 M. WHITEMAN, DIGEST OF INTERNATIONAL LAW 35-40 (1970).

27. Department of State control over negotiators goes beyond issuing full powers.
"The receipt or possession of a 'full power' is never to be considered as a final authorization to sign [a treaty]. That authorization is given by the Department by a written
or telegraphic instruction, and no signature is affixed in the absence of such instruction." 11 Foreign Affairs Manual, Dep't of State, 730.3 (Oct. 25, 1974).

Kaye Holloway argues:

[W]here treaty-making is a joint competence under the constitution, the
government is under obligation to consult other competent organs . . . .

    . . . .

    In spite of doctrinal divergence, there seems to be a clear indication that
in the minds of the framers of the Constitution, Article 2, cl. 2, associated
the Senate with the making of treaties and not just empowered it to approve or reject a treaty concluded by the President.

K. HOLLOWAY, *supra* note 9, at 54.

Whether or not the executive branch is legally required to consult with the Senate
during the negotiating process, such consultation is often helpful in obtaining Senate
approval of the treaty. Secretary of State Vance made the following remarks at hearings before the Senate:

Indeed, SALT II as presented significantly reflects the influence of the
Senate.

    Throughout these negotiations, we have consulted closely with this com-
mittee and with individual Members of the Senate at every stage. Twenty-
seven Senators traveled to Geneva to observe the negotiations firsthand.
We have strongly encouraged that process. Secretary Brown, General
Seignious, his predecessor, Ambassador Warnke, and I have discussed
SALT issues in nearly 50 separate congressional hearings since January
1977. Most of those have been in the Senate.

    In the same period, there have been over 140 individual SALT briefings
of Senators by responsible officials of the administration, and another 100
briefings of members of Senators' staffs. The consultation and cooperation
between the Executive and the Congress on this treaty have been extensive.

    Those sessions have been held to receive your advice as well as to report
on our progress. Time and again, issues raised by Members of the Senate
have been taken up directly in the negotiations. Our negotiators were conscious of the need to meet a number of specific objectives of the Senate.

*The Salt II Treaty—Part 1: Hearings on Ex. Y Before the Senate Committee on
Foreign Relations*, 96th Cong., 1st Sess. 94-95 (1979). *See also* FOREIGN AFFAIRS AND

number of international decisions. In the *Advisory Opinion on Reservations to the Convention on the Prevention and Punishment of the Crime of Genocide*,[28] the International Court of Justice was concerned, among other things, with the effect to be given to certain objections to other states' reservations made by signatories and nonsignatories to an unratified multilateral convention. In that context the court stated:

> Without going into the question of the legal effect of signing an international convention, which necessarily varies in individual cases, the Court considers that signature constitutes a first step to participation in the Convention.
>
> It is evident that without ratification, signature does not make the signatory State a party to the Convention; nevertheless, it establishes a provisional status in favour of that State. . . .
>
> . . . Pending ratification, the provisional status created by signature confers upon the signatory a right to formulate as a precautionary measure objections which have themselves a provisional character. These would disappear if the signature were not followed by ratification, or they would become effective on ratification.[29]

Objections made by a state which had not signed the Convention to reservations made by other states were held to be without legal effect.[30] The *Reservations* case thus recognizes signature as conferring certain legal rights on a signatory. The purpose of the conferral of such rights would appear to be to enable the signatory to continue to participate in the on-going process whereby the final balance of rights and obligations of all the parties is struck. In this sense the court is providing legal protection for the process of agreement leading to eventual ratification and entry into force.

The *Mavrommatis Palestine Concessions (Jurisdiction)*[31] case also provides support for attributing legal consequences to signature. In that case, Greece filed an application in the Permanent Court of International Justice claiming certain rights against Great Britain under the Treaty of Lausanne[32] and a supplementary Protocol.[33] When Greece filed its application in the court, the Treaty had

---

NATIONAL DEFENSE DIVISION, CONGRESSIONAL RESEARCH SERVICE, LIBRARY OF CONGRESS, 96TH CONG., 1ST & 2D SESS., CONGRESS AND FOREIGN POLICY—1978 47-50 (Comm. Print 1979); SENATE COMM. ON FOREIGN RELATIONS, 96TH CONG., 1ST SESS., SENATE DELEGATION REPORT ON SALT DISCUSSIONS IN THE SOVIET UNION (Comm. Print 1979).

28. [1951] I.C.J. 15.

29. *Id.* at 28.

30. *Id.* at 30.

31. [1924] P.C.I.J., ser. A, No. 2, *reported in* 1 WORLD COURT REPORTS 297 (M. Hudson ed. 1934).

32. Treaty of Lausanne, July 24, 1923, 28 L.N.T.S. 11.

33. Protocol Relating to Certain Concessions Granted in the Ottoman Empire and Declaration, July 24, 1923, 28 L.N.T.S. 203.

been signed by both Greece and Great Britain, but it had not yet entered into force. Great Britain sought dismissal on that ground. In rejecting Great Britain's contention, the Court said that "[e]ven . . . if the application were premature because the Treaty of Lausanne had not yet been ratified, this circumstance would now be covered by subsequent deposit of the necessary ratifications."[34] By regarding the Greek filing as legally effective, even though the Treaty had not yet entered into force, the court in effect accorded provisional status to the signed but unratified Treaty.

Judge Moore dissented:

> The treaty was at length ratified (August 6, 1924); but, in the interval of nearly two months that elapsed after the Court met, the application evidently was, as it stood, subject to dismissal on the ground that the enforcement of unratified treaties, whether by the award of damages for their alleged infraction or otherwise, is beyond the Court's jurisdiction. On this point Article 36 of the Statute limiting compulsory jurisdiction to matters specially provided for "in treaties and conventions *in force*", is definite and conclusive. The doctrine that governments are bound to ratify whatever their plenipotentiaries, acting within the limits of their instructions, may sign, and that treaties may therefore be regarded as legally operative and enforceable before they have been ratified, is obsolete, and lingers only as an echo from the past.[35]

The court would certainly not have retained jurisdiction and rendered a decision if the Treaty had not been subsequently ratified. But by refusing to accede to the British position, the court did give legal effect to mere signature.

The importance of eventual ratification is highlighted by two other international decisions. In the *Case concerning the Territorial Jurisdiction of the International Commission of the River Oder,*[36] the Permanent Court of International Justice considered whether Poland should be bound by the provisions of the Barcelona Convention on the Régime of Navigable Waterways of International Concern[37] which Poland had signed but not ratified. The court concluded that the Barcelona Convention could not be relied on as against Poland, saying that "it cannot be admitted that the ratification of the Barcelona Convention is superfluous. . . ."[38] A similar result was reached by the International Court of Justice in the

---

34. [1924] P.C.I.J., ser. A, No. 2, *reported in* 1 WORLD COURT REPORTS 293, 319 (M. Hudson ed. 1934).

35. *Id.* at 293, 333-34.

36. [1929] P.C.I.J., ser. A, No. 23, *reported in* 2 WORLD COURT REPORTS 609, 611 (M. Hudson ed. 1935).

37. For the text of the Barcelona Convention, see Convention and Statute on the Régime of Navigable Waterways of International Concern. Barcelona, April 20, 1921, 7 L.N.T.S. 35 (1921); 1 INTERNATIONAL LEGISLATION 638-44 (M. Hudson ed. 1931).

38. 2 WORLD COURT REPORTS, *supra* note 36, at 623.

North Sea Continental Shelf Cases,[39] where the court refused to hold the Federal Republic of Germany bound by the provisions of the Geneva Convention on the Continental Shelf[40] which the Federal Republic had signed but not ratified.

2. *The Legal Obligation.* The only decision of an international tribunal which clearly rests on the rule imposing an obligation not to defeat the object or purpose of a treaty between signature and entry into force is *Megalidis v. Turkey,* decided by a mixed Greco-Turkish Arbitral Tribunal in 1928.[41] In that case, a Greek claimant sought the return of certain items taken forcibly by Turkish authorities from a strong-box which he rented in the Crédit Lyonnais in Smyrna. The seizure occurred on August 14, 1923. The claimant relied on various provisions of the Treaty of Lausanne,[42] which was signed on July 24, 1923, but which did not enter into force until August 6, 1924. Article 65 of the Treaty provided:

> Property, rights and interests which still exist and can be identified in territories remaining Turkish at the date of the coming into force of the present Treaty, and which belong to persons who on the 29th October, 1914, were Allied nationals, shall be immediately restored to the owners in their existing state.[43]

To recognize the forced expropriation of the property of an allied national by Turkish authorities subsequent to the signature of the Treaty but prior to its entry into force would, of course, severely limit the scope and effectiveness of Article 65. In holding the Turkish seizure to be a violation of international law, the tribunal stated: "[A]lready with the signature of a Treaty and before its entry into force there exists for the parties an obligation to do nothing which may be prejudicial to the Treaty by diminishing the significance of its provisions. . . ."[44] The precedential value of the decision in establishing the obligation not to defeat the purpose or object of a signed but unratified treaty is somewhat reduced, however, by the high probability that the Turkish seizure was illegal under international law as an unlawful expropriation of alien-owned property.[45] Nevertheless, the tribunal did not base its decision on that ground and did regard the rule under consideration as an established princi-

---

39. [1969] I.C.J. 3.

40. Convention on the Continental Shelf, *done* April 29, 1958, 499 U.N.T.S. 311, 15 U.S.T. 471.

41. 8 Recueil des Décisions des Tribunaux Mixtes 386 (1928).

42. See note 32 *supra.*

43. See note 32 *supra,* at 55.

44. 8 Recueil des Décisions des Tribunaux Mixtes 386, 395 (1928).

45. Chorzow Factory Case, [1926-1929] P.C.I.J. ser. A, Nos. 7, 9, 17, 19 *reported in* 1 WORLD COURT REPORTS 510 (M. Hudson ed. 1934) and 2 WORLD COURT REPORTS 23, 508, 691 (M. Hudson ed. 1935); Norwegian Shipowners Claim, (United States v. Norway), *reprinted in* 17 AM. J. INT'L L. 362, 388 (Perm. Ct. Arb. 1922). *See generally* B. WORTLEY, EXPROPRIATION IN PUBLIC INTERNATIONAL LAW 33-36 (1959).

ple of international law.[46]

There are several international decisions that appear to accept the existence of a legal obligation not to defeat the object or purpose of a signed but unratified treaty, but which do so only arguendo or in dicta. The principal case in this category is the *Case concerning Certain German Interests in Polish Upper Silesia*, decided by the Permanent Court of International Justice in 1926.[47] That case, so far as pertinent here, involved the legality of a transfer by sale by Germany of property, located in territory that Germany was required to cede to Poland, to a corporation formed for the purpose of acquiring the property. Poland denied the legality of the transfer, relying on Article 256 of the Treaty of Versailles.[48] That Article provided that "Powers to which German territory is ceded shall acquire all property . . . situated therein belonging to the German Empire. . . ."[49] The Treaty of Versailles was signed by Germany on June 28, 1919, and was ratified on January 20, 1920. The contract of sale for the transfer of the property was entered into on December 24, 1919, between the date of signature and the date of ratification. The court upheld the German transfer as not violating Article 256:

> Germany undoubtedly retained until the actual transfer of sovereignty the right to dispose of her property, and only a misuse of this right could endow an act of alienation with the character of a breach of the Treaty; such misuse cannot be presumed, and it rests with the party who states that there has been such misuse to prove his statement.[50]

It should be noted that the court deemed that under German law the actual transfer took place on January 28-29, 1920, when the Treaty of Versailles was already in force. In the court's view, the

---

46. In the *Megalidis* case, the tribunal supported its imposition of the obligation by reference to the fact that "this principle . . . has received a certain number of applications in various treaties." 8 Recueil des Décisions des Tribunaux Mixtes 386, 395 (1928). The tribunal then refers to a treaty provision which is apparently Article 8 of the protocol annexed to the Treaty of Neutrality, Conciliation and Judicial Settlement, May 30, 1928, Greece-Italy, 95 L.N.T.S. 185. That provision does not provide support for the tribunal's contention.

Whereas the *Megalidis* case provides some support for the rule under discussion, the *Iloilo Claims* decision may be regarded as authority for a contrary view. F. NIELSEN, AMERICAN AND BRITISH CLAIMS ARBITRATION 382 (1926). In that case, before a British-American Claims Commission in 1925, claimants suffered damage at Iloilo caused by Filipino insurgents during the interval between the signature and ratification of the Treaty of Paris, December 10, 1898, Spain-United States, 30 Stat. 1754.

47. [1926] P.C.I.J., ser. A, No. 7, *reported in* 1 WORLD COURT REPORTS 475, 510 (M. Hudson ed. 1934).

48. Treaty of Versailles, June 28, 1919, art. 256, 2 TREATIES AND OTHER INTERNATIONAL AGREEMENTS OF THE UNITED STATES 43, 161 (C. Bevans ed. 1968).

49. *Id.*

50. [1926] P.C.I.J. ser. A, No. 7, at 30, *reported in* 1 WORLD COURT REPORTS 510, 530 (M. Hudson ed. 1934).

Treaty, even after its entry into force, did not impose on Germany an obligation to refrain from making the sort of transfer involved in the case. "In these circumstances," the court said that it "need not consider the question whether, and if so how far, the signatories of a treaty are under an obligation to abstain from any action likely to interfere with its execution when ratification has taken place."[51]

The Permanent Court of International Justice was faced with a similar problem in the *German Settlers in Poland* case.[52] In that case, the court allowed the German Government and the Prussian State to undertake transactions falling within the normal administration of the country during the period between the signing and entry into force of the Treaty of Versailles. The court approved the transactions even though the effect of those transactions was to finalize the transfer of property owned by the German State to private individuals, thereby removing the property from the operation of the Treaty which called for its passage to Poland.

Another decision containing dicta approving the imposition of pre-ratification obligations on the signatories to a treaty is *Ignacio Torres v. The United States,* decided by Francis Lieber as umpire in 1871.[53] In that case American troops attacked, sacked, and burned the town of Zacualtipan, Mexico, thereby causing damage to the property of a Mexican citizen. The military action occurred subsequent to the signing of the peace treaty of Guadalupe Hildago[54] by the United States, but before it had been ratified by the Senate. The umpire rejected the damage claim of the injured party:

> How is it, however, when a treaty of peace has been signed, but has not yet been ratified? Many of the best authorities hold that peace begins *de jure* when it is signed, and not from the day it is ratified

---

51. *Id.* at 40, *reported in* 1 WORLD COURT REPORTS at 538. *See* Law of Treaties, [1965] 2 Y.B. INT'L L. COMM'N 3, 44, U.N. Doc. No. A/CN.4/Ser.A/1965/Add.1 (Waldock, Special Rapporteur):

> In the *Polish Upper Silesia* case the treaty had entered into force and the State concerned had ratified the treaty; moreover, the Court itself appears to have approached the matter from the point of view of whether the acts done prior to ratification constituted a breach of the treaty. One point of view might therefore be that the "good faith" obligation of a negotiating State not to frustrate in advance the objects of the proposed treaty is merely inchoate until the treaty enters into force with respect to that State; but that then it becomes complete on the State's entering into the obligations of the treaty. In drafting article 17, however, the Commission took the position that an independent obligation not to frustrate the objects of a proposed treaty attaches to a State when it takes part in the negotiations or in the drawing up or adoption of the text; and *a fortiori* when it ratifies, accedes to, accepts or approves the treaty. (footnote omitted).

52. [1923] P.C.I.J., ser. B, No. 6, *reported in* 1 WORLD COURT REPORTS 297 (M. Hudson ed. 1934).

53. 4 J. MOORE, INTERNATIONAL ARBITRATIONS 3798 (1898).

54. Treaty of Peace, Friendship, Limits and Settlement with the Republic of Mexico, Feb. 2, 1848, United States-Mexico, 9 Stat. 922 (1848).

by the two supreme belligerent powers or the authorities which by
the law of the land have alone the right to ratify. This, however, is
far from being unconditional. If a peace were signed with a moral
certainty of its ratification and one of the belligerents were, after
this, making grants of land in a province which is to be ceded,
before the final ratification, it would certainly be considered by
every honest jurist a fraudulent and invalid transaction. But it is
well understood that a peace is not a complete peace until ratified;
that, as a matter of course, the ratifying authority has the power of
refusing unless, for that time, it has given up this power
beforehand. . . .[55]

B.   State Practice

Numerous treaties have included provisions placing obligations on
the signatories prior to entry into force.[56] Such provisions oblige the

---

55. 4 J. MOORE, *supra* note 53, at 3800-01.

56. There are conceptual problems with the establishment of legally binding pre-
ratification obligations. "Any arrangement, whether expressed or implied, that a
treaty is to take effect for any purposes prior to the completion of the contractual
relationship between the signatory parties, is obviously subject to the condition that
that relationship be perfected." 2 C. HYDE, INTERNATIONAL LAW CHIEFLY AS INTER-
PRETED AND APPLIED BY THE UNITED STATES § 522, at 1451 (2d rev. ed. 1945). Briggs
comments that "[i]t is not inconceivable, however, that certain provisions of a treaty
may be intended by the signatory parties to come into force upon signature, although
the treaty as a whole is intended to come into force only upon the exchange of ratifications." THE LAW OF NATIONS: CASES, DOCUMENTS, AND NOTES 867 (2d ed. H. Briggs
ed. 1952). One possible solution to this problem is to regard the pre-ratification undertaking as a separate agreement that enters into force at the time of signature. *See*
Vienna Convention, arts. 12(1), 24(1), *supra* note 10, at 287; Bolintineanu, *Expression of Consent to be Bound by a Treaty in the Light of the 1969 Vienna Convention*, 68 AM. J. INT'L L. 672 (1974). From the point of view of domestic American law,
such an agreement may be regarded as an executive agreement, which does not require Senate participation. *See* Memorandum of Law from Monroe Leigh to Senator
James Abourezk (October 31, 1975), *reprinted in* [1975] DIGEST OF UNITED STATES
PRACTICE IN INTERNATIONAL LAW 307-16; State Department Circular No. 175 Procedure, *Dept. of State Foreign Aff. Manual*, Vol. 11, ch. 700, *reprinted in* A. ROVINE,
[1974] DIGEST OF UNITED STATES PRACTICE IN INTERNATIONAL LAW 199-215. *See also*
McDougal & Lang, *Treaties and Congressional-Executive or Presidential Agreements: Interchangeable Instruments of National Policy I & II*, 54 YALE L.J. 181, 534
(1945). As regards SALT see section 33 of the Arms Control and Disarmament Act of
1961 § 33, 22 U.S.C. § 2573 (1976):

>   [N]o action shall be taken under this chapter or any other law that will
>   obligate the United States to disarm or to reduce or to limit the Armed
>   Forces or armaments of the United States, except pursuant to the treaty
>   making power of the President under the Constitution or unless authorized
>   by further affirmative legislation by the Congress of the United States.

The most frequently cited example of a treaty provision which imposes obligations
on the signatories from the date of signature is Article 38 of the General Act of the
Conference of Berlin, Feb. 26, 1885, 165 CONSOLIDATED TREATY SERIES 485, 502 (C.
Parry ed. 1978). For citations to other treaty provisions, see *Research in Interna-
tional Law*, *supra* note 21, at 786; Lauterpacht, *The Contemporary Practice of the
United Kingdom in the Field of International Law—Survey and Comment*, *III*, 6

signatories to adhere to the terms of the treaty or not to take action that would interfere with the operation of the treaty once it entered into force. It is not uncommon for responsible government officials to make similar representations with respect to treaties signed by

---

INT'L AND COMP. L. Q. 301, 320-21 (1957). *See also* 5 G. HACKWORTH, DIGEST OF INTERNATIONAL LAW 213-15 (1943). A recent example may be found in the two Common Understandings appended to the two Salt I agreements. *See* Treaty on the Limitation of Anti-Ballistic Missile Systems, May 26, 1972, United States-Union of Soviet Socialist Republics, 23 U.S.T. 3437, 3459, T.I.A.S. No. 7503 (1972); Interim Agreement on Certain Measures with Respect to the Limitation of Strategic Offensive Arms, May 26, 1972, United States-Union of Soviet Socialist Republics, 23 U.S.T. 3463, 3479, T.I.A.S. No. 7504 (1972). Common Understanding E of the ABM Treaty and Common Understanding C of the Interim Agreement read as follows:

STANDSTILL

On May 6, 1972, Minister Semenov made the following statement: In an effort to accommodate the wishes of the U.S. side, the Soviet Delegation is prepared to proceed on the basis that the two sides will in fact observe the obligations of both the Interim Agreement and the ABM Treaty beginning from the date of signature of these two documents.

In reply, the U.S. Delegation made the following statement on May 20, 1972: The U.S. agrees in principle with the Soviet statement made on May 6 concerning observance of obligations beginning from date of signature but we would like to make clear our understanding that this means that, pending ratification and acceptance, neither side will take any action prohibited by the agreements after they had entered into force. This understanding would continue to apply in the absence of notification by either signatory of its intention not to proceed with ratification or approval.

The Soviet Delegation indicated agreement with the U.S. statement.

ABM Treaty, *supra* note 2, 23 U.S.T. at 3459; Interim Agreement, *supra* note 2, 23 U.S.T. at 3479.

As to the legal effect of the Common Understandings, see the exchange between Senator Percy and Secretary of State Rogers:

II. Question. Will these clauses [understandings and interpretations made available to this Committee by the Administrator when it forwarded this treaty for consideration] have exactly the same force as if they were included in the text of the agreements?

Answer. The agreed interpretations will clearly be binding on both parties.

Strategic Arms Limitation Agreements: Hearing on Ex. L and S.J. Res. 241 and S.J. Res. 242 Before the Senate Comm. on Foreign Relations, 92d Cong., 2d Sess. 53 (1972)(questions of Senator Percy to Secretary of State Rogers).

Concerning the Agreed Statement and Common Understandings appended to the SALT II Treaty, the following exchange took place at hearings of the Senate Committee on Foreign Relations:

The Chairman. Then do the agreed statements and/or the common understandings represent binding obligations of the two parties?

Secretary Vance. The answer is clearly yes. They were signed by the leaders of the two governments involved and there is no question about it.

The Chairman: So, they will not be regarded simply as negotiating history from which to interpret the obligations contained in the treaty, but will have equal, binding force with the treaty itself?

Secretary Vance: That is correct.

The SALT II Treaty: Hearings on Ex. Y Before the Senate Committee on Foreign Relations, 96th Cong., 1st Sess. 121 (1979).

their countries but which have not yet entered into force.[57] Article

---

57. For example, President Carter has repeatedly indicated that the United States regards itself bound by the provisions of the SALT II agreement. In his State of the Union Message in January 1980, he called for "observing the mutual constraints imposed by the terms of [SALT I and SALT II.]" The State of the Union Address of January 23, 1980, 16 WEEKLY COMP. OF PRES. DOC. 194, 196 (Jan. 28, 1980). In his news conference of March 14, 1980, he said:

> SALT II has been signed by me and President Brezhnev. I consider it binding on our two countries . . . .
>
> . . . .
>
> But my present intention, within the bounds of reciprocal action on the Soviet Union and consultations with the Senate and, to some degree, the House leadership, I intend to comply with the provisions of SALT II.
>
> . . . .
>
> Ordinarily, when a treaty is signed between the heads of two nations, the presumption is that the treaty will be honored on both sides absent some further development. One further development that would cause me to renounce the treaty would be after consulting with the Members of the Senate to determine an interest of our Nation that might cause such a rejection, in which case I would notify the Soviet Union that the terms of the treaty were no longer binding.
>
> So, there will be two provisos in the continued honoring of the SALT II treaty. One is that the Soviets reciprocate completely, as verified by us, and secondly, that the consultations that I will continue with the Senate leadership confirm me in my commitment that it's in the best interests of our country to do so.

The President's News Conference of March 14, 1980, 16 WEEKLY COMP. OF PRES. DOC. 488-89 (Mar. 14, 1980).

On March 19, talks commenced in Geneva between the United States and Soviet governments to discuss plans for carrying out the provisions of SALT II. Soviet representatives refused, however, to engage in discussions on procedures for complying with the treaty in apparent reaction to President Carter's news conference statement that there might be circumstances under which the United States would renounce the agreement even if the Soviet Union continued to adhere to its terms. *See* Burt, *Soviet Balks at Geneva Discussions on Carrying Out the Arms Accord*, N. Y. Times, March 20, 1980, at 1; Whitney, *Complying with Arms Pact*, N. Y. Times, March 24, 1980, at A8.

See also the letter of June 15, 1979, of Elliot Richardson, Ambassador at Large, Special Representative of the President for the Law of the Sea Conference, to Congressman Gerry Studds, concerning the legal effect of signature by the United States of a Law of the Sea treaty on United States unilateral deep seabed mining legislation:

> *Question 24.* What is the legal effect of signature of the treaty on unilateral ocean mining?
>
> *Answer.* United States signature of a Law of the Sea treaty would not necessarily have an effect on unilateral ocean mining undertaken pursuant to U.S. legislation now pending before Congress. The United States would be bound by the treaty only upon deposit of its instrument of ratification and the treaty's entry in force pursuant to final clauses contained in the treaty itself. Signature only serves as a preliminary indication of intent to become a party and, under customary international law, imposes no obligation other than refraining from acts which would defeat the object and purpose of the treaty. This very general obligation continues only until such time as it becomes clear that the State no longer intends to become a party to the treaty. Signature would not impose any obligation to abide by the

38(1)(b) of the Statute of the International Court of Justice provides that "international custom, as evidence of a general practice accepted as law" shall be a source of law for the court.[58] Clive Parry has called international custom a "practice followed in the persuasion that it is binding."[59] Treaty provisions may be evidence of such a practice and in that way "may . . . exercise their effects, *qua* evidence of customary international law, upon nonparties."[60] The statements of responsible government officials may also be evidence of what practices states regard as legally obligatory. While certainly not conclusive, the treaty provisions and the public statements of government officials do provide further support for the existence of a pre-ratification obligation upon the signatories to a treaty.

C. *The Vienna Convention on the Law of Treaties*

The Vienna Convention on the Law of Treaties[61] provides in Article 26 that "every treaty in force is binding upon the parties to it

---

substance of the treaty itself, and the United States would still be free to regulate United States activities undertaken as high seas rights. Moreover, refusal or likely refusal of the U.S. to ratify would probably influence the ratification decisions of other major powers, and thus could affect customary international law.

The legislation now pending before Congress is designed to be compatible with the eventual ratification and entry into force for the United States of a Law of the Sea treaty. Seabed mining undertaken pursuant to it will not in any way defeat the object or purpose of the treaty.

Letter from Elliot Richardson to Gerry Studds (June 15, 1979), *reprinted in Law of the Sea: Hearings on H.R. 2759 Before the Subcomm. on Oceanography of the Comm. on Merchant Marine and Fisheries*, 96th Cong., 1st Sess. 206 (1979).

McNair reproduces a Report by the Attorney-General and the Queen's Advocate dated May 15, 1857 to the same effect. That report contains the following language:

That Altho' the Convention between Her Majesty and the Republic of Honduras has not yet been ratified, yet the ratifications, when exchanged, will relate back to, and confirm the Convention, as from the 27th of August 1856. No Act can in the mean time be properly done by Her Majesty . . . which may at all affect any of the stipulations of the Treaty.

McNAIR, *supra* note 21, at 201.

There are, however, examples of official statements to the contrary. *See, e.g.,* Statement of Secretary Hull to the British Ambassador:

This Government considers that, in the case of any treaty or convention to which it is a signatory, it has not accepted any obligations or acquired any rights until it has duly ratified such instrument in accordance with its constitutional procedure and until the requirements of the treaty or convention with reference to exchange or deposit of ratification also have been fulfilled by it.

Reprinted in 5 G. HACKWORTH, *supra* note 56, at 199.

58. I.C.J. STATUTE, art. 38(1)(b).

59. C. PARRY, THE SOURCES AND EVIDENCES OF INTERNATIONAL LAW 56 (1965).

60. Baxter, *Treaties and Custom*, 129 RECUEIL DES COURS 25, 31 (1970). *See also* North Sea Continental Shelf Cases, [1969] I.C.J. 3, 225 (Lachs, J., dissenting).

61. *See* Vienna Convention, *supra* note 10.

and must be performed by them in good faith."[62] This principle, *pacta sunt servanda*, is described by the International Law Commission as "the fundamental principle of the law of treaties."[63] Since the obligation of good faith performance is dependent upon a treaty's being in force, the determination of when a treaty enters into force with respect to a party is critical. Article 24 (1) specifies the basic rule that "a treaty enters into force in such a manner and upon such date as it may provide or as the negotiating States may agree,"[64] and Article 24 (2) provides that "failing any such provision or agreement, a treaty enters into force as soon as consent to be bound by the treaty has been established."[65] Article 28 denies retroactive effect to a treaty, "unless a different intention appears from the treaty or is otherwise established."[66] These provisions, read together, express the general principle that treaties do not have legal effect before their entry into force.

The Vienna Convention also contains an exception to this general principle in Article 18:

> A state is obliged to refrain from acts which would defeat the object and purpose of a treaty when:
> (a) it has signed the treaty or has exchanged instruments constituting the treaty subject to ratification, acceptance or approval, until it shall have made its intention clear not to become a party to the treaty; or
> (b) it has expressed its consent to be bound by the treaty, pending the entry into force of the treaty and provided that such entry into force is not unduly delayed.[67]

Article 18 represents the codification of a rule of customary international law, as it was developed in the decisions of international tribunals and state practice, and was refined in the work of the International Law Commission and the Vienna Conference on the Law of Treaties.

The provision which became Article 18 of the Vienna Convention has its origin in Article 9 of the Harvard Draft Convention on the Law of Treaties. The Harvard Draft reads as follows:

> Unless otherwise provided in the treaty itself, a State on behalf of which a treaty has been signed is under no duty to perform the obligations stipulated, prior to the coming into force of the treaty with respect to that State; under some circumstances, however, good faith may require that pending the coming into force of the

---

62. *Id.* at 292.
63. Commentary to Draft Article 23, *United Nations Conference*, Documents, *supra* note 12, at 30.
64. Vienna Convention, *supra* note 10, at 292.
65. *Id.*
66. *Id.* at 293.
67. *Id.* at 291.

treaty the State shall, for a reasonable time after signature, refrain from taking action which would render performance by any party of the obligations stipulated impossible or more difficult.[68]

The Comment to Article 9 states that the Article "does not envisage a legal duty, e.g. a duty under international law . . . . Under Article 9 a signatory is only under a duty of good faith to refrain from the action referred to therein."[69] The Comment continues:

> The essential distinction between the two kinds of duty is that non-performance of the former involves important legal consequences—the responsibility of the non-performing party and its liability to make reparation for any losses or damages sustained by the other party or parties; whereas non-performance of the latter produces no such legal results. It may expose the non-performing State to the charge of bad faith or may impair its good name and reputation, but it does not render such State liable to damages for violation of a legal obligation, because no legal obligation existed which could be violated.[70]

Professor Brierly, Special Rapporteur on the Law of Treaties, adopted Article 9 of the Harvard Draft Convention (with inconsequential alterations) in the Draft Convention he submitted to the Third Session of the International Law Commission in 1951.[71] In his Comment, Professor Brierly made clear his belief that the Article states a moral rather than a legal obligation.[72] In his report the following year, the provision was omitted.[73] Professor Brierly commented that:

> A certain amount of material exists concerning an alleged obligation on the part of States not to do anything, between the signature of a treaty on their behalf and its ratification, that would render ratification by other States superfluous or useless. This material is, however, of too fragmentary and inconclusive a nature to form the basis of codification.[74]

Sir Hersh Lauterpacht succeeded Professor Brierly as Special Rapporteur on the Law of Treaties. In his report for the Fifth Session of the International Law Commission in 1953, Lauterpacht included an Article entitled *Signature*.[75] The Comments to this Arti-

---

68. *Research in International Law, supra* note 21, at 778.

69. *Id.* at 781.

70. *Id.*

71. Law of Treaties, [1951] 2 Y.B. INT'L L. COMM'N 70, 73, U.N. Doc. A/CN.4/Ser.A/1951/Add.1 (Brierly, Special Rapporteur).

72. *Id.*

73. Law of Treaties, [1952] 2 Y.B. INT'L L. COMM'N 50, U.N. Doc. A/CN.4/Ser.A/1952/Add.1 (Brierly, Special Rapporteur).

74. *Id.* at 54.

75. Law of Treaties, [1953] 2 Y.B. INT'L L. COMM'N 108, U.N. Doc. A/CN.4/Ser.A/1953/Add.1 (Lauterpacht, Special Rapporteur). The Article contained the following provision:

cle make it clear that Lauterpacht's views differ significantly from those expressed by the Harvard Draft and Professor Brierly. Lauterpacht regarded signature as having "the effect of obliging the signatories to abstain, prior to ratification, from a course of action inconsistent with the purpose of the treaty" and believed "that obligation constitute[d] a legal, and not merely a moral, duty."[76] In response to Professor Brierly's contention that the relevant legal material was of "too fragmentary and inconclusive a nature to form the basis of codification,"[77] Lauterpacht maintained that "judicial practice . . . is as complete as can be desired in the circumstances."[78] The next Special Rapporteur, Sir Gerald Fitzmaurice, followed the Lauterpacht approach.[79]

Sir Humphrey Waldock, who succeeded Sir Gerald Fitzmaurice as Special Rapporteur, concurred in the views of Lauterpacht and Fitzmaurice regarding the existence of a legal obligation during the period following signature and prior to the entry into force of a treaty. That obligation was extended to the negotiating period, prior to signature, in the Draft Articles of 1962[80] and 1965.[81] The pertinent article which was the immediate predecessor of Article 18 of the Vienna Convention, reads:

> A State is obliged to refrain from acts tending to frustrate the object of a proposed treaty when:
>
> (a) It has agreed to enter into negotiations for the conclusion of the treaty, while these negotiations are in progress;
>
> (b) It has signed the treaty subject to ratification, acceptance or approval, until it shall have made its intention clear not to become a party to the treaty;

1. The signature of a treaty constitutes an assumption of a binding obligation in all cases in which the parties expressly so agree or where, in accordance with Article 6, no confirmation of the signature is necessary.

2. In all other cases the signature, or any other means of assuming an obligation subject to subsequent confirmation, has no binding effect except that it implies the obligation, to be fulfilled in good faith:

    (a) To submit the instrument to the proper constitutional authorities for examination with the view to ratification or rejection;

    (b) To refrain, prior to ratification, from any act intended substantially to impair the value of the undertaking as signed.

76. Law of Treaties, [1953] 2 Y.B. INT'L L. COMM'N 110, U.N. Doc.A/CN.4/Ser.A/1953/Add.1 (Lauterpacht, Special Rapporteur).

77. See note 74 *supra*.

78. Law of Treaties, [1953] 2 Y.B. INT'L L. COMM'N 111, U.N. Doc. A/CN.4/Ser.A/1953/Add.1 (Lauterpacht, Special Rapporteur).

79. Law of Treaties, [1956] 2 Y.B. INT'L L. COMM'N 113, U.N. Doc. A/CN.4/Ser.A/1956/Add.1 (Fitzmaurice, Special Rapporteur).

80. Law of Treaties, [1962] 2 Y.B. INT'L L. COMM'N 46, U.N. Doc. A/CN.4/Ser.A/1962/Add.1 (Waldock, Special Rapporteur).

81. Report of the Commission to the General Assembly, [1965] 2 Y.B. INT'L L. COMM'N 161, U.N. Doc. A/CN.4/Ser.A/1965/Add.1.

(c) It has expressed its consent to be bound by the treaty, pending the entry into force of the treaty and provided that such entry into force is not unduly delayed.[82]

The Commentary of the International Law Commission to this article, Draft Article 15, notes, "that an obligation of good faith to refrain from acts calculated to frustrate the object of the treaty attaches to a State which has signed a treaty subject to ratification appears to be generally accepted."[83] Discussion of Draft Article 15 in the nineteenth and twentieth meetings of the Committee of the Whole evidences a general agreement that the portion of the Draft Article (subparagraphs (b) and (c)) which eventually became Article 18 "were acceptable and conformed to general rules of international law"[84] and were "accepted . . . both in doctrine and in practice."[85]

The Vienna Convention on the Law of Treaties was the product of a conference in which 110 nations participated.[86] The Draft Articles presented to the conference were the result of twenty years of study and debate. As the foregoing discussion has shown, Article 18 underwent considerable discussion and modification, although from the time of the Lauterpacht draft in 1953, there was general agreement that the obligation contained in Article 18 existed as a matter of customary international law. When and if the Vienna Convention enters into force, states that are parties will of course be subject to the obligations imposed by Article 18. But the Vienna Convention has not yet entered into force. Even as an unratified multilateral convention, though, it may be regarded as evidence of a customary rule. Judge Baxter of the International Court of Justice has argued persuasively that there are good reasons for regarding multilateral conventions that propose to codify rules of customary international

---

82. *United Nations Conference,* Documents, *supra* note 12, at 22. For a thorough discussion of Draft Article 15, see Morvay, *The Obligation of a State Not to Frustrate the Object of a Treaty Prior to its Entry into Force,* XXVII ZEITSCHRIFT FÜR AUSLÄNDISCHES ÖFFENTLICHES RECHT UND VÖLKERRECHT 451 (1967)(Special Number, Comments on the Law of Treaties).

83. *United Nations Conference,* Documents, *supra* note 12, at 22.

84. *United Nations Conference,* First Session, Comments of Mr. Bindschedler of Switzerland, *supra* note 10, at 97.

85. *United Nations Conference,* First Session, Comments of Mr. Jagota of India, *supra* note 10, at 98. Interestingly, a Soviet Representative believed that "subparagraphs (b) and (c) had a perfectly sound basis in positive international law" and that "no provision of the article was prejudicial to the sovereign right of a State to withdraw from the treaty at any time before it finally became binding." *United Nations Conference,* First Session, Comments of Mr. Lukashuk of the Ukrainian Soviet Socialist Republic, *supra* note 12, at 100.

86. For general background to the organization and work of the Vienna Conference, see Reports of the Committee of the Whole, Chapter 1, *United Nations Conference,* First Session, *supra* note 10, at 107-09. *See also* G. A. Res. 2166, 21 U.N. GAOR, Supp. No. 9, part II, U.N. Doc. A/6309/Rev.1 (1966); Kearny & Dalton, *The Treaty on Treaties,* 64 AM. J. INT'L L. 495, 495-502 (1970).

law as evidence of those rules.[87] While the Vienna Convention has not yet entered into force, good reasons also exist for giving weight to those of its provisions that the drafters regarded as codifying existing customary rules. Judge Lachs, writing in dissent in the *North Sea Continental Shelf Cases*, said: "It is generally recognized that provisions of international instruments may acquire the status of rules of international law. Even unratified treaties may constitute a point of departure for a legal practice."[88]

Finally, the process of hammering out the Convention's text may, in itself, lead to clarification of a norm of customary international law. In the *North Sea Continental Shelf Cases*, Denmark and the Netherlands advanced the argument, concerning the status of a certain rule embodied in the Geneva Convention on the Continental Shelf, that "the process of the definition and consolidation of the emerging customary law took place through the work of the International Law Commission, the reaction of governments to that work and the proceedings of the Geneva Conference. . . ."[89] Although the court rejected this argument, it did so primarily because the Article in question "was proposed by the Commission with considerable hesitation, somewhat on an experimental basis, at most *de lege ferenda*, and not at all *de lege lata* or as an emerging rule of customary international law."[90] In this respect Article 18 is quite different because the prevalent view in the International Law Commission from at least 1953 on was that Article 18 codified an existing rule of customary international law.

III. Basis of the Obligation: The Theory of Abuse of Rights

There is growing agreement that the obligation not to defeat the object or purpose of a treaty after signature but prior to its entry into force is legal in nature. It has come to be regarded not simply as a moral admonition, but as a binding obligation whose breach entails legal consequences. This is certainly the opinion of the last three International Law Commission Special Rapporteurs on the law of treaties.[91] That such an obligation exists is the import of Article 18 of the Vienna Convention.[92] While this view also finds support in recent scholarly literature,[93] the primary legal materials on which it

---

87. Baxter, *supra* note 60, at 36-56.
88. [1969] I.C.J. 3,225 (Lachs, J., dissenting). Tentative Draft No. 1 of the Restatement (Revised) of the Foreign Relations Law of the United States of the American Law Institute specifically follows Article 18 of the Vienna Convention. *See* Restatement (Revised) of the Foreign Relations Law of the United States, *supra* note 20.
89. Quoted by the Court in North Sea Continental Shelf Cases, [1969] I.C.J. 3, 38.
90. *Id.*
91. See text accompanying notes 61-90 *supra*.
92. *Id.*
93. *See* notes 20 & 22 *supra*.

is based are fragmentary and ambiguous. No international tribunal has ever provided an analysis of the principle or given it more than the most cursory treatment. Although the principle is cited with approval in several cases,[94] it appears to have provided the rule of decision only once, and in that case the actions of the offending state were reprehensible and probably illegal on other grounds.[95] State practice is also fragmentary and inconclusive.[96] Various theoretical bases have been advanced for the obligation. The principle of good faith is mentioned. The principle of abuse of rights has been invoked. The thesis of this Article is that the obligation under consideration is a legal obligation, as demonstrated in the preceeding part. Clarification of the theoretical basis of the obligation is necessary to allow the contours of the obligation to be defined.

The obligation can logically derive from only two sources: the signed treaty itself or general international law. Since the treaty is not yet in force, and assuming that it contains no provisions giving it either retroactive or provisional effect, it is difficult to see how any pre-ratification obligations can flow directly from it. To impute binding force to a treaty not yet in force would run counter to the principle of *pacta sunt servanda*. Leaving the signed treaty aside as a basis of obligation, one possible basis for finding an obligation would be a presumed agreement of the signatories to the effect that it was their intent that such an obligation be imposed. Intent to enter into what would amount to a side agreement might be inferred from the context of the negotiations. For example, the SALT II agreement is part of an on-going process of negotiations. That process began more than ten years ago and in the contemplation of the parties is to extend into the future. If one of the signatories were to take actions prior to ratification that violated the terms of the agreement and perhaps made execution of its provisions impossible, the larger process of negotiations might be detrimentally affected. Thus an agreement to be bound by the legal obligation not to defeat the treaty's purpose might be inferred. While this theory is superficially attractive, international tribunals are reluctant to find that a state has entered into binding consensual arrangements without the clearest expressions of intent to be bound.[97]

---

94. See text accompanying notes 41-55 *supra*.

95. Megalidis v. Turkey, 8 Recueil des Décisions des Tribunaux Mixtes 386 (1928).

96. See text accompanying notes 56-60 *supra*.

97. In the *North Sea Continental Shelf Cases*, Denmark and the Netherlands argued:

> [T]he Convention [on the Continental Shelf] or the regime of the Convention, and in particular of Article 6, has become binding on the Federal Republic [of Germany] . . . because, by conduct, by public statements and proclamations, and in other ways, the Republic has unilaterally assumed the obligations of the Convention . . . .

290   *MAINE LAW REVIEW*   [Vol. 32:263

In the *Megalidis* case, the tribunal indicated that it regarded the obligation to be based on the principle of good faith.[98] Good faith, however, cannot impose a legal obligation on a state. An obligation which a state undertakes or which is imposed by some other general principle of international law may carry with it the additional obligation of good faith performance. Or it may be said that the reason an assumed obligation must be performed at all rests on the principle of good faith. Whatever is meant by the term good faith, a state is clearly not obliged to do or refrain from doing an act simply because that act is required or forbidden by notions deriving from the general principle of good faith. From one point of view, it may even be argued that "good faith requires first and foremost scrupulous respect for the freedom which international law grants to sovereign States."[99]

The International Court of Justice has recognized that the principle of good faith alone is not sufficient to give rise to an international obligation. In the *Nuclear Tests Case*,[100] the court held that a state could be bound by a unilateral declaration. The state was bound because the court found that the state officials making the declarations intended that the state should become bound by the declarations. According to the court, it is the intention to be bound that confers on a declaration the character of a legal undertaking. Once the obligation has been assumed, it may be appropriate to say that the obligation is binding because of the principle of good faith. Thus, the court in the *Nuclear Tests Case* said that "[j]ust as the very rule of *pacta sunt servanda* in the law of treaties is based on

---

As regards these contentions, it is clear that only a very definite, very consistent course of conduct on the part of a State in the situation of the Federal Republic could justify the Court in upholding them; and, if this had existed—that is to say if there had been a real intention to manifest acceptance of recognition of the applicability of the conventional régime—then it must be asked why it was that the Federal Republic did not take the obvious step of giving expression to this readiness by simply ratifying the Convention. In principle, when a number of States, including the one whose conduct is invoked, and those invoking it, have drawn up a convention specifically providing for a particular method by which the intention to become bound by the régime of the convention is to be manifested—namely by the carrying out of certain prescribed formalities (ratification, accession), it is not lightly to be presumed that a State which has not carried out these formalities, though at all times fully able and entitled to do so, has nevertheless somehow become bound in another way. [1969] I.C.J. 3, 25. *See also* Nuclear Tests Case, [1974] I.C.J. 253; A. McNair, *supra* note 21, at 6; D. O'Connell, 1 International Law 205-06 (2d ed. 1970): Bolintineanu, *Expression of Consent to Be Bound by a Treaty in Light of the 1969 Vienna Convention*, 68 Am. J. Int'l L. 672 (1974).

98. Megalidis v. Turkey, 8 Recueil des Décisions des Tribuneaux Mixtes 386, 395 (1928).

99. Schwarzenberger, *supra* note 24, at 291.

100. [1974] I.C.J. 253.

good faith, so also is the binding character of an international obligation assumed by unilateral declaration."[101]

States have an obligation, however, not to act in such a way as to injure other states.[102] Such obligations are not consensual, but are imposed by general principles of international law. International tribunals have applied such principles with specific reference to the obligation under consideration.[103] Professor Schwarzenberger regards the dicta of international tribunals as "justify[ing] the prognosis that . . . a fraudulent exercise of a right, which is alleged to be based on rules underlying the principle of sovereignty, amounts to an illegal disappointment of the expectations of the other contracting party and constitutes an international tort."[104] The Permanent Court of International Justice in the *Case concerning Certain German Interests in Polish Upper Silesia*[105] adopted a similar approach, making use of the theory of abuse of rights to evaluate the legality of certain actions of the German government during the period between the signature of the Treaty of Versailles and its entry into force. Allegedly, the acts were contrary to the terms of the Treaty and would have interfered severely with the operation of the Treaty once it did enter into force. In that case, Germany had the legal right to effect transfers of property that it owned in territories which were then under German sovereignty. Since the Treaty was not yet in force, German transfers could not be illegal as in violation of treaty obligations. The court, however, thought it proper to evaluate the legality of the German acts under the abuse of rights theory. If the German transfer could be shown to be an abuse of rights, it would be illegal. The court held, however, that an abuse of rights could not be presumed, thus placing the burden on Poland, the state alleging that an abuse of rights had occurred.[106] The court regarded the German transfer as part of the normal administration of its sovereign territory.

Resort by international tribunals to the abuse of rights theory

---

101. *Id.* at 268. *See also* Rubin, *The International Legal Effects of Unilateral Declarations,* 71 Am. J. Int'l L. 1 (1977).

102. An act of a State injurious to another State is nevertheless not an international delinquency if committed neither wilfully and maliciously nor with culpable negligency. . . . The *Corfu Channel* case between Great Britain and Albania provided an instructive example of the affirmation of the principle that there is no liability without fault.

L. Oppenheim, 1 International Law 343 (8th ed. H. Lauterpacht 1955). *See also* Corfu Channel Case, [1949] I.C.J. 4; Trail Smelter Case (United States v. Canada), 3 R. Int'l Arb. Awards 1905 (1949).

103. See text accompanying notes 41-55 *supra.*

104. Schwarzenberger, *supra* note 24, at 299. *See also* L. Oppenheim, *supra* note 102, at 345-47.

105. [1926] P.C.I.J. ser. A, No. 7, *reported in* 1 World Court Reports 510 (M. Hudson ed. 1934).

106. *Id.* at 30, 1 World Court Reports at 530.

raises two questions. Is the theory a "general principle of law recognized by civilized nations" so that it is properly part of international law, and, if so, what acts are proscribed by the theory?

The theory of abuse of rights developed in France during the second half of the nineteenth century.[107] According to the usual formulation of the theory, the use of a right may be susceptible of abuse, and thus constitute a fault giving rise to legal liability.[108] The doctrine originally developed in connection with a property owner's use of his property to cause intentional harm.[109] Thus, in an early French decision it was held to be an abuse of rights for a property owner to construct a false chimney for the sole purpose of interfering with his neighbor's view.[110] The doctrine was later extended into other areas, like abusive use of legal process,[111] and expanded to include inconsiderate, negligent, or selfish behavior as sufficient to constitute wrongful acts.[112] The abuse of rights doctrine was later

---

107. *See generally* M. PLANIOL, 2 TREATISE ON THE CIVIL LAW 476-85 (11th ed. 1959); Catala & Weir, *Delict and Torts: A Study in Parallel, Part II*, 38 TUL. L. REV. 221 (1964); Crabb, *The French Concept of Abuse of Rights*, 6 INTER-AM. L. REV. 1 (1964); de la Morandière, *Preliminary Report of the Civil Code Reform Commission of France*, 16 LA. L. REV. 1, 27-28 (1955); Guttridge, *Abuse of Rights*, 5 CAMBRIDGE L.J. 22 (1935); Walton, *Motive as an Element in Torts in the Common and in the Civil Law*, 22 HARV. L. REV. 501 (1909).

108. Professor Planiol strongly disagrees with this formulation of the theory:

This new doctrine [abusive use of rights] is based entirely on language insufficiently studied; its formula "abusive use of rights" is a logomachy, for if I use my right, my act is licit; and when it is illicit, it is because I exceed my right and act without right . . . . One must not be misled by the use of words; the right ceases where the abuse commences . . . .

What is true is that rights are almost never absolute; for the most part they are limited in their scope, and submitted, as to their exercise, to divers conditions. When one exceeds such limits, or when one does not observe the conditions, one acts in reality without right.

M. PLANIOL, *supra* note 107, at 477.

But see Walton, *supra* note 107, at 503-05. Professor Walton disagrees with Planiol and argues that the traditional formulation correctly places emphasis on the *end* sought to be achieved by the exercise of a right. "It is the intention to injure, or the want of a lawful motive, which converts an act otherwise lawful into one which is unlawful." *Id.* at 505.

Professor Politis formulates the doctrine in these terms: "[T]here is an abuse if the general interest is injured by the sacrifice of a very strong individual interest to another interest which is weaker." Politis, *Le Problème des Limitations de la Souveraineté et la Théorie de L'Abus des Droits dans Les Rapports Internationaux*, 6 RECUEIL DES COURS 5, 81 (1925) (trans. by author).

109. *See* Catala & Weir, *supra* note 107, at 222-25.

110. Court of Appeal at Colmar, May 2, 1855, [1856] D.P.II 9, *cited in* Catala & Weir, *supra* note 107, at 222-23 n.3.

111. *See* Catala & Weir, *supra* note 107, at 226; M. PLANIOL, *supra* note 107, at 480-84.

112. [I]ntentional harm as the test of liability for the abuse of a right has today secured the approval of both the judges and the legislature.

. . . .

adopted by other civil law countries.[113]

In 1925 Professor Politis presented a series of lectures at The Hague Academy of International Law in which he argued that the French doctrine of abuse of rights constituted a general principle of international law and thus could be applied by international tribunals.[114] In his book *The Function of Law in the International Community,* published in 1933, Sir Hersh Lauterpacht also enthusiastically embraced this view:

> The essence of the doctrine is that, as legal rights are conferred by the community, the latter cannot countenance their anti-social use by individuals; that the exercise of a hitherto legal right becomes unlawful when it degenerates into an abuse of rights; and that there is such an abuse of rights each time the general interest of the community is injuriously affected as the result of the sacrifice of an important social or individual interest to a less important, though hitherto legally recognized, individual right. For the determination of such abuse of rights the question of subjective fault and intention may, but need not always, be material.[115]

> [But] insistence on the presence of an intention to cause harm greatly restricts the scope of liability. . . . In many cases, indeed, the sense of what is fair and reasonable requires that a sanction be imposed on the author of the damage even though he had no intention to harm his neighbor. The defendant merely conducted himself in a negligent, imprudent or careless manner, without having been really motivated by the desire to cause damage to others.

Catala & Weir, *supra* note 107, at 227. *See also* Draft Article 147 of the Preliminary Report of the Civil Code Reform Commission of France, which extends liability beyond intentional harm:

> Every act or every fact which, by the intention of its author, by its object or by the circumstances in which it occurred, manifestly exceeds the normal exercise of a right, is not protected by the law and ultimately incurs the responsibility of its author.
>
> This provision does not apply to rights which by their nature or by virtue of the law can be exercised in a discretionary manner.

Quoted in de la Morandière, *supra* note 107, at 27 n.13. In commenting on this proposal de la Morandière notes: "[This article] is but legislative incorporation of a well-established jurisprudence which finds application in all the fields of private law (family law, property law, law of contracts and obligations, law of judicial proceedings . . .)." *Id.* at 28.

113. *See, e.g.,* Swiss Civil Code, Art. 2 which provides in pertinent part: "Every person is bound to exercise his rights and to fulfill his obligations according to the principles of good faith. The law does not protect the manifest abuse of a right." THE SWISS CIVIL CODE § 2 (I. Williams trans. 1925). *See also* German Civil Code, Article 226: "The exercise of a right is unlawful, if its purpose can only be to cause damage to another." THE GERMAN CIVIL CODE § 226 (I. Forrester, S. Goren & H. Ilgen trans. 1975). *See also* Bolgar, *Abuse of Rights in France, Germany and Switzerland: A Survey of a Recent Chapter in Legal Doctrine,* 35 LA. L. REV. 1015 (1975); Brunner, *Abuse of Rights in Dutch Law,* 37 LA. L. REV. 729 (1977); Sono & Fujioka, *The Role of the Abuse of Rights Doctrine in Japan,* 35 LA. L. REV. 1037 (1975).

114. Politis, *supra* note 108.

115. H. LAUTERPACHT, THE FUNCTION OF LAW IN THE INTERNATIONAL COMMUNITY

Lauterpacht thought that "there is . . . no difference of substance between English law and other legal systems. The major part of the law of torts is nothing else than the affirmation of the prohibition of abuse of rights."[116]

There is some disagreement as to whether the principle of abuse of rights is a general principle of law capable of application by an international tribunal. Professor Guttridge regarded the doctrine as quite unsettled in French law.[117] "[I]t must still be considered," he wrote, "to be uncertain both as regards its basis and the degree to which it is applicable to the exercise of legal rights."[118] Moreover, he regarded the doctrine as a "dangerous expedient, which should only be utilized to prevent manifest injustice,"[119] and as incompatible with the common law.[120]

While Professor Guttridge may be correct in cautioning against wholesale reliance on a doctrine that is ill-defined and provides little guidance for a court, this should not mean that in certain limited situations, clearly demarcated and understood, an international tribunal should not make use of certain aspects of the doctrine. Although approaches to problems may differ, and the abuse of rights doctrine might not fit into the scheme of common law jurisprudence, policy outcomes in similar situations do not markedly differ under common law tort concepts and the continental abuse of rights doctrine.[121] Professor Catala posited that the test for the abusive exercise of a right which has emerged in French law "compares the defendant's conduct with that of a prudent and careful citizen. The exercise of a right is unlawful when the *bonus paterfamilias* would not have exercised it in the same way as the defendant."[122] In a companion portion of the same article, Professor Weir argued that in English law "rights tend to contain their own qualifications. Very often this is in terms of 'reasonableness.' "[123]

The doctrine of abuse of rights has been specifically accepted by international tribunals.[124] The Permanent Court of International Justice has utilized the principle in the *Upper Silesia* case, already discussed,[125] and in the *Free Zones* case.[126] Furthermore, interna-

---

286 (1933).

116.   *Id.* at 295.

117.   Guttridge, *supra* note 107.

118.   *Id.* at 42.

119.   *Id.* at 43.

120.   *Id.* at 30.

121.   R. SCHLESINGER, COMPARATIVE LAW 713-15 (4th ed. 1980).

122.   Catala & Weir, *supra* note 107, at 230.

123.   *Id.* at 258.

124.   *See generally* B. CHENG, *supra* note 22, at 121-36.

125.   See text accompanying notes 41-55 *supra*.

126.   [1932] P.C.I.J., ser. A/B, No. 46, *reported in* 2 WORLD COURT REPORTS 562 (M. Hudson ed. 1935). *But see* [1927] P.C.I.J., ser. A, No. 10, *reported in* 2 WORLD

tional tribunals have accepted the more general principle that the discretionary rights of action traditionally regarded as inherent in state sovereignty may be limited in certain situations.

In the *Anglo-Norwegian Fisheries* case,[127] for example, the International Court of Justice regarded Norway's delimitation of an exclusive fisheries zone as necessarily a unilateral act. But "the validity of the delimitation with regard to other States depends upon international law."[128] Judge Alvarez, in his individual and dissenting opinions, had been the most persistent proponent of a theory limiting the discretionary rights of states. In his view, international law has moved beyond what he characterizes as the traditional individualistic regime to a regime of social interdependence. The international law of social interdependence is characterized by, among other things, a concern with both delimiting and harmonizing the rights of states, while condemning the abuse of these rights.[129]

Other individual and dissenting opinions of the International Court of Justice have supported the notion of the relativity of sovereign rights and in that context have elaborated the theory of the abuse of rights. Judge de Castro, in his separate opinion in the *Fisheries Jurisdiction* case, speaks of the abuse of rights theory as a "safety valve" rule which provides flexibility and permits more just solutions in individual cases.[130] In his separate opinion in the *Legal Consequences for States of the Continued Presence of South Africa in Namibia* case, Judge Ammoun sought to define a standard for evaluating the legality of the exercise of discretionary power:

> [T]he international judge cannot be denied the right of determining in all circumstances whether proper use has been made of the discretionary power. . . . To pass an opinion in these various situations, a judge cannot rely on his personal judgment, which is bound to be subjective and vary according to the mentality of each judge, his legal, philosophical and ethical outlook, his views on natural law and his cultural and social background. An objective criterion or standard is clearly necessary. Such a criterion is afforded by the general conduct of States and international organizations as a whole. Should the judge further decide to derive criteria from municipal precedents, which abound in such examples as the notion of the *bonus paterfamilias* . . ., or from powerful moral trends in a given country, they must still be acceptable to other countries in general or be already enshrined in the universal conscience of mankind.[131]

A state's breach of an obligation arising from the application of

---

COURT REPORTS 23 (M. Hudson ed. 1935).

127. [1951] I.C.J. 116.
128. *Id.* at 132. *See also* [1955] I.C.J. 20-21.
129. [1951] I.C.J. at 149.
130. [1974] I.C.J. 3, 96 (separate opinion of de Castro, J.).
131. [1971] I.C.J. 16, 88-89 (separate opinion of Ammoun, J.).

the abuse of rights doctrine will cause the state to be held internationally responsible. The Draft Articles on State Responsibility of the International Law Commission provide that "An Act of a State which constitutes a breach of an international obligation is an internationally wrongful act regardless of the origin, whether customary, conventional or other, of that obligation."[132]

Whatever the limitations of the theory of abuse of rights as a general principle of international law, that theory has been elaborated with sufficient specificity and has obtained sufficient support with respect to the obligation not to defeat the object or purpose of a signed but unratified treaty to provide a firm theoretical legal justification for that obligation. The following portion of this Article will examine the scope and content of that obligation.

IV. THE EXTENT OF THE OBLIGATION

The obligation not to defeat the object or purpose of a treaty commences when a state signs the treaty.[133] Draft Article 15 provided that the obligation commenced when a state "has agreed to enter into negotiations for the conclusion of the treaty,"[134] but there was general agreement at the Vienna Conference that this was clearly not a rule of international law,[135] and it was accordingly deleted from the final document.[136] While domestic law in some nations has been moving in the direction of imposing certain obligations on the parties to negotiations,[137] there is no evidence of a comparable trend at the international level.

Any obligations imposed on a signatory should terminate when that state indicates that it will not ratify the treaty, since a signatory is under no obligation to ratify a signed agreement, and may refuse ratification for any reason.[138] The Vienna Convention regards the obligation as terminated when a signatory state "shall have made its intention clear not to become a party to the treaty . . . ."[139] This provision may lead to uncertainty in application, since, as the French delegate pointed out, "the most obvious way for a State to make clear its intention not to become a party to the

---

132. Report of the International Law Commission on the Work of Its Thirtieth Session, [1978] 2 Y.B. INT'L L. COMM'N 1, 79, U.N. Doc. A/CN.4/SER.A/1978/Add.1 (Part 2).

133. Vienna Convention, *supra* note 10, at 291.

134. *United Nations Conference*, Documents, *supra* note 12, at 22.

135. *United Nations Conference*, First Session, *supra* note 10, at 97-106.

136. *United Nations Conference*, Documents, *supra* note 12, at 132.

137. *See, e.g.,* Henderson, *Promissory Estoppel and Traditional Contract Doctrine*, 78 YALE L.J. 343 (1969); Kessler & Fine, Culpa in Contrahendo, *Bargaining in Good Faith, and Freedom of Contract: A Comparative Study*, 77 HARV. L. REV. 401 (1964); Knapp, *Enforcing the Contract to Bargain*, 44 N.Y.U.L. REV. 673 (1969).

138. See note 11 *supra.*

139. Vienna Convention, *supra* note 10, at 291.

treaty was for it to frustrate the object of the treaty."[140]

The content of the obligation as it emerges from application by international tribunals is extremely uncertain and there are few interpretational guides.[141] Various principles, however, may be discerned from the relevant legal materials. First, the obligation in its present form imposes no affirmative duty upon a signatory to do certain acts or to carry out specific provisions of the treaty. The formulation of Article 18 of the Vienna Convention is thus expressive of the general rule: "A state is obliged to refrain from acts which would defeat the object and purpose of a treaty. . . ."[142] The obligation is phrased in purely negative terms—*not* to do certain acts. In the *Iloilo Claims*[143] decision, for example, an arbitral tribunal refused to impose the affirmative obligation of keeping order upon the United States in the Philippines during the period between the signing of the Treaty of Peace Between the United States and Spain and its subsequent entry into force.

Second, a signatory may engage in normal activities incident to its sovereignty after signature but prior to entry into force, even though the effect of a particular activity may be to reduce the benefit of the bargain for the other signatory or signatories. In the *Upper Silesia* case, for example, German transfers of property were upheld as coming within the state's normal administration of territory over which it had sovereignty.[144] Under this principle, the United States or Canada could engage in the fishing of stocks governed by the provisions of the East Coast Fishery Resources Agreement if such fishing were of the type and magnitude normally engaged in by that country.[145]

Third, a signatory state may do those acts whose consequences would not render provisions of the treaty impossible of performance when the treaty enters into force. The Reporter's Note to section 314 of Tentative Draft No. 1 of the American Law Institute *Restatement of the Foreign Relations Law of the United States (Revised)*

---

140. *United Nations Conference,* First Session, *supra* note 10, at 100.

141. "[T]he legal effect of sub-paragraph (b) [of Draft Article 15] was so uncertain that its application would be extremely difficult." Statement of Mr. Chang Choon Lee (Republic of Korea). *Id.* at 101.

142. Vienna Convention, *supra* note 10, at 291.

143. AMERICAN AND BRITISH CLAIMS ARBITRATION 382 (F. Nielsen reporter 1926).

144. German Interests in Polish Upper Silesia, [1926] P.C.I.J., ser. A, No. 7, *reported in* 1 WORLD COURT REPORTS 475 (M. Hudson ed. 1934). *See also* German Settlers in Poland, [1923] P.C.I.J. ser. B, No. 6, *reported in* 1 WORLD COURT REPORTS 207 (M. Hudson ed. 1934).

145. Canadian fishermen have in fact increased their catches in disputed areas of the Georges Bank fishing grounds, protesting U. S. delays in the ratification of the East Coast Fishery Resources Agreements and the related boundary settlement agreement. Kramer, *Canadian Fishermen Increase Catch,* Portland Press Herald, June 17, 1980, at 24. *See also* Irwin, *Canadians on Georges? No Worry, but —,* Portland Press Herald, June 19, 1980, at 1.

gives the following example:

> Issues have been raised as to the application of these principles to
> the Strategic Arms Limitation Treaty signed in 1979. Testing a
> new weapon in contravention of a clause prohibiting such a test
> would presumably violate the purpose of the agreement since the
> test's consequences might be irreversible. Failing to dismantle a
> weapon scheduled to be dismantled under the treaty might not de-
> feat its object since the dismantling could be effected later.[146]

There is some confusion concerning whether intentional action in
bad faith is required for a violation of the obligation or whether the
rule incorporates an objective standard. Sir Hersh Lauterpacht, in
his 1953 Report on the Law of Treaties to the International Law
Commission, said that "the purpose of that rule is to prohibit action
in bad faith deliberately aiming at depriving the other party of the
benefits which it legitimately hoped to achieve from the treaty and
for which it gave adequate consideration."[147] In Draft Article 15, the
obligation was stated in the following manner: "A state is obliged to
refrain from acts tending to frustrate. . . ."[148] The final wording of
Article 18 is: "A State is obliged to refrain from acts which would
defeat. . . ."[149] The American delegate, Mr. Kearney, favored
changing "tending to" to "which" because that change would, in his
view, emphasize the element of intent required for a violation.[150] Mr.
Riphagen of the Netherlands, however, thought that this change
would have precisely the opposite effect.[151] Subsequently, when
Draft Article 15 was referred to the Drafting Committee for further
consideration,[152] the Committee replaced the words "acts tending to
frustrate the object of a treaty" with "acts which would defeat the
object and purpose of a treaty."[153] The Committee stated that "it
wished to emphasize that that was a purely drafting change, made in
the interests of clarity. . . . The change in no way affected the substance of the provision and did not widen the obligation imposed on
States by article 15."[154]

The most likely conclusion to be drawn from the discussions in
Vienna, the prior work of the International Law Commission, and
the decisional law is that the purpose of the rule is to prevent a
signatory from claiming the benefits to which it is entitled under the
treaty while at the same time engaging in acts that would materially

---

146. RESTATEMENT (REVISED) OF THE FOREIGN RELATIONS LAW OF THE UNITED
STATES, Reporters' Note § 314, at 111 (Tent. Draft No. 1, 1980).
147. [1953] Y.B. INT'L L. COMM'N 110, U. N. Doc. A/CN.4/Ser.A/1953/Add.1.
148. *United Nations Conference*, Documents, *supra* note 12, at 22.
149. Vienna Convention, *supra* note 12, at 291.
150. *United Nations Conference*, Documents, *supra* note 12, at 131.
151. *United Nations Conference*, First Session, *supra* note 10, at 99.
152. *United Nations Conference*, Documents, *supra* note 12, at 132.
153. *United Nations Conference*, First Session, *supra* note 10, at 361.
154. *Id.*

reduce the benefits to which the other signatory or signatories are entitled. Actual proof of state of mind is probably difficult or impossible in most situations, especially since the burden of proving a violation is on the state claiming that a violation has occurred.[155] Therefore, an objective standard is necessary, and one like that proposed by Judge Ammoun, which incorporates the general conduct of both states and international organizations, would serve well to effectuate the purpose.[156]

V. Conclusion

In giving content to international obligations, like the one under consideration, extreme care must be taken not to impose legal responsibilities that exceed the reasonable expectations of the states involved. Rather than discourage actions contrary to the spirit of a signed but unratified treaty, the imposition of such legal obligations may in fact deter states from signing treaties in order to preserve their freedom of action when delay in ratification is considered a possibility. Such a consequence would be generally harmful to the process of international agreement and might especially inhibit the conclusion of multilateral agreements. The reasonable expectations of states must be ascertained and evaluated on a case-by-case basis in light of a full appreciation of the history of the particular negotiations and with a view toward effectuating the real long-term objectives of the states involved. One major consideration must be the preservation and furtherance of the particular negotiating process itself, for it is ultimately the fostering and strengthening of the process by which nations eventually reach mutually satisfactory agreements that is the real challenge facing international law.

---

155. The Free Zones Case, [1932] P.C.I.J., ser. A/B, No. 46, *reported in* 2 WORLD COURT REPORTS 562 (M. Hudson ed. 1935); German Interests in Polish Upper Silesia, [1926] P.C.I.J., ser. A, No. 7, *reported in* 1 WORLD COURT REPORTS 475 (M. Hudson ed. 1934).

156. See text accompanying note 131 *supra*, describing the test proposed by Judge Ammoun. A similar development occurred in the French doctrine of abuse of rights, where originally an evil intention had to be shown, but later such intention could be inferred from the acts themselves. See note 112 *supra*.

Part III
Treaty Integrity

[7]

UNIVERSALITY OR INTEGRITY? SOME REFLECTIONS ON RESERVATIONS TO GENERAL MULTILATERAL TREATIES*

By CATHERINE REDGWELL‡

Acceptance of and objections to reservations to general multilateral treaties raise many complex issues of international law. Notwithstanding an advisory opinion from the International Court of Justice (ICJ),[1] fifteen years of deliberation by the International Law Commission (ILC),[2] the conclusion of an international convention,[3] and extensive literature on the subject,[4] the legal effect of an objection to a reservation on the basis that it

* © Catherine Redgwell, 1994.
‡ Senior Lecturer in Law, University of Nottingham. Particular thanks are due to Gillian White, David Harris, Michael Bowman and Stephen Weatherill for their helpful comments and suggestions. The author would also like to thank Tony Aust, Frank Berman and Nigel Parker for their assistance and encouragement.

[1] *Reservations to the Convention on the Prevention and Punishment of the Crime of Genocide*, *ICJ Reports*, 1951, p. 15.

[2] For discussion of the work of the ILC on this topic, see in particular Anderson, 'Reservations to Multilateral Conventions: A Re-Examination', *International and Comparative Law Quarterly*, 13 (1964), p. 450 at pp. 463–76, and Ruda, 'Reservations to Treaties', *Recueil des cours*, 146 (1975–III), p. 97 at pp. 148–51 and 156–75.

[3] The 1969 Vienna Convention on the Law of Treaties, UN Doc. A/CONF.39/27; *UK Treaty Series*, No. 58 (1980), Cmnd 7964; *American Journal of International Law*, 63 (1969), p. 875; *International Legal Materials*, 8 (1969), p. 679. For the preparatory materials see *United Nations Conference on the Law of Treaties, Official Records*, First Session, A/CONF.39/11; Second Session, A/CONF.39/11/Add.1; Documents of the Conference, A/CONF.39/11/Add.2. See also Rosenne, *The Law of Treaties: A Guide to the Legislative History of the Vienna Convention* (1970).

[4] See in particular Anderson, loc. cit. above (n. 2); Bowett, 'Reservations to Non-Restricted Multilateral Treaties', this *Year Book*, 48 (1976–7), pp. 67–92; Elias, *The Modern Law of Treaties* (1974), ch. II; Fenwick, 'Reservations to Multilateral Treaties', *American Journal of International Law*, 45 (1951), pp. 145–8; Fitzmaurice, 'Reservations to Multilateral Conventions', *International and Comparative Law Quarterly*, 2 (1953), pp. 1–26, and 'The Law and Procedure of the International Court of Justice 1951–4: Treaty Interpretation and Other Treaty Points', this *Year Book*, 33 (1957), p. 203, at pp. 272–90; Gamble, 'Reservations to Multilateral Treaties: A Macroscopic View of State Practice', *American Journal of International Law*, 74 (1980), pp. 372–94; Gore-Booth (ed.), *Satow's Guide to Diplomatic Practice* (5th edn., 1979), ch. 3, pp. 284–92; Holloway, *Modern Trends in Treaty Law* (1967), Book 3, Part 1; Horn, *Reservations and Interpretative Declarations to Multilateral Treaties* (1988); Imbert, *Les Réserves aux traités multilatéraux* (1978); Jennings and Watts (eds.), *Oppenheim's International Law*, vol. 1 (9th edn., 1991), pp. 1241–8; Kearney and Dalton, 'The Treaty on Treaties', *American Journal of International Law*, 64 (1970), p. 495 at pp. 509–14; Koh, 'Reservations to Multilateral Treaties: How International Legal Doctrine Reflects World Vision', *Harvard International Law Journal*, 23 (1982), pp. 71–116; Lauterpacht, *The Development of International Law by the International Court* (1958), pp. 186–90 and 372–4; Malkin, 'Reservations to Multilateral Treaties', this *Year Book*, 7 (1926), pp. 141–62; McNair, *The Law of Treaties* (1961), ch. 9; Reuter, *Introduction au droit des traités* (2nd rev. edn., 1985); Rosenne, *Developments in the Law of Treaties 1945–1986* (1989), and op. cit. above (n. 3); Ruda, 'Reservations to Treaties', loc. cit. above (n. 2); Schwarzenberger, *International Law as applied by International Courts and Tribunals* (3rd edn., 1957), vol. 1, pp. 442–5; Sinclair, 'Vienna Conference on the Law of Treaties', *International and Comparative Law Quarterly*, 19 (1970), p. 47 at pp. 53–60, and *The Vienna Convention on the Law of Treaties* (2nd edn., 1984).

246   RESERVATIONS TO MULTILATERAL TREATIES

is incompatible with the object and purpose of the treaty is unclear. It is the purpose of this article to examine this issue in light of the development of this difficult area of treaty law over the past several decades.[5] Such examination reveals inconsistent State practice and continuing confusion regarding the legal effect of an objection to a reservation as incompatible with the object and purpose of the treaty, thus indicating a need for the reconsideration of this topic in a neutral forum such as the International Law Commission. Such reconsideration may be imminent since in its 1993 Report the ILC has proposed the topic of reservations to general multilateral treaties for inclusion in its current programme of work.

I. THE TRADITIONAL RULE

Traditionally a reservation[6] made subsequent to the conclusion of a treaty required the unanimous acceptance of all other treaty parties, unless the treaty otherwise provided. If any State entitled to object to the reservation did so, either the reservation was withdrawn or the reserving State was not regarded as a party to the treaty. The traditional unanimity rule was 'based on the concept of the integrity of the terms of the treaty which had been freely negotiated by the prospective parties, and it provided an unambiguous answer to the question whether a State which had submitted an instrument of ratification or accession, accompanied by a reservation, had become a party to the treaty generally'.[7] This approach is similar to that adopted in the law of contract, where once negotiations are concluded the contract may only be modified with the consent of the parties. In a contract theory of treaty formation, the reserving State offers to become a party to a treaty without abiding by certain provisions, an offer which must be

---

[5] This paper is not concerned with reservations to treaties which are the constituent instrument of an international organization nor with treaties where 'a reservation requires acceptance by all the parties' because 'it appears from the limited number of the negotiating States and the object and purpose of the treaty that the application of the treaty in its entirety between all the parties is an essential condition of the consent of each one to be bound by the treaty' (Article 20(2) and (3) V.CLT). Nor is it concerned with bilateral treaties where the unanimity rule operates satisfactorily in a reciprocal context: on this point see Fitzmaurice, *The Law and Procedure of the International Court of Justice*, vol. 1 (1986), at p. 412, n. 3.

[6] A definition of 'reservation' is found in Article 2 of the Vienna Convention on the Law of Treaties, which states:
'reservation means a unilateral statement, however phrased or named, made by a State when signing, ratifying, accepting, approving, or acceding to a treaty, whereby it purports to exclude or modify the legal effect of certain provisions of the treaty in their application to that State . . .'
It is beyond the scope of this article to discuss the difficulties in determining when a unilateral statement amounts to a reservation, and of distinguishing between reservations and interpretative declarations. See, generally, Bowett, loc. cit. above (n. 4), at pp. 67–70; on the latter point see McRae, 'The Legal Effect of Interpretative Declarations', this *Year Book*, 49 (1978), pp. 155–73, and Horn, op. cit. above (n. 4).

[7] *Official Records*, First Session, loc. cit. above (n. 3), at p. 113, para. 71 (Sinclair). For further discussion of the traditional rule, see McNair, op. cit. above (n. 4), ch. 9; Ruda, loc. cit. above (n. 2), ch. 4; Malkin, loc. cit. above (n. 4); and Fitzmaurice, loc. cit. above (n. 4) (*ICLQ*), at pp. 11–12. See also the four-judge dissent in the *Genocide* case, *ICJ Reports*, 1951, pp. 31 ff., who put the integrity of the Convention before universal participation in it and espoused the unanimity rule.

accepted by the other parties in order to constitute that reserving State a party to the treaty.[8]

Another view which gained currency throughout the decades of the 1950s and 1960s was the importance of widespread participation in the treaty.[9] The use of reservations was viewed as facilitating the process of States becoming parties to treaties notwithstanding widely divergent political and economic systems. With a larger number of States negotiating multilateral treaties, the desirability of universal participation was weighed against maintenance of the integrity of the treaty. It was argued that without the flexibility necessary to accommodate diverse State interests, the process of multilateral treaty-making would prove increasingly difficult with adverse consequences for international co-operation.[10] In addition, the use of the majority principle to facilitate the conclusion of multilateral treaties increased the need for certain States to make reservations.[11] A flexible system which does not require the consent of all contracting States to a reservation was viewed as meeting some of these concerns. It was this view which ultimately prevailed in the International Law Commission and the International Court of Justice, and is reflected in the 1969 Vienna Convention on the Law of Treaties.

II. THE *GENOCIDE* CASE

The first major departure from the unanimity rule is found in the advisory opinion of the International Court of Justice in the *Genocide* case.[12] In 1950 the General Assembly became seised of the problem of

---

[8] Indeed, the reserving State may be viewed as making a counter-offer to the other parties, which must be accepted by them in order to constitute the reserving State a party to the treaty. However, unlike traditional contract analysis, the counter-offer does not extinguish the original offer. Thus should the other parties refuse to accept the reservations it is still open to the reserving State to become a party to the treaty without the reservations. For brief discussion of the contract theory of formation, see Sinclair, loc. cit. above (n. 4) (*ICLQ*), at p. 54; McNair, op. cit. above (n. 4), p. 160. See also the submission of M. Charles Rousseau to the ICJ in the *Genocide* case (14 April 1951), reproduced in Kiss, *Répertoire de la pratique française en matière de droit international public*, vol. 1, p. 280, para. 557; Rousseau, *Droit international public* (1970), vol. 1, pp. 121–4; Jennings, 'Les Traités', in Bedjaoui (ed.), *Droit international: bilan et perspectives* (1991), ch. 6, p. 151, para. 18.

[9] See, for example, the UNITAR study by Schachter, Nawaz and Fried entitled *Towards Wider Acceptance of UN Treaties* (1971). Chapter 8 examines the issue of the relation of reservations to acceptance. It opens with the statement that '[i]t is reasonable to assume that the right to make reservations to multilateral treaties facilitates their wider acceptance' and quotes the following observation by the ILC in its commentary on draft Articles on the Law of Treaties:
'a power to formulate reservations must in the nature of things tend to make it easier for some States to execute the act necessary to bind themselves finally to participating in the treaty and therefore tend to promote a greater measure of universality in the application of the treaty.' (*General Assembly Official Records*, 21st session, Supplement No. 9, A/6309/Rev.'1, p. 38)

[10] The United Kingdom representative at the Vienna Conference, whilst noting that his Government had been a strong advocate of the traditional unanimity doctrine, accepted that the doctrine 'might in modern times be a counsel of perfection, since it had been rendered less practicable by the great expansion of the membership of the international community in recent years': loc. cit. above (n. 3), at p. 114, para. 72 (Sinclair). See also ILC Report, ibid., p. 38, para. 12.

[11] *Genocide* case, loc. cit. above (n. 1), p. 22.

[12] An exception to the unanimity rule, which was drawn upon by the ICJ in its advisory opinion, was the practice of the Pan American Union, the precursor of the Organization of American States. In 1932

248   RESERVATIONS TO MULTILATERAL TREATIES

reservations to multilateral conventions because of the imminent entry into force of the 1948 Convention on the Prevention and Punishment of the Crime of Genocide, which contained no provision regarding reservations.[13] As the depositary the Secretary-General was required by Article XIII of that Convention to draw up a procès-verbal on receipt of the twentieth instrument of ratification or accession, with the Convention coming into force 90 days thereafter.[14] The issues confronting the Secretary-General were whether instruments with reservations should be included within this total, and the legal effect of objections to reservations. Discussion of these issues within the International Law Commission, which had commenced the codification of the law of treaties as one of its first topics, was brief (one meeting) and inconclusive. The Commission's 1950 Report simply notes with respect to reservations that whilst there was general agreement that a reservation required the consent of all parties to become effective, application of the general principles to the wide range of specific circumstances encountered in international treaty-making required further consideration.[15]

the Governing Board of the PAU approved the following three rules on the juridical effects of reservations:

'With respect to the juridical status of treaties ratified, with reservations, which have not been accepted, the Governing Board of the Pan American Union understands that:

1. The treaty shall be in force, in the form in which it was signed, as between those countries which ratify it without reservations, in the terms in which it was originally drafted and signed.

2. It shall be in force as between the governments which ratify it with reservations and the signatory States which accept the reservations in the form in which the treaty may be modified by said reservations.

3. It shall not be in force between a government which may have ratified with reservations and another which may have already ratified, and which does not accept such reservations' (ibid., p. 17). There is no requirement for a reservation to be compatible with the object and purpose of the treaty. For a fuller description of the Pan American practice, see Ruda, loc. cit. above (n. 2), at pp. 115–33; Rosenne, op. cit. above (n. 4), at pp. 354 ff.; Fitzmaurice, loc. cit. above (n. 4) (*ICLQ*), pp. 13–22; Fenwick, loc. cit. above (n. 4), at pp. 145–8; and Koh, loc. cit. above (n. 4), at pp. 80–4.

The 1932 PAU approach was modified by a new set of OAS standards in 1973 in accordance with the VCLT: *United States Digest of International Law*, 1973, p. 179; see Harris, *Cases and Materials on Public International Law* (4th edn., 1991), p. 754, n. 66. The standards are also reproduced as Documents 19 and 23 respectively in Horn, op. cit. above (n. 4), at pp. 501 and 503. However, neither the 1932 nor the 1973 standards contain a reference to the compatibility test. In 1985 the Inter-American Juridical Committee proposed new standards viewed as more consistent with the VCLT with explicit reference therein to compatibility with the object and purpose of the treaty: cf. Horn, ibid., at pp. 504 ff.

[13] Adopted by GA Res. 260 (III) of 9 December 1948; *UN Treaty Series*, vol. 78, p. 277; *UK Treaty Series*, No. 58 (1970), Cmnd 4421. The Convention entered into force on 12 January 1951, four months before the ICJ rendered its opinion in the *Genocide* case, having received the requisite number of ratifications and accessions without reservation. See further n. 21, below.

[14] For a fuller account of the depositary practice of the UN, see Rosenne, op. cit. above (n. 4), at pp. 424–36; see also Imbert, 'A l'Occasion de l'entrée en vigueur de la Convention de Vienne sur le droit des traités: réflexions sur la pratique suivie par le secrétaire général des Nations Unies dans l'exercice de ses fonctions de dépositaire', *Annuaire français de droit international*, 26 (1980), pp. 524–41 (practice pre- and post-VCLT); and Horn, 'Certain Questions Relating to the Functions of Depositaries of Treaties', *Finnish Yearbook of International Law*, 1 (1990), p. 145.

[15] *Yearbook of the International Law Commission*, 1950, vol. 2, p. 381, para. 164. The Commission had before it the First Report on the Law of Treaties prepared by the Special Rapporteur, James Brierly, which was based on the principle of unanimous consent. See Rosenne, ibid., at p. 425.

The matter was also debated in the Sixth Committee, which failed to achieve consensus. The Secretary-General's Report[16] and the attached UK memorandum[17] advocated the unanimity rule, whilst a Uruguayan memorandum[18] set forth the more flexible Latin American practice which did not require unanimity.[19] Indeed, the 'profound divergence of views' expressed in the Sixth Committee was referred to in the advisory opinion of the ICJ in support of the proposition that the conception of the absolute integrity of a convention had not been transformed into a rule of international law.[20] In any event the need for an immediate answer to the Secretary-General's dilemma disappeared when, on 16 October 1950, the Secretary-General informed the Sixth Committee that the obligation to draw up a procès-verbal could be met without determining the effect of reservations.[21] With more time to consider the matter, the General Assembly adopted a resolution[22] on 16 November 1950 which requested the following:

(i) an advisory opinion from the International Court of Justice on certain questions concerning the Genocide Convention;[23]
(ii) that the International Law Commission, in the course of its work on the codification of the law of treaties, should 'study the question of reservations to multilateral conventions both from the point of view of codification and from that of progressive development' and give priority to this study; and
(iii) in so far as the depositary practice of the UN was concerned, that the Secretary General should follow previous practice 'without prejudice to the

---

[16] UN Doc. A/1372 (20 September 1950). The Secretary-General summarized his position as follows: 'A State may make a reservation when signing, ratifying or acceding to a convention, prior to its entry into force, only with the consent of all States which have ratified or acceded thereto up to the date of entry into force; and may do so after the date of entry into force only with the consent of all States which have theretofore ratified or acceded': *General Assembly Official Records*, Fifth Session, Agenda item 56, A/1372, at p. 8, para. 46. See further Fenwick, loc. cit. above (n. 4), at pp. 146–7.

[17] Ibid., UN Doc. A/1372, Annex II.

[18] Ibid., UN Doc. A/C.6/L.117.

[19] See above, n. 2.

[20] Loc. cit. above (n. 1), at p. 26. For further discussion of debates in the Sixth Committee, see Liang, 'Notes on Legal Questions Concerning the United Nations', *American Journal of International Law*, 46 (1952), pp. 483–503.

[21] He had received a further five instruments of ratification or accession, bringing the total to 22 such instruments, only 2 of which contained reservations (the Philippines and Bulgaria). The Convention required 20 ratifications to enter into force.

[22] GA Res. 478(V), *General Assembly Official Records*, Fifth Session, Supplement No. 20, at p. 74, UN Doc. A/C.6/L.125 (16 November 1950).

[23] The following questions were put to the International Court of Justice:
'In so far as concerns the Convention on the Prevention and Punishment of the Crime of Genocide, in the event of a State ratifying or acceding to the Convention subject to a reservation made either on ratification or on accession, or on signature followed by ratification:
I. Can the reserving State be regarded as being a party to the Convention while still maintaining its reservation if the reservation is objected to by one or more of the parties to the Convention but not by others?
II. If the answer to question I is in the affirmative, what is the effect of the reservation as between the reserving State and: (*a*) The parties which object to the reservation? (*b*) Those which accept it?
III. What would be the legal effect as regards the answer to question I if an objection to a reservation is made: (*a*) By a signatory which has not yet ratified? (*b*) By a State entitled to sign or accede but which has not yet done so?'
(Ibid.)

250   RESERVATIONS TO MULTILATERAL TREATIES

legal effect of objections to reservations as it may be recommended by the
General Assembly at a later session'.[24]

On 18 May 1951 the International Court of Justice rendered its opinion
on *Reservations to the Convention on the Prevention and Punishment of the
Crime of Genocide*.[25] The substance of the opinion, and reaction to it, is
well known. By a majority of seven votes to five the Court rejected the
unanimity rule, which it viewed as directly inspired by a notion of contract
inappropriate to a multilateral convention of the nature of the Genocide
Convention.[26] In respect of such a convention 'one cannot speak of individual advantages or disadvantages to States, or of the maintenance of a perfect
contractual balance between rights and duties'.[27] This is because 'the contracting States do not have any interests of their own; they merely have,
one and all, a common interest, namely, the accomplishment of those high
purposes which are the raison d'être of the convention'.[28] The Court there-

---

[24] Ibid. See Fenwick, 'Reservations to Multilateral Conventions: The Report of the International
Law Commission', *American Journal of International Law*, 46 (1952), pp. 110–23. In 1952 the General
Assembly directed the Secretary-General to conform with the opinion of the ICJ in the *Genocide* case in
respect of future multilateral conventions, without passing upon the legal effect of documents containing reservations or objections but communicating them to all States concerned, 'leaving it to each State
to draw legal consequences from such communications': GA Res. 598 (VI), *General Assembly Official
Records*, Sixth Session, Supplement No. 20, at p. 84. In 1959, when the issue of India's reservation to
the IMCO Convention arose, the General Assembly affirmed this practice and extended it to pre-1952
treaties which did not contain contrary provisions: GA Res. 1452 B (XIV), *General Assembly Official
Records*, Fourteenth Session, Supplement No. 16, at p. 56. See Schachter, 'The Question of Treaty
Reservations at the 1959 General Assembly', *American Journal of International Law*, 54 (1960),
p. 372; and Mendelson, 'Reservations to the Constitutions of International Organizations', this *Year
Book*, 45 (1971), pp. 141–69. See also Rosenne, op. cit. above (n. 4), at pp. 431–3, and Holloway, op.
cit. above (n. 4), at pp. 510–14 and 519–27.
[25] Loc. cit. above (n. 1).
[26] Ibid., p. 22. For similar reasoning, see advisory opinion No. OC-2/82 of 24 September 1982,
requested by the Inter-American Commission on Human Rights of the Inter-American Court of
Human Rights in *The Effect of Reservations on the Entry into Force of the American Convention on
Human Rights (Arts. 74 and 75)*, *International Legal Materials*, 22 (1983), p. 37, at pp. 46–8, paras.
28–31. Under consideration there was Article 75 of the American Convention on Human Rights, which
provides that: 'This Convention shall be subject to reservations only in conformity with the provisions
of the Vienna Convention on the Law of Treaties signed on May 23, 1969'. The Inter-American Court
held that the effect of this article was expressly to authorize States to make appropriate reservations to
the Convention 'provided the reservations are not incompatible with the object and purpose of the
treaty. As such', the Court continued, 'they can be said to be governed by Article 20(1) of the Vienna
Convention and, consequently, do not require acceptance by any other State Party': ibid., p. 49, para.
35. Since the advisory opinion was restricted to consideration of questions bearing on the entry into
force of the Convention, other matters arising from Article 75 were not addressed (ibid., para. 39). In
particular, there was no discussion of what amounts to an incompatible reservation and upon whom a
determination of compatibility should fall. If, however, a State viewed a reservation as incompatible
and wished to dispute its validity, the Court clearly envisaged such a State making use of the advisory or
adjudicatory mechanisms of the Convention: Davidson, *The Inter-American Court of Human Rights*
(1992), at p. 144.
[27] Loc. cit. above (n. 1), p. 23.
[28] Ibid. 'As a result', notes Imbert, 'one of the basic principles governing convention-based relations
and the system of reservations, that of reciprocity, would seem to disappear': Imbert, 'Reservations and
Human Rights Conventions', *Human Rights Review*, 6 (1981), p. 28, at p. 33. This article is a translation of a report presented by Imbert at the Fifth International Colloquy on the European Convention on
Human Rights in Frankfurt, 1980.

fore opined that a reserving State could be considered a party to the Genocide Convention notwithstanding objections to its reservation by one or
more parties but not by others, so long as the reservation was compatible
with the object and purpose of the Convention. The Court sought to
achieve a compromise between universal participation, slavish adherence to
which risked frustrating the purposes of the Convention, and the absolute
integrity of the treaty, which precluded even minor reservations compatible
with the purpose of the Convention unless accepted by all other contracting
parties. While it was inconceivable, said the Court, that an objection to a
minor reservation should lead to the complete exclusion from the Convention of one or more States, contrary to the goal of universal participation in
the Convention sought by the General Assembly, 'even less could the contracting parties have intended to sacrifice the very object of the Convention
in favour of a vain desire to secure as many participants as possible'.[29]

The foundation of the Court's opinion is the criterion of compatibility
with the object and purpose of the treaty, which functions as a limiting factor upon the freedom both to make reservations and to object to them.[30] If a
reservation is compatible, but a State none the less objects to it, the Court
considered that an understanding between the reserving and objecting
States could be achieved with the effect that the treaty entered into force
between them, but for the clauses affected by the reservation.[31] If incompatible, the reserving State could not be regarded as a party and a party
objecting to a reservation as incompatible would be entitled to consider that
the reserving State was not a party.[32] In the event of a divergence of views
as to the compatibility of a reservation, the Court suggested recourse to the
dispute settlement provisions of the Convention or special agreement.[33]

The opinion has been criticized on a number of grounds, including the
failure of the Court to adhere to *lex lata*, perceived as the unanimity rule,
and the uncertainty and subjectivity of the 'object and purpose' criterion.[34]
The joint dissenting opinion of Judges Guerrero, McNair, Read and Hsu

[29] Loc. cit. above (n. 1), p. 24. Exclusion, said the Court, would not only restrict the scope of application of the Convention 'but would detract from the authority of the moral and humanitarian principles
which are its basis'.

[30] 'It follows', said the Court, 'that it is the compatibility of a reservation with the object and purpose
of the Convention that must furnish the criterion for the attitude of the State in making the reservation
on accession *as well as for* the appraisal by the State in objecting to the reservation': ibid., emphasis
added. But see the ILC's abandonment of the application of the compatibility criterion to objections to
reservations, below, n. 52.

[31] Loc. cit. above (n. 1), p. 27. The four-judge minority (Judges Guerrero, McNair, Read and Hsu
Mo) objected to this solution as they could not 'regard the admissibility of a reservation as a private
affair to be settled between pairs of States' which might come to different understandings in respect of
the same reservations (p. 45).

[32] Ibid., p. 29.

[33] Article IX of the Genocide Convention provides for the compulsory jurisdiction of the Court;
however, as the four-judge minority points out, eight States had already made reservations against or in
relation to this article: ibid., p. 45.

[34] Referring to the advisory opinion, Satow notes that 'This sibylline pronouncement was initially
greeted with less than enthusiasm': op. cit. above (n. 4), at p. 288, para. 33.14. For reaction in the
Sixth Committee and the ILC, see Liang, loc. cit. above (n. 20).

Mo[35] is a thorough and scholarly defence of the unanimity rule as an existing rule of international law. They criticize the majority for articulating a
new rule devoid of any legal basis which, moreover, is so difficult to apply
that finality and certainty are lost.[36] This view was widely shared in contemporaneous literature by, amongst others, Fitzmaurice,[37] Schwarzenberger[38] and Brierly.[39] Less condemnatory is Sir Hersch Lauterpacht, who
regards the *Genocide* case as a significant example of judicial legislation.
Such legislation should not 'attempt to lay down all the details of the application of the principle on which it is based', since it 'is not, and ought not to
be, like legislative codification by statute'.[40] On a general basis, Fitzmaurice
is prepared to find value in the Court's clear indication 'that the right of
reservation, even where it exists, is never an unlimited one' and 'the nature
of one important element, amongst others, that the parties should bear in
mind in deciding whether to object to a given reservation or not'.[41] He
accepts that some mitigation of the unanimity rule may be appropriate
where 'general multilateral conventions of a humanitarian or sociological
type' are concerned, which possess 'markedly non-contractual elements as
to their substance and are not "reciprocal" in their mode of application'.[42]
Thus normative types of treaties with obligations owed *erga omnes*, such as
the Genocide Convention, could be distinguished from contractual types of
treaties with specific obligations owed to specific States where the unani-

[35] Loc. cit. above (n. 1), at pp. 31 ff. Writing in 1957, Schwarzenberger referred to this as 'one of the
most powerful and hard-hitting dissenting opinions in the whole history of the World Court'. See
volume 1 of his *International Law as applied by International Courts and Tribunals* (3rd edn., 1957),
at p. 445. Judge Alvarez arrived at the same conclusions as the four-judge minority, but for different
reasons delivered in a jointly dissenting opinion: see *ICJ Reports*, 1951, pp. 49–55.
[36] Ruda highlights five difficulties with the new rule identified in the joint dissenting opinion:
'(i) What was to be understood by "the object and purpose of the convention"?
(ii) There would be no legal certitude, because every State would be free to arrive at the conclusions
most convenient to itself; only a judicial decision could reach a solution.
(iii) It had been said that in the Genocide Convention there were rules indicating the judicial procedure
for settlement of such a controversy; but these were precisely the provisions that had been the object of
most reservations.
(iv) The suggestion of the Advisory Opinion that the Convention could enter partially into effect
between the reserving and the objecting State if there is an understanding to this effect, would create a
chaotic situation because "different pairs of States may come to different understandings upon the same
reservations and . . . some States may consider a reserving State to be a party while others do not".
[p. 45]
(v) The new rule created many problems for the depositary as to whether or not a State was a party
when some States accepted the reservation and others rejected it' (loc. cit. above (n. 2), at pp. 146–7).
[37] The compatibility criterion was uncertain, subjective and unworkable in his opinion: see loc. cit.
above (n. 4) (*ICLQ*), including the authorities noted at p. 5, n. 10; and op. cit. above (n. 5), at p. 416,
n. 3.
[38] Op. cit. above (n. 4).
[39] *The Law of Nations* (5th edn., 1955), pp. 249–50. This is consistent with the view Professor
Brierly took in his preliminary report on the law of treaties for the ILC. He was appointed in 1949 as the
first Special Rapporteur on the topic. For further discussion of the ILC's work, see further section III,
below.
[40] Op. cit. above (n. 4), at pp. 189–90.
[41] Loc. cit. above (n. 4) (this *Year Book*), at p. 286.
[42] Ibid., p. 277.

mity rule might continue to be applied.[43] On the basis of this distinction, attempts were made to restrict the Court's reasoning to the Genocide Convention or to conventions of that type requiring by their nature universal participation.[44] In 1951 the International Law Commission stated in its Annual Report to the General Assembly that it 'believes that the criterion of the compatibility of a reservation with the objects and purposes of a multilateral convention, applied by the International Court of Justice to the Convention on Genocide, is not suitable for application to multilateral conventions in general'.[45]

III. THE ILC DRAFT ARTICLES AND THE 1969 VIENNA CONVENTION ON THE LAW OF TREATIES

Notwithstanding considerable criticism of the majority opinion in the *Genocide* case, support for the unanimity principle waned.[46] The ILC, initially a staunch supporter of the traditional rule, had kept under review the question of reservations to treaties,[47] and in the course of doing so it experienced a change of heart. This is reflected in a preliminary set of Articles in 1962 which proposed a flexible system for reservations. With respect to treaties silent as to reservations, 'the Commission was agreed that the Court's principle of "compatibility with the object and purpose of the treaty" is one suitable for adoption as a general criterion of the legitimacy of reservations to multilateral treaties and objections to them'.[48] This flexible

[43] See further Fitzmaurice, loc. cit. above (n. 4) (*ICLQ*), at p. 10, and (this *Year Book*) at p. 277. Unlike 'contractual treaties' which 'involve obligations moving between the parties *inter se* on a basis of reciprocity', normative conventions involve 'obligations assumed *erga omnes* on an absolute and self-existent basis', '[t]he parties to which do not so much acquire rights and enjoy reciprocal benefits as undertake to carry out obligations and observe certain standards of behaviour': ibid., p. 277, n. 2 and n. 1, respectively. He defines 'normative' as '[a] convenient term for that class of Convention . . . which lays down principles of conduct, sets up standards of behaviour, or creates new rules of law': loc. cit. above (n. 4) (*ICLQ*), p. 13, n. 23. The VCLT does not distinguish between normative and other types of treaties.

[44] The four-judge minority noted that the opinion sought to limit the new rule to the Genocide Convention but expressed some scepticism regarding identification of unique features of that Convention which would differentiate it from other humanitarian conventions: loc. cit. above (n. 1), at p. 47; for Sixth Committee discussions see Liang, loc. cit. above (n. 20). Fitzmaurice highlights the difficulties in applying the Pan American system to conventions of the normative type: loc. cit. above (n. 4) (*ICLQ*) at pp. 13 ff; a point echoed by Anderson, loc. cit. above (n. 2), at p. 473.

[45] *Yearbook of the International Law Commission*, 1951, vol. 2, p. 128, para. 24. This report was in response to a request from the UN General Assembly: see above, text accompanying nn. 23 and 24.

[46] Anderson, loc. cit. above (n. 2), at p. 456; see also Holloway, op. cit. above (n. 4), at p. 528.

[47] Reports were produced by Brierly (1950) and Lauterpacht (1953) supporting the traditional rule, though Lauterpacht also proposed four alternate texts which departed to some extent from the unanimity doctrine. Fitzmaurice (1956) produced a report supporting a modified unanimity rule, whilst Waldock (1962) embraced the more flexible approach of the *Genocide* case.

[48] *Yearbook of the International Law Commission*, 1962, vol. 2, pp. 178–9. The Commission proceeded to comment that the difficulty with the compatibility principle 'lies in the process by which that principle is to be applied, and especially where there is no tribunal or other organ vested with standing competence to interpret the treaty': ibid. After considering various solutions, including a collegiate system, the Commission in the end opted for the flexible system: see Sinclair, *The Vienna Convention on the Law of Treaties* (2nd edn., 1984), at pp. 60–1, and *Yearbook of the International Law Commission*, 1962, vol. 2, p. 180. The Commission considered that 'what is essential to ensure both the effectiveness and the integrity of the treaty is that a sufficient number of States should become parties to it, accepting

254   RESERVATIONS TO MULTILATERAL TREATIES

system became Articles 16[49] and 17[50] of the draft Articles on the Law of
Treaties adopted by the ILC at its eighteenth session in 1966,[51] which in
turn formed the basis for Articles 19 and 20 of the 1969 Vienna Convention
on the Law of Treaties.[52]

In the Commentary to draft Articles 16 and 17 the Commission indicated
that the Articles need to be read together 'because the legal effect of a reservation, when formulated, is dependent on its acceptance or rejection by the

the great bulk of its provisions': *Yearbook of the International Law Commission*, 1966, vol. 2, p. 38,
para. 12.
    [49] Article 18 in the 1962 and 1965 drafts. Article 16 reads as follows:
'A State may, when signing, ratifying, accepting, approving or acceding to a treaty, formulate a reservation unless:
(*a*) The reservation is prohibited by treaty;
(*b*) The treaty authorizes specified reservations which do not include the reservation in question; or
(*c*) In cases where the treaty contains no provisions regarding reservations, the reservation is incompat-
    ible with the object and purpose of the treaty.'
Article 16 became, in modified form, Article 19 of the Vienna Convention on the Law of Treaties,
which reads as follows:
'A State may, when signing, ratifying, accepting, approving or acceding to a treaty, formulate a reservation unless:
(*a*) the reservation is prohibited by the treaty;
(*b*) the treaty provides that only specified reservations, which do not include the reservation in question,
    may be made; or
(*c*) in cases not falling under sub-paragraph (*a*) and (*b*), the reservation is incompatible with the object
    and purpose of the treaty.'
    [50] Articles 19 and 20 in the 1962 draft and Article 19 in the 1965 draft. Article 17 read as follows:
'1. A reservation expressly or impliedly authorized by the treaty does not require any subsequent accept-
    ance by the other contracting States unless the treaty so provides.
2. When it appears from the limited number of the negotiating States and the object and purpose of the
    treaty that the application of the treaty in its entirety between all the parties is an essential condition
    of the consent of each one to be bound by the treaty, a reservation requires acceptance by all the par-
    ties.
3. When a treaty is a constituent instrument of an international organization, the reservation requires
    the acceptance of the competent organ of that organization, unless the treaty otherwise provides.
4. In cases not falling under the preceding paragraphs of this article:
    (*a*) Acceptance by another contracting State of the reservation constitutes the reserving State a party
        to the treaty in relation to that State if or when the treaty is in force;
    (*b*) An objection by another contracting State to a reservation precludes the entry into force of the
        treaty as between the objecting and reserving States unless a contrary intention is expressed by
        the objecting State;
    (*c*) An act expressing the State's consent to be bound by the treaty and containing a reservation is
        effective as soon as at least one other contracting State has accepted the reservation.
5. For the purposes of paragraphs 2 and 4 a reservation is considered to have been accepted by a State if
    it shall have raised no objection to the reservation by the end of a period of twelve months after it was
    notified of the reservation or by the date on which it expressed its consent to be bound by the treaty,
    whichever is later.'
Article 17 became, with modifications, Article 20 of the Vienna Convention on the Law of Treaties,
which states:
'1. A reservation expressly authorized by a treaty does not require any subsequent acceptance by the
    other contracting States unless the treaty so provides.
2. When it appears from the limited number of the negotiating States and the object and purpose of a
    treaty that the application of the treaty in its entirety between all the parties is an essential condition
    of the consent of each one to be bound by the treaty, a reservation requires acceptance by all the par-
    ties.
3. When a treaty is a constituent instrument of an international organization and unless it otherwise pro-
    vides, a reservation requires the acceptance of the competent organ of that organization.

other States concerned'.[53] One paragraph alone is devoted to commentary upon Article 16, wherein the Commission notes that the compatibility of a reservation with the object and purpose of a treaty 'is in every case very much a matter of the appreciation of the acceptability of the reservation by the other contracting States'.[54] For this reason, the Commission considered that Article 16 'has, therefore, to be read in close conjunction with the provisions of article 17 regarding acceptance of and objection to reservations'.[55] As is discussed further below, at the Diplomatic Conference this language gave rise to some understandable confusion as to whether an incompatible reservation under Article 16 was open to acceptance by States in accordance with Article 17.

Article 16 sets forth three prohibitions. A reservation may be formulated unless: (*a*) the reservation is prohibited by the treaty; (*b*) the treaty authorizes specified reservations, which do not include the particular reservation in question; or (*c*) the treaty contains no provisions regarding reservations, but the reservation is incompatible with the object and purpose of the treaty. These are the prohibitions found in Article 19 of the Vienna Convention, but with a significant change to the scope of paragraphs (*b*) and (*c*). The net effect of these changes is to expand the scope of permissible reservations subject only to the compatibility test under Article 19(*c*). It is

---

4. In cases not falling under the preceding paragraphs and unless the treaty otherwise provides:

    (*a*) acceptance by another contracting State of a reservation constitutes the reserving State a party to the treaty in relation to that other State if or when the treaty is in force for those States;

    (*b*) an objection by another contracting State to a reservation does not preclude the entry into force of the treaty as between the objecting and reserving State unless a contrary intention is definitely expressed by the objecting State;

    (*c*) an act expressing a State's consent to be bound by the treaty and containing a reservation is effective as soon as at least one other contracting State has accepted the reservation.

5. For the purposes of paragraphs 2 and 4 and unless the treaty otherwise provides, a reservation is considered to have been accepted by a State if it shall have raised no objection to the reservation by the end of a period of twelve months after it was notified of the reservation or by the date on which it expressed its consent to be bound by the treaty, whichever is later.'

[51] *Yearbook of the International Law Commission*, 1966, vol. 2; also reproduced in *United Nations Conference on the Law of Treaties, Official Records*, Documents of the Conference, A/CONF. 39/11/ Add.2.

[52] For the texts of Articles 19 and 20, compared with the ILC Draft Articles 16 and 17, see nn. 49 and 50, above.

One significant change occurred to the 1966 ILC text. The Commission had originally envisaged that the compatibility criterion would apply to objections as well as to reservations. However, Government responses to the draft Articles indicated a desire for more freedom of action, which the Commission accepted. The application of the compatibility criterion to objections was dropped, the Commission explaining that '[a]lthough an objection to a reservation normally indicates a refusal to enter into treaty relations on the basis of the reservation, objections are sometimes made for reasons of principle or policy without the intention of precluding the entry into force of the treaty between the objecting and reserving States': *Yearbook of the International Law Commission*, 1966, vol. 2, p. 207. See Sinclair, op. cit. above (n. 48), at p. 61.

[53] Documents of the Conference, loc. cit. above (n. 3), at p. 23.

[54] Ibid., p. 27. Some members of the Commission argued that the effectiveness of a reservation to a multilateral treaty should depend upon some measure of common acceptance by the other States concerned, a point raised again at the Diplomatic Conference.

[55] Ibid., emphasis added.

256   RESERVATIONS TO MULTILATERAL TREATIES

only in the case of reservations impliedly or expressly prohibited or permitted that no issue of compatibility will arise under Article 19.

Article 19(*b*) is to be read more narrowly because of the adoption of a Polish amendment adding the word 'only' before 'specified reservations'.[56] Thus the category of impermissible reservations under Article 19(*b*) is narrowed, particularly since 'specified *reservations*' is usually narrower than 'specified *articles*' to which reservations may be made.[57] This increases the flexibility of States in making reservations.[58] A reservations clause explicitly limiting reservations to particular wording precludes the application of the compatibility criterion, but a reservations clause which indicates, explicitly or implicitly, the range of articles to which reservations may be made would be subject to the compatibility criterion.[59] As for paragraph 19(*c*), the Commission's draft would have permitted the application of the

---

[56] A/CONF.39/C.1/L.163. The US delegation had recommended the deletion of sub-paragraph (*b*) 'which set out the unduly rigid rule that, where a treaty authorized specified reservations, no other reservations could be made': *Official Records*, Second Session, loc. cit. above (n. 3), at p. 108. See Kearney and Dalton, loc. cit. above (n. 4), at p. 511. A Polish amendment adding the word 'only' between 'authorized' and 'specified' reversed this rigid rule. As a consequence of this amendment, in order to exclude reservations not specifically mentioned it is necessary to use the word 'only' if Article 19(*b*) is to apply, otherwise a State may formulate other reservations subject only to article 19(*c*). See Ruda, loc. cit. above (n. 2), at pp. 181–2. Article 19(*c*) now refers to 'cases not falling under sub-paragraphs (*a*) and (*b*)' in place of 'cases where the treaty contains no provisions regarding reservations'. The cumulative effect of these changes is to expand the scope of paragraph 19(*c*).

[57] Bowett, loc. cit. above (n. 4), at p. 71. He draws upon the example of the European Convention on the Place of Payment of Money Liabilities of 16 May 1972, Article 7 of which precludes reservations save for that specified in Annex II, which provides: 'Any of the States mentioned hereafter may, at the time of signature or when depositing its instrument of ratification or acceptance of the Convention, declare that it reserves the right not to apply the provisions of Article 3 of Annex I: Italy, The Netherlands' (*European Treaty Series*, No. 75). This would fall under article 19(*b*) as a specific *reservation*; an indication by the parties in advance of what reservations will be permissible under the Convention. A specified *reservation* is thus not open to challenge as an impermissible reservation.

Article 12 of the 1958 Geneva Convention on the Continental Shelf, discussed in the *UK/France Continental Shelf* arbitration (first award), 54 ILR 6, para. 39, is an example of a provision specifying *articles* to which reservations may be made. Paragraph 12(1) provides: 'At the time of signature, ratification or accession, any State may make reservations to Articles of the Convention other than to Articles 1 to 3 inclusive'. Article 12 does not provide for specified reservations but only refers to specific *articles* to which reservations may be made. 'This distinction', notes Sinclair, 'is crucial . . . [I]n the the case of a reservations article article which confines itself to indicating expressly or by necessary implication the range of articles to which reservations may be made, any particular reservation may be open to challenge as being impermissible or may be objected to on other grounds': op. cit. above (n. 48), at p. 73. See also Bowett, loc. cit. above (n. 4), at p. 71, who states that 'if the treaty specifies as prohibited or permitted the actual reservations which may be formulated, there is no place for the "incompatibility" criterion: but if the treaty merely provides that reservations (unspecified as to type or kind) may be made to particular articles of the treaty, this does not exclude the "incompatibility" criterion in relation to such reservations.'

For further examples see Satow, op. cit. above (n. 4), at p. 285; Blix and Emerson (eds.), *The Treaty Maker's Handbook* (1973), section 14(A); and n. 59, below.

[58] Horn observes that '[t]he adoption of the Polish amendment was a further proof of the profoundly changed attitude to the capacity of States to formulate reservations': op. cit. above (n. 4), at p. 114.

[59] Reservations made under a clause indicating that 'reservations may be made to Articles other than to Articles 1 to 3' would be subject to the compatibility criterion, whereas a clause stating that 'reservations are only permitted to Articles 1 to 3' excludes the compatibility criterion. For an example of the former, see Article 19(1) of the 1958 Convention on Fishing and Conservation of the Living Resources of the High Seas, *UK Treaty Series*, No. 39 (1966), Cmnd 3028; and of the latter, see Article 17 of the 1961 UN Convention on the Reduction of Statelessness, ibid., No. 158 (1975), Cmnd 6364.

compatibility test only to those treaties entirely silent as to reservations. The Vienna Convention, however, allows the application of the test both to treaties silent as to reservations *and* to those which contain reservation clauses not covered by paragraphs 19(*a*) and (*b*).

At the Diplomatic Conference opinion was divided as to whether the flexibility under Article 20 could or should extend to impermissible reservations under Article 19, and specifically Article 19(*c*). It will be recalled that Article 20(4) provides that a treaty may enter into force as between the reserving State and another contracting State if the latter accepts the reservation or objects to it but does not oppose the entry into force of the treaty between them.[60] Is it possible for a State, where the treaty is silent on reservations, to accept a reservation which is incompatible with the object and purpose of the treaty? Or to object to the reservation as incompatible but not oppose the entry into force of the treaty as between it and the reserving State? It is not clear from the Commission's commentary that the effect of an objection to a reservation to a multilateral treaty as incompatible with its object and purpose *ipso facto* precludes the entry into force of the treaty as between the reserving and objecting States. Discussion at the Conference of this important issue appears to blur the distinction between the permissibility of a reservation under Article 19, and the effect of reservations and objections thereto under Article 20. If a reservation is made which is not permitted under Article 19, then the reservation is impermissible and no question of acceptance or objection to the reservation arises under Article 20. A reservation which is permissible under Article 19 may none the less be objected to under Article 20 on other grounds. There is thus a clear distinction between challenging a particular reservation on the grounds that it is impermissible (Article 19) and objecting to it on other grounds (Article 20).[61] Acceptance of an inadmissible reservation is theoretically not possible.[62]

Confusion may have arisen because of the element of appreciation by individual States required under both Articles. Consideration was given to independent adjudication of disputes arising under the Convention, including the effect of reservations, by both the ILC and the Diplomatic Confer-

---

[60] The presumption in Article 20(4)(*b*) was reversed in the Commission's draft Articles. The present wording was the result of a determined campaign by the Soviet Union which succeeded with a late amendment at the second Session. See further Sinclair, op. cit. above (n. 48), at pp. 62–3.

[61] Kearney and Dalton observe that Articles 19 and 20 concern the 'relationship between the substantive limitations on formulation and the procedural acts of accepting or objecting to a reservation': loc. cit. above (n. 4), at p. 512. It is submitted that these are separate and distinct processes. See further Horn, op. cit. above (n. 4), at pp. 112 ff.

[62] Horn views the VCLT as establishing 'a clear distinction between the admissability and opposability of a reservation': ibid., at p. 120. Jennings appears to view permissibility as the first hurdle, following which acceptance of or objection to the reservations follows. He states: 'A la question fondamentale de savoir *si* un État *peut faire* des réserves, la convention donne une réponse fondée sur le critère de la compatibilité avec le principe opératif . . . '. He goes on to discuss objections to and acceptances of reservations under Article 20, where 'chacune d'elles étant censée s'être formée une opinion sur la "compatibilité" ou non de la réserve avec le traité d'après la règle générale': loc. cit. above (n. 8), at p. 152, paras. 20–1 (emphasis added).

ence.[63] Many feared that the compatibility criterion would be unworkable in practice without jurisdiction vested in some international organ to determine compatibility, with that determination binding on all parties.[64] Whether such a view has been vindicated with the passage of time is considered below. In 1969, however, two substantial hurdles to such an approach existed: the first was the general reluctance of the Soviet Union and East European States to accept compulsory dispute resolution,[65] and the second was the general low esteem of the International Court of Justice.[66] Also considered but not adopted was some form of collective determination of compatibility. It was therefore left to individual States to determine whether a reservation is permissible under Article 19;[67] once such determination is made, and should the reservation be considered permissible, it may none the less be objected to on other grounds under Article 20 with the effects specified therein, including preclusion of the entry into force of the treaty as between the reserving and objecting States. Accept-

[63] On the ILC see Hogg, 'The International Law Commission and the Law of Treaties', *Proceedings of the American Society of International Law*, 1965, at p. 13 (advocating compulsory arbitration by an independent forum of disputes arising with respect to invalidity or termination of treaties, or regarding the interpretation of treaty obligations).

[64] See Jennings and Watts, op. cit. above (n. 4), at p. 1245; Fenwick, loc. cit. above (n. 24), at p. 122; and Anderson, loc. cit. above (n. 2), at pp. 467–8, who, writing in the 1960s, recognized that it was unlikely that States would favour such a provision. But even where such a body exists, it may be loath to take such decisions: see the discussion of the European Court of Human Rights, below, at n. 159.

[65] An attitude which, of course, does not prevail today. For example, Poland (21 September 1990), Bulgaria (26 May 1992) and Estonia (10 October 1992) have accepted the compulsory jurisdiction of the International Court of Justice. Reservations concerning the jurisdiction of the ICJ made on ratification or accession to a number of human rights treaties too numerous to mention in full have been removed by Belarus (e.g., the Convention on the Political Rights of Women, Art. IX), Bulgaria (e.g. the Genocide Convention, Art. 9); the former Czechoslovakia (e.g. the Convention on the Elimination of All Forms of Discrimination against Women, Art. 29(1)); Hungary (e.g. International Convention on the Elimination of All Forms of Racial Discrimination, Art. 22); Ukraine (e.g., ibid.); and the former USSR (e.g., Convention Against Torture, Art. 30). In addition, Belarus, Bulgaria, the former Czechoslovakia, Estonia, Hungary, Latvia, Lithuania, Poland, Romania, Slovenia, Ukraine, the former USSR and the former Yugoslavia have recently signed, ratified, acceded to, or accepted, treaty obligations including compulsory dispute settlement by the ICJ. Many have become a party to, for example, the 1985 Vienna Convention for the Protection of the Ozone Layer, which provides in Article 11 for compulsory dispute settlement by the ICJ.

[66] Rosenne notes the 'very widespread aversion to recognizing the International Court of Justice as the exclusive organ to be charged with these third party functions', an aversion which had 'become intensified following the widespread political dissatisfaction at the manner in which the Court handled the *South West Africa* case'. Final judgment was delivered by the ICJ in that case on the very same day that the ILC unanimously adopted the draft Articles on the law of treaties. See op. cit. above (n. 3), p. 81, n. 120.

[67] "[L]e critère de compatibilité est pour des raisons pratiques une question subjective pour chaque État partie, plutôt qu'une question qui exige une réponse objective . . .': Jennings, loc. cit. above (n. 8), at p. 153, para. 23. States may thus differ as to the view taken with respect to compatibility. The act of appreciation under Article 19(c) is threefold and complex: first, the object and purpose of the treaty must be identified; second, the nature of the reservation in question must be assessed; and finally, the relationship of the reservation to the object and purpose of the treaty must be ascertained. That neither the ILC, the ICJ nor the Diplomatic Conference saw fit to charge an independent body with the task has attracted some justifiable criticism. It was simply assumed by the Court in the *Genocide* case that the object and purpose of a treaty is self-evident. Nor is further guidance provided in the Vienna Convention, which simply reiterates the Court's compatibility criterion.

ance of or objection to reservations under Article 20 thus also involves an element of appreciation by individual States.

At the Diplomatic Conference there was little discussion of the effect of an impermissible reservation. However, some delegations did comment upon the relationship between paragraph 19(c) and paragraph 20(4), then paragraphs 16(c) and 17(4), respectively. The United States suggested an amendment to paragraph 17(4),[68] the stated purpose of which 'was to extend the applicability of the prohibited categories of reservations set out in article 16 to the decisions made by States under paragraph 4 of article 17 in accepting or objecting to a proposed reservation. In particular, the proposal would preclude acceptance by another contracting State of a reservation prohibited by the treaty, and the test of incompatibility with the object or purpose of the treaty set out in paragraph (c) of article 16 would then be applicable to such acceptance or objection.'[69] The US amendment was supported by Colombia,[70] the Republic of China[71] and Ireland.[72] Sweden pointed out that the US amendment 'had the merit of making it clear that the procedure for acceptance of admissible reservations prescribed in article 17, paragraph 4(c), did not apply to reservations prohibited under article 16'.[73] Sir Humphrey Waldock, in his capacity as Expert Consultant, indicated that the US amendment was compatible with the intention of the ILC in Article 16.[74]

The Irish representative said that '[h]is delegation considered that article 16 contained absolute rules and that consequently, if a State purported to become party to a treaty subject to a reservation which conflicted with those rules, its attempt to become a party would have no legal effect unless the reservation was withdrawn'.[75] He was prepared to go further and hold that

---

[68] The US delegation suggested several amendments to Article 17(4), including the addition of the words 'and unless the reservation is prohibited by virtue of Article 16' after the first phrase of paragraph 17(4), 'In cases not falling under the preceding paragraphs of this Article'. See Reports of the Committee of the Whole, in Documents of the Conference, loc. cit. above (n. 3), at p. 136, para. 179(v)(d). Although referred to the Drafting Committee by the Committee of the Whole, consideration of amendments to Article 17 was held over from the first to the second session and the amendment was withdrawn: see Report of the Committee of the Whole on Work at the Second Session of the Conference, 1 May 1969, Document A/CONF.39/15, ibid.

[69] *Official Records*, First Session, loc. cit. above (n. 3), at p. 108, para. 11. Although the use of the word 'extend' is unfortunate, the meaning of the US proposal is sufficiently clear.

[70] Ibid., p. 113, para. 69 (21st mtg).

[71] Ibid., p. 121, para. 5 (23rd mtg).

[72] Ibid., p. 122, para. 18 (23rd mtg). However, the Irish representative prefaced his support with the observation that 'it appeared from the last sentence of paragraph (17) of the commentary that the International Law Commission had not intended the rules in question to have that effect': ibid.

[73] Ibid., p. 117, para. 33 (22nd mtg).

[74] Ibid., p. 133, para. 4 (25th mtg). The function of the expert consultant was not defined. In his first intervention, Sir Humphrey said 'that he regarded himself as the servant of the Conference in the same way that he had served the Commission in his capacity as Special Rapporteur on the law of treaties. He was anxious to help in formulating the best possible draft convention and should not be thought of as someone who was attending the Conference simply to defend the Commission's work': *Official Records*, First Session, loc. cit. above (n. 3), at p. 20. See Kearney and Dalton, loc. cit. above (n. 4), at p. 509, n. 70.

[75] Ibid., p. 122, para. 18 (23rd mtg).

'tacit or even express acceptance of a reservation conflicting with the rules in article 16 would not make the reserving State a party to the treaty in relation to any other State, even an accepting State'.[76] The Australian representative considered that the Convention should 'make it absolutely clear that the purported reservations of the class referred to in article 16(c) were not susceptible of being accepted by the parties'.[77] However, at a later meeting the Australian representative appeared to support a collegiate system under which even an incompatible reservation might be accepted, likening the process to that during the negotiation of a treaty.[78]

Japan, the Philippines and the Republic of Korea jointly sponsored an amendment also designed to avoid the possibility that a State might make a reservation contrary to the object and purpose of the treaty that could be accepted by another State and upheld as valid under Article 17(4). Their suggested amendment included a collegiate system 'under which the views of the parties on the question of compatibility should be ascertained'.[79] A reservation would fail if, upon communication of the reservation to other contracting States, a majority thereof objected to the reservation within a stipulated time period. Switzerland, on the other hand, suggested amendments to the text to make it clear that the procedure in paragraph 4 of Article 17 would apply to two categories of reservations, those which are not prohibited under Article 16(*a*) and (*b*) and those contemplated in Article 16(*c*).[80]   .

None of the amendments was adopted. Though some were referred to the drafting committee, it declined to incorporate them, and others were withdrawn.[81] Article 19 was adopted by 92 votes in favour, 4 against and 7 abstentions, and Article 20 by 83 votes in favour, none against and 17 abstentions. Although the opportunity for desirable clarification of the relationship between Articles 19 and 20 of the Convention was lost, some support for an interpretation of Article 19(*c*) as distinct from the application of Article 20 may be found in the language of the adopted Convention:

(*i*) If a reservation incompatible with the object and purpose of the treaty may be accepted or objected to under Article 20, it is difficult to see what function additional to Article 20 is performed by Article 19(*c*). Ruda views Article 19(*c*) 'as a mere doctrinal assertion, which may serve as a basis for guidance to States regarding acceptance of reservations, but no more than

---

[76] Ibid.
[77] Ibid., p. 118. para. 49 (22nd mtg).
[78] Ibid., p. 132, paras. 72–5 (24th mtg).
[79] See the remarks by the Japanese representative, ibid., p. 110, para. 29 (21st mtg), and the more detailed proposal by the Indian representative, ibid., p. 128 (23rd mtg).
[80] Ibid., p. 111, para. 40 (21st mtg).
[81] See further Kearney and Dalton, loc. cit. above (n. 4), at p. 512; and n. 68, above. The Conference functioned as a Committee of the Whole, with each article considered seriatim by it, with a small Drafting Committee of fifteen members. A single Committee of the Whole was considered preferable for smaller States able to send fewer representatives: ibid., p. 500; see also Sinclair, loc. cit. above (n. 4) (*ICLQ*), at pp. 52–3.

that'.[82] But this does not accord with the principle of effectiveness according to which all provisions of a treaty are presumed to have significance and to be necessary to convey its intended meaning; 'an interpretation which reduces some part of the text to the status of a pleonasm, or mere surplusage, is prima facie suspect'.[83] At the Diplomatic Conference the United Kingdom representative pointed out that the ability to accept an incompatible reservation under Article 17(4) would nullify the compatibility test. 'If that was a correct interpretation of the combined effect of sub-paragraph (c) of article 16 and paragraph 4 of article 17 then clearly the compatibility test might prove in practice to be devoid of any real substance.'[84] As the foregoing discussion illustrates, this was not the intention of the ICJ in fashioning the compatibility criterion nor of the ILC in relying upon it in the draft Articles.

(*ii*) Article 19 is concerned with prohibited reservations; Article 20 refers to a second class of reservations, those expressly or impliedly authorized by the treaty. That a reservation must be made in accordance with these provisions before its legal effect may be considered is clearly stated in Article 21(1) governing the legal effects of reservations and objections to reservations. The first sentence of that Article refers to 'a reservation established with regard to another party in accordance with Articles 19, 20 and 23 . . . .'. This supports an interpretation of Article 19 as establishing those cases where a reservation may not be made.[85] If a prohibited reservation is made contrary to Article 19, it is not established 'in accordance with' that Article and Article 21 will not apply to it. Such an outcome would run contrary to the clear intent and meaning of Article 21, which is intended to govern the legal effect of all reservations and of objections to reservations under the preceding two Articles.

(*iii*) Article 19 establishes the general principle that States are entitled to formulate reservations, subject to the restrictions set forth therein. The choice of 'formulate', rather than 'make', was deliberate. The International Law Commission 'rejected the word "make" because it might imply that the State concerned had the right to participate in the treaty on the basis of the reservation'.[86] A proposed amendment replacing the word 'formulate' with

---

[82] Ruda, loc. cit. above (n. 2), at p. 190.

[83] This reflects the first of two aspects of the principle of effectiveness, the second being 'that the instrument as a whole, and each of its provisions, must be taken to have been intended to achieve some end, and that an interpretation which would make the text ineffective to achieve the object in view is, again, prima facie suspect': Thirlway, 'The Law and Procedure of the International Court of Justice 1960–1989: Part Three', this *Year Book*, 62 (1991), p. 1, at p. 44. The Principal Legal Secretary of the International Court of Justice acknowledges his terminological debt to Berlia, 'Contribution à l'interprétation des traités', *Recueil des cours*, 114 (1965–I), at pp. 306 ff.

[84] Loc. cit. above (n. 3), p. 114, para. 74 (21st mtg).

[85] Jennings and Watts, op. cit. above (n. 4), at p. 1243.

[86] *Per* Sir Humphrey Waldock, expert consultant at the United Nations Conference on the Law of Treaties, *Official Records*, First Session, Committee of the Whole, loc. cit. above (n. 3), at p. 126 (emphasis added). One objection which Fitzmaurice makes to 'mixed theories' 'is that they place the reserving and objecting State on a footing of equality of legal right'. Under the traditional system, an objecting State had an absolute right to object but there was no right of unilateral reservation: loc. cit.

'make' was not accepted at the Vienna Conference.[87] Ruda concludes that 'when the treaty does not contain a provision permitting certain reservations, a State only has the right to "propose" such reservations' and, consistently with the opposability approach he adopts, argues that these have no legal effect unless they are accepted.[88] Ruda is correct in so far as the legal effect of the reservation is dependent upon the response by other States. If a reserving State makes what it considers to be a compatible reservation which another State entitled to object views as incompatible with the object and purpose of the treaty, a genuine difference of opinion arises. But in addition to preventing any inference arising that a reserving State is entitled to participate in the treaty on the basis of that reservation, use of the word 'formulate' also indicates that certain criteria must be met in order for a reservation to be validly made, including compatibility with the object and purpose of the Convention.

The foregoing textual analysis of the VCLT may not wholly convince. This is unsurprising, since the text of the Convention possesses an ambiguity which is not wholly resolved even with recourse to the *travaux préparatoires*. The Convention fails directly to address the legal effect of an impermissible reservation. The core of the problem lies, it is submitted, in the attempt in the ILC draft Articles, subsequently incorporated in the 1969 Vienna Convention, to reconcile contradictory approaches. The purpose of Article 19(c) is to give effect to the criterion adopted by the International Court of Justice in the *Genocide* case which, it will be recalled, was of the opinion that an incompatible reservation entitled the objecting State to consider that the reserving State was not a party.[89] This reflects a view of multilateral treaties embodying a distinct essence with rational constraints upon States in entering treaty relations.[90] Article 20, in contrast, is based on the autonomy of sovereign States with the effect of a reservation dependent upon the reaction of other States.[91] These conflicting approaches existed in State practice, with the compromise reached in the ILC draft

above (n. 4) (*ICLQ*), at p. 13. See also the majority opinion in the *Genocide* Case, loc. cit. above (n. 1), at p. 24, wherein an absolute right to make and maintain reservations is rejected. For discussion of the Soviet view of the sovereign right to make reservations, see Chaumont, 'Cours général de droit international public', *Recueil des cours*, 129 (1970–I), ch. 3, pp. 447–8.

[87] A/CONF. 39/C.1/L.161

[88] Loc. cit. above (n. 2), at p. 180; see also Fitzmaurice, loc. cit. above (n. 4) (this *Year Book*), at p. 275.

[89] According to Fitzmaurice, the majority opinion in the *Genocide* case was itself a mixture of two theories corresponding with B,1 and B,2 (*d*) in his classification: loc. cit. above (n. 4) (*ICLQ*), at p. 10. The first is a limitation bearing on the application of the Convention, where a Convention is not in force as between the objecting and reserving States; the second is a limitation bearing on the nature of the reservations where 'reservations may be made as of right if "compatible with the object and purpose of the convention"' (ibid.).

[90] Koh, loc. cit. above (n. 4), at p. 74, n. 14.

[91] 'The system of the Convention on the admissibility of reservations is based on the recognition that the right to formulate reservations is a reaffirmation of a sovereign prerogative of the State': Ruda, loc. cit. above (n. 2), p. 183.

Articles[92] emerging relatively unscathed from the first session of the Vienna Conference to become embodied in the VCLT.[93]

IV. DOCTRINE

There is no clear consensus in the doctrine as to the legal effect under the Vienna Convention of an impermissible reservation. Indeed, commentaries on the law of treaties frequently share that Convention's silence on this issue in simply reiterating the Vienna Convention framework. There are exceptions, such as Jennings and Watts who argue that a '"prohibited" reservation is likely to be treated as a nullity, as is the act of consent which it accompanies'.[94] In general terms, two main approaches to the validity of reservations under the Convention may be identified in the doctrine, which Koh[95] labels as the permissibility and opposability schools. Proponents of the former, including Bowett, argue that under Article 19(c) incompatible reservations are invalid, whilst to adherents of the latter school, such as Ruda, the validity of a reservation depends upon its acceptance by other States. Underlying these differences of opinion lies a fundamental differ‐ ence in approach. The permissibility school gives effect to the ICJ's decision in the *Genocide* case which imposes a constraint, the test of compa‐ tibility, upon the freedom of States in making reservations to treaties silent on the point. The opposability school, on the other hand, finds its roots in the practice of the League of Nations and the supporters of the unanimity rule. It adopts a subjective approach which emphasizes the sovereign rights of States.

To state that a reservation which is incompatible with the object and pur‐ pose of a treaty is impermissible, or invalid, does not fully address the issue

[92] Sir Humphrey Waldock, the expert consultant at the Vienna Conference, observed: 'It was . . . not only for logical reasons, but also because of the divergent views of States that the Commission had dealt with reservations in two separate articles [19 and 20]. In doing so, it had sought to establish a balance between the interests of the reserving State and those of other negotiating States, and it was perhaps because that balance had been achieved that the divergent views had not manifested themselves too sharply during the present debate' (*Official Records*, First Session, loc. cit. above (n. 3), p. 126, para. 3).

[93] The adoption of the Soviet amendment to Article 20 (see above, n. 60) was the only significant development in connection with reservations at the second session: see Sinclair, loc. cit. above (n. 4) (*ICLQ*), p. 59. In his *Guide to the Legislative History of the Vienna Convention*, Rosenne observes that '[t]he proceedings, particularly in the Committee of the Whole, suggest that many delegations had been furnished with a general directive to support the International Law Commission's text save where some immediate national interest required otherwise': op. cit. above (n. 3), at p. 73; see also Kearney and Dalton, loc. cit. above (n. 4), at pp. 501–2 (position of developing and Communist States). This is not to suggest that the matter was without controversy; reservations to multilateral treaties was one of ten topics which gave rise to prolonged debates at the Diplomatic Conference: Rosenne, ibid., p. 75.

[94] Op. cit. above (n. 4), at p. 1247. They also observe that in the *Genocide* case the Court 'failed to provide a workable legal rule', the criterion of compatibility being unworkable in practice unless juris‐ diction is vested in some international organ to determine compatibility, with that determination bind‐ ing on all parties (p. 1245).

[95] Loc. cit. above (n. 4).

of the legal effect of such an impermissible reservation.[96] One of the few in-depth analyses of the legal effect of impermissible reservations is provided by Professor Bowett, written at the time he appeared as Counsel for the United Kingdom in the *Continental Shelf* arbitration with France.[97] He points out the 'patent contradiction in the expression of will by the State' which submits an instrument of ratification, accession or acceptance indicating an intention to be bound by the treaty but accompanies it with a reservation incompatible with the object and purpose of the treaty.[98]

According to Bowett, it is the intention to be bound which is, in theory, the primary intention and the one which should prevail, particularly since he presumes that the State making the reservation is unaware of its incompatibility. In his view, the difference between impermissible and permissible reservations lies both in the test of non-acceptance and in the effect of an objection thereto. In particular,

the effect of an impermissible reservation should not depend upon the reactions of the other Parties to the reservation in the same way as with a permissible reservation. For the issue of permissibility is determined by the treaty. It is a question whether the reservation is permitted by the treaty, and thus, though the Parties may have to form a view on that (or refer the question to independent adjudication), the test of permissibility is the treaty itself.[99]

To some extent, this is question-begging since, in the absence of independent adjudication, it is up to the individual appreciation of States whether a reservation is compatible with the object and purpose of the treaty.[100] Clearly reference must be made to the treaty itself in order to ascertain that object and purpose, and in this regard Bowett's distinction between permissibility and opposability is extremely useful. It is worth quoting his conclusions at length:

[96] 'The more serious aspect of the system propounded by the Court', affirms Fitzmaurice: op. cit. above (n. 5), at p. 421.

[97] *Delimitation of the Continental Shelf (United Kingdom of Great Britain and Northern Ireland and the French Republic)*, 30 June 1977, 54 ILR 6. Judgment was given before his article had gone to press, but an addendum states that his conclusions are largely unaffected by it: loc. cit. above (n. 4), at pp. 90–2.

[98] One could equally point to the 'patent contradiction in the expression of will by the State' which objects to a reservation as incompatible with the object and purpose of the treaty but does not oppose the entry into force of the treaty as between it and the reserving State. One contradiction is met with another. For an attempt at reconciling these contradictions in connection with the *Belilos* case, see Cameron and Horn, 'Reservations to the European Convention on Human Rights: The Belilos Case', *German Yearbook of International Law*, 33 (1990), p. 69, at p. 91.

[99] To fit reservations to treaties silent on the point within this model, Bowett states that '[i]f there is no reservations clause the presumption must be that reservations are permissible provided that they are not contrary to the object and purpose of the treaty': loc. cit. above (n. 4), at p. 81, n. 1. In this manner the question of permissibility of reservations to treaties silent regarding reservations is still 'governed' by the treaty itself. It is as if an implied term regarding compatibility is read into the treaty. This is consistent with the reasoning of the ICJ in the *Genocide* case, where the Court clearly proceeded on the basis that some limitation on the right of reservation must always be implied: see further Fitzmaurice, op. cit. above (n. 5), at p. 420.

[100] As Ago remarked in 1962, the compatibility of reservations is an objective criterion which can only be applied subjectively: *Yearbook of the International Law Commission*, 1965, vol. 1, p. 161.

RESERVATIONS TO MULTILATERAL TREATIES   265

The issue of 'permissibility' is the preliminary issue. It must be resolved by reference to the treaty and is essentially an issue of treaty interpretation; it has nothing to do with the question of whether, as a matter of policy, other Parties find the reservation acceptable or not. The consequence of finding a reservation 'impermissible' may be either that the reservation alone is a nullity (which means that the reservation cannot be accepted by a Party holding it to be impermissible) *or* that the impermissible reservation nullifies the State's acceptance of the treaty as a whole.

The issue of 'opposability' is the secondary issue and pre-supposes that the reservation is permissible. Whether a Party chooses to accept the reservation, or object to the reservation, or object to both the reservation and the entry into force of the treaty as between the reserving and objecting State, is a matter for a policy decision and, as such, not subject to the criteria governing permissibility and not subject to judicial review.[101]

Here Bowett distinguishes between two types of impermissible reservations: impermissible reservations which are a nullity and are severable from the principal act of ratification or accession;[102] and impermissible reservations which are fundamentally inconsistent with the object and purpose of the treaty where both the reservation and the whole acceptance of the treaty by the reserving State are nullities.[103] The latter type reflects the decision of the ICJ in the *Genocide* case, the approach in the final ILC draft Articles and in Article 19 of the VCLT, and is the view espoused by, *inter alia*, Jennings and Watts as mentioned above. Although at the time Bowett did not consider there to be any authority supporting the first possibility, namely, severance, the subsequent decision of the European Court of Human Rights in the *Belilos* case appears to provide such support.[104]

[101] Loc. cit. above (n. 4), at p. 88, emphasis added.

[102] Bowett acknowledges that 'no direct authority can be found for the proposition that an impermissible reservation is a nullity and severable from the principal act of ratification or accession': ibid., at p. 76. But as special rapporteurs both Lauterpacht and Fitzmaurice supported the severance of impermissible reservations: see *Yearbook of the International Law Commission*, 1953, vol. 2, at pp. 133–4, and ibid., 1956, vol. 2, at p. 115. See also n. 147, below.

Bowett is not suggesting that the *provisions* to which the impermissible reservation applies are severable. The severability of the provision to which the offending reservation attaches was clearly rejected by the Court in the *Anglo-French Continental Shelf* arbitration, loc. cit. above (n. 97), paras. 60–1; see further n. 146, below. This, however, is the approach a number of States have taken to impermissible reservations, including reservations to the VCLT itself. See, for example, the objection by the Netherlands to the Syrian Arab Republic's reservation to obligatory conciliation measures under the VCLT which, whilst not opposing the entry into force of the VCLT between them, 'considers that their treaty relations will not include the provisions of Part V of the Convention . . . ': *Multilateral Treaties Deposited with the Secretary-General, Status as at 31 December 1991*, UN Doc.ST/LEG/SER.E/10, p. 830 (hereinafter referred to as the *Index*).

[103] Loc. cit. above (n. 4), at pp. 77 and 84; see also Horn, op. cit. above (n. 4), at pp. 120, 121 and 219. Horn distinguishes between reservations 'not of primary concern to the reserving State' and reservations constituting 'an absolute condition for participation'. Horn is thus looking at the issue of incompatible reservations from the perspective of the reserving State, while Bowett appears concerned with reservations in relation to their effect upon the treaty and the network of treaty relations which result therefrom.

[104] Judgment of 29 April 1988. For comment, see Cameron and Horn, loc. cit. above (n. 98); McDonald, 'Reservations under the European Convention on Human Rights', *Revue belge de droit international*, 21 (1988), p. 429; and Marks, 'Reservations Unhinged: The *Belilos* Case Before The

In *Belilos* the Court gave primacy to the expression by Switzerland of its intention to be bound by the European Convention on Human Rights irrespective of the validity of its declaration, interpreted by the Court as a reservation, in respect of Article 6. The invalidity of the reservation meant that it did not modify Article 6 in its application to Switzerland. The Court rejected the option of considering Switzerland's ratification of the Convention as invalid; also rejected was the possibility that Article 6 would not take effect, to the extent of the reservation, against Switzerland. As Marks notes, the consequence of rejecting the latter possibility is that the Court avoided giving indirect effect to an invalid reservation, which would have been the outcome had the Court declined to apply Article 6 to the extent of the reservation.[105]

It is submitted that in accepting that an invalid reservation has no effect on either ratification or the provision it seeks to modify or exclude, the European Court has set an undesirable precedent with perhaps the most worthy of motives. It is important to consider the judgment since it is the first to consider a reservation invalid with the effect that the reservation is a nullity and the 'reserving State' is bound by the provision unaffected by the reservation. But the weight of this precedent must be carefully considered bearing in mind the fact that the Court was relying upon the wording of the European Convention on Human Rights within the context of a 'common European public order',[106] and not simply applying general principles of treaty law. It is perfectly understandable that there is a desire with normative conventions to ensure the fullest participation on the fullest possible

European Court Of Human Rights', *International and Comparative Law Quarterly*, 39 (1990), p. 300. Marks concludes (at p. 313) that the Court appears to have adopted Bowett's approach. It should be noted, however, that the European Court did not expressly consider the compatibility of the Swiss 'declaration' with the Convention.

[105] Ibid., pp. 313–14. This outcome is similar in effect to an objection to a reservation under Articles 20 and 21 of the VCLT. See Sinclair, op. cit. above (n. 48), at p. 76.

Rejection of the former possibility, i.e. considering Switzerland's ratification invalid, would have given rise to numerous practical problems which must have influenced the Court in arriving at the solution of treating the 'declaration' as invalid. What if, for example, individual petitions had already been lodged relating to events subsequent to the date of application? (The author is indebted to Professor Gillian White for this insight.)

[106] See Cameron and Horn, loc. cit. above (n. 98), at pp. 92–5. The Commission noted in its decision on the admissibility of Application No. 788/60 (*Austria v. Italy*) that when a High Contracting Party refers an alleged breach to the Commission it is not enforcing its own rights but bringing before the Commission an alleged violation of 'the public order of Europe': see *Yearbook of the European Convention on Human Rights*, 4 (1961), at p. 140.

Another point to bear in mind in the Commission and the Court's practice is that neither will apply to reservations the canons of effectiveness 'which they have consistently employed to widen the scope of the Convention': Robertson and Merrills, *Human Rights in Europe* (rev. 3rd edn., 1993), p. 205. Thus the Court's decision in the *Belilos* case may be viewed as based in part upon the need to preserve the 'vital safeguards' in Article 64 in accordance with the principle of effectiveness of interpretation applied to the reservations provision of the Convention. See Merrills, *The Development of International Law by the European Court of Human Rights* (2nd edn., 1993), at pp. 84 and 118. Indeed, the outcome in the *Belilos* case indicates the rigour with which the Court is now willing to preserve the effectiveness of Article 64 and of the Convention regime as a whole, to the extent of 'punishing' Switzerland for disregarding the clear provisions of Article 64 by overriding its lack of consent to be bound by Article 6 except in accordance with its reservation.

terms. However, the approach advocated by Bowett and apparently endorsed by the European Court raises certain difficulties if applied in a wider context. First and foremost, it is artificial to distinguish between an intention to be bound and an intention to modify certain provisions of the convention in their relation to the reserving State. Ratification, accession or acceptance of a convention is a voluntary act by a State indicating its intention to be bound on the terms stated; it is not to be interpreted nor should it be interpreted as a blanket acceptance of all the provisions of the convention where a contrary intention is clearly indicated. It was never the intention of the ICJ, the ILC or the VCLT that a State should be bound by a provision to which it had not indicated its consent. Rather, Articles 19 and 20 function to ensure that unless the parties have so provided a State cannot become a party to a convention on the basis of a reservation striking at the heart of the convention; otherwise the matter is one for the individual appreciation of States under the flexible system of Article 20. Article 21 of the VCLT does not permit an objecting State the option of disregarding the reservation and relying upon the provision to which it relates in its treaty relations with the reserving State.

Yet this is precisely the outcome of the Bowett approach in suggesting that the reservation alone may be a nullity if not in 'fundamental contradiction' with the object and purpose of the treaty. Thus a State meticulous in the observance of its treaty obligations, which makes a reservation to ensure that conflict between its domestic legal requirements and its international obligations is avoided,[107] may none the less find itself bound to the treaty in its entirety and potentially responsible for breach of the provisions to which it explicitly withheld consent. Denunciation or withdrawal, with all the attendant difficulties, may be its only recourse.[108] Indeed, in the *Belilos* case Switzerland threatened to denounce the European Convention on Human Rights, a threat nearly carried out after the Court's judgment, but the motion failed by one vote in the Swiss Federal Council.[109] Bearing in mind that Bowett is making his argument on the basis that the hypothetical reservation is neither 'fundamentally contradictory' to the object and purpose of the treaty nor prohibited under the terms of the treaty itself, such an outcome is clearly undesirable.[110] Nor does distinguishing between two types of impermissible reservations introduce greater certainty or workability into treaty relations since at least two (there may well be more)

[107] Either in the knowledge that there is incompatibility—in which case 'meticulous' is too generous a description—or inadvertently, with the incompatibility revealed only through other States' response to it.
[108] Imbert assumes that the reservation would not have been formulated without full consideration and in the belief that no other solution was possible. It is therefore probable that the only recourse for the State concerned will be to denounce the Convention. A secondary consideration is the effect of a finding of incompatibility upon other States which have made similar reservations: loc. cit. above (n. 28), at p. 45.
[109] Cameron and Horn, loc. cit. above (n. 98), at pp. 116 (veiled threats to denounce the Convention contained in the Swiss Memorial) and 117 (vote in Council).
[110] However, Bowett does advocate consultation with the declaring State where such problems arise.

undesirable consequences may arise: first, it is possible that the object and purpose of treaties will be interpreted more broadly to accommodate the two types of impermissible reservations; and second, States may be more willing to categorize reservations as contrary to the object and purpose of the treaty since such characterization would no longer have the necessary effect of denying treaty relations between the objecting and reserving State, because existing parties would treat the offending reservation as a nullity and sever it from what would then remain as a valid acceptance of the treaty. Moreover, as the outcome of the *Belilos* case itself demonstrates, the consequence of determining a reservation a nullity is not necessarily the desirable one of ensuring the full treaty participation of the reserving State. After the failed attempt to denounce the Convention, on 16 May 1988 Switzerland submitted a new declaration purporting to modify the language of the declaration found invalid by the Court. However, since Article 64, in common with most reservations clauses, permits reservations to be made only upon signature or ratification, the validity of this 'declaration' must also be in doubt. This leads Marks to suggest that a more desirable solution might be to require withdrawal of the reservation and re-ratification after a 'decent interval', rather than treating the reservation as a nullity.[111]

Finally, it is submitted that the compatibility criterion is difficult enough to apply without attempting further distinction on the basis of 'fundamental contradiction' with the object and purpose of the treaty. In the absence of independent adjudication or majority determination of compatibility, this enlarges the ambit of individual appreciation of the object and purpose of the treaty without necessarily any commensurate gain.

The fundamental importance of State consent underlies the criticism just made of the approach suggested by Bowett.[112] As Elias notes, the scheme of Articles 19 and 20 'is based on the consensual character of treaties'.[113] The overarching importance of consent is seen in the reluctance of commentators to exclude the legal possibility under Article 20 that other contracting States may unanimously accept a reservation incompatible with the object and purpose of the treaty.[114] Since the permissibility of a reservation is tested before its opposability arises, it is not possible under the VCLT to

---

[111] Marks, loc. cit. above (n. 104), at p. 314. Horn, relying on Bowett, states that the declaring State's view has to be ascertained because '[a] reserving State can hardly be asked to participate in the integral treaty against its will': op. cit. above (n. 4), at p. 120.

[112] 'Consent' in a multilateral treaty context clearly has 'a different and wider application'; it is clearly a stronger element in bilateral treaties. Cf. Fitzmaurice, op. cit. above (n. 5), at pp. 408 and 416.

[113] Elias, op. cit. above (n. 4), at p. 34. See also the *UK/France Continental Shelf* arbitration (First Decision) wherein the Court noted the 'principle of mutuality of consent in the conclusion of treaties': loc. cit. above (n. 97), at para. 60.

[114] Jennings and Watts, op. cit. above (n. 4), at p. 1244; Reuter, op. cit. above (n. 4), at p. 74, para. 131 *bis*. See also the Department of Trade Memorandum reproduced in this *Year Book*, 49 (1978), p. 379. By the same token, however, the acceptability of a reservation to other contracting States is an indication whether the reservation is compatible with the object and purpose of the treaty: Jennings and Watts, op. cit. above (n. 4), at p. 1244, n. 5.

RESERVATIONS TO MULTILATERAL TREATIES 269

'accept' an incompatible reservation. None the less, so long as it is argued that this possibility exists, it is difficult to speak of 'prohibited' reservations as *never* being effective.[115] However, in stating his preference for a waiver to be granted openly by a separate protocol rather than embracing fundamentally inconsistent reservations, Bowett quite rightly points out that the issue should not be treated as one relating to objections to reservations at all.[116]

V. State Practice

In practice the flexible system of the Vienna Convention is viewed as working reasonably well.[117] In part this is because of the nature of the treaty-making process, which seeks to ensure that consensus is achieved and cause to make reservations is concomitantly reduced. In a study published in 1980, Gamble concludes that 70% of reservations to multilateral treaties are insignificant in effect, with a mere 6% of reservations classified as 'major substantive' in his model.[118] In any event it is open to negotiating States to make express provision for reservations in the treaty, provided agreement can be reached on the subject.[119] Such provision might indicate certain key provisions against which no reservation may be made,[120] or

[115] Ibid., p. 1244.

[116] Bowett, loc. cit. above (n. 4), at p. 84.

[117] Brownlie, *Principles of Public International Law* (4th edn., 1990), at p. 611. Brownlie is here referring to the flexible system under Article 20(4).

[118] Gamble, loc. cit. above (n. 4), at p. 391. See also Reuter, who observes that States use reservations moderately, and objections thereto even less: op. cit. above (n. 4), at p. 73, para. 131(2). An earlier UNITAR study also concludes that many reservations to substantive clauses of treaties are of limited or marginal significance, and that 'the States would have accepted without reservations if reservations were not permitted, but this of course cannot be factually demonstrated': op. cit. above (n. 9), at pp. 154–5.

[119] Including express prohibition: cf. Article 309 of the 1982 United Nations Convention on the Law of the Sea. However, notwithstanding the political necessity for such a prohibition, based upon the 'package deal' approach of UNCLOS III, declarations made under Article 310 of the LOSC, and statements of other States in reply, 'evidence substantial disagreement over some issues': Churchill and Lowe, *The Law of the Sea* (rev. edn., 1988), at p. 17. For discussion of the genesis of Article 309 see White in Butler (ed.), *The Law of the Sea and International Shipping: Anglo-Soviet Post UNCLOS Perspectives* (1985), at pp. 22–6.

Reuter notes that instances of silence as to reservations are 'assez fréquent, surtout dans des situations difficiles ou l'on préfère ne pas soulever la question au cours des négociations à raison de son issue incertaine ou trop laborieuse; la CV fournit elle-même un exemple retentissant . . .': op. cit. above (n. 4), at p. 72, para. 129. The omission of a provision on reservations may thus be as indicative of disagreement as of inadvertence. Cf. *Official Records*, First Session, loc. cit. above (n. 3), at p. 114 (Sinclair). See also Jennings, loc. cit. above (n. 8), at p. 151, para. 18, where he notes that 'très souvent un traité ne contient pas de règles claires ou suffisantes sur la question, et ceci risque d'être le cas précisément lorsque la question des réserves s'est déjà avérée sujette à controverse. C'est pour cette situation difficile que des règles générales sont nécessaires.'

[120] Or, conversely, specify those provisions to which reservations may be made. See, for example, the 1975 Customs Convention on the International Transport of Goods under cover of TIR Carnets (Misc. No. 22 (1976), Cmnd 6492), Article 58 of which only permits reservations to paragraphs 57(2)–(6). For the discussion of the legal effect of such language, see Bowett, loc. cit. above (n. 4), and above, n. 59.

specify a collegiate system for determining the compatibility of a reservation
with the convention.[121] A rare example of the latter is found in Article 20(2)
of the 1966 International Convention on the Elimination of all Forms of
Racial Discrimination which provides that '[a] reservation incompatible
with the object and purpose of this Convention shall not be permitted, nor
shall a reservation the effect of which would inhibit the operation of any of
the bodies established by this Convention be allowed. A reservation shall be
considered incompatible or inhibitive if at least two-thirds of the States Parties to this Convention object to it.'[122] Article 20 thus operates as if there were
a presumption of validity in respect of the reservation with the onus upon the
other States parties to the Convention to object.[123] The purpose of Article 20
is to provide an objective test for the determination of the compatibility of a
reservation with the object and purpose of the Convention. If satisfied, that
is, if at least a two-thirds majority object to the reservation, it is deemed
incompatible as regards all contracting parties.

The advantage of a requirement of acceptance or non-objection on the part
of a pre-determined majority of contracting States is said to be its objectivity
and workability in practice.[124] The clear merit of such a system is the avoidance of a 'patchwork quilt' of relations between States party to the Convention. One rule applies to all, and automatically. Such merits were perceived
by the ILC, which considered a collegiate system in developing draft articles
on the law of treaties,[125] and a number of States proposed amendments to
this effect at the Diplomatic Conference in Vienna.[126] But even with such a
system a number of problems may none the less arise. In practice a majority

---

[121] See Article 20 of the 1954 Convention concerning Customs Facilities for Touring (*UN Treaty
Series*, vol. 276, p. 191; *UK Treaty Series*, No. 70 (1957)); Article 50(3) of the 1961 Single Drugs Convention (*UN Treaty Series*, vol. 529, p. 204; *UK Treaty Series*, No. 23 (1979)); and Article 32 of the
1971 Convention on Psychotropic Substances (Misc. No. 24 (1978), Cmnd 7330). In addition, the validity of a reservation may be the subject of a dispute under compulsory dispute settlement procedures
requiring disputes regarding the interpretation and application of the treaty to be submitted to the ICJ
or a court of arbitration. Horn maintains that disagreements regarding interpretation/application
encompass disagreements on the nature of a reservation: op. cit. above (n. 4), at p. 117.

[122] *UN Treaty Series*, vol. 660, p. 195. It will be noted that for the purposes of this Convention compatibility is not subject to the individual appreciation of States; instead, a pre-determined majority
objecting to the reservation on whatever basis is sufficient for the reservation to be considered incompatible with the Convention. The Committee on the Elimination of Racial Discrimination has concluded
that it does not have the authority to determine the admissibility of reservations: *United Nations Juridical Year Book*, 1976, pp. 219–21, UN Doc. CERD/C/SR.286. See also n. 158, below (CEDAW). For
general comment see Cassese, 'A New Reservations Clause', in *Recueil d' études de droit international
en hommage à Paul Guggenheim* (1986), at pp. 266–304. Cassese notes that 'Art. 20 establishes for the
first time in the field of positive law the criterion that reservations may be appended to a treaty if they
are not incompatible with the object and purpose of the said treaty' (p. 271). He views the clause as a
clear compromise between the 'universality of participation' and the 'integrity of agreement' (p. 267).

[123] Another form of majority determination would be to require a set number, perhaps two-thirds of
contracting parties, to *accept* the reservation. This would approach the issue of validity from a presumption of '*in*compatible unless', rather than the 'compatible unless' approach of Article 20.

[124] Fitzmaurice, loc. cit. above (n. 4) (this *Year Book*), at p. 286.

[125] See Satow, op. cit. above (n. 4), at p. 290.

[126] See comments at the 22nd meeting by Ecuador, Sweden, Australia, Ghana and Italy; Denmark
at the 23rd meeting; and the Japanese and Australian amendments.

will be difficult to achieve, particularly given the sluggishness with which States tend to respond to reservations.[127] It may also be questioned whether States are really concerned with the compatibility of reservations at all when an objection is made on the basis of 'incompatibility with the object and purpose of the treaty'. Imbert suggests that States are more likely to be motivated by the consequences of the reservation for them as contracting parties than by the effect of the reservation upon the general integrity of the treaty.[128]

Specific problems arise under the 1966 Convention. Though Article 20 specifies what constitutes a majority for the purposes of determining the compatibility of a reservation with the Convention, it does not state the legal effect of such a determination. Article 20 merely provides that an incompatible or inhibitive reservation is not permitted or allowed. But what consequence does a determination of incompatibility under the Convention have upon the State seeking to ratify or accede to the Convention? Is such accession or ratification inoperative? Or is the reservation simply inoperative, with the provision to which it applied unaffected by it in relations between the reserving State and other contracting parties?[129] And what if this pre-determined majority is not achieved? Does Article 20 prevent individual States determining for themselves the compatibility of a reservation and thus affecting 'bilateral' relations within a multilateral treaty framework? What if, for example, a State objects to a reservation on the basis of incompatibility with the object and purpose of the Convention, explicitly states that as a consequence the Convention is not considered in force between itself and the reserving State, and yet the required majority under Article 20 is not attained? It is inconceivable that individual State action would be curtailed on the basis of Article 20 to the extent of the Convention entering into force between the reserving and objecting State in the face of such explicit language of objection by the latter.[130]

[127] See Sinclair, op. cit. above (n. 48), at p. 63, who observes that 'Governments tend to be sluggish in their reaction to reservations, if only for the reason that many administrations are simply not equipped to keep under constant review reservations to multilateral conventions formulated by other States, whether on signature or ratification. This may be regrettable, but it is a fact of international life.' It would appear that States are not required to lodge objections to reservations as incompatible with the object and purpose of the treaty within the time period set forth in Article 21(5) with respect to objections to *permissible* reservations. Cameron and Horn are of the view that this provision does not constitute a legally binding rule in respect of impermissible reservations; other commentators have doubted the force of this rule at customary international law even in respect of permissible reservations: loc. cit. above (n. 98), at p. 89.

[128] Imbert, loc. cit. above (n. 28), at p. 42.

[129] Cassese suggests three alternatives: (1) the reserving State withdraws the offending reservation as required under Article 20(3) of the 1966 Convention; (2) the reserving State notifies its withdrawal altogether from the Convention; or (3) the reserving State remains silent, and 'consequently the reservation will have to be considered legally ineffective, so that the State in question will be bound by the Convention, including of course the provision or the provisions to which the reservation had been appended.': loc. cit. above (n. 122), at p. 280. His third option is in fact severance of the offending reservation.

[130] Cassese would support such a result only where the formulated objection explicitly provides that no treaty relations will result between the reserving and objecting States as a consequence of the reservation even if it is accepted under Article 20(2). Otherwise he considers that the Convention is applicable

272   RESERVATIONS TO MULTILATERAL TREATIES

In 1953, Fitzmaurice put forward his suggestion for an 'ideal system' which is not dissimilar to the arrangement under the 1966 Convention.[131] There are several key differences, however, most notably the attention paid by Fitzmaurice to the legal consequences arising from a determination of compatibility under such an arrangement. If not less than two-thirds of interested States entitled to object to the reservation do so within a stipulated time period, he suggests a further period within which the reserving State may withdraw the reservation, upon the expiry of which its instrument of ratification, accession or acceptance is regarded as inoperative. A fresh instrument of ratification, etc., without the reservation may be submitted at any time thereafter. If less than a two-thirds majority object to the reservation it is admissible and the reserving State becomes a party, subject to the right of objecting States not to apply the provision to which the reservation pertained as between themselves and the reserving State. Fitzmaurice would apparently restrict the application of this final point to treaties of the contractual kind where reciprocal rights and duties exist and may be so suspended.[132]

Without such attention to the legal consequences arising from an impermissible reservation the potential for confusion is obvious. A recent example of such potential, not realised in the event, is found in the responses to the Yemen Arab Republic's reservation to the Convention in 1989.[133] In addition to prohibiting reservations incompatible with the object and purpose of the Convention, and providing for majority determi-

---

even between the reserving and objecting States (save for the provision to which the reservation is appended, to the extent of the reservation) because such an approach, in his view, is most consistent with the aims of the Convention: loc. cit. above (n. 122), at pp. 283–4.

[131] Loc. cit. above (n. 4) (*ICLQ*), at pp. 23–6.

[132] A distinction supported by Anderson, loc. cit. above (n. 4), at p. 467. However, in his capacity as Special Rapporteur, Fitzmaurice favoured a system closer to the traditional unanimity principle than his earlier 'ideal proposal' in the *International and Comparative Law Quarterly*: see *Yearbook of the International Law Commission*, 1956, vol. 2, pp. 104–28 (Arts. 37–40). See also Lauterpacht's alternative drafts on reservations to multilateral treaties, particularly Drafts A and B: ibid., 1953, vol. 2, pp. 90–162.

[133] Accession was accompanied by the following reservation: 'Reservation in respect of article 5(*c*) and article 5(*d*)(iv), (vi) and (vii)'. See *Index* (above, n. 102), at p. 120, n. 7. The relevant provisions of Article 5 are:

'In compliance with the fundamental obligations laid down in Article 2 of this Convention, States Parties undertake to prohibit and to eliminate racial discrimination in all its forms and to guarantee the right of everyone, without distinction as to race, colour, or national or ethnic origin, to equality before the law, notably in the enjoyment of the following rights:

. . .

(*c*) political rights, in particular the rights to participation in elections—to vote and stand for election—on the basis of universal and equal suffrage, to take part in the Government as well as in the conduct of public affairs at any level and to have equal access to public service;

(*d*) other civil rights, in particular:

. . .

(iv) the right to marriage and choice of spouse;

. . .

(vi) the right to inherit;

(vii) the right to freedom of thought, conscience and religion.'

RESERVATIONS TO MULTILATERAL TREATIES 273

nation of compatibility, Article 20 also establishes a time period within which to object to a reservation. The period is 90 days from communication of the reservation. As at 31 December 1991, fifteen States had objected to the Yemeni reservation, twelve of them on the express basis of incompatibility with the object and purpose of the Convention.[134] Only six[135] of these twelve States made any reference to the legal effect of their objection, in each case providing that the objection was not an obstacle to the entry into force of the Convention between them. Three of these, Denmark, Finland and Sweden, did not consider the reservation to modify the obligations arising under the Convention. Of the remaining six States, three confined their objection to simply stating the incompatibility of the reservation with the object and purpose of the Convention;[136] two referred to the incompatible reservation as impermissible;[137] and one did not accept the reservation.[138] Since the two-thirds majority required under Article 20(1) was not achieved, the reservation was validly made thereunder and, since none of the objecting States had explicitly stated that their objection prevented the entry into force of the Convention between themselves and the reserving State,[139] it may be assumed that the Convention duly entered into force as between those States and the Yemen Arab Republic.

Where the treaty is silent as to reservations, it is clear that the VCLT accords a significant role to individual contracting States in determining their attitude towards particular reservations. This provides great scope for State practice to develop the law further. However, on the question of the legal effect of an objection to a reservation as incompatible with the object and purpose of the treaty, practice is inconsistent and/or unilluminating. The following discussion draws on a survey of State practice based on the status as at 31 December 1991 of multilateral treaties deposited with the Secretary-General.[140]

Starting with the Genocide Convention, of the five States which objected to reservations on the basis of incompatibility with the object and purpose

---

[134] Italy and Norway simply entered their formal objections to the reservation, whilst the United Kingdom did not accept it. However, since the Convention provides that a reservation will be considered incompatible with the object and purpose of the Convention if at least two-thirds of States Parties object to it, there was strictly speaking no need for States to do more than object to the reservation for the operation of this provision. Nor, indeed, is there any legal obligation to state the reasons for an objection (but see n. 130, above). Where such reasons may be relevant, as here, is in determining the effect of the reservation if the Convention rule does not apply. Since two-thirds of States Parties did not object to the Yemeni reservation within the allowed time period, it is not incompatible with the Convention for the purposes of Article 20(2).

[135] Denmark, Finland, France, Mexico, Netherlands and Sweden.

[136] Canada, Czechoslovakia and Germany.

[137] Australia and Belgium.

[138] New Zealand.

[139] This is assuming that such independent action is still open to objecting States where majority determination of compatibility is provided for in the Convention: see discussion above, at n. 130.

[140] *Index* (above, n. 102). The data upon which the following discussion is based is on file with the author. In examining State practice it should be borne in mind that a State may object to a reservation under Article 20(4) of the VCLT and indicate that the effect of such objection is to preclude the entry

274   RESERVATIONS TO MULTILATERAL TREATIES

of the Convention, only three States expressly stated the legal consequences
flowing from such an objection. Both China and the Netherlands observed
that they would not consider as parties to the Convention those States
which had made reservations incompatible with its object and purpose. On
4 June 1990 the Government of Mexico informed the Secretary-General
that it considered the effect of the United States' reservation to Article IX
to be incompatible with the object and purpose of the Convention, but did
not consider that the objection should be interpreted as preventing the
entry into force of the Convention between them.[141] The confusion
immediately following the advisory opinion of the ICJ in the *Genocide* case
is perhaps best summed up in the Brazilian objection, which expressly
referred to the 1951 advisory opinion and General Assembly Resolution
598 (VI), and said: 'The Brazilian Government reserves the right to draw
any such legal consequences as it may deem fit from its formal objection to
the above-mentioned reservations'.[142]

In 1990 Greece informed the Secretary-General that it could not accept
the United States' first reservation,[143] which it considered incompatible
with the Genocide Convention, but did not specify what legal effect such
objection was intended to have upon treaty relations between them. Such
an approach leaves unclear the matter of whether, and to what extent,
treaty relations exist between the objecting and reserving States. There are
three possibilities:[144]

(*i*) there are **no treaty relations** between the objecting and reserving
States;[145] or

into force of the treaty as between it and the reserving State. For example, the United Kingdom's objections to reservations by Syria and Tunisia to the VCLT read as follows:
'The United Kingdom does not accept that the interpretation of Article 52 put forward by the Government of Syria correctly reflects the conclusions reached at the Conference of Vienna on the subject to
coercion; the Conference dealt with this matter by adopting a Declaration on this subject which forms
part of the Final Act;
'The United Kingdom objects to the reservation entered by the Government of Syria in respect of the
Annex to the Convention and does not accept the entry into force of the convention as between the
United Kingdom and Syria.'
and
' . . . The United Kingdom objects to the reservation entered by the Government of Tunisia in respect
of Article 66(*a*) of the Convention and does not accept the entry into force of the Convention as between
the United Kingdom and Tunisia.'
(Ibid., p. 831.)
    [141] In any event, it could be argued that the Convention had already entered into force between them
by operation of Article 20(5) of the VCLT. However, although Mexico has ratified the VCLT the
United States has not, and it is doubtful whether the provisions of Article 20(5) reflect customary law.
    [142] *Index* (above, n. 102), at p. 101.
    [143] Ibid., at p. 100.
    [144] See also Cameron and Horn, loc. cit. above (n. 98), at p. 115.
    [145] If the reservation is considered fundamental to the reserving State's ratification of the treaty as a
whole, then the whole ratification would be invalid. This was the approach taken to invalid reservations
to Optional Clause declarations by Judge Lauterpacht in the *Norwegian Loans* case, *ICJ Reports*, 1957,
p. 9, at pp. 43–66. There he considered two alternatives to be open to the Court: it could 'treat as
invalid [the offending part] of the reservation or it may consider the entire Acceptance to be tainted with
invalidity'. See also the *Interhandel* case (*Preliminary Objections*), *ICJ Reports*, 1959, p. 6, at

RESERVATIONS TO MULTILATERAL TREATIES 275

(*ii*) the treaty is in force between them but for the provisions to which the offending reservation is attached; that is, **the provisions to which the reservation attached are severable;**[146] or

(*iii*) the treaty is in force between them with the effect of the objection being that the reservation does not modify any rights or obligations under the provision to which it applies; that is, **the reservation is severable.**[147]

Occasionally States will explicitly state the legal consequences of an objection made to a reservation on the basis of its incompatibility with the object and purpose of the Convention. There are but a handful of examples of the first possibility, namely, that the Convention does not enter into force as between the objecting and reserving State.[148] More frequently, but still in a minority of cases, States will object to a reservation as incompatible with the object and purpose of the Convention but will not view such objection

---

pp. 101–18, where Judge Lauterpacht expressed the same view in holding the United States declaration of acceptance invalid. His view may be contrasted with that of Judge Klaestad, the President of the Court, who in his separate opinion in the *Interhandel* case, while considering the US 'domestic jurisdiction' reservation contrary to Article 36(6) of the Statute of the ICJ, none the less stated that the compulsory jurisdiction of the Court depends upon the intention of the governments concerned. Examining US practice, including consideration of the declaration by the US Senate, he was 'satisfied that it was the true intention of the competent authorities of the United States to issue a real and effective Declaration accepting the compulsory jurisdiction of the Court, though—it is true—with far-reaching exceptions' (p. 77). He considered that the parts of the declaration of acceptance which were in conformity with Article 36(6) could still be given effect. It would appear therefore that Judge Klaestad's primary concern was to give effect to the United States' Optional Clause declaration and that he considered the United States' intention to accept the compulsory jurisdiction of the Court prevailed over the inconsistency with Article 36(6) of its domestic jurisdiction reservation.

However, the analogy with impermissible reservations to treaties is not a strict one: cf. Bowett, loc. cit. above (n. 4), at p. 76, n. 3. In establishing the compatibility criterion in the *Genocide* case, the Court established that the will to be bound cannot prevail over an impermissible reservation which is incompatible with the object and purpose of the treaty. Marks points out that in such a case there are not two issues of will, i.e. the will to be bound and the will to impose an impermissible condition, for 'a State which has subjected its acceptance of a treaty to a reservation which is fundamentally opposed to the objects and purposes of that treaty cannot be deemed to have intended its will to be bound to prevail over its will to impose the offending condition': loc. cit. above (n. 104), p. 313.

[146] Fitzmaurice points out that this may be tantamount to giving effect to a reservation and is an 'empty form of words': loc. cit. above (n. 4) (this *Year Book*), at p. 287; see discussion of *Belilos* case, above, n. 104 ff. Bowett states that whilst this view is the correct one with respect to permissible reservations, it is 'scarcely logical' to apply it to impermissible reservations (p. 78). Cameron and Horn refer to this as the 'surgical principle' and disapprove its application on the basis also that it fails to distinguish between valid and invalid reservations: loc. cit. above (n. 98), at p. 116. Judge Lauterpacht rejected this option in the *Norwegian Loans* case: loc. cit. above.

[147] The outcome in the *Belilos* case: loc. cit. above (n. 104). This approach is favoured by Lauterpacht, *Yearbook of the International Law Commission*, 1953, vol. 2, pp. 133–4, and is one of the two possibilities he mentions in the *Norwegian Loans* case, loc. cit. above (n. 145). See also Fitzmaurice, *Yearbook of the International Law Commission*, 1956, vol. 2, p. 115; Horn, op. cit. above (n. 4), at p. 412; and the United Kingdom's submission in the *Continental Shelf* arbitration, pp. 15–16, 9 February 1977, para. 1A (*f*) and 2 (*b*).

[148] See the objections by the United Kingdom and Israel to Burundi's accession to the 1973 Convention on the Prevention and Punishment of Crimes against Internationally Protected Persons, including Diplomatic Agents (*UK Treaty Series*, No. 3 (1980), Cmnd 7765); and by China and the Netherlands to reservations by a number of States to the 1948 Genocide Convention (*UN Treaty Series*, vol. 78, p. 277; *UK Treaty Series*, No. 58 (1970), Cmnd 4421).

as precluding the entry into force of the Convention between them.[149]
Further effects may be specified, such as the reservation not modifying any
rights and obligations between the parties,[150] or the provision to which the
offending reservation relates not applying as between the objecting and
reserving States.[151]

Most common, however, is an objection to a reservation as 'unlawful',
'impermissible', 'unacceptable', 'invalid', 'inadmissible', 'not recognized',
or 'one which the reserving State is not entitled to make'. The grounds for
objection are not stated and, though desirable, there is no rule of law
requiring States to do so.[152] With the possible exception of 'impermissible'
(assuming the residual rules of the VCLT are clear on this point—a rather
large assumption), such language leaves open the question whether treaty
relations arise between the reserving and objecting State. It is necessary to
determine the intention of the objecting State. Thus the legal effect of such
objection must be derived from a number of factors, not least of which concerns ascertaining whether the objection is based on impermissibility under
Article 19 or objection on other grounds under Article 20. If the latter, the
effect of the objection is reasonably clear and set forth in that Article and in
Article 21. The onus is then on the objecting State to indicate that the effect
of the objection is to preclude the entry into force of the whole, or a part
of,[153] the convention between them. However, since the rules embodied in

[149] For examples of State practice on this point, see: the objection by the Netherlands to the Chinese
reservation to the 1947 Convention on Privileges and Immunities of Specialised Agencies (*UN Treaty
Series*, vol. 33, p. 261; *UK Treaty Series*, No. 69 (1959), Cmnd 855); objections by France and Germany to reservations to the 1961 Vienna Convention on Diplomatic Relations (*UN Treaty Series*, vol.
500, p. 95; *UK Treaty Series*, No. 19 (1965), Cmnd 2565); German objections to reservations by Morocco and the UAR under the 1963 Vienna Convention on Consular Relations (*UN Treaty Series*, vol.
596, p. 261; *UK Treaty Series*, No. 14 (1973), Cmnd 5219); the Mexican objection to one of the US
reservations to the 1949 Genocide Convention (ibid.); objections to the Yemeni reservation to the 1966
Convention on the Elimination of Racial Discrimination (*UN Treaty Series*, vol. 60, p. 195; *UK Treaty
Series*, No. 77 (1969), Cmnd 4108) by Denmark, Finland, France, Mexico, the Netherlands, and Sweden; objections to the Algerian 'reservation' to the 1966 International Covenant on Economic, Social
and Cultural Rights (*UK Treaty Series*, No. 6 (1977), Cmnd 6702) by Czechoslovakia and the Netherlands; Finnish, German, Mexican and Dutch objections to reservations to the 1979 Convention on the
Elimination of Discrimination Against Women (Misc. No. 1 (1982), Cmnd 8444; *International Legal
Materials*, 19 (1980), p. 33). See *Index* (above, n. 102).
It is tempting to draw analogies here with repudiatory breach in the law of contract, the effect of
which is not automatically to terminate the contract but to give rise to a right of election exercisable by
the 'innocent party' either to treat the contract as at an end, or to affirm it and seek damages. See further
Cheshire, Fifoot and Furmston's *Law of Contract* (12th edn., 1991), at p. 541.

[150] See, for example, the objections by Australia, Belgium, Canada, Denmark, Ireland, Malta, New
Zealand, Thailand and the United Kingdom under the 1961 Vienna Convention on Diplomatic Rela-
tions (loc. cit. above, n. 149); and by Denmark and Sweden to reservations to the 1966 International
Convention on the Elimination of All Forms of Racial Discrimination (ibid.).

[151] See, for ecample, the United States' objections to reservations under the 1961 Vienna Convention
on Diplomatic Relations (ibid.) and the 1963 Vienna Convention on Consular Relations (ibid.).

[152] Bowett, loc. cit. above (n. 4), at p. 75. Indeed, an objection to a permissible reservation requires
no legal basis, a State being entitled to object on policy grounds. Where a State objects to a reservation
as impermissible, Bowett advocates a requirement to state the reasons why the treaty does not permit
that particular reservation (ibid.). This would bring much needed clarity to the whole vexed issue of the
legal effect of impermissible reservations.

[153] See Sinclair, op. cit. above (n. 48), at p. 68.

RESERVATIONS TO MULTILATERAL TREATIES 277

Articles 20 and 21 are residual, regard must be had to what provision, if any, the Convention in question makes in respect of reservations and objections thereto. Where the treaty itself deals with the question of reservations, as for example in Article 20 of the 1966 Convention on the Elimination of Racial Discrimination, the issue must be resolved in accordance with the provisions of that Convention. Thus an objection or lack of acceptance of a reservation under the 1966 Convention takes on added significance, since such lack of acceptance or objection may be counted towards a majority determination of the compatibility of the reservation.[154]

It is submitted that in the absence of a clear reference to incompatibility with the object and purpose of the Convention, it is not possible to interpret an objection to a reservation as 'unacceptable', 'unopposable', etc., as indicating a finding of such incompatibility. Even if it is presumed that the objection is on the basis of incompatibility (and wording such as 'impermissible' must surely give rise to such presumption, albeit a rebuttable one), it is still necessary to determine the legal effect of such an objection.[155] Since one such effect is the possible absence of treaty relations between the objecting and reserving States, some care must be taken in presuming that such is the intention of the objecting State in the absence of express language to that effect. That States wish to avoid stating that such drastic consequences flow from their objection is clear from State practice. There may be many reasons for such avoidance, including the reluctance of smaller States to oppose the entry into force of a convention between themselves and a more powerful reserving State.[156] On the other hand, strong objection to a reservation as contrary to the object and purpose of a treaty, irrespective of whether the objecting State indicates the legal consequence thereof, may have the salutary effect of causing the reserving State to withdraw the offending reservation.[157] There is also the reluctance of States entirely to exclude reserving States from treaty relations, even where an incompatible reservation is made, on the basis that more effective pressure

[154] Provided that the objection is couched in the terms required under the 1966 Convention, i.e. incompatibility with the object and purpose of the Convention, or impairment of the bodies to be established thereunder. Cf. Cassese, loc. cit. above (n. 122), at p. 275. A general objection would thus give rise to problems of interpretation for 'counting' purposes in a majority determination of compatibility.

[155] For example, Bowett interprets the UK's objection to the German Democratic Republic's reservation to Art. 30 of the 1946 Convention on Diplomatic Privileges and Immunities of the Untied Nations (*UN Treaty Series*, vol. 1, p. 15; *UK Treaty Series*, No. 10 (1950), Cmnd 7891) as unacceptable because it was not the kind they were entitled to make as follows: 'The objection clearly regarded the reservation as impermissible, and one can only presume this was on the ground of incompatibility with the object and purpose of the Convention. There is no indication of what consequence the United Kingdom attached to the objection': loc. cit. above (n. 4), at p. 75.

[156] This possibility is adverted to by Sinclair in the context of permissible reservations, where he notes that the reserval of the onus in Article 20(4) VCLT which was introduced by a Soviet amendment may have had the effect of 'inhibiting smaller States from asserting that their intention, in objecting to a reservation, is to refuse treaty relations with the reserving State': loc. cit. above (n. 4) (*ICLQ*), at p. 60, and op. cit. above (n. 48), at p. 63.

[157] See Chile's withdrawal of certain reservations to the Convention Against Torture in the *Index* (above, n. 102), at p. 190. Where a reservation is withdrawn, and the objection thereto was to the reservation and to treaty relations, Bowett assumes withdrawal establishes the treaty relationship (loc. cit.

may be applied to that State to conform with the treaty regime from within, rather than without, that regime.

VI. Conclusions

A number of conclusions may be drawn from the foregoing:

1. In the *Genocide* case the ICJ established the compatibility criterion and held that where a reservation was incompatible with the object and purpose of a treaty an objecting State 'may consider that' the reserving State had not become a party to that treaty.

2. The ILC initially resisted the compatibility criterion but later adopted it in draft Articles which formed the basis for consideration of the matter at the Diplomatic Conference at Vienna. While making it clear that the compatibility criterion was to apply to both normative and contractual types of conventions, the ILC did not elaborate upon the application of the criterion. In particular, the legal effect of an impermissible reservation is not explored in the ILC's 1966 draft Articles.

3. The Diplomatic Conference saw representatives resistant to changes in the draft Articles, with a majority of States expressing no view on the relationship between Articles 19 and 20. Of those that did, opinion differed as to the nature of the relationship and even as to whether further clarification was needed.

4. As adopted, the VCLT fails clearly to specify the legal consequences of an impermissible reservation.

5. State practice reveals no clear trend and continuing confusion as to the legal consequences of an objection to a reservation as incompatible with the object and purpose of the treaty.

VII. The Future: The Minimum Harmonization of International Law?

Recent debates within the United Nations underscore the importance and unresolved nature of this issue.[158] Occasions will be rare where an inde-

---

above (n. 4), at p. 87). The VCLT is silent on the effect of a withdrawal of a reservation in relation to another party who has objected to treaty relations. In the event the problem did not arise with respect to the Chilean reservations since no State objected to treaty relations arising with Chile; indeed, most of the 18 States which objected to the Chilean reservations in respect of Article 2(3) and Article 3 as incompatible with the object and purpose of the Torture Convention stated that this objection did not constitute an obstacle to the entry into force of the Convention between them. The United Kingdom objection was not based on impermissibility but upon opposability, stating that it 'is unable to accept the reservations[s]' to Articles 2 and 3 (*Index*, p. 193).

[158] See Committee on the Rights of the Child, *Summary Record*, CRC/C/SR/41, pp. 6–9; on the application of the VCLT regime to the 1979 Convention on the Elimination of All Forms of Discrimination against Women (CEDAW), see Clark, 'The Vienna Convention Reservations Regime and the Convention on Discrimination Against Women', *American Journal of International Law*, 85 (1991), pp. 281–321.

pendent body will be competent to determine the validity of a reservation as the European Court of Human Rights did in the *Belilos* case. And competence does not necessarily bring certainty to this issue since the ECHR had a record of timidity on this issue prior to the *Belilos* case.[159] Nor is it sufficient simply to exhort States to make provision for reservations during treaty negotiations, an exhortation which, in any event, has largely been ignored.

But should the matter be resolved? There is a very good reason why States have ignored exhortations to consider a reservations clause in treaty negotiations. Just as ambiguity in the language of contracts may facilitate the reaching of 'agreement',[160] silence on reservations to international treaties is a means of achieving agreement on the text without addressing the underlying political, cultural and/or economic reasons which may make adherence to the treaty in its entirety nugatory for some States. Such considerations apply with even more force to normative treaties. It was the reconciliation of competing objectives, namely, maximizing treaty participation by States with diverse cultural, economic and political conditions without sacrificing the integrity of the treaty, which led the ICJ to devise the object and purpose test in the first place. The ambiguity of the test may engender the flexibility necessary to enable States party to a convention to adjust gradually and progressively to rules which may not be precise in their application nor interpreted consistently over time.

Considering that the problem has most frequently been raised in connection with human rights conventions, it must additionally be asked whether it can be viewed solely as one for general treaty law. There are in effect two separate but related issues: should reservations to normative treaties be permitted, and should the validity of such reservations be assessed by a system other than that pertaining to treaties in general? On the first point, Cameron and Horn have pointed out that human rights treaties may not be ratified by States for purposes any higher than those applicable to other treaties. Indeed, it could be argued that there is a particular need for a margin of flexibility in respect of human rights treaties which tend to touch on matters of particular sensitivity to States and hence 'confront States with

---

[159] Cameron and Horn, loc. cit. above (n. 98). This reluctance is not confined to the European Court of Human Rights:
'The reluctance of the Court of the Hague and the international judicial bodies to pronounce upon the validity of reservations shows that these authorities were themselves aware of the danger [sc. of implicating themselves in a debate which is bound to have highly political overtones]. They have whenever ecessary interpreted reservations, given rulings about their scope and even examined their validity. In discussing validity, they have always shown great caution, not to say embarrassment, never to my knowledge declaring a single reservation null and void.'
(Imbert, loc. cit. above (n. 28), at p. 46 (endnotes omitted).)

[160] In *Prenn* v. *Simmonds*, [1971] 3 All E.R. 237, at p. 241, Lord Wilberforce observed that in contracts '[t]he words used may, and often do, represent a formula which means different things to each side, yet may be accepted because that is the only way to get "agreement" and in the hope that disputes will not arise'. For a discussion of the use of ambiguity by the European Court of Justice, see Plender, 'In Praise of Ambiguity', *European Law Review*, 8 (1983), pp. 313–24.

difficulties greater than any encountered in other fields'.[161] As for a separate system of appraisal, Imbert is unconvinced by the arguments that the absence of reciprocity in normative treaties provides a basis for a separate regime in respect of reservations; indeed, since the obligations owed thereunder are not reciprocal, the obligations of a non-reserving State are not affected by reservations entered by other States (nor, indeed, by whether other States become contracting parties at all).[162]

Imbert defends the application of general treaty principles to human rights treaties on a number of grounds, in particular the undesirability of creating two, potentially contradictory, systems. This does not, of course, preclude the use of organs established under the treaty to assess the validity of reservations where such organs have the authority to do so, as in the *Belilos* case. But not all human rights treaties have such well-developed institutions. Thus the Committees established under the 1966 Convention on the Elimination of Racial Discrimination and the 1989 Convention on the Elimination of Discrimination against Women have both denied competence to assess the validity of reservations, thus necessitating the application of the general residual principles of treaty law embodied in the 1969 Vienna Convention. Furthermore, the creation of two systems for reservations presupposes that the categories to which each system would apply are readily identifiable. This may not be so; indeed, the classification of a treaty as a 'human rights' instrument or otherwise could prove highly controversial, particularly given the increasing tendency to claim that there is a 'human right' to a clean environment and to development, for example.[163]

What must be borne in mind is that, particularly in the human rights context, while the language of discourse is treaty law the real issue is the incompatibility of different social and cultural traditions. The problem of reconciling different political, social and cultural traditions within a general treaty framework has been addressed by the European Community which, through progressive enlargement, has had to cope with an ever more diverse Community in terms of economic, political and social development. One legislative approach to reconciling such diversity is not to require uniformity of approach but to set minimum standards which must be adhered to by all States, with provision for upward derogation in prescribed circumstances. Additional provision is made for exceptions on the basis of, for example, different levels of development. Though clearly care must be taken in extrapolating from the specialized Community context to general international law, there may be tools for regional integration which may usefully be employed at the international level. A further problem lies in

---

[161] Imbert, loc. cit. above (n. 28), at p. 30.

[162] Assuming, of course, that the Convention is in force. Some commentators none the less view this as an inequitable and unfair result: see, for example, Cassese, loc. cit. above (n. 122), at p. 301; and the dissenting judges in the *Genocide* case (see Fitzmaurice, op. cit. above (n. 5), at p. 419, n. 1, who adds that the reserving States thus acquire all the kudos of participation and suffer no penalties since no benefits may be denied under a treaty regime non-reciprocal in nature).

[163] The author is indebted to Professor Gillian White for this insight.

RESERVATIONS TO MULTILATERAL TREATIES 281

the identification of those minimum standards, which presupposes a measure of member State agreement. As Cassese has noted in connection with the 1966 Convention on the Elimination of All Forms of Racial Discrimination, the 'best system' is undoubtedly one where the provisions of the Convention to which reservations may not be made are appended to the Convention, thereby indicating the irreducible minimum for participation in the treaty regime. He acknowledges that '[t]he advantages of such a system would certainly have compensated for the lengthy discussions which would necessarily have preceded its adoption'.[164] Where it is possible to identify the essential provisions, or package of provisions, necessary to be accepted to preserve the integrity of the treaty, this is clearly an attractive solution. The essential core of the treaty is encircled by a penumbra to which adherence is optional, depending upon factors such as the economic, social and cultural conditions of the State concerned.[165]

It is unlikely that this problem will be resolved through State practice, which is as inconsistent today as it was in 1977 when Bowett remarked upon it. Indeed, ever since the ICJ rejected the unanimity rule with respect to reservations to general multilateral treaties silent on the point, the law has been in a considerable state of flux. Much State practice has evolved, some of it contradictory, both in respect of responses to incompatible reservations and of new techniques in treaty-drafting to accommodate the diverse interests of the international community. The solution is ultimately a political one, requiring States to perceive a problem and seek to have it addressed. There is considerable advantage to consideration of the issue in more neutral forums, since matters such as reservations to CEDAW have become highly politicized. There are a variety of contexts in which the topic might be addressed, including the ILC (as a topic for consideration during the fast fleeting Decade of International Law),[166] the ICJ (as an

---

[164] Loc. cit. above (n. 122), at p. 304.

[165] Wide differences in the economic and social circumstances of the member States of the Council of Europe were taken into account in drafting the European Social Charter, which does not oblige States to accept all the provisions of the Charter before ratifying it (Article 20(1)). States are initially bound by a stated minimum with the expectation that additional obligations will be assumed over time: Robertson and Merrills, *Human Rights in the World* (rev. 3rd edn., 1989), at pp. 245–9. See also Harris, *The European Social Charter* (1984), esp. pp. 14–21.

This may be contrasted with the 'common but differentiated responsibilities' approach in recent environmental treaties such as the 1992 United Nations Framework Conventions on Climate Change (Art. 4) and Biological Diversity (Art. 6). Thus whilst both developed and developing States accept the same obligations in principle, their responsibilities with respect to achieving the objectives of the Convention are flexible, taking into account such factors as 'their national and regional development priorities, objectives and circumstances' (Art. 4, Climate Change). Recognition of the need to balance environment and development objectives is also found in Article 130 S (5) of the Treaty on European Union which permits, *inter alia*, temporary derogation from Community environmental measures where such measures would impose disproportionate costs on the public authorities of the member State concerned.

[166] For example, the Commission has established a working party to prepare a contribution to the UN Decade of International Law (1990–99) comprising the 'tentative outline of a publication constituting an overview of the main problems of international law on the eve of the twenty-first century, with chapters to be written by members of the Commission'. A chapter on the problems of reservations to

282   RESERVATIONS TO MULTILATERAL TREATIES

advisory opinion) and even the General Assembly (a resolution clarifying State practice, as was done in 1952 and 1959). Notwithstanding recent criticisms of the ILC, it may be the most appropriate forum for consideration of the matter; indeed, inclusion of the item on the ILC's work programme has been raised in recent debates.

general multilateral conventions would certainly be appropriate for inclusion. For further discussion of the work of the ILC at its forty-fourth session, see the report by Rosenstock (an ILC Member) in *American Journal of International Law*, 87 (1993), pp. 138–144, at p. 143.

In the context of the UN Decade of International Law, there have recently been proposals to hold a UN Congress on Public International Law in 1994 or 1995 which might usefully consider the subject of reservations to multilateral treaties. The idea of a Congress was suggested as a major new element in the second term (1993–4) of the UN Decade of International Law with the General Assembly to take a final decision at its next session (48th) on the basis of informal soundings of members of the Sixth Committee. See Morris and Bourloyannis, 'The Work of the Sixth Committee At The Forty-Seventh Session of the UN General Assembly', ibid., pp. 306–23, at p. 322.

Part IV
Treaty Interpretation

[8]

The International Law Commission's Draft Articles upon Interpretation: Textuality *Redivivus*

Myres S. McDougal

*Scire leges non hoc est verba earum tenere, sed
vim ac potestatem*—Celsus, *Dig.* 1.3.17

The great defect, and tragedy, in the International Law Commission's final recommendations about the interpretation of treaties is in their insistent emphasis upon an impossible, conformity-imposing textuality.[1] This unhappy emphasis makes an appearance in, and dominates, the goal for interpretation which the Commission implicitly postulates but never critically examines; the deprecatory appraisal which the Commission offers of the potentialities that inhere in the rational employment of principles of interpretation; and the content and ordering of the particular principles which the Commission puts forward for canonization as "obligatory" rules of law.

In explicit rejection of a quest for the "intentions of the parties as a subjective element distinct from the text," the Commission adopts a "basic approach" which demands merely the ascription of a meaning to a text.[2] The only justification offered, and several times repeated as if in an effort to carry conviction, is that "the text [of a treaty] must be presumed to be the authentic expression of the intentions of the parties" and hence that "the starting point of interpretation is the elucidation of the meaning of the text, not an investigation *ab initio* into the intentions of the parties."[3] This arbitrary presumption is described as "established law" because of approval by the Institute of International Law and pronouncements by the International Court of Justice. The Court, it is noted, "has more than once stressed that it is not the function of interpretation to revise treaties or to read into them what they do not, expressly or by implication, contain."[4]

In justifying the inclusion within its draft articles of any principles of interpretation—principles whose "utility and even existence" have been

---

[7] In the present volume of the JOURNAL one could point, for instance, to K. J. Keith, "Succession to Bilateral Treaties by Seceding States," 61 A.J.I.L. 521 (April, 1967).

The JOURNAL expects to prepare a similar collection of articles and comments concerning various problems of international legal protection of human rights for publication as one of its 1968 issues, probably that for October.

[1] The draft articles we criticize appear in Report of the International Law Commission, U.N. General Assembly, 21st Sess., Official Records, Supp. No. 9 (U.N. Doc. A/6309/Rev. 1) (1966), hereinafter referred to as "Report"; reprinted in 61 A.J.I.L. 248 (1967).   [2] Report at 49.

[3] *Ibid.* at 51.

[4] *Ibid.* at 52. What is ignored by the Court and the Commission is that a failure to apply an agreement because of some alleged verbal gap or inadequacy in the text may be equally a "revision" of the genuine shared expectations of the parties.

"sometimes questioned"—the Commission makes a distinction between "so-called canons" and "general rules" of interpretation.[5] The "so-called canons" are not "automatic" in their application, but depend upon discretion:

> They are, for the most part, principles of logic and good sense valuable only as guides to assist in appreciating the meaning which the parties may have intended to attach to the expressions that they employed in a document. Their availability for use in any given case hinges on a variety of considerations which have first to be appreciated by the interpreter of the document: the particular arrangement of the words and sentences, their relation to each other and to other parts of the document, the general nature and subject matter of the document, the circumstances in which it was drawn up, etc.[6]

It would "clearly be inadvisable," the Commission insists, to "attempt to codify the conditions of the application of those principles of interpretation whose appropriateness in any particular case depends on the particular context and on a subjective appreciation of varying consequences."[7] The "general rules" of interpretation are, in contrast, "obligatory" and presumably "automatic" in their application. As difficult as the task may be, "cogent reasons"—including promotion of the good faith interpretation of treaties, the taking of "a clear position in regard to the role of the text in treaty interpretation," the application of the convention itself, and advice to future draftsmen—require the isolation and codification of such principles.[8]

The framework of particular principles which the Commission in fact projects into its draft articles begins with that inevitable twin of textuality: "ordinary meaning." The first prescription in Article 27, the key article, is that "A treaty shall be interpreted in good faith and in accordance with the ordinary meaning to be given to the terms of the treaty in their context and in the light of its object and purpose."[9] Lest it be thought that the references to "context" and to "object and purpose" are intended to remedy the blindness and arbitrariness of "ordinary meaning," context is immediately defined as including mere text:

> The context for the purpose of the interpretation of a treaty shall comprise, in addition to the text, including its preamble and annexes:
>
> (a) Any agreement relating to the treaty, which was made between all the parties in connection with the conclusion of the treaty;
> (b) Any instrument which was made by one or more parties in connexion with the conclusion of the treaty and accepted by the other parties as an instrument related to the treaty.[10]

The Commentary makes clear, further, that "object and purpose" do not refer to the actual subjectivities of the parties, rejected as the goal of interpretation, but rather to the mere words about "object and purpose"

---

[5] *Ibid.* at 50.   [6] *Ibid.*
[7] *Ibid.*   [8] *Ibid.*
[9] *Ibid.* at 49.   [10] *Ibid.*

intrinsic to the text.[11] The Commission, in consistent stance, also explicitly refuses to recognize the principle of "effectiveness" by which decision-makers traditionally have assessed the relevance of many varying indices of the parties' shared purposes.[12]

In Subsection 3 of Article 27, the Commission adds three "elements," all "extrinsic to the text" and of an "obligatory character," which "shall be taken into account, together with the context" in interpretation.[13] These include:

> (a) Any subsequent agreement between the parties regarding the interpretation of the treaty;
> (b) Any subsequent practice in the application of the treaty which establishes the understanding of the parties regarding its interpretation;
> (c) Any relevant rules of international law applicable in the relations between the parties.[14]

Somewhat curiously, the Commission justifies the importance attached to "subsequent practice" by suggesting that "it constitutes objective evidence of the understanding of the parties as to the meaning of the treaty," and notes that "the value of subsequent practice varies according as it shows the common understanding of the parties as to the meaning of the terms."[15] Even more curious is the consideration of the Commission that "the relevance of rules of international law for the interpretation of treaties in any given case was dependent on the intentions of the parties."[16]

In modest concession to parties of unstandardized demands and expectations, and despite the reluctance of some of its members, the Commission provides in the final Subsection 4 of Article 27 that "A special meaning shall be given to a term if it is established that the parties so intended."[17] The Commentary emphasizes that "the burden of proof lies on the party

---

[11] *Ibid.* at 51. *Cf.* Rosenne, "Interpretation of Treaties in the Restatement and the International Law Commission's Draft Articles: A Comparison," 5 Columbia Journal of Transnational Law 205, at 221 (1966):

"The way the material is presented in articles 27 and 28 is designed to stress the dominant position of the text itself in the interpretation process, the material running in sequences from the text to related elements lying outside the text."

The context makes clear that "object and purpose," mentioned in the very first section of Art. 27, are regarded as part of the "text" and not of "related elements" lying outside the text.

It may be recalled that Professor Rosenne is a member of the International Law Commission.

[12] Report at 50.   [13] *Ibid.* at 51, 49.
[14] *Ibid.* at 49.   [15] *Ibid.* at 52, 53.

[16] *Ibid.* at 53. In a more explicit postulation of the goals of interpretation the Commission would have had to consider, beyond responsible effort to ascertain the content of the genuine shared expectations of the parties, the necessity, in any particular application of an agreement, both for supplementing incomplete and vague expectations by recourse to basic community policies and for appraising even genuine expectations for their compatibility with such policies. The Commission might have sought a more careful correlation of its principles of interpretation with its provision for *jus cogens* in Art. 50.   [17] *Ibid.* at 49.

invoking the special term," but nowhere indicates how, within the compass of the rules prescribed by the Commission and its "basic approach," such a burden is to be discharged and a special meaning established.[18]

The rigor of the Commission's insistency upon the "primacy of the text" is maintained in Article 28, which authorizes a minimum recourse to preparatory work and other features of the process of agreement prior to its culmination in the sacred words of commitment. This article reads:

> Recourse may be had to supplementary means of interpretation, including the preparatory work of the treaty and the circumstances of its conclusion, in order to confirm the meaning resulting from the application of Article 27, or to determine the meaning when the interpretation according to Article 27:
> (a) Leaves the meaning ambiguous or obscure; or
> (b) Leads to a result which is manifestly absurd or unreasonable.[19]

The Commission insists that it is establishing a hierarchy among the elements to which recourse is authorized in noting that the "word 'supplementary' emphasizes that Article 28 does not provide for alternative, autonomous, means of interpretation but only for means to aid an interpretation governed by the principles contained in Article 27."[20] The reason given for this creation of a hierarchy of relevance among potential indices of the parties' shared expectations is that, while the "elements of interpretation in Article 27 all relate to the agreement between the parties *at the time when or after it received authentic expression in the text*," preparatory work does not, since it comes before the culminating moment of text.[21] This appears to deprive it of "authentic character" and to make it more susceptible of discretion in appraisal. It is nowhere explained by what indices "meanings" which are "ambiguous or obscure" or "ordinary meanings" which are "manifestly absurd or unreasonable" are to be established.[22]

It is difficult to escape the assessment that the International Law Commission's entire formulation of principles of interpretation is based upon a conception of "ordinary meaning" which is impossible of application. Indeed, even with the aid of the *travaux préparatoires* of the proposed convention, it is difficult to ascertain what this conception is.[23] In a very

---

[18] *Ibid.* at 53.   [19] *Ibid.* at 49.

[20] *Ibid.* at 54.

[21] *Ibid.* at 51. It is difficult to understand why preparatory work is less "objective evidence of the understanding of the parties" than subsequent practice.

[22] *Cf.* Rosenne, note 11 above, at 222:

"In particular, it is our view that the formal limitation on the permission to employ what the Commission has entitled 'supplementary means of interpretation' in article 28 is artificial and has no basis either in practice or in law, and certainly cannot be supported by such international jurisprudence as there is on this question."

[23] *Cf.* Professor Briggs, speaking as a member of the Commission and recommending deletion of the concept, in 1966 I.L.C. Yearbook (I), Pt. II, at 188: "Such an approach would also have the advantage of deleting all reference to the 'ordinary' meaning, a term which he found just as objectionable as the former reference to the 'natural'

recent supplementary report, Sir Humphrey Waldock, the Special Rapporteur, objects to a reconstruction of Article 27 suggested by the United States upon the ground that such a reconstruction would "seem to recognize that terms have an ordinary meaning which is independent of their context and of the objects and purposes of the treaty." [24] "This," he adds, "may be true as a matter of pure linguistics but it may be doubted whether it is true as a matter of interpretation." [25] Yet, as we have seen, the references ascribed by the Commission to "context" and "object and purpose," as these words are employed in Article 27, are so limited it is difficult to know what "meanings" such words could be given apart from linguistics, pure or otherwise. The most "basic approach" of the Commission, in all the various articles, would appear to come close to Vattel's assumption that texts can have plain and natural meanings which do not require interpretation. Indeed, the Chairman of the Commission Professor Roberto Ago, has declared, not with whole-hearted approval, that "Vattel's rule" is "in fact implicit in the proposed articles." [26] Similarly, the suggestion that it is not the function of a decision-maker "to revise treaties or to read into them what they do not, expressly or by implication, contain" is at least mildly reminiscent of Mr. Justice Owle's insistence in the case of *Brigitte Bardot M.P.?* that "If

---

meaning. Words had no ordinary or natural meaning in isolation from their context and the other elements of interpretation."

The difficulties that other members of the Commission found with the concept are broadcast in the same volume. See, for example, pp. 189, 191, 194, 195, 196. Mr. Reuter at 194 is especially sharp in reference to the contradictions in the Commission's usage.

These difficulties were cogently anticipated by Professor Hyde. In 2 International Law Chiefly as Interpreted and Applied by the United States at 1470 (1945), he wrote:

"Accordingly, one must reject as an unhelpful and unscientific procedure the endeavor to test the significance of the words employed in a treaty by reference to their so-called 'natural meaning' or any other linguistic standard, and then to attempt to reconcile therewith the thought or conduct of the contracting parties. Such a method involves the implication that those parties must be deemed to have employed words in a sense that usage may have decreed, even though contrary to their common design. It transforms the function of the interpreter from a fact-probing endeavor to ascertain the actual sense in which the parties used the words of their choice, to an effort to find what usage appears to decree as to the significance of those words, and thereupon to reconcile the conduct of the parties therewith. In so far as the interpreter essays to make that effort he is diverted from the task of ascertaining the truth concerning the design of the parties as exemplified by the text of their agreement, and endangers the success of such an attainment."

[24] Sixth Report, U.N. Doc. A/CN.4/186/Add. 6 at 11.

[25] *Ibid.*

[26] 1964 I.L.C. Yearbook (I) at 280. *Cf.* Rosenne, note 11 above, at 219:

"Sir Humphrey appears to have regarded 'interpretation' as the process by which, *in cases of doubt only*, the correct meaning of the treaty is to be established. For that process and having that objective, the text to which the parties had set their hands constituted the only point of departure; not an investigation into the objectives which prompted them to subscribe to that text, or more teleological concepts having in mind the presumed objectives of the treaty."

Parliament does not mean what it says it must say so.'' [27] Even if it be assumed that by ''ordinary meaning'' the Commission refers to linguistic usages shared in some community of which the parties are members, it is nowhere indicated by what procedures, in aid of clairvoyance, such meaning is to be ascertained and related to a ''context'' and to ''object and purpose'' which are confined to a text and do not make reference to an extrinsic process of agreement, including identifiable particular parties, with all their unique demands and expectations and varying modalities of expression.[28]

It can scarcely be doubted, further, that the ''basic approach'' of the Commission in generally arrogating to one particular set of signs—the text of a document—the rôle of serving as the exclusive index of the shared expectations of the parties to an agreement is an exercise in primitive and potentially destructive formalism. The parties to any particular agreement may have sought to communicate their shared expectations of commitment by many other signs and acts of collaboration; and it is *hubris* of the highest order to assume that the presence or absence of shared subjectivities at the outcome phase of any sequence of communications, much less that of an international agreement, can be read off in simple fashion from a manifest content or ''ordinary meaning'' of words imprinted or embossed in a document.[29] It should be the task of decision-makers, representing a larger community dedicated to the shaping and sharing of values by persuasion and agreement with a minimum of coercion and violence, to honor and promote individuality, inventiveness and diversity, and to expand the alternatives in co-operation open to as many

[27] Herbert, Bardot M.P.? and Other Misleading Cases at 167–168 (1964).

[28] *Cf.* Professor Ago in 1966 I.L.C. Yearbook (I), Pt. II, at 189: ''The expression 'ordinary meaning' had been criticized. He agreed that no term had an inherent meaning, and that the meaning always depended on usage. That was why it was essential to use terms as far as possible in the sense in which they were customarily used, which was what was understood by their 'ordinary meaning' ''.

It may be noted that even this conception is not ''objective'' in the sense that it escapes inquiry about subjectivities. For the subjectivities of the particular parties to an agreement, it merely substitutes the subjectivities of the members of the larger community. The important question is by what indices inquiry is to be made about both kinds of subjectivities; they are not necessarily equivalent in the particular instance.

Despite its emphasis upon the ''ordinary meaning'' of text, the Commission cannot of course escape references to the intent of the parties. In addition to the tail-end reference in the concluding words of Art. 27 itself, there are many other instances in the proposed convention. I am indebted to Professor Frank Newman for the following itemization: Secs. 6 (1) (b), 24, 25, 31–33, 53, 56 (1) (a) and (2); also (in the guise of ''object and purpose'') 16 (c), 17 (2), and 55 (b). Unfortunately, the brief flash of insight in the words ''the intention underlying the treaty'' (Report at 23) does not seem often to recur.

[29] This ancient wisdom, confirmed by contemporary communication studies, was put into epigrammatic form by Mr. Justice Holmes in Towne *v.* Eisner, 245 U.S. 418, 425 (1918): ''A word is not a crystal, transparent and unchanged, it is the skin of a living thought and may vary greatly in color and content according to the circumstances and the time in which it is used.''

members of the community as possible on as many occasions as possible. It can only be a debasement of the basic values of such a community to seek to impose upon all parties, whatever their nuances in creativity, the lowest common denominator in conformity. To foreclose or impede inquiry about features of the process of making and performing agreements which in fact affect the parties' expectations about commitment, and to establish in advance of inquiry fixed hierarchies in significance among features of the process whose significance in fact is a function of the configuration of all other features in any particular context, may be to impose upon one or both of the parties an agreement they never made and completely to disrupt that stability in expectation which is indispensable to effective co-operation.[30] The truth is that in the absence of a comprehensive, contextual examination of all the potentially significant features of the process of agreement, undertaken without the blinders of advance restrictive hierarchies or weightings, no interpreter can be sure that his determinations bear any relation to the genuine shared expectations of the parties. If it be suggested that the Commission's formulations are so vague and imprecise and so impossible of effective application that a sophisticated decision-maker can easily escape their putative limits, surely it must be answered that not all decision-makers are so sophisticated and that it is not the expected function of the International Law Commission to create myth for cloaking arbitrary decision.[31]

The insight had appeared widespread, prior to the appearance of the Commission's formulations, that the most appropriate function of all principles of interpretation, including both "general rules" and "so-called canons," is that of guiding interpreters to potentially relevant features of the process of agreement and its context and, hence, of assisting in the making of that comprehensive and systematic examination regarded as indispensable to rational decision.[32] The great bulk of the principles

[30] The Commission itself purports to reject the notion of a hierarchy among the "elements of interpretation" it itemizes in Art. 27, but it does not carry this insight into its presentation of the allegedly "supplementary" elements in Art. 28, and its pervasive emphasis upon textuality qualifies even the modest insight asserted in relation to Art. 27. Report at 51. *Cf.* the appraisal by Lissitzyn in "The Law of International Agreements in the Restatement," 41 N.Y.U. Law Rev. 96, 108 (1966).

[31] If a dominant policy purpose of the Commission is, as a recurrent reference to "good faith" and "*Pacta sunt servanda*" might suggest, to preclude spurious or fraudulent interpretation, surely its overwhelming emphasis upon a single variable—the text—in the larger factual context is not the best instrumentality to its end. An open-eyed, systematic exploration of all relevant features of the context would appear to promise much the more effective protection against spurious and fraudulent claims. It is entirely gratuitous to assume that a departure in interpretation from somebody's notion of "ordinary meaning" is fraud.

[32] *Cf.* Waldock, Sixth Report, U.N. Doc. A/CN.4/L.116/Add. 18 at 8: "In a sense, all 'rules' of interpretation have the character of 'guide lines' since their application in a particular case depends so much on the appreciation of the context and the circumstances of the point to be interpreted."
There can of course be no comprehensive presentation or systematic ordering of principles in the absence of a clear postulation of goals for interpretation. The goal of "textuality"—with its deference to mere "shapes on paper"—yields no criteria for

historically employed by international and national tribunals, as well as by other interpreters, has in fact, with the exception of some formulations of the *travaux préparatoires* and the "ordinary meaning" principles, been primarily permissive, opening up features for inquiry, rather than restrictive in character; and expositions of relevant principles, whether by authoritative decision-makers or private scholars, have largely differed only in the comprehensiveness and systematization of their presentation. In such a context, it has made little difference whether principles of interpretation were regarded as "obligatory" prescriptions or mere optional aids; only occasional impediments to inquiry have been imposed by even the "obligatory" view.[33] The International Law Commission, in contrast, not only projects the highly restrictive principles which we have noted above, but also recommends that these principles be made obligatory prescription—which of course they will become if the states of the world accept in present form the proposed convention on the law of treaties. A broad sampling of past decision, practice and opinion would suggest that the Commission's formulations accurately reflect neither the aggregate flow of past decision and practice nor general expectations about the requirements of future decision.[34] Certainly, it would not appear to be in the common interest for a community, which depends upon agreement not merely as a modality for the peaceful shaping and sharing of values among members but even as a principal instrument for establishing its constitution and for the prescription of authoritative community policy, deliberately to accept and project as authoritative prescription, formulations so esoteric and potentially so destructive of the foundations of genuine agreement as those put forward by the Commission.

Fortunately, an excellent model both in statement of appropriate goal and in perception of relevant features of the process of agreement and its context is readily available for any critic who may choose to seek alternatives to the Commission's formulations. The Harvard Research in International Law, more than thirty years ago, put the essential understanding for such a model into black-letter nutshell:

> A treaty is to be interpreted in the light of the general purpose which it is intended to serve. The historical background of the treaty,

---

either identifying or organizing principles. The goal of seeking to approximate the genuine shared expectations of the parties to a particular agreement offers, in contrast, the criteria of potential relevance to communication (the factors that are commonly found to affect the mediation of subjectivities).

The differences between a bare textual and a genuinely contextual approach to interpretation are, hence, not merely in goals sought but also in the range of factors made relevant and the procedures recommended for inquiry.

[33] *Cf.* Liacouras, "The International Court of Justice and Development of Useful 'Rules of Interpretation' in the Process of Treaty Interpretation," 1965 Proceedings, American Society of International Law 161.

[34] For documentation, see McDougal, Lasswell, and Miller, The Interpretation of Agreements and World Public Order: Principles of Content and Procedure (1967).

The Commission formulations are based more upon what the International Court of Justice has said than upon what it has done, and ignore much other practice and opinion.

travaux préparatoires, the circumstances of the parties at the time the treaty was entered into, the change in these circumstances sought to be effected, the subsequent conduct of the parties in applying the provisions of the treaty, and the conditions prevailing at the time interpretation is being made, are to be considered in connection with the general purpose which the treaty is intended to serve.[35]

What the Harvard Research does not offer, in implementation of its insight about appropriate goal and necessary context, is a comprehensive and systematic set of principles of content and procedure designed effectively to assist interpreters in the economic examination of particular contexts in pursuit of their appropriate goal. Even the task of fashioning such a set of principles should not, however, be beyond the reach of contemporary scholars who enjoy the advantages both of a rich inheritance in tested principles and of access to modern studies in semantics, syntactics, and other aspects of communication.

[9]

VAE VICTIS OR WOE TO THE NEGOTIATORS! YOUR TREATY OR OUR "INTERPRETATION" OF IT?

(Review Article)
By Sir Gerald Fitzmaurice *

Bliss was it in that dawn to be alive;
But to be young was very heaven!
Wordsworth, *The Prelude*, Book 11.

Where Alph, the sacred river ran
Through caverns measureless to man
Down to a sunless sea.
Coleridge, *Kubla Khan*.

I

AIMS AND OBJECTS

The length of time which has unfortunately (owing entirely to the procrastinations and backslidings of this reviewer) elapsed since the date when this (by any standards) most original and arresting work was first published in April, 1967,[1] makes it scarcely necessary to supply that systematic description of its contents which, up to a point, any well-ordered review ought to seek to do,—for by this time all those who are interested in its subject matter will have read or at least looked through it. We shall therefore concentrate on those salient aspects of it which, even after the familiarity of three years has softened their outlines, still seem to stand out with special prominence.

Arresting and original—yes. But this is and remains a very difficult work to assimilate and, partly for that reason, to be fair to. We doubt whether we shall in fact succeed in being fair to it, and think it best to declare ourselves in that sense at the outset. Not only do the authors make the task exceptionally difficult, for reasons that will appear and which indeed constitute a major part of our complaint, but, in addition, the book is peculiarly well calculated to run foul of some of our most dearly cherished predilections! Having said this, however, we hope we can claim to have complied, or tried to comply, with at least one of the recommendations the authors make to "decision-makers," namely (p. 383), to carry out the operation of *"examining the self . . . for bias"* (italics in the original), as a first step towards modifying one's outlook.[2] If, however, having taken this step, and

---

* Judge of the International Court of Justice.

[1] The Interpretation of Agreements and World Public Order. Principles of Content and Procedure. By Myres S. McDougal, Harold D. Lasswell and James C. Miller. New Haven & London, Yale University Press, 1967. pp. xxii, 410. Index. $9.75; £3.60.

[2] Both the validity and the practical utility of such a recommendation, when addressed to persons acting in a judicial capacity, may be questioned in the context of

considered the results, we still find ourselves with a different outlook from that of our authors—indeed perhaps surveying a different scene—and if this is to be accounted unto us as bias—then we must suffer the imputation as best we may.

"Down to a sunless sea"—The title given to the last chapter of the book is, symbolically, "Past Inadequacies, and Future Promise." It is indeed a new dawn of treaty interpretation that is heralded by this promise, if we will only employ the recommended techniques. Gone will be the old confusions, uncertainties and inconsistencies, and it will be a case of

> The world's great age begins anew,
> The golden years return . . .[8]

Alas, it is to no smiling ocean, with all the winds and currents setting in the right direction, that the authors channel the sacred stream, but to a sunless sea without beacons, buoys or landfalls;—for this is one of the great paradoxes of this book, that, intended to place the "decision-maker" on a sort of conveyor belt which will lead him, as it were painlessly, if not always to the right spot precisely, then to some haven very close to it, an exactly contrary impression of near disorientation is left on the mind of the reader. It is a world in which almost anything can happen. One is told how to punch the cards, and in what order to feed them to the computer, but there is no knowing what will come out;—for although one of the chief aims professed by the authors is to give effect to the "shared expectations" of the parties and, for that purpose, to achieve a reasonable degree of certainty in the process of treaty interpretation (what they call the principle of "stable future expectations"), yet enough jokers and wild cards have been hidden in the machine to ensure that negotiators can never know what will happen,—until it does!

This matter we shall revert to later. But first we must take a look at those caverns, indeed "measureless to man"—or at least to this reviewer,—through which we are to be led on the way. There, insofar as the tenuous and uncertain light allows us to see them, we shall find, like Christian passing through the Valley of the Shadow, many new strange and repellent monsters lurking.

---

this work, and generally;—for (1) the "decision-makers'" duty of impartiality is elementary, though fundamental,—it exists in all circumstances and whatever the character of the dispute or point involved,—it is in no way peculiar to treaty law or interpretation as such; (2) a judge whose bias is presumable, because of some such thing as a concrete (*e.g.* financial) interest in the subject matter of the dispute, and so on, is in any case bound to stand down, and therefore ceases to be, for that case, a "decision-maker," so that *cadit quaestio*; (3) if the judge's prejudices are of a subjective character, but are not such that he could be successfully challenged in the given case, the matter must be left to his own conscience,—but simply as part of his normal judicial duty which involves other, hardly less important obligations, such as to study the applicable law, inform himself of the precedents, etc.

[8] Shelley, *Hellas.*

II

STYLE AND LANGUAGE

> Hence loathed Melancholy
> Of Cerberus [4] and blackest Midnight born,
> In Stygian caves forlorn,
> 'Mongst horrid shapes, and shrieks, and sights unholy.
> Milton, *l'Allegro*

Stygian waters [5] *and Cimmerian darkness,* [6] *or the new obscurantism*—We would never presume, and it would indeed be totally non-representative of our real attitude towards the three very distinguished authors of this book, to describe their own outlook as Stygian or Cimmerian,—yet it remains the fact that one reason why, as already mentioned, it is no easy task to be fair to this book, is that it is written in a highly esoteric private language,—we do not say jargon, but a kind of juridical code which renders large tracts of it virtually incomprehensible to the uninitiated (or at least to the unpracticed and unversed), short of a word by word "construe," such as we did in school with our Latin unseens. Even so, the reader, professional though he may be (and this is hardly a book that can have been intended for students), will frequently be left with a feeling of honest doubt as to whether he has really—or fully—grasped the intended significance of what he has been reading.

That these strictures are not merely the carpings of a disgruntled reviewer forced for once to study and reflect, instead of only to skim and to scold, will soon be demonstrated.[7] In passing, it is worth noticing that the offense with which Milton taxed Melancholy was the fact, not of her existence, but of her appearance in the wrong place. Indeed, in the *Penseroso* he commends her qualities of heart and mind which make for repose and *gravitas*. He even apostrophizes her as "divinest Melancholy,"—but he is quick to add

> Whose saintly image is too bright
> To hit the sense of human sight.

And this very neatly expresses the crux of the complaint we are making here; for a brilliant effulgence there may be, but it defeats its purpose if it

---

[4] This creature is defined in Chambers' Twentieth Century Dictionary (1962 ed.) as "the monster that guarded the entrance to Hades, a dog with (*at least*) three heads"—italics ours!

[5] The same source defines "Stygian" as "of the Styx, one of the rivers of Hades, across which Charon ferries the shades of the departed: hellish, infernal: black as the Styx." The 1965 Penguin English Dictionary says "of or like the underworld river Styx: dark, gloomy."

[6] The Cimmerii were a tribe fabled to have lived in perpetual darkness.

[7] The very title of the work (see note 1 above) gives rise to doubts,—for the category of general multilateral conventions that chiefly involves questions of "world order" is a comparatively small one, and the book is clearly not intended to be restricted to agreements of this kind. Equally there are doubts in respect of the subtitle: "Principles of Content and Procedure," for the *content* of a treaty is what the parties in fact put into it. There are no principles as to what they must put into it. And by principles of *procedure* is presumably meant methods or technique—of interpretation—yet interpretation is not a *procedural* but a substantive process.

is too bright "to hit the sense of human sight." In *l'Allegro*, therefore, Milton's point was that in a world in which all should be sweetness and light, Melancholy was not wanted—and so "Hence loathed Melancholy" of the Cerberean birth, etc.

Is it over-fanciful thus to perceive an analogy? Is an inspissated [8] obscurity any more justified in a work on treaty interpretation than melancholy in the realm of good cheer? The old saw is irresistible: *Quis custodiet ipsos custodes*? Who shall interpret the interpreters, and ought it to be necessary to do so? If a work on interpretation requires itself to be "interpreted" and practically transliterated into ordinary language before it can be understood, what value are we to attach to the views on interpretation expressed in this, itself most interpretation-requiring of works? [9]

The call is not for simplicity in the sense of absence of complexity, for interpretation, whether of treaties, contracts, statutes, wills, leases, conveyances, etc. is, and always will be, a difficult and complex matter;—which, however, renders clarity of exposition, and the use of terms that do not require a glossary for their elucidation, all the more important.

It is now time to show that these animadversions are not just the fuddy-duddy outpourings of a senile and saurian purism. To that end we shall cite (with, where possible, elucidations) a few passages from various parts of the work. We admit that these have not been chosen exactly at random, —nor have they been specially selected, except in respect of the final sentence of the last of them (for reasons which will appear). They are in fact matched by many other passages of a like nature, occurring in key places, thus showing that the use of this kind of language is no mere case of the occasional abstruse or difficult sentence or expression,—that it is in fact a deliberately employed technique. We also admit that the passages cited are taken out of context, but submit that the usual objection to this practice does not apply here,—for that objection is that, by so doing, the meaning is falsified or distorted. Here the issue is different, namely, whether there is any readily discoverable meaning at all.

The following passage taken from page 351 of the book, under the heading of "The Operation of Estimating Agreement Probability," [10] may be

---

[8] The—in the context—decidedly felicitous dictionary meaning of this adjective is "thickened"; "rendered more dense"—see references given in notes 4 and 5 above, and also R. H. Hill's Dictionary of Difficult Words (Arrow Books Edition, 1963).

[9] In fact, it would be difficult to find a better expression for describing the general style of the book than that of "linguistic esotericism" which the authors themselves use (p. 269, line 8) in alluding to an interpretative process they disapprove of,—an almost classic example of the pot and kettle syndrome!

[10] A not at all clear definition or attempted explanation of the notion of "estimating agreement probability" is given on p. 60 of the work. It is apparently intended to denote the process of having regard to the surrounding circumstances, and in particular to the presence or absence of other similar agreements in the field concerned, in order to judge whether it is likely that the parties would in fact have entered into an agreement on the lines alleged—(alleged that is to say, by one of them,—for if both allege it, there is no dispute on the point)—and whether the agreement is of the kind that would probably have been concluded in the given case.

regarded as a fairly typical example of the authors' methods of exposition:—

> The pragmatic dimension of communication analysis, to which agreement probability relates, has been examined in part by decision-makers as one aspect of the overall contextual approach. The contextual survey of the participants' shared demands and expectations, tracing these factors from early through current conditions, has nonetheless failed to make use of available operations in examining the "causes" of a communicated message. Past techniques developed for examining the "consequences" or "effects" of communication have failed to produce any more adequate results. The main references to the effects of communication have resulted, as we saw above, in analyses of its effects on the decision-making process and upon the participants as manifested in their subsequent courses of conduct. But the predominant emphasis of the pragmatic dimension of analysis has most frequently been limited to considerations of the "reasonableness" of reliance upon the communicated message. The operations designed to assess this feature of the agreement process, however, are scarcely representative of the operation of estimating agreement probability to which we refer.

Even though, after reading three hundred and fifty pages of the book, some skill may have been acquired in breaking the authors' cypher, this portentous passage frankly continues to baffle the present reviewer, if not as to its basic drift,[11] then as to the possibility of re-stating it in simpler and more readily comprehensible terms. We will not therefore here attempt such a re-statement, as we do in the case of certain other passages to be quoted later. True it may be that a number of the more recondite expressions employed are defined or explained, or attempted so to be, elsewhere in the book.[12] But an exegesis on interpretation should use terms that can be understood even when standing alone. Nor should writers assume that all utilizers of their work are going to be persons who will read it straight through as written. Quite as often,—and even habitually if they are practitioners—they will consult the table of contents, and/or index, and turn straight to the relevant paragraph.

We cite next the following, relatively speaking, much simpler but still highly elliptical passage, from page 42 of the book, in which the attempt to achieve synthesis by means of an advanced degree of compression is merely self-defeating:

> We may further specify our recommended integrative goals by emphasizing the consequences of interpretation for the aggregate agreement process. Since clarity of expectation may be encouraged in fu-

[11] From the authors' immediately following references to the 1962 South West Africa case (I.C.J. Reports, 1962, p. 319) it appears that the sort of problem envisaged was such a quite simply stated one as whether the Mandate for South West Africa amounted to an international agreement,—did those concerned treat it as such?—were other League of Nations Mandates regarded as treaties or agreements?—etc.

[12] The following expressions contained in the passage quoted would require elucidation by anyone coming upon them *for the first time* in such a context as that of this work: "pragmatic dimension"; "communication analysis"; "agreement probability"; "decision-makers"; "contextual approach"; "shared demands and expectations"; "communicated message"; "effects of communication"; "analyses of its effects [*i.e.* of the effects of the "effects of communication"] on the decision-making process"; etc.

ture agreement-making if decision-makers give deference to carefully worked out arrangements, we include among the objectives of interpretation the encouragement of deliberate efforts among the parties to future agreements to obtain definiteness of expectation.

This seems to mean (or does it?) that if you interpret agreements in the way the parties wanted (although the question of what they *then* (jointly) wanted is, of course, precisely what is in issue and now to be determined),[13] they will be encouraged in future agreements to make what they want clearer. It seems permissible to discern the lurking shadows of a *circulus inextricabilis* here, even though the exact meaning to be given to the expression "clarity (or "definiteness") of expectation" eludes the reviewer.

A further example of the same propensity for synthesis and compression, occurs on page 266 where the following sentence is to be found: "The absence of indicia of explicit rationality in the promulgative arena need not, thus, necessarily indicate that explicit rationality was not employed in the cameral arena." Being translated, this means no more than something like the following: "Because a tribunal does not give reasons for its findings, this does not entail that it did not have and discuss any during its private deliberations,"—same number of words but several magnitudes clearer, we hope.

It is of course obvious—and this is relevant to almost every sentence in the book—that when the authors use expressions such as "the promulgative arena," "the cameral arena," etc., their aim is to use terms which can cover any one of a number of different manifestations of the same process: thus one can seek to subsume under a single term such things as, for instance, (a) anything "handed down," be it judgment, decision, award, ruling, finding, order, decree, etc.; or (b) any "decision-making" *entity*, be it a court, a tribunal, a commission, a committee or even one man behind a desk sorting out an office squabble. But in the context of treaty interpretation such attempts to invest the subject with a pseudo-scientific aura are unrealistic and vain. It is as if an oculist should say to his client: "The fact that an aid to vision does not re-act adequately to normally-to-be-expected conditions of luminosity is not necessarily an indication of more than the existence of an adjustment-requiring situation." Such language may have the abstract virtue of applying to many more "aids to vision" than spectacles—for instance, telescopes, field glasses, opera glasses, microscopes,

---

[13] The difficulty is that the parties do not both, or all, want the same thing. If they did, there would be no dispute, and no occasion for any decision on interpretation. This fence, which constantly recurs, the authors seem to ignore. Phrases such as "the shared expectations" (whether "genuine" or not!) of the parties—or even the more traditional "intentions of the parties"—really only cause confusion, because the parties invariably appear in court as not *sharing* any expectations at all, and as having no common intentions. They may originally have done so, and this of course is what the court has to discover. But it would save a great deal of trouble if, instead of this unrealistic phraseology, reference were made to the intention or intentions, object or objectives, of the *treaty*, in which the parties are supposed to have embodied their (then) common desiderata. This, however, is something our authors are bound to dislike—see end of note 18 below.

reflectors, magnifiers, dioramas, view-finders, range-finders, telescopic sights and even, at a pinch, lighthouses, heliographs and cameras. But the client might well be forgiven for replying: "You mean I need different lenses."

Less defensible still, is the use of such an expression as "explicit rationality," which does not even have the (though quite superfluous) merit of being a portmanteau term. Since, in the context, the "absence of indicia of specific rationality" simply means a failure to give grounds for a decision, it has to be inferred, or guessed, that "specific rationality" means the process of giving such grounds. Even so, there is an element of uncertainty, for elsewhere (page 64) the authors indicate that what they mean is not so much stating the actual reasons, as stating the principles (of interpretation) upon which the actual reasons are based. In practice, no doubt, it comes to much the same thing,—but why use such an ambiguous expression as "rationality," the *primary* meaning of which is the quality or process of being rational? And where does "specific" come in?

We turn next to page 319, where the following passage is to be found:

> The most frequent application of the lexical operation has been in analyses of the cultural features of the largest shared audiences of particular communications made in the agreement process. In recent years a more general form of this concern has emerged in which the explicit specification of lexical operations in relation to the largest shared audiences has become paramount. . . .

It would seem (but only by reference to quite a different part of the book, page 216 *et seq.*) that the expression "the largest shared audiences" is intended to denote either the community at large or that part of it to which the particular agreement has reference. Thus the principle of interpretation according to the "plain" or "ordinary" meaning of terms, contemplates that meaning which would appear to be the "plain" or "ordinary" one to, say, the man in the street;—or if the agreement is about some health matter, that which members of the medical profession would regard as being, in the medical sense, the plain or ordinary meaning of the words used,—and so on. If that is the case, then, although the exact significance of the expression "the lexical operation" remains somewhat obscure,[14] it would seem that the first sentence of the paragraph under discussion can be explained in the following way, namely, that in the interpretation of an agreement it is necessary to analyze the linguistic usages of that section of the community to which the parties belong or to which the agreement has reference. The second sentence continues to be baffling. What, in particular, is the "specification" of the lexical operation? Perhaps the sentence simply means that in recent years there has been a tendency to make use of a wider context or frame of reference in carrying out the analyses necessary for the process of interpretation? Now in the ideas underlying this passage, the language of which we have been criticizing, there is much of quite acceptable substance. Why not therefore express it in a way which the normal intelligence can grasp without recourse to the so-called "lexical operation"?

[14] The dictionary meaning of "lexical" is "belonging to a lexicon." Is there an *operation* of belonging to a lexicon?

We shall finally cite the following passage taken from page 188:

> It should not be surprising that more extensive references by decision-makers to explicit anticipated solutions of subsequent disputes are seldom found, since in the degree to which solutions are spelled out either in the text or in preparatory work the probability of the dispute reaching the level of community decision obviously decreases. However, the increasing diversity in the various indices of expectations in modern multilateral agreements, as indicated by recent holdings of the International Court,[15] may serve to encourage litigation even in cases where one of these indices clearly outlines an anticipated solution. In addition, as Beckett has pointed out, participants may be induced to present claims, for various reasons of prestige or diplomatic advantage, even in the presence of explicitly communicated anticipations of present contingencies.

Before attempting any analysis of this passage it must be said in parenthesis that Sir Eric Beckett (then principal Legal Adviser to the Foreign Office, in London), who was well known for his exceptional clarity of thought and expression, could never possibly have said anything at all in the *form* here attributed to him by the authors. They do not give the reference, but we have identified it, as now set out in the footnote below,[16] —and if the authors' description of what Beckett said is read in conjunction with what he actually said, it seems to amount to this—that parties to a treaty may sometimes have political reasons for bringing a case under it, even though they have reason to anticipate that they will lose. But nothing as simple as that can be said to be apparent in the phrase "explicitly communicated anticipations of present contingencies."

Turning now to the first two sentences of the paragraph we are discussing (on page 188 of the book), it seems, from what immediately precedes them on pages 186–187, that the expression "anticipated solution" is intended to denote what may eventually come to pass, by way of outcome, in

---

[15] What "holdings" of the Court are being referred to is not specified, but the case of Reservations to the Genocide Convention is cited a paragraph earlier (pp. 187–188). It also seems from various passages elsewhere that another case the authors might have had in mind would be that of Certain Expenses of the United Nations. By "indices of expectations" the authors appear to mean the existence of pointers to what the parties to the agreement would have wanted, had they anticipated what subsequently occurred, which of course they did not, or the dispute, of which this non-anticipation constitutes the real issue, would not have arisen.

[16] The reference is to a passage on p. 440 of Vol. 43 (I, 1950) of the Annuaire of the Institut de Droit International (Bath Session). Beckett was answering (*inter alia*) a contention of Lauterpacht's to the effect that *ex hypothesi* there never *could* be a "plain sense of the words" in the case of disputed treaty clauses, for if the sense was really plain there would be no dispute about it. Beckett thought that it was not correct,

> as a matter of practice, and experience, to state that the meaning of a treaty provision cannot be clear or otherwise the States concerned would not be going to the trouble and expense of litigating about it. It certainly happens that the meaning of a treaty provision is perfectly clear but that one or another party to the treaty has for one reason or another found the provision inconvenient.

And, finding this inconvenient, it sees in a reference to adjudication (in which it may win but will be no worse off than before for losing) a possible solution. Beckett added: "The political position of the State concerned may be such that it can only give way on the basis of an international legal decision."

a position in which the parties, during their negotiations, discussed a possible course, which, however, without actually rejecting it, they did not eventually embody in the final text of their treaty. This could be either because they thought the situation it related to would not materialize, or because they were not really in agreement about it and trusted it would not. Or again—something to which both Hudson and Beckett [17] had drawn attention—it could be that the parties did not think about the matter at all, in which case there could not truly be even an "anticipated" solution.

In all these cases, however, whether the parties did not think about the matter, or did think about it but did not deal with it in the treaty, the so-called "anticipated solution" must evidently consist in practice of the view which the adjudicator himself takes as to what the parties *would* have done about the matter if they had both thought about it and dealt with it in the treaty.[18]

We shall comment later on the basic merits of this idea. The authors' defense of it is, however, far from convincing. In the first sentence of the paragraph which we are citing from page 188 of the book, it is admitted that there is not much judicial authority for the doctrine of the anticipated solution because, insofar as the parties did in fact anticipate a solution, the matter will probably not reach the "decision-makers" at all. This seems an obvious but a somewhat lame conclusion. However—so the authors hopefully continue (this is the second sentence of the quoted passage)—there may yet be some litigation if the courts are willing to have regard to the "increasing diversity" of pointers [19] to be found in "modern multilateral agreements,"—that is to say, pointers as to what the parties may or might have intended about something they did not clearly deal with, or

---

[17] Manley O. Hudson, The Permanent Court of International Justice (1943), p. 644; Beckett, Annuaire of the Institute of International Law, Vol. 43 (I, 1950), p. 438.

[18] There is only limited substance in the charge which the authors make against Beckett at the end of their note 226 on p. 187, namely, that he "failed to consider the possibility of determining, by an analysis of *travaux [préparatoires]*, just what issues were deadlocked and what anticipated conflicts were resolved or left unresolved by such a conference" [*i.e.*, a private meeting of heads of delegations];—for Beckett's whole point was that meetings of this kind, being private, nothing appeared about them in the official record. One may of course be justified in thinking that when the record peters out on a particular issue, this is because that issue has become deadlocked. But it may equally well be due to other causes: the issue has been overtaken in some way, or become secondary, or the participants have tacitly agreed to bypass or drop it. Beckett's point was that if an issue *is* deadlocked and is resolved at private off-the-record meetings, no indication of the *way* in which it was resolved will appear *except in the text of the treaty itself*. But, for our distinguished authors, to have to rely on the mere text of the treaty alone, without any other aid, amounts to a fate almost worse than death!

[19] Some such term as "pointers" seems preferable to the authors' favorite "indices" or "indicia," which are either ambiguous or incorrectly employed. The word "index" has two plurals, "indexes" and "indices," but the latter is strictly of mathematical connotation, meaning, in the exponential sense, the power to which a quantity is to be raised by successive multiplications of itself. "Indicia" is not a plural alternative to "indices" but the plural of the Latin *"indicium,"* which can mean an indication but has several other meanings such as disclosure, evidence, proof, and even permits or rewards given in connection with testifying.

did not deal with at all;—because, even if there is one pointer obviously tending in a particular direction that the parties, or some of them, do not like (and this is the implication), there will always remain the possibility for the court to decide on the basis of a different though *ex hypothesi* less clear but, to some at least of those interested, more welcome pointer.

The authors seem to see nothing strange in the idea that a court should deliberately act in this way,—that is to say, ignore a clear pointer in favor of others less clear but, presumably, leading to a better result for *some* of the parties. Here again the authors overlook the fact (see note 13 above) that the parties are not both or all wanting the same thing, or there would be no dispute, and that a decision in favor of the one side, on the basis of *less* clear pointers, must run counter to the right of the other side to succeed on the basis of the clearer pointer. The implication, in short, is that in the case to which the authors specifically refer in the sentence under discussion, namely, that of "modern multilateral conventions," a court, balancing the various legal factors involved, might be justified in reaching what would in effect be a policy decision not necessarily based on the real juridical weight of these factors. We cannot share that view.

III

DOCTRINE AND SUBSTANCE

With the concluding part of the last section we have moved over from the manner to the substance of what the authors say. If there is any single leit-motiv in what is an extremely complex theme, it seems to consist in a powerful plea for a completely "open-ended" technique of interpretation. In a sense it is the same plea that Sir Hersch Lauterpacht put forward fifteen years before this book was written,—but quite a different method is proposed for reaching the desired result. Lauterpacht's contention was, in essence, that principles or rules of interpretation were of little practical value, and should be disregarded, or at least used only as rough guides. The traditional rules tended to be contradictory and to cancel one another out. Each case involving the interpretation of a text was *sui generis,* and a conclusion should be arrived at only in the light of *all* the factors that might affect it.[20]

In the present work, exactly the opposite method is advocated. Every conceivable principle and rule of interpretation is instanced (including, it must be said, a number that one does not think one has ever heard of before), and these are listed in certain ordered categories, so that, whereas Lauterpacht wanted, paradoxically, to cover the ground by first clearing it of everything, in the present work the ground is, with equal paradox,

---

[20] See Lauterpacht's Report to the Institute of International Law in the Annuaire for 1950, Vol. 43(I). For a convenient summary of the controversy between Lauterpacht and Beckett (see note 16 above) on this and certain other questions of treaty interpretation, see Fitzmaurice and Vallat's article on Beckett and his work in 17 International and Comparative Law Quarterly (April, 1968) at pp. 302–313, more particularly pp. 303 and 310–313.

covered so comprehensively with everything that little of it remains visible —the wood cannot be seen for the trees.[21]

At the same time, Lauterpacht did think that if (contrary to his view) the traditional principles and rules of interpretation were to be retained, then at least an attempt should be made to place them in some kind of logical array, and to establish a short of hierarchy indicative of the order of weight or precedence which they should be regarded as having *inter se*.[22] In this, our authors seem to agree with him (as did Beckett at the time),[23] and this book consists indeed, in large measure, in a useful, if only partially effectual attempt at such an arrangement (see in particular at pages 35– 77),—a summary of recapitulation of the results arrived at being given towards the end (pages 382–390). But to this reviewer, these results appear to amount to little more than a listing of techniques of interpretation ("check-points") or goings through of motions, *all* of which are to be indiscriminately applied [24]—in a certain temporal order it may be—but not one adequately related to weight or precedence,[25] except that an overriding preponderance is given to certain notions of a very general, wide and far-reaching character which we shall discuss later (but these are notions which, as will be seen, are hardly in the nature of interpretation as such, but intended rather to go beyond that and, in effect, to amend the agreement or even cancel it altogether).

Vae victis—Hence therefore our cry of lamentation and foreboding: woe to the negotiators, for indeed would they be vanquished, and woe would it be unto them, if much that is contained in this book had to be taken literally. It would not be *their* treaty that would emerge from the fray, but another that someone else thought was the one they should have entered into. However, to start with something relatively minor, though not unimportant—for it is by its over-inclusiveness that much of this system errs— what, for instance, is to be made, and what are the implications, of the following passages read together?—

Page 372:

The *conception* of agreement as a process of communication, then, involves viewing *all signs and acts* (our italics here) of collaboration between the parties as an effort on their part to mediate all relevant subjectivities of commitment.[26] Seen in this way, communication involves the transmission of *signs . . . to targets* [27] or *audiences* (our italics) with the goal of mutual understanding on the part both of the sender and receiver of the messages. It is the possible inadequacies in transmission—usually through the inherent shortcomings in the capability

[21] It is tempting to make the contrast that in Lauterpacht's conception the wood hid the trees, but he really wanted to do away with the trees altogether!

[22] See Lauterpacht, *loc. cit.*, note 20 above, p. 367.

[23] *Ibid.*, p. 439; and see Fitzmaurice and Vallat, *loc. cit.*, note 20, p. 310.

[24] See Metzger in 61 A.J.I.L. at p. 1011 (1967).

[25] An example of the sort of operation that is really needed was given in *loc. cit.*, notes 20 and 23 above, at pp. 312–313.

[26] We do not know what this expression "subjectivities of commitment" really means.

[27] "Audiences" can be understood, but what "targets" are in mind here?—and, can a "sign" be transmitted to a target?

of words *and other signs* (our italics) to communicate shared subjectivities—that place the communications analyst on guard . . .

Ibid.:

It would be quite impossible, we believe, for a competent analyst who is acquainted with the study of language *and gesture* (our italics) to commit himself seriously to the one-sided assertions that clutter the literature of interpretation. . . .

And on page 388:

We do not neglect to note the operation of *assessing gestures and deeds* (italics in the original), since several techniques are already at hand for accomplishing this purpose, making it possible to choose among inferences that depend on judgment of the methods used. . . .

In the auction room, it is true, agreements are frequently reached, at least in principle, by means of signs and gestures. The bidder nods to the auctioneer, or raises a finger, and this commits him to his bid. The auctioneer brings down his hammer, and this commits his client to a sale, subject to any announced reservations or conditions. But treaties and other international agreements, and perhaps even more especially the general multilateral conventions the authors are mainly concerned with, are not and should not be concluded by the methods of the sale room, which are totally out of keeping with the occasion.

No doubt the doctrine of signs and gestures is not meant to be carried to extremes: yet if the passages just quoted were taken at their face value they could lead to some singular results. A negotiator, in accepting a certain condition or proviso, is seen to wink broadly; but the condition is written into the text, which is subsequently signed and ratified. Is evidence of the wink afterwards to be admitted to show that the condition was not really accepted, or that it is doubtful whether it was? The case may seem far-fetched, but the suppositions behind it are not; for it is very much part of the authors' philosophy—and a great deal of the book is concerned with this—that the text as written is inherently suspect: only by going behind it can the truth be arrived at. But if so, is there much point in reducing to writing what was supposedly agreed, and embodying it in a text?

It is not in reality signs and gestures—(for these constitute an altogether too uncertain and rickety basis on which to found any definite conclusion) —but the official acts and conduct of the parties that may be material. It is, for instance, now generally accepted that the conduct of the parties relative to a given provision, manifested in the ordinary course of the execution or application of the treaty, may be a very reliable and even the best guide as to the correct interpretation of that provision, *so long as* it is the mutual or common conduct of both or all of them, and not merely of one or some; —for in the latter case what may precisely be in issue, and calling for decision, is whether such conduct did not involve a *breach* of the treaty based on an incorrect interpretation of it.[28]

[28] In point of fact, however, it is not necessarily, or even principally, in the particular context of treaty interpretation that the acts and conduct of the parties may be material. In the case of the Temple of Preah Vihear (I.C.J. Reports, 1962, p. *6 et seq.*)

> But doth suffer a sea-change
> Into something rich, and strange [29]

The most striking feature of the authors' system is, however, that it subordinates the interpretation of a treaty—or rather (for the matter has little to do with interpretation *stricto sensu*) [30] its application—to the attainment of certain objectives,—a process which is summed up (see, for instance, page 41 of the book) under the head of the "policing . . . goal." This is defined in general terms (page 42) as "requiring the rejection of the parties' explicit expectations which [sc. if and insofar as they] contradict community policies." In other words the intentions of the parties, even if clear and ascertained and—what is even more important—common to them both, or all (in short the intentions of the *treaty*—see note 13 above), are not to be given effect to if, in the opinion of the "decision-maker," such intentions are inconsistent with (page 44) "the goals of public order." Since it is thus left to the adjudicator to decide not only whether there is such inconsistency but also what *are* the goals of public order (and of which public order) to be taken into account, it is evident that on this wide-ranging, indeed almost illimitable basis, the parties could never be sure how their treaty would be applied or whether it would be applied at all. The process would, in fact, confer on the "decision-maker" a discretion of a kind altogether exceeding the normal limits of the judicial function, amounting rather to the exercise of an administrative rôle.

This is well illustrated by the character of the only "community goal" which, so far as this reviewer can see, the authors themselves actually specify, namely, that of the preservation of "human dignity" which is coupled with what is called (page 383) "the operation of *examining the self* (italics in the original) for predispositions incompatible with the goal of human dignity"—an admirable desideratum, one aspects of which (the duty of impartiality) has already received some comment earlier herein.[31] No one of course can quarrel with the ideal of the preservation of human dignity, and the avoidance of action incompatible with it, as an essential objective. But without further and much more precise definition, this criterion and others like it which the authors specify, such as "overriding community goals" or "basic constitutive policies," etc. are too subjective to be of practical value to the adjudicator, or in the alternative would invest him with an almost arbitrary power. As Professor Leo Gross has well said,

---

the International Court relied markedly on such acts and conduct,—but this was not strictly with reference to the interpretation of the boundary treaty that underlay that case, but as affording evidence of the *acceptance* by the parties of a certain map line as constituting the correct boundary in the disputed area.

[29] Shakespeare, *The Tempest.*

[30] An agreement must already *be* interpreted in order to be "policed" (see below), for it is only on the basis of a particular and declared interpretation of it, that it can be shown to require policing in the authors' sense of that notion.

[31] See in particular note 2 above; but this might be the place to add something,—for certain of the events of the last few years and the many decided cases passed in review by the authors of this work from the standpoint of their doctrines, may suggest that examination of the self for bias is desirable not only for the decision-maker but also for those who comment upon the decision-maker's decisions!

such concepts "are pregnant with ambiguity far greater than ever confronted an international tribunal in interpreting . . . a treaty." [32] He adds, pointing to a further difficulty: "Reference is apparently made to communities of various orders ranging from a relatively compact community comprising the parties and the tribunal . . . to a world-wide community." [33] Everyone knows, for instance, that in private life some people will regard as an affront to their dignity things which others will not even notice; and in the international field also there is a wide range of possible variables. [34]

At bottom, the theory is one which proposes indirectly to import into treaty law an extensively conceived element of *ius cogens* without, however, any adequate definition of the *ius* which is to be *"cogendum."* The Vienna Convention on the Law of Treaties which, even so, is considered by some to go too far in this respect, does at least, in providing for the voidance of treaties if they conflict with "a peremptory norm of general international law (*ius cogens*)," define such a norm as being one that is "accepted and recognized by the international community of States as a whole as a norm from which no derogation is permitted and which can be modified only by a subsequent norm of general international law having the same character." [35] This definition may not itself be entirely satisfactory, [36] but it does give the adjudicator something to go by, at all events as to the *nature* of the notion involved.

Similarly, in the domestic field, the notion of "overriding community goals" is already to a limited extent reflected in the concept of "public policy," but in a highly modified, indeed quite different form. The latter policy is the policy of the law, and only indirectly of the community, considered apart from the law,—and it operates only within the confines of the law. [37] The law will not, for instance, enforce certain types of contracts,

---

[32] "Treaty Interpretation: The Proper Rôle of an International Tribunal," 1969 Proceedings, American Society of International Law at p. 114.   [33] *Ibid.*

[34] It would be easy, but it would be invidious to point to widespread practices sanctioned by law, religion and social usage, which would nevertheless be held by many to conflict with human dignity.   [35] Article 53.

[36] The expression "having the same character" at the end of this provision presumably means having the same character of being "a norm from which no derogation is permitted,"—for if it also included having the same character of being "a subsequent norm of general international law having the same character," an obvious element of circularity or infinite regress would be introduced. All the same there seems to be a latent ambiguity here. Furthermore, although even a *peremptory* norm can be rendered otiose or no longer applicable by a subsequent change of *circumstances* or conditions, there seems to be something a little queer about the idea of a norm that is peremptory, yet capable of being modified by another norm, also peremptory, but equally capable of modification, and so on *ad infinitum.* There would seem to be something dubious about the true peremptoriness of all such norms in the sense of being *ius cogens,* i.e., their peremptoriness would seem to be lent to them rather than inherent. There are of course norms that are *"higher"* than others, but this is a different thing. They do not conflict with or modify the "lower" norm, but on the contrary confer upon it a validity it might not otherwise have by its own force.

[37] On this subject see the interesting remarks of Professor Gross, citing Jenks, in *loc. cit.* note 32 above, at pp. 114–115.

as being usurious, as involving gambling transactions, as being directed to immoral purposes, etc. But, except in very special circumstances, these disqualifications are known to the parties in advance, not imposed *ex post facto* at the discretion of the adjudicator.

Nor is the policing of agreements in the sense of, in effect, voiding them for "conflict with community policies," by any means the only doom with which this work confronts the negotiators. An equal hazard, tending in certain circumstances to bring about, over the parties' heads, an even greater sea-change in a given treaty situation, is to be anticipated from what the authors call their second goal,—the first being (page 40) to make "a disciplined, responsible effort to ascertain the genuine shared expectations of the . . . parties . . . ," because (pages 40–41) "to defend the dignity of man is to respect *his* (authors' italics) choices and not, *save for overriding common interest* (our italics here), to impose the choices of others upon him,"—admirable sentiments of course, but we have seen where, in the pursuit of the third (policing) goal, that saving clause about the "overriding common interest" can lead.

The *second* goal contemplates the case where the search for (page 41) the "genuine shared expectations" of the parties "must falter or fail because of gaps, contradictions or ambiguities" in their "communication"—(an unclear term which might mean in the course of the negotiations leading up to the agreement, or in the agreement itself). In such event (*ibid.*) "a decision-maker should supplement or *augment* (our italics) the relatively more explicit expressions of the parties [sc. what they actually wrote into the agreement] by making reference to the basic constitutive policies of the larger community. . . ." Here again, therefore, community policies come in as a criterion, and also, once more, human dignity,—for (*ibid.*) "no conceivable alternative goal" could be "in accord with the aspiration to defend and expand a social system compatible with the overriding objectives of human dignity."

This, of course, however excellent, is not law but sociology; and although the aim is said to be "in support of search for the genuine shared expectations of the parties," it would in many cases have—and is perhaps subconsciously designed to have—quite a different effect, namely, in the guise of interpretation, to substitute the will of the adjudicator for that of the parties, since the intentions of the latter are, by definition (in the given circumstances) unascertainable because not sufficiently clearly or fully expressed,—and therefore presumed intentions, based on what the adjudicator thinks would be good for the community, or in accordance with "overriding objectives of human dignity" etc., must be attributed to them.

Now the process of, so to speak, curing the deficiencies of a text is, within certain limits, a perfectly legitimate one, constantly employed by courts and tribunals. For instance, where the intention or object of the agreement is plain, no court would allow a party to get out of what was a clear undertaking, merely on account of some drafting lapse, wrong reference, incorrect description or manifest omission, and such like deficiencies of a technical not substantive character—(this indeed, when the "explicit rationality" is cut away, can be seen to be the real basis of the decision of the International Court in the first (preliminary objection) phase of the *Temple* case).[88] Another example is afforded by the principle *ut res magis valeat quam pereat*, the effect of which is that where a text is ambiguous or defective, but a possible, though uncertain, interpretation of it would give the agreement some effect, whereas otherwise it would have none, a court is entitled to adopt that interpretation, on the legitimate assumption that the parties must have intended their agreement to have some effect, not none.

Significantly, however, the maxim *ut magis* is all too frequently misunderstood as denoting that agreements should always be given their *maximum possible* effect, whereas its real object is merely (*"quam pereat"*) to prevent them failing altogether. This affords a very good pointer to the limits of a doctrine which, if allowed free play, would result in parties finding themselves saddled with obligations they never intended to enter into, in relation to situations they never contemplated, and which often they could not even have anticipated. Is it unfair to ascribe to the authors of this work the championship of such a doctrine? Let them (page 388) be heard for themselves:

> Modern logical tools may disclose implications that were undreamed of when the parties were hammering out their understanding.

Of what use then is it to "hammer out" an understanding (not surely any casual process) if implications then "undreamed of" are later to be imported, and given obligatory force?

IV

VALEDICTORY

Despite its intrinsic interest, its stimulating character, and its many merits, of which the present review confessedly gives little indication, this is a work that leaves a somber impression on the mind. Aiming at order and liberality, its concepts, by their very breadth, open the door to anarchy and abuse. Down the centuries of close upon two millennia of years there come, still echoing, the lines of the great Mantuan:

> *Facilis descensus Averno;*
> *Noctes atque dies patet atri janua Ditis;*
> *Sed revocare gradum superasque evadere ad auras,*
> *Hoc opus, hic labor est.*[89]

[88] Cited in note 28 above.

[89] Vergil, *The Aeneid*, Book VI. A free rhyming translation might read:

Down to Avernus smooth and easy winds the trail,
Where noon and night the dark God's portals open stay:
But to return from thence into the light of common day,
Not ease nor rest but only striving can avail.

Apologies, however, to the memory of Wordsworth for this somewhat oblique use of his well-known figure of speech "the light of common day"—(Ode on Intimations of Immortality from Recollections of Early Childhood, verse V, last line).

[10]

VARIETIES OF APPROACH TO TREATY INTERPRETATION: WITH SPECIAL REFERENCE TO THE DRAFT CONVENTION ON THE LAW OF TREATIES BEFORE THE VIENNA DIPLOMATIC CONFERENCE

By

FRANCIS G. JACOBS *

OF all the issues raised by the Vienna Convention on the Law of Treaties, there can be few which combine theoretical interest and practical importance to the same degree as the question of treaty interpretation. The different approaches adopted in recent years by international lawyers not only reflect certain doctrinal differences, but raise fundamental questions of policy. And since questions of interpretation are involved in most legal disputes, it is not surprising that there has been a continuing controversy over the principles of treaty interpretation, culminating in considerable criticism of the articles on interpretation formulated by the International Law Commission in its Draft Convention.

The object of this paper is to analyse and assess the approach of the International Law Commission in the light of this controversy. It will be suggested that some of the criticisms of that approach are based partly on a misunderstanding both of its practical significance and of its theoretical justification. A detailed comparison with rival approaches is necessary to appreciate the precise implications of the articles in the Convention. But there is also room for argument about the proper function of rules of interpretation in international law. The paper ends, therefore, with an attempt to clarify the relevant issues of policy.

I

Modern approaches to interpretation can be classified in three broad groups: the subjective, the textual, and the teleological.[1] Although

* Lecturer in Law, London School of Economics and Political Science. This paper was prepared at the Centre for Studies and Research of the Hague Academy of International Law. The author takes this opportunity of expressing his appreciation to the Academy, to Professor I. Seidl-Hohenveldern (the Director of Studies of the English-speaking section), and to the other members of the section who participated in the discussions. However, this paper is the work exclusively of the present author and the views expressed are his own.

[1] This classification is used by Fitzmaurice, " The Law and Procedure of the International Court of Justice: Treaty Interpretation and Certain Other Treaty Points "

these approaches inevitably overlap, and the approach of international tribunals and of jurists often combines elements from each of them, a preliminary description of them will reveal some significant distinctions:

(1) The subjective approach looks primarily to the actual intentions of the parties. In the interpretation of treaties the principal question on this approach is concerned with the " real will " of the States. It attempts to elucidate the text of the treaty, which on this view is merely an expression of the will of the parties, by reference to the whole course of negotiations leading to the conclusion of the treaty, and seeks to investigate the actual intentions of the parties at the time of the adoption of the final text.

(2) The textual approach, of course, places the principal emphasis on the actual words of the treaty; while the subjective approach treats as the first question " What did the parties really mean? " the textual approach takes first the question " What did the parties say? " Inevitably, however, an excessive literalism has to be qualified, and every advocate of the textual approach readily admits certain qualifications: that extrinsic sources may be used if the text is ambiguous, or if the meaning of the words leads to a conclusion which is obviously absurd or unreasonable.

(3) The teleological approach seeks to interpret the treaty in the light of its objects and purposes. The first question on this approach is not about the meaning of the particular clause which is the subject of interpretation, but a broader inquiry into the objects and purposes of the treaty taken as a whole, and individual provisions of the treaty are construed so as to give effect to these objects and purposes. To a certain extent, this approach is simply a combination of elements of the first two approaches. In so far as it relies on the objects and purposes of the treaty as they are expressed in the text, and especially in the preamble, or can be gathered from a reading of the treaty as a whole, the teleological approach is essentially a variant of the textual approach. In so far as it goes beyond the text and seeks to ascertain the original aims of the parties in concluding the treaty by reference to the entire course of negotiations and the circumstances of its conclusion, it is the subjective approach in another guise. Certainly the classic controversies on interpretation are based on the antithesis between the textual and the subjective approaches, between the language used by the parties and their intentions. But

(1951) 28 B.Y.I.L. 1, and is also adopted in the Commentary of the International Law Commission on the Draft Convention on the Law of Treaties: see draft Articles on the Law of Treaties and Commentaries (cited below as I.L.C. Commentary), Report of the I.L.C. on its eighteenth session, May 4–July 19, 1966, p. 20 at p. 49.

recent developments in the teleological approach now seem to justify its inclusion as a separate category. It is now generally recognised, at least in the interpretation of constitutional documents and in particular of the United Nations Charter, that the objects and purposes of a treaty may have to be construed in the light of subsequent developments in international organisation. According to the doctrine of the " emergent purpose," the objects and purposes which determine the true interpretation of a treaty may be those which can be found to exist at the time of interpretation, not at the time of its conclusion. Clearly, this version of the teleological approach is not textual, since the emergent purpose cannot be gathered from the text; nor is it subjective, since it is independent of the original intentions of the parties, and perhaps also of their subsequent attitudes.[2] Rather, it regards the creation of the parties as having acquired a separate existence, at any rate within the necessary limits imposed by the original text.

The actual operation of these approaches can best be demonstrated by analysing the formulation in draft articles of principles of interpretation proposed by exponents of the different approaches. In each case it is possible to illustrate the effect of the approach by an appropriate text.

THE SUBJECTIVE APPROACH [3]

The subjective approach has received the support of many jurists representing very different schools of thought,[4] but was perhaps most

---

[2] See the dissenting Opinion of Judge Azevedo, *Admission to the United Nations Case* [1950] *I.C.J. Reports* 24: " Even long practice, usually a good guide in interpretation, cannot frustrate a pressing teleological requirement."

[3] A convenient text is provided by the draft resolution submitted by Lauterpacht to the Institute of International Law ((1950) 43 (1) *Annuaire de l'Institut de Droit International* 433). Paras. 1 and 2 read as follows:

1. La recherche de l'intention des parties étant le but principal de l'interprétation, il est légitime et désirable, dans l'intérêt de la bonne foi et de la stabilité des transactions internationales, de prendre le sens naturel des termes comme point de départ du processus d'interprétation. C'est à la partie qui prétend donner aux termes ou dispositions contestées du traité un sens différent du sens naturel ou qui leur attribue un sens apparemment clair qu'incombe le fardeau de la preuve. La clarté apparente ou supposée de ces termes ou dispositions ne saurait justifier le rejet de la preuve contraire ni la rendre indûment difficile.

2. Le recours aux travaux préparatoires, lorsqu'ils sont accessibles, est notamment un moyen légitime et désirable aux fins d'établir l'intention des parties dans tous les cas où, malgré sa clarté apparente, le sens d'un traité prête à controverse. Il n'y a aucun motif d'exclure l'usage de travaux préparatoires dûment consignés et publiés, à l'encontre d'Etats ayant adhéré au traité postérieurement à sa signature par les parties originaires.

[4] Among Continental writers see, *e.g.*, Guggenheim, *Traité de Droit international public*, Vol. I (1953) p. 133, Sørensen, *Les sources du droit international* (1946) p. 214; Verdross, *Völkerrecht* (5th ed. 1964) p. 173. For an American view see Hyde, *International Law, Chiefly as interpreted by the United States* (2nd ed.,

strongly advocated by Sir Hersch Lauterpacht and most clearly
formulated in his proposals to the Institute of International Law in
1950. His draft resolution laid particular stress on recourse to
travaux préparatoires as means of ascertaining the intentions of the
parties. Paragraph 2 of the draft resolution provided that such
recourse " *est notamment un moyen légitime et désirable* " in every
case where, in spite of its apparent clarity, the meaning of a treaty
gave rise to controversy. Lauterpacht naturally recognised that the
terms of the treaty must be used as a guide to the parties' intentions,
and paragraph 1 might be construed as a concession to the textual
approach in taking the natural meaning of the terms as the starting-
point of the interpretative process. The concession was limited,
however; for Lauterpacht's formulation was designed to show that the
text was the starting-point but nothing more.[5]

Of greater significance, perhaps, was a further qualification of the
subjective approach. According to paragraph 5 of the draft resolution, in the absence of any indication of the actual intentions of the
parties, the tribunal has the task of filling the gap in conformity with
the fundamental requirements of international law and justice. If
this provision is taken in conjunction with the wide scope given by
paragraph 4 to the principle of effective interpretation, the proposals
can be seen to embody an important teleological element. Although
the main emphasis is on the actual intentions of the parties, Lauterpacht himself fully recognised that, however conscientious and far-
ranging the search for a common intention, there would be many and
varied situations in which it could not be found.[6] In such circumstances full effect was to be given, within the terms of the agreement,
to the objects for which it was made.[7]

Although the subjective approach has received the consistent
support of jurists, and would indeed seem to be required by the theory
that international law is ultimately based on the will of States, it is
open to a number of formidable objections, which were ventilated in

---

1945) Vol. II, pp. 1468–1502. For support by recent Soviet writers of the
subjective approach, see Schweisfurth, *Der internationale Vertrag in der modernen
sowjetischen Völkerrechtstheorie* (1968) p. 262 *et seq.*

[5] See p. 341 below.

[6] (1950) 43 (1) *Annuaire de l'Institut de Droit International*, p. 423 *et seq.*; *cf.* the
same writer's article on " Restrictive Interpretation and the Principle of Effectiveness in the Interpretation of Treaties " (1949) 26 B.Y.I.L. 48 at 75 *et seq.*

[7] Elsewhere Lauterpacht recognised that the teleological approach was particularly
appropriate to the interpretation of constitutional instruments of international
organisations. In his Separate Opinion in the *South-West Africa: Voting Procedure Case*, he said: " A proper interpretation of a constitutional instrument
must take into account not only the formal letter of the original instrument, but
also its operation in actual practice and in the light of the revealed tendencies in
the life of the Organisation " [1955] *I.C.J. Reports* 106; *cf.* (1950) 43 (1) *Annuaire
de l'Institut de Droit International* 418 *et seq.*; (1949) 26 B.Y.I.L. 48 at 72 *et seq.*

the proceedings of the Institute of International Law and are considered further below.[8] It was these objections which led the
Institute ultimately to reject the subjective approach.

THE TEXTUAL APPROACH [9]

The resolution finally adopted by the Institute of International Law
in 1956 adopts the textual approach.[10] Having stated in Article 1 (1)
that " The agreement of the parties having been embodied in the text
of the treaty, it is necessary to take the natural and ordinary meaning
of the terms of this text as the basis of interpretation," the resolution
goes on to provide in Article 2 (1) that in the case of a dispute brought
before an international tribunal [11] it will be for the tribunal to decide
whether and to what extent there are grounds for making use of
other means of interpretation; these including, according to Article
2 (2), preparatory work, subsequent practice, and the objects of the
treaty.

Although the resolution undoubtedly places the principal emphasis
on the text, it appears to give considerable discretion to the court
on the use of other means of interpretation. It does not specify any
of the usual criteria for the admissibility of extrinsic sources, such as
the ambiguity or obscurity of the text. The scope of the resolution's
textuality is therefore somewhat uncertain.

The textual approach is based on the view epitomised in the
famous statement of Vattel [12]: " La première maxime générale sur
l'interprétation est, qu'il n'est pas permis d'interpréter ce qui n'a
pas besoin d'interprétation."

It has been adopted with relative consistency by the International
Court and was reaffirmed in 1950 in the following terms:

> The Court considers it necessary to say that the first duty of a
> tribunal which is called upon to interpret and apply the provisions
> of a treaty, is to endeavour to give effect to them in their natural and
> ordinary meaning in the context in which they occur. If the relevant
> words in their natural and ordinary meaning make sense in their
> context, that is an end of the matter. If, on the other hand, the
> words in their natural and ordinary meaning are ambiguous or
> lead to an unreasonable result, then, and then only, must the Court,

---

[8] See below, pp. 338–339.

[9] See Appendix (1).

[10] Sir Gerald Fitzmaurice had succeeded Sir Hersch Lauterpacht as Rapporteur.

[11] It is not clear whether it is intended that only international tribunals may use
other means of interpretation. There is an apparent inconsistency between the
wording of Article 2 (1) and the opening statement of the resolution that " States,
and international organisations and tribunals may be guided by the following
principles."

[12] Vattel, *Le droit des gens ou principes de la loi naturelle* (1758), Bk. II, ch. 17,
para. 263.

by resort to other methods of interpretation, seek to ascertain what the parties really did mean when they used these words.[13]

The textual approach, however has recently been the object of increasing criticism, especially by advocates of the teleological approach.[14]

THE TELEOLOGICAL APPROACH [15]

The clearest formulation of the teleological approach is to be found in the Draft Convention on the Law of Treaties prepared in 1935 as part of the Harvard Research in International Law. The relevant article of the Harvard Draft first provides that: " A treaty is to be interpreted in the light of the general purpose which it is intended to serve," and goes on to specify that the various sources of interpretation, whether prior to, contemporary with, or subsequent to the conclusion of the treaty, " are to be considered in connection with the general purpose which the treaty is intended to serve."

The various sources of interpretation are listed in the Article in chronological order, and no attempt is made, in contrast to the subjective and textual approaches, to establish any order of priority among them. The absence of any hierarchical system is indeed characteristic of the approach of many American writers, who adopt what might be described as an inclusive method, including all relevant sources of interpretation but refusing to admit any formal rules.[16]

While there may have been genuine policy considerations behind the American position, the denial by some English writers [17] of the

---

13 *Admission to the United Nations Case* [1950] *I.C.J. Reports* 8.

14 *Cf.* McDougal, Lasswell and Miller, *The Interpretation of Agreements and World Public Order* (1967), cited below as McDougal, *Interpretation.*

15 See Appendix (2), (3).

16 See *Harvard Research,* pp. 937–977. This approach seems to have been influenced, apart from the general trend of American " realist " jurisprudence, by Yü, *The Interpretation of Treaties* (1927); *cf.* Chang, *The Interpretation of Treaties by Judicial Tribunals* (1933). Hudson, *The Permanent Court of International Justice, 1920–1942* (1943), examined the practice of the Court but found " no rigid rule." *Cf.* Hyde, *International Law, Chiefly as interpreted by the United States* (2nd ed., 1945), Vol. II, pp. 1468–1502. Lauterpacht (1950) 43 (1) *Annuaire de l'Institut de Droit International,* p. 369, commented that " Le professeur Hyde, autorité considérable en la matière, a puissamment contribué à élucider ce chapitre du droit international, sans cependant proposer aucune règle précise d'interprétation."

The American approach can be further illustrated by an amendment to Arts. 27 and 28 submitted by the United States at the First Vienna Conference; see the Draft Report of the Committee of the Whole on its work at the first session of the Conference, A/Conf.39/C. 1/L.370, pp. 135–136. The amendment (defeated by 66 votes to 8, with 10 abstentions) would have substituted for these articles the following " inclusive " provision: " A treaty shall be interpreted in good faith in order to determine the meaning to be given to its terms in the light of all relevant factors, including in particular:" (a list of nine factors then followed).

17 Perhaps influenced by the statement with which Oppenheim opens his treatment of the subject, preserved by his editor (*International Law,* Vol. I (8th ed. 1955) p. 950): " There are no precise rules of customary or conventional International Law concerning the interpretation of treaties." Yet Oppenheim himself went on " to enumerate some rules of interpretation which commend themselves on account of their suitability " and proceeded to enumerate sixteen such rules (pp. 951–957).

very existence of rules of interpretation seems to be based on a confusion. They would not have accepted, to take just one example, that subsequent practice could be admitted where it conflicted with the express terms of the treaty. Yet to maintain that subsequent practice can only be admitted to elucidate the original intentions of the parties is of course to assert a rule of interpretation. Other writers, while recognising the existence of rules of interpretation, have denied that such rules could be classified as rules of law. Any doubts about the specifically legal character of rules of interpretation, however, should finally be resolved by the Convention itself.

The inclusive method is well illustrated by the *Restatement of the Foreign Relations Law of the United States* published by the American Law Institute in 1965. Paragraph 147 of the *Restatement* lists a large number of " factors to be taken into account by way of guidance in the interpretative process," in addition to the ordinary meaning of the words of the agreement in their context, but makes it clear that the list is not intended to be complete; and paragraph 147 (2) specifically provides that there is no established priority as between these factors " or as between them and additional factors not listed therein."

The inclusive method does not necessarily lead to a purely teleological approach. The inclusion of all relevant factors, and the rejection of an ordered hierarchy, does not determine the aim of interpretation. While the Harvard Draft is clearly teleological, the *Restatement* appears to combine subjective and teleological elements. According to paragraph 146 of the *Restatement*, " the primary object of interpretation is to ascertain the meaning intended by the parties for the terms in which the agreement is expressed . . .," while paragraph 147 (1) states: " International law requires that the interpretative process ascertain and give effect to the purpose of the international agreement which, as appears from the terms used by the parties, it was intended to serve." Although the *Restatement* thus emphasises the original purposes of the parties, the inclusive method, by readily admitting subsequent practice and subsequent changes of circumstances on an equal footing with earlier sources, naturally lends itself to a teleological approach.[18]

Similarly, Professor McDougal, in advocating the inclusive method, proposes, as the object of the interpretative process, the implementation of the " shared expectations " of the parties, a formula which also combines subjective and teleological elements, since although it takes account of the original intentions of the parties, it is wide enough to embrace subsequent changes in the attitudes and practice

---

[18] See especially *Restatement*, § 147 (1) (f) and (g).

of the parties. Subsequent practice may be admitted not merely as evidence of the original intentions of the parties, but on the contrary as displacing those intentions.[19] The apparent inconsistencies between these conflicting criteria of shared expectations are considered below.

The practical importance of the differences between these approaches is well illustrated by the controversial question whether the references to the use of force in the United Nations Charter should be interpreted to include economic pressure.[20] Recourse to the *travaux préparatoires* shows that a proposal to refer specifically to economic pressure was rejected; thus on the subjective approach it could be argued that economic pressure was not intended. This interpretation might be supported on the textual approach by reference to the ordinary meaning of the words used. On the other hand a teleological approach might lead to the opposite conclusion; it could be argued that subsequent developments in international law and the increasing significance of international economic relations justify a more extensive interpretation of the Charter which, even if it does not conform to the original intentions of the parties, is not explicitly excluded by their choice of words.

II

The question may now be considered what approach is adopted in the Draft Convention on the Law of Treaties prepared by the International Law Commission and accepted, without substantial modification, at the first session of the Vienna Conference.[21] From the point of view of the present classification, the first main characteristic of the draft articles on interpretation is the distinction drawn between what might be described as the principal means of interpretation enumerated in Article 27 and what Article 28 describes as "supplementary means of interpretation" which may be used only

---

[19] " Take into account the whole sequence of acts of communication and collaboration that have occurred since the outcome phase. Action by the parties in reliance upon asserted or implicit interpretations during the course of performing an agreement is appropriately regarded as reliable evidence of shared subjectivities and may be given priority over contradictory evidence even from the outcome phase." McDougal, *Interpretation*, pp. 58–59, *cf.* 143–144.

[20] In this connection it is interesting to compare the discussion both within the International Law Commission and at the First Vienna Conference on Art. 49, which provides that: " a treaty is void if its conclusion has been procured by the threat or use of force in violation of the principles of international law embodied in the Charter of the United Nations." At its first session the Vienna Conference adopted a draft declaration, to form part of the Final Act of the Conference, condemning " the threat or use of pressure in any form, military, political, or economic, by any State, in order to coerce another State to perform any act relating to the conclusion of a treaty in violation of the principles of sovereign equality of States and freedom of consent."

[21] See Appendix (4).

to confirm the meaning derived from the application of Article 27, or when the application of Article 27 fails to yield a clear and reasonable result. In its distinction between Article 27, "General rule of interpretation" and Article 28, "Supplementary means of interpretation," [22] the draft appears to establish a clear hierarchy in favour of the ordinary meaning of the words which suggests a textual approach.

This impression may be confirmed by the International Law Commission's Commentary to Article 27 which states: "The article as already indicated is based on the view that the text must be presumed to be the authentic expression of the intentions of the parties; and that, in consequence, the starting point of interpretation is the elucidation of the meaning of the text, not an investigation *ab initio* into the intentions of the parties." [23]

It is significant in this connection that, as the special rapporteur, Sir Humphrey Waldock observed in his commentary,[24] his original proposals to the International Law Commission, which embodied the distinction between supplementary and what are here called principal means of interpretation, were largely based on two sources: the 1956 resolution of the Institute of International Law, which embodied, as was seen above, the textual approach, and the formulation by Sir Gerald Fitzmaurice, who was then the Institute's Rapporteur, of the "major principles" of interpretation in an article on the law and procedure of the International Court of Justice.[25] At the same time, the Commentary pointed out that "the provisions of Article 28 by no means have the effect of drawing a rigid line between the 'supplementary' means of interpretation and the means included in Article 27." [26]

The second main characteristic of the Draft Convention, from the present viewpoint, is the inclusion of *travaux préparatoires* among the supplementary, not among the principal means of interpretation. This was a question on which doctrinal controversy had been particularly acute, and on which the alternative views could both find support in the pronouncements of the Permanent Court and the International Court of Justice. On the other hand, while not admitting *travaux préparatoires* as a principal source, the draft articles do not adopt the extreme solution of excluding them altogether, if the meaning of the words is clear; they are admitted for the purpose of "confirming" the meaning resulting from the application of Article 27. It is

---

[22] The Vienna Conference has not yet adopted headings for any of the draft articles.
[23] I.L.C. Commentary, p. 51.
[24] 1964 I.L.C.Y.B., Vol. II, p. 55.
[25] Sir Gerald Fitzmaurice, "The Law and Procedure of the International Court of Justice, 1951–4: Treaty Interpretation and Other Treaty Points" (1957) 33 B.Y.I.L. 203 at 211–212.
[26] I.L.C. Commentary, p. 51.

uncertain how they are to be regarded if, when admitted for that purpose, they lead unequivocally to the opposite interpretation.[27]

This subordinate role was accorded to the preparatory work in the first draft articles on interpretation submitted to the International Law Commission by Sir Humphrey Waldock,[28] and was retained with only verbal alterations throughout the successive drafts.[29]   Some justification is given in the International Law Commission's Commentary on the two articles,[30] but it is evidently required by the Commission's view that the text must be presumed to be the authentic expression of the intentions of the parties.

The most significant modification of the textual approach, however, is to be found in a further main characteristic of the Draft Convention, introduced as a result of the debate in the International Law Commission, relating to subsequent practice. In the draft articles originally formulated by Sir Humphrey Waldock, the subsequent practice of the parties was included among what were later described as the supplementary means of interpretation.[31]   Following some discussion in the Commission, the second draft articles included among the principal means of interpretation " any subsequent practice in the application of the treaty which clearly establishes the understanding of all the parties regarding its interpretation." [32]   With the omission of the words " clearly " and " all " the teleological element thus incorporated in the draft was further strengthened in the third draft,[33] which remained unchanged in the final draft [34] ultimately adopted [35] at the Vienna Conference.

Although it is proposed to consider below the various respects in which the apparent textuality of the Draft Convention is significantly qualified, the provision with regard to subsequent practice is undoubtedly the most striking innovation in the interpretative provisions of the Convention. On the traditional approaches to interpretation, subsequent practice is admissible, if at all, only to throw light on the original intentions of the parties; as such it may

---

[27] It is possible that Art. 27 (4) could be applied, which provides that a special meaning shall be given to a term if it is established that the parties so intended, but does not specify whether that intention may be established by the use of supplementary means of interpretation indicated in Art. 28. This was specifically provided by Art. 71 (2) of the original draft: see U.N.Doc. A/CN.4/167/Add.3 (cited below as first draft articles), Art. 71 (2).

[28] *Ibid.*

[29] See U.N.Doc. A/CN.4/L.107 (cited below as second draft articles), Art. 70; A/CN.4/L.117 and Add. 1 (cited below as third draft articles), Art. 70; A/CN.4/190 (cited below as final draft articles), Art. 28.

[30] I.L.C. Commentary, p. 51.

[31] First draft articles, Art. 71 (2).

[32] Second draft articles, Art. 69 (3) (b).

[33] Third draft articles, Art. 69 (3) (b).

[34] Final draft articles, Art. 27.

[35] With the substitution of the word " agreement " for " understanding."

serve either to confirm an interpretation reached by other means, or as a supplementary means of interpretation where other means fail to provide a clear and unambiguous result.[36] The Commentary of the International Law Commission itself cites [37] the formulation of the traditional view by the Permanent Court in its opinion on the *Competence of the ILO to Regulate Agricultural Labour* [38]: " If there were any ambiguity, the Court might, for the purpose of arriving at the true meaning, consider the action which has been taken under the Treaty." At the same time, as the Commentary adds, the Court referred [39] to subsequent practice in confirmation of the meaning which it had deduced from the text and which it considered to be unambiguous.

There was no suggestion, however, in the Court's opinion that subsequent practice might be applied as a principal means of interpretation, so that this opinion does not support the position taken by the Convention.[40]

The other citation in the Commentary is from the *Corfu Channel Case*,[41] where the International Court said : " The subsequent attitude of the Parties shows it has not been their intention, by entering into the Special Agreement, to preclude the Court from fixing the amount of the compensation."

Here, however, as the words of the quoted extract demonstrate, the subsequent attitudes of the parties were admitted as evidence of their original intentions. A similar inference was drawn, in more explicit terms, in the *Iranian Oil Case*, where the Court relied on a law passed between the date of signing a Declaration accepting the compulsory jurisdiction of the Court and the date of its ratification, as showing what the effect of the Declaration was; referring to a particular clause in the law, the Court said [42]: " This clause . . . is, in the opinion of the Court, a decisive confirmation of the intention of the Government of Iran at the time when it accepted the compulsory jurisdiction of the Court." In both these cases, the Court was using subsequent practice as evidence of prior intentions. In so doing, the Court was going no further than to apply the principle enunciated by the Permanent Court in the *Interpretation of Article 3, paragraph 2, of the Treaty of Lausanne* [43]: " The facts subsequent to the conclusion of the Treaty of Lausanne can only concern the Court in so far

[36] See comment upon Art. 19 of the Harvard Draft, at p. 966; McNair, *The Law of Treaties* (1961) p. 424.
[37] I.L.C. Commentary, p. 53.
[38] 1922 P.C.I.J. Ser. B, No. 2, p. 39.
[39] *Ibid.* pp. 40–41.
[40] *Report*, p. 53.
[41] [1949] *I.C.J. Reports* 25.
[42] [1952] *I.C.J. Reports* 107.
[43] 1925 P.C.I.J., Ser. B, No. 12, p. 24.

as they are calculated to throw light on the intention of the Parties at the time of the conclusion of that treaty."

A natural corollary of this principle is that if the intentions of the parties are clear, there is no need to have recourse to subsequent practice at all. It seems clear that it was this view which the Permanent Court was expressing in the words cited above, when it stated that *if there were any ambiguity* the Court might consider the action which has been taken under the treaty. The same view was taken by the Permanent Court in the *Serbian and Brazilian Loans Cases*,[44] where it expressly stated that the subsequent conduct of the parties was admissible only in the event of ambiguity.

Whereas in the case of the preparatory work the Court has frequently had recourse to it to confirm its conclusions as to the ordinary meaning of the text,[45] and has rarely refused to resort to it even if the text was clear,[46] the situation in the case of subsequent practice has been quite the reverse. It has rarely been admitted to confirm the meaning of the text, and only in the event of an ambiguity.

It seems, therefore, that the Draft Convention, in placing subsequent practice among the principal and preparatory work among the supplementary means of interpretation, represents a considerable departure from the practice of the Court.

But the significance of the Draft Convention does not rest only in its reversal of the relative importance of these two methods of ascertaining the original intentions of the parties. It is arguable that the main significance of subsequent practice in the Convention is not in clarifying the original intentions of the parties, but in enabling effect to be given to their subsequent intentions, at least within the framework of the original text.

Some support for this view can be derived from a comparison of the successive drafts in the workings of the International Law Commission. The relevant article in the first draft merely provided that " reference may be made to other evidence or indications of the intentions of the parties and, in particular, to the preparatory work of the treaty, the circumstances surrounding its conclusion and the subsequent practice of parties in relation to the treaty " for purposes

44 1929 P.C.I.J., Ser. A, Nos. 20/21, pp. 38, 119.
45 *Interpretation of the Convention of 1919 concerning Employment of Women during the Night*, 1932 P.C.I.J., Ser. A/B, No. 50, p. 380; *cf. Serbian and Brazilian Loans Cases*, 1929 P.C.I.J., Ser. A, Nos. 20/21, p. 30.
46 But see *Admission of a State to the United Nations* [1948] I.C.J. Reports 63; *cf. Competence of the General Assembly for the Admission of a State to the United Nations* [1950] I.C.J. Reports 8. " In a number of cases these courts have announced that as the text of the instrument under consideration is clear in itself there is no occasion to resort to preparatory work. Nevertheless, it is clear in numerous cases that before making such an announcement the court has in fact considered the preparatory work." McNair, *The Law of Treaties* (1961) p. 413; see, *e.g.*, *The Lotus*, 1927 P.C.I.J., Ser. A, No. 10, p. 16.

which the article enumerated.[47] This provision is clearly a formulation of the traditional role of subsequent practice. The corresponding article of the second draft stated:

> There shall also be taken into account, together with the context:
> (a) Any agreement between the parties regarding the interpretation of the treaty;
> (b) Any subsequent practice in the application of the treaty which clearly establishes the understanding of all the parties regarding its interpretation.[48]

In this draft subsequent practice was promoted to the status of a principal means of interpretation, but its primary function was apparently still that of elucidating the original intentions of the parties. It would perhaps have been arguable, however, that subsequent practice could also have been admitted under this article to establish the subsequent understanding of the parties. This argument acquires somewhat greater force in the final draft,[49] which, as amended by the Vienna Conference, provides:

> There shall be taken into account, together with the context:
> (a) any subsequent agreement between the parties regarding the interpretation of the treaty or the application of its provisions;
> (b) any subsequent practice in the application of the treaty which establishes the agreement of the parties regarding its interpretation;
> (c) any relevant rules of international law applicable in the relations between the parties.

The use of sub-paragraph (b) to establish the subsequent agreement of the parties, although the Commentary is silent on this point, can be supported by taking the paragraph as a whole. The reference in sub-paragraph (a) to any subsequent agreement between the parties clearly contemplates *inter alia* an agreement modifying their original intentions.

The reference in sub-paragraph (c) to any relevant rules of international law is less explicit, but seems sufficiently wide to include rules which were not applicable at the time when the treaty was concluded, but are applicable at the time of interpretation. The original draft specifically referred to " the rules of international law in force at the time of the conclusion of the treaty." [50] There was a division of opinion within the Commission; some members would have preferred to apply the rules in force at the time of interpretation; others supported the view that the rules applicable were those in

---

[47] First draft articles, Art. 71 (2).
[48] Second draft articles, Art. 69 (3).
[49] Third draft articles, Art. 69 (3); final draft articles, Art. 27 (3).
[50] First draft articles, Art. 70 (1) (b).

force at the time of the conclusion of the treaty.[51]   The Chairman proposed that the draft should not specify the temporal element, and this proposal was ultimately adopted.[52]

The Commentary also leaves this critical question open.   Referring to criticisms of the original draft, it merely states [53] that the Commission considered it unsatisfactory

> since it covered only partially the question of the so-called intertemporal law in its application to the interpretation of treaties and might, in consequence, lead to misunderstanding.   It also considered that, in any event, the relevance of rules of international law for the interpretation of treaties in any given case was dependent on the intentions of the parties, and that to attempt to formulate a rule covering comprehensively the temporal element would present difficulties.   It further considered that correct application of the temporal element would normally be indicated by interpretation of the term in good faith.

The Draft Convention thus avoids both a strictly textual approach which would naturally give the terms of a treaty their original significance, and a purely teleological approach which would allow for the effect of an evolution of the law on the interpretation of legal terms.[54]   But the omission of the original restriction to the law contemporary with the treaty supports the view that the sources of interpretation enumerated in the paragraph include subsequent developments not initially envisaged by the parties.

It seems, therefore, that the reference in Article 27 (3) (b) to " any subsequent practice in the application of the treaty which clearly establishes the agreement of the parties regarding its interpretation," taken in its context, includes an agreement which departs from their original intentions, and so may be used in effect to modify the treaty.[55] Further confirmation of this view is provided by comparing the wording of Article 27 (4), the following paragraph, which provides that " a special meaning shall be given to a term if it is established that the parties so intended "; this wording clearly implies: at the time of the conclusion of the treaty.

It is interesting to note, in this connection, that Article 38 of the Draft Convention, which provided for modification of treaties by subsequent practice, was deleted at the Vienna Conference.   Article 38 provided that " A treaty may be modified by subsequent practice

---

[51] See, *e.g.*, I.L.C.Y.B. 1964, Vol. I, p. 278, paras. 48–49 (Tunkin); p. 279, para. 57 and p. 281, para. 93 (Yasseen).

[52] I.L.C.Y.B. 1964, Vol. I, p. 280, para. 80; third draft articles, Art. 69 (3) (c).

[53] I.L.C. Commentary, p. 53.

[54] The Commission rejected, however, the reference in Art. 73 of the first draft articles to the emergence of any later rule of customary international law.

[55] See also I.L.C. Commentary, p. 51, in a different context: " The elements of interpretation in Art. 27 all relate to the agreement between the parties *at the time when or after it received authentic expression in the text*." (Original italics.)

in the application of the treaty establishing the agreement of the parties to modify its provisions." The use of subsequent practice, not merely to interpret a treaty, but to modify the rights and obligations of the parties, was illustrated in a recent arbitration [56] between France and the United States arising out of a bilateral air transport services agreement. Referring to the subsequent practice of the parties, the tribunal said [57]:

> This course of conduct may, in fact, be taken into account not merely as a means useful for interpreting the Agreement, but also as something more: that is, as a possible source of a subsequent modification, arising out of certain actions or certain attitudes, having a bearing on the juridical situation of the parties and on the rights that each of them could properly claim.

The rejection by the Vienna Conference of an explicit provision for modification of treaties by subsequent practice may appear to have detracted from its importance, or at least to counteract its significance in the process of interpretation. Such an impression, however, would be misleading; for while the failure to give subsequent practice a prominent position in the rules of interpretation would effectively have precluded its use in a case to which the Convention applies, the omission of an article providing for modification by subsequent practice will not preclude a party from relying on a general rule of international customary law recognising such modification, as evidenced by State practice and the decisions of international tribunals.

III

In the foregoing discussion of the role of subsequent practice in the interpretation of treaties, reference was made in passing to a number of other factors in the Draft Convention which preclude an exclusively literal interpretation and may be regarded as qualifying further its basic textual approach. These other factors include the reference in Article 27 (3) (c) to any relevant rules of international law applicable in the relations between the parties,[58] and the provision in Article 27 (4), that a special meaning shall be given to a term if it is established that the parties so intended.[59]

---

[56] Decision of the Arbitration Tribunal established pursuant to the Arbitration Agreement signed at Paris on January 22, 1963, between the U.S.A. and France, decided at Geneva on December 22, 1963; arbitrators R. Ago (President), P. Reuter, and H. P. de Vries: American Society of International Law, *International Legal Materials—Current Documents*, Vol. III, No. 4 (July 1964) p. 668.

[57] At p. 713.

[58] The principal question concerning the scope of this qualification is how far these rules include other treaty obligations of the parties.

[59] The main function of this provision in the earlier drafts, which required that this intention must be " established conclusively," appears to have been to emphasise the heavy burden of proof on a party alleging that a term had not been used in

It is now proposed to consider very briefly three further factors which may be regarded as additional modifications of the textual approach, and which all appear in the principal clause in Article 27 (1) which provides that a treaty shall be interpreted in good faith in accordance with the ordinary meaning to be given to the terms of the treaty in their context and in the light of its object and purpose.

1. *The Principle of Good Faith*

Taken in its broadest sense,[60] the principle of good faith when applied to the interpretation of treaties would amount to no less than a direct contradiction of the ordinary meaning rule. In its broadest sense the principle would require that the spirit of the agreement should prevail over the text, and it is invoked specifically to justify a departure from the literal terms of the document: *semper in fide quid senseris, non quid dixeris cogitandum.*[61]

Taken in the context of Article 27 of the Draft Convention, it is clear that the principle of good faith has a more restricted scope. What is less clear, at first sight, is what its precise significance is intended to be. Used as an integral part of the textual approach, it is presumably intended to restrain an excessive literalism. On the other hand, it is not to be construed so narrowly as merely to preclude a State from relying on an error in the wording of the text, since this eventuality is provided for by Article 74: nor even as simply precluding a State from relying on an error of substance in the treaty, a situation regulated by Articles 45 and 42.

The role of good faith between these extremes must remain, in the absence of any direct guidance from the Commentary or from the practice of international tribunals,[62] a matter for speculation. It might be taken more narrowly, as precluding a State from exploiting an ambiguity in the text or a genuine misunderstanding between the parties. Alternatively, more broadly, a State might be precluded, in certain circumstances, from advancing an interpretation contrary to its own previous practice, or contrary to the shared expectations of the parties.

its ordinary meaning; first draft articles, Art. 70 (3); second draft articles, Art. 71. As the provision now stands, it could have a different function; for since the means of proof are not specified, it may be regarded as a bridge between Art. 27 and Art. 28. Ordinarily the supplementary means indicated in Art. 28 are admissible only to confirm the meaning resulting from the application of Art. 27, or to determine the meaning in case of ambiguity, etc. If the supplementary means are also admissible under Art. 27 (4) to *contradict* the ordinary meaning, the very basis of the textual approach is undermined.

60 See Ehrlich (1928) 24 *Recueil des Cours* 12–32, and 80–94.
61 Grotius, *De Jure Belli ac Pacis* (1625), Bk. II, ch. 16.
62 For the limited extent of *jurisprudence*, see Guggenheim, *Traité*, Vol. I (1967) p. 250, n. 1; Bernhardt, *Die Auslegung völkerrechtlicher Verträge insbesondere in der neueren Rechtsprechung internationaler Gerichte* (1963) p. 24, n. 139; but *cf.* Judge Alfaro (Sep. op.), *Temple Case* [1962] *I.C.J. Reports* 41–42.

Although there is little discussion of the principle of good faith in the preparatory work of the International Law Commission, and no direct reference to it in the Commentary, the Commentary in its discussion of other rules of interpretation indirectly suggests a rather wider ambit for the principle. Discussing the principle expressed in the maxim *ut res magis valeat quam pereat*, the Commission states [63] that, in so far as this maxim reflects a true general rule of interpretation, " it is embodied in article 27, paragraph 1, which requires that a treaty shall be interpreted *in good faith* in accordance with the ordinary meaning to be given to its terms in the context of the treaty *and in the light of its object and purpose*." (Original italics.) The Commission adds that " when a treaty is open to two interpretations one of which does and the other does not enable the treaty to have appropriate effects, good faith and the objects and purposes of the treaty demand that the former interpretation should be adopted."

Again, in the Commentary dealing with Article 27 (3) (c) (any relevant rules of international law applicable in the relations between the parties), the Commission invokes the principle of good faith to supply the temporal element on which the draft is silent [64]; it considers that " correct application of the temporal element would normally be indicated by interpretation of the term in good faith."

In conclusion it may be suggested that the reference to good faith may have the function not merely of avoiding pure formalism but of making provision for a residuary category of cases which cannot be rigorously defined or exhaustively classified in advance. As such it represents a further qualification of the textual approach, but one which of its very nature is hardly open to abuse.

2. *Textuality and Contextuality*

It is hardly necessary to produce any authority for the principle that it is necessary, in any system of interpretation, to read the words in their context.[65] The principle follows not from any theory of interpretation, but from the fact that no meaning can be ascribed to words except in their context. The crucial question is how widely " context " is to be understood. McDougal cites some writers who " use the word to refer to the total range of relevant verbal and non-verbal behaviour," others who use it " to refer solely to the entire text of an agreement or of related agreements," and recognises that " the more consistent trend in international decision appears to favor the latter usage." [66]

---

[63] I.L.C. Commentary, p. 50.
[64] I.L.C. Commentary, p. 53.
[65] For references, see Jokl, *De l'interprétation des traités normatifs d'àpres la doctrine et la jurisprudence internationales* (1936) p. 41, n. 1.
[66] McDougal, *Interpretation*, p. 221, n. 341.

It is of course because McDougal adopts the wide sense of the word that he charges the Draft Convention with textuality [67] and himself advocates a contextual approach. If the word is used in its narrower sense the approach of the Draft Convention would be more correctly described as contextual than as textual.

The context for the purpose of interpretation is defined by Article 27 (2) as comprising

> in addition to the text, including its preamble and annexes:
> (a) any agreement relating to the treaty which was made between all the parties in connection with the conclusion of the treaty ;
> (b) any instrument which was made by one or more parties in connection with the conclusion of the treaty and accepted by the other parties as an instrument related to the treaty.

The definition embodies a compromise. On the one hand, it excludes a unilateral document unless it was not only made in connection with the conclusion of the treaty but its relation to the treaty was accepted in the same manner by the other parties.[68]

In this respect it differs from the American *Restatement*,[69] which expressly includes among its " Criteria for Interpretation " " unilateral statements of understanding made by a signatory before the agreement came into effect, to the extent that they were communicated to, or otherwise known to, the other signatory or signatories."

On the other hand, the context is not confined to the treaty alone. In the words of the Commentary [70] " What is proposed in paragraph 2 is that, for purposes of interpreting the treaty, these categories of documents should not be treated as mere evidence to which recourse may be had for the purpose of resolving an ambiguity or obscurity, but as part of the context for the purpose of arriving at the ordinary meaning of the terms of the treaty."

The relatively narrow scope of the context as defined in the Draft Convention is an inevitable consequence of its textual approach and cannot be evaluated independently of that approach. The significant feature of Article 27 in this connection is that the scope of this qualification of a narrowly textual approach is precisely delimited.

3. *Objects and Purposes*

Although the interpretation of a treaty by reference to its objects and purposes is associated especially with the teleological approach,

---

[67] McDougal, " The International Law Commission's Draft Articles upon Interpretation; Textuality *Redivivus* " (1967) 61 A.J.I.L. 992.
[68] In the first draft articles, the context included " any other instrument related to, and drawn up in connection with the conclusion of, the treaty ": Art. 71 (1) (c).
[69] *Restatement*, para. 147 (1) (e).
[70] I.L.C. Commentary, p. 52.

it is by no means confined to that. All methods of interpretation seem to accept some recourse to the objects and purposes of the treaty, but they differ on the question how these are to be ascertained. On the purely subjective approach they are determined primarily by reference to the intention of the parties and by examination of the preparatory work.[71] On the textual approach they are to be gathered from the text of the treaty itself; in practice, often from the preamble.[72] The teleological approach recognises that the objects and purposes of a treaty may be independent of the original intentions of the parties, and, in some measure, independent also of the text.

In his Dissenting Opinion on the *Interpretation of the Convention of 1919 concerning the Work of Women by Night*,[73] Judge Anzilotti appeared to adopt the teleological approach in two respects. First, he argued that it was not possible to say that an article in the Convention had a " clear " meaning until the object and purpose of the Convention had been ascertained.[74] Judge Anzilotti's attempt to give priority to the objects and purposes has been criticised as denying the circularity of reasoning which is a necessary feature of the logic of interpretation.[75] Secondly, in ascertaining the objects and purposes of the Convention, he apparently based himself not on the context of the article in question, but on the text of a different treaty, that of Part XIII of the Treaty of Versailles.[76] The majority of the Court, on the other hand, first read the article in the context of the Convention, and established that it was free from ambiguity or obscurity, and further that its clear meaning was not contradicted by the title,

---

[71] But *cf. Access to the Port of Danzig*, 1931 P.C.I.J., Ser. A/B, No. 43, p. 144: "The Court is not prepared to accept the view that the text of the Treaty of Versailles can be enlarged by reading into it stipulations which are said to result from the proclaimed intentions of the authors of the Treaty, but for which no provision is made in the text itself."

[72] See, *e.g., U.S. Nationals in Morocco Case* [1952] *I.C.J. Reports* 196: "The purposes and objects of this Convention were stated in its Preamble in the following words: ' the necessity of establishing, on fixed and uniform bases, the exercise of the right of protection in Morocco and of settling certain questions connected therewith . . .' In these circumstances, the Court cannot adopt a construction by implication of the provisions of the Madrid Convention which would go beyond the scope of its declared purposes and objects." *Cf.* 1922 P.C.I.J., Ser. B, Nos. 2/3, p. 23 *et seq.; id.* 1930, Ser. B, No. 17, p. 19 *et seq.*

[73] 1932 P.C.I.J., Ser. A/B, No. 50, p. 383.

[74] *Ibid.*; and *cf.* his Dissenting Opinion in *Diversion of Water from the Meuse*, 1937 P.C.I.J., Ser. A/B, No. 70, p. 46; " If the text is taken literally, it seems only to refer to ' feeders ' of the same sort as the one which the Treaty ordered to be constructed. But it is always dangerous to be guided by the literal sense of the words before one is clear as to the object and purpose of the Treaty; for it is only in this Treaty, and with reference to this Treaty, that these words— which have no value except in so far as they express the intention of the Parties— assume their true significance."

[75] See Neri, *Sull' interpretazione dei trattati nel diritto internazionale* (1958) pp. 104–105.

[76] See Jokl, *op. cit.*, pp. 44–45. For a contrary view, see Hyde, " Judge Anzilotti on the Interpretation of Treaties " (1933) 27 A.J.I.L. 502 *et seq.*

preamble, or other provisions of the Convention. Only then did it raise the question whether the Convention formed part of the Treaty of Versailles, and a consideration of this question confirmed its impression as to the clear meaning of the article.

This case shows that the basic problems of the scope to be given to the objects and purposes of a treaty are, first, that of priority: what significance is to be attached to them, in comparison with other factors? and, secondly, the method of ascertaining them: are they to be ascertained only by intrinsic means, *i.e.*, by reference to the text and related documents, or also by extrinsic means?

In the first draft articles presented by the Special Rapporteur, the objects and purposes of the treaty were only admitted as what were later called supplementary means of interpretation [77]; they were admitted only if the meaning of a term was not clear owing to its ambiguity or obscurity, or if the natural and ordinary meaning led to an interpretation which was manifestly absurd or unreasonable in the context of the treaty as a whole. This strictly textual approach was modified following discussion in the International Law Commission, and in the second draft [78] it was provided that the ordinary meaning should be given to each term " in the context of the treaty and in the light of its objects and purposes."

The change from " objects and purposes " to " object and purpose " in the final draft [79] may have been intended to give greater certainty, on the ground that there was less likely to be controversy on what was the principal object and purpose of a treaty than on which of several possibly conflicting objects and purposes should determine the meaning of a disputed term.

The inclusion of the phrase " in the light of its object and purpose " in the final draft of the principal interpretative provision of the Convention may be regarded as introducing an element of the teleological approach. It is true that in the context of the paragraph it is natural to infer that the object and purpose are to be gathered from the text. The Commentary [80] refers only to the fact that " the Court has more than once had recourse to the statement of the object and purpose of the treaty in the preamble in order to interpret a particular provision." But there is nothing in the articles or the Commentary to preclude consideration of the " emergent purpose " of the treaty.

---

[77] First draft articles, Art. 70 (2) (a). In this respect the draft followed the resolution of the Institute of International Law.

[78] Second draft articles, Art. 69 (1) (a). For the effecting of the amendment, see I.L.C.Y.B. 1964, Vol. I, p. 281.

[79] Third draft articles, Art. 69 (1); final draft articles, Art. 27 (1).

[80] I.L.C. Commentary, p. 52.

In this respect it may be contrasted both with the American *Restatement*, which states that " International law requires that the interpretative process ascertain and give effect to the purpose of the international agreement which, as appears from the terms used by the parties, it *was* [81] intended to serve [82] " and with the Harvard Draft, which states that " A treaty is to be interpreted in the light of the general purpose which it *is* [83] intended to serve." [84]

It is arguable that the silence of Article 27 (1) as between these alternatives introduces a further element of the teleological approach into the Convention.

Consideration of the object and purpose of the treaty, and of the other factors referred to above,[85] cannot under the draft Convention lead to an " interpretation " contrary to the express terms of the text. To this extent, the Convention adopts a textual approach. But it is not an absolute textuality; it is a textuality subject to a variety of important qualifications. At the same time, the formulation of clear rules of interpretation requires that these qualifications should themselves be delimited; and the main limiting factor adopted by the Convention is the text. The qualifications are themselves subject to the condition that they cannot be invoked to contradict the text. The Convention thus gives expression to the primacy of the text. But it is a qualified textuality. The concluding part of this paper attempts to assess, very tentatively, the merits and defects of this approach.

IV

Any critical assessment of the Draft Convention's approach to interpretation cannot refrain from critical appraisal of alternative approaches. The object of such appraisal is the constructive one of elucidating the principles on which a rational system of treaty interpretation can be based, and evaluating in the light of these principles the provisions of the Draft Convention.

The difficulties with the subjective approach are familiar, particularly from the proceedings of the Institute of International Law when

---

[81] Italics added.
[82] *Restatement*, para. 147 (1).
[83] Italics added.
[84] Harvard Draft, Art. 19 (a). The wording is repeated at the end of the paragraph.
[85] The list of qualifying factors so far mentioned is not intended to be exhaustive. Three further, minor, factors may be suggested here: (1) the choice of the expression " terms " of a treaty rather than " words ": " term " can include not only an individual word or phrase, but an entire provision of a treaty, which can thus be construed as a whole; (2) the first and second drafts referred to the ordinary meaning to be given to *each* term; the third and final drafts avoid this apparent literalism; (3) the first draft began " The terms of a treaty shall be interpreted . . ."; the second and subsequent drafts begin " A treaty shall be interpreted . . ."

Lauterpacht's draft resolution was debated.[86] The most immediate objection to the criterion of the parties' actual intentions is that in many cases there will be no common intention. In the first place there is the not infrequent case where there is no real agreement between the parties at all, except on a form of words chosen to conceal their differences. Secondly, even where there is real agreement, in many if not most cases the question at issue will simply not have been foreseen by the parties, and it will be necessary to extrapolate from the area of agreement to the unforeseen case. It is hard to find any greater justification for such a process than for simply applying the provisions of the treaty. Thirdly, even supposing a genuine agreement between the parties not recorded in the text, the very concept of the intentions of the parties, unless given effect in a formal agreement or in State practice, raises several problems. The subjective approach seems most appropriate to an informal unilateral document such as a deed or will drawn up by a private individual, where there is a real intention, where no one has relied upon the form of words used, where there has been no subsequent conduct based upon the document; here it is at least arguable that the clearly established intention of, say, the testator should prevail over a literal interpretation of the words. This analogy from private law is illuminating because there is almost nothing in common between such a document and a treaty concluded between States.

Recourse to *travaux préparatoires*, as a means of establishing the intentions of the parties, is fraught with practical difficulties too. It will often be possible for both parties to find in the protracted negotiations preceding the conclusion of a treaty, some support for their rival contentions.[87] " Moreover, it is beyond question that the records of treaty negotiations are in many cases incomplete or misleading, so that considerable discretion has to be exercised in determining their value as an element of interpretation." [88] These familiar practical difficulties raise an objection of principle to the use of *travaux préparatoires* as a primary means of interpretation: that it would prejudice the certainty and stability of treaty relations which must remain the overriding concern of contemporary international law. It is this concern for certainty and stability which is the true though unstated rationale of the textual approach adopted by the Draft Convention. Underlying this approach is the belief that this certainty and stability, required by the rule of law and the principle *pacta sunt servanda*, are the main goals of treaty

---

[86] See especially the criticism by Sir Eric Beckett (1950) 43 (1) *Annuaire de l'Institut de Droit International*, pp. 435–444.

[87] *Cf.* Beckett, *Annuaire*, p. 440.

[88] I.L.C. Commentary, p. 51.

interpretation in the present stage of the development of international society.

Criticisms of the textual approach can be divided into three main groups. Some critics deny the very possibility of a textual approach, and therefore seek to achieve the main goals of treaty interpretation by other means. Some critics, while not necessarily denying the possibility of a textual approach, argue that the goals of certainty and stability can be better achieved by different methods, by adopting, for example, the principle of giving effect to the shared expectations of the parties. And some question the assumption that certainty and stability are the main goals; this assumption, they would argue, simply enshrines the *status quo,* and does not take sufficient account of the need for change.

Those who deny the very possibility of a textual approach argue that interpretation is always necessary. But it is important at the outset to distinguish two forms which this argument may take. If it simply means that a tribunal is still in a sense " interpreting " when it gives words their ordinary meaning, then it is purely a matter of terminology.[89] We may speak of interpretation in this general sense, or we may confine it to the special case where the ordinary meaning does not yield an unambiguous answer, or where the ordinary meaning is for some other reason unsatisfactory. To adopt either usage [90] does not prejudge the substantive issue whether there are in fact two distinct types of case, one where the words can be given an ordinary meaning in their context, a second where interpretation in the special sense is required.

The argument that interpretation is always necessary is sometimes, however, a more fundamental objection to the textual approach; in this form, it rejects the underlying assumption that words have an " ordinary meaning." The philosophical considerations advanced in support of this argument, however, do not seem to establish any more than that words have no ordinary meaning *when detached from their context* (and therefore perhaps no " natural meaning "), which is in any case a qualification inevitably attached to the textual approach. Taken any further, the argument would lead to a denial of the very possibility of verbal communication, a somewhat unsatisfactory basis for any theory of interpretation whatever.

A related argument was presented in a more attractive form in

---

[89] *Cf.* in a related sense the *Pertulosa Claim* (1951) 18 *Int. Law Rep.* 415: " The abstract judicial norm, in order to be applied to a concrete instance, must always be interpreted in this sense, namely, the interpreter must by a process of reasoning determine its content." And see Yü, cited McDougal, *Interpretation,* p. 79, n. 5.

[90] The solution is perhaps to be found in the fact that when a tribunal gives a term its ordinary meaning, it can still be said to be engaged in interpreting *the treaty.*

Lauterpacht's original Report to the Institute of International Law.[91] Writing there of the view that if the words had a clear meaning, that was the end of the matter, he argued that the " clear meaning " should be the conclusion, not the starting-point, of the process of interpretation; and he denied that the words could be said to have a clear meaning until all the circumstances in which they had been adopted were exhaustively investigated.

It would be a *petitio principii*, however, to maintain that the meaning of words cannot be clearly established until all the different means of interpretation which Lauterpacht advocates have been exhausted. To say in this context that clarity is deceptive assumes precisely what requires to be proved, namely that this method of interpretation is alone correct.

A further objection to this argument is that, as has already been suggested above, obscurity rather than clarity may result from recourse to a wider set of sources, at any rate if there is no initial presumption of the primacy of the ordinary meaning of the text.

The principle of giving effect to the shared expectations of the parties, as advanced by McDougal, seems at some points identical with the subjective approach as outlined above. Thus when McDougal refers [92] to " the apparent acceptance by the vast majority of writers and decision-makers in past practice of the goal of seeking the genuine shared expectations of the parties," he appears to be identifying that criterion with the original intentions of the parties. Yet elsewhere [93] the principle is said to require giving effect to the subsequent expectations of the parties where these conflict with their original intentions.

The criterion of giving effect to the shared expectations of the parties, which combines subjective and teleological elements, is at first sight an attractive method of promoting the stability of treaty relations. If the parties to a treaty have for many years conducted their affairs on the basis of a certain interpretation, it would clearly be in the interest of stability for a tribunal to give effect to that interpretation. This approach would in any case be required by the doctrine of subsequent practice. The criterion is less satisfactory, however, when applied to a continuing disagreement of the parties which ultimately comes before a tribunal. It seems that here the only sense that could be given to the notion of shared expectations would

[91] (1950) 43 (1) *Annuaire de l'Institut de Droit International*, pp. 371–372, 387. *Cf. The Development of International Law by the International Court* (1958), p. 52.

[92] McDougal, *Interpretation*, p. 95. *Cf.* pp. 82–83 : " The recommended goal of interpreting international agreements to achieve the closest possible approximation to the genuine shared expectations of the parties . . . would appear . . . to have been given high deference in past practice and opinion. The most frequent emphasis in explicit formulation has been upon discovering the ' original intent ' of the participants."   [93] *e.g.*, pp. 58–59, 143–144.

be their prediction of the tribunal's decision (although in international litigation, for obvious reasons, it is most unlikely that the parties would have shared expectations even on this). In this sense, however, the criterion would clearly be vacuous as a principle for the tribunal itself to apply.

Equally, it gives no practical assistance to interpretation by the parties themselves. It would seem to require that the advisers of State A should consider how State B would expect them to interpret the treaty, while the advisers of State B simultaneously contemplate the converse problem.

The criterion of shared expectations as proposed by Professor McDougal seems intended primarily for the use of an international court; certainly the " inclusive method " and the emphasis on policy are generally associated with the judicial process. But principles of interpretation in the present stage of development of international law must be designed for the use of States. It is a truism of course that almost every dispute before an international tribunal involves a question of treaty interpretation. The interpretation of treaties is an important, and perhaps the characteristic, function of an international court. But no one could infer from this that treaty interpretation is primarily the function of the courts, rather than of States themselves. In due course, no doubt, the International Court of Justice will apply the provisions of the Convention, under Article 38 (1) of its Statute, in cases between parties which have ratified the Convention. The articles on interpretation may also be expressly adopted in treaties concluded between States which are not parties to the Convention. Ultimately these provisions may acquire the force of customary rules of international law binding on all States. But even then, it is safe to predict that judicial interpretation will be very much the exception rather than the rule. Since it is impossible to have a double standard, with States using one criterion and courts a different one, it follows that, even if the proposed criterion were workable as a basis for judicial interpretation, the appropriate principles must be determined by their suitability to State practice, not to the judicial process.

Further, in the present system of international relations, the primary aim of international law is not to provide the ideal method of resolving disputes, but to prevent disputes from arising. What is required for this purpose is a clear, simple, and precise principle of interpretation; and the principle of the primacy of the text is more appropriate for these reasons than the proposed alternatives.[94]

---

[94] It is arguable that such a principle is also preferable for an international court, since it is more likely to encourage States to settle their disputes by judicial means than vague criteria which make the decision more unpredictable.

Treaties can be drafted in the knowledge that the primary focus will be on the text; and the ability of States to interpret their treaty obligations in the ordinary case by reference to the text alone will greatly reduce the area of uncertainty and potential friction.

In some branches of municipal law it is arguable that the advantages of certainty, stability and security which are the primary aims of every legal system must be balanced by the need for flexibility.[95] Some elements of flexibility are introduced into the Draft Convention by the teleological aspects considered above. But for a variety of reasons the attempt to introduce notions of judicial policy into international law seems dangerous. Thus McDougal advocates not only that " in the absence of appropriate indices of genuine shared expectations, established decision-makers must have recourse to general community policies for supplementation," [96] but also that " established decision-makers must police even the genuine shared expectations of the participants in international agreements for their compatibility with basic constitutional community policies," [97] a formula which appears to go far beyond the limited and controversial recognition of *jus cogens* in Article 50 of the Draft Convention. The dangers and difficulties inherent in this type of formulation are evident. In the first place, apart from the obvious objection that there is generally no judge, it is notorious that there are no agreed conceptions of policy in the international community as there is often a general consensus in a municipal system. The delicate relations between States and the danger of hostilities make it unsafe to invoke policy considerations. In any case, given this instability in international relations, the principle of *pacta sunt servanda* would always be an important, if not overriding, policy consideration which could be invoked by the party wishing to maintain the *status quo*; the practical effect, therefore, would not be to solve the problem but to remove it on to a loftier and more intractable plane. Finally, the invocation of vague and widely formulated policy considerations in treaty interpretation, in common with all other departures from the textual approach, would lead to precisely the uncertainty which it is the chief object of legal codification to avoid.

[95] Justice is not considered here among the primary aims of a legal system because it is ambivalent on this point. On the one hand, justice requires an equitable solution to the individual case regardless of strict law: *summum jus, summa injuria*. On the other hand, justice also may be said to require that like cases be treated alike, the fulfilling of expectations, and the preservation of the rule of law.

[96] *Interpretation*, p. 104.

[97] pp. 105–106.

APPENDIX

(1) *Resolution on the Interpretation of Treaties Adopted by the Institute of International Law* (1956)

The Institute of International Law is of the opinion that when it becomes necessary to interpret a treaty, States, and international organisations and tribunals may be guided by the following principles:

Article 1

1. The agreement of the parties having been embodied in the text of the treaty, it is necessary to take the natural and ordinary meaning of the terms of this text as the basis of interpretation. The terms of the provisions of the treaty should be interpreted in their context as a whole, in accordance with good faith and in the light of the principles of international law.

2. If, however, it is established that the terms used should be understood in another sense, the natural and ordinary meaning of these terms will be displaced.

Article 2

1. In the case of a dispute brought before an international tribunal it will be for the tribunal, while bearing in mind the provisions of the first article, to consider whether and to what extent there are grounds for making use of other means of interpretation.

2. Amongst the legitimate means of interpretation are the following:

(a) Recourse to preparatory work;
(b) The practice followed in the actual application of the treaty;
(c) The consideration of the objects of the treaty.

(2) *Article 19 (a) of the Harvard Draft Convention on the Law of Treaties* [98]

A treaty is to be interpreted in the light of the general purpose which it is intended to serve. The historical background of the treaty, *travaux préparatoires*, the circumstances of the parties at the time the treaty was entered into, the change in these circumstances sought to be effected, the subsequent conduct of the parties in applying the provisions of the treaty, and the conditions prevailing at the time interpretation is being made, are to be considered in connection with the general purpose which the treaty is intended to serve.

(3) *Ss. 146, 147 of the Restatement (Second) of the Foreign Relations Law of the United States* [99]

§146. Basic Function of Interpretation. The extent to which an international agreement creates changes, or defines relationships under international law is determined in case of doubt by the interpretation of the agreement. The primary object of interpretation is to ascertain the meaning intended by the parties for the terms in which the agreement

[98] Harvard Research in International Law, "Law of Treaties" (1935) 29 A.J.I.L.Supp. 653 at 937, 971.
[99] American Law Institute, 1965.

is expressed, having regard to the context in which they occur and the circumstances under which the agreement was made. This meaning is determined in the light of all relevant factors.

§147. Criteria for Interpretation. (1) International law requires that the interpretative process ascertain and give effect to the purpose of the international agreement which, as appears from the terms used by the parties, it was intended to serve. The factors to be taken into account by way of guidance in the interpretative process include:

(a) the ordinary meaning of the words of the agreement in the context in which they are used;

(b) the title given the agreement and statements of purpose and scope included in its text;

(c) the circumstances attending the negotiation of the agreement;

(d) drafts and other documents submitted for consideration, action taken on them, and the official record of the deliberations during the course of the negotiation;

(e) unilateral statements of understanding made by a signatory before the agreement came into effect, to the extent that they were communicated to, or otherwise known to the other signatory or signatories;

(f) the subsequent practice of the parties in the performance of the agreement, or the subsequent practice of one party, if the other party knew or had reason to know of it;

(g) change of circumstances, to the extent indicated in § 153 [100];

(h) the compatibility of alternative interpretations of the agreement with (i) the obligations of the parties to other states under general international law and other international agreements of the parties, and (ii) the principles of law common to the legal system of the parties or of all states having reasonably developed legal systems;

(i) comparison of the texts in the different languages in which the agreement was concluded, taking into account any provision in the agreement as to the authoritativeness of the different texts.

(2) The ordinary meaning of the words of an agreement, as indicated in Subsection (1) (a), must always be considered as a factor in the interpretation of the agreement. There is no established priority as between the factors indicated in Subsection (1) (b)—(i) or as between them and additional factors not listed therein.

(4) *Articles 27 and 28 of the Convention on the Law of Treaties as Provisionally Adopted at the First Session (1968) of the Vienna Diplomatic Conference*

Article 27

1. A treaty shall be interpreted in good faith in accordance with the ordinary meaning to be given to the terms of the treaty in their context and in the light of its object and purpose.

2. The context for the purpose of the interpretation of a treaty shall comprise, in addition to the text, including its preamble and annexes:

[100] § 153: Rule of *Rebus Sic Stantibus*: Substantial Change of Circumstances.

(a) any agreement relating to the treaty which was made between all the parties in connection with the conclusion of the treaty;

(b) any instrument which was made by one or more parties in connection with the conclusion of the treaty and accepted by the other parties as an instrument related to the treaty.

3. There shall be taken into account, together with the context:

(a) any subsequent agreement between the parties regarding the interpretation of the treaty or the application of its provisions;

(b) any subsequent practice in the application of the treaty which establishes the agreement of the parties regarding its interpretation;

(c) any relevant rules of international law applicable in the relations between the parties.

4. A special meaning shall be given to a term if it is established that the parties so intended.

Article 28

Recourse may be had to supplementary means of interpretation, including the preparatory work and the circumstances of its conclusion, in order to confirm the meaning resulting from the application of article 27, or to determine the meaning when the interpretation according to article 27:

(a) leaves the meaning ambiguous or obscure; or

(b) leads to a result which is manifestly absurd or unreasonable.

[11]

THEORY AND PRACTICE OF TREATY INTERPRETATION*

by Maarten Bos**

  * This article will appear in two parts. The first part comprises sections 1-4 inclusive. The second part comprising sections 5 and 6 will appear in the next issue of this Review.
  ** Professor of International Law in the University of Utrecht; Vice-President, International Law Association; *Membre de l'Institut de Droit International;* Member of the Board of Editors.

1.   INTRODUCTION

Treaty interpretation is a matter of legal methodology, a comprehensive notion embracing a great variety of subjects. In the Diagram published together with this study, the present writer gives his own view of legal methodology as applied to international law. The "legal process" as shown therein is a complicated one, certain parts of which have been examined in earlier studies, viz., the principles of rational organization, the recognized manifestations of international law, and the existence of a hierarchy among them.[1] Treaty interpretation as dealt with, here, belongs to the wide category of problems designated in the Diagram as those of the ascertainment of the content (meaning, message) of the recognized manifestations of international law. For reasons/which, it is hoped, will become clear in the following pages, it is important to place treaty interpretation and the whole of ascertainment of content in the context of methodology generally, not isolated from the other questions involved in the application of recognized manifestations or from the problems surrounding the latter, such as the doctrine of "sources". As to the link between the present subject and that of the ascertainment of the content of recognized manifestations other than treaties, it is readily agreed that doctrinal treatment of the former would gain by a contrasting sketch of the latter, but since the present study already exceeds the limits of the habitual article, this writer has to forego what otherwise would be a legitimate pursuit.

For a better understanding of the attached Diagram, one should think of its Phase I as the "legislative" stage in the legal process, a process eventually leading to a legal finding at the end of Phase III and, possibly, its enforcement. Factual and moral elements in Phase I are the ingredients to which the principles of rational organization are applied according to a formal or informal procedure. The "legislative" stage traditionally results in the making of a treaty or the emergence of a customary rule, and in our times decisions of international organizations have come to join them when satisfying certain conditions. Depending on circumstances, judicial decisions, too, take their place among the recognized manifestations of international law, but their very nature precludes any "legislative" origin: they are there owing to a feed-back into the legal process as indicated in the Diagram. The remaining manifestations, viz., certain general principles of law and complementary natural law, stemming directly from the normative concept of law for international relations as they do, have a (purely) "intellectual" rather than a "legislative" or "judicial" origin. In Phase III, recognized manifestations of international law are process-

---

1. See "Principles of Rational Organization as Applied in the Process of Law", *Netherlands International Law Review*, vol. XXIV (1977) pp. 43-54, and in *Essays on International Law and Relations in Honour of A.J.P. Tammes* (Leyden 1977) pp. 43-54; "The Recognized Manifestations of International Law: A New Theory of 'Sources'", *German Yearbook of International Law*, vol. 20 (1977) pp. 9-76; and "The Hierarchy among the Recognized Manifestations (Sources) of International Law", *Netherlands International Law Review* (1978) pp. 334-344, also published in *Estudios de Derecho Internacional* (Homenaje al Profesor Miaja de la Muela), vol. I (Madrid 1979) pp. 363-374. Hereafter, these titles will be quoted in an abridged form as "Principles of Rational Organization", "The Recognized Manifestations", and "The Hierarchy".

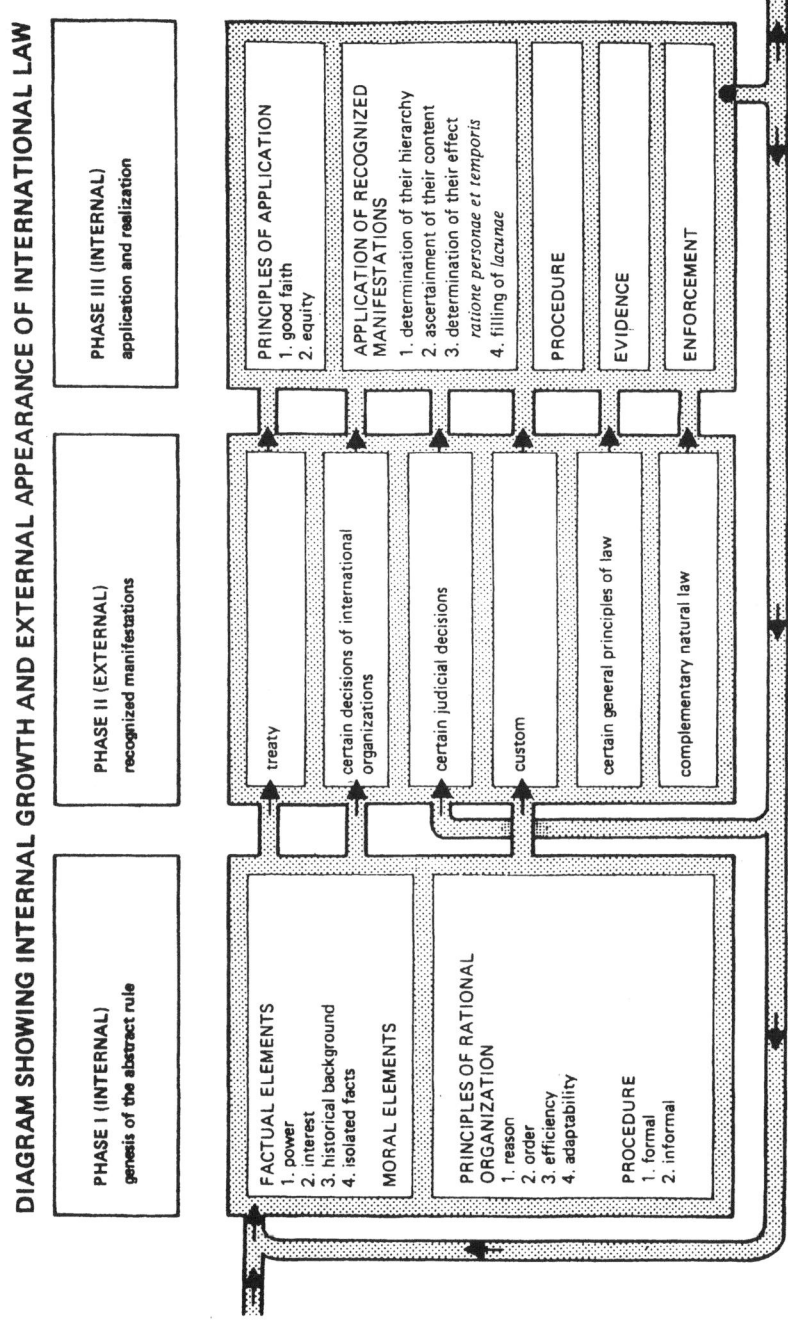

DIAGRAM SHOWING INTERNAL GROWTH AND EXTERNAL APPEARANCE OF INTERNATIONAL LAW

PHASE I (INTERNAL)
genesis of the abstract rule

PHASE II (EXTERNAL)
recognized manifestations

PHASE III (INTERNAL)
application and realization

FACTUAL ELEMENTS
1. power
2. interest
3. historical background
4. isolated facts

MORAL ELEMENTS

PRINCIPLES OF RATIONAL
ORGANIZATION
1. reason
2. order
3. efficiency
4. adaptability

PROCEDURE
1. formal
2. informal

treaty

certain decisions of international organizations

certain judicial decisions

custom

certain general principles of law

complementary natural law

PRINCIPLES OF APPLICATION
1. good faith
2. equity

APPLICATION OF RECOGNIZED MANIFESTATIONS
1. determination of their hierarchy
2. ascertainment of their content
3. determination of their effect
   ratione personae et temporis
4. filling of *lacunae*

PROCEDURE

EVIDENCE

ENFORCEMENT

5

ed until a verdict applying to a specific case is reached. At the centre of this final stage in the legal process is their "application". Since enforcement in the international legal order is usually a very diffuse activity and the verdict may be considerably changed in the course of it, it was thought inevitable to give enforcement a place within the range of the international legal process, contrary to what may apply in the national legal order.

The term "application of the recognized manifestations of international law" calls for a short comment. It is understood, here, to cover an activity marked by *respect du droit* as meant in Article 37, paragraph 1, of the First Hague Convention (1907). Where respect for the law begins and ends is, no doubt, a matter for discussion and a certain elasticity must, consequently, be inherent in the concept of application. Yet, here too, the Latin saying applies: *sunt certi denique fines,* to the effect that not every would-be "application" may deserve to be so named. No account will be taken, here, of applications not meeting the requirement of *respect du droit.*

The application of the recognized manifestations of international law necessarily starts with the determination of a possible hierarchy among them. Supposing the question of hierarchy either to be of no consequence *in concreto*, or to have been settled, the next stage in the legal process is that of the ascertainment of the content of the manifestation found applicable. To do this, the applier of that manifestation, living up to the requirement of *respect du droit,* is under an obligation to comply with certain methods and rules. The methods and rules relating to treaties will now be set forth.

First, however, two preliminary questions will have to be raised, viz., (1) what meaning should be given to the term "interpretation", so current in the present context, and (2) what is the origin and character of the methods and rules for the ascertainment of the meaning of treaties?

It is in the course of the discussion of the latter question that one will be able to appreciate to what extent there really is an "obligation" as suggested above. One may also draw nearer to answering the problem whether "method" generally speaking should be rated as "law", or should be distinguished from it, be it merely in the way of an atmosphere lying around it and permitting the law to breathe and live.

2.   WHAT IS INTERPRETATION?

2.1   Limitation to written manifestations

"Interpretation" is a term very differently understood by different authors and neither the scope nor content of it is commonly agreed upon.

The widest possible scope for the concept is seen by Professor Sur, author of a remarkable though controversial study entitled *L'interprétation en droit international public.*[2] In his view, interpretation extends to law and facts as well. He,

2. Paris, 1974.

6

indeed, refers to the "interpretation" of treaties, unilateral acts (both written and unwritten), and judicial decisions [3], of facts, situations, and unwritten law [4], of circumstances [5], of consent [6], and of attitudes (in their relation to custom).[7]

As to the content of interpretation, far from limiting it to "déterminer le sens et la portée juridiques du droit écrit, du droit coutumier, des circonstances" [8] (and of all the other things mentioned in the preceding paragraph), Professor Sur eagerly includes the determination of a possible hierarchy among contending rules of international law [9], and the filling of *lacunae*. [10] He proceeds farthest in this direction when pointing to the act of writing down a rule as a form of "interpretation": depending on the clarity of their text, parties to a treaty putting a rule into writing, to a degree, predetermine its interpretation, and in so doing perform an interpretative act.[11]

It is not surprising, therefore, that in the author's view interpretation is everywhere: "Elle [l'interprétation] concerne l'ensemble de l'ordonnancement juridique, quel que soit le domaine ou la nature de l'activité en cause".[12] Or, in the present writer's own words, "interpretation" as seen by Professor Sur extends to all that comes under the legal process, i.e., the legislative process as well as the process in which a more or less abstract rule contained in a recognized manifestation is being transformed into a rule indicating the exact legal relationship between two (or more) parties on a given point.

Looking for the reasons for this very wide view of interpretation, one cannot be far amiss when explaining it by Professor Sur's professed aim to promote the coherence of the international legal order by as broad an application of the methods of interpretation as possible.[13] Deeply imbued with the idea of the interaction between treaty, custom, and circumstances — "les trois domaines essentiels saisis par le droit international" [14] — he cannot but throw them together under one single heading: "interpretation". At the same time, however, he is keenly aware of the differences between methods used in the three fields indicated [15], but in order to avoid "methodological fragmentation", as he calls it, and to save the "unity of the

---

3. Op.cit., pp. 74-75; and see further on unilateral acts: ibid., pp. 222-232.
4. Ibid., pp. 157-158.
5. Ibid., pp. 159-160.
6. Ibid., p. 182.
7. Ibid., pp. 223-224.
8. Ibid., p. 317.
9. Ibid., p. 156.
10. Ibid., pp. 90 and 91.
11. Ibid., pp. 225, 363, and 365.
12. Ibid., p. 76; and see p. 317: "L'interprétation (. . .) est omniprésente dans l'activité judiciaire".
13. Op.cit., pp. 12 and 241.
14. Ibid., pp. 241-242.
15. Ibid., p. 242; and see ibid., p. 287, n. 121, on the difference, particularly, between the interpretation of written and that of unwritten (customary) law (quoting Ch. De Visscher and Huber); at p. 286, n. 120, the author already excluded the general principles of law from his observations, noting that their interpretation, though giving rise to no less difficulties than that of custom, on account of their declining importance is not of he same consequence as the latter.

7

legal system", he proposes to adopt a wide concept of "method" [16] embracing: (1) methods *stricto sensu,* being procedures of a technical character showing a certain amount of precision, as in the maxims *ut res magis valeat, contra proferentem eiusdem generis, expressio unius, generalia specialibus non derogant* [17], (2) principles [18], like good faith in the interpretation (Vienna Convention, Arts. 31 and 26) and application (United Nations Charter, Art. 2, para. 2) of treaties, (3) rules [19], like Vattel's famous one on the "sens clair" of a treaty provision [20] (as reflected in Art. 31, para. 1, of the Vienna Convention), and (4) "bases", or what one should turn to for purposes of interpretation, e.g., the text only of a treaty, or also the *travaux préparatoires.* [21]

A much narrower concept of interpretation was practised by Judge De Visscher. In his study of problems of judicial interpretation in international law he referred to "the interpretation of customary practices" [22] in addition to that of treaties. The same line was taken by Professor Barile, in whose opinion common law judges "interpret" the common law. The opposite view was propounded by Professor Bentivoglio for whom only those judges who are subject to *ius conditum (scriptum)* [23] "interpret".

Which of these terminologies is to be preferred? Above all, it should be realized that "interpretation" is a notion which throughout the history of law has had a number of meanings. As to classical Roman law, these meanings were examined by Dr. Archi in a recent study, and the author concluded there was a multiplicity of meanings all intimately connected with the requirements of the particular historical period.[24] Professor Coing, in a thought-provoking study of three historical forms of interpretation "of law", contrasted the medieval glossators' method with the man-

16. Ibid., p. 242, n. 2 (quoting the International Court of Justice, using a comparable set of expressions).

17. Ibid., p. 244 and n. 7.

18. Ibid., pp. 242-243: "On appellera principe ce qui domine très largement l'interprétation, sans être spécifique aux questions qu'elle pose, mais d'une application fort générale, et qui, par conséquent, ne saurait fournir clairement une solution équivoque".

19. Ibid., p. 243: "une directive juridique générale et spécifique au problème".

20. See p. 14 *infra.*

21. Op.cit., p. 244.

22. Charles De Visscher, *Problèmes d'interprétation judiciaire en droit international public* (Paris 1963) pp. 219-251. Although one would expect him to do so, Judge De Visscher does *not* refer to the "interpretation" of the general principles of law recognized by civilized nations.

23. See Bentivoglio, "Rilievi sulla natura della sentenza internazionale", *Comunicazioni e Studi,* vol. IV (1953), and Barile, "La rilevazione e l'integrazione del diritto internazionale non scritto e la libertá di apprezzamento del giudice", *Comunicazioni e Studi,* vol. V (1953), as quoted in Frosini, "Rilievi metodologici sulla posizione del giudice nel diritto internazionale", *Rivista di diritto internazionale,* vol. XXXIX (1956) pp. 523-525; and (for Dutch readers) the present writer's contribution "De betekenis van het rechterlijk proces voor de rechtsvorming" (The Significance of Judicial Proceedings in the Process of Law) in the volume *Quid Iuris* (Deventer 1977) p. 24. Comp. also Professor Emilio Betti, *Teoria generale della interpretazione,* vol. II (Milan 1955) p. 865: "interpretazione di norme consuetudinarie", with reference to his earlier book *Interpretazione della legge e degli atti giuridici* (1949), chapter XIV.

24. Gian Gualberto Archi, "Interpretatio iuris − interpretatio legis − interpretatio legum", *Zeitschrift der Savigny-Stiftung für Rechtsgeschichte,* 87. Band (Weimar 1970) pp. 1-49, at p. 32.

ner of the German pandectists of the nineteenth century and that of their French contemporaries, the members of the exegetical school.[25] In his terminology, "interpretation" clearly means "method of thought", and he offers the reader a lively picture of the striking differences in method between glossators, pandectists, and exegetics. If the term, therefore, is liable to vary with time, there is no historical reason to fix it for all time with one single connotation. But if from this standpoint no particular use of it is objectionable, this does not free one from the obligation, in the context of one's own thinking, to search for the *best* use of the term and, if need be, to be critical of the ways in which other publicists handle the expression.

In this writer's opinion, Professor Sur's far-reaching concept of "interpretation" should be rejected. Quite apart from the fact that from most of the examples of methods, principles, rules, and "bases" of interpretation given by Professor Sur it becomes clear that, actually, he thinks of the interpretation of *treaties*, it is submitted that the coherence of the international legal order, the unity of the legal system, he seeks is far better served by the conceptualist approach as advocated by the present writer than by the forcing of all and sundry steps in the application of the recognized manifestations of international law under one single and bleak generic title, "interpretation", and under one set of prescriptions the practicability of which varies greatly, as Professor Sur himself admits, from one manifestation to another.[26]

There is also good reason not to subscribe to the usage extending the term to unwritten manifestations. The reason lies in the circumstance that, technically speaking, the ascertainment of the meaning of unwritten manifestations is a procedure different from the one in which the message of a written manifestation is being determined. To illustrate the idea, reference is made, here, to Figure I.

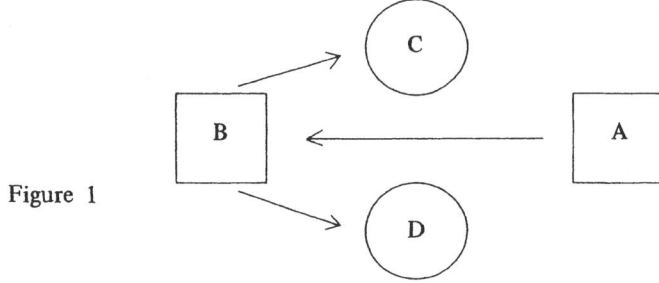

Figure 1

A : the facts to be put to the test of a treaty
B : the factural aspects of a treaty
C : definition of treaty
D : methods and rules of interpretation
arrow : direction of testing

25. Helmut Coing, "Trois formes historiques d'interprétation du droit: glossateurs, pandectistes, école de l'exégèse", *Revue historique de droit français et étranger* (Paris 1970) pp. 531-543.
26. Ibid., p. 287: in spite of the intrinsic equivalence of treaty and custom (see "The Hier-

In Figure I, A represents the litigious facts. The question to be elucidated is whether these facts are or are not in conformity with law, i.e., with an alleged treaty, B. In order to know whether there is actually such a thing as a treaty called B, a number of purely factual aspects are to be checked in the very first place: the authentication of its text, its signature, ratification, and entry into force (Arts. 11 and 24 of the Vienna Convention on the Law of Treaties). All this having been successfully performed, it then has to be examined whether the factual conglomerate B is a treaty. To that end, B is tested against C, holding a definition of a treaty (Art. 2 of the Vienna Convention). In the event of B corresponding to C, the message as expressed in the symbols used in B still has to be deciphered, an essential condition of any judgment on the legality or illegality of A. The ascertainment of B's message takes place in the shape of an application to B of the methods and rules of interpretation, D. "Interpretation" is here strictly limited to the latter operation: interpretation is *finding out the message of B,* not finding out whether B is a treaty.

Applying Figure I to custom instead of treaty, one will notice that the last phase in the operation – testing B against D – lapses. Indeed, for a *custom* to exist one merely has to ascertain the existence of the alleged factual aspects of it (B), i.e., its material and psychological components, and to put these to the test of the definition of custom (C). The message of B in this case does not have to be determined separately: with regard to custom, *content merges with existence.*

In order to bring out this operational difference between treaty and custom, it is proposed to restrict to treaty and the other written manifestations of international law the term "interpretation" [27], and to use the more general expression "ascertainment of the content (meaning, message)" with regard to custom and the other unwritten manifestations. Especially in connexion with the latter (the general principles of law recognized by civilized nations and complementary natural law), the undesirability of the term "interpretation" should be self-evident.[28]

Certainly, in a wide sense "every manifested instance of human behaviour is interpretable", as Professor Tammelo says, echoing Emilio Betti and other supporters of the idea, but when adding that "even in the legal sense, it is by no means inappropriate to speak of interpretation of every legally relevant act" [29] he is, for the reasons stated above, better not followed. Also, with regard to acts not to be identified with a recognized manifestation, his view runs the risk of confusion between interpretation and evidence: there is as little reason to reduce evidence to interpretation as there is to do the reverse.[30]

---

archy" p. 335) and their ensuing blending and profound unity, "la coutume n'en conserve pas moins un caractère très original qui confère à son interprétation des traits spécifiques"; and see ibid., pp. 78-80: the "interpretation" of custom is highly "creative", "quasi-legislative", and hence not strictly legal, work!

27. The same suggestion was made by J.H.W. Verzijl, *International Law in Historical Perspective,* vol. VI (Leyden 1973) p. 298.

28. See p. 8 n. 22 *supra* on Judge De Visscher.

29. Ilmar Tammelo, *Treaty Interpretation and Practical Reason: Towards a General Theory of Legal Interpretation* (Sydney 1967) p. 4.

30. See section 5.2 *infra* on Hyde's opinion on interpretation.

10

2.2 Interpretation and application

In this same context, another question may be mentioned, namely, the distance, indeed opposition, seen by some writers between "interpretation" and "application". As shown by Professor Coing in his article quoted above, the pandectists and exegetics both considered interpretation to be one thing, application another.[31] The school of exegesis, especially, saw application as a logical subsumption of the case under the terms of the law as interpreted beforehand in the logico-grammatical manner: no further interpretation starting from the case was admissible! This view was very much in harmony with the idea of the strictest obedience owed by the citizen to the French State's commands as contained in statute. The same gap between interpretation and application, though by no means the same obligation of obedience to the outcome of interpretation, was seen by Sir Humphrey Waldock in his Third Report on the Law of Treaties of 1964. Article 65 of his draft articles on that subject read as follows: "1. A treaty is to be *interpreted* in the light of the law in force at the time *when the treaty was drawn up*. 2. Subject to paragraph 1, the *application* of a treaty shall be governed by the rules of international law in force at the time *when the treaty is applied*".[32] It seems hardly possible to create a bigger gulf between interpretation and application than was done here. The International Law Commission in that same year dismissed the proposed provision. Two years afterwards, in 1966, Waldock maintained the validity of the distinction between interpretation and application, yet conceded that for purposes of codification it probably was "too subtle".[33] So it was that the proposed rule never reached the final text on the law of treaties prepared by the International Law Commission.

In his book on interpretation mentioned above, Professor Sur gives some thought to the relations between interpretation and application. First, he splits the concept of interpretation into a "doctrinal" and a "juridical" variety.[34] Doctrinal (or scientific) interpretation has for its aim the "understanding" of the legal order, juridical interpretation, i.e., interpretation by "qualified legal agents", its "functioning".[35] Juridical interpretation cannot avoid being influenced by doctrinal interpretation, but such influence is not properly to be considered as its object, unless doctrinal interpretation be moved by a "political doctrine". It is to juridical interpretation that Professor Sur wants to limit his argument. Juridical interpretation, as he sees it, far from being a merely preliminary activity, an act of "cognition" only, is in actual fact a composite notion harbouring both "cognition" and "will", i.e., the knowledge of all legally possible solutions together with the will to promote one particular solution to the exclusion of all the others.[36]

---

31. Coing, op.cit., pp. 540-541 and 542.
32. *Yearbook of the International Law Commission* (1964) vol. II pp. 8-9 (italics supplied).
33. Ibid., 1966, vol. I, Part II p. 199, para. 9.
34. Op.cit., p. 98: "interprétation doctrinale" and "interprétation juridique".
35. Ibid., p. 67; it is a bit odd to see doctrinal interpretation called "non juridique" at pp. 87, 94, and 98.
36. Ibid., pp. 98-99.

The author then recognizes four stages in the life of a rule of law: its coming into existence, its application, its modification, and its termination. Though no claim is laid to absoluteness, and the four compartments are not meant to be watertight, Professor Sur attributes a certain clarifying effect to his distinction: in his opinion, indeed, interpretation in each of the four stages has a role to play, and a different one at that. By "application", he understands the confrontation of a rule of law with the circumstances envisaged by it and with the legal consequences which the rule brings in its wake. "Modification" and "termination" he respectively defines as processes resulting in a change in the general meaning of a rule and its disappearance from the legal order, either formally, i.e., following a procedure expressly laid down to that end, or informally, i.e., subsequent to the interpretation of circumstances. In the integration of circumstances into the rule of law, Professor Sur holds, interpretation is not a passive catalyst, but an active and decisive agent.[37]

The only stage of interest being, here, that of the "application" of the rule of law, further references to Professor Sur's work are now to be limited to his observations on the relationship between interpretation and application. This relationship, in his view, seems to oscillate between the two poles of clear distinction and total merger, on the understanding, however, that interpretation and application constantly interact, except, of course, in the event of total merger. A clear distinction is feasible, for instance, when an organ of an international organization first interprets the rules regarding its own competence, then applies them in making a recommendation. But in case the rules on competence are obscure, their interpretation may merge with their application. Doctrine and treaties alike, therefore, speak of interpretation and application as equivalent or, at any rate, correlative concepts.[38]

Another sort of interaction, Professor Sur shows, is in the account the International Court of Justice takes of the impact its decisions may be expected to have in the political sphere. Occasionally, the Court cannot escape from allowing this to weigh in the scales of justice.[39]

Interpretative agreements between parties to a treaty blur the borderline between interpretation and application and, indeed, between the latter two and revision, bringing into existence, and termination of a rule of law.[40] Labelling them as agreements of "authentic interpretation" is, therefore, misleading. The borderline is definitively crossed when adaptation or peaceful change takes the place of application.[41]

It is submitted that the numerous complexities in the relationship between interpretation and application so well explained by Professor Sur must have been present in Sir Humphrey Waldock's mind when writing his Third Report on the Law of Treaties, but also that his proposed Article 65 (*supra*) was an unfortunate

37. Ibid., pp. 180-181.
38. Ibid., p. 193; and comp. Art. 31, para. 3(*b*), of the Vienna Convention on the Law of Treaties.
39. Ibid., pp. 335-339.
40. Ibid., pp. 362 and 388-389.
41. Ibid., pp. 343-344.

12

embodiment of one of the aspects of this relationship, viz., that of a clear distinction between interpretation and application which may sometimes have to be made. As the present writer sees it, it is simply impossible to divorce interpretation and application to a point where the outcome of the interpretation of a text would be nullified by the application given to it. That process would amount to treaty revision. Interpretation is an activity *in the context of the application* of the recognized manifestations of law.

There is one more weighty reason why interpretation and application should not be entirely disconnected, namely, the danger that otherwise in mere *questions de principe* too broad a judicial decision may be handed down. The danger was clearly recognized in the case of *Office de vérification et de compensation pour l'Alsace-Lorraine c. le Reichsausgleichsamt de Berlin* decided by the Franco-German Mixed Arbitral Tribunal on 19 October 1921.[42] Requested to pronounce on a *question de principe*, namely, whether certain payments made between French and German private parties were legally valid only if made at a certain rate of exchange, the Tribunal ruled that it had jurisdiction to deal with the matter notwithstanding the fact that no specific private parties were involved in the case. But the Tribunal would have to refrain, it observed, from laying down "a general and absolute principle which, being too comprehensive, might have unforeseen consequences and harm the solution of specific cases".[43]

2.3 Definition of interpretation

The third and last question is how exactly to define the concept of interpretation. Elements of a definition are to be found in a number of propositions made or referred to in the preceding section, viz., (1) the distinction made by Professor Sur between "doctrinal" and "juridical" interpretation [44], (2) the link between interpretation and application [45], and (3) the appropriateness of the exclusion from it of all interpretative agreements.[46] All these propositions are fundamentally sound, although some reservation must be made regarding Professor Sur's terminology in distinguishing a "doctrinal" from a "juridical" interpretation. Scholars representing one out of the three legal archetypes [47] are jurists in their own right and there is no reason, therefore, not to term their work "juridical" too. Consequently, it is better to refer to "practical" rather than to "juridical" interpretation, the more so since the expression "practical interpretation" aptly suggests the linkage of interpretation to application.

42. *Recueil des décisions des Tribunaux Arbitraux Mixtes,* vol. I p. 472.
43. Ibid., p. 478 (this writer's translation); and see on this case and on the question generally, the present writer's *Conditions du procès en droit international public* (Leyden 1957) pp. 66-75.
44. See p. 11 *supra.*
45. See p. 13 *supra.*
46. See p. 12 *supra.*
47. See this writer's "Legal Archetypes and the Normative Concept of Law as Main Factors in the Defining and Development of International Law", NILR (1976) pp. 76-77.

13

Are there any more elements to be worked into a definition of interpretation? One may think of two, namely, the use in the course of interpretation of specific methods, and the requirement of effectiveness (or: efficiency).[48] However, under the next heading it should become clear that specificness of method is too strong a claim [49] and that effectiveness is too much of a problem in itself [50] to be able to structure a definition of interpretation.

Keeping in mind the three elements retained, one might feel tempted to accept Professor Schwarzenberger's (still somewhat elliptical) formula: "Interpretation is the process of establishing *the legal character and effects of a consensus* achieved by the parties" [51], provided the consensus meant here was laid down in writing. But it follows from the foregoing that it cannot be considered correct to divide "interpretation" so understood from "application", as Professor Schwarzenberger does when adding: "In contrast, application is the process of determining *the consequences of such interpretation* in a concrete case".[52] For anybody recognizing the link between, if not the identity of, interpretation and application, it should be artificial to distinguish between the "effects" of a consensus and the "consequences" of the interpretation of a treaty. The present writer, therefore, rather agrees with Professor Gaudemet's view of interpretation. In this view, interpretation has a *dual* object, viz., clarification (*rendre clair*) and the recognition of sense (*donner un sens*), and the latter object he defines as the application of an abstract formula to the realities of daily life and practice.[53] With regard to clarification, the question may be asked whether it is true, as Vattel had it, that "it is not permissible to interpret what has no need of interpretation. When a deed is worded in clear and precise terms, when its meaning is evident and leads to no absurdity, there is no ground for refusing to accept the meaning which the deed naturally presents".[54] The usual and correct answer is that without interpretation one cannot know whether a text is clear or not. Consequently, one cannot do with-

48. See "Principles of Rational Organization" p. 52: "it is submitted that the judiciary (. . .) should (. . .) take efficiency as a guide (. . .) particularly in the interpretation of treaties".

49. But see Sur, op.cit., pp. 70-73.

50. Comp. Sur, ibid., pp. 59-60, quoting Ch. De Visscher who sees four categories of effectiveness.

51. Georg Schwarzenberger, "Myths and Realities of Treaty Interpretation", *Current Legal Problems* (1969) vol. 22 p. 212 (italics added).

52. Ibid. (italics added).

53. Jean Gaudemet, "L'interprétation des lois et des actes juridiques dans le monde antique", *Revue internationale des droits de l'antiquité*, 3e série, tome XVII (1970) p. 235. The expression "giving a meaning to a text" was previously used in the Harvard Law School's "Research in International Law", vol. III, Law of Treaties, AJIL Supplt. (1935) p. 946, and borrowed by Sir Humphrey Waldock, *Yearbook of the International Law Commission* (1964) vol. II p. 53.

54. Emer de Vattel, *The Law of Nations*, translated by Charles G. Fenwick (New York, reprint 1964), Book II, Chapter XVII, para. 263. The passage was relied upon in a number of judicial decisions, e.g., by the Mixed Claims Commission United States-Germany in its opinion in the *Lusitania* cases of 1 November 1923, *Reports of International Arbitral Awards*, vol. VII pp. 32-44, at p. 43, and by the Appeals Chamber of the Central Committee for the Navigation on the River Rhine in a case of 15 February 1969, reported in *Schip en Schade*, 1969, Nr. 67 (in German).

14

out interpretation, even in case the clarifying element in it amounts to no more than a declaration that a text "is" clear.[55]

As a result of the above observations, practical interpretation may defined as an activity (excluding all interpretative agreements) designed to clarify the text of a written manifestation of law and to recognize its sense with a view to its application to the realities of daily life and practice.

3. ORIGIN AND CHARACTER OF METHODS AND RULES OF INTERPRETATION

3.1 Historical origin

Generally speaking, modern authors studying the methods and rules relating to the ascertainment of the meaning of written manifestations of international law do not, or only fleetingly, refer to the *origin* of such methods and rules. Where do they come from, both historically and methodogically?

According to Sir Hersch Lauterpacht, one of the authorities to have given attention to the *historical* origin of the methods and rules of interpretation in international law, they were borrowed from national law, and national law took them from Roman law. To quote: "In fact it is through private law that most of the technical rules found their way into international law. Vattel's and Pothier's rules of interpretation, both remarkably similar, can each be traced in a striking manner to the Digest".[56] There is no reason to doubt the truth of this statement [57]. but what it actually says is that Vattel and all those who shared his ideas on treaty interpretation must have taken a private law approach to treaties. This is especially true of Lauterpacht himself who, as will be shown below, was unable to see why a treaty should not be interpreted in the same way as a private contract.[58] Nowadays, the exclusively private law approach to treaties is obsolete, witness the International Court's advisory opinion of 28 May 1951 (*Reservations to the Convention on the Prevention and Punishment of the Crime of Genocide*), in which the Court made a

55. On Vattel's *dictum*, see, *inter alios*, J.P. Fockema Andreae, *An Important Chapter From The History of Legal Interpretation* (Leyden 1948) p. 82; Sergio Neri, *Sull' interpretazione dei trattati nel diritto internazionale* (Milan 1958) pp. 94-95; Lord McNair, *The Law of Treaties* (Oxford 1961) p. 372; McDougal c.s., *The Interpretation of Agreements and World Public Order* (New Haven 1967) pp. 78-79; and Ilmar Tammelo, op.cit., p. 4.

56. Sir Hersch Lauterpacht, *International Law: Collected Papers* (Cambridge 1970) p. 361. In a footnote, Sir Hersch refers to Charles Fairman, "Interpretation of Treaties", *Transactions of the Grotius Society*, vol. 20 (1934) pp. 129-130, for an analysis. Professor Sur, op.cit., p. 251, n. 25, draws attention to Arts. 1156-1164 of the French *Code* Civil and their influence on international law.

57. Tammelo, op.cit., p. 9: "As an unsystematized collection of juristic wisdom, most principles of legal interpretation have come down to us from classical Roman *jurisprudentia*. All contemporary legal systems have drawn heavily from this source, either directly or through the mediation of continental civilists. Thus the application of international law has relied on a body of rules of common origin with which lawyers of all countries and civilizations are familiar and of which they have made constant use" (and see n. 23 and 24 for further literature).

58. See section 5.3.2 *infra*.

15

clear-cut distinction between treaties to which "the contractual conception of the absolute integrity of the convention as adopted" would apply [59], on the one hand, and treaties like the Genocide Convention, on the other hand, in which "one cannot speak of individual advantages or disadvantages to States, or of the maintenance of a perfect contractual balance between rights and duties".[60] As a result, it is no longer correct to attribute to the methods and rules of treaty interpretation an exclusively private law origin.

3.2   Methodological origin

Considerably more intriguing is the question of the *methodological* origin of the methods and rules of ascertainment. In his masterwork of 1758, Vattel taught that the rules of interpretation as formulated by him were accepted and prescribed by natural law on account of their being "founded upon right reason".[61] Phillimore, writing over a century later used the words "settled rules and fixed principles, originally deduced from right reason and rational equity".[62] Anzilotti saw interpretation as "a logical operation subject only to the laws of logic, the very general criteria inherent in the special character of a particular legal order being taken for granted".[63] Sir Humphrey Waldock, *Rapporteur* of the International Law Commission on the Law of Treaties, stated in his Third Report that the principles and maxims (as distinguished from the methods) of interpretation were, "for the most part, principles of logic and good sense valuable only as guides".[64] And Professor O'Connell, also in the sphere of logic, found the canons of interpretation to be "no more than logical devices for getting at the real area of treaty operation", characteristically adding, however, that "logic itself is a deceptive notion, for the mind will utilize different techniques of logic at different times, and the choice between them is not itself, often enough, dictated by logic".[65]

Besides these advocates of reason and logic, another school of thought sees the methods and rules of treaty interpretation flowing from good faith or equity (in the sense of the French word *équité*). Among its adherents, one finds such classics as Gentili and Grotius [66], both of whom, indeed, made the whole of international

---

59. ICJ Reports, 1951 p. 24.
60. Ibid., p. 23; and comp. Judge Alvarez' dissenting opinion, ibid., p. 51: the Genocide Convention is part of the new international *constitutional* law.
61. Emer de Vattel, op.cit., Book II, Chapter XVII, para. 268.
62. Sir Robert Phillimore, *Commentaries Upon International Law,* 3rd. ed. (London 1879) vol. II p. 95.
63. Dionisio Anzilotti, *Lehrbuch des Völkerrechts,* vol. I (1929) p. 82 (this writer's translation). Anzilotti's view was subscribed to by C.H. Cheng, *Essai critique sur l'interprétation des traités dans la doctrine et la jurisprudence de la Cour permanente de Justice internationale* (Paris 1941) p. 2.
64. Waldock, "Third Report on the Law of Treaties", *Yearbook of the International Law Commission* (1964) vol. II (New York 1965) p. 54.
65. D.P. O'Connell, *International Law,* vol. I (London 1965) p. 272.
66. Alberico Gentili, *De iure belli* (1598), lib. II, cap. IV; Hugo Grotius, *De iure belli ac pacis* (1625), lib. II, cap. XVI.

16

law subject to the principle of good faith.[67] They had modern followers in Ehrlich and Charles De Visscher: in their view, the basis of interpretation is in the principle *pacta sunt servanda*, itself founded in the requirement of good faith.[68] The accent is on equity in Professor Bernhardt's phrase that "one may take it that the rules of interpretation originated in considerations of natural law and equity".[69]

An attempt to combine the two trends was made by Degan when writing that "interpretation is a very complicated operation founded in logic, equity, and good faith, i.e., in extra-juridical categories".[70]

Which of these doctrines should one believe? It is submitted that an answer cannot be given without further theoretical reflection on the methods and rules of ascertainment. A valuable contribution in that direction was made by Professor Tammelo.

In his conception, the canons of treaty interpretation belong to rhetoric (in the Aristotelian sense of the term), i.e., to the principles and methods (*topoi*, maxims, canons, *dicta*) for the establishment of propositions which, in formal logic, do not follow from prior propositions, yet are likely, probable, or plausible enough to carry great conviction. In spite of the limited role of formal logic in rhetoric, the author still regards rhetoric as *rational* "in the extended sense which embraces other methods of disciplined thinking".[71] It is rational notwithstanding the acknowledged part played in rhetoric by intuition, provided intuition "can be placed into the moulds of principles and methods of composed thought".[72]

Within the framework of (rational) rhetoric, Professor Tammelo then lets the canons of interpretation be determined by *practical* reason, i.e., reason aiming at the attainment of chosen goals [73], as opposed to theoretical reason striving after assured knowledge. The canons of interpretation so understood are the rules of art governing the lawyer's skills, his "know-how". They are mostly practical principles of legal reasoning, challengeable, contradictory at times, which the interpreter is to evaluate and amongst which he has to make a choice as well-founded as possible on the basis of standards such as reasonableness and prudence. "Thus they can scarcely be principles for juristic *demonstratio*; they are rather principles for juristic *inventio*, that is, for discovery of legally relevant meanings".[74]

Legal interpretation, Professor Tammelo concludes, partakes of science and of art as well [75], and "since legal interpretation is an activity which tasks all human

67. Comp. Ludwik Ehrlich, "L'interprétation des traités", *Recueil de l'Académie de droit international*, 1928-IV pp. 70 and 16.

68. Ehrlich, op.cit., pp. 76 and 77; and Charles De Visscher, op.cit., p. 50.

69. Rudolf Bernhardt, *Die Auslegung völkerrechtlicher Verträge* (Cologne 1963) p. 28 (this writer's translation).

70. V.D. Degan, *L'interprétation des accords en droit international* (The Hague 1963) p. 163 (this writer's translation).

71. Tammelo, op.cit., p. 37.

72. Ibid., p. 41.

73. Ibid., p. 50: "The overall endeavour in the application of practical reason is to make use of, to preserve, and to enhance *order* in human affairs" (italics supplied).

74. Ibid., p. 48.

75. Ibid., pp. 49-50 (echoing Basdevant and Hambro — and so many others: see Degan, op. cit., p. 164, Sur, op.cit., pp. 82-83, 264, and 305-306).

faculties relevant to disciplined and circumspect reasoning he [the interpreter] must aspire not only to gain insight into the 'nature of things' encountered in interpretation but also to create conditions around himself enabling him to display not only *l'esprit de géométrie,* but also *l'esprit de finesse".*[76]

There is much to recommend itself in Professor Tammelo's *exposé*: his emphasis on reason while recognizing intuition; his portrayal of the canons of interpretation in the light colouring of an aquarelle banning all thoughts of the absolute; his reference to the nature of things [77] and the requisite insight into it; his suggestion with regard to the *esprit de finesse.* But there is also one drawback to it, namely, that it isolates the interpretation of treaties in a double sense, i.e., from the other forms of ascertainment as well as from that phase in the legal process that precedes the phase of ascertainment. Professor Tammelo does not seem to have been sufficiently aware of the fact that law is a "continuing process", i.e., that interpretation and all other forms of ascertainment are but the continuation of a process of growth which in the recognized manifestations of law only found its first and provisional expression.[78] Had he realized this, then he would have linked up his theory of interpretation with the driving force of growth already becoming apparent in the first phase of legal development. It is on this basis of law as a continuing process that the present writer proposes now to offer his own view of the origins of the methods and rules of ascertainment.[79]

In the matter of the existence of, and the hierarchy among, the recognized manifestations of international law it was stated that both existence and hierarchy are determined by the normative concept of law for international relations. It was added that the normative concept would, in time, also be held responsible for the methods and rules of interpretation.[80] In point of fact, the normative concept not only determines all interpretation, but all other forms of ascertaining the contents of the recognized manifestations as well.

Is it possible to specify the decisive influence thus exerted by the normative concept of law on all forms of ascertainment? It is submitted that it is, and in order to define this influence, it is recalled that rational organization on the basis of certain factual and moral elements was said to lend to law "its very own and inalienable character".[81] The implication is that the principles of rational organization are at the heart of the normative concept and that, the normative concept directing all as-

---

76. Ibid., p. 55. See Pascal, *Pensées,* ed. Brunschvicg, *Section première,* No. 1, on the difference between the two *esprits,* the relevance of which in treaty interpretation was already hint-. ed at by Charles De Visscher (Degan, op.cit., p. 164), and later was by Sur, op.cit., p. 264.

77. Sur, op.cit., pp. 27-28, has interesting observations to offer on the *nature des choses.*

78. See the annexed Diagram. In international law, the recognized manifestations not of a "legislative" origin (certain judicial decisions, the general principles of law recognized by civilized nations, and complementary natural law) are, nevertheless, considered to be included in this growing process: see pp. 4-6 *supra.*

79. Comp. Sur, op.cit., p. 11, who takes as the starting-point of his study of interpretation the question "what is law?".

80. See "The Hierarchy" p. 338. In the same vein, Sur, op.cit., p. 19, refers to the "idéologie intégrée" permeating the entire legal mecanism.

81. See "Principles of Rational Organization" p. 44.

18

certainment, the applier of the recognized manifestations is in the position of the law-giver, namely, that *he must let himself be directed by the principles of rational organization,* be it only to the extent compatible with the limitations inherent in all "application".[82] Interpretation and all other forms of ascertainment, therefore, are subject to the requirements of reason (absence of prejudice, objectivity, consistency, and clarity), order, and efficiency.[83] The principle of adaptability [84], however, although being one of the principles of rational organization the law-giver has to apply, appears to be naturally unsuited for observance in the application of the recognized manifestations: for the result of this application should aim at defining the legal relationship between two (or more) specific parties and, consequently, have a preciseness inconsistent with adaptability.[85] But if the applier's product cannot be required to be adaptable, therefore, it is he, precisely, who is in charge of the "adaptation" which "adaptability" is supposed to make possible, and one of his instruments to that end is equity.[86] The use of equity, however, may affect the requirement that there should be an "absence of prejudice" [87], for equity preeminently involves consideration of the interests of the parties concerned. And the same must be true, of course, regarding one of the *techniques* of order, viz., legal equality [88]: applying the law in an egalitarian manner may again be at variance with the essence of equity. These examples indicate the tension in using principles of rational organization when applying the recognized manifestations.

As to the link between the principle of efficiency and the application of the recognized manifestations, it may be recalled that, particularly in the interpretation of treaties, efficiency was held up as a guide for the judiciary.[89]

As in legislation, rationality in applying the recognized manifestations of international law should never be allowed to degenerate into rationalism.[90] Intuition will generally be involved, and the ultimate choice made by the applying agent may not

---

82. An analogous, though too unqualified, statement is to be found in Sur, op.cit., pp. 369-370, according to whom the methods of interpretation aim at establishing "le sens et la portée d'une disposition par reconstitution du travail des rédacteurs" and, in the end, are analogous to those used in the drafting of a treaty, "explication profonde de la maxime "ejus est interpretari cujus est condere"", and see ibid., pp. 205-206: both Lauterpacht and Charles De Visscher were of opinion that judges have the same discretionary power as legislative organs and contracting parties in determining the rational purpose of a treaty; and p. 53: "Aussi les problèmes politiques posés par la formation du droit se retrouvent-ils très souvent au moment de son application".

83. "Principles of Rational Organization" p. 45. The requirement of reason is clearly reflected in Art. 32(b) of the Vienna Convention on the Law of Treaties. An early example of the formula used there is to be found in the advisory opinion of the Permanent Court of International Justice of 16 May 1925 (*Polish Postal Service in Danzig*), Series B, No. 11 p. 39.

84. Ibid.

85. Adaptability not to be confused with the capability of generalization of judicial decisions: see "The Recognized Manifestations" p. 59. Nor with the tampering with judicial decisions the enforcement of which meets with obstacles.

86. See Diagram.

87. "Absence of prejudice" understood here as "an approach irrespective of persons", see "Principles of Rational Organization" p. 45.

88. Ibid., p. 50.

89. Ibid., p. 52 (and comp. p. 14 n. 50 *supra*).

90. Ibid., p. 47.

always be accountable in reason, but justifiable only in terms of the irrational components of the normative concept. In the end, there may be the irrational "leap" which in the Dutch legal philosopher Paul Scholten's view, indeed, was the concluding feature in all application of law.[91]

Looking back at the other theories on the subject and comparing them with the one presented here, one will find that the latter, apart from its extension to the entire process of growth, harmoniously unites the elements of the former into one comprehensive doctrine. Itself based particularly on reason, it takes logic into account through the requirement of consistency [92], while making an allowance for intuition. The nature of things is taken care of by another requirement of reason: objectivity.[93] Order, the first principle of organization [94], corresponds with the ultimate aim of practical reason as seen by Tammelo.[95] Good faith and equity are present as general principles of application.[96] The principle of efficiency appears to be the only feature not mentioned in the theories reviewed, but which, as a principle of rational organization, should have its place in any doctrine of ascertainment.

In addition to these similarities, there is a number of observations made by Professor Tammelo which are easily to be fitted into the present writer's conception. "Rhetorical reasoning", he states, "requires (. . .) the integrity of cognitive and emotive faculties".[97] He also refers to "the ability to find the 'places' or 'seats' of argument [i.e., the particular canon or canons of interpretation], from which reasons for a solution can emerge which may bring consensus" [98], and to "the basic dilemma which confronts any legal interpreter": legal certainty *versus* legal change.[99] Because of the decisive influence of the normative concept as upheld in the present writer's doctrine, it is believed that integrity, inventiveness, and a sense of history [100] are qualities indispensable in anyone applying the recognized manifestations of international law.

3.3   Character

It is a short step from here to the *character* of the methods and rules of ascertainment. The question has been amply discussed in the relevant literature. In particular, it was asked whether these methods and rules represent *rules of law* or mere

---

91. See Paul Scholten, "Algemeen Deel" (General Part) of Mr. C. Asser's *Handleiding tot de beoefening van het Nederlandsch Burgerlijk Recht,* 2nd ed. (Zwolle 1934) pp. 173-181; and comp. Gerard J. Wiarda, *Drie typen van rechtsvinding* (Three Types of Legal Method) (Zwolle 1972) pp. 70-71.

92. See "Principles of Rational Organization" pp. 47-48.

93. Ibid., p. 46.

94. Ibid., p. 48.

95. See p. 17, n. 73 *supra*).

96. See Diagram.

97. Op.cit., p. 46.

98. Ibid., p. 47.

99. Ibid., p. 53.

100. Comp. this writer's "Legal Archetypes and the Normative Concept of Law as Main Factors in the Defining and Development of International Law", NILR (1976) p. 86, on integrity and flexibility.

guides for the applier of the recognized manifestations of international law. It is submitted that their character as rules of law cannot be denied in so far as they have been laid down in a written text, whether general or particular, containing rules of law.[101] Articles 31-33 of the Vienna Convention on the Law of Treaties of 23 May 1969, once they have entered into force, will constitute such a text of a general nature.[102] But what are the methods and rules of ascertainment outside the cases of general or particular treaty law? Sir Hersch Lauterpacht, Professor Guggenheim, and Professor Bernhardt, for instance, claimed their character as customary law inasmuch as they established themselves in practice.[103] Others with equal emphasis denied their character as rules of law [104], while a third group stressed their character as guides. Lord McNair expressed himself in the following terms: "The many maxims and phrases which have crystallized out and abound in the textbooks and elsewhere are merely prima facie guides to the intention of the parties in a particular case. If they are allowed to become our masters instead of our servants these guides can be very misleading".[105] Sir Humphrey Waldock's partial subscription to this view has already been quoted [106]: as he put it, the principles and maxims of interpretation "for the most part" were principles of logic and good sense valuable only as guides. It was not these guides which he proposed to codify therefore, but "the comparatively few rules which appear to constitute *the strictly legal basis* of the interpretation of treaties".[107] In his opinion, some were guides, others were more than that.[108]

As a personal view, this writer suggests that the term "guide", if used at all, can best be applied to the normative concept of law for international relations, which, indeed, is the steering principle behind all ascertainment.[109] The methods and rules of ascertainment are aids at this guide's disposal, worked out over the centuries, tools designed to perform all imaginable jobs and, therefore, by times as contradictory among themselves as a hammer and a pair of pincers.

---

101. Comp. "The Recognized Manifestations" p. 23: those treaties only are "sources" of *law*, which augment or codify the body of already existing rules. The fact implies a qualification of the statement in the text above.

102. Note, however, that Arts. 31-33 are of an *optional* nature and, consequently, may be contracted away. Comp. Sur, op.cit., p. 367.

103. Sir Hersch Lauterpacht, *The Development of International Law by the International Court* (London 1958) p. 27; Paul Guggenheim, *Traité de droit international public* (Geneva 1967), vol. I pp. 247-248; Bernhardt, op.cit., p. 30.

104. Oppenheim-Lauterpacht, *International Law*, vol. I, 8th ed. (London 1955) pp. 950-951; Degan, op.cit., pp. 162-163; and see Bernhardt, op.cit., p. 26, for further examples.

105. McNair, *The Law of Treaties* (Oxford 1961) p. 366; in the same vein already the Harvard Law School's *Research in International Law*, vol. III, Law of Treaties, AJIL, Suppl. 1935 p. 947; and see Georg Dahm, *Völkerrecht*, vol. III (Stuttgart 1961) pp. 56-57, and Tammelo, op.cit., pp. 22 (quoting Basdevant) and 23.

106. See p. 16 *supra*.

107. Waldock, op.cit., p. 54 (italics supplied).

108. Sur, op.cit, p. 71 n. 9: Waldock himself meanwhile admitted the controversial and partly contradictory character of the rules belonging to this "strictly legal basis" of interpretation.

109. See p. 18 *supra*.

However, it would be wrong to consider the methods and rules of ascertainment as *nothing but* steering aids for the normative concept. To a limited extent, they also assist the normative concept in discovering itself and in coming to full consciousness of one or more aspects of the "many-faceted, gradually emerging, and ever-changing" entity it is. Methods and rules, in other words, are "two-way tools" of the normative concept.

This being so, the question is less whether *certain methods and rules* are obligatory, but whether *a certain normative concept* is to be put into practice to the exclusion of all other ones. The question is ambiguous, of course, to the extent that a normative concept is obligatory *per definitionem* for anybody believing in it. In an objective, not a subjective, sense, however, the question comes to mean, for instance, whether the International Court of Justice being "the principal judicial organ of the United Nations" (Art. 92 of the United Nations Charter) is free to operate on the basis of another normative concept than the one prevailing in the United Nations. The answer can only be in the negative, to the effect that the Court has to consider the United Nations' normative concept — a very different one from that of the League of Nations, for example — as obligatory in all its work.[110] But this entails the obligatory character also of those methods and rules of ascertainment which, in a given case, can help the Court to bring the United Nations' normative concept to fruition. Among other cases, one may think here of the Court's advisory opinion of 11 April 1949 (*Reparation for Injuries Suffered in the Service of the United Nations*).[111] Even so, however, a certain amount of discretion on the applier's side will always be indispensable: for it cannot be imagined that in all circumstances the normative concept can be realized only with the help of certain methods and rules and not through others.

Rules of law or mere guides, it was asked? Rules of law, the answer should be, in so far as a treaty as understood above consecrates one or more of the methods and rules. In all other cases, they are just part and parcel of legal method as such, and since legal method is not law, but belongs to the sphere of the normative concept, non-codified methods and rules cannot be law either. In particular, they are not customary law: the applier's indispensable discretion in their handling precludes this possibility.[112] As to their being guides, it was demonstrated that at most they are guides to a better understanding of the normative concept, and that the only real guide in the legal process is the normative concept itself. And with regard to their being obligatory, it was pointed out that any obligation to use a method or rule to the exclusion of another one is always a function of the normative concept, and that such obligation acquires an extra dimension in case the normative concept itself is obligatory within a given legal order.

---

110. Sur, op.cit., p. 338: the International Court of Justice is the principal judicial organ of an Organization the political *raison d'être* of which is the maintenance of peace. In terms of the normative concept of law of the Organization, this cannot fail to produce its effect.

111. ICJ Reports, 1949 pp. 174 et seq.

112. In "The Recognized Manifestations" pp. 32 and 74-75, this writer still advocated the customary law character of the methods and rules of interpretation. At pp. 74-75, however, he in fact already demonstrated to what absurdity this view must necessarily lead. This is why it is

4. MISCELLANEOUS QUESTIONS

From this personal viewpoint, a number of items raised in doctrinal writings may now be shortly examined, viz.,

(1) the impact on interpretation of the identity of the law-applying agent,

(2) the question of the freedom of interpretation, including the problems of the incoherence of the international legal order and the interpretation of *ius cogens*,

(3) the character of the eventual choice made by the interpreter, and

(4) the question of the use of codification in matters of interpretation.

4.1   The identity of the law-applying agent

In one of his earlier studies, the present writer concentrated on what he called the three "legal archetypes", namely, the lawgiver, the judge (or court), and the scholar, to each of whom he ascribed a typical attitude to law marked, respectively, by sovereignty, service, and the search for light, i.e., understanding.[113] The three legal archetypes gave rise to three legal functions of the same description, the members of which exert their minds in a way true to the relevant archetype.[114] Thus, a lawgiver, taking into consideration what Portalis called "les hommes en masse" [115], would above all be conscious of his sovereignty (*sic volo sic iubeo*). A judge, on the contrary, directing his mind to the "hypothèses privées", would chiefly think of his position as that of a servant of that sovereign. The possibility of a certain amount of osmosis between the functions and of a corresponding metamorphosis in the persons holding them was, however, noticed.[116] If, for instance, in a discussion on what is law *in a given case* a judge would refuse to be hypnotized by the mere "service" aspect of his activity and let in some of the cares and preoccupations of the sovereign, then there would be a degree of osmosis between the two functions. The same applies to the judicial and the scholarly professions whenever the judge allows himself to be influenced by the scholar's typical attitude to law.[117] And so on.

In that same study, examples were given of authors all feeling the same need the present writer felt to understand the legal process in terms of a typology of lawyers, legal agents, or whatever their name may be.[118] All of them —

---

now abandoned, and an additional argument to the same effect is that of the indispensable discretion proposed here.

113. "Legal Archetypes and the Normative Concept of Law as Main Factors in the Defining and Development of International Law", NILR 1976 pp. 74-77. Professor Sur, op.cit., p. 160, rightly speaks of the "compétence dérivée" of the judge, thus stressing the "service" character of his function.

114. Ibid., p. 81.

115. Jean Etienne Marie Portalis (1746-1807) took an active part in the drafting of the French *Code Civil*. The words quoted are from his celebrated speech made on the occasion of the presentation of the final draft of the Code. In this speech he, *inter alia,* analysed the different tasks of law-giver and judge. On this *discours préliminaire,* see Wiarda, op.cit., pp. 10-12.

116. "Legal Archetypes" p. 81.

117. Ibid., p. 76.

118. Ibid., pp. 79-81.

Oliver, Stone, Carlston, Falk, Schwarzenberger — were *international* lawyers, bearing witness to the fact that the *general* phenomenology of law as appearing in a number of characteristic attitudes towards law as such does not stop before that branch of the law called *international* law.

The immediate interest for international lawyers of a typology as understood here is in the answer it may provide to the question of the possible limits to the judicial function in a world legal system in which the legal archetypes of the law-giver and the judge did not, or did in an awkward manner only, materialize into the two corresponding functions. However, this aspect of the matter does not exhaust its importance which, in fact, extends to the wider problem of interpretation in international law. In order to illustrate this point, it is proposed to return to this writer's tenet of the modern State as the present-day representer of the *homo liber* of Old Germanic law.

Just like the Old Germanic freeman, it was argued, the modern State recognizes its subjection to law, yet claiming ultimately to be its own judge in the matter of the ascertainment of its meaning.[119] Like the freeman, however, the modern State is also its own law-giver inasmuch as law between States depends on its creation by those very States. Certainly, the State cannot create international law unilaterally, for as this writer observed, "in international law — being a law for the lineal descendants of the *homines liberi* of old — reciprocity is of the essence".[120] But what is important with regard to interpretation is that every State has the *frame of mind* of the law-giver, and when acting as its own judge, i.e., when unilaterally ascertaining the meaning of a rule of international law, will be guided by that particular, "legislative", frame of mind centred around its sovereignty rather than by the characteristics of the judicial attitude.

It is suggested that this situation is highly typical of the international legal order. In the absence of obligatory jurisdiction, and with a rarefied use made of compulsory jurisdiction, unilateral interpretation is the order of the day. Is it correct, here, to speak of the "usurpation" of the judicial function by the law-giver [121] (as understood above)? On reflection, it is thought not. In a society of modern *homines liberi*, naturally devoid of obligatory jurisdiction, there simply *is* no judicial function to usurp. In the international legal order, the two archetypes of the law-giver and the judge have so far failed to provoke the birth of two differentiated functions and professions as a regular feature of that order. As a rule, the international law-giver and the international judge, so to speak, still reside in a common matrix, or even worse: they there find themselves in the undifferentiated state of "the law-giver and judge in one". When in 1920 and 1946 the Permanent and International Courts were created, their existence only seemingly brought about a change, for through

---

119. "Old Germanic Law Analogies in International Law, or: The State as *Homo Liber*", NILR 1978 pp. 58-59 (also published in *Mélanges Fernand Dehousse*, vol. 1 (Les progrès du droit des gens) (Paris-Brussels 1979) pp. 25-30).

120. See "The Recognized Manifestations" p. 71; the phrase, of course, is not intended to do away with those recognized manifestations of international law which are not of the States' making.

121. As the present writer did in NILR 1976 p. 78.

the operation of Article 36 of their Statutes they were virtually emasculated at birth.[122] No real separation of powers took place. One may think, here, of Professor R.J. Dupuy's remark that the International Court of Justice, while operating in a "relational" world order, in fact belongs to an "institutional" system.[123] Clearly, in his view, the Court is a *corpus alienum* in today's world. Another quotation in place is that of Professor Decencière-Ferrandière who found the Court's predecessor a potentially dangerous body because of the absence of an international legislator of the institutional kind able to keep the Permanent Court of International Justice from exceeding the limits of its jurisdiction and becoming itself a legislator.[124] The author, apparently, had great difficulty in accepting a judge without a law-giver of that type. In this view, law-giver and judge are closely connected and should for ever remain so. In the present writer's mind there, indeed, is room for the question whether law-giver and judge, once having left their matrix and having reached a personal existence, should not for all future be considered as "identical twins".[125] In this way, only, the deeper sense of the maxim *eius est interpretari cuius est condere* can be grasped.[126] Looking at legal history, one finds historical evidence for this proposition in the royal origin of so many courts, sometimes reflected in their names. But it is not correct, as Decencière-Ferrandière did, to deny the non-institutional, and therefore diffuse, international law-giver — an ever varying conglomerate of States — all influence on the Permanent, and hence International, Court. One merely has to read Professor Sur's observations on the subject to be convinced of the opposite.[127]

With all the metaphors used — in particular those of the embryonic "law-giver and judge in one" and of their acting as sovereign and servant after birth — and which allowed the student to penetrate the role of States and international judges, it is time now to evaluate their respective positions in the matter of "practical interpretation". With regard to the State interpreting unilaterally it was already pointed out that its legislative frame of mind will be dominant in the undertaking.[128] Elsewhere, this writer observed that the State acting as *iudex in re sua* will not be given to the many niceties typical of a real court and that a rough-and-tumble law will be the result of it.[129] A much higher quality is to be recognized in the case-law of the Permanent and International Courts, not to mention the many other international judges called to the task of solving international disputes. However much they may have functioned in an institutional twilight, they

---

122. Comp. Sur, op.cit., pp. 347-359, on the fear of a "government by judges".

123. As quoted by Sur, op.cit., p. 318; and comp. p. 321 on the threefold weakness of the Court, and p. 383 on the risk involved in a premature development of institutions of international law.

124. See Sur, op.cit., p. 319; at pp. 178-179, the author himself already asked whether a without a legislator could remain a judge: did he not become a pseudo-legislator?

125. In a way, because they cannot be deemed identical to the point where they have an identical mission to accomplish. This is how this writer could say that, "to a point, the legislative and the judicial function must always remain separate" ("Legal Archetypes" p. 75).

126. Comp. p. 19, n. 82 *supra*.

127. Sur, op.cit., p. 321.

128. See p. 24 *supra*.

129. "Legal Archetypes" p. 78.

25

have generally shown themselves to be possessed of great professional conscience. There is an element of truth in Professor Sur's observation on the indissoluble link between judicial proceedings and evidence.[130] States interpreting unilaterally do so without the guarantees provided by the law of evidence, and the same applies to procedural law. Courts, on the contrary, are bound to abide with their rules forcing a meticulous working method upon them. The difference in outcome is striking.

This being so, it is believed that the fact that the judge just like the law-giver has to apply the principles of rational organization [131] does not prevent him from arriving at results very different from the verdicts reached by the State acting as *iudex in re sua*.

As to "doctrinal interpretation" aiming at "understanding" the legal order [132], it is clear that unanimity never has been a characteristic of interpreting scholars. If it is true that the scholar's objects are the presentation in a clear and critical picture of the law as produced by legislator and court, the discovery of the system underlying it, and the penetration into, and the unveiling of, the nature of law as such [133], then there is enough room for dissent among scholars alone. Nothing but the never ending struggle for the proper methods and rules of interpretation is an eloquent example. But it can also be easily shown how far "doctrinal interpretation" may be removed from the "practical" variety. The fact that the scholar, too, as this writer would submit, has to keep to the principles of rational organization cannot in the least impair this conclusion.

Although the impact on interpretation of the identity of the law-applying agent may be studied in greater detail, it is proposed to resist the temptation and to leave the matter with the above considerations, laying bare the principal *lignes de force* in interpretation. They should, at any rate, suffice to demonstrate how much, as Professor Sur has it, character and value of an interpretation may vary with the personality of the interpreter.[134] Apart from character and value, there also is the question of strength. Since doctrine is not a recognized manifestation of international law [135]. doctrinal interpretation is weakest in actual influence, yet is to be reckoned with because of its possible impact on practical, especially judicial, interpretation.[136] Judicial interpretation, though closely link-

---

130. Sur, op.cit., pp. 312-313.
131. See p. 19 *supra*.
132. See p. 11 *supra*.
133. "Legal Archetypes" p. 76.
134. Sur, op.cit., pp. 223-225. Comp. the present writer's Presidential Address to the International Law Association, Report of the Fifty-Fifth Conference, New York 1972 p. 6: "the lawyer is more important than the law especially in the kind of circumstances in which nowadays international law is supported to operate".
135. See "The Recognized Manifestations" p. 63.
136. On the influence of doctrine generally, see Fitzmaurice, *Yearbook of the International Law Commission*, 1957, vol. I p. 185: "It [international law] had always been made by the practice of States, but their debt to the professors was enormous; . . . admitted that States made international law, it must also be recognized that a very large part of their ideas came from professors and publicists"; and see J.P.A. François, "L'influence de la doctrine des publicistes sur le développement du droit international", *Mélanges Gilbert Gidel* (Paris 1961) pp. 275-281.

ed to application and carrying greater authority, therefore, suffers from the eccentric position of the judiciary in international relations. On account of the State's overbearing weight on the international scene, interpretation in the "legislative" manner must be considered, if not the best, at any rate the factually strongest variety. That the State also has an inherent *right* freely to interpret is something to be studied under the next heading.

4.2 The freedom of interpretation

One of the most fascinating strains in the theory of interpretation in international law is that of the "freedom to interpret" vested in the State and in the other subjects of international law. Professor Sur in his important study lays great stress on this freedom of interpretation, and rightly so, for it is highly characteristic of the international legal order as it is. Pondering the subject, one once more gains the impression of a legal order in which conditions still prevail that, in national law, belong to an ancient past. And do even the best of modern endeavours to regulate interpretation bring us any further than the stage of the medieval glossators and the freedom of interpretation they represented?[137]

The freedom of interpretation has its roots in the incoherence of the international community. It is this incoherence which brings in its wake concurrent powers for every single subject of international law to interpret the latter. The exercise of these powers in the international community is a matter of great consequence, and the role the freedom of interpretation is thus destined to play there finds itself enhanced considerably by another element of the same origin, viz., the technical imperfection of international law.[138]

The incoherence of the international community appears to be the backbone of Professor Sur's view of interpretation, and throughout his book he draws attention to it, making many an interesting observation. The main lines of his thought are the following. In order to be totally coherent, a legal order, whether national or international, should be possessed of "a precise and rigorous hierarchy of norms".[139] A coherent legal order includes a clear attribution of powers, clear as to the organs which will exercise them, as well as with regard to the scope and content of these powers and the procedural aspects of their use.[140] It also regulates interpretation in detail [141] — and at pp. 6-7 *supra* it was shown how comprehensive a view Professor Sur takes of the concept of interpretation. Incoherence already results from uncertainty over how to interpret "circumstances".[142] The more a legal order is inco-

---

137. Comp. p. 8 *supra* quoting Professor Coing.
138. Sur, op.cit., pp. 99 and 107; on the technical imperfection of international law, see ibid., pp. 375-380 (distinguishing three situations: contradictory rules, general imperfection of international law, and imperfection due to the impossibility to foresee future needs).
139. Ibid., pp. 54-55 (this writer's translation).
140. Ibid., p. 109.
141. Ibid., p. 245.
142. Ibid., p. 306

herent, the bigger a role interpretation has to play [143], until, in the final stage of incoherence, the legal order admits contradictory, yet equally valid interpretations.[144]

Coherence in the *international* legal order is incomplete [145] and seriously menaced by the freedom of interpretation, a sequel of sovereignty.[146] But interpretation may also *promote* international coherence, and Professor Sur enumerates a number of devices able to contribute to that end, namely, an interpretative statement relating to a written text of which that statement is a part, a device called *préconstitution écrite* in the author's terminology [147], – authentic (i.e., explicit) or quasi-authentic (i.e., tacit, as apparent in practice) interpretation by all parties to a rule [148], – and any interpretation harmonizing two seemingly contradictory treaties.[149] As a result of the ambiguous nature of the freedom of interpretation – a menace to, and an instrument towards, coherence – Professor Sur is compelled to acknowledge the existence in the international legal order of a permanent state of tension between coherence and incoherence, between efficiency and impotence.[150] But the emphasis is on incoherence and impotence and, hence, on the freedom of interpretation.

Professor Sur then develops his views of this freedom. As a sequel of sovereignty, its exercise nevertheless has its limitations in the requirements of good faith.[151] In the context of the United Nations, the consequences of the freedom of interpretation are most conspicuous. The organs of the Organization, indeed, have concurrent powers of interpretation *inter se*, to the effect that one organ may interpret the United Nations Charter in a manner contradicting the interpretation placed upon it by another organ of that same Organization, not excluding the International Court of Justice.[152] In addition, Member States are entitled to their own inter-

143. Ibid., p. 156.
144. Ibid., p. 99; but see ibid., p. 251, where Sur contradicts himself by saying: "L'interprétation unilatérale ne forme qu'une prétention de droit à l'égard des autres parties."
145. Ibid., p. 55.
146. Ibid., pp. 122-123.
147. Ibid., pp. 379-380; and see ibid., p. 366, for an explanation of the term intended for such phrases as "Nothing in this treaty may be interpreted as . . ."; Sur also recognizes a tacit (implied) form of *preconstitution:* the mere text of a treaty is considered to hold an interpretation (see p. 7 *supra*).
148. Ibid., p. 361; ibid.: in case not all parties partake in the interpretation, Sur speaks of "plurilateral" interpretation, a form of interpretation which he deems to be a sign of *incoherence* rather than a means to promote coherence; both (quasi-)authentic and plurilateral interpretation he unites under the name of *interpretation concertée,* in his opinion the most important form of interpretation in international law (ibid.).
149. Ibid., p. 175. The former two of these devices, in the present writer's opinion, are wrongly considered to represent forms of "interpretation". *Re vera,* they are nothing but agreements which *have to be* interpreted instead of interpreting themselves. Comp. p. 9 *supra* for this writer's rejection of Sur's wide concept of interpretation. Sur himself, op.cit., pp. 361-362, virtually acknowledges this writer's criticism when writing: "Authentique ou quasi-authentique, l'interprétation se laisse en dernière analyse malaisément dissocier de la formation d'une nouvelle règle de droit ou de la révision de l'ancienne".
150. Ibid., p. 239.
151. Ibid., p. 124, quoting the advisory opinion of the International Court of Justice of 11 July 1950 *(International Status of South-West Africa)*, ICJ Reports 1950 pp. 135-136.
152. But with the possible exception of the Secretary-General, supposing him to be the impersonation of the Secretariat which, under Art. 7, para. 1, of the Charter, is one of the princi-

pretation of the Charter, differing, if need be, from the one adopted by the organs of the United Nations, just as they have a right freely to interpret possible binding decisions of the Security Council and judgments pronounced by the International Court, whether in favour of, or against their claims.[153] Dramatic examples abound in the history of the Organization. Thus, the General Assembly ventured an interpretation of Article 4, paragraph 2, of the Charter which would have allowed it to admit States to membership in the United Nations without the co-operation of the Security Council. The claim was rejected in the International Court's advisory opinion of 3 March 1950 (*Competence of the General Assembly for the Admission of a State to the United Nations*).[154] In another bid for power, the Assembly initially was more successful: in its Uniting for Peace Resolutions of 3 November 1950, the Assembly took measures to take over the Security Council's primary responsibility for the maintenance of international peace and security in case the Council fails to exercise that responsibility because of a lack of unanimity of the permanent members of the Council, provided seven members, whether permanent or ordinary, vote in favour of a Council Resolution to that effect.[155] Interpretative clashes of opinion between the Organization and Members may be illustrated by reference to the International Court's advisory opinion of 20 July 1962 *(Certain Expenses of the United Nations)* [156], in which the scope of Article 17, paragraph 2, of the Charter was decided upon. Even after the advisory opinion, France and the Soviet Union who had refused to contribute towards the expenses of certain United Nations operations in the Congo and the Middle East kept to their own interpretation of Article 17 differing from the one adopted by the Court.[157] Interpretative wrangles between United Nations organs and Members were frequent, furthermore, with regard to Article 2, paragraph 7, of the Charter.[158]

In order to curb the freedom of interpretation, Professor Sur thinks of such means as "obligatory methods" of interpretation and the calling in of third persons to take upon them the task of interpretation.[159] He also stresses the need for custom and "circumstances" to be covered by those "obligatory methods".[160] As a third means, he quotes limitation by agreement as meant in Article 31, paragraph 2, of the Vienna Convention (an agreement contemporaneous with the treaty), or in the manner of the same article, paragraph 3 (a subsequent agreement).[161] As a combination of the second and a fourth method, the present writer

---

pal organs of the United Nations (and see Arts. 97-101 of the Charter). Secretary-General Dag Hammarskjöld, indeed, pursuing political power, claimed the freedom himself to interpret the Charter, but failed. See Sur, op.cit., p. 133.

153. Comp. Sur, op.cit., pp. 126-156; and see pp. 135-138 and 155-156, especially, for Professor Sur's interesting observations on the Members' right to challenge Security Council decisions on the strength of their freedom of interpretation.

154. ICJ Reports 1950 pp. 4 et seq.; and comp. Sur, op.cit., pp. 132 and 134.

155. Comp. Sur, op.cit., pp. 144-145.

156. ICJ Reports 1962 pp. 151 et seq.

157. Comp. Sur, op.cit., pp. 139-142.

158. Comp. Sur, op.cit., pp. 147, 150 and 152.

159. Ibid., pp. 237-238.

160. Ibid., pp. 245, 289, 299-302 and 312.

161. Ibid., pp. 238 and 386-387.

would like to quote Articles 53 and 66 of the Vienna Convention on the Law of Treaties. Article 53 (not being an agreement coming under Article 31) limits the freedom of interpretation by defining a rule of *ius cogens* as "a norm accepted and recognized by the international community of States *as a whole* . . . . . " etc. No unilateral interpretation seems to be in place here. Article 66 establishes compulsory jurisdiction for the International Court of Justice in the event of a dispute concerning "the application or the interpretation" of Article 53. But a reservation with regard to Article 66 may be entered by any signatory State in the moment of ratification [162], and the prohibition of unilateral interpretation in Article 53 then would lose much of its significance.

In spite of these different *techniques* to limit the freedom of interpretation, this freedom appears to be as fundamental as ever. Professor Sur may believe in "obligatory methods", or at least in their feasibility, even in the context of the interpretation of custom and "circumstances", but in the foregoing pages the normative concept was shown to be the only really "obligatory" element in interpretation [163], and below, when studying methods and rules in detail, it will become clear how liberal Articles 31-33 of the Vienna Convention actually are.[164]

The International Law Commission in the course of its preparatory work of these provisions may have stated how much, despite their rules, it remained attached to the freedom of the interpreter to handle them, but in view of the actual state of things this sounds like an understatement.[165] But however fundamental the freedom of interpretation therefore remains, it should be clear — as stated by Professor Sur (see p. 28 *supra*) — that all interpretation is bound by the requirements of good faith — one of the two great principles of application.[166]

4.3   The eventual choice made by the interpreter

At p. 19 *supra*, it was submitted that the interpreter should let himself be directed by the principles of rational organization to the extent compatible with the limitations inherent in all application. This requirement, coming on top of the need to act in good faith, is another bar against arbitrary constructions. But opin-

162. Comp. the questions raised in this respect by Sur, op.cit., p. 179; and see ibid., pp. 178-179: does not a Court empowered to decide whether a rule is a rule of *ius cogens* become a "pseudo legislator"? At p. 358, the author himself answers in the affirmative, and at p. 383, he sides with the International Law Commission which did not go beyond Art. 65, para. 3, of the Convention.
163. See p. 22 *supra*.
164. See section 5.2.2 *infra*.
165. Comp. Sur, op.cit., pp. 269-270: "En dernière analyse, les débats de la CDI révèlent que la liberté de l'interprète est pour la majorité de ses membres aussi importante à sauvegarder que la fixation d'une règle directrice leur semble nécessaire"; and ibid., p. 273: the ILC left many doors open and, thus, the interpreter's freedom came to take a place in the foreground; and ibid., p. 275: "C'est donc, toujours, la liberté de l'interprète qui apparaît, à côté de l'unité et de la souplesse des règles, la préoccupation principale de la Commission, ce qui ne va pas sans laisser nombre de problèmes peu ou mal résolus".
166. On good faith in interpretation, see Sur, op.cit., pp. 76-78 (quoting Ehrlich, Basdevant, Ch. De Visscher, and Lauterpacht).

ions on the dictates of good faith and rational organization may differ, as they may on a number of options the interpreter has even when staying within the boundaries of *bona fides* and the principles of rational organization. What then, in the end, is the character of the eventual choice made by the interpreter?

As an illustration of the possible options just mentioned, the following, all of a general nature, may be suggested:

(1) should everything be permissible unless prohibited?[167]

(2) should the concept of *ius aequum* be the interpreter's guiding star?[168]

(3) should the interpreting judge stick to the letter of the law or free himself from it, becoming a mature interpreter, or even be allowed to decide on the basis of equity *praeter* or *contra legem*?[169]

(4) should the International Court of Justice, in particular, operate on the basis of the United Nations' normative concept of law?[170]

(5) should all treaties be interpreted like private contracts?[171]

(6) should the text of a treaty be the only basis of interpretation, or should "extrinsic evidence" be admissible?[172]

(7) should party-intention be the interpreter's only object, or should "other factors" as well be taken into account?[173]

The answers to such general, as well as to the myriad case-bound, questions of interpretation which may crop up entirely depend on the interpreter's normative concept of law. At p. 18 *supra*, methods and rules were seen to rest in the normative concept, but options may also be open where no methods or rules exist, and the normative concept then, in a sort of "direct" manner, decides about the choice to be made. The positive answer to question (1) above given by the Permanent Court of International Justice in its judgment of 7 September 1927 (*The Case of the S.S. "Lotus"*)[174], for instance, most certainly was inspired by the Court's normative concept, or, in the words of Professor Bourquin, by "une certaine *conception* de l'ordre international, spécialement des rapports existant entre le droit des gens et la puissance étatique" [175], i.e., by one of the facets of the Court's normative concept.

The question now to be tackled is whether the eventual choice made by the interpreter may be called "political". Considering the role of the normative con-

---

167. See section 5.2.1 *infra*.

168. As advocated by Schwarzenberger, *International Law*, vol. I, 3rd Ed. (London 1957) p. 491; at p. 53, the author defines the "*ius aequum* rule" as "the exercise of judicially tempered discretion (. . . .) necessarily inspired by considerations of common sense, reasonableness and good faith or, in short equitable considerations".

169. The three classical types of the judicial officer: see Wiarda, *op.cit.*, p. 68; and comp. Tammelo, op.cit., pp. 53-54.

170. See p. 22 *supra*.

171. See p. 15 *supra* and section 5.3.2 *infra*.

172. See section 5.2.3 *infra*.

173. See section 5.2.3 *infra*.

174. Series A, no. 10.

175. Maurice Bourquin, "Règles générales du droit de la paix", Rec.A.D.I., 1931 — I p. 72 (author's emphasis).

cept in the process of interpretation, the question amounts to asking to what extent the normative concept itself may be termed "political". In order to answer that question, it should first be clear how the word "political" should be understood. It is meant, here, as the adverb to "policy" or "politics", and both of the latter expressions are supposed to connote an activity designed to organize human group life and to administer public affairs within a human group thus organized. There is no doubt that the "administration of justice" is part of the administration of public affairs, i.e., of affairs interesting the community as such, even in cases which themselves are of a private law character. The administration of justice, consequently, is a *political* activity, as is anything concomitant with it, such as, e.g., interpretation.

There are, however, *degrees* to which public affairs may be "political". In national communities, most political of all is the constitution. Constitutions, indeed, embody the most fundamental facets of the nation's normative concept of law. The remainder of national law does no more have to worry about them, takes them for granted, and to that extent is "de-politicized". But national law by no means loses its political content, for that matter, which, in varying degrees, is ever present, even in utterly technical branches of the law. In the national community, therefore, interpretation, too, is "political", though hardly noticeable anymore with regard to certain legal questions, for instance in the field of traffic law.

In the international community, things differ considerably owing to the fact that no international constitution exists. The fundamental options, there, are still open. As a result, they have to be made over and over again by anyone involved in the application of international law, the interpretation of which, therefore, must be far more "political " than the average interpretation of national law. The situation is not sensibly affected by the existence of the Charter of the United Nations. First of all, the Charter technically is in no way to general international law what a national constitution is to the rest of national law. Second, in its substantive (as distinguished from its formal) aspects the Charter is so full of contradictions and *lacunae* that it cannot possibly be deemed to contain the main lines upon which to build an international legal order in the way in which a national constitution provides a "legitimacy" within the confines of which national "legality" can take shape.[176]

But if interpretation in international law, as stated, is "far more" political than in the national legal order, can there be room for a *totally* political interpretation? If this were so, and if law thus could occasionally identify itself with pure politics, all difference in principle between law and pure politics would fall to the ground. All those, however, who believe in the general concept of law must deny the possibility of such identification and, therefore, of a purely political interpretation. Anyone purporting to "interpret", i.e., to exercise a *legal* activity, must be conscious of the fact that he never can be allowed to overstep the boundaries drawn by

---

176. Dutch readers may at this point be referred to the present writer's "Van Panhuys' 'Carnaval des Animaux'", *Nederlands Juristenblad,* 1975 pp. 1120-1123, where the same ideas are expressed in a slightly more detailed way.

the general concept of law. If in the international legal order interpretation may be *more* political than in national law, it cannot be *entirely* so. Even *legislation* has to respect the general concept of law, and realizing that interpretation as an activity is more restricted than legislation, one must agree that interpretation *a fortiori* may be expected to live up to its requirements. Two of these requirements, good faith and observance of the principles of rational organization, have already been quoted above. In addition, the methods and rules of interpretation may once more be referred to, here. At p. 22 *supra*, their character as "two-way tools" was set forth: not only are they aids for interpretation in the light of the normative concept, but they were also said to have an effect in the opposite direction, namely, in establishing the content of the normative concept itself. In the present context, the latter aspect of the methods and rules may be differently rendered as follows: they assist the interpreter in finding his own *juridicité*, as the French call it. And acting on the basis of that *juridicité*, the interpreter cannot but conclude that purely political interpretations are precluded. A purely political interpretation *is* no interpretation, but a political act, gratuitous if emanating from someone devoid of political power; in other conditions a possible instrument of usurpation of power as for instance the interpretation of the United Nations Charter in the Uniting for Peace Resolutions.[177]

The (limited) political character of interpretation is another argument in favour of this writer's opinion that the interpreter is free to choose the methods and rules best suited to realize the normative concept of law.[178] This is what Professor Verzijl must have had in mind when writing: "Every judge — this is never more clearly realized until oneself is confronted by difficult decisions — is already prejudiced before he draws up his sentence, in the sense that at that moment — led by an intuitive, uncontrollable and to himself probably obscure preference — he has already chosen the starting-point decisive to the judgment."[179] Judge Lauterpacht was on the same wavelength. "As a rule", he stated, "they [the rules of interpretation] are not the determining cause of judicial decision, but the form in which the judge cloaks a result arrived at by other means".[180] Within the limits of the interpreter's freedom, therefore, no objection can be made against comparing him to "a cunning marksman, who first shoots a bullet through the wall and subsequently draws the target around it"[181], provided aim was taken as directed by the normative concept. One of the foremost commentators on Dutch Supreme Court deci-

---

177. See p. 29 *supra*, and comp. Sur, op.cit., p. 145, calling the interpretation of 3 November 1950 "éminemment politique"; and see ibid., pp. 143-145, for further observations and references to doctrine.

178. See p. 22 *supra*.

179. J.H.W. Verzijl, "Vijftien jaren internationale rechtspraak" (Fifteen Years of International Case-Law), *Mededeelingen der Koninklijke Nederlandsche Akademie van Wetenschappen*, Afd. Letterkunde, Nieuwe Reeks, vol. I, no. 2 (Amsterdam 1938) p. 146, in the translation appearing in J.P. Fockema Andreae, *An Important Chapter from the History of Legal Interpretation* (Leyden 1948) pp. 75-76.

180. Sir Hersch Lauterpacht, "Restrictive Interpretation and the Principle of Effectiveness in the Interpretation of Treaties", BYIL 1949 p. 53.

181. J.P. Fockema Andreae, op.cit., p. 74.

sions, D.J. Veegens, once in a doctrinal note submitted that this Court's wealth of interpretative methods was now such that it enabled the Court to justify any decision it deemed desirable [182], but the fact, of course, does not entitle the *Hoge Raad* to *take* any decision it pleases! The essentially tributary character of methods and rules of interpretation made Professor Pitlo write: "It is not difficult to catch in the act of apparent contradiction someone frequently called to sit in judgment. Now the same interpreter is heard saying that this is but the outward appearance of the words, and that he cannot be expected to abide with them since they would lead to socially unacceptable results; now, emphatically upholding a text in defence of a finding, he argues that the words are unmistakably clear, and that he cannot evade them. It is for incompetents only to save the appearance of consistency."[183]

Finally, the present writer's limited conception of interpretation makes him unable to agree with Professor Sur's description of interpretation as a *concept charnière*, the "hinge" between politics and law [184], the *locus* where politics is "transformed" into law.[185] Interpretation is actually the continuation of a process — the "legal process" — started long before interpretation sets in. It is not the interpreter, but the law-giver who is first in that process to think "in the legal manner", as a lawyer, instead of politically, and in saying so it is fully realized that legal thinking inevitably has a political *element* in it. Sur's idea of interpretation obviously was born from his all-embracing definition of interpretation, including in that concept even the legislative activity. In light of this, he apparently intended to say that *the legal process* is the transition from (pure) politics to law. This, of course, is correct, but he more or less contradicts himself when stating that "law is the continuation of politics by other means".[186] For law is above all the continuation of politics by *more limited* means, viz., means limited by the general concept of law, and which will still further be limited in the event of an interpreter being subject himself to functional limitations, such as a judge.[187]

Above, politics was understood to be "an activity designed to organize human group life and to administer public affairs within a human group thus organized". Politics *strives after* power permitting the order characteristic of all organization. Law *acknowledges* power as a factual element in its proper texture, and, as an extension of politics, may at times endeavour to *promote* power as a factor of organizational cohesion or strength, but its calling essentially is not in the promotion

182. Doctrinal note appended to the *Hoge Raad*'s decision of 24 February 1950, *Nederlandse Jurisprudentie* 1950, no. 742.

183. A. Pitlo, *Evolutie in het privaatrecht* (Evolution in Private Law) (Haarlem 1969) p. 129 (this writer's translation).

184. Sur, op.cit., pp. 18, 83-84, and 313.

185. Ibid., p. 85.

186. Ibid., p. 51: "le droit est la continuation de la politique par d'autres moyens".

187. It is with these observations in mind that one has to read the present writer's contribution to the *Festschrift* for L.J. Hijmans van den Bergh, *Met eerbiedigende werking* (Deventer 1971), under the title "Het politiek karakter van het zogenaamd intertemporaal volkenrecht" (The Political Character of so-called Intertemporal International Law) pp. 53-66, especially p. 63.

of power: it is in the pursuit of truth in the sense of a legal order which by the participants in that order for a longer or shorter period of time will be recognized as the "true" one.[188] In this perspective, the eventual choice made by the interpreter, less than with politics, has to do with the higher ideal of a lasting form of collective satisfaction: the feeling to be in tune with historical developments, or better still, with the stage of development of human intelligence.

4.4   The use of codification in matters of interpretation

The observations made under the three preceding headings naturally lead to the last question posed, namely, that of the use of codification in matters of interpretation. For, indeed, if the identity of the law-applying agent is an element in interpretation, if there is his freedom when interpreting, and if the eventual choice made by him in the process of interpretation in part is a political one, one easily comes to wonder to what advantage methods and rules of interpretation may be codified. The question is the more pressing since the Vienna Convention on the Law of Treaties, including its Articles 31-33, was adopted, although it has not entered into force, so far. At p. 21 *supra*, it was intimated that codifying methods and rules of interpretation means making *rules of law* out of former guides, and at p. 22 *supra*, it was submitted that non-codified guides belong to legal method and, consequently, are *not law*. The present question, therefore, boils down to this one: is there any sense in making law out of method, in letting method crystallize into law? The question may also be placed in a wider context: does not the codification of methods and rules of interpretation bear witness to a certain amount of overestimation of the idea of codification?[189] Not only for reasons of subject-matter, however, but also for reasons of logic one may feel puzzled, here. Codified methods and rules of interpretation, indeed, in time will have themselves to be interpreted [190] — and anyone doing so *on the basis of those very rules* risks meeting the same incredulity as provoked by the famous Baron von Münchhausen when boasting that he lifted both himself and his horse from a swamp by the tail of his wig.

As to the suitability or unsuitability of methods and rules of interpretation for purposes of codification, it may be recalled that Sir Humphrey Waldock himself

---

188. Comp. this writer's "De betekenis van het rechterlijk proces voor de rechtsvorming" (The Significance of Judicial Proceedings in the Process of Law), in *Quid Iuris* (Deventer 1977) p. 33.

189. The International Law Commission in codifying "secondary" rules only on State responsibility, and no "primary" rules, showed some restraint in this matter, at least. "Secondary" rules are those regarding imputability, the consequences of imputation, and the implementation of responsibility. "Primary" rules are rules holding the basic obligations the violation of which gives rise to the questions answered in the "secondary" ones. See *Yearbook of the International Law Commission*, 1969, vol. II p. 233 (paras. 80-82), and 1978, vol. II, Part Two pp. 75-76 (paras. 82-84). On the problem of codification generally, see this writer's *Rondom de codificatie van het volkenrecht* (Around the Codification of International Law) (Leyden 1959).

190. Tammelo, op.cit., p. 34, and Lachs, "The Law of Treaties (Some General Reflections on the Report of the International Law Commission)" in *Recueil d'études de droit international en hommage à Paul Guggenheim* (Geneva 1968) p. 401.

in his capacity as a Special Rapporteur of the International Law Commission on the Law of Treaties gave considerable attention to the subject. Paragraphs 1-8 of his Commentary to Articles 70-73 as proposed in his 1964 Draft were entirely devoted to it.[191] Distinguishing "principles and maxims" on the one hand, "methods" on the other, he included in the former category a number of Latin precepts such as *ut res magis valeat quam pereat*, in the latter "all the different approaches to interpretation — textual, subjective and teleological". Principles and maxims, Sir Humphrey wrote, "are, for the most part, principles of logic and good sense valuable only as guides to assist in appreciating the meaning which the parties may have intended to attach to the expressions which they employed in a document. Their (. . . . .) application is not automatic but depends on the conviction of the interpreter that it is appropriate in the particular circumstances of the case. In other words, recourse to many of these principles is *discretionary rather than obligatory*, and the interpretation of documents is to some extent an art, not an exact science". A clearly different view he had of methods. As he put it, "the jurisprudence of international tribunals (. . . . . .) shows that, if the textual method of interpretation predominates, none of these approaches is exclusively the correct one, and that their use in any particular case is to some extent a matter of choice and appreciation. This does not necessarily mean that there is no obligatory rule in regard to methods of interpretation; but it does mean that there is *a certain discretionary element* also on this point".[192] The contrast seen, here, is one between "predominantly discretionary" and "predominantly obligatory", as it seems. The conclusion drawn from it by the Special Rapporteur was that principles and maxims are not codifiable, whereas an attempt *may* be made at the codification of methods or, as he had it, of "the comparatively few rules which appear to constitute the strictly legal basis of the interpretation of treaties". The reasons why such an attempt also *should* be made are threefold, in his mind, the principal one of which appears to be "that the interpretation of treaties without arbitrariness and according to law is a necessary linch-pin of the *pacta sunt servanda* rule".

There certainly is great merit in Sir Humphrey's observations. Insight and modesty vie with a constructive desire to bring some order, at least, in one of the most delicate subjects of international law. In particular, he proves to have an eye for the interpreter's indispensable discretion. One may, yet, wonder whether he did not underestimate this and other factors of the same order and, as a result, did not overrate the "legal" element in interpretation, i.e., did not see more "law" than there actually is. For apart from the interpreter's inherent discretion, one may point at the following aspects of Articles 31-33 of the Vienna Convention, being the final outcome of Sir Humphrey's epoch-making endeavour:

(1) The Articles themselves leave the interpreter considerable freedom. Below, a short commentary on them is to be inserted, and it will be seen that, while

191. See *Yearbook of the International Law Commission,* 1964, vol. II pp. 53-55.
192. Italics in these quotations are the present writer's.

starting with the text of a treaty, the interpreter may branch off in different directions without violating their terms or their spirit.[193]

(2) The Articles, though not codifying "principles and maxims" of interpretation as understood by the Special Rapporteur, also refrain from prohibiting their use. It is submitted that they may have a far from negligible influence.

(3) Neither do Articles 31-33 contain any indication on how to ascertain the meaning of custom. Being equivalent to treaty [194], custom has an undeniable bearing on the content of treaties. Professor Sur goes as far as saying that in the absence of rules providing for the "interpretation" of custom and "circumstances" any codification of rules on treaty interpretation is of only marginal interest, or even has no sense at all.[195]

Considering, in addition, the three items studied in paragraphs 4.1-4.3 *supra*, one may rightfully question the use of codifying methods and rules of interpretation. Putting aside his own hesitations and scepticism, the present writer, however, in the end wants to take a positive stand in this matter. There are two important reasons to do so. First, reference is made to the character of methods and rules of interpretation as "two-way tools" of the normative concept of law. If methods and rules, as set forth above [196], are not only steering aids for the normative concept, but are also instrumental in making the interpreter conscious of his own normative concept, there is reason enough, already, to put them into writing. But secondly, putting them into writing one renders a considerable service to treaty as a separate manifestation of international law, a service going well beyond safeguarding the *pacta sunt servanda* rule (see Waldock as quoted *supra*). Codified methods and rules of interpretation, indeed, above all *confirm the proper nature of treaty* as against custom. Recognized manifestations of international law, as the present writer stated, all are recognized on their own and inalienable merits.[197] It is part and parcel of the very concept of treaty that there be methods and rules for its interpretation, provided they are not too permissive. Articles 31-33 satisfy the condition: though allowing the interpreter the discretion as defined above — i.e., of branching off in different directions — they appear to have enough backbone to prevent the arbitrary, — which, of course, is not to say that custom would necessarily lead thereto. And this, it is thought, is a powerful reason, overriding any argument to the contrary, to salute their presence precisely in a codification of the law of treaties.

POSTSCRIPT

On 28 December 1979, the thirty-fifth instrument of ratification of, or accession to, the Vienna Convention on the Law of Treaties was deposited with the Secre-

---

193. See section 5.2.2 *infra*.
194. See "The Hierarchy" p. 337.
195. Sur, op.cit., pp. 245 and 285.
196. See p. 22 *supra*.
197. See "The Recognized Manifestations" p. 73.

tary-General of the United Nations. Under Article 84, paragraph 1, the Convention was to enter into force on the thirtieth day following the date of deposit of the thirty-fifth instrument. On 27 January 1980, the Convention may, therefore, be deemed to have become treaty-law between the ratifying or acceding Parties. However, some reservations made at the moment of ratification or accession or afterwards (see *Multilateral Treaties in Respect of Which the Secretary-General Performs Depositary Functions*, List of Signatures, Ratifications, Accessions, etc. as at 31 December 1978, ST/LEG/SER.D/12, pp. 581-586) do not make it easy to establish which provisions should be considered as not binding between certain Parties. The Articles 31-33 appear not to have been objected to by any Party.

THEORY AND PRACTICE OF TREATY INTERPRETATION

by Maarten Bos*

5. THE INTERPRETATION OF TREATIES

5.1 Introduction

At p. 10 *supra*, it was proposed to limit the use of the term "interpretation" to the *written* manifestations of law, i.e., to treaty (as defined in Article 2, paragraph 1(a), of the Vienna Convention on the Law of Treaties), certain decisions of international organizations, and certain judicial decisions. The present study is concerned with the interpretation of treaties only. With regard to *unwritten* agreements (not coming under the said definition of treaty), it remains to be seen whether the methods and rules of interpretation also apply to them.[198]

5.2 Methods and rules of treaty interpretation

What means are to be used to reach the objectives of treaty interpretation as defined in para. 2.3 *supra*? Judge Waldock, when still a member of the International Law Commission and its *Rapporteur* on the Law of Treaties, wrote as follows in his Third Report: "Writers (. . .) differ to some extent in their basic approach to the interpretation of treaties according to the relative weight which they give to —

(a) the text of the treaty as the authentic expression of the intentions of the parties;

(b) the intentions of the parties as a subjective element distinct from the text; and

(c) the declared or apparent objects and purposes of the treaty".[199]

---

*Concluding part (first part in NILR (1980) pp. 3-38). In the first part, the following printer's errors are to be corrected: p. 9, line 4 from the bottom of the text, ˙'factual" instead of "factual"; p. 25, n. 124: insert "judge" at the end of the first line; p. 26, n. 134: "supported" on the last line should read "supposed".

198. In so far as unilateral declarations should be deemed to produce unwritten agreements, the following *dictum* of the International Court of Justice may be quoted in passing: "When states make statements by which their freedom of action is to be limited, a restrictive interpretation is called for" (judgment of 20 December 1974 in the *Nuclear Tests Case*, ICJ Reports, 1974 p. 267, para. 44). Cf. pp. 166-167 *infra*.

199. *Yearbook of the International Law Commission*, 1964, Vol. II (New York 1965), p. 53.

As examples of each of these three schools of thought he quoted Sir Hersch Lauterpacht, who emphasized (b) and, therefore, was in favour of using all forms of evidence, including *travaux préparatoires*, of the intentions of the parties [200]; Cavaré and Alvarez laying stress on (c) and, for that reason, inclined sooner than others to admit teleological interpretation, especially of multilateral treaties; and the majority of modern authors preferring (a), but prepared to accept corrections of, and to a limited extent amendments to, the text through "extrinsic evidence of the intentions of the parties" or on account of "the objects and purposes of the treaty". The same tendencies were found by Judge Waldock in international judicial decisions: "The jurisprudence of international tribunals furnishes examples of all the different approaches to interpretation — textual, subjective and teleological. But it also shows that, if the textual method of interpretation predominates, none of these approaches is exclusively the correct one, and that their use in any particular case is to some extent a matter of choice and appreciation".[201]

In the present writer's opinion, it should be possible for doctrinal purposes to push the theory of interpretation somewhat further than the learned *Rapporteur* was able to do. First of all, a distinction between "methods" and "rules" of interpretation may be in place.

5.2.1 Methods

The methods of interpretation are the same for national and international law and may be classified under three headings each of which represents a criterion of its own:

(1) methods of interpretation according to the approach taken:
  (a) grammatical (textual, literal),
  (b) historical (subjective),
  (c) systematic,
  (d) teleological,
  (e) sociological;

(2) methods of interpretation according to the intellectual instrument used:
  (a) logical,
  (b) comparative;

(3) methods of interpretation according to their effect:
  (a) restrictive,
  (b) extensive.

It is impossible, of course, to go into the details of each of these methods, and a short comment should, therefore, suffice.

---

200. Note here the influence on the extent of proof to be given. According to Professor Charles Cheney Hyde, "The Interpretation of Treaties by the Permanent Court of International Justice", AJIL (1930) p. 19, interpretation, indeed, merges with the handling of evidence of the intentions of the parties. With Professor Sur, one sees the opposite happening: evidence becoming interpretation (see p. 7 *supra*).

201. Op.cit., p. 54.

As to the five methods of interpretation under the first heading, they are very much a part of continental European legal history, bound up as they are with the development of legal method in the codification countries. Their importance nevertheless extends beyond the boundaries of continental Europe because of their general methodological potential. Professor Pitlo's thumbnail sketches of them, written in his own very pungent manner, may, therefore, also be of interest to the international lawyer, in spite of their being inspired in the first place by continental legal orders. With regard to the *grammatical* method, Professor Pitlo observes that in the first decades after the introduction of the great codifications "legism" reigned supreme, i.e., total subservience to the letter of the law: one lived in "the pseudo-certainty of the written word which, in actual fact, only carries insecurity (. . .). A fortuitous text, before its intelligent construction and insertion into a larger context, decides in a concrete situation, and the result can but be arbitrary".[202] On the *historical* method, he has this to say: "There always were jurists who dug their way into the past in order to learn whether the drafting process of a text, or the history of the relevant legal institution, possibly holds the solution for a text the obscurity of which no merely grammatical interpretation can dispel".[203] The *systematic* method Professor Pitlo puts in the following perspective: referring to the arbitrariness resulting from the grammatical method (see *supra*), he sets forth that "arbitrariness can only come to an end — and certainty be substituted for insecurity — once the all-embracing context has been perceived, the cohesion between the many written rules *inter se*, and between the latter and what remained unwritten"[204]; "there is no gainsaying that systematic interpretation to a certain extent presupposes an overall view of the law: for this method has for its basis the combination, the interconnecting, of texts which topographically speaking may be far apart"[205]; "orderly minds feel attracted to this method".[206] The *teleological* method "aims at the intellectual penetration of the purpose which the law-giver had in mind when making a rule".[207] Finally, Professor Pitlo offers a number of remarks to illustrate the concept of *sociological* interpretation: "To the extent that the written rule becomes obsolete and the letter of it ceases to correspond with the needs of society, the emphasis [in interpretation] will shift

202. A. Pitlo, op.cit., pp. 123-124 (this writer's translation; the other quotations from Pitlo to follow were likewise translated by him).

203. Ibid., pp. 124-125; Dutch readers may be reminded, here, of Professor Scholten's incisive observations on historical interpretation under the title "Eggens' Bewijsrecht" (Eggens on Evidence), *Weekblad voor Privaatrecht, Notarisambt en Registratie* (16-23 February 1935) Nos. 3399-3400.

204. Ibid., p. 124.

205. Ibid., p. 125.

206. Ibid., p. 158.

207. Ibid., p. 125. On teleological interpretation in international law, see Sur, op.cit., pp. 228-231. According to the author, p. 229, interpretation is teleological whenever the interpreter himself rationally constructs the purpose of the treaty and, in interpreting its text, derives conclusions from it. To the interpreter, the purpose of a treaty almost constitutes a pretext for developing the law and opposing himself to the sovereignty of States. "Objectivist" authors, therefore, mostly favour the teleological method, whereas "voluntarists" seek to limit recourse to it.

towards the need for a socially acceptable result (. . .). Then, the doctrine of judicial freedom arises, the doctrine that the judge is not a mere mouth-piece of the legislator, but autonomously, creatively, intervenes in the social process. Thus, a barrier is broken through, and one, indeed, recognizes the feasibility of making law contrary to the letter or the spirit of the written rule".[208] But the author hastens to add that "the number of cases in which the law is applied *contra legem* is extremely low − and should remain so".[209] It may be noted in passing that the unfamiliar expression "sociological interpretation" is not one invented by himself, but had previously been coined by Paul Scholten.[210]

Coming now to the methods of interpretation according to the intellectual instrument used, one meets with two subjects belonging to the most intriguing ones in the theory of law, logic and analogy. They have been discussed in legal literature on a correspondingly large scale, but the present writer cannot pretend even to start a critical analysis of them in the limited context of this study. Especially with regard to *logic* and its *rôle* in interpretation, he proposes to include in the concept anything coming under the term in what might be called common legal parlance [211] and having the colouring of a process of thought characterized by automatism. In this sense, one may think of the *a contrario* reasoning, as well as of the more or less related slogan *expressio unius est exclusio alterius* which Lord Asquith of Bishopstone held to be "mere common sense" in his arbitral award of 1951 in *Petroleum Development (Trucial Coast) Ltd. and the Sheikh of Abu Dabi.*[212] Furthermore, the arguments *a fortiori, a minori,* and *ad majus* may be mentioned [213], together with a number of *argumenta* in the same bracket which, like the others, are already to be found in the writings of ancient authors who faced identical problems, problems which apparently are of all ages.[214] An interesting question, here, is whether the argument that "all is permissible unless prohibited" does equally belong to the sphere of logic. One will remember that in its judgment of 7 September 1927 (*The Case of the S.S. "Lotus"*) the Permanent Court of International Justice found in favour of the Turkish view " that Article 15 [of the Convention of Lausanne of 24 July 1923 respecting conditions of

---

208. Ibid., p. 126.
209. Ibid., p. 127.
210. See Wiarda, op.cit., p. 25. A proponent of sociological interpretation as a regular feature of judicial practice is Professor H.C.F. Schoordijk, *Oordelen en vooroordelen* (Judgment and Prejudice) (Deventer 1972) p. 13, n. 3.
211. Tammelo, op.cit., p. 39: philosophically speaking, the arguments *a simili, a fortiori,* and *a contrario* are "formally invalid" (and see p. 43: "quasi-logical arguments") "but nevertheless have obtained through intelligent use by reputable men in appropriate contexts a [certain?] cogency and dignity".
212. ICLQ, 1952 p. 251.
213. On these arguments, see, e.g., Marcelle Jokl, *De l'interprétation des traités normatifs d'après la doctrine et la jurisprudence internationales* (Paris 1935) pp. 109 et seq.
214. See, e.g, the *argumentum ab absurdo* developed by the famous Dutch jurist Everaerts (1462-1532), as quoted by Professor J.P.A. Coopmans, "Vrijheid en gebondenheid van de rechter vóór de codificatie" (Freedom and Limitations of the Judiciary before the Codification), in the volume *Rechtsvinding* (Deventer 1970) pp. 90-91.

residence and business and jurisdiction] allows Turkey jurisdiction whenever such jurisdiction *does not come into conflict with* a principle of international law".[215] The Court, indeed, saw no "principle of international law *precluding Turkey from* instituting the prosecution which was in fact brought against Lieutenant Demons".[216] In so doing, the Court adhered to the thesis of all being permissible unless prohibited. But did the Court's position, and its ensuing interpretation of Article 15 of the Lausanne Convention, have anything to do with logic? A similar question may be asked regarding a passage in the International Court's advisory opinion of 28 May 1951 (*Reservations to the Convention on the Prevention and Punishment of the Crime of Genocide*), worded as follows: "In this state of international practice, it could certainly not be inferred from the *absence* of an article providing for reservations in a multilateral convention that the contracting States are *prohibited* from making certain reservations".[217] To answer this question, it may be of interest to have a look at the International Court's advisory opinion of 13 July 1954 (*Effect of Awards of Compensation Made by the United Nations Administrative Tribunal*) dealing with the alleged right for the United Nations General Assembly "to refuse to give effect to awards of compensation made by the Administrative Tribunal".[218] The Court held that, "in order that the judgments pronounced by such a tribunal could be subjected to review by anybody other than the tribunal itself, it would be necessary, in the opinion of the Court, that the statute of that tribunal or some other legal instrument governing it *should contain an express provision to that effect* (. . .). But as no such provisions are inserted in the present Statute, there is no legal ground upon which the General Assembly could proceed to review judgments already pronounced by that Tribunal".[219] It is clear that the Court in the latter pronouncement said exactly the reverse of what the 1927 and 1951 decisions proclaimed, namely, that *no* express provision was required for the exercise of a competence under international law. Can it be argued, therefore, that the 1954 opinion was wrong — and possibly that it violated the logical precept that all is permissible unless prohibited? The answer is no. In this writer's opinion, there is no such "logical" precept, and whether one adopts the 1927-1951 thesis or the 1954 formula depends not on logic, but on an utterly fundamental choice one has to make as to the basic assumption underlying the legal order.[220] Is the legal order to be a liberal one in which freedom is the paramount value, or a strait jacket from which no escape is allowed outside the case of an express authorization to that effect? Here lies an option which is very real, even if, at times, it may lose some of its drama and be reduced to the antithesis of two types of legal order each as respectable as the other. In the three cases referred to above, two types of legal order are, indeed, evoked, viz., the unorganized legal

---

215. *Publications of the Permanent Court of International Justice. Collection of Judgments,* Series A, No. 10 p. 18 (italics supplied).
216. Ibid., p. 31 (italics supplied).
217. ICJ Reports 1951 p. 22 (italics supplied).
218. ICJ Reports 1954 p. 55.
219. Ibid., p. 56 (italics supplied).
220. Comp. Bourquin as quoted at p. 31 *supra.*

system of sovereign States as against (what the International Court in 1954 called) "the organized legal system of the United Nations".[221] The idea which the Court in 1954 wished to convey is that in the latter system because of its being "organized" the methods of the former do not always prevail. The Court's 1954 decision was a very wise one, and it had everything to do with the basic features of the United Nations as an organization, but nothing at all to do with logic. The Permanent Court's decision in the *Lotus* case was considerably less commendable as future developments proved [222], and from the start was subjected to severe criticism, but if there was one point at which no criticism was justified it is precisely the Court's basic tenet that in the unorganized society of States to which it directed its attention everything is permissible unless prohibited.[223] The Court went astray only when it placed a very positivist construction on the word "prohibited".[224] Until present times, differing so radically from the *interbellum*, this "spirit of the *Lotus*" lives on, as is evidenced by the individual opinions appended by Judges Gros and Petrén to the International Court's judgment of 20 December 1974 (*Nuclear Tests Case*).[225] In that same case, a really modern approach was shown by Judges Oneyama, Dillard, Jiménez de Aréchaga, and Waldock in their joint dissenting opinion.[226]

The second intellectual instrument in interpretation is *comparison*. The comparative method may involve a comparison either of factual situations (analogy), or of treaties.

In the first hypothesis, a factual situation not, or not clearly, covered by a treaty is compared with situations clearly coming under its terms. The object and purposes of the comparison is to examine whether the former situation is analogous enough to the latter to warrant the extension of the treaty to it.[227] In the second hypothesis, a treaty is interpreted with an eye to (past interpretations of) other treaties of a comparable character.[228]

---

221. ICJ Reports, 1954 p. 56.

222. See Art. 1 and 3 of the Brussels International Convention for the Unification of Certain Rules Relating to Penal Jurisdiction in Matters of Collision and Other Incidents of Navigation of 10 May 1952, and Art. 11, para. 1, of the Geneva Convention on the High Seas of 29 April 1958. On the Brussels Convention, comp. Professor François' Fifth Report to the International Law Commission, *Yearbook of the International Law Commission* (1953), Vol. II pp. 51-53.

223. For such unwarranted criticism, see, e.g., Judge Loder's dissenting opinion in the *Lotus* case, Series A, No. 10 pp. 34-35, and Louis Delbez, *Les principes généraux du droit international public*, 3rd ed. (Paris 1964) p. 172: "La Cour se décida en faveur de la thèse turque, en partant du principe — très discutable — que tout ce qui n'est pas défendu est permis".

224. See on the Permanent Court's positivism Sir John Fischer Williams, "L'affaire du 'Lotus'", *Revue générale de droit international public* (1928) pp. 361-376, as well as Louis Cavaré, "L'arrêt du "Lotus" et le positivisme juridique", in *Travaux juridiques et économiques de l'Université de Rennes*, Tome X (1930) pp. 144-194.

225. ICJ Reports, 1974 pp. 286 and 306, respectively.

226. Ibid., pp. 365-366 (para. 109).

227. It comes very close to the *technique* of comparing situations in the light of a rule of law of an outspokenly general nature, as, e.g., a rule on tort. On the comparative method then used, and on the result of a *ius in causa positum*, see Wiarda, op.cit., pp. 62-63 and 65-67.

228. In its advisory opinion of 13 July 1954 (*Effect of Awards of Compensation Made by the United Nations Administrative Tribunal*), ICJ Reports, 1954 p. 62, the International

The use of the term "analogy" in the present context gives rise to the following observation. In the text above, it was limited to the first hypothesis. In so doing, the writer followed in the footsteps of Judge De Visscher who thus defined the concept of analogy: "L'analogie est un procédé de raisonnement qui permet à l'interprète d'étendre une norme qui régit certains rapports à des rapports nouveaux juridiquement semblables à ceux que visait son contenu originaire."[229]

Others are less reticent in using the term. Degan, for instance, speaks of analogy in the second sense reported above, and his problem appears to be whether only treaties concluded between the same parties may be compared with each other or also treaties between partly or wholly different parties. He himself opts for the latter, most liberal, course.[230] Since there is no use applying the same term of art to two so divergent operations as comparing factual situations and comparing treaties, it is proposed to restrict the application of the term "analogy" to operations in the former sense, on the understanding, however, that the term may also apply outside the interpretation of treaties, e.g., to the application (not: interpretation) of precedents, as indicated by Black, quoting Francis Wharton: "Where there is no precedent in point, in cases on the same subject, lawyers have recourse to cases on a different subject-matter, but governed by the same general principle. This is reasoning by analogy."[231]

Basically, applying analogy in treaty interpretation means applying the principle behind the rule and extending the words of the latter to a case not expressly covered by them.[232] There is no reason, however, to identify the principle behind the rule as a general principle of law, either in the sense of Article 38, paragraph 1(c), of the International Court's Statute, or in the connotation of a principle belonging to the general concept of law [233]: for such principles, indeed, one may always apply, and analogy is not the device needed to bring them into operation.[234]

In the opinion of some writers, analogy serves to fill *lacunae* in the law.[235] This raises the question of the definition of a *lacuna*. President Wiarda has one for

---

Court, invited to interpret (not a treaty, but) the Statute of the United Nations Administrative Tribunal, refused to do so in the light of an alleged precedent under the League of Nations.

229. De Visscher, op.cit., p. 38. Comp. *Dictionnaire de la terminologie du droit international* (Paris 1960) p. 44, *sub voce* Analogie: "Procédé d'interprétation consistant à pourvoir à une lacune ou à l'obscurité d'une règle de droit en se référant à ce qui est admis dans une situation ressemblant à celle qui est considérée."

230. Degan, op.cit., p. 100. See also Sergio Neri, op.cit., p. 230.

231. Black, *Law Dictionary*, 4th ed. (St. Paul, Minn. 1951) p. 110. Wharton's version of analogy differs from Wiarda's *technique* (see p. 140, n. 227 *supra*) in that instead of statute law it concerns judge-made law.

232. Michael Akehurst, "The Hierarchy of the Sources of International Law", BYIL, 1974-1975 p. 279, n.1.

233. Comp. "The Recognized Manifestations" p. 38.

234. But see De Visscher, op.cit., p. 39: the International Court does not distinguish between analogy and the general principles of law.

235. See, e.g., Lammasch, *Die Lehre von der Schiedsgerichtsbarkeit in ihrem ganzen Umfange*, in *Handbuch des Völkerrechts*, Vol. III-3 pp. 180-181. Professor Verzijl, *International Law in Historical Perspective*, Vol. I (Leyden 1968) pp. 50-51, subscribes to the view, as does

national law to the effect that a *lacuna* exists when written law offers no point of contact (D. *aanknopingspunt*, Fr. *point de rattachement*).[236] In other words, no *lacuna* exists where analogy still is available. Owing to the central *rôle* of the normative concept of law and to all it entails [237] , the present writer, on his part, would like to propose a definition in the same spirit, namely, that there is a *lacuna* when within a certain normative concept of law no rule exists applicable to a certain factual situation. In his opinion, the event materializes when analogy is no longer reasonably possible. The implication is that analogy cannot serve to fill *lacunae*.

Finally, on analogy, it should be clear that by the use of it a result may be obtained which is the obverse of the outcome of logical interpretation, especially of the *argumentum a contrario*.[238] Herein, analogy as a separate *technique* finds its own *raison d'être*.

The two methods indicative of the effect of interpretation, either restrictive or extensive, are at all events leading to opposite results.

The concept of restrictive interpretation includes what Paul Scholten called the "refining" of the law, i.e., the fact of finding new exceptions to existing rules drafted in a broad and comprehensive style.[239]

Extensive interpretation, also called "liberal construction", is often motivated by a desire for efficiency, being the second principle of rational organization.[240] Writers usually refer to "the rule of effectiveness", not of "efficiency", but although effectiveness and efficiency are not identical concepts since it may be utterly inefficient to give effect to a freakish treaty, they may generally be supposed to have efficiency in mind when using the term "rule of effectiveness".

The International Law Commission in its commentary to Articles 27-28 of its Draft Articles on the Law of Treaties was rather explicit about the rule of effectiveness, often expressed in the words *ut res magis valeat quam pereat*. It worked the principle into its Draft Article 27, paragraph 1 (now Article 31, paragraph 1, of the Vienna Convention), "which requires that a treaty shall be interpreted *in good faith* in accordance with the ordinary meaning to be given to its terms in the context of the treaty *and in the light of its object and purpose*".[241]

Siorat, *Le problème des lacunes en droit international* (Paris 1958) p. 148. And comp. p. 141, n. 229, *supra*.

236. Wiarda, op.cit., p. 13.

237. See pp. 18-20 *supra*.

238. See the judgment handed down by the Permanent Court of International Justice on 17 August 1923 (*The S.S. "Wimbledon"*), Series A, No. 1 p. 24; and comp. J.P. Fockema Andreae, op.cit., pp. 64 and 134.

239. Scholten, op.cit., p. 6.

240. See p. 19 *supra*.

241. *Yearbook of the International Law Commission*, 1966, Vol. II p. 219 (para. 6). Comp. Sur, op.cit., p. 203: extensive interpretation, instead of denying it, only waters down the principle that interpretation should abstain from *modifying* a treaty (quoting Professor Monaco); and see ibid., pp. 203-206, 269, and 276, on extensive interpretation (*effet utile*). Tammelo, op.cit., p. 13, sees the principle embodied in what now is Article 32(b).

5.2.2   Rules

As to the "rules" of the interpretation of treaties which were distinguished from its "methods" [242], they stand for something more definite than the mere possibilities offered by the latter.[243] The overall theme here is the question whether a treaty should be interpreted only with a view to the discovery of the intention of the parties, or whether other factors as well should be taken into account. Those in favour either of the first or of the second *modus operandi* will speak of a "rule", not of a "method". Other, more technical, rules proposed in this sense are that treaties should be interpreted *ex tunc,* not *ex nunc* [244]; that treaty interpretation should not become a revision of the treaty concerned [245]; that, "if the wording of a treaty provision is not clear, in choosing between several admissible interpretations, the one which involves the minimum of obligations for the Parties should be adopted" [246]; and that an obscure provision should be interpreted *contra proferentem,* that is, against the party invoking it.[247]

It is submitted that Judge Waldock when proposing for codification "the comparatively few rules which appear to constitute the strictly legal basis of the interpretation of treaties" [248] above all had in mind one rule, namely, that the interpreter should seek to ascertain the intention of the parties, a rule of which the *ex tunc* rule and the rule that no treaty revision is allowed may possibly be considered to be but implications. Waldock's texts eventually led to the Articles 31-32 of the Vienna Convention. Article 33 embodies Waldock's second and third rule relating to the interpretation of treaties authenticated in two or more languages. But it should also be clear that a choice of a rule of interpretation often includes a choice of one or more methods, as will be shown hereafter, particularly when considering the Articles 31-33 of the Vienna Convention.

The ILC Draft articles on interpretation of 1966 as amended by the 1969 Vienna Conference on the Law of Treaties ultimately came to be worded as follows:

242. See p. 136 *supra.*
243. For all practical purposes, attention is drawn to the fact that the present distinction of "methods" and "rules" bears no relation to Professor Sur's as reported at p. 8 *supra.*
244. Permanent Court of International Justice, advisory opinion of 15 May 1931 (*Access to German Minority Schools in Upper Silesia*), Series A/B No. 40 p. 19.
245. International Court of Justice, advisory opinion of 18 July 1950 (*Interpretation of Peace Treaties with Bulgaria, Hungary, and Romania*), ICJ Reports, 1950 p. 229; judgment of 27 August 1952 (*Case Concerning Rights of Nationals of the United States of America in Morocco*), ICJ Reports, 1952 p. 196; and judgment of 18 July 1966 (*South West Africa Cases* – Second Phase), ICJ Reports, 1966 p. 48.
246. Permanent Court of International Justice, advisory opinion of 21 November 1925 (*Article 3, Paragraph 2, of the Treaty of Lausanne*). Series B, No. 12 p. 25.
247. See Lord Asquith's award as quoted at p. 138 *supra.*
248. See p. 21 *supra.* Endeavours preceding those made by Waldock and the International Law Commission were those of the Harvard Law School, op.cit., pp. 937-977, of the *Institut de Droit International, Annuaire,* 1956 p. 359, of the American Law Institute, *Second Restatement of the Law: Foreign Relations Law of the United States* (St. Paul Minn. 1965) pp. 449-456, and of Sir Gerald Fitzmaurice, BYIL, 1957 pp. 210-212. Comp. Tammelo, op.cit., pp. 18-25, on the *Institut* Draft.

Article 31
General rule of interpretation

1. A treaty shall be interpreted in good faith in accordance with the ordinary meaning to be given to the terms of the treaty in their context and in the light of its object and purpose.
2. The context for the purpose of the interpretation of a treaty shall comprise, in addition to the text, including its preamble and annexes:
    (a)   any agreement relating to the treaty which was made between all the parties in connexion with the conclusion of the treaty;
    (b)   any instrument which was made by one or more parties in connexion with the conclusion of the treaty and accepted by the other parties as an instrument related to the treaty.
3. There shall be taken into account, together with the context:
    (a)   any subsequent agreement between the parties regarding the interpretation of the treaty or the application of its provisions.
    (b)   any subsequent practice in the application of the treaty which establishes the agreement of the parties regarding its interpretation;
    (c)   any relevant rules of international law applicable in the relations between the parties.
4. A special meaning shall be given to a term if it is established that the parties so intended.

Article 32
Supplementary means of interpretation

Recourse may be had to supplementary means of interpretation, including the preparatory work of the treaty and the circumstances of its conclusion, in order to confirm the meaning resulting from the application of article 31, or to determine the meaning when the interpretation according to article 31:
    (a)   leaves the meaning ambiguous or obscure; or
    (b)   leads to a result which is manifestly absurd or unreasonable.

Article 33
Interpretation of treaties authenticated in two or more languages

1. When a treaty has been authenticated in two or more languages, the text is equally authoritative in each language, unless the treaty provides or the parties agree that, in case of divergence, a particular text shall prevail.
2. A version of the treaty in a language other than one of those in which the text was authenticated shall be considered an authentic text only if the treaty so provides or the parties so agree.
3. The terms of the treaty are presumed to have the same meaning in each authentic text.
4. Except where a particular text prevails in accordance with paragraph 1, when a comparison of the authentic texts discloses a difference of meaning which the application of articles 31 and 32 does not remove, the meaning which best reconciles the texts, having regard to the object and purpose of the treaty, shall be adopted.

Article 31, paragraph 1, proclaims the rule of the intention of the parties as the central object of all treaty interpretation: it is the interpreter's duty first and foremost to determine this intention. In order to enable the interpreter to attain the goal thus set, Article 31 then refers him to the *concurrent* use of no less than three methods, viz., the grammatical ("the ordinary meaning to be given to the terms of the treaty"), the systematic ("in their context"), and the teleological method ("in the light of its object and purpose"). One may wonder at once whether these methods, virtually so different in outcome [249], were rightly combined, and whether the suggestion that their amalgamation is the best possible guarantee of an acceptable interpretation is entirely warranted. But the general principle of application, good faith [250], also set forth in Article 31, paragraph 1, and which was even given pride of place, may possibly hold the key to a solution.

Paragraph 2 of the same article subsequently clarifies the concept of "context", and in so doing underlines the importance of the systematic method. This method once more is emphasized in paragraph 3 (c), a provision which as originally drafted had in view the settlement of intertemporal problems, but gradually evolved into its present, far more general, shape.[251] The words *"together with* the context" in paragraph 3 are no impediment to the view that "any relevant rules of international law applicable in the relations between the parties" actually are *part of* that context, and that a further form of systematic interpretation is envisaged, here. But what about subparagraphs (a) and (b)? Those who consider "authentic" and "quasi-authentic interpretation" as forms of "interpretation" will have difficulty in reading into (a) and (b) suggestions as to method: for how can that which already *interprets* be supposed to hold a mere *suggestion on how to* interpret? Those, however, who, like the present writer, consider "subsequent agreements" and "subsequent practice" as explicit and tacit agreements, respectively, which *have to be* "interpreted" [252] are in a better position to understand (a) and (b), too, as further hints in the direction of systematic interpretation.

The implied reference in Article 31, paragraph 3 (c), to the doctrine of "sources", i.e., of the recognized manifestations of international law, is an illustration of the fundamental problems which systematic interpretation as meant here may encounter.[253] The further implication as to the possibility of considerable divergence in interpretation depending on the fundamental views of the interpreter is obvious. Drawing the "context" of a treaty as wide as was done in paragraph 3 (c) no doubt brings great insecurity to its interpretation. The imperative "shall" in all of the paragraphs of Article 31 this way loses much of its meaning, drawing nearer to the permissive "may" in Article 32.

---

249. Comp. Sur, op.cit., p. 278.
250. See Diagram.
251. See p. 11 *supra* on Waldock's Draft Article 65, and this writer's book-review in *Rechtsgeleerd Magazijn Themis*, 1978 pp. 31-35, for details of the development from this article to Art. 31, para. 3(c), of the Vienna Convention.
252. See p. 28 n. 149 *supra*.
253. On the scope of Art. 31, para. 3(c), see Sur, op.cit., p. 284: the provision "consacre le principe de la réintégration du traité dans l'ensemble du droit international".

After the mandatory amalgam of the grammatical, systematic, and teleological methods in Article 31, with its heavy emphasis on the systematic method,
the next article gives leave to use the historical method as a means to ascertain
the intention of the parties.[254] On the terms there specified, the methods designed to bring the rule of party-intention into operation again find themselves
enriched — or should one rather say that still more is being left, here, to the interpreter's free judgment? That it becomes ever more clear that the Vienna Convention fails to "bring us any further than the stage of the medieval glossators and
the freedom of interpretation they represented"?[255] If so the distinction between
treaties and custom may be seriously jeopardized [256] — and the interpreter not
wishing to do so may, therefore, have good reason to interpret (or: apply) Articles
31-32 in a restrictive rather than in an extensive manner.[257] This merely shows that
articles on interpretation, besides *solving* problems of interpretation, may also
provoke them!

A second rule of interpretation is contained in Article 33, paragraphs 1 and 2. It
is the rule of "equal authority" for all languages in which a treaty was authenticated, and for any additional language if so provided. A third, related, rule is the
one in paragraphs 3 and 4 and which may be called the rule of "equal meaning"
of the terms in each authentic text. According to paragraph 4, in case no "equal
meaning" results from an application of the amalgamated (grammatical-systematic-
teleological-historical) method of Articles 31 and 32, an exclusively teleological
approach shall decide.[258]

5.2.3   Methods and rules evaluated

It may be of interest now to investigate some observations to which the methods
and proposed rules of interpretation gave rise. Opinions, on this score, are kaleidos-
copic. Not all of them can be reviewed here and one has to be satisfied with a small
selection only. It is proposed to start from the alleged rules, not from the methods,
because, as stated, an alleged rule in many cases automatically leads to one or more
methods. The rules to be discussed, here, are those enumerated at p. 143 *supra*.
The two rules in Article 33 of the Vienna Convention do not call for any special
comment.[259]

(1) *Party-intention and other factors.* — There is an important rift in learned
opinion on the question whether the interpreter should limit himself to the discovery of the will (intention) of the parties to a treaty, or whether this will at

---

254. On a possible hierarchy among Arts. 31 and 32, see Sur, op.cit., pp. 277-278.
255. See p. 27 *supra*.
256. Comp. p. 37 *supra*.
257. A similar opinion may be Professor Sur's, according to whom, even under Arts. 31-33
of the Vienna Convention, "la liberté de l'interprète doit connaître des butoirs". See op.cit., p.
276.
258. Comp. Sur, op.cit., pp. 226-227, quoting from practice.
259. On Art. 33, comp. Sur, op.cit., pp. 273-275. The International Law Commission dismissed the idea of a necessarily *restrictive* interpretation to solve the problems arising from
authentication in two or more languages (ibid. p. 274).

times may be diminished in favour of other factors. It must be clearly understood at the outset what is meant by "party-intention". It is submitted that the term may be used in four different connotations: (1) the party-intention as expressed solely in the text of the treaty, (2) this intention as apparent not only in the text, but also elsewhere, as in the *travaux préparatoires*, (3) this intention as a construct arrived at on the basis of the declared or implied object and purpose of the treaty, and (4) this intention as a rational construct. On each of these connotations, a short comment appears to be in place.

Choosing to rely upon nothing else but the text of the treaty, one delivers oneself up to all its possible shortcomings. The danger is apparent as soon as one realizes that the choice automatically leads to another one, viz., that of the grammatical method so eloquently conjured up by Professor Pitlo.[260] A particularly dramatic example of a deficient text is the Declaration of The Hague of 29 July 1899 prohibiting "the use of projectiles the sole object of which is the diffusion of asphyxiating or deleterious gases".[261] When on 22 April 1915, in the course of the First World War, Germany launched a large-scale cylinder attack with chlorine against the Allied positions in the Ypres salient, it could claim that cylinders were not projectiles. But could it also claim the lawfulness of its attack?[262]

Concentrating on the text, one also has to cope with the doctrine of the "ordinary meaning" of the terms of the treaty. It may be useful here to quote at some length the commentary to Article 31 (then still 27) published by the International Law Commission in 1966 and in which, in addition to the first, also the second and third connotations (see *supra*) of the expression "party-intention" come to be mentioned:

(11) The article as already indicated is based on the view that the text must be presumed to be the authentic expression of the intentions of the parties; and that, in consequence, the starting point of interpretation is the elucidation of the meaning of the text, not an investigation *ab initio* into the intentions of the parties. The Institute of International Law adopted this — the textual — approach to treaty interpretation. The objections to giving too large a place to the intentions of the parties as an independent basis of interpretation find expression in the proceedings of the Institute. The textual approach, on the other hand, commends itself

---

260. See p. 137 *supra*.
261. Louis Le Fur and Georges Chklaver, *Recueil de Textes de Droit International Public*, 2nd ed. (Paris 1934) pp. 165-166. And see an English translation as prepared by the United States Department of State in Dietrich Schindler and Jiri Toman, *The Laws of Armed Conflicts* (Leyden 1973) pp. 99-100.
262. At the time of the attack, all belligerents were parties to the Declaration which, to all intents and purposes, was to be considered as a treaty. The United States of America never acceded to the Declaration. Since the United States did not enter the First World War before 6 April 1917, the reservation that the Declaration "shall cease to be binding from the time when, in a war between the Contracting Powers, one of the belligerents shall be joined by a non-Contracting Power" was not operative on 22 April 1915. Comp. Eberhard Spetzler, *Luftkrieg und Menschlichkeit* (Göttingen 1956) p. 93: "Nach seinem Wortlaut untersagt es [das II. Haager Abkommen vom 29.7.1899] auch nicht (....) den Giftgaseinsatz vermittels anderer Verfahren als durch Verschiessen", and n. 37 (supporting the legality of the German attack). But see also Wil D. Verwey, *Riot Control Agents and Herbicides in War* (Leyden 1977) pp. 222-225.

by the fact that, as one authority [Footnote 128: *Annuaire de l'Institut de droit international*, vol. 44, tome I (1952), p. 199.] has put it, *"le texte signé est, sauf de rares exceptions, la seule et la plus récente expression de la volonté commune des parties"*. Moreover, the jurisprudence of the International Court contains many pronouncements from which it is permissible to conclude that the textual approach to treaty interpretation is regarded by it as established law. In particular, the Court has more than once stressed that it is not the function of interpretation to revise treaties or to read into them what they do not, expressly or by implication, contain. [Footnote 129: E.g., in the *United States Nationals in Morocco* case, *I.C.J. Reports* 1952, pp. 196 and 199.]

(12) *Paragraph 1* contains three separate principles. The first — interpretation in good faith — flows directly from the rule *pacta sunt servanda*. The second principle is the very essence of the textual approach: the parties are to be presumed to have that intention which appears from the ordinary meaning of the terms used by them. The third principle is one both of common sense and good faith; the ordinary meaning of a term is not to be determined in the abstract but in the context of the treaty and in the light of its object and purpose. These principles have repeatedly been affirmed by the Court. The present Court in its Advisory Opinion on the *Competence of the General Assembly for the Admission of a State to the United Nations* said [Footnote 130: *I.C.J. Reports 1950*, p. 8.]:

'The Court considers it necessary to say that the first duty of a tribunal which is called upon to interpret and apply the provisions of a treaty, is to endeavour to give effect to them in their natural and ordinary meaning in the context in which they occur. If the relevant words in their natural and ordinary meaning make sense in their context, that is an end of the matter.'

And the Permanent Court in an early Advisory Opinion [Footnote 131: *Competence of the ILO to Regulate Agricultural Labour, P.C.I.J.* (1922), Series B, Nos. 2 and 3, p. 23.] stressed that the context is not merely the article or section of the treaty in which the term occurs, but the treaty as a whole:

'In considering the question before the Court upon the language of the Treaty, it is obvious that the Treaty must be read as a whole, and that its meaning is not to be determined merely upon particular phrases which, if detached from the context, may be interpreted in more than one sense.'

Again the Court has more than once had recourse to the statement of the object and purpose of the treaty in the preamble in order to interpret a particular provision. [Footnote 132: E.g., *United States Nationals in Morocco* case, *I.C.J. Reports 1952*, pp. 183, 184, 197 and 198.] [263]

It was to this textuality approach that Professor McDougal opposed his own view in the following strong language: "The great defect, and tragedy, in the International Law Commission's final recommendations about the interpretation of treaties is in their insistent emphasis upon an impossible, conformity-imposing textuality. This unhappy emphasis makes an appearance in, and dominates, the goal for interpretation which the Commission implicitly postulates but never critically examines; the deprecatory appraisal which the Commission offers of the potentialities that inhere in the rational employment of principles of interpretation; and the content and ordering of the particular principles which the Commission puts forward for canonization as "obligatory" rules of law."[264]

263. *Yearbook of the International Law Commission*, 1966, Vol. II pp. 220-221.
264. Myres S. McDougal, "The International Law Commission's Draft Articles Upon Interpretation: Textuality Redivivus", AJIL, 1967 p. 992.

It is proposed to revert to this clash of opinions below, save for the "ordinary meaning" concept which, as the International Law Commission stated, is "the very essence of the textual approach". For, as one might have expected, it is not immediately clear what the implications of the concept are: what, indeed, is the ordinary meaning of "ordinary meaning"? One opinion may be cited, here, because of its succinctness: "The meaning according to ordinary usage is such meaning as at the date of the treaty. Language constantly varies and meanings may fluctuate from one age to the next. To interpret old treaties, it is necessary to attain the ordinary usage at the time when the treaty was concluded and for this end, comparison should be made with documents and other writings of the same period. This is the only reliable method. Etymological and grammatical bases are arbitrary and unreliable; their use is of limited theoretical value and fruitless as a method of proof".[265] Once more, Vattel's rule of the *sens clair* as codified in Article 31 of the Vienna Convention (interpretation "in accordance with the ordinary meaning to be given to the terms of the treaty") may be said to be of doubtful value.[266]

The second connotation of "party-intention" as indicated admits recourse to extrinsic evidence of that intention, i.e., to evidence outside the text. One imagines the mistrust such evidence may provoke with lawyers inclined to stick to a text considered as a well-balanced result in a sometimes lengthy process of negotiation. But Judge Lauterpacht was very much in favour of *travaux préparatoires* as a means of discovering the parties' real intentions.[267] In terms of methods, he thus opted for the historical method.[268] Lord McNair saw its usefulness, yet expressed himself rather cautiously on the subject: "no litigant before an international tribunal can afford to ignore the preparatory work of a treaty, but (. . .) he would probably err in making it a main plank in his argument. Subject to the limitations indicated in this chapter it is a useful make-weight but in our submission it would be unfortunate if preparatory work ever became a main basis of interpretation. In particular, it should only be admitted when it affords evidence of the common intention of both or all parties".[269]

Extrinsic evidence in a different shape is the "context" of a treaty as described in paragraph 2 of Article 31, while its paragraph 3, defining what "shall be taken

265. R.D. Klinger in Tammelo, op.cit, p. 87.
266. Comp. pp. 14-15 *supra*.
267. See p. 136 *supra*.
268. In his dissenting opinion, Section IV (The Historical Background of the Drafting of the Mandate), as appended to the International Court's judgment of 18 July 1966 (*South West Africa Cases* — Second Phase), ICJ Reports, 1966 pp. 352-373, Judge Jessup showed himself to be a strong supporter of the historical method.
269. McNair, op.cit., pp. 422-423. And see Sur, op.cit., pp. 256-259, for a careful analysis of the arguments *pro* and *contra* the use of *travaux préparatoires*. Ibid., p. 279, the author rightly observes that the Vienna Convention, though permitting the use of *travaux préparatoires*, left the problems surrounding it unsolved. In particular, a definition of *travaux préparatoires* is sorely missed (do ILC documents and transactions qualify, for example?), and their opposability as to third States adhering to a treaty is an open question. Comp. Tammelo, op.cit., pp. 14-15 (a number of judicial pronouncements on *travaux préparatoires*), and 18-22 (references to Lauterpacht, Beckett, McNair, Huber).

into account together with the context", in fact places an extensive interpretation upon the word "context".[270]

The extrinsic evidence as admitted by Articles 31 and 32 of the Vienna Convention testifies to a method of mixed historical and systematic character.

"Party-intention" as a construct arrived at on the basis of the declared or implied object and purpose of the treaty — its third connotation — may take the interpreter still further afield. It is remarkable that Article 31, paragraph 1, of the Vienna Convention, textuality-oriented as it is, makes room for it. The International Law Commission itself in its commentary called it a principle "both of common sense and good faith" that "the ordinary meaning of a term is not to be determined in the abstract but in the context of the treaty and in the light of its object and purpose".[271] In support of the latter words, it quoted the example of the International Court's judgment of 27 August 1952 (*Case Concerning Rights of Nationals of the United States of America in Morocco*) referring to the preamble of the treaty in question stating its object and purpose and using it as an aid in interpretation.[272] But it is obvious that parties with an object and purpose in mind do not invariably agree to anything conducive to it. In addition, object and purpose may not have been explicitly stated. In the International Law Commission's view, the "object and purpose" phrase in Article 31, paragraph 1, is the consecration of the maxim *ut res magis valeat quam pereat*.[273]

Meanwhile, the expression "object and purpose" leaves some doubt as to its significance. Are "object" and "purpose" synonyms, or do they each connote something different? The Permanent and International Courts sometimes treated them as synonyms, or almost [274], whereas Article 60, paragraph 3 (*b*), of the Vienna Convention dissociates the two terms by referring to "the object *or* purpose of the treaty". Professor Sur proposes to interpret the "object" of a treaty as its *"contenu matériel, par opposition aux éléments formels"*, in other words as "that which the treaty is about". But what the treaty "is about", he says, first has *to be* determined by interpretation before it can itself help to determine the intention of the parties.[275] The same, of course, applies to the term "purpose" [276], which leads the present writer to believe that the interpretation of "object" will necessarily affect that of "purpose", and the reverse, and that the best solution of this question of semantics, therefore, is to consider the expression "object and purpose" as a unitary one reflecting two closely interrelated aspects of a single idea.

---

270. See p. 145 *supra*.

271. Op.cit., p. 221 (as quoted at pp. 147-148 *supra*).

272. ICJ Reports, 1952 pp. 183, 184, 197 and 198. And see already the Permanent Court of International Justice, judgment of 26 April 1928 (*Rights of Minorities in Upper Silesia — Minority Schools*), Series A, No. 15 p. 33: "The Treaty would fail in its purpose if it were not to be considered as an established fact that persons who belonged *de facto* to such a minority must enjoy the protection which had been stipulated."

273. *Yearbook of the International Law Commission*, 1966, Vol. II p. 219, para. 6.

274. See Sur, op.cit., p. 228.

275. Ibid.

276. Ibid., p. 229, and Tammelo, op.cit., p. 34. And see Sur's further observations on "object" and "purpose" of a treaty, op.cit., pp. 227-231.

The method employed under this third connotation of "party-intention" is the teleological one.[277] The International Law Commission, also making the link with methods, commented as follows on the said maxim: "Properly limited and applied, the maxim does not call for an "extensive" or "liberal" interpretation in the sense of an interpretation going beyond what is expressed or necessarily to be implied in the terms of the treaty".[278] Below, it will be shown that authorities to the contrary may be quoted (see pp. 159-160 *infra*).

The fourth meaning attached *supra* to "party-intention", that of a rational construct, is illustrated by Professor Tammelo on the basis of observations made by Castberg and Radbruch. Party-intention, in this view, is not to be understood in the psychological sense, but in a special technical sense, viz., that of a "rational intention" (Castberg). "In jurisprudential treatment of the problem of legal interpretation, the same idea has found strong support from Gustav Radbruch, who takes the view that the goal of interpretation is "the objectively valid meaning of a legal rule". The so-called legislator's intention is constructively to be regarded as his intention. "It is therefore possible to determine as the legislative will what never existed in the conscious wills of the authors of the law." "The law may be wiser than its authors — indeed, it must be wiser than its authors"."[279]

It is clear that the fourth meaning must appeal to all those who, as does the present writer, consider that the interpreter should let himself be directed by the principles of rational organization.[280] It is equally clear that this connotation of "party-intention" is closely bordering on the second *modus operandi* hinted at above (pp. 146-147 *supra*), the one, namely, taking into account other factors than the intention of the parties alone. And as to the method the fourth meaning entails, it is suggested that the suitable method, here, is a composite one partaking of the systematic, the teleogical, and the sociological at a time.

Proceeding now to the view of party-intention *not* as the sole object of treaty interpretation, but as an object together with "other factors", one should above all refer, here, to Professor McDougal's opposition as reported.[281] He, Lasswell, and Miller in their collective work on treaty interpretation see the interpreter's mission "in determining the parties' genuine shared expectations and identifying relevant general community policies".[282] But others, too, evolved in this direction, like Professor Bernhardt [283] , who suggested recognizing the "proper life" of a treaty and placing it in its normative and factual context in order to enable the interpreter to take into account customary law, social conditions, etc. How far remote this opinion is from Lauterpacht's idea, dating back to 1937, of a treaty as indistin-

277. See pp. 135-136 *supra* (Waldock on Cavaré and Alvarez).
278. See n. 273 at p. 150 *supra*.
279. Tammelo, op.cit., p. 51 (quotations are from Gustav Radbruch, *Rechtsphilosophie*, 5th ed. (Stuttgart 1956), pp. 210 and 214).
280. See p. 19 *supra*. And comp. McDougal as quoted at p. 148 *supra* on "the rational employment of principles of interpretation".
281. See p. 148 *supra*.
282. McDougal, Lasswell, and Miller, *The Interpretation of Agreements and World Public Order* (New Haven 1967) p. 111.
283. Rudolf Bernhardt, *Die Auslegung völkerrechtlicher Verträge* (Cologne 1963) p. 31.

guishable from a private contract![284] At the same time, however, one should realize that in national law the same current away from party-intention is to be observed.[285]

As it appears, this doctrine must lay heavy emphasis on the sociological method.

(2) *Interpretation* ex tunc. — The first among the more technical rules enumerated above is the rule that a treaty should be interpreted *ex tunc*, not *ex nunc*. The meaning of the rule is that the interpretation is supposed to hold good from the beginning of the treaty, and not just from the moment of its interpretation. The character of the judge as a "servant" of the "sovereign" [286] is underlined in this rule. But, as the present writer had occasion to observe elsewhere, two factors tend to mitigate the austerity of it, namely, that applying the law is a creative activity itself, and that the sovereign may allow, or oblige, the servant to adapt the law to modern conditions.[287] As a very special branch of the latter activity, one may think of the judicial *rôle* with regard to the so-called "intertemporal problems". The rule discussed here, in other words, has to be applied *cum grano salis*. It, nevertheless, remains essential because of its relevance to the basic attitude to be taken towards interpretation. Professor Tammelo takes a different attitude. If the Permanent Court in its advisory opinion of 15 May 1931 [288] held that, "in accordance with the rules of law, the interpretation given by the Court to the terms of the Convention [of 15 May 1922 between Germany and Poland concerning Upper Silesia] has retrospective effect — in the sense that the terms of the Convention must be held to have always borne the meaning placed upon them by this interpretation" [289], he wonders whether this declaration is "anything more than expression of pious wishes or attempts to give some reassurance and comfort to the litigants under the cover of which *ex nunc* interpretation may still take place. For by what criteria is it possible to test whether a convention has "always borne the meaning" placed upon it by interpretation?"[290] For the reasons *supra*, this scepticism appears to be ill-considered, and in reply to the author's question regarding criteria, he may be referred to what the present writer called the lawyer's prime virtue: his personal integrity, and to what he proposed to consider as an integral part of it: mental flexibility.[291]

The thought may be alluring that interpretation *ex tunc* has something special to do with the historical method. Actually, it is submitted that any of the five

---

284. Sir Hersch Lauterpacht, *International Law: Collected Papers* (Cambridge 1970) p. 365. And comp. p. 15 *supra*.

285. As a partisan of this new current in the Netherlands, see J.M. van Dunné and his book *Normatieve uitleg van rechtshandelingen* (Deventer 1971).

286. See this writer's "Legal Archetypes" (as quoted at p. 20, n.100 *supra*) pp. 74-75.

287. Ibid., p. 74. Comp. Tammelo, op.cit., p. 58, n. 30: "*Ex nunc* interpretation enters into the decisions of international courts above all through their allowing for equitable considerations", with reference to Georg Schwarzenberger, *International Law*, Vol. I, 3rd. ed. (London 1957) p. 494.

288. Quoted at p. 143, n. 244 *supra*.

289. Series A/B, No. 40 p. 19.

290. Tammelo, op.cit., p. 10.

291. See "Legal Archetypes" p. 86.

methods of interpretation may be used in order to find out how a provision at the time of its coming into force was meant to be read.

(3) *No revision*. — The rule that treaty interpretation should avoid becoming a revision of the treaty concerned seems to be closely related to the preceding one, and it may even be asked whether the *ex tunc* rule is not at the origin of the present prescription or, indeed, whether the two of them are not identical.[292] The no revision-rule, too, provoked Professor Tammelo's doubts. In its advisory opinion of 18 July 1950 [293] , the International Court stated: "It is the duty of the Court to interpret the Treaties, not to revise them" [294] , and in its judgment of 27 August 1952 [295] , the Court was satisfied with repeating its own words.[296] "By these statements", Professor Tammelo then wrote, "the Court has wanted to emphasize that its interpretative activity can be only *intra legem* and under its cover no judicial legislation can take place. However, such declarations are no warrant that *praeter* and even *contra legem* interpretations do not take place in actual fact nor that the international courts have succeeded in making the intangible borderline between treaty interpretation and judicial legislation visible in the cases they have decided".[297]

It is believed that the same rebuttal is in place, here, as with respect to the learned author's view regarding the *ex tunc* rule.[298]

(4) *Minimum of obligations*. — The rule of the minimum of obligations as found by the Permanent Court of International Justice [299] is curiously reminiscent of Antoine Pillet's doctrine of the least sacrifice.[300] Rejecting Bentham's postulate of "the greatest happiness of the greatest number" because of its inapplicability to an international community consisting of States which are relatively few, Pillet conceived another norm which would best serve the commonwealth of the world, namely, that, in a hierarchy of interests, the higher interest has precedence over the lower, and that, in the event of a choice between interests being unavoidable, the sacrifice should be as small as possible. Every State, Pillet held, should respect every other State's "external sovereignty", being its right to partake in "commerce" as understood since the Congress of Vienna, including communications, progress of civilization, solidarity, interdependence. The dynamic character of this "commerce" made conflicts inevitable, and the formula devised by Pillet to meet them was that of a reasonable weighing of interests. But where no ordinary reasonableness would lead to a result, in particular in cases where a weaker interest is doubled by

292. As suggested by Georg Schwarzenberger, op.cit., pp. 489-490, and Sur, op.cit., p. 202..
293. See p. 143, n. 245 *supra*.
294. ICJ Reports, 1950 p. 229.
295. See p. 143, n. 245 *supra*.
296. ICJ Reports, 1952 p. 196.
297. Tammelo, op.cit., p. 10, once more referring to Schwarzenberger, op.cit., p. 488.
298. See further Sur, op.cit., pp. 200-210, 343-344, and 348 on the no revision-rule.
299. See p. 143, n. 246 *supra*.
300. Antoine Pillet, "Recherches sur les droits fondamentaux des états dans l'ordre des rapports internationaux et sur la solution des conflits qu'ils font naître", *Revue générale de droit international public,* 1898 pp. 55-89, and 236-264; and 1899 pp. 503-532. And see Professor Arnold Tammes' comments in his study *De wet van het geringste offer* (The Law of the Least Sacrifice) for the Royal Academy of Sciences of the Netherlands (Amsterdam 1963).

an unquestionable right under international law to thwart the other party's better interest (e.g., to have a corridor to an enclave), Pillet suggested his *loi du moindre sacrifice*.[301]

It is a conjecture, but it may well be that the Permanent Court's statement as reproduced above [302] has a link with the intellectual world of Pillet, notwithstanding the reference it makes to "the minimum of obligations for *the Parties*", instead of for one party only. For is it not inherently the same *technique* whether one convinces one or both parties with an argument based upon the minimal weight of an obligation? And interpretation, too, is a matter of conviction.[303]

The Court's statement as such is not to be overrated: as an *obiter dictum*, it did not contribute towards the grounding of its opinion. However, the idea behind it is sound, resting on reasonableness as it does, and its attractiveness is in the *rôle* it can play in the interpretative application of the principles of rational organization in psychologically difficult situations.

As to methods, the rule of minimal obligations naturally leads to restrictive interpretation.

(5) *Interpretation* contra proferentem. – This rule is referred to by Lord McNair in an entirely non-committal way.[304] He is satisfied with the indication of three cases in which it was applied, including the judgment handed down by the Permanent Court of International Justice on 12 July 1929 (*Case Concerning the Payment in Gold of Brazilian Federal Loans Contracted in France*) and in which the Court said that "there is a familiar rule for the construction of instruments that, when they are found to be ambiguous, they should be taken *contra proferentem*".[305]

Lord Asquith of Bishopstone, on the other hand, having approved of the maxim *expressio unius est exclusio alterius,* in his decision quoted at p. 138 *supra* then went on to say: "Much more dubious to my mind is the application to this case of certain other English maxims relied on by one or the other party in this case. For instance, *verba chartarum fortius accipiuntur contra proferentem*: or the rule that grants by a sovereign are to be construed against the grantee. The latter is an English rule which owes its origin to incidents of our own feudal polity and royal prerogative which are now ancient history; and its survival, to considerations which, though quite different, seem to have equally little relevance to conditions in a protected State of a primitive order on the Persian Gulf".[306] The Arbitrator clearly sounded a note of warning against an indiscriminate use of the rule.

Contrary to rules (1) and (4), the rule *contra proferentem* does not seem to bring a particular method of interpretation in its wake.[307]

---

301. See Professor Tammes' *résumé*, op.cit., pp. 1-4.
302. See p. 143 *supra*.
303. Comp. this writer's contribution "De betekenis van het rechterlijk proces voor de rechtsvorming" (The Significance of Judicial Proceedings in the Process of Law) (as quoted at p. 35, n. 188 *supra*) p. 33, and p. 18 *supra* on the *esprit de finesse*.
304. McNair, op.cit., pp. 464-465.
305. Series A, No. 21 p. 114.
306. Op.cit., p. 251.
307. Further on this rule, see Ch. De Visscher, op.cit., pp. 110-112.

5.3 Interpretation and the character of a treaty

5.3.1 A comparison with national legal orders

A question now to be examined is to what extent, if any, the character of a treaty may influence, or determine, the use of the different methods and rules of interpretation. In order to answer the question, it is proposed first to look for an analogy to national legal orders.

In national legal orders, it is a well-known feature that one branch of the law may differ more or less considerably from another with respect to the legal method applied to it. As a rule, private law provisions, for instance, may be interpreted far more strictly than prescriptions of a public law nature, and *travaux préparatoires* may be much more important with regard to the former than in the interpretation of the latter. Occasionally, however, the reverse may be true, and a private law rule may receive an interpretation as liberal as any placed upon a rule of public law, whereas a provision of constitutional or administrative law may at times be construed on very strict lines. Opinions on when a strict or a liberal approach in either of the two branches of the law is desirable diverge, and in the Netherlands, especially, there is no consensus among public law scholars as to the permissible measure of liberality in interpreting the Dutch Constitution.[308]

On the national plane, there also is a current conviction on the interpretation of criminal law and procedural law provisions. According to it, no analogy should be allowed in the interpretation of criminal law [309], and procedural law should always be strictly construed. As Professor Pitlo has it, procedural law represents "the last means for getting one's due" [310], and the Courts, therefore, deal with it with extra circumspection, interpreting it less flexibly than other sections of the law.[311]

The same sort of distinction as in national law is to be found in international law with regard to treaties. The questions, here, are whether all treaties should be interpreted as private law contracts, or whether some should receive a public law construction, — how multilateral treaties as distinguished from bilateral agreements should be read, — how one should approach "normative" treaties, military treaties,

---

308. See a survey of learned opinion in Professor Jeukens' "De interpretatie van de grondwet" (The Interpretation of the Constitution), in *Rechtsvinding* (Finding the Law) (Deventer 1970) pp. 173-177; and comp. Prakke, "Constitutional Interpretation in the Netherlands", Netherlands Reports to the VIIIth International Congress of Comparative Law, Pescara, 1970 (Deventer 1970) pp. 267-287.
309. See a curious example in Akehurst, "The Hierarchy of the Sources of International Law", *The British Yearbook of International Law*, 1974-1975 (Oxford 1977) p. 279, n. 1.
310. Pitlo, op.cit., p. 147 (this writer's translation).
311. Ibid. p. 148. In so far as jurisdiction may be considered a matter of procedure, there is an important exception to be made, here, concerning the Netherlands, the Dutch *Hoge Raad* not basing its case-law regarding jurisdiction on the text of statutory provisions, nor on any expressed legislative intent, but autonomously seeking to establish a *reasonable system* of jurisdiction. See that Court's judgment of 15 December 1950, *Nederlandse Jurisprudentie*, 1951, No. 221.

treaties creating an objective situation, treaties carrying a limitation of sovereignty,
– and how to deal with agreements reached through "consensus".

A preliminary question, however, is whether, actually, one should distinguish
treaties, or rather *clauses* in treaties on the basis of their character. One single
treaty, indeed, may contain clauses of a very divergent nature. Professor Georges
Scelle rightly pointed out that the Treaty of Versailles included a number of "contractual" clauses, besides clauses of a clearly "legislative" intent. Therefore, depending on the clause under consideration, the Versailles Treaty was sometimes to be
interpreted as a *traité-contrat*, sometimes as a *traité-loi*. Hence Professor Scelle's
view that treaties are but "anonymous forms" (*un moule anonyme*), and that no
treaty *as a whole* may be deemed to entail one specific manner of interpretation.[312]

The present writer, who in an earlier study adopted, and now maintains, a position similar to Professor Scelle's on the separate consideration of every single
clause [313], nevertheless prefers not to subscribe to that great scholar's idea of an
interpretative "anonymousness" of treaties, nor to Professor Sur's logical conclusion derived from it, viz., that of a total fragmentation of method in which circumstances established *a posteriori* would most of the time be decisive on what
method to apply.[314] It is submitted that an over-all characterization of treaties continues to make sense, particularly as a first step towards systematic interpretation.
And did not Sir Humphrey Waldock himself observe: "It is true that the character
of a treaty may affect the question whether the application of a particular principle, maxim or method of interpretation is suitable in a particular case"?[315]

5.3.2   The private as against the public law approach: constitutional documents of international organizations

One of the first things to be realized in this context is that not all treaties contain "law". Some, indeed, as expounded before, instead of "law" carry "obligations".[316] The difference was said to be of importance precisely in the matter of
interpretation, for treaties carrying "obligations" may be expected to be interpreted with a very heavy emphasis on the will of the parties, in contrast with treaties
containing "law", the construction of which to a degree may be influenced by the
collective state-interest.[317] It is believed that the distinction between the two sorts
of treaties takes care of at least some of the private *versus* public law dichotomy in

---

312. Georges Scelle, *Précis de droit des gens,* Vol. II (Paris 1934) p. 334.
313. See his "Kartels en Euromarkt" (Trusts and Common Market) in *De kartelbepalingen in het EEG-Verdrag* (The Anti-Trust Provisions in the European Common Market Treaty) (Zwolle 1960) pp. 11, 17-18, and 39-40.
314. Sur, op.cit., pp. 262-263 and 264.
315. *Yearbook of the International Law Commission,* 1964, Vol. II p. 55 (para. 9). And comp. McNair, *The Law of Treaties* (Oxford 1961) pp. 739-754 ("The Functions and Differing Legal Character of Treaties"), and Tammelo, op.cit., p. 24.
316. See "The Recognized Manifestations" p. 23 (and comp. p. 21, n. 101 *supra*).
317. Ibid., p. 24.

the interpretation of treaties. For does not a treaty carrying "obligations" show the features of a private law contract?[318]

There is more, however, militating in favour of a private law approach to some, a public law approach to other treaties. According to Judge Lauterpacht, all treaties should be interpreted in the way of private law contracts, whatever their subject or the number of participants. He was a believer in "the essential identity of consensual agreements in municipal and international law". Regretting that so much between States had to be settled by agreement, he proposed to "minimize the inconvenience (. . .) by at least putting such agreement within the firm orbit of the general principles of the law of contract which the legal history of mankind has abundantly developed through the ages".[319] But, as stated above [320], this exclusively private law approach to the interpretation of treaties is antiquated, now, and the *Reservations Case* was quoted in support: in its advisory opinion of 28 May 1951, the International Court could not think of the Genocide Convention as a contract, but clearly intimated the public law nature of it.

Most apparent is the public law character of the constitutive documents of the great international organizations, such as the Covenant of the League of Nations and the Charter of the United Nations. Being public law instruments they are by some considered to be self-contained entities evolving with the times, "living constitutions" which may be liberally construed as needs command. Interpretations of this sort of treaties may diminish the rigour of their terms as well as extend their meaning. An example in the first category are the Resolutions adopted in 1921 by the Assembly of the League of Nations intending to obviate the extravagant results of a literal interpretation of Article 16, paragraphs 1 and 2, of the Covenant on sanctions. The sanctions against Italy in 1935 rested on these Resolutions rather than on the literal text of Article 16.[321] An example of an interpretation adding to the text of a constitutive treaty is the one placed by the International Court of Justice on the Charter in its advisory opinion of 11 April 1949 (*Reparation for Injuries Suffered in the Service of the United Nations).* [322] One of the questions asked of the Court by the United Nations General Assembly was as follows: "In the event of an agent of the United Nations in the performance of his duties suffering injury in circumstances involving the responsibility of a State, has the United Nations, as an Organization, the capacity to bring an international claim against the responsible *de jure* or *de facto* government with a view to obtaining the reparation due in respect of the damage caused (a) to the United Nations, (b) to the victim or to persons entitled through him?" The Court observed as follows:

"In order to answer this question, the Court must first enquire whether the Charter has given the Organization such a position that it possesses, in regard to its

318. It is realized that the nomenclature used here and below – private *versus* public law – is by no means ideal, but there seems to be no better one at hand.

319. Sir Hersch Lauterpacht, *International Law: Collected Papers* (Cambridge 1970) p.366.

320. See p. 15 *supra.*

321. See J.L. Brierly, *The Law of Nations,* 3rd. ed. (Oxford 1942) pp. 240-244; ibid. p. 243: "though these Resolutions [had] only a moral authority, that authority [was] a high one".

322. ICJ Reports, 1949 pp. 174 et seq.

Members, rights which it is entitled to ask them to respect. In other words, does the Organization possess international personality? (. . .)

To answer this question, *which is not settled by the actual terms of the Charter*, we must consider what characteristics it was intended thereby to give to the Organization".[323]

Having examined the Charter and the 1946 Convention on the Privileges and Immunities of the United Nations, the Court found that the Organization exercised and enjoyed "functions and rights which can only be explained on the basis of the possession of a large measure of international personality and the capacity to operate upon an international plane".[324] Reverting to the question asked by the General Assembly, the Court then was able to state that the sum of international rights of the Organization comprised the right to bring the kind of international claim described in the Request for an advisory opinion:

"Whereas a State possesses the totality of international rights and duties recognized by international law, the rights and duties of an entity such as the Organization must depend upon its purposes and functions as specified or *implied in its constituent documents* and developed in practice. The functions of the Organization are of such a character that they could not be effectively discharged if they involved the concurrent action, on the international plane, of fifty-eight or more Foreign Offices, and the Court concludes that the Members have endowed the Organization with capacity to bring international claims when necessitated by the discharge of its functions".[325]

Herewith, the public law doctrine of "implied powers" had received its consecration in international law.[326] But it cannot possibly be maintained that the International Court in all questions of a public law character applied the public law method. In its advisory opinions of 28 May 1948 (*Conditions of Admission of a State to Membership in the United Nations – Article 4 of the Charter*)[327] and 3 March 1950 (*Competence of the General Assembly for the Admission of a State to the United Nations*)[328], the Court applied a strict method of interpretation in two questions of an undeniable public law character, viz., the rights under the United Nations Charter of Member States and the General Assembly, respectively, in the matter of the admission of new Members. In the former of these two opinions, the Court held that "the text of this paragraph [Article 4, paragraph 1, of the Charter], by the enumeration which it contains and the choice of its terms, clearly demonstrates the intention of its authors to establish a legal rule which, while it fixes the conditions of admission, determines also the reasons for which admission may be refused".[329] So clear was the text in the Court's eyes

323. Ibid., p. 178 (italics supplied).
324. Ibid., p. 179.
325. Ibid., p. 180 (italics supplied).
326. See also the Court's advisory opinion of 13 July 1954 (*Effect of Awards of Compensation Made by the United Nations Administrative Tribunal*), ICJ Reports, 1954 pp. 56-57.
327. ICJ Reports, 1948 pp. 57 et seq.
328. ICJ Reports, 1950 pp. 4 et seq.
329. ICJ Reports, 1948 p. 62.

that it rejected all recourse to its *travaux préparatoires*.[330] In the latter advisory opinion, the Court found "no difficulty in ascertaining the natural and ordinary meaning of the words in question [Article 4, paragraph 2, of the Charter] and no difficulty in giving effect to them".[331] Here, too, the Court deemed resort to the preparatory documents to be superfluous.[332] But no lesser jurists than Judges Basdevant, Winiarski, McNair, and Read, in a joint dissenting opinion appended to the advisory opinion of 28 May 1948, came to a result diametrically opposed to the Court's. It is impossible here to quote more than paragraphs 9 and 10 from their dissenting opinion, which as a whole should be recommended as first class reading in the methodology of international law:

"9. The resolutions which embody either a recommendation or a decision in regard to admission are decisions of a political character; they emanate from political organs; by general consent they involve the examination of political factors, with a view to deciding whether the applicant State possesses the qualifications prescribed by paragraph 1 of Article 4; they produce a political effect by changing the condition of the applicant State in making it a Member of the United Nations. Upon the Security Council, whose duty it is to make the recommendation, there rests by the provisions of Article 24 of the Charter "primary responsibility for the maintenance of international peace and security" — a purpose inscribed in Article 1 of the Charter as the first of the purposes of the United Nations. The admission of a new Member is pre-eminently a political act, and a political act of the greatest importance.

The main function of a political organ is to examine questions in their political aspect, which means examining them from every point of view. It follows that the Members of such an organ who are responsible for forming its decisions must consider questions from every aspect, and, in consequence, are legally entitled to base their arguments and their vote upon political considerations. That is the position of a member of the Security Council or of the General Assembly who raises an objection based upon reasons other than the lack of one of the qualifications expressly required by paragraph 4 of Article 4.

That does not mean that no legal restriction is placed upon this liberty. We do not claim that a political organ and those who contribute to the formation of its decisions are emancipated from all duty to respect the law. The Security Council, the General Assembly and the Members who contribute by their votes to the decisions of these bodies are clearly bound to respect paragraph 1 of Article 4, and, in consequence, bound not to admit a State which fails to possess the conditions required in this paragraph.

But is there any other legal restriction upon the freedom which in principle these organs enjoy in the choice of the reasons for their decisions, that is to say, upon the liberty which in principle a State enjoys in choosing the reasons for its decisions, and in this case, for its vote? Is there in this case a restriction consisting in a prohibition to oppose an application for admission on grounds foreign to the qualifications required by paragraph 1 of Article 4?

10. We must therefore decide whether there exists such a restriction upon the principle of law stated above.

330. Ibid., p. 63.
331. ICJ Reports, 1950 p. 8.
332. Ibid.

There is a rule of interpretation frequently applied by the Permanent Court of International Justice, when confronted with a rule or principle of law, to the effect that no restriction upon this rule or principle can be presumed unless it has been clearly established and that in case of doubt it is the rule or principle of law which must prevail. In the present case, before acknowledging the existence of any restriction upon the principle of the widest examination of requests for admission by the Security Council, the General Assembly and their members, it is necessary to show that such a restriction has been established beyond a doubt.

Can it therefore be said that the application of this principle is subject to a clearly established restriction precluding the putting forward, in the course of the examination of requests for admission, of considerations not expressly specified in paragraph 1 of Article 4?"[333]

The answer given by the dissenting judges to the first question asked by the General Assembly was as follows:

A Member of the United Nations which is called upon, in virtue of Article 4 of the Charter, to pronounce itself by its vote either in the Security Council or in the General Assembly, on the admission of a State which possesses the qualifications specified in paragraph 1 of that Article, is participating in a political decision and is therefore legally entitled to make its consent to the admission dependent on any political considerations which seem to it to be relevant. In the exercise of this power the Member is legally bound to have regard to the principle of good faith, to give effect to the Purposes and Principles of the United Nations and to act in such a manner as not to involve any breach of the Charter."[334]

They manifestly applied what this writer would call a public law approach which, in itself, is no better or worse than the private law method. It is a matter of preference which of them one would choose, but in no circumstances could one, as Professor Verzijl does, cast aside the public law approach as a mere *petitio principii*.[335]

In this writer's personal opinion, treaties for the regulation of constitutional subjects all deserve a special approach.[336] First of all, there is a close analogy between their interpretation and that of *traités-loi*, and it even seems to be a legitimate question whether an institutional treaty is not a species of the latter.[337] At any rate, *travaux préparatoires* cannot play the same *rôle* in interpreting *traités-loi*, or institutional treaties, as in interpreting a *traité-contrat*, for in neither of the two cases (*traité-loi* or institutional treaty) can one speak of a transaction the

---

333. ICJ Reports, 1948 pp. 85-86.
334. Ibid., p. 92. And see Sur, op.cit., p. 85: "les Etats membres, interprétant les conditions juridiques posées par l'article 4 de la Charte des Nations-Unies, feront de considérations politiques les éléments de l'appartenance juridique de l'Etat à l'organisation".
335. J.H.W. Verzijl, *The Jurisprudence of the World Court*, Vol. II, (Leyden 1966) p. 16. For further reading on the subject, see Ch. De Visscher, op.cit., pp. 148-149, Gordon, "The World Court and the Interpretation of Constitutive Treaties", AJIL 1965 pp. 794 et seq., and Joyce Gutteridge, *The United Nations in a Changing World* (Manchester 1969).
336. See "Kartels en Euromarkt" (Trusts and Common Market) (as quoted at p. 156 n. 313 *supra*) pp. 7-20.
337. Ibid., pp. 10-11 (but see Ch. De Visscher, op.cit., p. 140: "règle de droit" *versus* "action commune"); and on *traités-loi*, comp. this writer in "The Recognized Manifestations" p. 24, McNair, op.cit., pp. 749-752, and Sur, op.cit., pp. 88-89, 249-250, 261-262, 270, and 304.

confines of which the States parties to it were able completely to determine.[338] Secondly, although all law belongs to cybernetics [339], institutional treaties more than any other kind of law serve to "administer" international relations, and the difficult art of "administration" is subject to "laws" of its own which no administrator can afford to neglect. Obviously, both features — the inevitable lack of precision, the subjection to political contingency — must bear upon the interpretation of institutional traties, and the only question is the extent to which their influence may be admitted without betraying the requirement of *respect du droit* adopted for all "application" worth the name.[340] There is a border-line where "judicial" interpretation changes into "legislative" interpretation, as when on 3 November 1950 the General Assembly of the United Nations voted the "Uniting for Peace" Resolutions making armed intervention, *inter alia*, recommended by the Assembly legal where, in cases coming under Article 39 of the Charter, the Security Council on account of a veto was prevented from acting in the interest of the maintenance of international peace and security.[341]

Even Judge Lauterpacht, as staunch a defender of the private law approach as he might have been, saw the necessity at times of a more liberal interpretation of constitutional instruments. "It must be borne in mind", he observed in one of his last writings, "in particular in relation to treaties of a constitutional and legislative character, that the true intentions of the parties may on occasions be frustrated if exclusive importance is attached to the meaning of words divorced from the social and legal changes which have intervened in the long period following upon the conclusion of those treaties".[342] One may ask by what means these "true intentions" after such a "long period" are to be ascertained, and whether, consequently, it is not artificial still exclusively to cling to the private law approach.

5.3.3   Bilateral and multilateral treaties

At pp. 135-136 *supra*, Sir Humprey Waldock was seen quoting Professor Cavaré and Judge Alvarez as advocates of teleological interpretation, especially of multilat-

---

338. "Kartels en Euromarkt" p. 11. Sur, op.cit., p. 128: the *travaux préparatoires* of the UN Charter "n'ont pas en principe de valeur juridique, et leur pertinence en ce qui concerne l'interprétation est très contestée". But see the International Court in its advisory opinion of 21 June 1971 (*Legal Consequences for States of the Continued Presence of South Africa in Namibia (South West Africa) Notwithstanding Security Council Resolution 276 (1970)*), ICJ Reports, 1971 p. 34, para. 62: "The records of the San Francisco Conference show that . . .".

339. See "Principles of Rational Organization" p. 44: "The essential vocation of law, indeed, is to be an instrument of government, and its essential nature, therefore, is to be part of cybernetics".

340. See p. 6 and pp. 159-160 *supra*. And comp. Ch. De Visscher, op.cit., p. 141: with regard to institutional treaties, "on ne saurait leur appliquer dans toute leur rigueur les règles courantes de l'exégèse des textes".

341. "Kartels en Euromarkt" pp. 14-16. See also Judge Fitzmaurice's dissenting opinion as appended to the International Court's advisory opinion of 21 June 1971 (*Legal Consequences for States of the Continued Presence of South Africa in Namibia (South West Africa) Notwithstanding Security Council Resolution 276 (1970)*), ICJ Reports, 1971 p. 220: "I cannot *as a jurist*accept the reasoning on which ⌊the Opinion of the Court⌋ is based" (italics supplied).

342. Lauterpacht, op.cit., p. 133.

eral treaties. All treaties in which three or more parties participate are "multilateral", regardless of their content.[343] The greater the number of parties, the more difficult it becomes for the interpreter to trace a common intention, and to base a pronouncement on what he is convinced represents the indubitable will shared by all. In these circumstances, it is only natural that interpreters should move away from the *travaux préparatoires*, and draw nearer to an "objective" method of interpretation. As an "objective" method, the teleological method for some time was particularly popular with reference to one category of multilateral treaties, viz., the constitutional documents of international organizations. A prime example, here, is the International Court's advisory opinion of 11 April 1949 (*Reparation for Injuries Suffered in the Service of the United Nations*).[344] But in 1962, the teleological method as applied to the United Nations Charter suffered a serious set-back when France and the Soviet Union refused to comply with the Court's advisory opinion of 20 July of that year (*Certain Expenses of the United Nations*)[345], and ever since, as it appears, one has learnt to be more reticent with regard to it.[346]

5.3.4   Law-making treaties, military treaties, treaties creating an objective situation, treaties carrying a limitation of sovereignty

Unlike the preceding paragraph, the present paragraph is concerned with the content of treaties. The first class of treaties to be dealt with, here, are the law-making treaties, called in French *traités normatifs* or *traités-loi* (as distinguished from *traités-contrat*). It was observed above that in interpreting *traités-loi*, the *travaux préparatoires* cannot play the same *rôle* as with respect to *traités-contrat*.[347] This was said to be due to the fact of their confines not being completely determined. Are there any other features of their interpretation to be identified? Judge Charles De Visscher defines law-making treaties as treaties the object of which is the laying down of common rules of conduct (*normes de conduite communes*).[348] In the International Court's advisory opinion of 28 May 1951 (*Reservations to the Convention on the Prevention and Punishment of the Crime of Genocide*), he finds an accurate account of the characteristics of the law-making treaty, he says.[349] In a convention like the one under consideration, indeed, the Court held that "the contracting States do not have any interests of their own; they merely have, one and all, a common interest, namely, the accomplishment of those high purposes which are the *raison d'être* of the convention. Consequently, in a convention of this type one cannot speak of individual advantages or disadvantages to States, or of the maintenance of a perfect balance between rights and

---

343. See McNair, op.cit., p. 30.
344. See pp. 157-158 *supra*.
345. See p. 29 *supra*.
346. See Sur, op.cit., pp. 230-231.
347. See pp. 160-161 *supra*.
348. Ch. De Visscher, op.cit., p. 128.
349. Ibid., p. 133.

duties".[350] In De Visscher's own words, the Convention under consideration was less a manifestation of free will than a calling to mind of principles obligatory for every civilized State, less a contract than a universally valid regulation of objective law.[351] In the matter of interpretation, the learned author then also places the validity of the Convention outside the sphere of the will of the Contracting Parties.[352] In the present writer's view, it is questionable whether the personal scope of a treaty may really be considered a problem of "interpretation". Practical interpretation was defined as "an activity designed to *clarify* the text of a written manifestation of law and to *recognize* its sense *with a view to its application to the realities of daily life and practice.* "[353] The determination of the personal sphere of action of the text is not included herein, and this writer, therefore, would prefer to accommodate this activity elsewhere in the legal process. The same applies to the effect of retroactivity De Visscher attributes to a "normative" treaty in the event of its being declaratory of existing customary law.[354] Retroactivity is an intertemporal problem of law, no problem of interpretation. Both problems – a treaty's sweep *ratione personae* and *ratione temporis* – are entitled to a common bracket of their own (see Diagram). Genuine features of interpretation of law-making treaties as suggested by De Visscher are the non-applicability of the rule *contra proferentem* because of the absence of "interests of their own", i.e., of the contracting States (see *supra*), the predominance of "object and purpose", i.e., of the teleological method [355], and the admissibility of reasoning by analogy in the interpretation of law-making treaties which are declaratory of existing customary law.[356] Nobody will have any difficulty in accepting these suggestions, fundamentally sound as they are.

Military treaties are treaties of alliance and actual warfare. How very differently they have to be interpreted may be illustrated in one example of each.

At p. 147 *supra*, the Declaration of The Hague of 29 July 1899 was termed "a deficient text" – deficient because of the most unsatisfactory protection it proved to offer against the use of gas in war. Or was that text comprehensive enough, and should it only have been interpreted in a more generous way? Asking this is posing the anguishing problem of the interpretation of all texts designed to subject to law an activity which by its very essence aims at discretion rather than legal regulation. In this context, the present writer is always reminded of the sneering words of Sir G. Sherston Baker introducing his fourth edition of Halleck's

350. ICJ Reports, 1951 p. 23; and comp. p. 16 *supra*.
351. De Visscher, op.cit., pp. 134-135.
352. Ibid., p. 135.
353. See p. 15 *supra*.
354. De Visscher, op.cit., p. 135. It is submitted that retroactivity as suggested by De Visscher is questionable: all "restatement" of customary law is *creative*, and why should the resulting *new* formula be retroactive?
355. Ibid.
356. Ibid., p. 41. Gaetano Morelli, "Cours général de droit international public", Rec. ADI, 1956-I p. 467, denies the existence of any general norm authorizing analogy in the interpretation of agreements.

International Law. Writing shortly after the Hague Rules on Land Warfare had been adopted at the Second Hague Peace Conference, he expressed as follows his lack of appreciation of that document: "No general or admiral worth the name would pause in difficult strategy, or at the moment of victory, because some effeminate Article of the Second Hague Convention or other grandmotherly Conference forbade him to do so and so. All that can be hoped for is the exercise of well known, plain, and intelligent rules which do not interfere with the act of war, but cause it to be waged with more humanity. Elaborate rules prescribed by delegates sitting at ease in the Palace of Peace, or any other place, will never be followed at a moment when the safety of an empire or life or liberty is in serious jeopardy".[357]

With all its sarcasm, and extravagance, there is a ring of realism in this view which is not to be neglected. One may add that military leaders gathered around a conference-table never will give up means they still intend to use if circumstances would so demand. Another observation making sense is that never again they will be brought to agree on any military subject at all in case their agreements, instead of being interpreted in the strictest manner possible, would be construed on different lines, such as by analogy, reading "cylinders" for "projectiles", for example. The inevitable conclusion, therefore, seems to be that this sort of military treaty is viable only when interpreted literally, i.e., according to the grammatical method.

Exactly the opposite should be true with regard to treaties of alliance. As an eloquent example of such treaties, the North Atlantic Treaty, signed in Washington (D.C.) on 4 April 1949 and entered into force on 24 August of that year, may be quoted.[358] Ambassador Lambert Schaus of Luxemburg aptly characterized this treaty in the following words: "Sur le plan des principes, il faut rester fidèle à l'application des règles du droit dans l'exécution des traités internationaux, même si ces règles sont souvent sujettes à controverse. Mais il faut être conscient aussi que les traités politiques – et celui de l'Atlantique Nord est certainement à ranger dans cette catégorie – ont pour objet des matières qui relèvent plutôt du domaine de la politique que de celui du droit. Ce seront donc finalement les considérations d'ordre politique qui prédomineront, dans l'optique de la finalité des traités."[359] This military treaty is a political treaty in that its performance is intimately tied up with the Parties' most vital interests. The ultimate decision on military co-operation and action rests with the individual Parties, therefore, and resolutions taken by the Council in pursuance of Article 9 of the Treaty cannot be binding in law: they do not constitute anything beyond decisions of policy. A potentially different view was held by Professors Éric Stein and Dominique Carreau, writing in 1968 after France's withdrawal from the North Atlantic Treaty Organization. In their own words, "although the Council has not made any formal provision concerning the *effect* of its acts, and the members apparently have sought to avoid any discussion

357. Halleck's *International Law*, 4th Ed. by Sir G. Sherston Baker, Bt., Vol. I (London 1908) p. VI.
358. See *Tractatenblad van het Koninkrijk der Nederlanden*, 1954, No. 176.
359. Lambert Schaus, "Le Conseil de l'Atlantique Nord: son fondement et ses structures, ses compétences et ses missions", *Chronique de politique étrangère*, Vol. XXIV (No. 3: mai 1971) p. 372.

or confrontation on this subject, consistent practice has evolved, pursuant to which the member states have in fact accorded to these acts such legal effect as their substance and form warranted. Thus one must analyze and interpret each Council act in its context in order to determine its normative impact. To the extent that a resolution *purported* to impose an obligation, member states in principle have acted as if they were bound by reason of their concurrence."[360] And further on the authors asserted that: "even if one takes the view that the NATO Council, unlike the OEEC-OECD Councils, is nothing more than a conference of member states and has no power to make authoritative decisions, there can be no question, and General de Gaulle seems to concur, that certain resolutions agreed upon unanimously by the national representatives in the Council would constitute *international agreements* creating international obligations for the member states. At the very least, "the agreements, arrangements and decisions", to use the French Government's own terms, and the behavior of all the member states, based thereon over a period of years, must be viewed as having brought into being *implied obligations* on France. If nothing else, considering the extensive expenditures and investments made in reliance on these arrangements, France may be held *estopped* from denying the obligations to the serious detriment of the Organization and the other members."[361] Later events, especially the LRTNF (Long Range Theatre Nuclear Forces) crisis in late 1979 in the Netherlands, proved that not all NATO Member States were at ease with regard to the legal nature of Council resolutions.

Treaties creating objective situations are treaties the performance or non-performance of which affects the interests of third parties. As an example, one may think, here, of the London Treaties of 19 April 1839 signed by the Great Powers, the Netherlands, and Belgium, in different combinations.[362] Article IX, paragraph 2, of the Treaty between the Netherlands and Belgium, still in force, provides, *inter alia*, that "Les deux Gouvernements s'engagent à conserver les passes navigables de l'Escaut et de ses embouchures et à y placer et y entretenir les balises et bouées nécessaires, chacun pour sa partie du fleuve". It is obvious that such an engagement of a territorial nature is of the highest import to other nations as well, and that its interpretation must take their interests into account. Another celebrated instance is Article 380 of the Treaty of Versailles of 28 June 1919, providing that "The Kiel Canal and its approaches shall be maintained free and open to the vessels of commerce and war of all nations at peace with Germany on terms of entire equality". When on 21 March 1921 the *Wimbledon*, an English merchantman carrying munitions and artillery stores consigned to the Polish Naval Base at Danzig, presented itself at the entrance to the Kiel Canal, the Director of Canal Traffic refused to allow it to pass, basing his refusal upon the neutrality Orders issued by Germany in connection with the Russo-Polish war then in progress, and upon in-

360. Eric Stein and Dominique Carreau, "Law and Peaceful Change in a Subsystem: 'Withdrawal' of France from the North Atlantic Treaty Organization", AJIL, 1968 p. 608.
361. Ibid., p. 613. Comp. Frederic L. Kirgis, "Nato Consultations as a Component of National Decisionmaking", AJIL , 1979 pp. 372 et seq.
362. De Martens, *Nouveau Recueil*, Vol. XVI pp. 770-791.

structions which he had received. The Permanent Court of International Justice, called upon to decide as to the legality of the refusal under international law, in its judgment of 17 August 1923 (*The S.S. "Wimbledon"*) was of opinion that Article 380 had changed the Kiel Canal into "an international waterway intended to provide under treaty guarantee easier access to the Baltic for the benefit of all nations of the world".[363] Saying so, the Court endorsed Professor Basdevant's argument of a *"statut objectif"*.[364] Rejecting the German plea of neutrality in the Russo-Polish war, it declared "that the German authorities on March 21st, 1921, were wrong in refusing access to the Kiel Canal to the S.S. "Wimbledon"."[365]

The *Wimbledon* case is also of relevance in the context of treaties carrying a limitation of sovereignty and the question whether they should be interpreted restrictively.

The rule proposed by the Permanent Court of International Justice "that in case of doubt a limitation of sovereignty must be construed restrictively" [366] could not count on Sir Hersch Lauterpacht's sympathy. After having traced back the history of the doctrine of restrictive interpretation in the Permanent Court of International Justice, he concluded in 1958 that the Court attached in practice little importance to it.[367] "The preponderant practice of the Court itself has, as we have seen, been based on principles of interpretation which render the treaty effective rather than ineffective. These principles are not easily reconcilable with restrictive interpretation conceived as the governing rule of construction."[368]

Before entering upon the question whether Judge Lauterpacht rightly dismissed the rule of restrictive interpretation with regard to limitations of sovereignty, a number of preliminary remarks must be made. First of all, the rule of "the minimum of obligations" discussed above [369] should not be considered as identical with the present one. The rule of "the minimum of obligations for *the Parties*" certainly should not be confused with another one tending to restrict the *obligations* of one party and, symmetrically, the *rights* of the other party. In the second place, a limitation of sovereignty is of such a special and incisive character that it cannot simply be treated the same way as any other agreement resulting in obligations for sovereign States. Not every agreement brings a limitation of sovereignty with it, as was often held, and by far the greatest number of them will just be *expressions* of sovereign power rather than *limitations* of it. But where a State concedes to another State *rights to be exercised upon its territory* which correspondingly limit the territorial State's right to act contrarily, there certainly is a limitation of the latter

363. *Publications of the Permanent Court of International Justice*, Series A, No. 1 p. 22 (italics supplied).
364. As quoted by De Visscher, op.cit., p. 132.
365. Series A, No. 1 p. 33.
366. As expressed by the Court in its judgment of 7 June 1932 (*Case of the Free Zones of Upper Savoy and the District of Gex*), Series A/B, No. 46 p. 167.
367. Sir Hersch Lauterpacht, *The Development of International Law by the International Court* (London 1958) p. 304.
368. Ibid., p. 305.
369. See pp. 153-154 *supra*.

State's sovereignty involved. The question then is whether the maxim *exceptiones sunt strictae interpretationis* applies. This question can never arise with regard to the situations contemplated when dealing with the rule of "the minimum of obligations". The exception envisaged here is one to the *plenitudo potestatis* under international law of the modern *homo liber*, the State, in his own territory. As a prime example of such a situation, attention may again be drawn to Article 380 of the Treaty of Versailles (see *supra*) and to the Permanent Court's judgment of 17 August 1923 (*Case of the S.S. "Wimbledon"*). The Court agreed that an important limitation of the exercise of sovereign rights "constitutes a sufficient reason for the restrictive interpretation of the clause which produces such a limitation", adding, however, that this applied only "in case of doubt". In the Court's mind, no such doubt existed.[370]

For the two reasons stated, the two rules discussed here cannot possibly be thought of as identical, nor even be put on a par. Judge Lauterpacht, it is suggested, failed to appreciate the difference between them. This is how he could quote the Permanent Court's *obiter dictum* of 1925 [371] together with cases in which a limitation of sovereignty was discussed.[372] And this too is how in both contingencies he could equally speak out against restrictive interpretation.

In point of fact, there may be something to be said in favour of restrictive interpretation in case of a limitation of sovereignty, provided always that, as the Court said, there is doubt about the meaning to be attached to the provision concerned. Judge Lauterpacht acknowledged that the Court took exactly the same attitude, but this he interpreted as nothing but "a courteous obeisance to the tradition of respect for State sovereignty", as "a concession to form".[373] In the present writer's opinion, there must have been more to it. It is also hardly consistent when the learned author then continues his argument by saying that, "if the case calls for restrictive interpretation, it may not be difficult to find in support of it a principle of law of greater generality and persuasiveness", namely, that a State claiming special rights and privileges in the territory of another, for instance, must be able to prove them.[374] However, there is no use in shifting the problems of interpretation to the sphere of evidence, nor in obliterating the borderline between the two provinces of interpretation and of evidence.[375]

5.3.5   Agreements through consensus "UN-style"?

This final paragraph is devoted to a modern phenomenon the contour and significance of which still are very much a question-mark, namely, the practice of "consensus".

370. Series A, No. 10 pp. 24-25.
371. See p. 154 *supra*.
372. Op.cit., p. 302, n. 8.
373. Op.cit., p. 302.
374. Op.cit., p. 304.
375. Comp. p. 136, n. 200 *supra*. See further on the restrictive method in interpreting treaties limiting State sovereignty: McNair, op.cit., pp. 765-766, Tammelo, op.cit., pp. 13-14, and Sur, op.cit., pp. 87, 121, 244, and 354-355. In Judge De Castro's opinion, *privileges* (the oppo-

The word "consensus" may be old, the practice it nowadays connotes is rather new, extending well beyond its traditional meaning of an identity of *opinions*. Professor Jennings, in the footsteps of Dr. C. Wilfred Jenks, thought of consensus in the modern sense as the normal working method of the Governing Body of the International Labour Office, for instance, the gist of which is in the *absence of voting* in the process of *decision*.[376] Limiting his observations on consensus to the framework of international organizations, he concluded " that here is a quasi-legal problem of the first order, and far too little attention has been paid even to the theory of it".[377] The problem became the more pressing since the method of consensus found its way to the Third United Nations Conference on the Law of the Sea, which opened on 3 December 1973 and is still continuing. Conferences of this kind, with their massive global participation, are faced with the danger of the steam-roller majority forcing its will upon the minority by sheer numbers, and possibly regardless of its own weight in legal matters on a world scale. In the event of a conference launched with an eye to the conclusion of a world treaty, the outcome of such conduct may be that no treaty of an universal character may prove to be feasible. In these circumstances, new style consensus appeared to many to represent a way out.

Professor De Lacharrière, writing on consensus inside the United Nations Organization shortly after Professor Jennings' statement, pointed at the two ways in which the expression may be understood, viz., as a *method* used in an international organization in order to reach a conclusion, and as the *conclusion itself*. As a method, consensus as practised in the United Nations hesitates between unanimity and the greatest number of members who agree; as a conclusion it is something less than a resolution: proposed by the Chairman, it is deemed adopted without voting, provided nobody voices his dissent. The binding force of a consensus – in the sense not of method, but of conclusion – is subject to doubt, Professor De Lacharrière noted.[378]

Outside the United Nations, it may be asked which is the possible connexion between consensus and treaty. Either as a method or as a result, consensus certainly may *lead to* a treaty. But what about suggesting that consensus as a result may as well be *equivalent* to treaty? The importance of the question is that, in the affirmative, such treaty – or agreement, to give it a less solemn title – would have to be interpreted, and according to which methods and rules?

It is submitted that the answer to the first question must depend on circumstances. In the course of the Third Law of the Sea Conference, for instance, one cannot escape the impression that little by little, from the single Negotiating Text

---

site of limitations), too, are to be interpreted restrictively. See his separate opinion in the case of *Legal Consequences for States of the Continued Presence of South Africa in Namibia (South West Africa) Notwithstanding Security Council Resolution 276 (1970)*, ICJ Reports, 1971 p. 186.

376. Robert Y. Jennings, *General Course on Principles of International Law*, Rec. ADI, 1967-II p. 594.

377. Ibid., p. 595.

378. Guy de Lacharrière, "Consensus et Nations Unies", *Annuaire français de droit inter-*

of 1975 to the Revised Informal Composite Negotiating Text of 1978, the participating States gave in to developments as reflected in these Texts representing a growing consensus. Rather than the conscious "intention" to bring about a new law of the sea of one's own making, there seems to be a sort of "insight" that one has to acquiesce in the unavoidable, based on an evaluation of political realities within the Conference.[379] The question thus boils down to another one, viz., whether a common "insight" like this could be the basis of an agreement. Anyone tempted to admit such novel procedure should, of course, first of all deal with the fact that, formally, the Negotiating Texts are nobody's responsibility but the President's and that of the three Chairmen of the three principal Committees. In the second place, it should be explained why the Vienna Convention on the Law of Treaties adopted on 23 May 1969, before entering into force on 27 January 1980 could not be rated a recognized manifestation of international law [380], but far less developed "Negotiating (!) Texts" should be admitted as agreements. In the latter context, however, an element to be studied is the difference in subject-matter: whereas the Vienna Convention is concerned with the conclusion of treaties by States, the Law of the Sea Conference seeks to regulate less esoteric activities in which States and individuals alike may take part and which, therefore, may generate pressures of an earthly character not felt in the context of treaty-law. An agreement can more readily be seen in the event of a certain amount of practice coming on top of a consensus. Reference may be made, here, to the generally accepted seaward extension of their jurisdiction by coastal states in conformity with the Informal Composite Negotiating Text.

An agreement based on consensus as meant here, supposing its existence can be admitted, may well give rise to considerable difficulties with regard to its interpretation. Professor Koers calls attention to the low drafting quality and, indeed, emptiness of too many provisions in the Informal Composite Negotiating Text, as well as to the fact that the Third Conference on the Law of the Sea practically consists of nothing but informal meetings, to the effect that no *travaux préparatoires* properly speaking will be available.[381] Therefore, if ever the International Court of Justice recognizes an international law of the sea as laid down in texts of this particular nature construed as (the basis of) agreements and has to pronounce on it, it should not let a golden opportunity pass by to be "wiser than its authors".[382] Where so many loose ends were left by a legislature operating under most unorthodox rules of procedure, and where the absence of *travaux préparatoires* stands in the way of an application of the historical method, one has no other choice but to search for "the objectively valid meaning" of what was agreed upon. And this is about all there is to be said about the subject at this moment.

---

national, Vol. XIV (1968) pp. 9-14.

379. Comp. Albert W. Koers, *Het internationale recht van de zee* (The International Law of the Sea) (Deventer 1979) p. 9.

380. See "The Recognized Manifestations" p. 65.

381. Koers, op.cit., p. 17, n. 36 and 37.

382. See p. 151 *supra*.

6. FINAL OBSERVATIONS

If the writer may be allowed to indicate the salient features of his contribution, he would, first of all, like to point to the fact that he placed the subject of the ascertainment of the content of the recognized manifestations of international law in the widest possible context: that of the methodology of law in general, and of international law in particular. Delivering it from the shackles isolating it as a merely technical activity, and recognizing it as part and parcel of the legal process, it was exposed to the decisive and beneficial influence of the normative concept of law for international relations. The core of this concept being the principles of rational organization, it was shown that ascertainment as a form of rhetoric, though subject to functional limitations, basically has to follow the same precepts as legislation.

Out of necessity, the subject was, furthermore, limited to the ascertainment of the content of treaties, i.e., their "interpretation", an expression most intentionally reserved for the ascertainment of the content of written manifestations of law. A drawback caused by this limitation was that no attention could be paid to the ascertainment of the content, e.g., of custom, yet so important for the functioning of treaties.

Methods and rules of treaty interpretation were detailed, and the character of treaties examined as an important element in the decision on what methods and rules should be applied. Should methods and rules be applied as an "obligation"? And generally speaking, i.e., apart from the character of a treaty, can they be said to be "obligatory"? The answer was that methods and rules, being a function of the normative concept, can be deemed obligatory only inasmuch as the normative concept causes them to be so. The use of their codification was found in their being a means to strengthen the proper nature of treaty as distinguished from the other recognized manifestations.

Finally, the close relationship seen between methods and rules on the one hand, the normative concept on the other hand, must have made it clear that, as already intimated in the beginning, interpretation, as a part of legal method in general, in this writer's opinion essentially belongs to the "atmosphere" lying around the law. As such, it is not to be identified with the law, but neither should interpretation be separated from it, for like all method it is a *sine qua non* of its object, permitting it to "breathe and live".

Zeist, 29.1.1980.

Part V
Invalidity, Suspension and
Termination of Treaties

[12]

PROBLEMS CONCERNING THE VALIDITY OF TREATIES

by

T.O. ELIAS

INTRODUCTION: GROUNDS OF INVALIDITY OF A TREATY

In accordance with section 13 of the Charter of the United Nations and as more particularly enjoined upon it by Articles 1 (1) and 18 of its Statute, the International Law Commission has since its establishment in 1949 been engaged in a series of studies[1] based upon the principle of "progressive development of international law and its codification". Conscious of the need to make international law meet the requirements of a changing international society, the Commission, in its report for 1949,[2] listed the law of treaties as one of those considered as suitable for codification. Both Mr. J. L. Brierly and Sir Hersch Lauterpacht, the first and second Special Rapporteurs appointed by the Commission on the law of treaties envisaged that the Commission's work would take the form of a draft convention,[3] but the third Special Rapporteur, Sir Gerald Fitzmaurice, preferred an expository code in his five successive reports.[4] When the Commission, at its 1961 session, appointed Sir Humphrey Waldock as its fourth British Special Rapporteur on the law of treaties, it decided that "its aim would be to prepare draft articles on the law of treaties intended to serve as the basis for a convention".[5] The Commission accordingly took the definitive decision to prepare draft articles which would form a basis for an international convention which would be legally binding once adopted, instead of its being a mere series of articles in the form of an expository statement of the law on the subject of treaties. The Commission's explanation of its change of plan was expressed as follows:

---

1. The Conventions on the Territorial Sea and the Contiguous Zone, the High Seas, Fishing and Conservation of the Living Resources of the High Seas, and the Continental Shelf; the Vienna Convention on Diplomatic Relations; the Vienna Convention on Consular Relations; and the Convention on the Reduction of Statelessness.

2. *Official Records* of the General Assembly, Fourth Session, Supplement No. 10 (A/925), para. 16.

3. *Yearbook of the International Law Commission* 1950, Vol. II, p. 223; 1951, Vol. II, pp. 1, 70; 1953, Vol. II, p. 90; 1954, Vol. II, p. 123.

4. *Yearbook of the International Law Commission* 1956, Vol. II, p. 104; 1957, Vol. II, p. 16; 1958, Vol. II, p. 20; 1959, Vol. II, p. 37; 1960, Vol. II, p. 69.

5. *Yearbook of the International Law Commission* 1961, Vol. II, p. 128, para. 39.

"First, an expository code, however well formulated, cannot in the nature of things be so effective as a convention for consolidating the law; and the consolidation of the law of treaties is of particular importance at the present time when so many new States have recently become members of the international community. Secondly, the codification of the law of treaties through a multilateral convention would give all the new States the opportunity to participate directly in the formulation of the law if they so wished; and their participation in the work of codification appears to the Commission to be extremely desirable in order that the law of treaties may be placed upon the widest and most secure foundations".[6]

On the basis of the comments from two governments that the draft articles should be cast in the form of a code rather than a convention, the Commission in 1965 re-examined the whole question and re-iterated its earlier views in favour of a convention, and—

"recalled that at the seventeenth session of the General Assembly the Sixth Committee had stated in its report that the great majority of representatives had approved the Commission's decision to give the codification of the law of treaties the form of a convention. The Commission, moreover, felt it to be its duty to aim at achieving the maximum results from the prolonged work done by it on the codification of the law of treaties. Accordingly, it reaffirmed its decision of 1961 to prepare draft articles 'intended to serve as the basis for a convention'".[7]

A related problem which has troubled the Commission since it submitted its 1959 report concerns the question whether the draft articles should ultimately be in the form of "a code of a general character"[8] or as a series of international conventions. Towards the end of its work on the law of treaties in 1965, the Commission "concluded that the legal rules set out in the different parts are so far inter-related that it is desirable that they should be codified in a single convention. It considered that, while certain topics on the law of treaties may be sus-

---

6. *Yearbook of the International Law Commission* 1962, Vol. II, p. 160, para. 17.

7. *Official Records* of the General Assembly, Twentieth Session, Supplement No. 9 (A/6009), Chap. II, para. 16.

8. *Reports of the International Law Commission* 1966, para. 14.

ceptible of being dealt with separately, the proper co-ordination of the rules governing the several topics is likely to be achieved only by incorporating them in a single, closely integrated set of articles. Accordingly, it decided that in the course of their revision the draft articles should be re-arranged in the form of a single convention".[9] It was accordingly in the form of one single draft convention that the final 75 draft articles were presented to the General Assembly[10] and considered by the Vienna Conference on the Law of Treaties in 1968 and 1969.

There can be no doubt that the Vienna Convention on the Law of Treaties is a landmark in the whole history of modern international law.[11] The Commission's draft articles, which have emerged with only a few changes, can rightly be claimed as constituting both codification and progressive development of international law in terms of Article 15 of the Statute of the Commission, which provides—

"In the following articles the expression 'progressive development of international law' is used for convenience as meaning the preparation of draft conventions on subjects which have not yet been regulated by international law or in regard to which the law has not yet been sufficiently developed in the practice of States. Similarly, the expression 'codification of international law' is used for convenience as meaning the more precise formulation and systematisation of rules of international law in fields where there already has been extensive State practice, precedent and doctrine".

In the Vienna Convention on the Law of Treaties, as in the Commission's previous draft conventions, it is not possible to separate the several provisions into one or the other categories, but a careful study will soon reveal which contains elements of "progressive development" and which "codification".[12] It is, however, in Part V of the Convention

---

9. *Official Records* of the General Assembly, Twentieth Session, Supplement No. 9 (A/6009), Chap. II, p. 18.

10. *Report of the International Law Commission* 1966, para. 27.

11. See, e.g., W. Friedmann's "The United Nations and the Development of International Law", in *International Journal*, Vol. XXV, No. 2, Spring 1970, pp. 272-286, at p. 275.

12. *Report of the International Law Commission* 1966, para. 35. See also *Yearbook of International Law* 1956, Vol. II, pp. 255-256, paras. 25-26, and 1961, Vol. II, p. 91, para. 32.

on invalidity, termination and suspension of the operation of treaties
that the elements of progressive development in treaty law will be
found to be most marked. This is because the issues dealt with in
Part V are of such crucial importance to the stability of treaties and the
assurance of confidence in contemporary inter-State relations that the
Commission felt the need to reassess certain traditional practices and
assumptions in the light of present-day values and realities. If we accept
that the Vienna Convention on the Law of Treaties has to "grapple with
the fundamentals of constructing a world legal order",[13] the reforming
character of the provisions in this Part of the Convention is obvious,
especially from the point of view of the new States.

The various grounds of invalidity of a treaty have had to be
enumerated by the Commission with reasonable fullness, even though
certain of them will scarcely arise for consideration in practice or may
elude precise definition. The "treaty on treaties" must be logically
complete, leaving no gaps for the free play of the continued application
of certain inadmissible practices hitherto sanctioned by customary
international law. It is not sufficient that such practices are rare today
or that evidence of them in the past has sometimes been oblique. It is
necessary to emphasise at the outset that, although Part V of the Vienna
Convention on the Law of Treaties also deals with questions of termination and suspension of the operation of a treaty, it is only with
invalidity that the present series of lectures is concerned. The grounds
of invalidity covered in the Convention are the effect of a limitation of
internal law upon the competence of a State to conclude treaties, restrictions on the authority of a State's representative to express its
consent to be bound by a treaty, essential error in a treaty, inducement
of a State to conclude a treaty by the fraudulent conduct of another
State, corruption of a State's representative in expressing that State's
consent to be bound by a treaty, coercion of a State's representative to
express that State's consent to be bound by a treaty, coercion of a
State to conclude a treaty by the threat or use of force, and treaties that
conflict with a peremptory norm of general international law *(jus
cogens)*.

Before we go into these specific grounds of invalidity, however,
there are some problems of a preliminary but important nature which
are common to the three issues of invalidity, termination and sus-

---

13. R. D. Kearney and R. E. Dalton's "The Treaty on Treaties", in *AJIL,*
Vol. 64, No. 3, July 1970, p. 495.

The Validity of Treaties 345

pension of the operation of a treaty that must be examined, even if only briefly, in order to get our perspective right. The first of these preliminary problems is to warn that any impeachment of the validity of a treaty, its termination, denunciation, suspension of its operation or a party's withdrawal from it must be strictly in accordance with the provisions set out in the Convention.[14]

As the Commission itself emphasised:

> "The substantive provisions of the present part of the draft articles concern a series of grounds upon which the question of the invalidity or termination of a treaty or of the withdrawal of a party from a treaty or the suspension of its operation may be raised. The Commission accordingly considered it desirable, as a safeguard for the stability of treaties, to underline in a general provision at the beginning of this part that the validity and continuance in force of a treaty is the normal state of things which may be set aside only on the grounds and under the conditions provided for in the present article".[15]

It must also be noted that the provisions of Part V of the Convention regarding the various grounds of invalidity do not affect any other obligations placed upon a party under general principles of international law, that is, apart from any particular treaty obligations.[16]

Until fairly recently, treaty provisions were considered separable almost only where there had been a breach by one party which gave the other a right to terminate it. But, in the light of certain observations in certain cases such as the *Free Zones Case*[17] and the *S.S. Wimbledon Case*,[18] which really related to the interpretation of self-contained parts of treaties, some jurists have suggested that separability should be possible in cases of invalidity or when determining the effect of war on treaties so long as the balance of interests and obligations of the parties

---

14. Article 42 of the Vienna Convention.

15. *ILC 1966 Report*, p. 66 (para. 1).

16. Article 43: The invalidity, termination or denunciation of a treaty, the withdrawal of a party from it, or the suspension of its operation, as a result of the application of the present Convention or of the provisions of the treaty, shall not in any way impair the duty of any State to fulfil any obligation embodied in the treaty to which it would be subject under international law independently of the treaty.

17. *Series A/B, No. 46*, p. 140.

18. *Series A, No. 1*, p. 24.

under the treaty remains undisturbed. This view has since been re-inforced by individual opinions of some judges in the *Norwegian Loans Case*[19] and the *Interhandel Case*[20] in both of which the invalidity of a reservation was raised and the principle of separability of treaty pro-visions was held to be applicable to a case in which the nullity of a unilateral declaration under the Optional Clause had been alleged. It seems odd that a treaty should be invalidated, terminated or have its operation suspended in its entirety simply because the alleged ground of invalidity relates only to an unimportant provision in it. It should sometimes be possible to strike out such provisions without altering the basis on which the parties gave their orginal consent to the treaty. If the treaty itself contains provisions for the exercise of a right to terminate, denounce or suspend parts only of the treaty, then the definitive conditions must be stated; otherwise, it will be presumed that the right for which provision is made in the treaty may be exer-cised only in respect of the treaty as a whole unless the treaty other-wise provides or the parties otherwise agree.[21] Also, only the clauses affected by an alleged ground of invalidity, termination or suspension, if distinct and separable and not an essential basis of the treaty, may be eliminated, the remainder being kept in force.[22] A distinction is, however, made in cases of fraud and corruption. Only the State which was the victim of the fraud or corruption can invoke the ground of invalidity, and then it has the option either to nullify the treaty in its entirety or only the clauses involving the alleged fraud or corruption.[23]

---

19. *ICJ Reports 1957*, at pp. 55-59.

20. *ICJ Reports 1959*, at pp. 57, 77-78, and 116-117.

21. Article 44 provides: "1. A right of a party, provided for in a treaty or arising under Article 56, to denounce, withdraw from or suspend the operation of the treaty may be exercised only with respect to the whole treaty unless the treaty otherwise provides or the parties otherwise agree.

2. A ground for invalidating, terminating, withdrawing from or suspending the operation of a treaty recognised in the present Convention may be invoked only with respect to the whole treaty execept as provided in the following paragraphs or in Article 60 (i.e., termination or suspension of the operation of a treaty in consequence of its breach)".

22. Article 44 (3): "If the ground relates solely to particular clauses, it may be invoked only with respect to these clauses where:

(*a*) the said clauses are separable from the remainder of the treaty with regard to their application;

(*b*) it appears from the treaty or is otherwise established that acceptance of those clauses was not an essential basis of the consent of the other party or parties to be bound by the treaty as a whole; and

(*c*) continued performance of the remainder of the treaty would not be unjust."

23. Article 44, para. 4.

The Validity of Treaties 347

In the case of coercion, whether exerted on the State or its representative, the treaty is absolutely void,[24] since it is only in this way that it would "be possible to ensure that the coerced State, when deciding upon its future treaty relations with the State which had coerced it, would be able to do so in a position of full freedom from the coercion".[25] Similarly, the principle of separability does not apply to a treaty which conflicts with a rule of *jus cogens*.[26] The Commission was of the opinion that "rules of *jus cogens* are of so fundamental a character that, when parties conclude a treaty which conflicts in any of its clauses with an already existing rule of *jus cogens,* the treaty must be considered totally invalid".[26] If it is only particular clauses that are affected, separability is permitted provided that it is feasible and equitable and the continued performance of the remainder of the treaty would not be unjust in the circumstances of the case.

Finally, a party to a treaty may lose the right to invoke a ground for invalidating, terminating, withdrawing from or suspending the operation of a treaty if, on becoming aware of the facts, it expressly agrees that the treaty is valid or remains in force or continues in operation or if the party must necessarily be deemed to have acquiesced by its conduct.[27]

It is generally agreed that international law functions on the basis of good faith and fair dealing, and this is sometimes expressed by the maxim *allegans contraria non audiendus est.* In the recent cases of *The Arbitral Award made by the King of Spain*[28] and *The Temple of Preah Vihear,*[29] the principle was expressly affirmed.[30] It cannot be denied that the various grounds of invalidity, termination or suspension are open to abuse. Thus, after a party to a treaty has become aware of, e.g., a breach by the other party, a fundamental error in the conclusion of a treaty, lack of competence or excess of authority on the part of the other's representative, it may nevertheless treat the treaty as still in force until an occasion arises later which might make it convenient for that party to want to resile from its obligations under the treaty. In such cases, the principle should apply to limit the occasions or the

---

24. Article 44, para. 5:
25. *ILC 1966 Report,* p. 68.
26. Article 44, para. 5.
27. Article 45.
28. *ICJ Reports 1960,* pp. 213-214.
29. *ICJ Reports 1962,* pp. 23-32.
30. At pp. 39-51 by Judge Alfaro and at pp. 62-65 by Judge Fitzmaurice in *The Temple of Preah Vihear, ICJ Reports 1962.*

circumstances of claims that can validly be made by the party desiring to invalidate, terminate or suspend the operation of a treaty. And although the two cases just cited support the view that the principle of good faith and fair dealing is of general application in international law, it is of particular importance in the law of treaties. No State that has expressly acknowledged the continuance in force of a treaty after becoming aware of any of the grounds of invalidity, termination, withdrawal from or suspension of the operation of the treaty, should be allowed to invoke it at a later date. Equally, a State must be precluded from subsequently invoking any ground of which it has become aware but in which it has acquiesced. This would amount to what in certain legal systems is called estoppel by conduct. The Commission, in its commentary, has given the following reason for avoiding the use of this term:

> "The Commission noted that in municipal systems of law this principle has its own particular manifestations reflecting technical features of the particular system. It felt that these technical features of the principle in municipal law might not necessarily be appropriate for the application of the principle in international law. For this reason, it preferred to avoid the use of such municipal law terms as 'estoppel'".

It is clear that the principle, however phrased, is based upon good faith and that, as such, it will not operate against a State that has not been aware of all the facts of the case or that was not in a position at the relevant time freely to raise the question of nullity, termination, or suspension of the operation of a treaty. Accordingly, coercion of a State or of its representative must make the resulting treaty absolutely void. The position is the same in all cases of *jus cogens*. It is to be noted that the principle does not apply if the treaty itself specifically provides for termination or if the parties agree to its termination.

Given the seven grounds of invalidity and the antecedent conditions outlined in the preceding paragraphs, the problems of general acceptability remain. In view of the relatively novel or imprecise character of some of the grounds of invalidity, such as fraud, corruption and *jus cogens,* almost all the Western European States and some non-Western ones expressed themselves forcefully against their inclusion in the Convention unless adequate procedural machinery was at the same time provided for the settlement of any dispute that might arise about the

The Validity of Treaties 349

interpretation or the application of the various invalidating criteria. Not a few of these delegations said quite firmly that, without a satisfactory procedure of adjudication, their governments would neither sign nor accede to any convention that the conference might ultimately adopt.[31] The newer States of Africa, Asia and many Latin American ones as well as the East European group of States would, however, have preferred the International Law Commission text which did little more than to incorporate the provisions of Article 33 of the United Nations Charter on the various modes of peaceful settlement of disputes. The compromise that was reached in the end is contained in Articles 65 and 66 of the Convention. It is only when a *jus cogens* is invoked to invalidate a treaty that the compulsory jurisdiction of the International Court of Justice may be resorted to. In all other cases, arbitration and conciliation are the procedures provided for, as the parties may agree in particular cases.

It should be emphasised, once again, that the present study is concerned only with the problems of invalidity of treaties, not of termination, suspension, denunciation of or withdrawal from, treaties. It is only for the sake of clarity that the general provisions relating to all have been disposed of together in these introductory remarks. The remainder of our study will concentrate on the various grounds of invalidity of treaties and the problems raised by these.

---

31. *Official Records* of the United Nations Conference on the Law of Treaties, First Session, 1968, pp. 472-473; also *AJIL*, Vol. 64, 1970, at p. 551.

350

CHAPTER I

CONSTITUTIONAL LIMITATIONS UPON TREATY-MAKING POWER

Article 46 of the Vienna Convention provides:

"1. A State may not invoke the fact that its consent to be bound by a treaty has been expressed in violation of a provision of its internal law regarding competence to conclude treaties as invalidating its consent unless that violation was manifest and concerned a rule of its internal law of fundamental importance. 2. A violation is manifest if it would be objectively evident to any State conducting itself in the matter in accordance with normal practice and in good faith".

The problem raised by this article relates to the extent to which a State may by its internal law impose constitutional limitations that would affect the validity under international law of a consent to a treaty given by a State agent having ostensible authority to give it. Now, international law does not impose upon a State possessing treaty-making capacity any restriction on the exercise of that power apart from the requirement that every member of the international community should do nothing which might hamper it from fulfilling its international obligations. As Hyde has put it:

"In making such decisions and in taking such action a State finds itself unhampered by any requirement of international law other than by that which obliges each member of the international society not to render itself impotent to respond as it should to the duties which its owes to the other members thereof".[1]

But States act through the instrumentality of agents. All States having capacity to make treaties must provide in one form or another for the designation of the organ or organs and a definition of the limits of their powers in expressing the State's consent to be bound by a treaty.

---

1. C. C. Hyde, *International Law*, Vol. 2, p. 1383.

The Validity of Treaties 351

There are various ways in which States make such provisions, but three main ones may be noted here. A State may by its internal law provide that its treaties shall have no effect internally until they have sub-sequently received Parliamentary approval or ratification. A State may make such legislative approval or confirmation a condition precedent to the conclusion of any treaty, thus precluding its executive from entering into treaties or into particular kinds of treaties on its own initiative. Yet a third variation is that certain fundamental provisions are entrenched in the constitution requiring stated majorities and pro-cedures before they can be altered, thus restricting the executive in the exercise of its power to enter into treaties.[2]

We must, however, distinguish between the invalidity of a treaty concluded by a State in its external relations and the incapacity to implement it under its internal law after its conclusion. To quote Hyde again:

> "So it happens that as a matter of fact, the self-imposed restrictions which some States have been disposed to establish through the instrumentality of written constitutions do not serve to interfere with, or necessarily retard the performance of international obli-gations; constitutional checks upon treaty making thus prove to be mere manifestations of an endeavour by the individual State to choose the pattern of its governmental life in the international community and to regard the making of its choice as a domestic matter".[3]

In this connection, it is pertinent to refer to this passage in the Advisory Opinion of the Permanent Court of International Justice in the *Treatment of Polish Nationals in Danzig*:[4]

> "It should, however, be observed that, while on the one hand, according to generally accepted principles, a State cannot rely, as against another State, on the provisions of the latter's Constitution, but only on international law and international obligations duly

---

2. Cf. the practice in the United Kingdom and most of the Commonwealth countries of not requiring Parliamentary approval of most treaties entered into by the executive—McNair, *Law of Treaties*, 1960, OUP, p. 69. There are, of course, certain exceptions, e.g., treaties involving changes in municipal law or the imposition of financial obligations (*ibid.*, pp. 83-94).

3. *Op. cit.*, pp. 1383-1384.

4. (1932) *Series A/B, No. 44*, at p. 24.

accepted, on the other hand and conversely, a State cannot adduce
as against another State its Constitution with a view to evading
obligations incumbent upon it under international law or treaties
in force".

This analysis brings into focus the doctrinal controversy between the
monist and the dualist schools of thought in international jurisprudence.
According to the monists, municipal law and public international law
are one, so that the one is a part of the other in a unified legal order.
International law is part of the municipal law of each State without any
Parliamentary intervention. In the sphere of treaty law, the unitary
character of both systems lies in the fact that the conclusion of a treaty
by a State organ in excess of its authority or not in accordance with the
procedures prescribed by internal law renders such a treaty void not
only in municipal law but also, *ipso facto,* in international law. The
consent of a State representative to a treaty given on the international
plane in disregard of a constitutional limitation is a nullity[5] since,
according to this view, the internal laws of the State which limit the
power of its agents to enter into treaties must be regarded as part of
international law. The trouble with the monistic school is that its
approach lays an intolerable burden upon other States to satisfy themselves in every case that the constitutional limitations of a State with
which they desire to enter into a treaty are not breached; they can no
longer rely on the apparent or ostensible authority of State agents as a
normal incident in diplomatic intercourse between States. The International Law Commission once adopted this view in Article 2 of its
draft in these words:

> "A treaty becomes binding in relation to a State by signature,
> ratification, accession or any other means of expressing the will
> of the State, in accordance with its constitutional law and practice
> through an organ competent for that purpose".[6]

---

5. See, in this connection, Article 21 of the Harvard Draft Convention on The
Law of Treaties: "A State is not bound by a treaty made on its behalf by an organ
or authority not competent under its law to conclude the treaty; however, a State
may be responsible for an injury resulting to another State from reasonable
reliance by the latter upon a representation that such organ or authority was
competent to conclude the treaty". (*AJIL,* Vol. XXIX, Supplement, October
1935, p. 661.)

6. *Yearbook of the International Law Commission*, 1951, Vol. II, p. 73. Cf.
Lauterpacht's draft Article 11 (para. 1): "A treaty is voidable, at the option of

The Validity of Treaties 353

A number of the Commission's members frowned upon the idea that provisions of international law in the form of constitutional limitations are to be considered as incorporated into international law.

A variant of the monistic school accepts the view that constitutional limitations under internal law are incorporated into international law, but holds that if the stability of treaties is not to be undermined, only those constitutional limitations that are notorious need be taken into account by other States when entering into a treaty with the State concerned. It is only the notorious ones that other States can reasonably be expected to be aware of or be acquainted with.[7] There are clearly certain difficulties with this qualification of the strict monistic doctrine. One is how to determine which particular limitations are notorious and which are not. Who is to decide the question of notoriety—the party invoking the particular limitation as a ground of the invalidity of the treaty in question or the State that has imposed it as part and parcel of its internal law? If neither, by what objective standard is the issue to be resolved?

The advocates of this view argue that good faith requires that only notorious limitations should be regarded by international law. But it may be that the State's internal law makes no such distinction between notorious and "non-notorious" constitutional limitations in respect, for instance, of the authority of a State organ or agent to express its consent to enter into a treaty. Besides, some constitutional limitations are sometimes not clear as to whether they relate to the agent's power to conclude a treaty or to its implementation in internal law. Even where some limitations appear to be straightforward and unambiguous on the face of them, they may bear such subjective connotations or interpretations as would cast doubt on their supposedly notorious character. The constitution of a State may say one thing, while "conventions" or practices may follow a different or modified procedure. For these and other reasons, this view about notorious constitutional limitations in internal law being capable of incorporation into international law is, on balance, untenable.

---

the party concerned if it has been entered into in disregard of the limitations of its constitutional law and practice". (First Report to ILC.)

7. See, e.g., Lord McNair's *The Law of Treaties*, 1960, OUP, p. 60: "...a treaty which purports to be concluded on behalf of a State and which is made by an organ lacking the necessary power to bind that State, or by a procedure that fails to observe the constitutional requirements of that State, is, subject to certain qualifications to be studied later, not binding on that State".

We now turn to the dualist school which, in strict theory, regards municipal law and public international law as two separate systems of law each functioning within its own sphere. According to this view, international law concerns itself only with the external relations of States, leaving it entirely to each State to order its own internal affairs, including the allocation of functions among its various organs and agents as well as the limitations on the exercise of those functions. The conditions and procedures subject to which States enter into treaties at the international level and also the conditions for the recognition of the several classes of State agents as competent to express the consent of their States to be bound by treaties are matters for international law. If, therefore, an agent who is regarded as competent under international law to express the consent of a State to be bound by a treaty does so in accordance with the proper procedures, the State so committed is regarded as bound by the treaty, whatever may be that State's internal legal requirements. The effect of a failure to observe any constitutional limitations in such a case may be to render invalid that treaty under its municipal law;[8] it may even entail the application of internal sanctions against the erring State agent. It does not, however, affect the validity of the treaty in question under international law, so long as it is clear that the agent acted in the course of his employment, that is, within the scope of his authority as such agent.

In order to avoid the obvious consequences of the application of this doctrine, a qualification has been introduced by some jurists to the effect that a State which is aware of the other State's agent's failure to comply with internal law, or which is deemed to have been aware of the agent's manifest lack of competence to commit its State, should not be able to claim the validity of the resulting treaty. Since the underlying assumption is that the maxim *omnia praesumuntur acta rite sunt* applies in international transactions, good faith demands that States should not take advantage of a situation when they know or ought to be aware of the agent's lack of competence to express the consent of its State to be bound by a treaty.

Although there has not been much direct judicial precedent on the relevance of constitutional provisions to the validity of treaties under

---

8. Hans Blix, in his *Treaty-Making Power*, 1960, p. 303, has found that the constitutions of most States have not gone so far as to say what consequences of the violation of a restriction in internal law would be on the international level, because the ostensibly competent organs were normally clothed with the necessary authority to commit their States.

The Validity of Treaties 355

international law, nevertheless a number of *dicta* in certain decided cases[9] would seem to support the view that if a State agent, who is competent under international law to commit the State, expresses that State's consent to a treaty through a proper procedure, the State is bound by the treaty unless the other party is in fact aware of any disregard of internal law or there is a manifest lack of constitutional authority on the agent's part. The agent must, of course, have acted within the scope of its ostensible authority. The two leading cases often cited in support are, however, the *East Greenland Case*[10] and the *Free Zones Case*.[11] In the one case Mr. Ihlen, the Norwegian Foreign Minister, while in the other an Agent in the proceedings in question were held entitled to make declarations to other States which were binding upon their respective States, and it is clear that international law will not concern itself with any question of constitutional limitations in the internal law of States. The International Law Commission observed:

> "State practice furnishes examples of claims that treaties were invalid on constitutional grounds, but in none of them was that claim admitted by the other party to the dispute. Moreover, in three instances—the admission of Luxembourg to the League, the Politis incident and the membership of Argentina—the League of Nations seems to have acted upon the principle that a consent given on the international plane by an ostensibly competent State agent is not invalidated by the subsequent disclosure that the agent lacked constitutional authority to commit his State".[12]

It will be agreed on all hands that, in diplomatic intercourse, State agents have not made it their practice to go beyond the report of Credentials Committees attesting the authority of delegates to international conferences and sessions, in order to investigate whether there are constitutional limitations imposed upon such delegates by rules of their State's internal laws with respect to signing treaties or depositing instruments of ratification, acceptance and the like. The alternative would be chaos, as States might look upon any attempt by

---

9. E.g., *The Cleveland Award* (1888) and *George Pinson's Case* (1928), cited in footnotes to para. 6, on p. 70 of *1966 ILC Report*.

10. *PCIJ, Series A/B, No. 53*, pp. 56-71, 91.

11. *PCIJ, Series A/B, No. 46*, p. 170.

12. *1966 ILC Report*, para. 7, p. 70.

their partners to a treaty to probe into their municipal arrangements as an unwarranted interference with their domestic affairs.

States have a number of procedures by which they can protect their interests against the possibility that a State agent might sometimes lack the necessary constitutional authority to express the consent of his State to a treaty. States have on occasions agreed to signature *ad referendum,* and there are the procedures of ratification, acceptance, approval and accession—all designed to give States sufficient time not only to ponder on the treaty provisions and their implications, but also to examine questions of domestic law likely to affect the validity of the treaty.

Every State having treaty-making capacity which duly authorises its agent to express consent to enter into a treaty does so at its own peril if, through no fault of the other States parties to it, it should turn out that there has been a failure to comply with its internal law in that regard. It is the responsibility of a State to ensure the regularity of its internal affairs, including the fact that States dealing with anyone held out by it as having ostensible authority are entitled reasonably to assume the latter's constitutional competence.

If a State, after entering into a treaty, should discover that it is faced with certain constitutional difficulties, the proper thing to do is not to seek to get out of these by a unilateral invocation of the invalidity of the treaty on the ground of constitutional limitations, but promptly to notify the other States parties about the real nature of the problem and seek to obtain its revision or amendment if the particular difficulties cannot be got rid of by its own internal legislative or executive action.[13] Good faith requires that this be done in preference to a resort to a claim of invalidity on the ground of limitations of internal law.

The International Law Commission, at its Fifteenth Session, gave further thought to the matter. While some of its members took the line that the agent's lack of authority under internal law to give the consent of his State to a treaty should render the treaty invalid under international law, "the majority, however, considered that the complexity and uncertain application of provisions of internal law regarding the conclusion of treaties creates too large a risk to the security of trea-

---

13. Cf. M. O. Hudson's *International Tribunals,* 1944, at p. 130: "In the *Eastern Greenland Case,* the Court having held that a Norwegian declaration of occupation of territory in Greenland was unlawful and invalid, the Norwegian Government proceeded two days later to revoke the decree impugned".

The Validity of Treaties   357

ties".[14] This preoccupation of the Commission with the maintenance of the integrity of treaties against an all too easy invocation of constitutional limitations as a ground of invalidity is worth noting as showing the Commission's genuine concern for a balanced and progressive development of international law. It accordingly "considered that the basic principle of the present article should be that non-observance of a provision of internal law regarding competence to enter into treaties does not affect the validity of a consent given in due form by a State organ or agent competent under international law to give that consent".

The question then arose as to whether this basic principle should be weakened by the admission of an exception to it. The view that prevailed, however, is that an exception should be made in a case where there has been a manifest violation of internal law regarding competence to enter into treaties, whether generally or in respect of specified types of which the treaty in question is one. This is because cases have occurred in the past when a Head of State entered into a treaty with another State in sheer disregard or contravention of the State's clear constitutional provisions. The latter State must surely know that the Head of State's want of authority to express consent to conclude the treaty is so manifest that the treaty should. be regarded as *ipso facto* invalid. Most of the governments that have commented on the Commission's draft article approved of it in the form it took as draft Article 43 as follows:

> "A State may not invoke the fact that its consent to be bound by a treaty has been expressed in violation of a provision of its internal law regarding competence to conclude treaties as invalidating its consent unless that violation of its internal law was manifest".

Two inter-related suggestions for the amendment of this Article had been made in their comments by some governments: one was to make it quite clear to whom the violation must be "manifest", and the other was to delimit the meaning of the expression "manifest violation". While regarding the first point as unnecessary, the Commission explained the second point by elaborating the purport of the article thus:

---

14. *1966 ILC Report*, para. 10, p. 71.

"The rule embodied in the article is that, when the violation of internal law regarding competence to conclude treaties would be *objectively evident to any State dealing with the matter normally and in good faith,* the consent to the treaty purported to be given on behalf of the State may be repudiated".[15]

The objective character of the criterion to be applied is sufficiently indicated in the ordinary meaning of the word "manifest", and no useful purpose would be served, in the Commission's view, by any attempt to state in advance the circumstances and the occasions when a violation of internal law is to be regarded as "manifest". The negative form in which the rule was expressed was to underline the rarity of the occasions on which constitutional limitations may be invoked as a ground of the invalidity of treaties.

During the First Session of the Vienna Conference in 1968, two significant amendments, one suggested by the Peruvian delegation and the other by the United Kingdom delegation, were accepted as improvements to the text of the article. The Peruvian amendment[16] would want it included in the rule that the rule of internal law, the violation of which would make it manifest that the State should not be bound by a treaty concluded by its agent, must be of fundamental importance was approved, although the idea is already implicit in the basic principle embodied in the Commission's draft Article. The conference saw no reason for not making explicit what is so obviously necessary to delimit the scope of this ground of invalidity more precisely, since not every violation of any rule of internal law can be regarded as bringing the principle into play. The United Kingdom amendment[17] was intended to clarify the idea of what constitutes "manifest violation", a point to which the Commission itself had devoted much anxious thought. The suggested definition was that "manifest violation" should mean, in the words of the Commission's own commentary,[18] objectively evident to any State dealing with the matter in accordance with normal practice "and in good faith". It will be noticed that this is only a slight reformulation of the italicised portion of the statement contained in the commentary, to which we have just referred above. It was thought that

---

15. *1966 ILC Report,* para. 11, p. 71. The italicising was done by the Commission.
16. UN Doc. A/Conf. 39/C.1/L228. 1968.
17. *Official Records,* First Session, at p. 246.
18. *1966 ILC Report,* para. 11, p. 70.

the notion ought to be expressed in the article itself, since that would make it clearer and more acceptable. Accordingly, the Conference voted for it.

To the other extreme was the proposal put forward by both Pakistan and Japan to exclude from the article the requirement of "manifest violation" as an element of the basic principle enunciated therein. This suggestion would have reversed the position in the conference by taking the delegates back to the extreme dualist standpoint. We need not dilate any further here on the implications of this amendment which, when put to the vote, was easily defeated. The Commission was thus confirmed in its view that claims of invalidity on the ground of constitutional limitations should be limited to cases of manifest violation of a fundamental provision of internal law.

The resulting Article 46 of the Vienna Convention on the Law of Treaties was formulated as stated at the beginning of this chapter.

Specific Internal Restrictions

An ancillary principle to that dealt with in Article 46 will be found in the Commission's draft Article 44 which provides as follows:

> "If the authority of a representative to express the consent of his State to be bound by a particular treaty has been made subject to a specific restriction, his omission to observe that restriction may not be invoked as invalidating a consent expressed by him unless the restriction was brought to the knowledge of the other negotiating States prior to his expressing such consent".[19]

Here we are dealing with the case where a State's representative has purported to do an act by which his State is bound when in fact he had no authority to do so because he omitted to observe some specific restrictions imposed upon his authority in the particular case.

If a treaty requires ratification, acceptance or approval in order to become binding upon the parties to it, any excess of authority on the part of a State's representative will automatically be dealt with when the moment arrives for its ratification, acceptance or approval. In that case, States parties to the treaty have an option either to repudiate or adopt the treaty. Where a State elects to adopt the treaty, it will be con-

---

19. See *1966 ILC Report*, p. 72.

sidered to have thereby endorsed its agent's unauthorised act.

It is important to note that the article has a limited application. It covers only cases where the agent's lack of authority relates to the execution of an act by which a State's representative purports finally to establish his State's consent to be bound. This means that the article applies where a representative, whose authority to express his State's consent to be bound by a treaty is made expressly subject to specific conditions, reservations or limitations, exceeds his authority by omitting to observe those restrictions upon his authority. But notice of any such restriction must be given to the other States parties to the particular treaty. This point was thus stressed in the Commission's commentary:[20]

> "The Commission considered that in order to safeguard the security of international transactions, the rule must be that specific instructions given by a State to its representative are only effective to limit his authority *vis-à-vis* other States, if they are made known to them in some appropriate manner before the State in question concludes the treaty".

Instances are rare in which States have sought to disavow the acts of their representatives on the ground of undisclosed restrictions upon their authority. There is a duty upon States to disclose to other parties to a treaty such restrictions upon their representatives' authority as may be relevant to the particular transaction in hand; and the representative must himself take care not to omit to observe any specific limitation upon his authority to bind his State. A representative must realize that specific restrictions on his authority will not in any way affect a consent which he has expressed unless, prior to his expressing such consent, those restrictions had been notified to the other negotiating States.

The Commission's draft Article 44 was, at the Vienna Conference, improved upon by the substitution of the words "notified to" for "brought to the knowledge of" herein, so that as Article 47 it now reads:

> "If the authority of a representative to express the consent of a State to be bound by a particular treaty has been made subject to a specific restriction, his omission to observe that restriction may

---

20. See para. 3, p. 72 of the *1966 ILC Report*.

not be invoked as invalidating the consent expressed by him unless the restriction was notified to the other negotiating States prior to his expressing such consent".

The reason for the modification is that it is often better to lay a duty to give notice upon a State imposing such restriction on its representative than to leave it to the other negotiating States to have the restriction brought to their knowledge. Is such knowledge to be actual or constructive, and how is its communication to be carried out? It is to obviate these and similar problems that notification was preferred in the context of this article.

Finally, it is necessary to observe that the restrictions referred to in the present article are not the constitutional limitations dealt with in the preceding Article 46, or there would be no need to insist on notification being given to the other negotiating States. Such restrictions, it would be reasonable to suppose, must be those provided for in executive instruments or administrative regulations of a kind not otherwise specifically provided for in constitutional documents. If it were otherwise, Article 47 would in the light of its immediate predecessor, be otiose.

362

CHAPTER II

ERROR AND FRAUD

It is proposed to discuss each of these two related topics here as separately as possible, although certain well-known writers have tended to discuss them together. Thus, Lord McNair treated the subjects together under the sub-title "Mistake, including Mistake induced by Fraud";[1] W. E. Hall remarked: "Freedom of consent does not exist where the consent is determined by erroneous impressions produced through the fraud of the other party to the contract",[2] and went on to cite the example of a forged map. Schwarzenberger appears to have made short shrift of the matter in these words:

"A party which by its fraud has induced another party to enter a treaty is estopped from invoking the treaty. . . . Where a State has not contributed to the error of the other, such error cannot affect the validity. This is the distinguishing mark between *unilateral* mistake and fraud".[3]

Some other writers like C. C. Hyde even relegated the subject of fraud to a footnote, observing that, as far as he knew at that time, there had been no recorded instance where fraud has been invoked to vitiate consent to be bound by a treaty on the part of either the United States or another party "on account of wilful misrepresentation on the part of itself or of any other party".[4] But a few like C. W. Jenks have treated the topics of mistake and fraud as two independent grounds of invalidity of treaties under certain conditions.[5]

The International Law Commission was, therefore, right to have

---

1. *Law of Treaties,* p. 211, OUP, 1961.
2. *Treatise on International Law,* p. 342, 4th ed., OUP, 1895.
3. *A Manual of International Law,* 5th ed., 1967, pp. 158-159.
4. *International Law,* Vol. II, 1951, 2nd Revised ed., Boston, part of footnote 4 on p. 1382. Hyde cited 29 Harvard Draft to the effect that a tribunal may declare a treaty as not binding but grant the complainant the privilege of provisional suspension subject to specified conditions. The author also noted that fraud is dealt with in Article 3 of Harvard Draft Convention on the Law of Treaties: id., 663, and the Comment thereon, id., 1144.
5. *The Prospects of International Adjudication,* Stevens, London, p. 196.

considered error and fraud in separate draft Articles 45 and 46 in its Report on its Eighteenth Session in 1966,[6] while the United Nations Conference on The Law of Treaties saw no reason to adopt either a different approach or even a different formulation for both draft Articles which now appear respectively as Articles 48 and 49 of the Vienna Convention. We will accordingly deal with each separately.

Error

The first problem is one of terminology, involving mainly a choice between the English word "mistake" and the Latin word "error", although both carry almost the same connotation. Indeed, they are so synonymous that they are used interchangeably; but English-speaking writers would seem on the whole to prefer "mistake", while the non-English-speaking normally use "error". The Commission wisely adopted "error" as the more general, less imprecise word to denote the use and nuances of the legal concept.

The incidence of error as a vitiating element in the conclusion of a treaty has been as infrequent as it has been indirect in the jurisprudence of international courts and tribunals.[7] There are one or two reasons for this. The first is that the kinds of error with which national legal systems have to deal are quite different from those that usually occur in disputes under international law; for example, almost all the known cases so far have involved geographical errors, especially about maps. The second reason is that the established processes by which treaties are negotiated and concluded in the practice of States have been and are such as to eliminate as far as possible most of the pitfalls into which negotiating parties tend to fall in private law contracts. If, despite all precautions, errors have very occasionally occurred in the past, States parties to a treaty might have overcome them either by re-negotiating a fresh one or by agreeing to treat the error as relating only to the interpretation rather than the validity of the treaty.[8]

The International Law Commission itself mentioned three leading cases as supplying certain important *dicta* with reference to the problem

---

6. At pp. 72-74.

7. See, e.g., McNair, *op. cit.,* p. 211: "It is, however, not easy to find much direct arbitral or judicial authority on the matter".

8. C. C. Hyde, *op. cit.,* p. 1382 (text) also refers to maps showing boundaries being an error common to both sides as not having the effect of invalidating the treaty, but that in interpreting it regard must be had to material circumstances subsequently discovered after the conclusion of the treaty concerned.

of error in treaties. In the first of these, the *Legal Status of Eastern Greenland*,[9] the Foreign Minister of Norway, Mr. Ihlen, had in answer to a specific question put to him by the Danish Minister made a declaration regarding the extent of Danish sovereignty over Greenland which turned out to be mistaken and which was claimed as not having been authorised by the Norwegian Government. The Permanent Court of International Justice took the view that there was no relevant question of error raised in the case, as Mr. Ihlen's statement was couched in definitive and categorical terms. It was this important *dictum* of Judge Anzilotti that contained a useful clarification on the issue of error:

> "But even accepting, for a moment, the supposition that Mr. Ihlen was mistaken as to the results which might ensue from an extension of Danish sovereignty, it must be admitted that this mistake was not such as to entail the nullity of the agreement. If a mistake is pleaded it must be of an excusable character; and one can scarcely believe that a Government could be ignorant of the legitimate consequences following upon an extension of sovereignty . . .".[10]

This clearly indicates the circumstances in which error does not invalidate consent, namely, that a plea of error, in order to be successful, must go to the root of the matter. The observation does not help us in determining when error will vitiate consent. Similarly, in the second case, the *Temple of Preah Vihear*,[11] we get but little guidance on the subject. The issue in controversy concerned the delimitation of a particular boundary along the line of a water shed, as to which the parties were agreed in the original treaty; there was no question of any error about it. The trouble arose, however, when the agreed boundary came later to be shown on a map. During the earlier stage of the case, the International Court of Justice observed:

> "Any error of this kind would evidently have been an error of law, but in any event, the Court does not consider that the issue in the present case is really one of error. Furthermore, the principal

---

9. (1933) *PCIJ, Series A/B, No. 53*, p. 71.
10. *Ibid.*, p. 92.
11. *ICJ Reports 1961*, p. 30.

juridical relevance of error, where it exists, is that it may affect the reality of the consent supposed to have been given".[12]

In the course of its judgment in the subsequent stage of the case with reference to the geographical error, the Court pointed out:

"It is an established rule of law that the plea of error cannot be allowed as an element vitiating consent, if the party advancing it contributed by its own conduct to the error, or could have avoided it, or if the circumstances were such as to put that party on notice of a possible error".[13]

The importance of this cogent statement of principle of international law concerning the effect of error will be seen when we come to consider the eventual formulation of the rule as adopted by the International Law Commission in 1966.

If these two cases could not have been more forthcoming on the question of invalidity arising from error, the third case cited by the Commission[14] gave some guidelines, although the problem there was one relating to the grant of concessions and not a treaty. In the *Readaptation of the Mavrommatis Jerusalem Concessions,*[15] it was decided that only an error relating to an essential element of a State's consent to a treaty can be invoked to vitiate that State's consent.

If the matter does not constitute a condition upon which the agreement or treaty was based, it will not be regarded as sufficient to vitiate the consent. Thus, Hyde, quoting Professor Garner's comment[16] as Reporter on Article 29 of the Harvard Law Research Institute draft, wrote:

---

12. Here, the ICJ would seem to be saying much the same thing as Lord Atkin had said in the leading English case of *Bell* v. *Lever Brothers Ltd.* (1932) A.C. 161, at p. 217: "If mistake operates at all, it operates so as to negative or in some cases to nullify consent".

13. *ICJ Reports 1962,* p. 26.

14. *Report of the International Law Commission,* 1966, pp. 72-73.

15. *PCIJ, Series A, No. 11.* Also in the *Mavrommatis Palestine Concessions (Merits) Case (Series C, No. 7, ii,* p. 212), M. Mavrommatis was described as an Ottoman subject when he was not and Britain also claimed that he obtained the concessions in that capacity. The Court noted that the identity of the person had never been in doubt and concluded that the reference to M. Mavrommatis as an Ottoman subject in the agreements concerning the Jerusalem concessions, is not intended to represent a condition on which the grant of the concession is dependent ... *(Series A, No. 5,* pp. 30-31).

16. *Op. cit.,* p. 1382. and *AJIL.* XXIX. Supplement, Oct. 1935, p. 1129.

366   *T. O. Elias*

"If a treaty was based upon material error and created obligations
for a party which it clearly would not have assumed if the real
facts had been known to it before ratification, such party is not
bound by the treaty".

This leads us to the consideration of certain distinctions between
types of error which some municipal legal systems make. Anglo-
American legal systems, for example, distinguish between *unilateral* and
mutual mistakes, while some English writers [17] make the further distinction between *mutual* and *common* mistakes. Schwarzenberger probably best illustrates this approach as applied to international law when
he writes:

"In the case of *mutual* mistake, where parties are mistaken about
each other's intention so that there is disagreement as to the object
of their consent—as, for instance, the identity of two places with
the same name—it depends on the circumstances of each case
whether the treaty must, in good faith, be treated as void.
    Where there has been a *common* mistake on an essential of the
treaty, for instance, by concluding an agreement for the cession
of an island which at the time of the conclusion of the treaty, but
unknown to both parties, had already ceased to exist, this amounts
to dissent, and the treaty is void. On the other hand, parties may
agree on the identity of an object which, unfortunately they mis-
described in the treaty. In such a case, the common mistake can
be ignored: *falsa demonstratio non nocet*".[18]

From this analysis Schwarzenberger deduces that, since municipal law
is only a question of fact to be proved before international tribunals, a
mistake as to the law is one of fact: "If, on the international level,
municipal law is considered merely as a legally relevant set of facts,
a mistake regarding municipal law is probably as relevant as any other
mistake of fact".[19] It follows from this that a mistake as to international
law is irrelevant, and the treaty in which it occurs is valid.

---

17. E.g., Cheshire and Fifoot's *Law of Contract*, 1st ed., pp. 137-158, which
Sir Gerald Fitzmaurice cited in his Third Report—see *ILC Yearbook 1958*, p
27, at p. 37.
18. *A Manual of International Law*, 5th ed., 1967, pp. 158-159.
19. *Op. cit.*, p. 159.

The Validity of Treaties 367

In this connection it is interesting to recall that even Sir Humphrey Waldock in his Second Report made a distinction between mutual and unilateral mistakes, no doubt thereby following the example of one of his predecessors as Rapporteur, Sir Gerald Fitzmaurice. But such was the opposition from the civil lawyers and others in the Commission to any such distinction that it had to be abandoned altogether.[20] The draft Article 45 as finally formulated by the Commission and as eventually adopted by the Vienna Conference without any alteration as Article 48 is as follows:

> "1. A State may invoke an error in a treaty as invalidating its consent to be bound by the treaty if the error relates to a fact or situation which was assumed by that State to exist at the time when the treaty was concluded and formed an essential basis of its consent to be bound by the treaty.
>
> 2. Paragraph 1 shall not apply if the State in question contributed by its own conduct to the error, or if the circumstances were such as to put that State on notice of a possible error.
>
> 3. An error relating only to the wording of the text of a treaty does not affect its validity; Article 79 then applies".

The principles enunciated in this article may be thus summarised. There is no distinction between unilateral and mutual mistake, at least for the purposes of international law, whatever may be the position under particular legal systems. It does not matter whether the error is made by only one party, or by both or all parties, so long as the error relates to a fact or situation assumed by the party invoking it as in existence at the time of the conclusion of the treaty. The error must constitute an essential basis of the consent of that party to be bound by the treaty. If it is shown or if the circumstances were such as to put it on notice of a possible error, that party is precluded[21] from invoking such an error as a ground of the invalidity of the treaty in question.[22]

---

20. See *1963 ILC Yearbook*, Vol. I, 43-45 (para. 60), UN Doc. A/C.N.4/ Sec. A/1963.

21. Sir Gerald Fitzmaurice observed in the *Temple of Preah Vihear Case*, *ICJ Reports 1962*, at p. 62, that the concept of preclusion is "the nearest equivalent in the field of international law to the common-law's rule of estoppel, though perhaps not applied under such strict limiting conditions (and it is certainly applied as a rule of substance and not merely as one of evidence or procedure)".

22. The United States representative sought to stress this rule of preclusion

A close look at paragraph 2 will disclose that, while the exceptions have been based on those given by the Court itself in the *Temple of Preah Vihear Case,* the Commission deliberately limited the ambit of the Court's statement of the principle by omitting in particular the words "or could have avoided it", if it were to be made applicable to cases other than those dealt with in the instant case. We may also note in passing that the article does not speak of errors of law or of fact, a distinction that has already proved intractable in domestic law. Instead, the article refers simply to errors relating to a "fact" or "situation", and so avoid introducing the idea that an error of law may ever be invoked as a ground of invalidity. There is no doubt that a treaty may in practice involve mixed questions of law and fact, and that it may not always be easy to distinguish between the two.[23]

Again, if we compare the text of this article with that of the Harvard Law Institute Draft Article 29 *(a),* there will be found a number of similar provisions. That article reads:

> "A treaty entered into upon an assumption as to the existence of a state of facts, the assumed existence of which was envisaged by the parties as a determining factor moving them to undertake the obligations stipulated, may be declared by a competent international tribunal or authority not to be binding on the parties, when it is discovered that the state of facts did not exist at the time the treaty was entered into".[24]

While the general intendment seems to be essentially similar, the Harvard draft differs in *(a)* providing for adjudication by a tribunal, and *(b)* being limited to *mutual* mistake, an Anglo-American predilection to which reference has been made earlier in the present chapter.[25]

It remains to note the provisions of Article 48, paragraph 3, which are two-fold: the sub-paragraph makes it clear that the Article as a

---

where the State's own conduct contributed to the error by adding the clause "or could have avoided it by the exercise of reasonable diligence", but the proposed amendment was rejected on the ground that the idea was already implicit in the Commission's draft. See *Official Records,* First Session, pp. 250-254 (1968).

23. E.g., in the *Orinoco Steamship Company* Case (see J. B. Scott's *The Hague Court Reports,* 1916, pp. 226-239), where there arose mixed questions of law and fact, the tribunal had to determine the matter in accordance with justice and equity" (at p. 237, *id.*).

24. See 29 *AJIL,* Supplement 653, p. 1126 (1935).

25. Kearney and Dalton, *op. cit., AJIL,* July 1970, Vol. 64, No. 3, at p. 529.

whole does not cover cases of errors in the text and in certified copies of treaties; and it draws attention to Article 79 in which are contained detailed and fairly straight-forward rules for the correction of such errors. *Textual errors:* The rules set out in Article 79 may be stated as follows. Where, after due authentication of the text of a treaty, the contracting and the signatory States agree that it contains an error or an inconsistency, rectification may be effected by duly amending the text, by executing or exchanging a corrective instrument or a series of instruments or by re-executing the corrected text of the treaty as a whole.[26] The particular method adopted in any given case depends upon whether or not there is a depositary for the treaty in question. If there is a depositary and the treaty is multilateral, the procedure will be affected by the number of States parties involved and the type of depositary. On the basis of the *Summary of the Practice of the Secretary-General as Depositary of Multilateral Agreements,*[27] the depositary notifies all the signatory States and the contracting States of the error or inconsistency and of the proposal to correct the text. If no objection has been raised within the specified time-limit, the depositary makes the correction, records the fact in a *procès-verbal* which he causes to be circulated to all the interested parties and to those entitled to become parties to the treaty. Where an objection has been raised by any of the contracting States, it must be promptly communicated to the signatory States and to the contracting States.

The procedure thus outlined applies also in cases where there appears to be a discordance between two or more authentic language versions one of which all the parties agree to correct. The article does not make any specific provision for the correction of errors of translation since the parties can agree to modify them without much formality.

Once a treaty is duly corrected, the corrected text replaces the defective one *ab initio* in the absence of any decision to the contrary by the signatory and the contracting States. It is also necessary that the correction of the text of a duly registered treaty should be notified to the Secretariat of the United Nations.

If the discovery of an error or inconsistency occurs not in the text of the treaty itself but in a certified copy of it, the depositary is required to draw up a *procès-verbal* specifying the rectification that has

---

26. Other methods adopted in practice are to be found outlined in Hackworth's *Digest of International Law*, Vol. 5, pp. 93 ff.

27. See especially pp. 8-10, 19-20, and the Annexes.

been duly made and communicating a copy of it to the signatory and
to the contracting States.[28] This rule is made necessary by the fact that,
in the case of multilateral treaties, the individual State parties have
only the certified copies as the texts of the treaty.

We may now conclude our study of the invalidity of treaties on the
ground of error with an observation on the relationship between Articles
48 and 79. The line of demarcation between essential error that affects
a State's consent to be bound and textual error that can be rectified
by those concerned may sometimes need to be drawn with care if confusion is to be avoided. The Commission recognised this when it
observed in its commentary on its Article 74 (i.e., Article 79 of the
Vienna Convention) as follows:[29]

> "Errors and inconsistencies are sometimes found in the texts of
> treaties and the Commission considered it desirable to include
> provisions in the draft articles concerning methods of rectifying
> them. The error or inconsistency may be due to a typographical
> mistake or to a misdescription or misstatement due to a misunder-
> standing and the correction may effect the substantive meaning
> of the text as authenticated. If there is a dispute as to whether or
> not the alleged error or inconsistency is in fact such, the question
> is not one simply of correction of the text but becomes a problem
> of mistake which falls under Article 45. The present article only
> concerns cases where there is no dispute as to the existence of
> the error or inconsistency".

It may be recalled that draft Article 45, paragraph 3, expressly excludes
cases of error in the wording of the text of a treaty from its consideration of the effect of error on the question of the validity of the treaty
itself. In that connection, the Commission had insisted:[30]

> "Paragraph 3, in order to prevent any misunderstanding, dis-
> tinguishes errors in the wording of the text from errors in the

---

28. The Vienna Conference in the new Article 79 made two important modifications to Article 74 in the Commission's draft by adding "Signatory States"
to "contracting States" throughout the text and by requiring the depositary to
multilateral treaties to communicate the *procès-verbal* not only to the parties but
also to "the States entitled to become parties to the treaty". (UN Conference on
The Law of Treaties. First Session. *Official Records,* 1968, pp. 468-469, 487).

29. *1966 ILC Report,* p. 99, para. 1.

30. *Ibid.,* p. 73, para. 9.

The Validity of Treaties 371

treaty. The paragraph merely underlines that such an error does not affect the validity of the consent and falls under the provisions of Article 74 relating to the correction of errors in the texts of treaties".

These two comments complement each other in delimiting the scope of Article 48 in particular, in relation to the problem of error as a ground of invalidity of a treaty. Occasionally, a situation might arise which could raise in an interesting form the intermingling of questions of substantive error in the treaty, error in the text due to differing language versions that are authentic, and even fraud in the conclusion of the treaty.

In this connection we may cite a solemn episode during the Fifty-seventh Meeting of the Committee of the Whole at the Vienna Conference on The Law of Treaties. The Ethiopian representative said that, since the Treaty of Uccialli of 2 May 1899, between Ethiopia and Italy (*British and Foreign State Papers*, Vol. 81, p. 733) had been cited by the USSR representative at the forty-fifth meeting as an example of a treaty procured by fraud, he would like "to add a few details". He regretted the Russian reference to the incident between Italy and Ethiopia and observed that the "charge of fraud was harmful to the dignity of both States". He continued:

"In denouncing the Treaty of Uccialli the Emperor Menelik II had not made any allegation of fraud in so many words: indeed for him to have done so would have been quite out of character. The treaty had been one of friendship and alliance, drawn up in Amharic and in Italian, both texts being considered equally authentic. After its conclusion, differences had arisen concerning the meaning to be given to Article VII of the Treaty. . . . It was thus clear that the starting-point in the chain of events that had led the Emperor Menelik to denounce the treaty had been the difference between the Amharic and the Italian texts, a difference which must have arisen from an error striking at the very root of the treaty and therefore representing an absence of *consensus ad idem* on a highly important point of that instrument".

He then added the postscript:

"But the Emperor had had an even stronger ground for denouncing the treaty in connection with which he had not alleged fraud, and that was that Article XVII had been interpreted by the other party in a sense which could have implied the surrender of Ethiopia's treaty-making capacity. The Emperor's denunciation of the treaty had been prompted by a love of independence which, from the modern standpoint, might be regarded as an assertion of a principle of *jus cogens*".[31]

Fraud

Let us follow up here what we have mentioned briefly at the beginning of this chapter concerning the attitude of text writers to the treatment of error in relation to fraud. We there accepted that the Commission had been right to have kept error and fraud distinct in separate articles. After careful deliberations, it reached this conclusion because: "Fraud, when it occurs, strikes at the root of an agreement in a somewhat different way from innocent misrepresentation and error. It does not merely affect the consent of the other party to the terms of the agreement; it destroys the whole basis of mutual confidence between the parties".[32]

The significance of this passage lies in the fact that it supplies not only the rationale for the Commission's methodology but also the real point of departure between error and fraud. Although mistake and misrepresentation are distinct legal concepts in nearly all legal systems, mistake may be induced by misrepresentation, whether innocent or fraudulent; but unilateral mistake and fraud still differ in their essentials. The concept of fraud is present in most legal systems, although the details and the application may vary. As Jenks has put it:[33] "Fraud is clearly a ground of invalidity of a treaty obligation induced thereby, but the principle is so elementary that it does not apear to have become an issue in any international adjudication"; and, after citing several arbitral awards based on successful allegations of fraud, he concluded: "A broad generalisation that international law, like every responsible legal system, regards fraud as vitiating any legal act or transaction induced or materially affected thereby would not appear to be too wide".[33]

---

31. *Official Records,* First Session, pp. 264-265, paras. 14-17.
32. *Ibid.,* p. 73, para. 1.
33. *The Prospects of International Adjudication.* 1964. p. 519.

The Validity of Treaties 373

Yet, probably all the legal systems that recognise fraud as a ground of invalidity have failed to achieve a precise definition of the word fraud (in English), *dol* (in French), or *dolo* (in Spanish). For all its technical details and nuances in the various systems of domestic law, fraud in its international usage has or should have a common or universal connotation; it should denote one standard concept of moral turpitude in the legal sense.[34] Faced with the difficulty of formulating an acceptable definition and moved by a felt need for recognising the invalidity of treaties affected by fraud, the Commission hit upon the next best thing and decided upon establishing a rule against "fraudulent conduct", an expression "designed to include any false statements, misrepresentations or other deceitful proceedings by which a State is induced to give a consent to a treaty which it would not otherwise have given".[35]

The Commission considered that, amidst the lack of uniformity of internal law concepts, of State practice and of the jurisprudence of international tribunals, it would not be wise to attempt a definition of fraud at this stage.[36] It "concluded, however, that it would suffice to formulate the general concept of fraud applicable in the law of treaties and to leave its precise scope to be worked out in practice and in the decisions of international tribunals".[37] The Commission's draft Article 46 finally read as follows:

> "A State which has been induced to conclude a treaty by the fraudulent conduct of another negotiating State may invoke the fraud as invalidating its consent to be bound by the treaty".

At the Vienna Conference in 1968, various and valiant attempts were made to discredit or, at least, attenuate the effectiveness of the article. Two main groups pressed for the deletion of Article 49: one group, made up of Chile and Malaysia,[38] asked that it be deleted as unnecessary in view of the lack of precedent either in State practice or in the

---

34. Sir Humphrey Waldock's First Report contained a draft article on fraud based on English common law notions, but the definition was later narrowed down to meet the objections of the civil lawyers in the Commission. But even this narrow definition was finally abandoned: *1963 ILC Yearbook*, Vol. I, p. 37, UN Doc. A/CN4/Ser. A 1963.

35. *1966 ILC Report*, pp. 73-74, para. 3.

36. It is noteworthy that the Harvard Draft Article 31 did not attempt to define fraud (see 29 *AJIL*, Supp. 653, p. 1145 (1935)).

37. *Ibid.*, para. 2.

38. *Official Records*, First Session, p. 265.

374   *T. O. Elias*

jurisprudence of international tribunals, as already admitted by the
Commission in the commentary previously quoted; a second group,
consisting of Chile, Japan and Mexico,[39] would like to see it retained
in some form but only on condition that Article 50 (on corruption of a
representative of another negotiating State) was deleted, the reason
being that the point in the latter article would be adequately covered
by that on fraud. The United States representative, on the other hand,
would only like to see the draft article amended by introducing the
idea that there must have been reasonable reliance upon the alleged
fraudulent conduct and that the consent of the other party must have
been induced by fraudulent conduct of a material nature.[40] All the three
proposed amendments were rejected.

It may be pointed out that in the Commission's draft Article 46, the
effect of fraud is not to render the treaty void *ab initio,* but only voidable at the option of the other party. Until the latter invokes the fraud
as invalidating its consent to be bound, the treaty remains valid. But
the representatives of Venezuela and Congo (Brazzaville) introduced
amendments which would have had the effect of making treaties procured by fraud or corruption void *ab initio* rather than merely voidable
at the option of the injured party.[41] Both these amendments were
defeated.

Article 49 of the Vienna Convention finally emerged in the following form:

> "If a State has been induced to conclude a treaty by the frau-
> dulent conduct of another negotiating State, the State may invoke
> the fraud as invalidating its consent to be bound by the treaty".

The formulation will be seen to be almost without a change in the
Commission's text, except that the Conference considered it more
appropriate to express the idea in the form of a conditional, rather than
a positive rule. This seems right in view of the consensus reached that
the treaty is only voidable, and not void, at the option of the injured
party, who is therefore expected to raise the issue of invalidity on the
ground of an alleged fraud.

---

39. *Official Records, op. cit.,* pp. 256-257.
40. UN Doc.A/CONF.39/C.1/L276 (1968).
41. See UN Doc. A/CONF.39/C.1/L239 and Add. 1; Doc. A/CONF.39/C.1/
261 and Add. 1. (1968).

375

CHAPTER III

CORRUPTION AND COERCION

Corruption

As we have seen when discussing what is now Article 49 of the Vienna Convention on Fraud, a number of representatives of States[1] strenuously opposed the inclusion of an article on Corruption of a State's representative in the conclusion of a treaty. One of the main reasons adduced was that it was unnecessary because it was already covered by the article on fraud. They were no doubt using the same argument as had been employed by some members of the Commission when it proposed an article on Corruption for the first time at its Eighteenth Session in 1966, in connection with which the Commission commented as follows:

> "At the present session certain members of the Commission were opposed to the inclusion in the draft articles of any specific provision regarding 'Corruption'. These members considered such a provision to be unnecessary especially since the use of corruption, if it occurred, would in their view fall under the present article 46 as a case of fraud. Corruption, they maintained, is not an independent cause of defective consent but merely one of the possible means of securing consent through 'fraud' or 'dol'. It would thus be covered by the expression 'fraudulent conduct' in article 46".[2]

We should remember that, in the Commission's provisional draft articles on invalidity of treaties in its 1963 Report, there was no provision on the subject of corruption of a State's representative as one of the vitiating elements of the State's consent to be bound by a treaty. Only Article 33 as then provisionally drafted could be regarded as capable of being stretched to cover the case of corruption of a State's representative. It was during its extraordinary winter meeting in Monaco

---

1. See the earlier reference to the *Official Records,* First Session, pp. 256-257, particularly paras. 56 and 57.
2. *1966 ILC Report,* p. 74, para. 2.

376   *T. O. Elias*

in January 1966 that the Commission re-examined its 1963 draft
articles in the light of comments by governments thereon, and came to
the conclusion that the matter deserved further consideration. Some
members doubted whether corruption of a State's representative "can
properly be regarded as a case of fraud". The majority later took the
line that "the corruption of a representative by another negotiating
State undermines the consent which the representative purports to
express on behalf of his State in a quite special manner which differentiates the case from one of fraud".[3] Equally, the majority did not
see why acts of coercion directed against the person of a representative
should be equated in all cases with those designed or used to corrupt
him. Coercion is of such distinct nature and gravity that it should be
dealt with on its own in a separate article. The Commission considered
that the corruption of a representative is more likely in practice than
coercion, and that it deserves an independent article of its own placed
between that on fraud and that on coercion of a State's representative.
The article finally adopted by the Commission read:

> "If the expression of a State's consent to be bound by a treaty
> has been procured through the corruption of its representative
> directly or indirectly by another negotiating State, the State may
> invoke such corruption as invalidating its consent to be bound by
> the treaty".

As is usual in such cases, the real problem is to determine what constitutes "corruption", especially in regard to the infinite circumstances
in which the first steps are taken towards the initiation of the idea of a
possible treaty, its negotiation and its conclusion. Inducements of varied
kinds might be offered at different stages and for different purposes,
according to the nature of each particular case and the personal predilections of the representative concerned. Certainly, the term corruption
cannot be used to cover ordinary civilities and normal exchanges incident to legitimate diplomatic intercourse. As the Mexican representative, who otherwise opposed the article on corruption, rightly pointed
out at the Vienna Conference:[4]

> "Representatives of States often received decorations at the end

---

3. *1966 ILC Report*, p. 74, para. 3.
4. *Official Records, op. cit.*, p. 257.

The Validity of Treaties 377

of important negotiations. In the eyes of a true diplomat, however, that was not a small courtesy or favour, but rather a mark of esteem. There could be no question of corruption in such cases, for the State giving the decoration was not rewarding the representative for his docility, but for his honesty and good faith".

The same speaker had just a little earlier observed:

"It is true that there had been cases in the past in which the representatives of certain States had received valuable gifts as an inducement to act against the interests of the State they represented, so that the rule was not unnecessary in itself.... Nobody could maintain that corruption was a legal act—a lawful means of negotiation".

In discussing the scope of the meaning to be given to the word "corruption" for purposes of the international law of treaties, the Commission found it necessary to attempt something approaching a definition, if not of the word, at least of its application within the rule enunciated in the Article, in these words:

"The strong term 'corruption' is used in the article expressly in order to indicate that only acts calculated to exercise a substantial influence on the disposition of the representative to conclude the treaty may be invoked as invalidating the expression of consent which he has purported to give on behalf of his State. The Commission did not mean to imply that under the present article a small courtesy or favour shown to a representative in connection with the conclusion of a treaty may be invoked as a pretext for invalidating the treaty".[5]

Thus, the Commission was concerned to base the new rule within strictly acceptable limits. In furtherance of this purpose, the article carries the phrase "directly or indirectly by another negotiating State" so as to ensure that the alleged acts of corruption can be proved to be directly or indirectly those of the accused negotiating State. Corruption is scarcely ever effected by overt acts, but it is not enough, under the article merely to establish the fact that the representative had

---

5. *1966 ILC Report,* p. 74, para. 4.

been corrupted; it must be shown that the corruption had been effected directly or indirectly by the other negotiating State. Finally, in order to emphasise that corruption is more akin to fraud rather than coercion of a representative, corruption cases have, as we have seen, been treated in the same way as those of fraud: it will be recalled that, in the Introduction, separability of treaty provisions in Article 44 (para. 4), loss of a right to invoke a ground of invalidity in Article 45, and consequences of the invalidity of a treaty in Article 69—have all been treated in that way.

Coercion of a State's Representative

Coercion may take two forms, *either* of a representative in negotiating a treaty or expressing consent to be bound, *or* of the State itself. The Commission was itself aware that it may not always be easy to distinguish between coercion of a Head of State or a Minister as a means of coercing the State itself and coercion exerted against a State's representative in his personal capacity. It recalled "the shocking case" of Dr. Hacha, as Lord McNair has described it,[6] where President Hacha and the Foreign Minister of Czechoslovakia had been coerced by the Hitlerite German Government in 1939 into signing a treaty imposing a German protectorate over Bohemia and Moravia. It would seem that this personal coercion also entailed the gravest possible threats to Czechoslovakia itself should its august representatives fail to comply.[7] It was nevertheless considered desirable to treat both types of coercion in separate articles.

Text-writers have sometimes tended to treat both together. Thus, Lord McNair wrote:

> "The traditional opinion accepted by the majority of writers has, at any rate until recently, been that a treaty becomes and remains binding upon a State in spite of the fact that that State was acting under coercion in concluding the treaty, and that the invalidating

---

6. *Op. cit.*, p. 208.

7. *1966 ILC Report*, pp. 74-75, para. 1. D. P. O'Connell, *International Law*, Vol. I, p. 261, explained the situation as follows: "The classical instance is the Czech-German Treaty of March 1939, concerning which opinions differ. Actually, this is a very extreme instance, and the physical occupation of Czechoslovakia at the time by German forces probably rendered the treaty invalid as involving no real consent. A case of a very different order is the denunciation by Pakistan of the Indus River Agreement with India of 4 May 1948, on the ground of duress".

The Validity of Treaties 379

effect of coercion must be confined to cases where it is applied to the representative of a State engaged in the final act which concludes the treaty, either signature in the case of a treaty not requiring ratification, or ratification where that is required".[8]

Jenks expressed himself in a similar vein:

"The rule that coercion does not invalidate the consent of a State to a treaty obligation unless the coercion was applied to the person of its representative was until recently the established rule of international law . . .".[9]

Whatever the case, it is generally agreed that coercion, actual or threatened, against the person of a State's representative or in their personal capacity to compel him to sign, ratify, accept or approve a treaty renders any consent so procured absolutely void.[10] The Commission recalled: "History provides a number of instances of the employment of coercion against not only negotiators but the members of legislatures in order to procure the signature or ratification of a treaty".[11]

Article 48 of the Commission's draft reads as follows:

"The expression of a State's consent to be bound by a treaty which has been procured by the coercion of its representative through acts or threats directed against him personally shall be without any legal effect".[12]

---

8. *Op. cit.*, p. 207. But it is obvious that the learned author does make the distinction on the following page when he said "We speak now of coercion applied to the State itself, not of personal intimidation applied to its representatives".

9. Jenks, *op. cit.*, pp. 421-422.

10. Hall, *International Law*, 4th ed., p. 342.

11. *1966 ILC Report*, p. 74, para.1.

12. According to Art. 32 of Harvard Draft Convention on The Law of Treaties: "*(a)* As the term is used in this Convention, duress involves the employment of coercion directed against the persons signing a treaty on behalf of a State or against the persons engaged in ratifying or acceding to a treaty on behalf of a State; provided that, if the coercion has been directed against a person signing a treaty on behalf of a State and if with knowledge of this fact the treaty signed has later been ratified by that State without coercion, the treaty is not to be considered as having been entered into by that State in consequence of duress (C. C. Hyde, *International Law*, Vol. 2, 2nd Revised ed., p. 1380).

380   *T. O. Elias*

As thus stated, the rule is intended to cover all types of constraint of or threat against a representative as an individual and not as an organ or agent of the State he represents. It embraces physical threat to his person and psychological or a moral pressure regarding his private acts of indiscretion a disclosure of which might ruin his career. Nor does the article exclude other forms of subtle pressure exerted against close relatives of a State's representative which it would be difficult for the latter to resist. These and other forms of coercion involving improper pressure against the person of the representative are covered.

The article renders null and void a treaty procured by the coercion of a representative, and does not give the State concerned a choice to treat the matter as voidable at its option. The gravity of an act of coercion done in such circumstances and to secure such ends makes it imperative that the treaty be regarded as *ipso facto* void. Yet, this result was called in question by *inter alios* the representatives of the United States of America, France and the United Kingdom,[13] who would like to see the omission of the words "without any legal effect" from the text of Article 48, since, they argued, the other articles on invalidity (e.g., fraud, corruption of a representative) give the injured party an option whether to ratify or repudiate. The United States representative, in introducing the United States amendment,[14] claimed that the text of Article 48 could be improved in three ways: it should be made clear that the injured State alone could invoke coercion to invalidate the treaty, but that the expression "shall be without any legal effect" would seem to make it possible for the guilty party also to invoke its own turpitude to invalidate the treaty; it should also be made clear that the coercion was that of another negotiating State, and not possibly a third State or even a third person; and, finally, the article would be better if it had the effect of making the treaty voidable at the option of the injured State, and not void *ab initio*. All the proposed amendments were rejected, and the Commission's draft Article 48 emerged unchanged as Article 51 of the Vienna Convention.

Coercion of a State by the Threat or Use of Force

It is now generally agreed that contemporary international law regards all treaties concluded by the threat or use of force against the

---

13. *Official Records,* First Session, pp. 266-268.

14. A/CONF.39/C.1/L.277; the French amendment was contained in Doc. A/CONF.39/C.1/L.300; the United Kingdom did not submit a written amend-

sovereign independence and territorial integrity of States as absolutely void. But this was not the position under customary international law before 1919 when the Covenant of the League of Nations first prohibited the use of force as means of settling international disputes. This was later followed by the Kellogg-Briand Pact (or the Pact of Paris) of 1928 which, under its full title of International Treaty for the Renunciation of War As An Instrument of National Policy, forbids "recourse to war for the solution of international controversies" and prescribes that "the settlement or solution of all disputes or conflicts of whatever nature or whatever origin they may be, . . . shall never be sought except by peaceful means". The Charter of the Allied Military Tribunals and the principles enunciated in consequence of the Nuremberg trials and the express prohibition of the threat or use of force in Article 2(4) of the United Nations Charter serve to crystallise an already developing body of international opinion against treaties obtained by force.[15] Against this background it is impossible to deny that it is part of modern international law that treaties procured by the threat or use of force are invalid.

The objection commonly given in the past against the acceptance of this rule of invalidity of treaties based on coercion of a State was that it would encourage States lightly to impugn the integrity of treaties, and that it would unsettle things done under the peace treaties at the option of the defeated parties. But this is only a sad reflection of the era when the legality of the threat or use of force was recognised in relations between States.

The article formulated by the Commission is accordingly a simple and categorical one using as its temporal frame of reference the date of the coming into force of the United Nations Charter. Article 49 reads:

"A treaty is invalid if its conclusion is procured by the threat or use of force in violation of the principles of the Charter of the United Nations".

There are a number of points calling for comment. For instance,

---

ment, but supported the other two in debate. The Australian amendment was in Doc. A/CONF.39/C.1/L.284.

15. Lord McNair, *op. cit.*, at p. 210, has given a full arcana of the progressive stages of elimination of enforced treaties and other transactions up to the *Corfu Channel Case* (Merits), *ICJ Reports 1949*, pp. 4, 35.

the phrase used is "in violation of the *principles* of the Charter", not "in violation of the Charter itself", an alternative formulation that would have limited the application of the article to only member States of the United Nations, thereby depriving it of any legal force in respect of non-member States. By emphasising the *principles* of the Charter, the article implies all those rules and practices of international law which underlie the Charter provisions and which are of general application today. The rule enunciated in the article applies with equal force to a case where even an individual State is alone being coerced into giving its consent to be bound by a multilateral treaty. Again, the article expresses the idea of coercion in terms of a "threat or use of force" in violation of the principles of the Charter, in the belief in the words of the Commission in its commentary, "that the precise scope of the acts covered by this definition should be left to be determined in practice by interpretation of the relevant provisions of the Charter".[16] So pervasive is the influence of the United Nations and its agencies that few would dare to flout its Charter provisions with impunity. The Commission by a narrow majority refused to formulate the article so as to include "other forms of pressure, such as a threat to strangle the economy of a country" within the concept of coercion mentioned in the article. As we shall soon see, this was not the end of the matter.

Another question that the Commission had to deal with was whether to make void or merely voidable a treaty that has been procured by a threat or use of force. Some members were of the view that the treaty should be voidable at the instance of the party coerced which might wish to maintain the treaty after its release from the act of coercion. The majority, however, considered that the threat or use of force to extort the consent of a State to be bound by a treaty must be considered a matter of such depravity as to call for complete voidness and not mere voidability. Once nullified, the subject-matter of such a treaty could be revived only by means of another treaty freely entered into when *all* the parties are once again on an equal footing with regard to treaty-making.

Let us now turn to a consideration of the temporal element in the application of the article. Should it be retrospective in its effect? If so, from what date should the new rule be deemed to have come into operation? It is clear that the only sensible solution is to make the rule take effect in the future so as not to unsettle things done or purported

---

16. *1966 ILC Reports*, p. 75, para. 3.

The Validity of Treaties 383

to be done at a time in the past when it was lawful and perhaps also appropriate that they should have been so done or purported to have been so done. The Commission made the following pertinent observation:

"The rule codified in the present article cannot therefore be properly understood as depriving of validity *ab initio* a peace treaty or other treaty procured by coercion prior to the establishment of the modern law regarding the threat or use of force. ... Moreover, whatever differences of opinion there may be about the state of the law prior to the establishment of the United Nations, the great majority of international lawyers today unhesitatingly hold that Article 2, paragraph 4, together with other provisions of the Charter, authoritatively declares the modern customary law regarding the threat or use of force".[17]

The article is, therefore, expressed in a form that recognises that the rule it embodies applies only in respect of treaties concluded since the United Nations Charter came into force. Despite its comparative modernity, the new rule has been formulated in the present article with a reasonable degree of perspicacity and caution.

At the Vienna Conference, however, the Commission's draft Article 49 had a rough passage. The expression "threat or use of force" was subjected to the same controversial interpretation by both the Western group of States and the "new States" made up of Africans, Asians and Latin Americans as had characterised their debates in the counsels of the Special Committee on Principles of International Law Concerning Friendly Relations and Co-operation among States since the latter was first set up in 1963 by the United Nations General Assembly and since it began its deliberations in Mexico in 1964. One of the seven principles which were contained in the relevant resolution 1966 (XVIII) referred to the Committee for study was "the principle that States shall refrain in their international relations from the threat or use of force against the territorial integrity or political independence of any State, or in any other manner inconsistent with the purposes of the United Nations".[18] The Committee had at its 1964, 1966 and 1967 sessions

---

17. *Ibid.*, p. 76, paras. 7 and 8.
18. *Yearbook of the International Law Commission*, 1966, Vol. II, p. 19, para. 3.

384   *T. O. Elias*

discussed in great detail and with much heat the question whether the provision of Article 2 (4) of the United Nations Charter which forbids "the threat or use of force" means only "armed force" or whether it embraces "economic and political pressure". The representatives of the Western States supported the former interpretation, while those of the newer States favoured the latter.[19] Each group espoused its cause with equal eloquence and vehemence. On the one hand, reference was made to the *travaux préparatoires* in respect of the formulation of Article 2 (4) of the Charter at the San Francisco Conference where the Brazilian proposal to include an express reference to economic pressure had been rejected, to which the Afghan representative retorted:[20] "but not because the Conference had refused to recognise economic pressure; if that had been so, the Charter would not have mentioned the economic and political measures referred to in Article 41".

The International Law Commission had earlier observed that if it were itself to attempt to elaborate the rule in the article by detailed interpretations of the principle, it would encroach on a topic which had been remitted by the General Assembly to the Special Committee.[21] The United States representative among others at the Vienna Conference insisted that:

> "the Conference of Plenipotentiaries on the Law of Treaties was not charged with formulating the principle stated in Article 49 of the International Law Commission's text. The sponsors of the nineteen-State amendment had claimed that, as the Conference would be defining the use of force for the purposes of the present convention, there would be no conflict with the work undertaken by other United Nations organs. But the Conference was not called upon to interpret the United Nations Charter, particularly parts of it having an important and dangerous political content . . . Attempts to resolve questions of definition or political issues relating to the Charter in the context of a convention on the law of treaties might cause States which disagreed with the proposed definition to refuse to adopt the convention".[22]

19. *Official Records,* First Session, 1968, pp. 269-293, *passim.*
20. *Ibid.,* at p. 293.
21. *Yearbook of the International Law Commission,* 1966, Vol. II, p. 19, para. 5.
22. *Official Records,* First Session, p. 292.

The Validity of Treaties 385

The nineteen-State amendment,[23] to which reference was thus made, had been intended to define the scope of draft Article 49 and to stipulate that the expression "threat or use of force" included economic and political pressure. The Uruguayan representative gave the following five reasons why he could not support the amendment:

1. That "the notion of economic and political pressure was too vague to rank as a defect in consent".
2. That the expression "the threat or use of force" was a "time-honoured and broad term embodied in the United Nations Charter, which did not exclude particularly serious cases of economic or political coercion, such as economic blockade . . .".
3. That the amendment, "by expressly introducing a reference to economic and political pressure, might give the impression *a contraria* that those forms of pressure, if of a grave character, were not at present covered by Article 2, paragraph 4, of the Charter. On the other hand, the wording used by the International Law Commission was flexible enough and did not prejudge the content of the Charter. It could be interpreted progressively in accordance with the particular circumstances of each case, in harmony with the conditions and opinions prevailing from time to time".
4. That "the reference by the sponsors of the amendment to the principle of non-intervention laid down in the Charter of the Organisation of American States had no relevance to Article 49, and the need for expressly specifying economic and political pressure in that article as a ground for the voidance of a treaty was not deduced from it".
5. That, "in a conference for the codification of international law, the legitimate economic and social claims of the developing countries—claims which were fully supported by Uruguay—were out of place".[24]

The Algerian representative, on the other hand, stated the popular view of "the new States" when he observed: [25]

---

23. Doc. A/CONF.39/C.1/L.67/Rev.1/Corr. 1 was submitted by Afghanistan, Algeria, Bolivia, Congo (Brazzaville), Ecuador, Ghana, Guinea, India, Iran, Kenya, Kuwait, Mali, Pakistan, Sierra Leone, Syria, United Arab Republic, United Republic of Tanzania, Yugoslavia and Zambia.

24. *Official Records,* First Session, pp. 276-277.

25. *Ibid.,* p. 276.

"Economic pressure took many forms, and its effects on the victim were obviously of the same nature as those of the threat or use of force. It was true that the era of the colonial treaty was past or disappearing, but there was no overlooking the fact that some countries had resorted to new and more insidious methods, suited to the present state of international relations, in an attempt to maintain and perpetuate bounds of subjection. Economic pressure which was a characteristic of neo-colonialism, was becoming increasingly common in relations between certain countries and the newly independent States. Political independence could not be an end in itself; it was even illusory if it was not backed by genuine economic independence".

To some extent, the Spanish representative, took a similar view when, in speaking to another amendment co-sponsored by Spain (A/CONF.39/C.1/L.289 and Add. 1), he said that, while he could not support the thirteen-State amendment, the phrase "threat or use of force" did not refer only to physical force or war, and added: "But that was not the case, for a proper interpretation of the spirit of the Charter condemned all unlawful use of force of any kind whatever, and might in some cases include the abuse which consisted in exploiting the development needs of nations".[26]

As the debate became more and more acrimonious, it was decided that the work of the Committee of the Whole should be suspended to allow for informal consultations between the representatives of the various groups in an effort to reach agreement on a resolution to accompany Article 49, which would facilitate its adoption by all sides. When the debate was resumed a few days later, the Draft Declaration on the Prohibition of the Threat or Use of Economic or Political Coercion in Concluding a Treaty[27] was unanimously adopted.[28] The draft declaration condemns threat or use of pressure in any form by one State to coerce another to conclude a treaty. The Committee of the Whole, having accepted a Bulgarian co-sponsored amendment[29] to insert the words "international law embodied in" between the words

---

26. *Official Records, op. cit.,* p. 291.

27. See Annex I for the text of this Declaration which now forms part of the Final Act of the Vienna Convention. A/CONF.39/26.

28. *Official Records, op. cit.,* p. 329.

29. A/CONF.39/C.1/L.289 and Add. 1. There were twelve other States. It was adopted by 49 votes to 10, with 33 abstentions.

The Validity of Treaties 387

"principles of" and "the Charter of the United Nations", proceeded to dispose of all other amendments, including the nineteen-State one the co-sponsors of which agreed not to press it to a vote.

Article 52 (i.e., the International Law Commission's draft Article 49) as finally adopted by the Vienna Conference now reads as follows:

> "A treaty is void if its conclusion has been procured by threat or use of force in violation of the principles of international law embodied in the Charter of the United Nations".

Bulgaria, Czechoslovakia and Ecuador[30] put the case for the addition of the words "principles of international" admirably when they pointed out that the prohibition of the threat or use of force was already *lex lata* before the San Francisco Conference and that all that the United Nations Charter has done in its Article 2 (4) is no more than to emphasise the obvious fact that the principles codified in the article are not those of the Charter *per se*, but also those of the customary international law on which the Charter itself is based.

---

30. *Official Records*, First Session, 1968, pp. 271, 273 and 276.

388

CHAPTER IV

JUS COGENS

The concept of *jus cogens* is a relatively new one in customary international law. The international community has not, until recently, become sufficiently organised to accept the notion of public policy or *ordre public* as commonly understood and applied in municipal law. Even in those legal systems, whether based on the common law or on the civil, that law has long recognised the principle of public policy, it has not been possible to give the notion a satisfactory precise definition. It has been described as "an unruly horse", although domestic courts have come to identify with a reasonable degree of success those hard cases (involving, e.g., illegal contracts) in which to set their face against certain forms of agreements that should be regarded as positively harmful to the body politic if permitted by law. Nevertheless, the lack of a clear and acceptable definition of the concept has not prevented its recognition and enforcement by domestic courts in appropriate cases. While it is possible to stretch this analogy with municipal law too far, the inference to be drawn is obvious when we come to consider the formulation of the rule of *jus cogens* as conceived both by the International Law Commission and by the Vienna Conference on the Law of Treaties.

Let us begin with the premise that some jurists have denied the existence in international law of any rules of *jus cogens* which forbid States to enter into certain types of treaties. Jenks has put the case thus:

> "Except where they apply, or any similar principle is applicable in other international organisations, the *jus dispositivum* consisting of the treaty stipulations agreed between the parties thereto is not generally regarded as being governed by any *jus cogens* consisting of principles of law or policy which are binding on the negotiators of such treaties or can be ignored by them only at the risk of the invalidity of their agreement. There have been isolated judicial dicta suggesting the existence of an international public order which the provisions of treaties must respect".[1]

---

1. *Op. cit.*, p. 504.

The Validity of Treaties 389

Their contention is based on the idea that to admit that there are such rules would be contrary to the supposedly unlimited sovereign powers of States to conclude any type of international agreement that they might wish, a proposition that is out of tune with contemporary international law thinking and development. Thus, in the *Oscar Chinn Case*,[2] Judge Schucking, in endorsing Judge van Eysinga's opinion specifically introduced the concept of international public policy in these words:

> "I think that the case in which a convention has to be regarded as automatically null and void is not an entirely isolated case in international law. The Covenant of the League of Nations, as a whole, and more particularly in Article 20, in which the Members undertake not to enter into obligations or understandings *inter se* inconsistent with its provisions, would possess little value unless treaties concluded in violation of that undertaking were to be regarded as absolutely null and void, that is to say, as being automatically void. And I can hardly believe that the League of Nations would have already embarked on the codification of international law if it were not possible, even today, to create a *jus cogens,* the effect of which would be that, once States have agreed on certain rules of law, and have also given an undertaking that these rules may not be altered by some only of their number, any act adopted in contravention of that undertaking would be automatically void".

To the above *dicta* must now be added Lord McNair's pertinent observation:

> "It is difficult to imagine any society, whether of individuals or of States, whose law sets no limit whatever to freedom of contract. In every civilised community there are some rules of law and some principles of morality which individuals are not permitted by law to ignore or to modify by their agreements. The maxim *modus et conventio vincunt legem* does not apply to imperative provisions of the law or of public policy".[3]

The learned author then went on to give examples of rules of cus-

---

2. (1934) *PCIJ, Series A/B, No. 63*, pp. 134-136 and 149-150.
3. *Ibid.*, pp. 213-214.

tomary international law in respect of which States may conclude
treaties to the contrary, for instance, States may agree by treaty to
confer diplomatic privileges and immunities upon consuls within their
borders, and they may equally agree by treaty to waive their right to
exercise jurisdiction over persons and things on board foreign private
vessels in their harbours. Both of these would constitute a derogation
from the normal rules of customary international law which States may
achieve by treaty. Lord McNair thereafter added:

> "There are, however, many rules of customary international law
> which stand in a higher category and which cannot be set aside
> or modified by contracting States; it is easier to illustrate these
> rules than to define them. They are rules which have been
> accepted, either expressly by treaty or tacitly by custom, as being
> necessary to protect the public interests of the society of States
> or to maintain the standards of public morality recognised by them.
> For instance, piracy is stigmatised by customary international law
> as a crime, in the sense that a pirate is regarded as *hostis humani
> generis* and can lawfully be punished by any State into whose
> hands he may fall. Can there be any doubt that a treaty whereby
> two States agreed to permit piracy in a certain area, or against
> the merchant ships of a certain State, with impunity, would be
> null and void? Or a treaty whereby two allies agreed to wage a
> war by methods which violated the customary rules of warfare,
> such as the duty to give quarter?"[4]

Although in the *Oscar Chinn Case,* Judge Schucking would appear
to have regarded Article 20 of the League of Nations Covenant as
possessing the character of a rule of *jus cogens,* the International Law
Commission had contented itself with the assertion that "the law of the
Charter [of the United Nations] concerning the prohibition of the use
of force in itself constitutes a conspicuous example of a rule in international law having the character of *jus cogens*".[5] It was encouraged to
pursue its task of formulating a rule of *jus cogens* by the fact that, of
all the Governments of the United Nations member States that had
submitted comments on its first draft article, only one had questioned
the existence of rules of *jus cogens* in the international law of today,

---

4. *(1934) PCIJ, Series A/B, No. 63,* pp. 214-215.
5. *1966 ILC Report,* para. 1, p. 76.

although a number would accept the draft only if satisfactory provision were also included for independent adjudication. In view of this, the Commission concluded that "in codifying the law of treaties it must start from the basis that today there are certain rules from which States are not competent to derogate at all by a treaty arrangement, and which may be changed only by another rule of the same character".[5] It realised that it is not every provision in a treaty that forbids any derogation from it which possesses the character of *jus cogens,* and that it is not enough to say that a treaty is void if any of its provisions is in conflict with a general rule of international law. If a treaty were to forbid the parties from entering into a later treaty with a provision in conflict with that of the earlier treaty, the party acting thus might be guilty of a breach resulting in its international responsibility, but not guilty of any rule of *jus cogens.* "It is not the form of a general rule of international law but the particular nature of the subject-matter with which it deals that may, in the opinion of the Commission, give it the character of *jus cogens*".[6]

As with Lord McNair, the Commission took the view that, rather than embark upon a task of definition or enumeration, it was better "to provide in general terms that a treaty is void if it conflicts with a rule of *jus cogens* and to leave the full content of the rule to be worked out in State practice and in the jurisprudence of international tribunals".[7] Some members thought that examples of the new rule should be given, such as a treaty to employ an unlawful use of force in contravention of the United Nations Charter or to engage in acts that are criminal under international law or to practise slave trade, piracy or genocide—acts clearly forbidden by international law. Other examples given were treaties in violation of fundamental rights, the principle of the equality of States or that of self-determination. The Commission, however, decided not to give examples, as the maxim *expressio unus exclusio est alterius* would apply and, in any case, to attempt a list would entail "a prolonged study of matters which fall outside the scope" of the draft articles.

The Commission, therefore, formulated draft Article 50 as follows:

"A treaty is void if it conflicts with a peremptory norm of general international law from which no derogation is permitted and which

---

6. *Ibid.,* para. 2.
7. *Ibid.,* para. 3.

can be modified only by a subsequent norm of general international law having the same character".

This provision clearly contemplates the voidness of a treaty only if
it is in conflict with a *peremptory* rule of general international law from
which States are forbidden to derogate by another treaty. Such a rule
should be capable of being modified from time to time by a *general*
multilateral treaty, and not by particular States or a group of States
inter se.

There were two other matters raised in the process of formulating the
draft article. The first was the insistence of governments on the inclusion of an explicit and satisfactory provision for adjudication of
disputes in respect of claims of invalidity based on an alleged conflict
with a rule of *jus cogens*. The Commission did not consider that it
need go beyond the provision contained in its draft Article 62 [8] which
was based on Article 33 of the United Nations Charter, since the problem posed by a claim of invalidity arising out of an allegation of *jus
cogens* must be regarded as identical with that raised by other grounds
of invalidity such as the termination, suspension or withdrawal from
the operation of a treaty. Besides, contemporary international opinion
was not ready to accept compulsory machinery for the peaceful settlement of disputes. The procedure set out in Article 62 was considered
by the Commission to be sufficient to "exclude the arbitrary determination of the invalidity, termination or suspension of a treaty by
an individual State . . .".[9]

The other matter relates to the question whether or not the rule
stated in the draft Article 50 is retroactive in nature. The Commission
was quite emphatic that there could be no question of any retroactive
effect as the article "concerns cases where a treaty is void *at the time
of its conclusion* by reason of the fact that its provisions are in conflict with an already existing rule of *jus cogens*".[10]

It is suggested that the draft Article 50 should be read along with
draft Article 61 which provided:

"If a new peremptory norm of general international law of the
kind referred to in Article 50 is established, any existing treaty
which is in conflict with that norm becomes void and terminates".

---

8. See footnote at p. 4.
9. *Ibid.*, para. 5, p. 77.
10. *Ibid.*, para. 6, p. 77.

The Validity of Treaties 393

This draft article[11] clearly envisages a situation in which a treaty which was valid at the time of its conclusion but which becomes void and terminates because it conflicts with a new rule of *jus cogens* subsequently established. This makes it obvious that the emergence of a new rule of *jus cogens* is not intended to have any retrospective effect, as it becomes void only from the time that the new rule is established. The Commission also drew attention to the provision of its draft Article 67, paragraph 2,[12] that no retroactive effect should result from the termination of a treaty on the emergence of a new rule of *jus cogens*.

Draft Article 61 will be seen to complement Article 50 in that it invalidates existing as well as future treaties. It does not make void *ab initio* a treaty which conflicts with a newly established rule of *jus cogens*; it merely prohibits the future existence or performance of such a treaty. That was why the Commission decided not to put the rules in Articles 50 and 61 in one article on invalidity, but to place the latter among the articles on termination of treaties. Also, we have noted in Chapter I, that, whereas under Article 50 a treaty is void *ab initio* and its provisions are not separable if any of them is found to conflict with the rule of *jus cogens,* under Article 61 the principle of severability applies because when first concluded the treaty was entirely valid but some of its provisions are later found to be void on the ground that they conflict with a newly established rule of *jus cogens*. In such

---

11. Draft Article 62 of the Commission provided:

    1. A party which claims that a treaty is invalid or which alleges a ground for terminating, withdrawing from or suspending the operation of a treaty under the provisions of the present articles must notify the other parties of its claim. The notification shall indicate the measure proposed to be taken with respect to the treaty and the grounds therefor.

    2. If, after the expiry of a period which, except in cases of special urgency, shall not be less than three months after the receipt of the notification, no party has raised any objection, the party making the notification may carry out in the manner provided in Article 63 the measure which it has proposed.

    3. If, however, objection has been raised by any other party, the parties shall seek a solution through the means indicated in Article 33 of the Charter of the United Nations.

    4. Nothing in the foregoing paragraphs shall affect the rights or obligations of the parties under any provisions in force binding the parties with regard to the settlement of disputes.

    5. Without prejudice to Article 42, the fact that a State has not previously made the notification prescribed in paragraph 1 shall not prevent it from making such notification in answer to another party claiming performance of the treaty or alleging its violation.

12. The whole of Article 67 will be considered in Chapter V.

a case, the severable clauses may be omitted as invalid while the remainder are left intact.

At the Vienna Conference, draft Articles 50 and 61 on *jus cogens,* as had been expected, generated heated controversy. Four main lines of attack were canvassed. The first was that the international society had not evolved to the stage of having a concept of international law based on the idea of public policy or morality comparable to what had obtained in the municipal jurisprudence of States. The second was that the proposed rule of *jus cogens,* even if such a concept could be deemed to exist, lacked precision or definition necessary to recommend it for general acceptance; besides, precedents hardly existed, nor were there illustrations of the new rule numerous and positive enough to warrant the inference that a clear rule of *jus cogens* had emerged in international law to govern the treaty relations of States. The third and the most persistent criticism of the rules stated in both draft Articles 50 and 61 was the inadequacy of the disputes settlement procedure set out in draft Article 62 in cases of an allegation of invalidity of a treaty, especially on the ground of a breach of the rule of *jus cogens.* The fourth was that the rule as stated did not contain a specific indication that it was non-retroactive in character.

The attitudes of the representatives of States varied from that of those (a very few) that wanted Article 50 deleted to that of those (a large number) that wanted the Commission's draft adopted without change.[13] The main amendments, however, were those proposed by the United States,[14] Finland,[15] Mexico,[16] Finland-Greece-Spain,[17] the United Kingdom,[18] and Romania and the USSR.[19] The United States amendment was in two parts. It proposed the addition of the words "at the time of its conclusion", an idea which was, as we have seen above, explained by the International Law Commission as clearly implicit in its draft article though not explicitly stated therein. This amendment was accepted by the Conference. The second limb of the amendment would add "which is recognised in common by the national and

---

13. An Indian amendment (Doc. A/CONF.39/C.1/L.254) which would merge Articles 50 and 61 into one was withdrawn fairly early in the debate.

14. UN Doc. A/CONF.39/C.1/L.302.

15. Doc. A/CONF.39/C.1/L.293, later withdrawn (see *Official Records,* First Session, pp. 328, 330).

16. Doc. A/CONF.39/C.1/L.266, later withdrawn, *ibid.,* p. 325.

17. Doc. A/CONF.39/C.1/L.306 and Add. 1 and 2.

18. Doc. A/CONF.39/C.1/L.312, later withdrawn, *ibid.,* p. 330.

19. Doc. A/CONF.39/C.1/L.258 and Corr. 1.

regional legal systems of the world", a suggestion which was criticised by many delegates as likely to subordinate the principle of *jus cogens* to "national legal systems"; it was also questioned whether the expression "regional legal systems" had any more precise connotation than the wording of the text of the article itself. This part of the United States amendment was, therefore, rejected. The Finnish amendment wanted the principle of separability to be applicable to the clauses of a treaty that conflicted with a rule of *jus cogens*. This was withdrawn in view of the several objections that were raised against it. The Mexican amendment would like the article to specify that it has no retrospective effect, a point also stressed in the Commission's commentary, though not stated in the draft article. The three-nation amendment by Finland, Greece and Spain would specify that [20] "the peremptory norms in question were the norms recognised by the international community as those from which no derogation was permitted".[21] As the Greek representative put it: "A *jus cogens* rule in the meaning of Article 50 in principle prevailed over a treaty. But there was an exception: the treaty would prevail if it was a general multilateral treaty. The essential element of international *jus cogens* therefore lay in the universality of its acceptance by the international community".[22] The United Kingdom sub-amendment to the United States amendment proposed that there should be a definition of the *jus cogens* rule by means of protocols in which would be stated a list of such rules, a proposal which would require the convening of a Conference after the drafting by another body of the text of those protocols and after their entry into force. This would undoubtedly have the effect of maintaining in force a clause that was in conflict with a *jus cogens* rule. This amendment was later withdrawn conditionally when the United States representative offered an explanation of their own proposed amendment and suggested that the essence of their proposal and not necessarily its particular formulation (to which objections had been made by several other delegates) be referred to the Drafting Committee for a better reformulation. The amendment by Romania and the USSR proposed to clarify the text of

---

20. E.g., Monaco, Turkey and Switzerland.
21. *Per* Mr. de Castro, the Spanish representative: *Official Records*, First Session, p. 316.
22. *Ibid.*, at p. 295. Compare this with the Mexican representative's suggestion that "the rules of *jus cogens* were those rules which derived from principles that the legal conscience of mankind deemed absolutely essential to co-existence in the international community at a given stage of its historical development" (p. 294).

the Commission's draft by giving greater prominence to the character and legal nature of peremptory rules, thereby establishing a link between its two parts and making its second part explain the words "peremptory norm of general international law". As it seemed to be a drafting point, it was referred to the Drafting Committee.

After various consultations in the corridors and in the regional groups, the Conference left the matter in the hands of the Drafting Committee with certain directions. Since it had adopted a United States amendment that the opening words of Article 50 should read: "A treaty is void if, at the time of its conclusion, it conflicts . . .," this was reflected in the final draft. The Romanian and USSR amendment as well as that of Finland, Greece and Spain were also taken into account as they had been referred to the Drafting Committee. The Committee of the Whole had specified that it had approved the principle of *jus cogens* as enunciated in the draft article, so that only drafting improvements had been made.[23] The text of the revised version of the Commission's draft Article 50 (now Article 53 of the Vienna Convention) then read as follows:

> "A treaty is void if, at the time of its conclusion, it conflicts with a peremptory norm of general international law. For the purposes of the present Convention, a peremptory norm of general international law is a norm accepted and recognised by the international community of States as a whole as a norm from which no derogation is permitted and which can be modified only by a subsequent norm of general international law having the same character".

When this re-draft was put to the vote, 72 were in favour, 3 were against and there were 18 abstentions.[24] Thus was ended the highly controversial debate on the principle of *jus cogens,* a debate in which acid references had been made to the favourable views of Lord McNair and other eminent jurists on the one hand, and to the critical opinion of Schwarzenberger on the other. The latter had written in an article that "apparent progressiveness can readily be made to serve sectional interests not apparent at first sight"; he added a warning that the

---

23. *Official Records, op. cit.,* at p. 334, a ruling by the present writer as Chairman of the Committee of the Whole.
24. *Ibid.,* at p. 472.

"publication" of Article 50 would make it easy for any State to invoke the invalidity of any inconvenient treaty and thus "provide splendid opportunities for the expression of moral indignation by third parties on matters which, otherwise, would clearly not be their business".[25] Verdross's[26] and Schwelb's[27] convincing rebuttals of this line of argument were also cited by the proponents of the article. In this connection, it is pertinent to refer to the 1966 Lagonissi Conference Papers and Proceedings entitled *The Concept of* Jus Cogens *In International Law* published in 1967 by the Carnegie Endowment for International Peace, in which the conclusion had been reached that the existence of peremptory rules in international law could no longer be doubted. Accordingly, the representative of the Federal Republic of Germany noted "that only a few speakers had denied the existence of certain rules of *jus cogens* in international law and said that his delegation was equally of the opinion that such rules existed in international law. The growing interdependence of States had brought about an international public order which had led to the establishment of certain fundamental rules as peremptory norms from which no derogation was permitted".

Article 61 (now Article 64 of the Convention) on the emergence of a new *jus cogens* provoked little discussion as the rule embodied in it had already been fully debated. The only justification for it as a separate article lies in the differing legal effects of each, and these will be considered in the concluding Chapter V.

Judicial Settlement Procedure

It now remains to deal with the outstanding question of a satisfactory settlement procedure. As has been indicated earlier in this Chapter, the objections of some delegations to Article 50, both in its original form from the Commission and in its revised version by the Conference, had been based largely on the inadequacy of the provisions contained in Article 62 as set forth by the Commission. The point of view of the critics may be summed up in these words of the United Kingdom representatives:

---

25. See his article entitled "International *Jus Cogens*", in *Texas Law Review*, March, 1965, p. 455, at p. 477.

26. "*Jus Dispositivum* and *Jus Cogens* in International Law", in (1966) *AJIL* 55, Vol. 60, No. 1, pp. 55-63.

27. "Some Aspects of International *Jus Cogens* as Formulated by the ILC", (1967) *AJIL* 946, Vol. 61, No. 4, pp. 946-975.

398   *T. O. Elias*

"The Conference would be failing in its duty if it did not prescribe some clear-cut mechanism whereby the existence and content of peremptory rules of general international law could be properly identified and defined. The dangers of Article 50 as it stood would be very much greater for old-established and developed States than for others. Treaties concluded between, or applying as between, newly independent States might also be placed in jeopardy by the operation of that article".[28]

On the other hand, several delegations, especially of the newer States Members of the United Nations, considered the Commission's draft Article 62 satisfactory in that it did not impose compulsory judicial settlement of disputes arising out of Part V of the Convention but instead provided for a procedure requiring a party which invoked the nullity of a treaty to notify the other parties and give them appropriate opportunity to state their own views, and, in case of an objection by the other parties, to resort to the procedure laid down in Article 33 of the United Nations Charter. Those favouring this approach pointed out that the Geneva Conventions on the Law of the Sea and the two Vienna Conventions on Diplomatic and Consular Relations respectively did not contain provisions for compulsory judicial settlement by the International Court of Justice. The Commission took into consideration the discussions in the Special Committees on Principles of International Law concerning Friendly Relations and Co-operation between States,[29] the Charter and the Protocol of the Organization of African Unity, and other evidence of recent State practice in deciding that draft Article 62 "represented the highest measure of common ground that could be found among governments as well as in the Commission on this question".[30] After all, the International Court of Justice decision in the Second Phase of the *South West Africa Cases* (Liberia and Ethiopia *v.* South Africa),[31] which had astonished African and world opinion, was still fresh enough in the memory to excite opposition to the Court and even to undermine confidence in it. It, therefore, follows that the Commission finally took this position:

---

28. *Official Records,* First Session, p. 305.
29. The 1964 Report of the Special Committee (A/5746), Ch. IV and the 1966 Report (A/6230), Ch. III.
30. *1966 ILC Report,* para. 4, p. 90.
31. *ICJ Reports 1966,* p. 6.

The Validity of Treaties 399

"Even if, for the reasons previously mentioned in this commentary, the Commission felt obliged not to go beyond Article 33 of the Charter in providing for procedural checks upon arbitrary action, it considered that the establishment of the procedural provisions of the present article as an integral part of the law relating to the invalidity, termination and suspension of the operation of treaties would be a valuable step forward. The express subordination of the substantive rights arising under the provisions of the various articles to the procedure prescribed in the present article and the checks on unilateral action which the procedure contains would, it was thought, give a substantial measure of protection against purely arbitrary assertions of the nullity, termination or suspension of the operation of a treaty".[32]

These conclusions of the Commission were, however, not acceptable to a number of delegations from the Western European States and Japan. A Japanese amendment[33] sought to provide a safe guarantee for the settlement of *any* dispute that might arise under Part V. It provided that disputes arising in respect of *jus cogens* should be submitted to the International Court of Justice at the request of any of the parties, while in all other cases, if there was no settlement within twelve months through the means indicated in Article 33 of the United Nations Charter, the dispute should be submitted to arbitration unless the parties themselves agreed to submit it to the International Court of Justice. Of the various other amendments proposed, reference should be made to the thirteen-nation amendment[34] to Article 62. While agreeing with the provision in paragraph 3, the sponsors considered that the nature of the disputes likely to arise made it necessary to establish special procedures of a compulsory character. It, therefore, proposed that if the parties were unable to reach agreement *ad hoc* on a means of settlement and if no solution was reached within twelve months, either party could request the United Nations Secretary-General to set in motion the settlement procedures laid down in a proposed annex to the Convention. A conciliation phase should be followed by one of

---

32. *Ibid.*, para. 6, p. 90.
33. Doc. A/CONF.39/C.1/L.338 and L.339. A somewhat more extreme position in favour of the compulsory settlement of disputes under Part V was taken by Switzerland—see A/CONF.39/C.1/L.347. See also a proposed new Article 62 *bis* (Doc. A/CONF.39/C.1/L.348) and a new Article 76 (Doc. A/CONF.39/C.1/L.250).
34. UN Doc. A/CONF.39/C.1/L.352/Rev.1/Corr.1.

arbitration if no solution had been found after the first phase. A conciliation commission and an arbitral tribunal should be constituted, each allowing for either party to the dispute to designate two conciliators or arbitrators, as the case may be, and to appoint the chairman jointly. A permanent list of conciliators should be established for the purpose by the Secretary-General. The expenses of both bodies, but not the cost of the parties' pleadings, should be borne by the United Nations. The United States amendment[35] was a variant of this elaborate thirteen-States amendment. It proposed a commission of twenty-five on treaty disputes as well as a sub-commission, which should have the power to order provisional measures to preserve the rights of the parties pending settlement of the dispute. The Commission should be an organ of the United Nations, with power to request an advisory opinion from the International Court of Justice which, if requested by either party, should establish a chamber under Article 26 of its Statute for an expeditious settlement of the dispute. The commission should also have a reporting function with a view to effecting a friendly settlement of disputes. If the commission should fail, the dispute should be referred to an arbitral tribunal. The example of the Protocol of the Commission of Mediation, Conciliation and Arbitration of the Organization of African Unity was cited in support of this two-tier arrangement. The United States amendment finally proposed a procedure for a "stay of execution" where an objection had been raised to a measure proposed to be taken by a party invoking the invalidity of a treaty. No such measure could be carried out until final settlement unless the parties agreed otherwise or the commission or tribunal seized of the matter gave a provisional order.

After an adjournment of the debate and some days' further negotiations and consultations among the various groups of delegations, the text of Article 62 (now Article 65 of the Convention) as finally adopted reads as follows:[36]

> 1. A party which, under the provisions of the present convention, invokes either a defect in its consent to be bound by a treaty or a ground for impeaching the validity of a treaty, terminating it, withdrawing from it or suspending its operation, must notify the other parties of its claim. The notification shall indicate the measure proposed to be taken with respect to the treaty and the reasons therefor.

---

35. Doc. A/CONF.39/C.1/L.355, annex Articles 1-7 and parts 1-3.
36. *Official Records*, First Session, p. 489.

2. If, after the expiry of a period which, except in cases of special urgency, shall not be less than three months after the receipt of the notification, no party has raised any objection, the party making the notification may carry out in the manner provided in Article 67 [37] the measure which it has proposed.

3. If, however, objection has been raised by any other party, the parties shall seek a solution through the means indicated in Article 33 of the Charter of the United Nations.

4. Nothing in the foregoing paragraphs shall affect the rights or obligations of the parties under any provisions in force binding the parties with regard to the settlement of disputes.

5. Without prejudice to Article 45, the fact that a State has not previously made the notification prescribed in paragraph 1 shall not prevent it from making such notification in answer to another party claiming performance of the treaty or alleging its violation.

It was then agreed that the thirteen-States amendment [38] should be considered at the 1969 Session of the Conference as a proposed new Article 62 *bis,* and that all the amendments to Article 62, paragraph 3, could be recast and submitted in respect of the new article. [39]

When the second session of the Conference resumed its consideration of the new Article 62 *bis,* the position of the two main groups had hardly changed. There were repetitions of the old arguments for and against the inclusion of a form of compulsory conciliation or adjudication in the proposed new article. The Japanese and Swiss amendments of 1968 were rejected, while the thirteen-States amendment which after a revision had in the interval attracted six additional co-sponsors to become a nineteen-States amendment [40] was carried by a majority of 54 against 34, with 14 abstentions. An attempt by India, Yugoslavia,

---

37. Article 67 provides that the notification must be made in writing through an instrument communicated to the other parties. Unless the instrument is signed by the Head of State, Head of Government or Minister for Foreign Affairs, the representative of the State communicating the notification may be asked to produce full powers.

38. Doc. A/CONF.39/C.1/L.352/Rev.1/Corr.1.

39. See *Official Records*, p. 474.

40. Doc. A/CONF.39/C.1/L.352/Rev.3 and Add. 1 and 2 and Corr. 1 (1969). The original 13 States were Central African Republic, Colombia, Dahomey, Denmark, Finland, Gabon, Ivory Coast, Lebanon, Madagascar, Netherlands, Peru, Sweden and Tunisia. The six additions were Austria, Bolivia, Costa Rica, Malta, Mauritius and Uganda.

402   *T. O. Elias*

Tanzania and Indonesia to turn the amendment into an optional protocol was, however, defeated.[41]

Two issues which had been postponed from the 1968 to the 1969
Session of the Conference were the so-called "all-States" proposal[42] by
the Eastern European countries and the French proposal concerning
so-called "restricted multilateral treaties" which would permit a limited
group of States to have the right to restrict membership only to States
of their choice. The "all-States" proposal would give a right to all
States to participate in multilateral treaties, although the International
Law Commission had felt unable to define both concepts.[43] In the
end, the French withdrew their series of amendments, but the Soviet
group and a number of Asian and African delegations fought hard to
trade in acceptance of a disputes settlement procedure for the inclusion of a provision on the "all-States" formula. The various amendments[44] in connection with the "all-States" formula were nevertheless
finally rejected by the Conference.

The nineteen-States amendment could not, however, be adopted because it soon became clear that the necessary two-thirds majority could
not be achieved.[45] The impasse could not be overcome in view of the
insistence of the Western group of States that they would not be parties
to the Convention on the law of treaties unless a satisfactory disputes
settlement procedure was included in it. Equally, the opponents of this
idea would not budge. Indeed, strenuous efforts were made to incorporate the "all-States" formula in the Final Clauses.[46] This amendment,
if accepted, would have permitted split but unrecognised States like
the two Germanies, the two Koreas and the two Viet-Nams to become
parties to the convention through the signature and the accession
clauses. The Conference eventually rejected the proposal[47] in favour of
the so-called "Vienna formula" which limited participation to all
States Members of the United Nations or of its Specialised Agencies,
or of the International Atomic Energy Agency or parties to the Statute
of the International Court of Justice, and to any other State invited by

---

41. Doc. A/CONF.39/C.1/S.R.99, at 7 and 8.
42. Doc. A/CONF.39/C.1/L.74 and Add. 1 and 2.
43. *1966 ILC Report,* para. 8, pp. 22-23; para. 14, p. 38.
44. Doc. A/CONF.39/C.1/S.R. 104; S.R. 105.
45. Doc. A/CONF.39/S.R. 27, at 8.
46. Doc. A/CONF.39/S.R. 34; A/CONF.39/C.1/L.394.
47. Doc. A/CONF.39/C.1/S.R. 104, pp. 13-14.

the General Assembly of the United Nations to become a party to the convention.[48]

The impasse on settlement procedure was broken when a group of African and Asian delegations led by Nigeria put forward a compromise proposal in a new article entitled *Procedures for Judicial Settlement, Arbitration and Conciliation.*[49] In introducing the article sponsored by Ghana, Ivory Coast, Kenya, Kuwait, Lebanon, Morocco, Nigeria, Sudan, Tunisia and Tanzania, the present writer said that the plenary must adopt it as a "package deal" which could not be voted on in separate parts, and invited delegations to proceed to a vote on it without any undue delay. It was the last day of the Conference and the occasion was solemn. Up to that moment, it looked as if no convention would be adopted at the end of the day. Then, the Conference rose to the level of the occasion by adopting the new article by 61 votes in favour, 20 against and 26 abstentions. The main elements of the new Article 66 are that it enables a party to a dispute involving *jus cogens* to submit it to the International Court of Justice for adjudication in all cases in which Article 33 procedures have failed to produce a solution within twelve months, unless the parties to the dispute have agreed to refer it to arbitration. A dispute relating to the application or the interpretation of any of the other articles in Part V may be submitted by a party to the conciliation procedures embodied in the annex to the article by making a request to the United Nations Secretary-General in that behalf. In the annex is a provision for the establishment of a panel of jurists as conciliators, from among whom a conciliation commission would be constituted from time to time by the United Nations Secretary-General on the receipt of a request from a party to a dispute.

Article 66 provides as follows: [50]

> "If under paragraph 3 of Article 65, no solution has been reached within a period of 12 months following the date on which the objection was raised, the following procedures shall be followed:
>
> (a) any one of the parties to a dispute concerning the application or the interpretation of Article 53 or 64 may, by a written application, submit it to the International Court of Justice for a decision unless the parties by common consent agree to submit the dispute to arbitration;

---

48. See Articles 81-83 of the Convention.

49. Doc. A/CONF.39/S.R. 34, at 27.

50. This article must be read in conjunction with Article 65 of the Convention the provisions of which have been set out earlier in this chapter.

404   *T. O. Elias*

> *(b)* any one of the parties to a dispute concerning the application
> or the interpretation of any of the other articles in Part V of
> the present convention may set in motion the procedure
> specified in the Annex[51] to the convention by submitting a
> request to that effect to the Secretary-General of the United
> Nations".

This compromise solution will be found to combine certain features of
the Japanese and of the thirteen-nations amendments. What is new,
apart from the acceptance of the jurisdiction of the International Court
of Justice in cases of *jus cogens,* is the express provision for a conciliation commission with power to make findings of fact and of law.[52]
None of the previous conciliation-arbitration procedure proposals included such a provision.[53] This is a concession to the Western group
that had insisted on a commission having power to determine the legality of any allegation of invalidity of a treaty. Another new feature of
Article 66 is the change from requiring the commission to establish the
facts and make proposals for amicable settlement to requiring the commission to "hear the parties, examine the claims and objections and
make proposals to the parties". The commission's task thus goes beyond
that of being a mere mediator and amounts to its acting as a tribunal.
Where there is to be no arbitration, the conciliation stage should have
the character of a judicial settlement. There remains, however, one
weakness which the new Article 66 shares with the International Law
Commission's original draft, and that is the absence of any express
provision for the situation arising after the conciliation commission's
report has been submitted. Should the commission find that a claimant
State's allegation of invalidity of a treaty on the ground, say, of *jus
cogens* is established, that State could invoke the procedure laid down
in Article 65. But if the finding should be that a case of invalidity has
not been established, the accused State should be able to pursue the
remedy provided for in Article 69. The principle of *pacta sunt servanda*
under Article 26 should apply to enable the accused State to insist that
the claimant State remains bound under the treaty by considerations of
good faith.

---

51. The Annex is herewith reproduced as Annex II for ease of reference.
52. See Annex II, para. 6.
53. Except, perhaps, the United States amendment, Doc. A/CONF.39/C.1/
L.355, Article 5, para. 2, of the Annex.

CHAPTER V

CONSEQUENCES OF THE INVALIDITY OF A TREATY

The Commission's draft Article 65 on the consequences of the invalidity of a treaty read as follows:

"1. The provisions of a void treaty have no legal force.
2. If acts have nevertheless been performed in reliance on such a treaty:
   (a) Each party may require any other party to establish as far as possible in their mutual relations the position that would have existed if the acts had not been performed;
   (b) Acts performed in good faith before the nullity was invoked are not rendered unlawful by reason only of the nullity of the treaty.
3. In cases falling under Articles 46, 47, 48 or 49, paragraph 2 does not apply with respect to the party to which the fraud, coercion or corrupt act is imputable.
4. In the case of the invalidity of a particular State's consent to be bound by a multilateral treaty, the foregoing rules apply in the relations between that State and the parties to the treaty".

The Vienna Conference adopted amendments by the United States, France, Australia, Bulgaria and Poland[1] which were designed to make it clear that the article deals only with treaties proved to be invalid under the convention. The consequences of invalidity provided for therein will, therefore, follow only in such cases. As the Conference considered some of the proposed amendments to be useful in principle, paragraph 1 was in the end re-drafted as follows: "A treaty the invalidity of which is established under the present Convention is void. The provisions of a void treaty have no legal force". The United States proposal to delete sub-paragraphs 2 and 3 on the ground that it was strictly a matter of State responsibility which is put outside the scope of the Convention by the provisions of Article 73, was defeated. The

---

1. UN Doc. A/CONF.39/C.1/L.360; A/CONF.39/C.1/L.363; A/CONF.39/C.1/L.297; A/CONF.39/C.1/L.278. See also *Official Records*, 1968, p. 447.

406   *T. O. Elias*

Swiss representative had also proposed the deletion of paragraph 2 *(a)* and (3) of the draft article,[2] on the ground that the sanctions stipulated therein were a matter of State responsibility and would not always prove satisfactory in practice. He added:

> "Such a limited range of sanctions, with their possibly harsh results, might discourage the parties from settling their disputes amicably and encourage them to seek the maximum benefit from the invalidity. Moreover, it was an underlying principle of the Convention that treaties should continue to be performed until invalidity was established. But the parties would be disinclined to perform their obligations gratuitously while the invalidity was being discussed, if they knew that paragraph 3 denied them any right of recovery".[3]

This proposal was also rejected.[4] The only slight change made in Article 2 *(b)* was to substitute the word "invalidity" for the word "nullity" in the last line. This article was adopted as amended only after a prolonged and sometimes heated debate, even after its having been reported from the Drafting Committee to the Committee of the Whole.[5] The wording of paragraph 1 was as follows: "A treaty the invalidity of which is established under Articles 43 to 50 and 61, and in accordance with the procedures laid down in Article 62, is void". This rewording was intended to make the text clearer without affecting the substance. Several delegations, however, complained that the proposed change would have the effect of confining the section on invalidity to the specified articles, which constituted an unnecessary limitation of the scope of Article 65. The invalidity of a treaty could be raised not only as regards the conclusion of a treaty, but also as regards its implementation or its consequences. The Conference finally agreed to replace the reference to named articles by one to "the present Convention".

Article 69 does not concern itself with questions of State responsibility for acts that cause the invalidity of a treaty; rather, it relates only to the legal effects of the invalidity of a treaty. Once the nullity of a treaty is established, it is void *ab initio* and not from the date that the

---

2. A/CONF.39/C.1/L.358.
3. *Official Records*, 1968, p. 446.
4. *Ibid.*, p. 447.
5. See *Official Records*, First Session, pp. 490-492.

invalidity was invoked. The position is different where the treaty becomes void and terminates under Article 64; the treaty is not invalid from the date of its purported conclusion. The point is made explicit in paragraph 1.

The parties may have assumed the validity of a treaty and may have acted upon it in that belief for sometime before discovering its invalidity *ab initio*. What should the parties do in such a case? Much would depend on the position of the parties. If neither has been guilty of fraud, coercion or corruption, regard must be had for that fact, and there should as far as possible be a return to the *status quo ante*. It is necessary, however, to prevent parties from taking unfair advantage of one another if an apparently valid treaty turns out to be void *ab initio*. Where the act in question is for any other reason unlawful apart from the nullity or invalidity of the treaty itself, the provision in paragraph 2 *(b)* will not save it. In clear cases of the fraud, coercion or corruption of a party which has caused the invalidity of the treaty, it is not given any quarter. The last paragraph of the article deals with the case where the consent of a State to be bound by a multilateral treaty is nullified but acts have been performed on the basis of its assumed validity. The same principles governing the re-establishment of the *status quo ante* apply only in the relations between that particular State and the parties to the treaty.

The rules governing the consequences of the invalidity of a treaty which conflicts with a peremptory norm of general international law are laid down in Article 71 of the Convention as follows:

> "1. In the case of a treaty which is void under Article 53, the parties shall:
>
>   *(a)* eliminate as far as possible the consequences of any act performed in reliance on any provision which conflicts with the peremptory norm of general international law; and
>
>   *(b)* bring their mutual relations into conformity with the peremptory norm of general international law.
>
> 2. In the case of a treaty which becomes void or terminates under Article 64, the termination of the treaty:
>
>   *(a)* releases the parties from any obligation further to perform the treaty;
>
>   *(b)* does not affect any right, obligation or legal situation of the parties created through the execution of the treaty prior to its termination; provided that those rights, obliga-

tions or situations may thereafter be maintained only to
the extent that their maintenance is not in itself in conflict with the new peremptory norm of general international
law".

The Vienna Conference adopted this article as Article 71 of the
Convention with the substitution of the word "performed" for the word
"done" in paragraph 1 *(a)*, a tribute to the skill and wisdom of the
International Law Commission. Article 69 deals with consequences of
invalidity in the case of innocent parties as well as in the case where
one or more parties have been guilty of fraud, coercion or corruption
or, at least, where these acts are imputable to them. The case of *jus
cogens* was expressly reserved for separate treatment under the present
article.[6] The Commission had observed:

> "The nullity of a treaty *ab initio* by reason of its conflict with a
> rule of *jus cogens* in force at the time of its conclusion is a special
> case of nullity. The question which arises in consequence of the
> invalidity is not so much one of the adjustment of the position of
> the parties in relation to each other as of the obligation of each of
> them to bring its position into conformity with the rule of *jus
> cogens*".[7]

In the same way, the termination of a treaty which becomes void and
terminates under Article 64 because it is in conflict with a new rule of
jus cogens is a special case of termination as well as of invalidity,
especially as the invalidity does not operate *ab initio*. The consequences
of invalidity under Article 64 ought logically to be governed by the
provisions of Article 69. It would at first sight seem strange to assert,
as does Article 71, that the nullity of a treaty will not affect rights,
obligations or legal situations brought about by the execution of the
treaty prior to its termination, because the emergence of a new rule of
jus cogens operates to release the parties from any obligation to perform the treaty. There is no doubt that, since the new rule of *jus
cogens* will not operate *ex tunc*, it will not affect any right, obligation
or legal situation created *before* the treaty becomes void; but, unless
the parties agree, it cannot be said that such a right, obligation or

---

6. *1966 ILC Report*, para. 4, p. 92.
7. *Ibid.*, para. 1, p. 93.

legal situation can be maintained *after* the treaty has become void.

It will be generally agreed that acts, which have been performed in good faith in reliance on a treaty considered by the parties to be valid at the time, do not become illegal by reason of the fact that the treaty is subsequently shown to be invalid. But this has reference only to acts the performance of which had already been completed, not to acts which have been performed while the treaty is valid but which continues in existence after the treaty has become void. The doctrine of acquired rights clearly cannot be invoked in such a case.

A Finnish amendment[8] would introduce the concept of separability to this article but had to be withdrawn in the face of widespread criticism that it was an attempt to re-introduce a proposal already rejected by the Conference.[9] A Mexican amendment[10] proposed that the question arising as a result of the invalidity of a treaty was not so much one of the adjustment of the position of the parties in their mutual relations as one of the obligation incumbent upon each to bring its position into conformity with the *jus cogens* rule. Several delegations pointed out that the proposed amendment was already implicit in the Commission's draft article, and it too was rejected. The draft article was accordingly adopted without amendment as Article 71 of the Convention.

Conclusions

On the basis of our fairly detailed examination of the problems of validity of treaties in international law, certain broad inferences and conclusions would seem to have emerged. The Convention clearly contained large elements of progressive development and codification in this area of treaty law.[11] The various grounds of invalidity dealt with represent the first detailed treatment of the rules in any treaty, bilateral or multilateral. Also, neither State practice nor the writings of publicists afford us any such comprehensive and analytic study of the topics of

---

8. UN Doc. A/CONF.39/C.1/L.295.

9. *Official Records,* First Session, pp. 449, 483.

10. UN Doc. A/CONF.39/C.1/L.356.

11. The seventh paragraph of the preamble to the Convention expresses the belief "that the codification and progressive development of the law of treaties achieved in the present Convention will promote the purposes of the United Nations set forth in the Charter, namely, the maintenance of international peace and security, the development of friendly relations and the achievement of co-operation among nations".

410   *T. O. Elias*

error, fraud, corruption, coercion (use or threat of force) and, above all, *jus cogens*. Decisions and dicta of international tribunals and judges have sometimes alluded to some of these grounds of invalidity of treaties and even occasionally attempted to clarify certain notions and principles relating to them. But the international community had had to await the fruits of the twenty-year labours of the International Law Commission as embodied in the 1966 draft articles.

The pioneering character of the text of the Convention explains why the tripartite partnership of the International Law Commission, the governments that had commented on the drafts at different stages and the Vienna Conference on the Law of Treaties took so long to produce results which at least two-thirds of the Member States of the United Nations and others found it expedient, and even necessary, to adopt in May 1969. The final adoption took place, however, only after the various draft articles submitted by the International Law Commission had been subjected to some of the most cogent and acute analyses of which contemporary knowledge is capable. This was especially the case with the use or threat of force and the rule of *jus cogens* on both of which there was the greatest divergence of views as between the older and the newer States Members of the United Nations. While the former resisted the incorporation in the Convention of the relatively novel rules and their formulation, the latter insisted that there must be new universally accepted standards of international behaviour in the field of treaty relations that had remained hitherto unsystematised by any concerted international effort.[12]

Of the several grounds of invalidity, the *jus cogens* rule has proved to be the most controversial, if because the most important. Here, for the first time, has been articulated the previously latent and imprecise principle that there exists an over-riding, peremptory norm of general international law which invalidates all treaties inconsistent with it because States are not permitted to derogate from it. It is a form of international public policy or *ordre public* for the community of States. There has thus been recognised a transition from the concept of an international *society* to that of an international *community,* ever more closely integrated and inter-dependent.

In certain cases, a treaty is void, while in others it is merely voidable. Certain types of error make treaties generally voidable, but fraud,

---

12. The fifth preambular paragraph recalls "the determination of the peoples of the United Nations to establish conditions under which justice and respect for the obligations arising from treaties can be maintained".

The Validity of Treaties 411

corruption, coercion and conflict with a *jus cogens* rule have the effect of voiding treaties. Where the alleged ground of invalidity is fraud or corruption of a representative, the Convention renders the clauses of a treaty severable if the clauses in question are separable or if a severed clause does not go to the root of the treaty and if the continued performance of the remainder of the treaty would not be unjust. Where, on the other hand, fraud, corruption, coercion or original *jus cogens* is involved, the entire treaty is void and no severance of the clauses of any treaty is allowed.[13]

The Vienna Convention on the Law of Treaties ensures that, from now on, *all* States are required to conduct their external relations according to ascertainable and established rules of international conduct. This necessarily implies that, for all its novelty, the Convention also makes express provisions for the maintenance of the integrity of treaties, and insists in several instances that no undue advantage may be taken by *any* State, old or new, of the newly adopted grounds of the invalidity of treaties. Thus, a State loses its right to invoke a ground of invalidity in the case of constitutional limitation of or specific restriction on the treaty-making powers of its representative, error, fraud or corruption if, on becoming aware of the facts, the State concerned has *either* agreed to treat the treaty as valid or as remaining in force, *or* acquiesced in the validity of the treaty.[14] Again, the Convention applies only to treaties concluded between States after its entry into force in respect of such States, unless it is expressly provided otherwise in the Convention.[15] This provision of the non-retroactivity of the grounds of invalidity is a realistic safeguard against possible abuse. Nor must we under-rate the importance and value of the disputes-settlement procedure built into the fabric of the Convention, involving as they do recourse to conciliation, arbitration and, in the case of *jus cogens,* the International Court of Justice.[16] The ultimate acceptance of this necessary mechanism of determining the existence and the nature of an alleged ground of invalidity is a tribute to the sense of realism and maturity of all the participants in the Vienna Conference. It is partly for this reason that the Convention has been rightly described as the "treaty on treaties".[17]

---

13. Article 44.
14. Article 45 of the Convention.
15. Article 4.
16. Articles 65 and 66.
17. Kearney and Dalton, *op. cit.*

412

ANNEX I

DECLARATION ON THE PROHIBITION OF THE THREAT OR USE OF ECONOMIC OR POLITICAL COERCION IN CONCLUDING A TREATY

"The United Nations Conference on the Law of Treaties

Upholding the principle that every treaty in force is binding upon the parties to it and must be performed by them in good faith;

Reaffirming the principle of sovereign equality of States;

Convinced that States must have complete freedom in performing any act relating to the conclusion of a treaty;

Mindful of the fact that in the past instances have occurred where States have been forced to conclude treaties under pressures in various forms exercised by other States;

Deprecating the same;

Expressing its concern at the exercise of such pressure and anxious to ensure that no such pressures in any form are exercised by any State whatever in the matter of conclusion of treaties;

1. Solemnly condemns the threat or use of pressure in any form, military, political or economic, by any State, in order to coerce another State to perform any act relating to the conclusion of a treaty in violation of the principle of sovereign equality of States and freedom of consent;

2. Decides that the present declaration shall form part of the Final Act of the Conference on the Law of Treaties."

413

ANNEX II

1. A list of conciliators consisting of qualified jurists shall be drawn up and maintained by the Secretary-General of the United Nations. To this end, every State which is a Member of the United Nations or a party to the present Convention shall be invited to nominate two conciliators, and the names of the persons so nominated shall constitute the list. The term of a conciliator, including that of any conciliator nominated to fill a casual vacancy, shall be five years and may be renewed. A conciliator whose term expires shall continue to fulfil any function for which he shall have been chosen under the following paragraph.

2. When a request has been made to the Secretary-General under Article 66, the Secretary-General shall bring the dispute before a conciliation commission constituted as follows:

The State or States constituting one of the parties to the dispute shall appoint:

(a) one conciliator of the nationality of that State or of one of those States, who may or may not be chosen from the list referred to in paragraph 1; and

(b) one conciliator not of the nationality of that State or of any of those States, who shall be chosen from the list.

The State or States constituting the other party to the dispute shall appoint two conciliators in the same way. The four conciliators chosen by the parties shall be appointed within sixty days following the date on which the Secretary-General receives the request.

The four conciliators shall, within sixty days following the date of the last of their own appointments, appoint a fifth conciliator chosen from the list, who shall be chairman.

If the appointment of the chairman or of any of the other conciliators has not been made within the period prescribed above for such appointment, it shall be made by the Secretary-General within sixty days following the expiry of that period. The appointment of the chairman may be made by the Secretary-General either from the list or from the membership of the International Law Commission. Any of the periods within which appointments must be made may be extended by agreement between the parties to the dispute.

Any vacancy shall be filled in the manner prescribed for the initial appointment.

3. The Conciliation Commission shall decide its own procedure. The Commission, with the consent of the parties to the dispute, may invite any party to the treaty to submit to it its views orally or in writing. Decisions and recommendations of the Commission shall be made by a majority vote of the five members.

4. The Commission may draw the attention of the parties to the dispute to any measures which might facilitate an amicable settlement.

5. The Commission shall hear the parties, examine the claims and objections, and make proposals to the parties with a view to reaching an amicable settlement of the dispute.

6. The Commission shall report within twelve months of its constitution. Its report shall be deposited with the Secretary-General and transmitted to the parties to the dispute. The report of the Commission, including any conclusions stated therein regarding the facts or questions of law, shall not be binding upon the parties and it shall have no other character than that of recommendations submitted for the consideration of the parties in order to facilitate an amicable settlement of the dispute.

7. The Secretary-General shall provide the Commission with such assistance and facilities as it may require. The expenses of the Commission shall be borne by the United Nations.

415

BIBLIOGRAPHY

INTRODUCTION

General problems relating to Validity of Treaties, Yearbooks of the International Law Commission 1950, 1956, 1961, 1962.
The Report of the International Law Commission, 1966.
W. Friedmann's "The United Nations and the Development of International Law", *International Law Journal,* Vol. XXV, No. 2, 1970, pp. 272-286.
R. D. Kearney and R. E. Dalton's "The Treaty on Treaties", *AJIL,* Vol. 64, No. 3, July 1970, p. 495.
Free Zones Case, PCIJ, Series A/B, No. 46, p. 140.
S.S. Wimbledon, PCIJ, Series A, No. 1, p. 24.
Norwegian Loans Case, ICJ Reports 1957, at pp. 55-59.
The Interhandel Case, ICJ Reports 1959, at pp. 57, 77-78 and 116-117.
The Arbitral Award made by the King of Spain, ICJ Reports 1960, pp. 213-214.
The Temple of Preah Vihear, ICJ Reports 1962, pp. 23-32, 39-51, 62-65.
The Official Records of the United Nations Conference on the Law of Treaties, First Session, 1968, pp. 472-473.

CHAPTER I

C. C. Hyde, *International Law,* Vol. 2, p. 1383-1384.
Lord McNair, *The Law of Treaties,* 1960, OUP, pp. 60, 69, 83-94.
Treatment of Polish Nationals in Danzig (1932), *PCIJ, Series A/B, No. 44,* p. 24.
"The Harvard Draft Convention on the Law of Treaties", in *AJIL* (1935), Vol. XXIX, Supplement, p. 661.
The Yearbook of the International Law Commission, 1951, Vol. II, p. 73.
Hans Blix, *Treaty-Making Power,* 1960, p. 303.
The Legal Status of Eastern Greenland Case, PCIJ, Series A/B, No. 53, pp. 56-71, 91.
The Free Zones Case, PCIJ, Series A/B, No. 46, p. 170.
M. O. Hudson, *International Tribunals,* 1944, at p. 130.
The Official Records, First Session, p. 246.

CHAPTER II

Lord McNair, *Law of Treaties,* OUP, 1961, p. 211.
W. E. Hall, *A Treatise on International Law,* 4th ed., OUP 1895, p. 342.
G. Schwarzenberger, *A Manual of International Law,* 5th ed., 1967, pp. 158-159.
C. C. Hyde, *International Law,* Vol. II, 1951, 2nd ed., p. 1382.
C. W. Jenks, *The Prospects of International Adjudication,* Stevens, London, pp. 196-519.
The Legal Status of Eastern Greenland (1933), *PCIJ, Series A/B, No. 53,* pp. 71, 92.
The Temple of Preah Vihear (Preliminary Objections), *ICJ Reports 1961,* p. 30.
Bell v. *Lever Brothers Ltd.* (1932) A.C. 161, at p. 217.
The 1966 Report of the International Law Commission, pp. 72-73.
Readaptation of the Mavrommatis Jerusalem Concessions, PCIJ, Series A, No. 11.
The Mavrommatis Palestine Concessions (Merits) Case, PCIJ, Series C, No. 7, ii, p. 212.

416   *T. O. Elias*

Cheshire and Fifoot's *Law of Contract*, 1st ed., pp. 137-158.
Yearbook of the International Law Commission, 1963, Vol. I, pp. 43-45.
The Orinoco Steamship Company Case (see J. B. Scott's *The Hague Court Reports*, 1916, pp. 226-239).
"The Harvard Law Institute Draft Articles on Law of Treaties" (1935) *AJIL*, Vol. 29, Supplement 653, p. 1126.
Hackworth, *Digest of International Law*, Vol. 5, pp. 93 ff.
Summary of the Practice of the Secretary-General as Depositary of Multilateral Agreements, pp. 8-10, 19-20 and the Annexes.
The Official Records, First Session, pp. 256, 264-265, paras. 14-17.

CHAPTER III

The 1966 International Law Commission's Report, pp. 74, 75, 76.
The Official Records, First Session, pp. 256-257, 266-268, 269-293.
D. P. O'Connell, *International Law*, Vol. I, p. 261.
Lord McNair, *Law of Treaties*, p. 207.
C. W. Jenks, *The Prospects of International Adjudication*, pp. 421-422.
W. E. Hall, *International Law*, 4th ed., p. 342.
C. C. Hyde, *International Law*, Vol. 2, 2nd ed., p. 1380.
The Corfu Channel Case (Merits), *ICJ Reports 1949*, pp. 4, 35.
Yearbook of the International Law Commission, 1966, Vol. II, p. 19.

CHAPTER IV

C. W. Jenks, *The Prospects of International Adjudication*, Stevens, London, at p. 504.
The Oscar Chinn Case (1934) *PCIJ, Series A/B, No. 63*, pp. 149-150.
Lord McNair, *Law of Treaties*, pp. 213-215.
1966 International Law Commission's Report, pp. 76-77.
G. Schwarzenberger, "International *Jus Cogens*", *Texas Law Review*, March 1955, p. 455 at p. 477.
A. Verdross, "*Jus Dispositivum* and *Jus Cogens* in International Law" (1966) *AJIL* 55, Vol. 60, No. 1, pp. 55-63.
E. Schwelb, "Some Aspects of International *Jus Cogens* as Formulated by the International Law Commission", (1967) *AJIL* 946, Vol. 61, No. 4, pp. 946-975.
South West Africa Cases (Liberia and Ethiopia v. *South Africa), ICJ Reports 1966*, p. 6.

CHAPTER V

The Text of the Vienna Convention on the Law of Treaties, 1969.
Official Records, First Session, pp. 446-447, 449, 483, 490-492.
1966 Report of the International Law Commission, pp. 92-93.

[13]

DOWN THE DANUBE: THE VIENNA CONVENTION ON THE LAW OF TREATIES AND THE *CASE CONCERNING THE GABCÍKOVO-NAGYMAROS PROJECT*

DANIEL REICHERT-FACILIDES*

OVER the last 30 years, the Vienna Convention on the Law of Treaties[1] has emerged as one of the most influential instruments of modern international law. The Convention, which was adopted at the UN Conference on the Law of Treaties on 23 May 1969, entered into force on 27 January 1980 and has meanwhile been ratified by more than 80 States.[2] Yet, as it does not operate retroactively,[3] the scope of application is growing only slowly and its practical importance stems, rather, from the fact that the Convention is widely considered a restatement of customary international law. As early as 1971 the International Court of Justice referred to the articles governing termination for breach of treaty as a codification of the existing law on the subject.[4] Since then both international tribunals and national courts have more and more habitually relied on the material provisions of the Convention to ascertain traditional rules of the law of treaties.[5]

The success of the Vienna Convention on the Law of Treaties clearly reflects the virtues of codification, viz. to provide an easily accessible and comprehensive source of the law.[6] At the same time, it has exposed the Convention to the problems of ageing legislation earlier than its drafters may have expected: while they adopted some new tendencies such as the concept of *jus cogens* and a compulsory procedure for the peaceful settlement of disputes, most articles restate the law as it stood in the late 1960s. Moreover, the International Law Commission deliberately excluded a number of topics that appeared to be either too contentious or too com-

---

* Rechtsanwalt, Berlin. My thanks go to Philippe Sands and Benedict Kingsbury.

1. 1155 U.N.T.S. 331.

2. By 31 Dec. 1996, 81 States were parties to the Convention; see *Multilateral Treaties Deposited with the Secretary-General, Status as at 31 December 1996*, UN Doc.ST/LEG/SER.E/15, p.869.

3. See Art.4 of the Convention.

4. *Legal Consequences for States of the Continued Presence of South Africa in Namibia (South West Africa)* I.C.J. Rep. 1971, 47.

5. For some recent examples see e.g. *Opel Austria GmbH* v. *Council of the European Union* [1997] E.C.R. II-43, 70; *R.* v. *Secretary of State for the Home Department, ex p. Flynn*, Queen's Bench Division CO/2310/93, *The Times*, 23 Mar. 1995; *Sale* v. *Haitian Centers Council, Inc.* 509 U.S. 155, 191 (1993).

6. See Brierly, *The Law of Nations* (6th edn, 1963), pp. 78–80, and, for a recent comprehensive overview on codification in international law, Jennings and Watts (Eds), *Oppenheim's International Law* (9th edn, 1992), Vol.I/1, pp.96–115.

plex.[7] This approach may have helped to ensure widespread acceptance, but it also contradicts the claim for comprehensiveness that is inherent to any codification.

As becomes clear from the Preamble, which explicitly reserves the role of customary law for the areas not covered, the drafters of the Convention were, of course, aware of these problems. Yet the International Court's recent judgment in the *Case Concerning the Gabcïkovo-Nagymaros Project* probably demonstrates the full extent of the methodological implications for the first time.[8] Taking some of the specific issues decided by the Court as examples, the following comments will focus mainly on how the Court has addressed the difficulties of an ageing and fragmentary codification, which are by no means peculiar to international law.[9]

I.   THE CASE AND THE JUDGMENT OF 27 SEPTEMBER 1997

THE *Case Concerning the Gabcïkovo-Nagymaros Project* arose from a dispute between Hungary and Slovakia over the construction of a system of locks on the Danube, which for some 140 kilometres forms the common boundary of the two States. The main purpose of the project that had been agreed in a treaty of 16 September 1977[10] was the joint operation of two hydroelectric power plants with a total output of 878 megawatts. While the technical and scientific details are highly complex, some basic understanding of the scheme is essential for the evaluation of the judgment.

According to the 1977 Treaty, the Danube was first to be dammed near the Hungarian village of Dunakiliti, where it becomes the boundary river of the two States after a short passage through Slovakia. At the dam, most of the water was to be diverted to a by-pass canal on Slovak territory, leaving only a small portion to the old river bed. A hydroelectric barrage halfway on the by-pass canal near Gabcïkovo would then generate the energy for the main 720-megawatt power plant before returning the water to the old river bed some 30 kilometres downstream from Dunakiliti.

A second barrage was to be built another 115 kilometres downstream near Nagymaros, where the Danube finally enters Hungarian territory. The Nagymaros structure was supposed to generate another 158 megawatts of electric energy, but its main purpose was to attenuate the effects of the so-called peak mode operation of the Gabcïkovo plant: according to the original plan, the water to be diverted to the by-pass canal would be

---

7. (1966) II Y.B.I.L.C. 176–177.

8. Judgment of 27 September 1997 (1998) 37 I.L.M. 162.

9. As the emphasis of this article lies on methodological questions, the treatment of substantive issues is not meant to be exhaustive even as regards the law of treaties: in particular, the role of new norms of international environmental law for the interpretation of treaties will be considered only occasionally; the question of State succession, dealt with at paras.117–124 of the judgment, *idem*, is entirely omitted.

10. For the complete text of the Treaty see (1993) 32 I.L.M. 1249

kept back at the Dunakiliti reservoir most of the day in order to obtain maximum output at times of peak energy demand, notably in the morning and the early afternoon. If they were left unregulated, the flood-waves resulting from the sudden release of the water could have affected water management and navigation down to the estuaries. Hence the need for a second barrage.[11]

While a second barrage can attenuate the downstream effects of peak mode operation, the ecological impacts on the section of the river immediately affected are both inevitable and, in principle, self-evident. They range from the quality of ground and surface water to the fauna and flora, the micro-climate and local water resources. Some of these effects were already known when Hungary and Czechoslovakia entered into the 1977 Treaty, which, indeed, includes specific provisions for the protection of water quality, fishing interests and the natural environment.[12] However, the extent of the environmental impact became clear only as scientific knowledge and public awareness increased in the late 1980s. During the same period ecological issues emerged as a purportedly unpolitical topic of democratic protest throughout Eastern Europe. As a result, the Hungarian government decided to reassess the environmental implications and, in May 1989, suspended the works a few weeks after the parties had agreed finally to complete the project within five years by a protocol of 6 February 1989. While the works at Dunakiliti and Gabcïkovo were well advanced at that time, the construction of the Nagymaros barrage (on which the Hungarian environmentalist groups had focused) had hardly begun.

The suspension of the works led to an immediate protest from Czechoslovakia followed by a series of fruitless talks between the two governments. As it became evident that Hungary was more or less determined to abandon the project for both ecological and political reasons, Czechoslovakia proceeded to what it called the "provisional solution" or "Variant C": in order to operate the Gabcïkovo barrage notwithstanding Hungary's refusal to complete the works at Dunakiliti, another dam was built a few kilometres upstream on Czechoslovak territory at Cunovo, whence the waters of the Danube could be diverted to the by-pass canal without Hungary's consent. In reply, on 16 May 1992 Hungary unilaterally denounced the 1977 Treaty, invoking, *inter alia*, environmental necessity, fundamental change of circumstances and material breach of treaty.[13]

---

11. The minimum distance between the two barrages depends on the drop of the river, which is extremely low on the relevant section of the Danube. This explains why the Nagymaros barrage had to be situated more than 100 km downstream from Gabcïkovo.

12. See Arts.15, 19 and 20 of the Treaty.

13. For the text of the Declaration of 16 May 1992 see (1993) 32 I.L.M. 1260.

Czechoslovakia rejected the declaration and continued construction of Variant C. In November 1992 the Gabčikovo power plant finally started operations—albeit not at peak power mode but as a regular run-of-the-river hydroelectric power station—with most of the waters of the Danube being diverted to the by-pass canal.

As this stand-off between the two neighbouring States was evidently not sustainable in the long run,[14] the governments of Hungary and Slovakia[15] submitted the dispute to the International Court by a Special Agreement of 28 June 1993.[16] During the ensuing proceedings both sides produced extensive scientific evidence supporting their respective views on the environmental implications of the original project. In a nutshell, the Court generally admitted the ecological impact but found no sufficient proof to support Hungary's case.[17] Consequently, it ruled that the suspension and abandonment of the works in 1989 had been illegal and that Hungary's environmental concerns constituted no valid grounds for the denunciation of the Treaty.

However, the Court also rejected Slovakia's argument that Variant C, which deprived Hungary of its share in the Danube up to the point where the by-pass canal rejoined the old river bed, could be justified as a legitimate countermeasure or as an approximate application of the Treaty. At the same time, it refused to give effect to Hungary's denunciation for breach of treaty because the Declaration of 16 May 1992 had preceded the actual deviation of the river. Consequently, the Treaty was held to be still in force although both parties had breached their respective obligations.

If the findings on the past conduct of the parties are remarkable for their frequent references to the Vienna Convention on the Law of Treaties—which did not apply directly to the case—the Court took an almost opposite approach when it came to determine the legal consequences of the dispute: leaving the wording of the Treaty aside, the Court suggested that Slovakia would not insist on the construction of the Nagymaros barrage if Hungary agreed to a common regime for the operation of Variant

14. Both countries had already expressed their aspiration for membership of the EU.

15. On 1 Jan. 1993 the Czech and Slovak Republics had succeeded to former Czechoslovakia as two independent States.

16. For the text of the Special Agreement see (1993) 32 I.L.M. 1294; under Art.2, the ICJ was requested (1) to decide: (a) whether Hungary had been entitled to suspend and later abandon the works at Nagymaros and Dunakiliti; (b) whether Czechoslovakia had been entitled to proceed to and put into operation Variant C; (c) whether the Hungarian notification of termination was effective; and (2) to determine the consequences arising from these legal findings.

17. More precisely, the ICJ based its decision on the assumption that Hungary's pleadings did not meet the standard of environmental necessity, see judgment, *supra* n.8, at paras.55–56. While this corresponds with a general tendency among judges to avoid contentious findings on the scientific facts, it is all the more understandable if one takes into account that the ICJ is rather used to historical maps and diplomatic documents as means of factual evidence.

C. Moreover, the adversaries were called upon to reconsider and accommodate the environmental effects of the project. In practical terms, this means that the Treaty now has to be renegotiated along the guidelines set forth in the judgment.

The outcome of the case as reported above clearly reflects an attempt to strike a reasonable balance between the interests of the two parties: the Court neither ordered Hungary to build the Nagymaros barrage nor did it deprive Slovakia of the benefits of the enormous investment in the construction of the Gabcïkovo power plant and the by-pass canal. Moreover, the judgment lays the foundations for a sustainable environmental regime that accommodates the project and for the normalisation of relations between the two countries, which had only recently emerged from Soviet domination. Yet there is no doubt that the Court was perfectly aware that its decision will also be read as an authoritative statement on a number of previously unresolved legal issues, both in international environmental law and in the law of treaties. The striving to reconcile abstract policy considerations and concrete dispute resolution probably accounts for the somewhat meandering line of argument in the judgment. The statements on the law of treaties to be analysed below, therefore, should not be weighed individually but in the context of the three central issues put before the Court, viz. Hungary's environmental concerns (*infra* Part II), Czechoslovakia's proceeding to Variant C (Part III) and the consequences of the dispute for the future relations between the two States (Part IV).

II. HUNGARY'S ENVIRONMENTAL CONCERNS

IN the proceedings before the International Court, Hungary had invoked its environmental concerns both as a justification for the suspension and later abandonment of the works in 1989 and as a ground for the denunciation of the Treaty in 1992. Following the order suggested by Article 2 of the Special Agreement, the Court first dealt with the suspension and abandonment of the works.[18] In the eyes of the Court these measures had been illegal because Hungary had shown no grave and imminent peril that would exclude responsibility under Article 33 of the Draft Articles on State Responsibility. Under these factual premises, it is not surprising that the later passages of the judgment rejecting Hungary's environmental arguments with regard to the termination of the Treaty are rather short.[19]

Short as they may be, the Court's answers to Hungary's environmental arguments—which were conceptually framed as necessity, impossibility

---

18. Judgment, *idem*, paras.49–57.
19. Idem, paras.101–104, 112; however, it should also be kept in mind that allowing for unilateral termination of the Treaty by Hungary would practically have excluded the possibility of a later settlement and, thus, would have put the entire burden of the conflict on Slovakia.

and fundamental change of circumstances—are interesting for their literal reliance on the Vienna Convention on the Law of Treaties. As Hungary and Czechoslovakia had become parties to the Vienna Convention only in 1987,[20] it did not apply directly to the 1977 Treaty.[21] However, there was no doubt that the Court would take the pertinent provisions of the Convention into consideration, which it had on several occasions already endorsed as a codification of existing customary international law.[22] What is more remarkable is the general statement that Articles 60 to 62 of the Vienna Convention define the conditions under which a treaty may lawfully be terminated or suspended without the other parties' consent "in a limitative manner".[23]

If the last proposition holds true, any denunciation of a treaty henceforth has to be framed under one of the three headings suggested by the Vienna Convention, viz. material breach, supervening impossibility of performance or fundamental change of circumstances. On its face this seems to imply a policy decision favouring legal security over substantive justice, since the latter may call for the admission of new grounds of termination in special cases. Yet, if the primary object of codification is indeed to provide a comprehensive source of law (as opposed to the regulatory focus of statutory legislation), the gains must not necessarily be offset by a loss of flexibility. In this respect, Hungary's attempt to invoke environmental necessity as a cause for termination lends itself as a good example.

A. Necessity

In its treatment of the Hungarian argument on immediate ecological danger, the Court strictly limited the concept of necessity to the law of State responsibility. Accordingly, a state of necessity may serve as an excuse for the temporary non-compliance with a party's obligations under a treaty,

20. The two States acceded to the Vienna Convention on 19 June 1987 and 29 July 1987 respectively; see *Multilateral Treaties, loc. cit. supra* n.2.
21. See Art.4 of the Convention.
22. See judgment, *supra* n. 8, at para.46, referring to the *South West Africa* case, *supra* n.4, the *Fisheries Jurisdiction* case (*Jurisdiction of the Court*) I.C.J. Rep. 1973, 18, and the *WHO and Egypt case*, I.C.J. Rep. 1980, 95–96. Nevertheless, the ICJ did not rely exclusively on the concept of codification: instead, it also recalled that "it had not lost sight of the fact" that the Vienna Convention directly applied to the Protocol of 6 Feb. 1989, by which the two governments had agreed on a new time schedule for the remaining works. Since this peculiarity may, indeed, have justified a more literal approach, one may regret that the ICJ has wrapped the argument into a somewhat nebulous formula which does not allow one to ascertain its exact significance for the judgment. However, the remark indicates that a subsequent agreement governed by the Vienna Convention also enhances its authority with regard to the underlying treaty.
23. Judgment, *idem*, para.47.

but it can never be called upon as a ground for unilateral termination.[24] Since the Court had already denied the existence of a grave and imminent peril at this stage,[25] the practical implications of the argument are not immediately evident from the judgment. However, supposing that a state of necessity had been established, one may wonder whether the parties should be bound indefinitely by a dormant treaty, as the Court suggested; for, although it is true that a treaty may always be terminated by mutual consent to accommodate this situation, the law cannot limit itself to an appeal to common sense where the latter has been lost.

Another answer to the problem, which attempts to reconcile the desire for a limited set of legal rules with the diversity of the real world, is to address necessity within the concept of a fundamental change of circumstances once it comes to the termination of treaties.[26] In fact, the conditions determining necessity under the law of State responsibility can roughly be equated to the elements of a fundamental change of circumstances as set forth in Article 62 of the Vienna Convention, provided that the different perspectives are taken into account: whereas Article 33 of the Draft Articles on State Responsibility[27] defines necessity by reference to the *occurrence* of the incident that gives rise to the claim for termination, the circumstances that may become relevant under Article 62 have to be evaluated in the light of the parties' *expectations* at the time when they entered into the treaty.

Subject to this qualification, the two concepts largely overlap. Thus it can be assumed that the absence of grave peril to an essential interest of the State regularly constitutes part of the basis for the consent of the parties, and that the later emergence of such peril radically alters the nature of the parties' obligations under the treaty within the meaning of Article 62 of the Vienna Convention. The negative condition that necessity may not be relied upon where it has been anticipated by a treaty[28] finally correlates with the requirement that the change of circumstances must be unforeseen.

As the comparison of the two provisions reveals, necessity and fundamental change of circumstances are not mutually exclusive concepts but

---

24. *Idem*, para.101; it should be noted that necessity was never universally accepted as a ground for the unilateral termination of treaties by a majority of States; see Vamvoukos, *Termination of Treaties under International Law* (1985), p.202, and De Visscher, *Théorie et Réalités en Droit International Public* (3rd edn, 1960), pp.338–340.

25. Judgment, *idem*, paras.55–56.

26. Interestingly, the subchapter dealing with necessity as a ground for unilateral termination in the 3rd edition of De Visscher, *op. cit. supra* n.24, was replaced with the discussion of fundamental change under the Vienna Convention in the 4th edition (1970), pp.297–298.

27. International Law Commission Draft Articles on the International Responsibility of States (1980) II Y.B.I.L.C. 34.

28. See *idem*, Art.33, para.2(b).

simply relate to different remedies, viz. the excuse for non-compliance with international obligations and the right to unilateral termination of treaties.[29] If the Court has not failed to make this distinction,[30] it would have been preferable to note also the substantive overlap, and to extend the later analysis under Article 62 of the Vienna Convention to the facts underlying Hungary's claim for necessity. In the absence of the emergence of a grave and imminent peril qualifying as a fundamental change, this would not have affected the outcome of the case but it could have attenuated the apparent rigour of the Court's statement on the limitative function of Articles 60 to 62 of the Vienna Convention.

B. Impossibility

Of the three grounds for termination related to Hungary's environmental concerns, the claim of impossibility of performance was probably most far-fetched. Article 61 of the Vienna Convention limits the concept of impossibility to cases in which an object indispensable to the execution of the treaty has been destroyed or permanently disappeared. According to the International Law Commission's Commentary, the provision addresses instances such as the submerging of an island, the drying-up of a river or the destruction of a dam.[31] Evidently this does not include the deliberate abandonment of the works explicitly undertaken by Hungary in the 1977 Treaty.

The Court, however, did not rule out a broader interpretation of Article 61 that would extend to the environmental and economic sustainability of the project.[32] Rather, it confined itself to the argument that the 1977 Treaty provided for consultation procedures to address these concerns; if consultation had failed and joint exploitation of the project was no longer possible, this was essentially due to Hungary's refusal to comply with its obligations under the Treaty. In such cases, the party responsible for the event of impossibility is, indeed, barred from invoking it as a ground for termination under Article 61, paragraph 2, of the Vienna Convention.

C. Fundamental Change

Whereas the concept of impossibility relates to the proper *object* of a treaty (either in a physical or in a more abstract sense), Article 62 of the

29. For a general discussion of the relationship between the law of treaties and State responsibility see Reuter, *Introduction to the Law of Treaties* (1989), pp.150–153.

30. Judgment, *supra* n.8, at para.47.

31. (1966) II Y.B.I.L.C. 256.

32. For similar tendencies in the private law of contract, see Zweigert and Kötz, *An Introduction to Comparative Law* (2nd edn, 1992), pp.559, 566, 570, and Posner and Rosenfield, "Impossibility and Related Doctrines in Contract Law: An Economic Analysis" (1977) 6 J.Leg.Stud. 83. In English law the problem is discussed under the notion of impracticability; see Treitel, *Frustration and Force Majeure* (1994), pp.255–265.

Vienna Convention allows for termination if the *circumstances* prevailing at the time when the treaty was concluded have fundamentally changed. As the circumstances relied upon must have constituted an essential basis of the consent of the parties, they can be understood as an intermediate layer between the proper object of the treaty and the irrelevant sphere of the outside world. In the present case Hungary had claimed, *inter alia*, fundamental changes in scientific knowledge and international environmental law.[33] Although both factors had indeed undergone profound transformations between 1977 and 1992, the Court rejected the argument on the ground that these developments were not completely unforeseen.[34]

To demonstrate its point, the Court referred to Articles 15, 19 and 20 of the Treaty providing for the protection of water quality, fishing interests and the natural environment as part of the joint management of the project. At first sight this appears convincing because an explicit treaty provision indicates that the parties have anticipated the later developments and agreed on how they should be dealt with. Yet the argument ignored the fact that the core problem of the case was the dimension of change: whereas the procedures provided for by the Treaty were meant to accommodate environmental concerns *within* the original scheme, Hungary had questioned the environmental sustainability of the entire project and, in particular, of peak mode operation. At this level the articles relied upon indicated that the parties had, in fact, attached some importance to environmental issues and thus that sustainability was part of the basis of their consent.

One may, of course, speculate whether the Court was at all willing to let environmental arguments prevail over the binding force of treaties. But there is also a more dogmatic explanation for the reluctance to apply Article 62 of the Vienna Convention to the present case. Under most domestic laws that recognise the *clausula rebus sic stantibus*, the burden of the change calling for termination has to be weighed against the countervailing interests of the other party.[35] The need to take these interests into account was all too evident in the present case since Czechoslovakia had already made enormous investments in the project when Hungary first raised its environmental concerns in May 1989. However, as the Vienna

33. Hungary had also argued the relevance of the political changes in Eastern Europe, and the diminishing economic viability of the project. According to the ICJ, neither of these changes had radically altered the obligations under the Treaty within the meaning of Art.62, para.1(b) of the Vienna Convention; see judgment, *supra* n.8, at para.104.

34. *Ibid*; as the ICJ had already stated in *Fisheries Jurisdiction, supra* n.22, at p.17, both factual and legal developments may constitute a fundamental change of circumstances within the meaning of Art.62 of the Vienna Convention.

35. See e.g. the Netherlands Ministry of Justice (Ed.), *The Netherlands Civil Code, Book 6, The Law of Obligations, Draft Text and Commentary* (1977), pp.582–583, referring to Art.6.5.3.11 of the Dutch Civil Code, the German revalorisation case RGZ 100, 130, 133 (1920), and Art.1467 of the Italian Civil Code, under which the other party can avoid termination for fundamental change by an offer to adapt the terms of the contract.

Convention does not provide for a balancing test, the Court would have had to add it to the conditions set forth in Article 62 as a further element of law.

At first sight, a more liberal approach seems rather unproblematic in a case which was not directly governed by the Convention in any event. But there is an intrinsic danger in this reasoning. For a differentiation between the proper application of the Vienna Convention as a treaty and its role as a codification of customary law would have seriously undermined the Court's attempt to establish a uniform regime for the law of treaties. In the long run it might even jeopardise the entire concept of codification through treaties because customary law would continue to develop outside the codifying treaties, while the latter became fossils of legal history.

If this is not to happen, one must accept that codifying treaties differ from other international agreements just as national codes differ from statutes in that they require more leeway in their application. Therefore, rather than squeezing the case into the concept of foreseeability, the Court should have acknowledged the gap in Article 62 and added the balancing test under the heading of interpretation. This would have been all the more justifiable as Article 62 provides only that a fundamental change of circumstances "*may not be invoked unless*" the conditions explicitly set forth are met. The negative wording reflects the widespread scepticism against the reception of *clausula rebus sic stantibus* in international law and was meant to prevent an excessive use of the provision that would corrupt the binding force of treaties.[36] Under these circumstances, it is difficult to see why the introduction of a balancing test as a further *restrictive* element of law should be inconsistent either with the text of the Convention or with the intentions of its drafters.

As under domestic law, the starting point of the proposed balancing test is an evaluation of the other party's interest in the preservation of the treaty as opposed to the burden resulting from the transformation of the obligations, which is explicitly addressed in Article 62, paragraph 1, clause (b) of the Vienna Convention. As a third element, the interest of the international community as a whole in the stability of treaties establishing a territorial or local regime may be taken into account. This concern is reflected in Article 62, paragraph 2, clause (a) of the Vienna Convention, which categorically excludes termination of boundary treaties for fundamental change, and in Article 11 of the Vienna Convention on Succession of States with respect to Treaties[37] providing for the continuity of bound-

36. See e.g. the ILC Commentary on Draft Article 59 of the Vienna Convention (1966) II Y.B.I.L.C. 257, 259.
37. For the text of the Convention that was adopted on 23 Aug. 1978, see (1978) 17 I.L.M. 1488.

ary treaties in cases of State succession. Moreover, Article 12 of the Convention on State Succession lists some other territorial regimes to which a new State succeeds *ipso jure*. While these categories are not mentioned in Article 62 of the Convention on the Law of Treaties, the enhanced need for continuity may still be relevant for a balancing test.

Since the balancing test operates as a result-orientated check on the application of Article 62, the relevant positions have to be evaluated and weighed objectively. Yet it is quite evident that there is no common scale for ecological danger, economic damage and the stability interests of the international community. Objective evaluation, therefore, cannot be identified with proper quantification, but is limited to a rough categorisation of values.[38] Where similarly grave interests are affected on both sides, the general principle of *pacta sunt servanda* would probably prevail, as it did in the present case.

III.   CZECHOSLOVAKIA'S PROCEEDING TO VARIANT C

IF the International Court rejected Hungary's environmental concerns as a legal ground for the abandonment of the works and the later denunciation of the Treaty, it did not approve of Czechoslovakia's response either. In fact, Variant C evidently violated the Treaty because it differed substantially from the original project; it also conflicted with general international law because the diversion of the Danube deprived Hungary of some 80 to 90 per cent of its share of the waters up to the point where the by-pass canal rejoined the old river bed. The Slovakian government tried to justify the implementation of Variant C against this background by invoking the right of reprisal, the principle of approximate application and the duty to mitigate damages. Of these three arguments, the treatment of approximate application in the judgment is of particular interest because it demonstrates how legal development can take place within the framework of the Vienna Convention.[39]

A.   Approximate Application

According to the principle of approximate application, a legal instrument which cannot be applied literally due to the conduct of one party should

---

38. The need for objective evaluation makes the balancing test almost inoperable without a neutral judicial authority. Although there is no authority to this effect in the *travaux préparatoires*, the objectivity requirement may in part explain the silence of the Vienna Convention on the issue: for, since adjudication is still the exception in international law, the Convention primarily addresses the State parties themselves. These can hardly be expected to balance their own interests objectively against each other; see also (1996) II Y.B.I.L.C. 260.

39. The two other arguments were rejected on the grounds that Variant C was disproportionate as a countermeasure, and that the duty to mitigate damages does not authorise an act that would otherwise be illegal under international law; see judgment, *supra* n.8, at paras.80, 85.

instead be applied in a way approximating most closely to its primary object.[40] Although its supporters claim that this proposition remains within the scope of interpretation, it clearly goes beyond the textual approach underlying Articles 31 and 32 of the Vienna Convention, which is also predominant in the Court's earlier jurisprudence.[41] The relevant passages in the judgment of 27 September 1997 now seem to indicate the Court's willingness to adopt the new concept if need should arise in the future: while avoiding a definitive statement on the matter, the Court prospectively defined the possible scope of approximate application in stating that it could operate only "within the limits of the treaty in question".[42]

More precisely, the basic characteristics of the original agreement—such as joint ownership and management of the barrage system in the present case—must remain intact. Since Variant C was exclusively owned and operated by Slovakia, it differed sharply from these features. Consequently, the Court refused to accept approximate application as a justification for the unilateral diversion of the Danube.[43] Nevertheless, the argument shows that the codifying character of the Vienna Convention does not exclude the reception of new legal trends within its scope.

The contrast between the relatively open approach towards approximate application and the literal reference to the articles governing the termination of treaties raises the question whether the judgment of 27 September 1997 actually contains a methodological lesson beyond the pragmatism of a trial court and a general endorsement of the Vienna Convention. However, there is at least a tendency favouring the rigid application of the more specific provisions of the Convention and, in particular, of those governing formalities.

B.   Formalities of Termination

Since the implementation of Variant C by Czechoslovakia constituted a material breach of treaty, it could in principle have been invoked as a ground for unilateral termination under Article 60 of the Vienna Convention. Nevertheless, the Court rejected Hungary's denunciation as premature although the Declaration of 16 May 1992 explicitly referred to the illegality of the "provisional solution".[44] From a formal point of view this was a pertinent conclusion because the works at Cunovo were carried out exclusively on Czechoslovak territory and the diversion of the Danube to

---

40. See *Admissibility of Hearings of Petitioners by the Committee on South West Africa,* separate opinion of Sir Hersch Lauterpacht, I.C.J. Rep. 1956, 46

41. See e.g. Reuter, *op. cit. supra* n.29, at pp. 74–75; *Interpretation of Peace treaties (Second Phase)* I.C.J. Rep. 1950, 229; *US Nationals in Morocco* I.C.J. Rep. 1952, 196; *South West Africa (Second Phase)* I.C.J. Rep. 1966, 47–48

42. Judgment, *supra* n.8, at para.77.

43. *Idem,* para.78.

44. *Idem,* para.108.

the by-pass canal started only in November 1992. More realistically, the breach was already imminent in May 1992 since the construction of the second dam clearly demonstrated that Czechoslovakia was determined to proceed on its own. Under these circumstances it would hardly have made any difference to the later developments if Hungary had held back its declaration for another six months, or if it had repeated the denunciation after Variant C was put into operation in November 1992.

Although there were good reasons to uphold the Treaty as a bond between the two neighbouring States, the Court's statement on premature termination at first appears unfortunate because it largely excludes the concept of anticipatory breach from Article 60 of the Vienna Convention. This is even more surprising as the Court could have left the issue open, relying instead on the legal maxim that no one may discharge himself from an obligation by invoking a breach of duty that was prompted by his own illegal conduct:[45] if it is true that the implementation of Variant C was disproportionate as a countermeasure and therefore illegal, allowing for termination on this ground finally would have sanctioned Hungary's initial breach of the Treaty. As the Court actually raised this argument to underline its conclusion,[46] one wonders why there was any need to dwell on the timing of the declaration of termination.

A plausible explanation may start from the observation that the Court also rejected Hungary's denunciation of the Treaty on the further ground that it purported to take effect after a mere six days, whereas Article 65 of the Vienna Convention provides for a regular notice period of three months.[47] The entire argument thus seems to reflect an attempt to strengthen the role of formalities in the law of treaties.[48] There are, in fact, good reasons to adopt such a policy as long as most international disputes are not subject to the jurisdiction of an impartial tribunal. For, under these conditions, formalities as set forth in Article 65 of the Vienna Convention provide the main framework for the peaceful resolution of treaty disputes. This role would be corrupted if the Court was willing to excuse the violation of formal rules too easily.

IV.   LEGAL CONSEQUENCES OF THE DISPUTE

THUS, when it came to determining the legal consequences of the dispute, the International Court was faced with a situation in which the underlying Treaty had been violated by both parties but was still in force. This did not pose any particular problems as far as the reciprocal claims for damages

---

45. See e.g. (1966) II Y.B.I.L.C. 260.
46. Judgment, *supra* n.8, at para.110.
47. *Idem*, para.109.
48. See also *idem*, para.48, where the ICJ rejected Hungary's argument that the suspension and later abandonment of *works* in 1989 implied a tacit suspension of the *Treaty* within the meaning of the Vienna Convention.

were concerned;[49] however, the Court also had to decide on the future of the Treaty, which had been questioned both by Hungary's refusal to build the Nagymaros barrage and by Czechoslovakia's unilateral implementation of Variant C. If the parties were to honour the original agreement, the Court would have had to enjoin the completion of the works on the Hungarian side and the return to joint operation. In more practical terms, there was no doubt that the final structure would have to be managed jointly and that the Dunakiliti dam had become obsolete due to the construction of the Cunovo reservoir. Thus the Nagymaros barrage, which was essential for peak mode operation, re-emerged as the central issue of the case.

As one will recall, the Court finally suggested that Slovakia would not insist on the construction of the Nagymaros barrage if Hungary agreed to a common regime for the operation of Variant C. Although the Court formally confined itself to the ruling that the parties had to renegotiate the Treaty, the proposed formula certainly sets the standard for the fulfilment of this obligation. On the other hand, the Court did not explicitly rely on any legal concept to justify its solution. While this increases the speculative element of any interpretation, the relevant parts of the judgment are quite coherent if they are seen within the general framework of international adjudication.

A. Specific Performance under International Law

First, there is no serious doubt that a State can validly undertake to perform or tolerate specific acts on its territory, and that such an obligation cannot be challenged at a later stage—on the principle of national sovereignty.[50] What is much less clear is whether an international tribunal can actually order specific performance of an act that affects sovereignty over natural resources as deeply as the construction of the Nagymaros barrage would have done.[51] In fact, declaratory judgments and compensatory damages remain the principal judicial remedies under international law, and awards implying specific performance have so far only been granted either to *re-establish* a prior state of affairs in cases of State responsibility or to *delimit* the geographical scope of sovereignty in territorial disputes.[52]

49. *Idem*, paras.151–154.
50. See e.g. the *Wimbledon* case, where the PCIJ confirmed the right of the Allies to free passage through the Kiel Canal under Art.380 of the Treaty of Versailles, P.C.I.J. Rep., Ser.A, No.1, pp.24–25. Considering sovereignty over natural resources, the award in the *Aminoil* arbitration (63 I.L.R. 586–591) upheld the stability clause in an oil concession agreement, but gave it a rather restricted meaning.
51. See the *BP Exploration Co. (Libya) Ltd* arbitration (53 I.L.R. 346–349), where the sole arbitrator explicitly ruled out a right to specific performance of a concession agreement under international law, and Gray, *Judicial Remedies in International Law* (1987), pp.16–17, 95–108.

Neither of these categories concerns the political core of sovereignty, that is, the right of a people to decide its own future.

The absence of any precedent for an award requiring specific performance of a treaty obligation[53] clearly reflects the reluctance of States to submit such disputes to adjudication. Notwithstanding this reservation, international tribunals are probably also aware that awards directly interfering with central issues of domestic policy are particularly prone to disregard, and that any such instance undermines their authority in the settlement of international disputes. This, of course, is not to say that the Court could not have restated Hungary's obligation to build the Nagymaros barrage; but it may in part account for the Court's decision not to insist on the original wording of the Treaty.

Besides, it should be recalled that the Court, when dealing with Hungary's environmental concerns, had admitted a fundamental change in scientific knowledge and international environmental law, and had rejected the termination of the Treaty under Article 62 of the Vienna Convention only because these changes (allegedly) had not been unforeseen.[54] It is, therefore, not surprising that the Court called upon the parties to reassess the environmental effects of the project as part of the implementation of a new regime for Variant C.[55] Nevertheless, the Court did not explicitly rely on the concept of fundamental change to support its conclusions. It merely referred to the fact that the Gabcïkovo barrage had been in operation in a run-of-the-river mode for five years, implying that both parties had "effectively discarded" peak mode operation.[56] While this reasoning led to an equitable result, the question whether it was justifiable under the law remains.

B. Judicial Adjustment

In the absence of any reference to positive law, one may try to conceptualise the Court's solution with the help of general notions of treaty and contract law. The assumption that both Hungary and Slovakia had effectively abandoned peak mode operation clearly evokes the concept of *desuetudo*, according to which the parties may tacitly amend or terminate a legally binding agreement through continuous diverging practice.[57] Yet, in the

---

52. See e.g. Brownlie, *Principles of Public International Law* (4th edn, 1990), p.463, and the *Temple* case, I.C.J. Rep. 1962, 36–37; the fact that the ruling calling for specific performance usually takes the form of a declaratory judgment reflects the default of judicial enforcement procedures in international law.

53. See also Mann, "The Consequences of International Wrong in International and Municipal Courts" (1976–77) 48 B.Y.B.I.L. 13.

54. Judgment, *supra* n.8, at para.104.

55. *Idem*, para.140.

56. *Idem*, para.134.

57. For an account of the relevant international jurisprudence see Vamvoukos, *loc. cit. supra* n.24.

The Law of Treaties

present case, the parties to the dispute evidently disagreed on their respective obligations under the Treaty. To rely explicitly on the concept of *desuetudo* therefore would have cast some serious doubt on the soundness of the result. What seems more adequate is to interpret the relevant passages of the judgment as a judicial adjustment of a treaty that had become unsustainable due both to the unilateral implementation of Variant C and to the changes in scientific knowledge and environmental law.

The concept of judicial adjustment derives from the private law of contract.[58] It operates as a remedy for fundamental change of circumstances in cases where termination appears inadequate because it would charge one party with the entire burden of the conflict, and thus compensates for the restrictive character of the balancing test that favours the stability of contractual relationships.[59] The doctrine was first adopted during the postwar periods and is meanwhile widely recognised in civil law systems and in American law. Its basic rule is restated in Article 6.5.3.11, paragraph 1, of the Dutch Civil Code, which reads:

> The court may at the suit of one of the parties vary a contract or set it aside in whole or in part on account of unforeseen circumstances which are of such a nature that the other party is not entitled to expect, according to the standards of reasonableness and equity, that the contract should be maintained unchanged. The court has the power to allow the demand conditionally.

Even if the judgment of 27 September 1997 does not mention this parallel, it can be assumed that the Court was aware of it, not least because the Dutch member of the Court, Judge Kooijmans, also sat on the drafting committee. At the same time, an explicit discussion of the private law doctrine may have appeared inappropriate; for, given the more restrictive approach of the common law towards interference with the terms agreed upon by the parties,[60] the Court could hardly have claimed judicial adjust-

---

58. For a comparative overview from the common law perspective see Treitel, *op. cit. supra* n.32, at pp.530–537; as the concept is not part of the common law, there is no established terminology in English. Treitel, *ibid*, uses the terms "adaptation" and "alteration". The term "adjustment" is used here because it has occasionally been employed to describe the function of *clausula rebus sic stantibus* under international law; see Lauterpacht, *The Function of Law in the International Community* (1933), p.283.

59. See text accompanying *supra* nn.37, 38.

60. The difference is exemplified by the revalorisation cases that gave rise to the doctrine of judicial adjustment in Continental Europe after the First World War (see e.g. RGZ 100, 130, 133): thus, when faced with the impact of hyperinflation on a life insurance policy in *Anderson* v. *Equitable Assurance Society of United States* [1926] All E.R. Rep. 93, 95, Bankes LJ stated: "One cannot help feeling ... that one is bound to give a decision which, in this particular case, works great hardship upon the plaintiff. Speaking for myself, I hope ... that this rich and powerful company may see its way to do something eventually to mitigate the hardship to plaintiff. That is, of course, by the way; all we have to do is to deal with questions of law which are raised by this appeal."
Half a century later, the Court of Appeal sanctioned unilateral termination of a water supply contract that had become economically unsustainable due to inflation but, again, left adaptation of the terms to the parties: "Rather than force such unequal terms on the parties,

ment as a general principle of law under Article 38, paragraph 1(c) of its Statute. On the other hand, the Vienna Convention, while adopting the concept of fundamental change as a ground for termination, does not provide for judicial adjustment either. Since the Convention does not govern judicial remedies,[61] the omission is not surprising. Yet, under these circumstances, it seems difficult to reconcile the concept of judicial adjustment with the earlier jurisprudence according to which the Court may in no event disregard the wording of a treaty or reformulate its provisions in order to remedy a violation by the parties.[62] This restraint is founded predominantly on the binding force of treaties, but it also reflects the distinction between proper adjudication and decisions *ex aequo et bono* under Article 38, paragraph 2 of the ICJ Statute.

What is left is the possibility of justifying the Court's solution (which was doubtless an equitable one) under the notion of equity. Indeed, the Court has repeatedly relied on equity as a general principle of law in cases where customary law did not provide an appropriate rule to dispose of the dispute.[63] As in these earlier instances, the judgment of 27 September 1997 indicates only the guidelines of an equitable solution, leaving the final determination to the parties. While this is a striking parallel, the present case would have been the first one in which the concept had been employed to discard the express provisions of a treaty, thus questioning one of the most sacred and sensitive principles of international law. It is, therefore, hardly surprising that the Court preferred to mask its solution with the assumption that the parties themselves had effectively discarded peak mode operation.[64]

If the analogy with the Court's earlier use of the notion of equity is correct, judicial adjustment would operate as an instrument to modify the express provisions of a treaty in accordance with what the parties might

the court should hold that the agreement could be and was properly determined in 1975 by the reasonable notice of six months. This does not mean, of course, that on the expiry of the notice the water company can cut off the supply to the hospital. It will be bound to continue it. All that will happen is that the parties will have to negotiate fresh terms of payment ... The hospital should be entitled to 5,000 gallons a day free of charge and pay for the excess at a rate which is 70 per cent. of the current market rate. I would recommend this solution to these two public authorities in the hope that it will settle their difficulties without troubling the courts further": *Staffordshire Area Health Authority* v. *South Staffordshire Waterworks Co.* [1978] 1 W.L.R. 1387, 1397–1398 (*per* Lord Denning MR).

61. See e.g. the express reservation for the law of State responsibility in Art.73 of the Convention.

62. See e.g. *Interpretation of Peace treaties* (*Second Phase*), *supra* n.41, rejecting the idea that the right of the Secretary-General to appoint the chairman of an arbitral tribunal extends to the case where one of the parties fails to nominate its own arbitrator and *US Nationals in Morocco* and *South West Africa* (*Second Phase*), both *supra* n.41.

63. See e.g. the *North Sea Continental Shelf* cases, I.C.J. Rep. 1969, 46–52 and *Fisheries Jurisdiction* (*Second Phase*), I.C.J. Rep. 1974, 30–35.

64. As one may recall, the concept of fundamental change originally derives from the assumption of a tacit *clausula rebus sic stantibus* as part of the agreement of the parties; see (1966) II Y.B.I.L.C. 258.

reasonably have agreed upon if they had foreseen the later change of circumstances. Notwithstanding its fictional character, this formula implies that an international court or tribunal applying the remedy should, as far as possible, be guided by the purpose of the treaty and by the original intention of the parties. Within this framework, it is up to the judge to devise a solution that will best promote a sustainable relationship between the parties for the future.

V. CONCLUSIONS

NOTWITHSTANDING the predominance of pragmatic dispute resolution, the judgment in the *Case Concerning the Gabcïkovo-Nagymaros Project* has certainly strengthened the role of the Vienna Convention on the Law of Treaties as a restatement of customary international law. At the same time, the case has revealed the fragmentary character of the Convention. If the latter is not to impair the project of codification, the Vienna Convention must be understood as a framework of legal rules that is not governed by the traditional rules of subjective treaty interpretation. While the International Court may be criticised for its tendency to mask these implications, it has disposed of the substantive conflict in an adequate manner. The judgment thus demonstrates that the Convention can operate as a reliable and flexible tool for the resolution of treaty disputes in an increasingly complex international environment.

[14]

THE CONCEPT OF JUS COGENS IN THE VIENNA CONVENTION ON THE LAW OF THE TREATIES

MERLIN M. MAGALLONA*

I. *Introduction*

In the general theory of law, every legal system is said to contain general norms of imperative character which the subjects of law cannot modify or set aside in their contractual relations. They constitute the irreducible minimum principles in the legal system. These norms are called *jus cogens;* they are to be distinguished from *jus dispositivum* rules which can be derogated by private contracts.[1] In the interest of the community as a whole, *jus cogens* norms are set above the wills of the parties to a contract and are absolutely binding on them in restricting their freedom to determine the content of their agreement.[2] They serve as a medium through which the individuated legal relations are subordinated to what are considered as superior interests of the community.

But as thus formulated, the concept of *jus cogens* is identified with the notion of *ordre public* in municipal law, understood as an aggregate of fundamental norms on "public policy and good morals", which unify particular rules and principles in the legal order.

Whether there exist in international law general norms in the nature of *jus cogens* has been the subject of theoretical treatment for years.[3] It is implied in Grotius' hierarchy of norms in which

---

* *Senior Lecturer in Law*, University of the Philippines and *Senior Research Fellow*, U.P. Law Center.

Modified for this publication, this paper forms part of a larger research work undertaken by the author on the law of treaties as Research Fellow of the U.P. Law Research Council.

[1] See Marek, *Contribution a l'etude du jus cogens en droit international,* in GENEVA UNIVERSITE FACULTE DE DROIT, RECUEIL D'ETUDES DE DROIT INTERNATIONAL HOMMAGE A PAUL GUGGENHEIM 429 (Geneva, 1968): "Ce principe apparait en effet comme necessaire. Il est d'abord d'une necessite d'ordre politique et social: il permet de proteger les interets essentiels et les bases fondamentales d'une societe donne. Il est ensuite d'une necessite d'ordre logique: un systeme juridique ne serait pa concevable si les sujets de cet ordre pouvaient le bouleverser a leur gre". Also at 426 and 447.

[2] *Id.,* at 427-429.

[3] For a review of international law literature on *jus cogens,* see Suy, *The Concept of Jus Cogens in Public International Law,* in CARNEGIE ENDOWMENT FOR INTERNATIONAL PEACE, THE CONCEPT OF JUS COGENS IN INTERNATIONAL LAW (Papers and Proceedings of Conference on International Law, Lagonissi, Greece, April 3-8, 1966) 17, 26-49 (1967).

the immutability of natural law even applied to God.[4] As far back as Vattel, the concept of *jus cogens* has been given its natural-law rationale.[5] But while a broad agreement among reputable publicists supports the view that such norms exist on the international plane,[6] many of their *de lege ferenda* prescriptions on the nature of *jus cogens* norms are quite apart from the historical realities and practices of States and are not in keeping with the legal nature of the international community itself. Serious questions may precisely arise from an uncritical transference of *jus cogens* as a municipal-law concept into international law, which many theories seem to assume. The logic of the municipal-law analogy may lend support to "the existence of an international public order overriding state sovereignty",[7] implying that international *jus cogens* could acquire validity as legal norms independent of the consent of the individual members of the international community. From the municipal-law concept of *ordre public* it is a short step to transforming the "interest of the community" into a "common will" that stands above the wills of the individual States and creates norms binding upon them. This would then place the concept of *jus cogens* along the thinking which rejects the juridical equality of States, namely, that a group or a majority of States may dictate international-law rules binding upon the rest of the international community.[8]

---

[4] "The law of nature, again, is unchangeable—even in the sense that it cannot be changed by God. Measureless as is the power of God, nevertheless it can be said that there are certain things over which that power does not extend; . . . DE JURE BELLI AC PACES, LIBRI TRES, 40 (Classics of Int'l Law, Kelsey trans., 1925).

[5] "Since, therefore, the necessary Law of Nations consists in applying the natural law to states, and since the natural law is not subject to change, being founded on the nature of man, it follows that the necessary Law of Nations is not subject to change.

"Since this law is not subject to change and the obligations which it imposes are necessary and indispensable, Nations can not alter it by agreement, nor individually or mutually release themselves from it.

"It is by the application of this principle that a distinction can be made between lawful and unlawful treaties or conventions and between customs which are innocent and reasonable and those which are unjust and deserving of condemnation". 3 THE LAW OF NATIONS OR THE PRINCIPLES OF NATURAL LAW 4 (Classics of Int'l Law, No. 4, Fenwick trans., 1915).

[6] See Suy, *op. cit.*, *supra*, note 3.

[7] See, for example, the statement of Mr. Milan Bartos (Yugoslavia) at the 683rd meeting of the International Law Commission. 1963-I ILC YRBK 66.

[8] For example, see Quadri, *Le fondement du caractere obligatoire du droit international public*, 80 RECUEIL DES COURS 579, 624-625 (I, 1952): 'En effet, dans chaque societe les elements individuels qui la composent entrouvent etre subordonues a l'entite collective dont la volonte et l'action sont decisives pour eux. Devant et au-dessus de chaque entite individuelle il y a l'entite collective, le corps social, dont la force irresistible est appelee autorite. D'autre part il n'est pas necessaire que l'entite collective soit organisee dans le sens d'une distribution consciente des differentes fonctions juridiques entre un ensemble d'organes specialises. Il suffit la volonte, la decision et l'action commune d'une ensemble etant en mesure d'imposer le cas echeant son autorite".

A misplaced municipal-law analogy has also been made a basis for rejecting international *jus cogens*. Upon the assumption that the international legal community lacks the constituent elements which characterize the municipal legal system, it may be argued, as does Schwarzenberger, that *jus cogens* could not yet mature in the field of international law, because this concept "presupposes the existence of an effective *de jure* order" which is envisaged in the model of the municipal legal order.[9]

The emergence of the concept of *jus cogens* in positive international law is by no means merely a *lex lata* transformation of this concept as understood in such abstract, logical or natural-law sense, particularly in its strict municipal-law analogy. It is rather defined by the peculiar nature of international law, *i.e.*, by the condition that in the international legal order the subjects (States) of the law are themselves the creators of the law on the basis of sovereign equality. As is the case with the whole corpus of international law rules, *jus cogens* norms are strictly *inter*-national law and reject a supranational source.

It is in the Vienna Convention on the Law of Treaties[10] that the concept of *jus cogens* is introduced into positive international law for the first time. As shown in the discussion below, the process of identifying a general norm of international law as *jus cogens* is definitively a consensual mechanism. Which norms in international law are characterized as *jus cogens* is not determined by the Convention in a ready-made fashion by an explicit listing of those norms. In terms of specific content, *jus cogens* norms are to be identified by the State themselves in their actual experience of struggle and cooperation. Thus, it is the intention of the International Law Commission (ILC) in drafting the Convention rule on *jus cogens* "to leave the full content of this rule to be worked out in State prac-

---

[9] A MANUAL OF INTERNATIONAL LAW 29-30 (1967): "Unlike municipal law, international customary law lacks rules of *jus cogens* or international public policy, that is, rules which, by consent, individual subjects of international law may not modify. In fact, *jus cogens*, as distinct from *jus dispositivum*, presupposes the existence of an effective *de jure* order, which has at its disposal legislative and judicial machinery, able to formulate rules of public policy and, in the last resort, can rely on overwhelming physical force." See also his *International Jus Cogens*, 43 TEXAS L. REV. 455 (1965).

[10] By an overwhelming majority of 79 votes in favor, 1 against, with 19 abstentions, the Convention was adopted on May 22, 1969 by the United Nations Conference on the Law of Treaties which was convened in Vienna in two sessions, from March 26 to May 24, 1968 and from April 9 to May 22, 1969. The Philippines voted in favor of the Convention. It was opened for signature on May 23, 1969. By its Article 84, the Convention enters into force after the ratification or accession of 35 States. As of December 31, 1976, 27 States have deposited instruments of ratification or accession. A signatory, the Philippines ratified the Convention on November 15, 1972. [The Convention is hereinafter referred to as the Vienna Convention.]

tice and in the jurisprudence of international tribunals."[11] While made the basis of criticism against the inclusion of *jus cogens* provisions in the Convention on ground of basic ambiguity, the approach of the ILC emphasizes the more the fact that the identification of *jus cogens* norms is determined by the very real and concrete interests of States and therefore springs from necessity internal to the system of their inter-relationships, and not from some abstract considerations extraneous to international life.

Hence, the acceptance of *jus cogens* by the international community in its present stage of development reflects a recognition of necessity on the part of the member States,[12] born out of historical

---

[11] Commentary of the Commission on its draft Article 50, U.N. CONFERENCE ON THE LAW OF TREATIES, OFF. REC., DOCUMENTS OF THE CONFERENCE, first and second sessions, Vienna, 26 March-24 May 1968 and 9 April-22 May 1969 (New York, 1971), A/CONF. 39/11/Add. 2, p. 67. [Hereinafter referred to as ILC COMMENTARIES].

Jus cogens norms are illustrated in the following examples cited by the Commission: "(a) a treaty contemplating an unlawful use of force contrary to the principles of the [U.N.] Charter, (b) a treaty contemplating the performance of any other act criminal under international law, and (c) a treaty contemplating or conniving at the commission of acts, such as trade in slaves, piracy or genocide." ILC COMMENTARIES, pp. 67-68.

[12] In the process of codification, a representative opinion was that expressed by the Hungarian delegate, E. Ustor, in the Sixth Committee (Legal) at the 18th session of the U.N. General Assembly: "..., although the members of the [International Law] Commission disagreed on the origin of the peremptory rules of international law, they had nevertheless agreed to recognize their existence, and their ideological differences had not prevented them from reaching a solution that met the needs of practice." U.N. GEN. ASS. OFF. REC., 18th Sess., Sixth Committee, p. 40. While the members of the Commission expressed differences on the nature of *jus cogens* norms, it is true that, as Suy summarized, "The most striking feature of the record of the Commission is the unanimity with which the members of the Commission accepted the idea of *jus cogens*." *Op. cit., supra*, note 3 at 50. Mr. Mustafa Kamil Yassein (Iraq), for example, stressed that to have the character of *jus cogens*, a rule of international law must not only be accepted by a large number of States, but must also be found necessary to international life and deeply rooted in the international conscience. Mr. Manfred Lachs (Poland) in effect said that the limitation imposed by *jus cogens* on the treaty-making freedom of States was necessary to protect the interests not only of third parties, but of the international community as a whole. Mr. Antonio de Luna (Spain) commended the Special Rapporteur's definition of *jus cogens* because it satisfied moral, economic and social requirements, which were essential for the existence of an international society. See 1963 ILC YRBK. 62, 68, 72.

Although certain delegations doubted the efficacy of the draft article on *jus cogens*, "Without exception all the members of the [Sixth] Committee of the [U.N. General] Assembly welcomed the introduction of the *jus cogens* article into the [International Law] Commission's draft." Suy, *op. cit., supra*, note 3, at 54.

The text in Convention Article 53 was adopted by the Committee of the whole of the U.N. Conference on the Law of Treaties by 72 votes to 3, with 18 abstentions, and by the Plenary Meeting of the Conference, by 87 votes to 8, with 12 abstentions. The text in Convention Article 64 was adopted in that Committee without formal vote, which means that there was very substantial or overwhelming support for the text; it was adopted in the Plenary Meeting by 84 votes to 8, with 16 abstentions. In each voting, the Philippines voted in favor of Articles 53 and 64. U.N. CONFERENCE ON THE LAW OF TEATIES, OFF. REC. DOCUMENTS OF THE CONFERENCE, A/CONF. 39/11/Add. 2 (1971), pp.

experience common to them. Historically, this has been given impetus by the moral principles that grew out of the struggle against fascism in the Second World War and those that have consolidated in international relations as a result of the influence of the socialist community of States and the newly independent States that emerged from colonialism. The prohibition against the use or threat of force, the Nuremberg principles,[13] human rights, sovereign equality of States, non-intervention, and right of self-determination are among the norms and principles which have formed part of contemporary international law founded on a new social base.

The accelerated pace in the internationalization of economic activities in the last four decades has increasingly interlinked the interests of States by a system of cooperative efforts, many aspects of which have been institutionalized in international organizations. The expansion and deepening of mutuality, brought about by rapid technological and scientific progress, has developed multilateralism as the most appropriate medium of achieving international cooperation, limiting the effectiveness of bilateral relations in meeting the requirements of a State's international relations.[14] The widening scope of multilateralism predisposes States to conduct their relations in the light of principles and norms already established in general multilateral treaties or conventions in which their interests are more substantially linked to a greater number of States. A State is thus less inclined to deal bilaterally with other States in terms that may be inimical to its multilateral commitments to which, in the first place, the latter may also subscribe as signatory to general multilateral treaties. It is in this context that States achieve agreement to structure their obligations into a hierarchy, thus up-

---

173-175; SUMMARY RECORDS OF THE PLENARY MEETINGS & MEETIINGS OF THE COMMITTEE OF THE WHOLE, A/CONF. 39/11/Add. 1(1970), pp. 102-107; 122-125.

13 The Nuremberg principles relate to crimes against peace, war crimes, and crimes against humanity, for which international law imposes criminal responsibility on individuals. The concept of crimes against humanity led to the adoption of the Convention on the Prevention and Punishment of the Crime of Genocide. In Resolution 95(I), adopted on December 11, 1946, the U.N. General Assembly affirmed the principles of international law recognized by the Charter and the Judgment of the International Military Tribunal at Nuremberg.

14 See Lachs, Recognition and Modern Methods of Cooperation, 35 BRIT. YRBK. INT'L. L. 252 (1959), for an appropriate description of international relations in the context of mutilateralism. Along the same context, Mr. Manfred Lachs (Poland) pointed out as member of the International Law Commission that in recent years two perhaps conflicting trends had become discernible: on the one hand an enormous increase in the number of treaties being concluded and on the other a growing number of general principles that were becoming part and parcel of jus cogens and thus constituting a limitation on the freedom of States in drafting treaty provisions if they were to comply with such binding rules and to respect the interests not only of third parties, but of the international community as a whole. 1963 ILC YRBK. (684th meeting), p. 68.

holding some norms or principles of law as superior to others. For example, under Article 103 of the United Nations Charter, it is the position of the Member States that their obligations in the Charter shall prevail in case these come into conflict with their obligations under any other international agreement.

In this sense, the rise of *jus cogens* in positive international law goes hand in hand with the concrete historical development of the international society, but not in the direction drawn by a teleological doctrine which makes the emergence of *jus cogens* dependent on the degree of development of the international society toward a world State in the model of a well-developed municipal legal order. Conditions for the reception of international *jus cogens* have matured in the relations of States not for reason of abstract rationality but out of concrete political interests and social or economic requirements involved in the struggle and cooperation of States, in the pursuit of solution to compelling problems of the moment. The maturation of such conditions is hastened by the deliberate and systematic work in the codification and progressive development of international law now carried on within the United Nations system.[15]

II. *Definition of* Jus Cogens *under the Vienna Convention*

The Vienna Convention transforms the concept of *jus cogens* into concrete norms of law by providing this as a ground for invalidating or terminating treaties. Article 53 of the Convention states that —

> A treaty is void if, at the time of its conclusion, it conflicts with a peremptory norm of general international law. For the purposes of the present Convention, a peremptory norm of general international law is a norm accepted and recognized by the international community of States as a whole as a norm from which no derogation is permitted and which can be modified only by a subsequent norm of general international law having the same character.

A companion provision is set forth in Article 64:

> If a new peremptory norm of general international law emerges, any existing treaty which is in conflict with that norm becomes void and terminates.

---

[15] A specific function of the U.N. General Assembly relates to "encouraging the progressive development of international law and its codification." See U.N. CHARTER, Art. 13(1) (a). As a subsidiary organ of the General Assembly, the International Law Commission undertakes this work, which provides the basis for international conferences and the resulting general mutilateral conventions.

So broad a definition of a *jus cogens* norm amounts only to a statement of general concept: it is a peremptory norm of general international law accepted and recognized by the international community as a whole as a norm from which no derogation is permitted. It differentiates a *jus cogens* norm of general international law from a *jus dispositivum* norm of general international law. The latter category of norms is not qualified to nullify a treaty despite its general character. A *jus cogens* norm contains two elements: (1) it is a norm of general international law, and (2) it is accepted and recognized by the international community of States as a whole as a norm from which no derogation is permitted. While a *jus cogens* norm is held to be superior to other norms, these two elements project the consensual nature of such norm. The first requires that this norm should express the will of at least a broad majority of States as a rule binding upon them. The second calls for the expression of their consent on the specific character of a general norm as *jus cogens* norm, *i.e.*, as a norm accepted by them as restricting their treaty-making competence and having the effect of invalidating their agreements contrary to its mandate. That it is the agreement of States which invests a norm with peremptory character is concretized as an objective basis for the identification of such norm within the framework of the Convention. The procedure prescribed by the Convention for the settlement of dispute, for example, as to the *jus cogens* character of a norm being invoked as a ground for invalidating or terminating a treaty in question, should serve to stress the consent of the parties to the dispute as a specific requirement in the operation of the concept of *jus cogens* in the law of treaties. This procedure actually becomes an objective method by which a norm with which a treaty is in conflict is determined to be *jus cogens* or not. As shown below, unless the parties to a treaty agree to its nullity, it cannot legally be considered void as conflicting with a *jus cogens* norm.

However, the consensual nature of a *jus cogens* norm should not lead to the formalism that the character of *jus cogens* finds explanation in the mere expression of the States' consent. In the preparation of its final draft articles on the law of treaties, the International Law Commission considered the possibility that parties to a treaty may stipulate with respect to any subject-matter and for any reason that no derogation from that stipulation is to be permitted, with the intended result that another treaty which conflicts with that provision would be void. The mere fact that the parties have so stipulated does not lend *jus cogens* character to that treaty provision.[16] As the Commission clarified: "It is not the form of a general rule of international law but the particular nature of the

---

[16] ILC COMMENTARIES, p. 67.

subject-matter with which it deals that may, ... give it the character of *jus cogens.*"[17] This clarification does not suggest a departure from the consensual nature of *jus cogens* norms. The "particular nature of the subject-matter'" which determines the *jus cogens* character of general norms does not refer to some jusnaturalistic factors outside the consensual regime of States; instead, this is to be interpreted as indicating the level of importance or special relevance by which the States regard the function of a particular norm of general international law, *vis-a-vis* the maintenance of an international legal order as a system of "interconditionality of wills" of its members,[18] based on necessity.

As a norm of general international law, it is to be assumed that a *jus cogens* norm is either a customary or conventional rule. Also, it is either a universal one, in that it is accepted as binding by all members of the international community, or it is so recognized by a great majority of States. In defining a *jus cogens* norm, Article 53 of the Convention carries the requirement that it be recognized and accepted as such by the international community of States *as a whole.* The effect of the words "as a whole" is intended to preclude the possibility that an objection on the part of any one State may operate as a veto to the characterization of a norm as *jus cogens,* despite its recognition as a peremptory norm by a broad majority of States.[19] This should serve to emphasize the point that universal consent or unanimity is not intended as a basis for the determination of a *jus cogens* norm. A dissenting State cannot stop the bind-

---

[17] *Ibid.*

[18] TUNKIN, THEORY OF INTERNATIONAL LAW 216 (1974): "The concordance of the wills of states includes the interconditionality of wills, reflected in the fact that the consent of a state to recognize a particular norm as norm of international law is given on condition of analogous consent by another or other states."

[19] The words "as a whole" were added by the Drafting Committee of the Committee of the Whole in the Vienna Conference on the Law of Treaties. The Chairman (Mr. Yassen) of the Drafting Committee explained this change at the 80th Meeting of the Committee of the Whole, as follows—

It appeared to have been the view of the Committee of the Whole that no individual State should have the right to veto, and the Drafting Committee had therefore included the words "as a whole" in the text of Article 50.

x x x   x x x   x x x

... by inserting the words "as a whole" in Article 50 the Drafting Committee had wished to stress that there was no question of requiring a rule to be accepted and recognized as peremptory by all States. It would be enough if a very large majority did so; that would mean that, if one State in isolation refused to accepted the peremptory character of a rule, or if that State was supported by a very small number of States, the acceptance and recognition of the peremptory character of the rule by the international community as a whole would not be affected. (U.N. CONFERENCE ON THE LAW OF TREATIES, OFFICIAL RECORDS, 1st Sess., 80th Meeting, Committee of the Whole, A/CONF. 39/11, pp. 471-472).

ing operation of a general norm as *jus cogens* with respect to the great majority of States which have so recognized it. This should not mean, however, that such norm binds the dissenting State. Norms of international law are created by agreement of States and *jus cogens* norms are not in any way distinct in this respect. It is not realistic, however, to think that a State would set itself apart from a *jus cogens* norm which corresponds with the interests of the great majority of States. Its relations with the rest of the members of the international community may precisely operate through the acceptance of that *jus cogens* norm.

III. *Function of Convention Rules on* Jus Cogens

The specifiic function of *jus cogens* norms under the Convention is to limit the freedom of the parties to a treaty in determining the content of their agreement. Any treaty provision that contravenes a *jus cogens* norm is either declared void or voidable, depending on whether the case falls within Article 53 or 64 of the Convention.

It is to be noted that both articles belong to Part V of the Convention, which is entitled "Invalidity, Termination and Suspension of the Operation of Treaties." But within this format, the two articles part ways: Article 53 is subsumed under Section 2, dealing with *invalidity* of treaties, and Article 64 forms part of Section 3, governing *termination and suspension* of the operation of treaties. Accordingly, while Article 53 declares that "a treaty is void" if it clashes with a *jus cogens* norm, Article 64 merely says that in such case "a treaty becomes void and terminates."

As a ground of invalidity of treaties, Article 53 renders a defective treaty a nullity.[20] As explained below, however, this article does not produce this effect automatically; its concrete operation is determined by other provisions of the Convention, which limit to a great extent its function in the law of treaties. However, if declared void through the procedure prescribed in the Convention, the illegal treaty under Article 53 is extinguished.

The consequences of invalidating a treaty on the basis of incompatibility with a *jus cogens* norm under Article 53 are set out in paragraph 1, Article 71 of the Convention, under which the parties to that treaty have the duty to —

> (a) eliminate as far as possible the consequences of any act performed in reliance on any provision which conflicts with the peremptory norm of general international law; and

---

[20] However, the Commission considered this "a special case of nullity." ILC COMMENTARIES, p. 86, See *infra*, at 530-531.

(b) bring their mutual relations into conformity with the peremptory norm of general international law.

From the language of paragraph 1(a) above, it may be appropriate to raise the problem as to how far indeed should the parties go in eliminating the consequences of a void treaty. May the referent of the phrase "as far as possible" be circumscribed by an agreement that may result from negotiation between them as may be done under Article 65(3) of the Convention in relation to Article 33(1) of the United Nations Charter?[21] It is suggested that whatever discretion this phraseology may allow the parties is restricted by their related duty under paragraph 1(b), namely, that they have to adjust their mutual relations in conformity with the *jus cogens* norm. Clearly, the intention of paragraph 1(b) is to prevent the existence of treaty relations that is inconsistent with the peremptory norm of general international law, a situation that may result from too liberal an interpretation of paragraph 1(a) in favor of the individual interests of the parties.

Again, under paragraph 1(a) the words "any act performed in reliance on any provision which conflicts with the peremptory norm of general international law" are susceptible to the interpretation that the provisions of an invalid treaty are separable and that the duty of the parties to eliminate the consequences of any act arising from the treaty may not extend to those provisions which are not directly affected by illegality. Such interpretation would seem to come to an inevitable conflict with Article 44(5) which does not permit separation of the provisions of a treaty violative of a *jus cogens* norm.[22] In this case, together, paragraph 1(a) of Article 71 and Article 44(5) would create an absurd situation: separable consequences springing from non-separable provisions of an illegal treaty.

At any rate, the sense of paragraph 1, Article 71, on the whole, carries the implication that some consequences arising from a treaty

---

21 Under Art. 65(3) of the Vienna Convention, if there is a dispute with respect the invalidity of a treaty, on ground, for example, of conflict with a *jus cogens* norm, "the parties shall seek a solution through the means indicated in Article 33 of the Charter of the United Nations," which enumerates modes of peaceful settlement of dispute, including negotiation.

22 The pertinent provisions of Art. 44 on "separability of treaty provisions" read:

        x x x   x x x   x x x

2. A ground for invalidating, terminating, withdrawing from or suspending the operation of a treaty recognized in the present Convention may be invoked only with respect to the whole treaty ...

        x x x   x x x   x x x

5. In cases falling under Articles 51, 52 and 53, no separation of the provisions of the treaty is permitted.

which is illegal under Article 53 may be saved from the nullifying effect of a *jus cogens* norm. In this sense, it may have the effect of qualifying the concept of nullity as applied in Articles 53 and 69(1) of the Convention.[23]

The interpretation of paragraph 1, Article 71 that illegality based on conflict with a *jus cogens* norm does not totally wipe out the consequences of a void treaty is reinforced by paragraph 2(b), Article 69 in which it is made explicit that there are acts which are performed in good faith in reliance of the invalidated treaty and these acts "are not rendered unlawful by reason only of the invalidity of the treaty." This line of thought may provide us with an approach for resolving the conflict between paragraph 1 of Article 71 and paragraph 5 of Article 44, as pointed out above. Given the premise that there are indeed consequences of the invalidated treaty which are not affected by its illegality, such consequences, or "acts performed in good faith", should be deemed as valid and subsisting on the basis of a new agreement, expressly or tacitly made, which the parties may bring about as part of their effort to bring their mutual relations in line with the relevant *jus cogens* norm, as prescribed in paragraph 1(b), Article 71. Any attempt to maintain the validity of these acts cannot be anchored on any of the provisions of the invalidated treaty because invalidity based on violations of a *jus cogens* norm affects the entire treaty or each and every provision of it;[24] in fact, in this case, the ground of invalidity may be invoked only with respect to the whole treaty and no separation of its provisions is permitted, as prescribed in paragraphs 2 and 5 of Article 44.

---

[23] That a treaty is *void* under Art. 53 meant to the Commission a "nullity" or "wholly void." See ILC COMMENTARIES, p. 68.

The pertinent part of Art. 69 on "consequences of the invalidity of a treaty" provides:

1. A treaty the invalidity of which is established under the present Convention is void. The provisions of a void treaty have no legal force.
2. If acts have nevertheless been performed in reliance on such a treaty:
   (a) each party may require any other party to establish as far as possible in their mutual relations the position that would have existed if the acts had not been performed;
   (b) acts performed in good faith before the invalidity was invoked are not rendered unlawful by reason only of the invalidity of the treaty.

x x x   x x x   x x x

Under the draft article on which Art. 69 was based, the Commission commented that nullity here "attaches to the treaty *ab initio*, and not merely from the date when the ground of nullity was invoked. See ILC COMMENTARIES, pp. 67-68, 84.

[24] See Art. 44, *supra*, note 22. The Commission rejected the separability of treaty provisions on the ground that violation of a *jus cogens* norm under Art. 53 is so fundamental that it affects the treaty in its entirety. See 1963-II ILC YRBK. 199.

Under Article 45 of the Convention, a State may lose the right to invoke a ground for invalidating, terminating, withdrawing, or suspending the operation of a treaty, through confirmation or acquiescence. This may result in the event that if, after becoming aware of the relevant facts —

(a) it shall have expressly agreed that the treaty is valid or remains in force or continues in operation, as the case may be; or

(b) it must be by reason of its conduct be considered as having acquiesced in the validity of the treaty or in its maintenance in force or in operation, as the case may be.

Article 45, however, expressly limits its application to Articles 46 to 50, and Articles 60 and 62. The omission of Articles 53 and 64 from the coverage of Article 45 points to the conclusion that the invalidity of a treaty arising from violation of *jus cogens* norms cannot be cured by confirmation or acquiescence of the parties, or, in other words, by their consent. This serves to reinforce the objective character of *jus cogens* norms as criterion of illegality and to project their importance over the narrow individual interests of States.

Article 64 of the Convention is a ground for termination of a treaty and is a logical corollary of the *jus cogens* rule in Article 53. Its effect does not avoid the treaty from the time of its conclusion, "but only from the date when the new rule of *jus cogens* is established; in other words it does not annul the treaty, it forbids its further existence and performance."[25] Until the treaty is terminated on the basis of the emergence of a new *jus cogens* norm, all situations created by the treaty are of full validity. This feature of termination of a treaty, which distinguishes it from invalidity under Article 53, is spelled out in paragraph 2, Article 71 in which it is provided that when a treaty "becomes void and terminates," the termination —

(a) releases the parties from any obligation further to perform the treaty;

(b) does not affect any right, obligation or legal situation of the parties created through the execution of the treaty prior to its termination; provided that those rights, obligations or situations may thereafter be maintained only to the extent that their maintenance is not in itself in conflict with the new peremptory norm of general international law.

The other point of distinction is that unlike invalidity under Article 53, the case of termination under Article 64 admits of separability of treaty provisions, and those which are not tainted

---

[25] ILC COMMENTARIES, p. 81.

with illegality continue to be valid.[26] In this case, the terms of paragraph 3, Article 44 apply:

> If the ground relates to particular clauses, it may be invoked only with respect to the those clauses where:
> (a) the said clauses are separable from the remainder of the treaty with regard to their application;
> (b) it appears from the treaty or is otherwise established that acceptance of those clauses was not an essential basis of the consent of the other party or parties to be bound by the treaty as a whole; and
> (c) continued performance of the remainder of the treaty would not be unjust.

IV. *Operation of Convention Rules on* Jus Cogens

A treaty in conflict with a *jus cogens* norm is invalid in international law. But under the present state of the law, it can only be invalidated on that ground within the framework of the Vienna Convention. Article 2 of the Convention provides that the validity of a treaty may be impeached "only through the application of the present Convention." The basic limitation in the effective enforcement of *jus cogens* norms in the regime of the law of treaties is that this ground of invalidity may be invoked only by the parties to the Convention.

A *jus cogens* norm does not automatically invalidate a treaty conflicting with it. The Convention prescribes a particular procedure to be followed by a party to a treaty in establishing its invalidity. This is provided in paragraphs 1 and 2 of Article 65 in the following terms:

> 1. A party which, under the provisions of the present Convention, invokes either a defect in its consent to be bound by a treaty or a ground for impeaching the validity of a treaty, terminating it, withdrawing from it, or suspending its operation, must notify the other parties of its claim. The notification shall indicate the measure proposed to be taken with respect to the treaty and the reasons therefor.
> 2. If, after the expiry of a period which, except in case of special urgency, shall not be less than three months after the receipt of the notification, no party has raised any objection, the party making the notification may carry out in the manner provided in Article 67 the measure which it has proposed.

---

[26] The relevant comment of the Commission reads:
Similarly, although the Commission did not think that the principle of separability is appropriate when a treaty is void *ab initio* under Article 50 by reason of an existing rule of *jus cogens*, it felt that different considerations apply in the case of a treaty which was entirely valid when concluded but is now found with respect to some of its provisions to conflict with a newly established rule of *jus cogens*. If those provisions can properly be regarded as severable

As is clear from paragraph 1 above, this procedure is compulsory upon the parties to a treaty, not only with respect to invalidation based on *jus cogens* ground but to all cases of invalidity, termination, withdrawal from or suspension of the operation of a treaty on all possible grounds under the Convention. Note that the procedure leaves no room for a party to unil'terally establish the invalidity of a treaty in conflict with a *jus cogens* norm. It cannot deviate from the requirement that it must send to the other parties a written notification of its claim as to the illegal character of the treaty based on *jus cogens* ground, stating the measure proposed to be taken by the contesting party and the reasons therefor.[27] With respect to invalidity under Article 53 and termination under Article 64, the claim of the contesting party is that the treaty is illegal because it violates a *jus cogens* norm, and the "measure to be taken" by him is the invalidation or termination of that treaty.

Unless the treaty under question provides otherwise, it is required under the Convention that the notification be transmitted directly by the contesting party to the other party, but if the treaty has appointed a depositary, transmission to the latter is instead the rule. Notification shall be considered as having been made only upon receipt by the party to which it was transmitted or by the depositary, as the case may be. If it was transmitted to a depositary, notification shall be considered as having been received by the party for which it was intended only when the latter has been so informed by the depositary.[28] Article 67 prescribes that the notification must be in an instrument normally signed by the Head of State, Head of Government or Minister for Foreign Affairs.

It is only after the expiration of at least three months from the receipt of notification, as understood in the procedure described above, that the contesting party may legally carry out the measure which it has proposed to any of the other parties, but this step can only be taken if the latter has not raised objection against the proposal within that period. In the absence of such objection, the contesting party can then proceed to effectuate the invalidation or termination of the treaty by a declaration to that effect embodied in an instrument communicated to the other parties. The instrument as thus communicated to the other parties establishes the invalidity or termination of the treaty in question.[29] The absence of objection within the minimum period prescribed should be taken as an im-

---

from the rest of the treaty, the Commission thought that the rest of the treaty ought to be regarded as still valid. ILC COMMENTARIES, p. 81.

[27] Vienna Convention, Arts. 65(1) and 67.

[28] Vienna Convention, Arts. 77 and 78.

[29] Vienna Convention, Arts. 65(2) and 67(2).

plied consent on the part of the other parties to the measure proposed by the contesting party with respect to the invalidation or termination of the treaty.

If any of the other parties to the treaty has raised objection to the measure proposed in the notification, the matter becomes a dispute and the parties are obliged under paragraph 3, Article 65 of the Convention to seek solution "through the means indicated in Article 33 of the Charter of the United Nations." This requires them to settle their dispute by negotiation, inquiry, mediation, conciliation, arbitration, judicial settlement, resort to regional arrangements or other peaceful means of their own choice.[30] In case the parties have failed to reach a solution through these means within 12 months from the date the objection was raised, Article 66 of the Convention requires the parties to submit the dispute to (1) the International Court of Justice, with respect to the application or interpretation of Article 53 to 64 of the Convention, or to (2) the conciliation procedure annexed to the Convention concerning the application or interpretation of any of the other articles in the Convention relating to invalidity, termination and suspension of the operation of treaties.[31]

The import of the procedural requirements outlined above is that the right to establish the invalidity of a treaty or bring about its termination may be invoked only by the parties to the treaty under question, in addition to the restriction that they be parties to the Convention.[32] Outside of the Convention, the only possibility that

---

[30] Article 33 of the U.N. Charter reads in full:
    1. The parties to any dispute, the continuance of which is likely to endanger the maintenance of international peace and security, shall, first of all, seek a solution by negotiation, inquiry, mediation, conciliation, arbitration, judicial settlement, resort to regional agencies or arrangements, or other peaceful means of their own choice.
    2. The Security Council shall, when it deems necessary, call upon the parties to settle their dispute by such means.

[31] Under Art. 66 of the Convention, any of the parties may set in motion the procedure specified in the Annex to the Convention by submitting a request to the U.N. Secretary General to that effect. The Secretary General shall then bring the dispute before a Conciliation Commission, which shall be composed of five conciliators, appointed as follows. The State constituting one of the parties shall appoint one conciliator of the nationality of that State, who may or may not be chosen from the list of conciliators and another conciliator not of the nationality of that State, who shall be chosen from that list. The State constituting the other party to the dispute shall also appoint two conciliators in the same way. The four conciliators chosen by the parties shall appoint a fifth conciliator who shall be chairman of the Commission. There shall be a list of conciliators which shall consist of names nominated by every State which is a member of the United Nations or a party to the Convention. (For complete procedure, see text of Annex given in U.N. CONFERENCE ON THE LAW OF TREATIES, OFFICIAL RECORD, DOCUMENTS OF THE CONFERENCE, A/CONF. 39/11/Add. 2, p. 301.)

[32] See Vienna Convention, Art. 65(1), *supra*, pp. 14-15. This provision makes available the procedure for invalidation of a treaty only to a party to that treaty.

may broaden the effectivity of *jus cogens* norms is for the States not parties to the Convention to adopt the system of invalidation or termination each time that they conclude a treaty. While it may be possible to regard the rules on *jus cogens* as applicable just the same to non-parties to the Convention in the character of customary law, their enforceability outside of the Convention's framework is problematical, lacking the procedure for invalidation or termination established by the Convention.

The other basic limitation to invalidation or termination on *jus cogens* ground is the fact that the Convention in effect requires that this be established by the consent of the parties to the treaty in question. In fact, the serious implication of this consensual requirement is that in the event that no agreement is reached by the parties to invalidate or terminate the treaty by authority of Article 53 or 64 of the Convention, it would seem that nothing can be done about the treaty in question on the part of the international community. Consequently, the treaty in conflict with the peremptory norm of international law would continue to subsist. It should be borne in mind that, considering the nature and function of *jus cogens* norms in the international community, the invalidation or termination of a treaty in conflict with these norms objectively subserves the interests of the community and not only the interests of the parties to that treaty. The latter interests should be deemed as merely incidental to the larger issue of protecting the regime of *jus cogens* from the encroachment of treaties or agreements incompatible with its norms. As an objective ground of invalidity, conflict with a *jus cogens* norm may thus theoretically be invoked by any State. Despite these considerations, however, the law under the Convention stands, namely, it is not possible for a third State (not party to the treaty under question) to invoke the *jus cogens* ground in the attempt to establish its invalidity or bring about its termination.

In taking this position, the Convention resolves the issue in favor of the claim that a more liberal system of protecting the regime of *jus cogens* norms, at the present stage in the development of international society, may jeopardize the stability of treaties. Procedural safeguards, particularly those in Article 65 of the Convention, as quoted above, are intended to ward off arbitrariness in unilateral assertion of invalidity, termination or suspension of the operation of treaties. In formulating the final draft of what is now Article 65, the International Law Commission expressed the apprehension of its members that "some of the grounds upon which treaties may be considered invalid or terminated or suspended under those sections, if allowed to be arbitrarily asserted in face of objection from the other party, would involve real dangers for the security of treaties." Thus, the Commission reached the conclusion that the relevant articles of the Convention "should contain procedural safeguards against the possibility that the nullity, termination or suspension of the operation of a treaty may be arbitrarily asserted as a mere pretext for getting rid of an inconvenient obligation."[33]

V. *Non-Retroactivity of Convention Rules on* Jus Cogens

Article 28 of the Convention lays down the general rule that—

> Unless a different intention appears from the treaty or is otherwise established, its provisions do not bind a party in relation to any act or fact which took place or any situation which ceased to exist before the date of the entry into force of the treaty with respect to that party.

While this rule establishes the non-retroactive operation of treaties in general, it provides for flexibility in that the parties themselves may expressly stipulate the retroactive effects of treaty provisions. Article 4 of the Convention makes it doubly clear that in the application of the Convention itself, such general rule is followed, *i.e.,* its provisions do not apply retroactively to *treaties concluded by States before it has entered into force* as to them.[34] In this light, the provisions of Article 53 and 64 may be understood as applicable only to treaties that may be concluded after the entry into force of the Convention.

There is no question that treaties concluded *after the entry into force of the Convention* which are in conflict with a *jus cogens* norm are void under Article 53, or become void and terminate under Article 64 if in conflict with a new *jus cogens* norm which has emerged. In this case, note that both the conclusion of the treaty in question and the time of conflict between that treaty and the relevant *jus cogens* norm necessarily occur after the Convention's entry into force. A problem may be raised, however, whether Articles 53 and 64 may still apply in a situation where the treaty in question has been concluded *before* the Convention's entry into force but the time of conflict between that treaty and a *jus cogens* norm comes *after* its entry into force. A plain application of the non-retroactivity

---

[33] ILC COMMENTARIES, p. 81.

[34] Article 4 on "non-retroactivity of the present Convention" reads in full:

> Without prejudice to the application of any rules set forth in the present Convention to which treaties would be subject under international law independently of the Convention, the Convention applies only to treaties which are concluded by States after the entry into force of the present Convention with regard to such States.

rule in the Convention would seem to exclude such situation from the coverage of the Convention's rules on *jus cogens,* for the reason that under Article 4, the Convention "applies only to treaties which are concluded by States after the entry into force of the present Convention." However, this same situation could perfectly come within the normal operation of Article 64 at least: an existing treaty, validly concluded before the Convention's entry into force becomes void and terminates for the reason that it comes into conflict with a new *jus cogens* norm which emerges after the Convention comes into force.

The non-retroactivity rule contemplated in Article 4 may be concretized in the application of Article 53. Since it is to be understood that a treaty under the latter article is one which is concluded after the Convention enters into force, a *jus cogens* norm cannot possibly reach a treaty concluded *before* the Convention comes into force because the point of conflict defined by this article is "the time of its [the treaty's] conclusion." Treaties concluded before the Convention's entry into force are perforce saved from the operation of Article 53, even if they conflict with a *jus cogens* norm. Here, the date of Convention's entry into force draws the dividing line between treaties which are affected by the non-retroactivity rule and those which are not.

But Article 4 bears a different level of relevance with respect to Article 64. Commenting on the issue of retroactivity in regard to its draft Article 61, which is now Article 64, of the Convention, the Commission explained:

> Manifestly, if a new rule of that character—a new rule of *jus cogens* —emerges, its effect must be to render void not only future but *existing* treaties. This follows from the fact that a rule of *jus cogens* is an overriding rule depriving any act or situation which is in conflict with it of legality. An example would be former treaties regulating the slave trade, the performance of which later ceased to be compatible with international law owing to the general recognition of the total illegality of all forms of slavery.[35]

It is suggested that by "existing treaties" the Commission necessarily had in mind treaties already concluded at the time it submitted its report to the United Nations General Assembly in 1966, together with its final articles on the law of treaties. In other words, it was referring to treaties already concluded before the Convention enters into force. It would be reasonable to interpret the Commission's view as meaning that existing treaties, *although concluded before the Convention's entry into force,* are affected by

---

[35] ILC COMMENTARIES, p. 81. Italics in word "existing" supplied.

the invalidating force of a *jus cogens* norm when it is given binding force as such by the entry into force of the Convention. In this case, the non-retroactivity rule in Article 4 does not relate so much to the fact that a treaty in question was concluded before the Convention's entry into force—which is the literal requirement of that article—as to the non-retroactive effect of a particular *jus cogens* norm on a treaty concluded before the Convention's entry into force. To determine the correct application of the non-retroactive rule under Article 4 in relation to Article 64, the relevant issue is *not* whether the treaty in question was concluded before or after the Convention's entry into force, but from what point of time after the Convention's entry into force should a *jus cogens* norm invalidate that treaty. On the basis of the nature of the *jus cogens* rule in Article 64, the more precise non-retroactivity rule applicable is not Article 4, but paragraph 2(b), Article 71, which provides, *inter alia*, that the termination of a treaty under Article 64 "does not affect any right, obligation or legal situation of the parties created by the execution of the treaty prior to its termination."

Hence, while under Article 53 the point of reference for the operation of the non-retroactivity rule is the *date the Convention enters into force*, under Article 64 it is the *time of emergence of the jus cogens norm*.

One more point relating to Article 64 deserves comment. The peremptory norm which this Article speaks of is described as "new". This word introduces an issue which may affect the range of effectivity of the *jus cogens* rules in the Convention. It gives rise to the suggestion that the Convention contemplates two categories of *jus cogens* norms: (1) those general norms of international law existing on the date of the Convention's entry into force, the acceptance and recognition of which as *jus cogens* norms by the international community, at that time, takes on binding force upon the entry into force of the Convention; and (2) those general norms which become *jus cogens* norms only sometime later after the Convention has entered into force.

If the term "new peremptory norm of general international law" in Article 64 refers only to the second category, treaties existing at the time the Convention enters into force are not affected by the operation of that "new" *jus cogens* norm. Neither are these treaties affected by the application of Article 53, because they were concluded before the Convention comes into force. The result is that they continue to subsist despite their incompatibility with *jus cogens* norms which come into effect as such upon the entry into force of the Convention. The lacunae may be so seriously broad as to nullify the whole rationale of introducing the concept of *jus cogens* into positive international law through the Convention. In effect, the former legal regime, in conflict with the *jus cogens* norms at the time the Convention takes effect, cannot be brought into conformity with the peremptory norms of the new international legal order. It is submitted that a norm of general international law which is deemed accepted and recognized as *jus cogens* norms upon the entry into force of the Convention constitutes "a new peremptory norm of general international law" under Article 64 as of that time, in relation to the treaties existing then, such that the invalidating effect of a *jus cogens* norm upon such treaties would operate as a mechanism of adjusting the old regime of treaties along the imperatives of the new international legal order. In this respect, the correlation between Article 53 and 64 is that treaties concluded prior to the Convention's entry into force, which thus escape the coverage of the former Article, are caught by the invalidating effect of the latter Article. This would seem to be the understanding of the Commission when it stated that the effect of a new rule of *jus cogens* under its draft Article 61 (which is the present Article 64 of the Convention) "must be to render void not only future but existing treaties."

VI. *Modification of* Jus Cogens *Norms*

A *jus cogens* norm is not immutable.[36] It is subject to change in keeping with societal developments of global scale. This is clearly implied in Article 53 of the Convention. However, it is required that a *jus cogens* norm "can be modified only by subsequent norm of general international law having the same character." Only a *jus cogens* norm can totally supersede or partially change an existing peremptory norm.

Generally, the process of modification of a *jus cogens* norm follows the same mechanism as its formation, which is on the same consensual basis as any other norm of general international law. This may occur both in terms of customary or conventional norm-formation. The modification process may present the least difficulties when it operates through a general multilateral treaty or convention. In that case, the terms of change can be precise and the moment of modification exactly determined. While, as the International Law Commission anticipated, "a modification of a rule of *jus cogens* would today most probably be effected through a general multilateral treaty", in the field of customary rules the requirement of Article 53 may pose a problem. Much that can be said on this point may pertain

---

[36] For comment of the Commission on the modification of *jus cogens* norms, see ILC COMMENTARIES, p. 6.

to abstract possibilities, but at any rate certain State practices may develop contrary to an existing *jus cogens* norm and, in the absence of significant protest, broaden into a customary rule adhered to by the majority of States, thus gaining the status of a norm of general international law. However, at that stage, it may lack peremptory character in the sense that it is not yet "accepted and recognized by the international community of States as a whole as a norm from which no derogation is permitted". Under Article 53, it cannot therefore yet modify the existing *jus cogens* norm on the matter, even if it is established as a norm of general international law (*jus dispositivum*). The result would be that a norm retains its *jus cogens* character formally, despite the fact that its content as a norm of general international law is contradicted by a new customary norm among the majority of States. However, the real world does not develop along the sequence of theoretical analysis; the two elements of *jus cogens* norm, pointed out above,[37] would most likely occur as one process in reality.

VII. *Concluding Remarks*

In providing *jus cogens* as a ground of invalidity or termination of treaties, the Vienna Convention on the Law of Treaties puts an end to the regime of *laissez-faire* in treaty-making. That the competence of States in this field has ceased to be unlimited is in itself one of the most significant features of progressive development in contemporary international law. It is a landmark that may shift the whole perspective of the theory of international law, and determine its future course on the basis of the same social forces that ushered in the concept of *jus cogens* into the modern law of treaties. However, as shown by the terms of the Convention, recognition of *jus cogens* by the international community of States does not mean at all the existence of superior norms independent of the wills of States, contrary to the hypothesis of publicists represented by Verdross.[38] That certain rules are normatively superior to others is brought about only by the concordance of wills of States themselves.

The introduction of *jus cogens* in the Vienna Convention can serve as a transformative mechanism for discarding out-moded rules in the old international law and for replacing them with progressive

---

[37] See *supra*, at
[38] *Forbidden Treaties in International Law*, 31 AM. J. INT'L L. 571, 572 (1937): "These principles concerning the conditions of the validity of treaties cannot be regarded as having been agreed upon by treaty; they must be regarded as valid independently of the will of the contracting parties. That is the reason why the *possibility* of norms of general international law, norms determining the limits of the freedom of the parties to conclude treaties, cannot be denied *a priori*."

principles that contribute to the making of a qualitatively new legal order. It may be recalled that the major capitalist powers whose exploitative interests are subserved by those obsolete rules indicated their opposition to a provision on *jus cogens* in the Convention or opted for the restriction of its application; on the other hand, the Third World States and the socialist community firmly supported the principle of *jus cogens* in all the stages toward the conclusion of the Convention.[39]

Despite the fact that the overwhelming majority of States have recognized the existence of international *jus cogens,* the operation of *jus cogens* rules under the Convention is seriously restricted, largely on account of the stand taken by the Western powers. But what remains as an achievement is that the Convention has succeeded in laying down the framework within which the international community can develop the fuller content of *jus cogens* norms, through the auspices of the new forces which have a stake in strengthening the conditions for detente, national independence and self-determination of peoples.

---

[39] For a discussion of this confrontation, see Sinclair, *Vienna Convention on the Law of Treaties,* 19 INT'L & COMP. L.Q. 47, 66-68 (1970); Tunkin, *Jus Cogens in Contemporary International Law,* 1971 TOLEDO L. REV. 107, 112-114; Abi-Saab, *The Third World and the Future of International Law,* 29 REV. BELGE DROIT INT'L 27, 51-53 (1973).

[15]

Unilateral Denunciation of Treaties: The Vienna Convention and the International Court of Justice

By Herbert W. Briggs [*]

The final preambular paragraph of the 1969 Vienna Convention on the Law of Treaties affirms "that the rules of customary international law will continue to govern questions not regulated by the provisions of the present Convention;" and Article 4 of the Convention, establishing the nonretroactivity of the Convention by providing that it "applies only to treaties which are concluded by States, after the entry into force of the present Convention with regard to such States," stipulates that this nonretroactivity is "[w]ithout prejudice to the application of any rules set forth in the present Convention to which treaties would be subject under international law independently of the Convention." [1]

The combined effect of the preambular passage and Article 4 is to affirm that the rules of customary international law applicable to treaties and to the parties to them will continue to govern (1) questions not regulated by the provisions of the Vienna Convention (e.g., the effect of war on treaties [2]), as well as (2) matters on which the Vienna Convention does contain substantive provisions, but where, because it has not yet entered into force or has not become binding on a particular state, the Convention as such is not applicable. [3]

It follows that the restrictive effects arising from requirements of entry into force, [4] consent to be bound, or nonretroactivity [5] are considerably

---

[*] Of the Board of Editors.

[1] UN Doc. A/Conf. 39/27, 23 May 1969; 63 AJIL 875 (1969). On the drafting of this preambular provision, see United Nations Conference on the Law of Treaties, Official Records, Vienna, Second Sess., 1969, A/Conf.39/11/Add.1 (cited hereafter as Vienna, O.R.II), 169–77 (31st and 32d plenary meetings) and A/Conf.39/11/Add. 2, (cited hereafter as Vienna, O.R., III) 263, 271. On Art. 4, see Vienna, O.R.II, 310–41 (100th–104th meetings, C.1), 165–66 (30th plenary meeting) and Vienna, O.R.III, 252–53. Consult also, Shabtai Rosenne, The Law of Treaties—A Guide to the Legislative History of the Vienna Convention (1970).

[2] Cf., Art. 73, Vienna Convention.

[3] Cf., also Art. 43, Vienna. On the general problem, see R. R. Baxter, Multilateral Treaties as Evidence of Customary International Law, 41 Brit. Y. B. Int. L. 275–300 (1965–66); R. R. Baxter, Treaties and Custom, Hague Academy of International Law, 129 Rec. des Cours, 25–105 (1970–71); Anthony A. D'Amato, The Concept of Custom in International Law (1971); H. W. A. Thirlway, International Customary Law and Codification (1972).

[4] Cf., Art. 84, which requires 35 ratifications or accessions for the Convention to enter into force.

[5] Cf., Art. 4.

52   THE AMERICAN JOURNAL OF INTERNATIONAL LAW   [Vol. 68

mitigated because the Vienna Convention is so largely a consolidation of the existing customary international law of treaties.

Like the International Law Commission, the Vienna Conference on the Law of Treaties refrained in most cases from indicating whether a particular provision was regarded as a codification of existing law or as a development of the law. The penultimate preambular clause of the Convention refers to "the codification *and* progressive development of the law of treaties achieved in the present Convention." [6] The size of the affirmative votes at Vienna, while certainly not conclusive on the point, may provide some indication of familiarity with a rule or principle which led to its relatively easy acceptance.

All articles in the Vienna Convention required adoption by a two-thirds vote of the states present and voting.[7] Of 85 articles, 60 were adopted unanimously (with abstentions on 23 of them, running from 1 to 17 abstentions).[8] Of 25 articles on which there were negative votes, there was but one negative vote on each of 8 articles, and only 2 on 4 more. The largest number of negative votes were on Article 15 (accession, but no universal participation, 73–14–8); Article 38 (treaty rules becoming customary law, 83–13–7); Article 45 (estoppel, 84–17–6); Article 66 (procedure for judicial settlement, 61–20–26); and Articles 81 and 83 (because no "all-States" formula included, 84–11–5 and 83–13–6, respectively). The lowest number of affirmative votes were recorded on Article 66 (procedure for judicial settlement, 61–20–26) and Article 67 (declarations of invalidity, etc., 68–1–29).

There was widespread acceptance at Vienna of the view expressed by Hans Blix (Sweden), a well-known authority on the law of treaties:

> It was generally agreed that most of the contents of the present convention were merely expressive of rules which existed under customary international law.[9]

Mustafa Kamil Yasseen (Iraq), the distinguished chairman of the Drafting Committee at Vienna, similarly observed:

> The purpose of the draft articles was not only to create new rules, but in the main to formulate existing rules which were already part of positive international law. It had to be realized that non-retroactivity, which was the principle that should be adopted, could not impair the binding force of those rules, since, in general international law, customary rules, for instance, or rules deriving from some other source of international law did not lose their character of positive law by the mere fact of their being codified in an international convention.[10]

[6] *Italics* added.

[7] Rules of Procedure 35 and 36. *Loc. cit.*, Vienna, O.R., I, xxviii.

[8] Of the articles adopted unanimously, significant numbers of abstentions were recorded on Art. 20 (objection to reservations, 83–0–17) and Art. 30 (effect of successive treaties, 90–0–14). Other significant abstentions occurred on articles on which there were negative votes, as indicated above. For the voting, consult the Official Records. *See also* ROSENNE, cited *supra* note 1.

[9] *Loc. cit.*, Vienna, O.R.II, 321, par. 43.

[10] *Ibid.*, 325, par. 20.

Sir Humphrey Waldock, to whose wise and expert guidance the Vienna Convention on the Law of Treaties is eloquent testimony, observed at Vienna that:

> he had been very comforted to hear many representatives at the Conference speak of the convention as essentially a codifying instrument. That was the right view if the convention was regarded essentially as a consolidating instrument which took account of differences of opinion but found a common agreement as to the lines to be followed in the law of treaties. . . .
>
> . . . He had been very glad to hear the representative of Switzerland emphasize the inter-temporal element in international law, because that element was his particular preoccupation. Conventions such as the one under consideration have their consolidating force and even matters which might or might not have been international law . . . at the time of the convention might be so considered at a later date.[11]

While the observations made above should not be regarded as an argument against the necessity or desirability of widespread ratification and the early entry into force of the Vienna Convention as such, it will be interesting to examine with some attention the attitude of the International Court of Justice towards the Vienna Convention and its content as revealed by the most recent jurisprudence of the Court.

Although the Court has had no occasion to pronounce upon the current status or effect of the Vienna Convention as a whole, it has already made observations upon, or followed implicitly,[12] particular provisions of the Convention. It is noteworthy that the articles of the Vienna Convention on which the Court has made explicit observations have all concerned claims to terminate treaties unilaterally on grounds such as breach, coercion, or changed conditions, and it is to these aspects of the cases to be examined that our attention will be largely confined.

UNILATERAL DENUNCIATION OF TREATIES FOR BREACH

Namibia: *The Court's Unfortunate Dictum*

In the *Namibia* case,[13] the International Court of Justice was requested by the United Nations Security Council to give an advisory opinion on the legal consequences for states of the continued presence of South Africa

---

[11] *Ibid.*, 337, pars. 77, 80.

[12] Although it will not be further discussed here, the manner in which the Court proceeded to interpret the 1961 Exchanges of Notes between the United Kingdom and Iceland and the Federal Republic of Germany and Iceland in the Fisheries Jurisdiction cases, Judgments of Feb. 2, 1973 on the Jurisdiction of the Court, ICJ REPORTS, 1973, pars. 13–23 (U.K. v. Iceland) and pars. 14–23 (F.R.G. v. Iceland), provides an admirable example of the way in which Arts. 31 and 32 of the Vienna Convention on the Law of Treaties were intended by their draftsmen to be applied in order to discover the intentions and expectations of the parties through an examination of text, context, object, and *travaux préparatoires*. *See further*, 65 AJIL 707–12 (1971).

[13] Legal Consequences for States of the Continued Presence of South Africa in Namibia (South West Africa) notwithstanding Security Council Resolution 276 (1970), Advisory Opinion of June 21, 1971. ICJ REPORTS, 1971, at 16.

in Namibia. In examining the action of the United Nations General Assembly in terminating the Mandate exercised by South Africa over South West Africa because of the failure of South Africa to fulfill its obligations thereunder, the Court noted (par. 90) that "with the entry into force of the Charter of the United Nations a relationship was established between all Members of the United Nations on the one side, and each mandatory Power on the other,"[14] and observed (par. 91):

> One of the fundamental principles governing the international relationship thus established is that a party which disowns or does not fulfil its own obligations cannot be recognized as retaining the rights which it claims to derive from the relationship.[15]

Seeking further justification for the General Assembly action, the Court thought it "appropriate to have regard to the general principles of international law regulating termination of a treaty relationship on account of breach" (par. 94), because, even if the Mandate is of a special institutional character, it "incorporates a definite agreement," as the Court itself observed in an earlier judgment,[16] and the Mandate, "in fact and in law, is an international agreement having the character of a treaty or convention."

Referring to Article 60 [17] of the Vienna Convention, the Court's *Namibia*

[14] *Ibid.*, 45.   [15] *Ibid.*, 46.

[16] South West Africa cases (Ethiopia v. South Africa; Liberia v. South Africa), Preliminary Objections, Judgment of December 21, 1962, ICJ REPORTS, 1962, 319 at 331 and 330.

[17] Article 60 reads as follows:

Termination or suspension of the operation of a treaty as a consequence of its breach

1. A material breach of a bilateral treaty by one of the parties entitles the other to invoke the breach as a ground for terminating the treaty or suspending its operation in whole or in part.

2. A material breach of a multilateral treaty by one of the parties entitles:

(a) the other parties by unanimous agreement to suspend the operation of the treaty in whole or in part to terminate it either:

(i) in the relations between themselves and the defaulting State, or

(ii) as between all the parties;

(b) a party specially affected by the breach to invoke it as a ground for suspending the operation of the treaty in whole or in part in the relations between itself and the defaulting State;

(c) any party other than the defaulting State to invoke the breach as a ground for suspending the operation of the treaty in whole or in part with respect to itself if the treaty is of such a character that a material breach of its provisions by one party radically changes the position of every party with respect to the further performance of its obligations under the treaty.

3. A material breach of a treaty, for the purposes of this article, consists in:

(a) a repudiation of the treaty not sanctioned by the present Convention; or

(b) the violation of a provision essential to the accomplishment of the object or purpose of the treaty.

4. The foregoing paragraphs are without prejudice to any provision in the treaty applicable in the event of a breach.

opinion continues (pars. 94–95):

> 94. The rules laid down by the Vienna Convention on the Law of Treaties concerning termination of a treaty relationship on account of breach (adopted without a dissenting vote) may in many respects be considered as a codification of existing customary law on the subject. In the light of these rules, only a material breach of a treaty justifies termination, such breach being defined as:
>
> (a) a repudiation of the treaty not sanctioned by the present convention; or
>
> (b) the violation of a provision essential to the accomplishment of the object or purpose of the treaty. (Art. 60, para. 3).
>
> 95. General Assembly resolution 2145 (XXI) determines that both forms of material breach had occurred in this case. By stressing that South Africa "has, in fact, disavowed the Mandate", the General Assembly declared in fact that it had repudiated it. The resolution in question is therefore to be viewed as the exercise of the right to terminate a relationship in case of a deliberate and persistent violation of obligations which destroys the very object and purpose of that relationship.[18]

Had the Court stopped here in its discussion of the right to terminate a treaty for breach, one might have little with which to quarrel, although the Court might usefully have stated more explicitly that it was applying the principles set forth in paragraph 2(a) of Article 60, *i.e.*, the right of the other parties to the treaty collectively to terminate it for material breach.[19]

Most unfortunately, however, the Court proceeds (par. 96) to refer to a supposed

> general principle of law that a right of termination on account of breach must be presumed to exist in respect of all treaties, except as regards provisions relating to the protection of the human person contained in treaties of a humanitarian character (as indicated in Art. 60, para. 5, of the Vienna Convention). The silence of a treaty as to the existence of such a right cannot be interpreted as implying the exclusion of a right which has its source outside of the treaty, in general international law, and is dependent on the occurrence of circumstances which are not normally envisaged when a treaty is concluded.[20]

The Court produces no evidence to support its allegation that a general principle of law establishes "a right of termination on account of breach." Moreover, it fails to note that even had such a supposed right existed in general international law, it finds no recognition in Article 60 of the Vienna Convention (which the Court properly regards as "in many respects . . . a codification of existing customary law" on termination of a

---

5. Paragraphs 1 to 3 do not apply to provisions relating to the protection of the human person contained in treaties of a humanitarian character, in particular to provisions prohibiting any form of reprisals against persons protected by such treaties.

[18] ICJ REPORTS, 1971, at 47.

[19] Would the fact that Portugal joined South Africa in voting against General Assembly resolution 2145 (XXI) be sufficient to defeat the purpose of par. 2(a) of Art. 60 of the Vienna Convention, which refers to "the other parties by unanimous agreement?"

[20] *Loc. cit.*, 47. The concluding clause appears, confusingly, to add the *rebus sic stantibus* principle in support of the alleged rule.

56   THE AMERICAN JOURNAL OF INTERNATIONAL LAW   [Vol. 68

treaty relationship on account of breach), except with regard to joint action by other parties to terminate a multilateral convention.

More explicitly, the only recognition of such an alleged right in the Vienna Convention is found in par. 2(a) of Article 60. No such alleged "right of termination" is recognized for bilateral treaties, where a material breach may only be *invoked as a ground for termination or suspension*; and pars. 2(b) and 2(c) permit invocation of a material breach of a multilateral treaty only as a ground for suspension, not termination, of the treaty.

In a legal sense, the distinction between "a right to terminate" and "a right to invoke as a ground for termination" is not entirely dependent upon the availability of a forum with compulsory jurisdiction.[21] In its official Commentary on Article 57 (Art. 60, Vienna) the International Law Commission observed in part:

> (5) The Commission was agreed that a breach of a treaty, however serious, does not *ipso facto* put an end to the treaty, and also that it is not open to a state simply to allege a violation of the treaty and pronounce the treaty at an end . . .
>
> (6) . . . The formula "invoke as a ground" is intended to underline that the right arising under the article is not a right arbitrarily to pronounce the treaty terminated. . . .[22]

That the distinction was understood at the Vienna Conference on the Law of Treaties is clearly demonstrated by the rejection, by votes of 52–4–34 and 51–3–38, of Venezuelan proposals to substitute a right "to terminate" for the right to invoke a breach as a ground for termination or suspension set forth in the International Law Commission's draft.[23] After amending the Commission's text of Article 57(2)(c) [Art. 60(2)(c), Vienna] to substitute a right "to invoke the breach as a ground" for suspension for the right "to suspend" which had crept into the Commission's text,[24] the Vienna Conference adopted the article by a vote of 88–0–7.

The Vienna Convention contains its own procedures for settlement of disputes arising, *inter alia*, from claims of a unilateral right to terminate or suspend treaties.[25] It is true that the Vienna Convention is not yet in force and the Court was not purporting to apply it as such in the *Namibia* case. However, the elaborate care with which the International Law Commission and the Vienna Conference in their restatement of the law of

---

[21] *Cf.* the observation of Judge de Castro in his Separate Opinion in the ICAO Council (Jurisdiction) case (ICJ REPORTS, 1972, 46, at 133 n.), inveighing against "what is a fairly common source of confusion, namely the belief that the absence of any tribunal having compulsory jurisdiction arbitrarily leaves States free to terminate or suspend treaties," whereas "The true position is that a declaration of termination or suspension must be objectively justified to be valid."

[22] INTERNATIONAL LAW COMMISSION, REPORT ON ITS 18TH SESS. (1966) 83 (GAOR, 21st sess. (A/6309/Rev. 1); 61 AJIL 424 (1967).

[23] *See* discussion in the Committee of the Whole, *loc. cit.*, Vienna, O.R. I, 352 *ff.*; O.R., III, 181 *ff.*

[24] *Ibid.*, O.R. II, 111 *ff.* (21st plenary meeting); O.R. III, 269.

[25] *See* Arts. 42, 65, 66, and Annex.

treaties restricted any claim of a unilateral right by a state to terminate a treaty for breach to a right to invoke the breach as a ground for termination or suspension should have given pause to the Court, particularly before it indulged in *obiter dicta* and made undiscriminating generalizations not essential to the case before it. It should be carefully noted that no question of a claim by a state of a unilateral right to terminate a treaty for breach was before the Court in this case. In *Namibia* the Court was dealing incidentally with the revocation by a collective supervisory organ of a multilateral treaty having institutional characteristics because of nonperformance. The only analogy with Article 60 of the Vienna Convention is with the collective right of termination set forth in paragraph 2(a).

The failure of the Court to confine its observations to the point actually before it led it to make unsupported generalizations about "a right [of termination] which has its source outside the treaty, in general international law" (par. 96)—*obiter dicta* which appear to have misled counsel for India in its dispute with Pakistan over the *Jurisdiction of the ICAO Council.*

Jurisdiction of the ICAO Council Case: India Misled

In the *Appeal relating to the Jurisdiction of the ICAO Council* (India v. Pakistan),[26] the issue of the right of a state unilaterally to terminate or suspend multilateral treaties for breach arose in two ways: in regard to the jurisdiction of the ICAO Council and in regard to the jurisdiction of the International Court of Justice itself. The case came before the Court on an appeal brought by India (on the basis of jurisdictional clauses in the 1944 Chicago Convention on International Civil Aviation and the 1944 Chicago International Air Services Transit Agreement, and Articles 36 and 37 of the Court's Statute) against decisions of the Council of the International Civil Aviation Organization taking jurisdiction over an Application and Complaint brought by Pakistan (under the jurisdictional clauses of the same Chicago Treaties) on the ground that India had violated provisions of those treaties by unilaterally suspending flights of Pakistan aircraft over Indian territory.

The Indian *Memorial*[27] requested the Court to reverse as "illegal, null and void, or erroneous" the assumption of jurisdiction by the ICAO Council over the claim of Pakistan on the ground (*inter alia*) that, since the Chicago treaties had "been terminated or suspended as between the two States," the Council's jurisdiction, which rested only on the jurisdictional clauses of those treaties, no longer existed. Although, in its *Counter-Memorial*, Pakistan asked the Court to reject the Indian appeal and to confirm the decisions of the ICAO Council,[28] in oral pleadings, counsel for Pakistan proceeded to challenge the jurisdiction of the Court,[29] in part

---

[26] Judgment of August 18, 1972, ICJ REPORTS, 1972, at 46.

[27] Since the Court's documentation is not yet available, I have followed the Indian *Memorial* and the Pakistan *Counter-Memorial* as reprinted in 12 INDIAN J. OF INT. L. 421–62 (*Memorial*) and 463–89 (*Counter-Memorial*) (1972). *See also* ICJ REPORTS, 1972, at 49.

[28] ICJ REPORTS, 1972, at 50.   [29] *Ibid.*, 52 *ff.*

58   THE AMERICAN JOURNAL OF INTERNATIONAL LAW   [Vol. 68

on the ground that

> since it is one of India's principal contentions that the Treaties are not
> in force at all (or at any rate in operation) between the Parties, (a)
> India cannot have any *ius standi* to invoke their jurisdictional clauses
> for the purpose of appealing to the Court, and (b) India must admit
> that the Court in any event lacks jurisdiction under its own Statute
> because . . .

according to the Indian argument, the treaties are no longer "treaties and
conventions *in force*" within the terms of Article 36, par. 1, of the Court's
Statute.[30]

The Court decisively rejected the Pakistan challenge to its jurisdiction
and, among other interesting observations, made one pertinent to the
present study:

> (b) Nor in any case could a merely unilateral suspension *per se*
> render jurisdictional clauses inoperative, since one of their purposes
> might be, precisely, to enable the validity of the suspension to be
> tested. If a mere allegation, as yet unestablished, that a treaty was
> no longer operative could be used to defeat its jurisdictional clauses,
> all such clauses would become potentially a dead letter, even in cases
> like the present, where one of the very questions at issue on the merits,
> and as yet undecided, is whether or not the treaty is operative—i.e.,
> whether it has been validly terminated or suspended. The result would
> be that means of defeating jurisdictional clauses would never be
> wanting.[31]

After establishing its own jurisdiction, the Court turned to the issue of
the jurisdiction of the ICAO Council. The jurisdictional clauses[32] were
limited to "any disagreement between two or more contracting States relating to the interpretation or application" of the Chicago Treaties. Consequently, observed the Court, unless the dispute "is one that can be resolved without any interpretation or application of the relevant Treaties
at all . . . then the Council must be competent." [33]

India, maintaining that the Council lacked jurisdiction because the dispute could be resolved without any reference to the treaties, relied on two
principal contentions: (1) that the treaties were no longer in force or
were suspended as between India and Pakistan; and (2) that, even if
they were in force between the parties, the dispute related to the termination or suspension of the treaties, not to their interpretation or application,
and therefore did not fall within the jurisdictional clauses.[34]

Although India contended as regards the first point that "the question
of justification for termination or suspension of the Convention or the
Transit Agreement is not within the scope of the Council's jurisdiction

---

[30] *Ibid.*, 52–53.   [31] *Ibid.*, 53–54.
[32] Art. 84 of the Chicago International Civil Aviation Convention and Art. II, Section 2, of the International Air Services Transit Agreement. For texts, *see ibid.*, 55.
[33] *Ibid.*, 62.   [34] *Ibid.*, 62, par. 29.

and does not arise as an issue" in its appeal to the Court,[35] India nevertheless proceeded to present the Court with arguments that either (a) the treaties were or became terminated or suspended as between the parties because of the outbreak of hostilities between India and Pakistan in 1965, and had never been revived; or (b) India "had the right to suspend them unilaterally, and it should be regarded as having suspended them unilaterally"[36] in 1971 under general principles of international law permitting unilateral termination or suspension for breach (in particular, the hijacking of an Indian plane, allegedly involving Pakistan complicity).

This allegation of a unilateral right of termination or suspension of treaties for breach under general principles of international law was also advanced by India to support its second main contention that the termination or suspension of a treaty making no provision therefor could not involve the interpretation or application of that treaty and was consequently not within the jurisdictional clauses. In other words, Indian behavior was not under the treaties, but outside them.[37]

In support of the alleged right "to unilateral termination or suspension of a multilateral treaty due to material breach,"[38] India placed undiscriminating reliance on, *inter alia*, paragraphs 94 and 96[39] of the *Namibia* opinion of the International Court of Justice, on Article 60 of the Vienna Convention on the Law of Treaties,[40] and on an Indian author, whose major thesis, if not all the evidence, supported the Indian contention.[41]

What position did the Court take on this asserted right? The Court first noted that the issue belonged to the merits of the dispute into which the Court could not go. However, there were certain preliminary points which were relevant to the jurisdictional issue before the Court and a correct appreciation of the Indian position thereon.[42] The contention relied on most prominently by India was that its behavior was outside the treaties and justified by a general principle of international law, and therefore the ICAO Council, whose jurisdiction arose under the treaties, was incompetent. This contention, said the Court,

> involves a point of principle of great general importance for the jurisdictional aspects of this—or of any—case . . . . The Court considers however, that for precisely the same order of reason as has already been noticed in the case of its own jurisdiction in the present case, a mere unilateral affirmation of these contentions—contested by the other party—cannot be utilized so as to negative the Council's jurisdiction. The point is not that these contentions are necessarily wrong but that their validity has not yet been determined. Since therefore the Parties are in disagreement as to whether the Treaties ever were (validly) suspended or replaced by something else; as to whether they are in force

---

[35] Indian *Memorial,* par. 30, cited *supra* note 27.

[36] *Ibid.,* and pars. 33 *ff.*   [37] *Ibid.,* pars. 75 *ff.*

[38] *Ibid.,* pars. 37 *ff.,* 75.   [39] Quoted *supra* at notes 18 and 20.

[40] *Supra,* note 17.

[41] BHEK PATI SINHA, UNILATERAL DENUNCIATION OF TREATY BECAUSE OF PRIOR VIOLATIONS OF OBLIGATIONS BY OTHER PARTY (1966).

[42] ICJ REPORTS, 1972, at 62.

between the Parties or not; and as to whether India's action in relation to Pakistan overflights was such as not to involve the Treaties, but to be justifiable *aliter et aliunde;*—these very questions are in issue before the Council, and no conclusions as to jurisdiction can be drawn from them, at least at this stage, so as to exclude *ipso facto* and *a priori* the competence of the Council.[43]

The Court continued by observing that it would be "destructive of the whole object of adjudicability" and "a wholesale nullification of the practical value of jurisdictional clauses" if a party were allowed "first to purport to terminate, or suspend the operation of a treaty, and then to declare that the treaty being now terminated or suspended, its jurisdictional clauses were in consequence void, and could not be invoked for the purpose of contesting the validity of the termination or suspension . . ."[44]

The importance of what the Court is saying here is not to be minimized because the Court, by limiting the issue to treaties containing jurisdictional clauses, failed to clear up the ambiguity of its *Namibia obiter dicta* about the unilateral right of a state under general international law to terminate a treaty for breach, which had misled counsel for India in this case.[45] Indeed, the Court may have invited further claims to such an alleged right by observing (as noted above) that "The point is not that these contentions are necessarily wrong . . ."

However, the Court proceeded to limit further the scope of the Indian contention by holding that a dispute as to the termination or suspension of a treaty for alleged material breach by the other party

> is inherently and by its very nature, one that must involve the examination of the Treaties in order to see whether, according to the definition of a material breach of a treaty contained in Article 60 of the 1969 Vienna Convention on the Law of Treaties, there has been (paragraph 3(*b*)) a violation by Pakistan of a "provision essential to the accomplishment of the object or purpose of the Treaty."[46]

This holding that a dispute as to termination or suspension of a treaty for breach is necessarily one as to its interpretation or application (and thus comes within the ICAO Council's competence under the jurisdictional clauses) is all the more interesting because of the Court's reliance on the Vienna Convention on the Law of Treaties as an authoritative statement of international law, even prior to the entry into force of that Convention.

The Court properly confined itself to upholding its own jurisdiction and that of the ICAO Council;[47] but it may be noted that much of the rationale advanced by the Court to restrict claims of a unilateral right under general international law to terminate or suspend jurisdictional treaties for breach

---

[43] *Ibid.*, 64, par. 31.   [44] *Ibid.*, 64–65.

[45] Judge de Castro saw the point clearly when he observed in his Separate Opinion that "The Advisory Opinion in the *Namibia* case does not support India's contention" (*ibid.*, 130, n.1) and that "It is not correct that the principle laid down in Article 60 of the Vienna Convention is *dehors* the Chicago Convention" (*ibid.*, 129).

[46] *Ibid.*, 67.

[47] *Ibid.*, 70. By votes of 13 to 3 and 14 to 2, respectively.

would appear to have cogency in relation to all treaties, whether or not they contain jurisdictional clauses.

OTHER CLAIMS OF A RIGHT OF UNILATERAL DENUNCIATION

The Fisheries Jurisdiction Cases: Iceland Defaults

The next occasion on which the Court had to deal with a claimed unilateral right to terminate, or consider terminated, a treaty arose in the *Fisheries Jurisdiction* cases (the United Kingdom of Great Britain and Northern Ireland v. Iceland and the Federal Republic of Germany v. Iceland).[48] Unlike the cases discussed above, here the alleged right was based not upon breach by the other party, but upon a variety of arguments including duress, *rebus sic stantibus*, and rights allegedly derived from the nature of certain treaties.

On April 14, 1972, the United Kingdom filed an Application before the International Court of Justice instituting proceedings against Iceland challenging the proposed extension of Iceland's exclusive fisheries jurisdiction from 12 to 50 miles around its shores. The United Kingdom founded the Court's jurisdiction on Article 36, paragraph 1, of the Court's Statute and a March 11, 1961, Exchange of Notes between the two countries under which the United Kingdom recognized Iceland's claim to a 12-mile fisheries limit in return for Iceland's agreement that any dispute as to the extension of Icelandic fisheries jurisdiction beyond the 12-mile limit "shall, at the request of either party, be referred to the International Court of Justice."[49]

Despite the clarity of this jurisdictional clause, the Government of Iceland notified the Court by letter dated May 29, 1972 that Iceland was not willing "to confer" jurisdiction on the Court and would not appoint an Agent. Thereupon, the Government of the United Kingdom requested the Court to grant interim measures of protection under Article 41 of the Court's Statute, which the Court proceeded to do, while ordering hearings on the question of its jurisdiction to deal with the merits.[50]

In its decision of February 2, 1973, the Court, finding by 14 to 1 that it had jurisdiction, regretted the absence of Iceland in the proceedings, noted its obligations under the Statute to establish its own jurisdiction, and observed that in so doing it would "consider those objections with might, in its view, be raised against its jurisdiction."[51]

---

[48] Fisheries Jurisdiction (United Kingdom v. Iceland) Jurisdiction of the Court, Judgment of February 2, 1973, ICJ REPORTS, 1973, at 3. The comparable Judgment of Fisheries Jurisdiction (Federal Republic of Germany v. Iceland), Judgment of February 2, 1973, ICJ REPORTS, 1973, at 49, is in many, but not all, respects identically worded. For the purposes of this study reference is made only to the United Kingdom case.

[49] ICJ REPORTS, 1973, at 8.

[50] *See* Fisheries Jurisdiction (United Kingdom v. Iceland), Interim Protection, Order of August 17, 1972, ICJ REPORTS, 1972, at 12. For the comparable Order in Federal Republic of Germany v. Iceland, *ibid.*, 30.

[51] ICJ REPORTS, 1973, par. 12, citing Art. 53 of the Court Statute under which the Court may give default judgments where it is satisfied that it has jurisdiction.

Although Iceland had refused to submit written or oral pleadings, in fact, as Judge Sir Gerald Fitzmaurice observed in his Separate Opinion:

> Iceland has sent to the Court a series of letters and telegrams on the subject, often containing material going far beyond the question of competence and entering deeply into the merits, and has lost no opportunity of doing the same thing through statements made or circulated in the United Nations, and by other means, all of which have of course been brought to the attention of the Court in one way or another as, doubtless, they were intended to be.[52]

In an aide-mémoire of February 24, 1972, the British Government was informed that "The Government of Iceland, therefore, considers the provisions of the [1961] Notes exchanged no longer to be applicable and consequently terminated." [53] As noted above, the grounds upon which Iceland justified a unilateral right of termination were varied. At least five were identified by the Court: (1) duress; (2) so-called "perpetual" treaties; (3) jurisdictional treaties; (4) treaties whose object has been fulfilled; (5) changed conditions.

Duress: In a letter addressed to the Registrar of the Court on May 29, 1972, the Minister for Foreign Affairs of Iceland stated that:

> The 1961 Exchange of Notes took place under extremely difficult circumstances, when the British Royal Navy had been using force to oppose the 12-mile fishery limit established by the Icelandic Government in 1958.[54]

On this the Court observed:

> This statement could be interpreted as a veiled charge of duress purportedly rendering the Exchange of Notes void *ab initio,* and it was dealt with as such by the United Kingdom in its *Memorial.* There can be little doubt, as is implied in the Charter of the United Nations and recognized in Article 52 of the Vienna Convention on the Law of Treaties, that under contemporary international law an agreement concluded under the threat or use of force is void.[55]

It was equally clear, however, that the Court could not consider so serious an accusation on the basis of vague charges unsupported by evidence, particularly when the history of the negotiations leading up to the 1961 Exchange of Notes revealed that they had been "freely negotiated by the interested parties on the basis of perfect equality and freedom of decision on both sides." [56]

What is significant for present purposes is the Court's unhesitating acceptance as a principle of contemporary international law of the rule "recognized" in Article 52 of the Vienna Convention, providing that "A treaty is void if its conclusion has been procured by the threat or use of force in violation of the principles of international law embodied in the Charter of the United Nations." This was not the traditional view under which treaties

---

[52] *Ibid.,* 35.   [53] *Ibid.,* 39.

[54] *Ibid.,* 14, par. 24.   [55] *Ibid.*

[56] *Ibid., Cf.,* the Court's review of the negotiations, pars, 18–23 (U.K. v. Iceland), and of the German-Icelandic negotiations, *ibid.* (F.R.G.–Iceland), pars. 19–23.

procured through the coercion of a state by the threat or use of force were nevertheless considered valid in international law. Since the Court found no factual basis for the charge of duress, it found it unnecessary to consider any procedural problems raised by the wording of Article 52.

Implied Right of Unilateral Denunciation Supposedly Derived From the Nature or Character of Certain Treaties: In his letter of May 29, 1972, to the Registrar of the Court, the Minister for Foreign Affairs of Iceland asserted that the 1961 Exchange of Notes "was not of a permanent nature" and that "an undertaking for judicial settlement cannot be considered to be of a permanent nature." [57]

From these assertions the Court concluded that Iceland was contending that "perpetual" treaties and treaties containing jurisdictional clauses were by their nature subject to a right of unilateral termination.[58] The Court found no need to pronounce upon the existence of such alleged principles of treaty law and contented itself with denying the perpetual nature of the 1961 Exchange of Notes and with distinguishing general treaties and declarations of judicial settlement of unpredictable future disputes from the specific compromissory clause in the 1961 Exchange of Notes "establishing the jurisdiction of the Court to deal with a concrete kind of dispute which was foreseen and specifically anticipated by the parties." When precisely the type of dispute contemplated by the *compromis* was referred to the Court, "the contention that the compromissory clause has lapsed, or is terminable, cannot be accepted." [59]

A third contention of Iceland, based upon assertions of its Foreign Minister, that "the object and purpose of the provisions in the 1961 Exchange of Notes for recourse to judicial settlement in certain eventualities have been fully achieved" and, therefore the agreement is no longer in force,[60] was clearly indefensible, held the Court, in the light of the reciprocal nature of the agreement reached in the Exchange of Notes, the terms of the compromissory clause, and the intentions and expectations of the parties.[61]

However, continued the Court, Iceland's argument might be that since Iceland in 1961 had traded the jurisdictional clause for a recognition of the right to a 12-mile fisheries limit, and since today the 12-mile limit is generally recognized, there is a "failure of consideration" which entitles Iceland to claim that the object and purpose of the agreement have been fulfilled and it is therefore no longer binding on Iceland. The Court unhesitatingly rejected such a contention because the very purpose of the 1961 Exchange was "not merely to decide upon the Icelandic claim to fisheries jurisdiction up to 12 miles, but also to provide a means whereby the parties might resolve the question of the validity of any further claims." [62]

These three contentions based upon alleged principles supposedly derived from the nature of treaties find no specific counterpart in the Vienna Convention on the Law of Treaties, although, ironically, an unfortunate British amendment to Article 56 opened the door to the type of claim made by

---

[57] *Ibid.*, 14.
[59] *Ibid.*, 16.
[61] *Ibid.*, 9–14, *Cf.*, *supra* note 12.

[58] *Ibid.*, pars. 25 *ff.*
[60] *Ibid.*, 39.
[62] *Ibid.*, 16–17.

64   THE AMERICAN JOURNAL OF INTERNATIONAL LAW   [Vol. 68

Iceland. After careful debate, the International Law Commission had rejected the proposal of its Special Rapporteur, Sir Humphrey Waldock, that certain treaties, by their nature, were to be regarded as limited in duration or as subject to a right of unilateral denunciation—a view supported by some British authors.[63] The Commission decided that the rules of international law governing the termination of treaties, were fully applicable to commercial treaties, treaties of alliance, treaties of judicial settlement, and so-called "perpetual" treaties without the necessity for any special rules based upon the "nature" or "'character" of a treaty—a pseudo-scientific notion which refers not to the juridical nature of treaties but to their content or political purpose. The Commission therefore adopted an article (Art. 53) providing:

> 1. A treaty which contains no provision regarding its termination and which does not provide for denunciation or withdrawal is not subject to denunciation or withdrawal unless it is established that the parties intended to admit the possibility of denunciation or withdrawal.

At the Vienna Conference in 1968, there were some mutterings about "perpetual" treaties and the Committee of the Whole unwisely adopted, by a vote of 26–25, with 37 abstentions, a British proposal to add to the above "unless" clause: "or (b) a right of denunciation or withdrawal may be implied by the nature of the treaty." [64]

Since the Vienna Convention applies only to treaties which are concluded by states after its entry into force with regard to such states,[65] there may be little occasion to imply a right of denunciation of "perpetual" treaties. Nor has the abusive practice by which some states have claimed a right to terminate on notice their unilateral declarations accepting the compulsory jurisdiction of the International Court of Justice found any lodgement in the law of treaties. The attitude of the Court in the *Fisheries Jurisdiction* cases suggests that any claim by a state of a unilateral right of denunciation implied from the nature of a treaty will be received with reserve.

Fundamental Change of Circumstances: The contention of changed circumstances as a ground for invoking the termination or suspension of a treaty (or, as Iceland presented it, of conferring a unilateral right to terminate) was considered by the Court to have been advanced both in relation to changes in the law and as to changed factual circumstances such as improved fishing techniques and depletion of resources.

---

[63] *See* 2 Y.B. INT. L. COMM., 1963, at 64–70, *Second Report on the Law of Treaties,* by Sir Humphrey Waldock, Arts. 16 and 17, with Commentary. For the debate in the International Law Commission, *see* 1 *ibid.,* 98–107 (688th-89th meetings), 239–41 (709th meeting), 293–94 (717th meeting); and (as Art. 39), 1 *ibid.,* 1966, Part I, 43–48 (829th meeting).

[64] As rephrased by the Drafting Committee. *See* Vienna, O.R. III, 177–78 (on Art. 53 of the ILC text). For the debate in the Committee of the Whole, *ibid.,* O.R. I, 336–43 (58th and 59th meetings, May 8, 1968); and in plenary, *ibid.,* O.R. II, 108–10 (20th and 21st meetings, May 12–13, 1969), where the amended text of Art. 53 was adopted by a vote of 95–0–6, and became Art. 56 of the Vienna Convention.

[65] Art. 4. *Cf.,* Art. 28.

As regards the Icelandic contention that the law had changed (the 12-mile fisheries limit had become generally accepted since Iceland had bargained the jurisdictional clause for British recognition of it in 1961, and therefore the 1961 Exchange of Notes was no longer applicable), the Court observed that "While changes in the law may under certain conditions constitute valid grounds for invoking a change of circumstances affecting the duration of a treaty," the contention was not relevant to the present case since, as noted above, the purpose of the 1961 agreement was not merely to recognize an Icelandic claim of 12 miles but also to provide a means for the settlement of claims to exclusive fisheries jursidiction beyond that limit.[66] Said the Court:

> Clearly it then becomes incumbent on Iceland to comply with its side of the bargain, which is to accept the testing before the Court of the validity of its further claims to extended jurisdiction. Moreover, in the case of a treaty which is in part executed and in part executory, in which one of the parties has already benefited from the executed provisions of the treaty, it would be particularly inadmissible to allow that party to put an end to obligations which were accepted under the treaty by way of *quid pro quo* for the provisions which the other party has already executed.[67]

On the general principle of *rebus sic stantibus*,[68] the Court made the following carefully worded observation:

> International law admits that a fundamental change in the circumstances which determined the parties to accept a treaty, if it has resulted in a radical transformation of the extent of the obligations imposed by it, may, under certain conditions, afford the party affected a ground for invoking the termination or suspension of the treaty. This principle, and the conditions and exceptions to which it is subject, have been embodied in Article 62 of the Vienna Convention on the Law of Treaties, which may in many respects be considered as a codification of existing customary law on the subject of the termination of a treaty relationship on account of change of circumstances.[69]

[66] ICJ REPORTS, 1973, at 17.   [67] *Ibid.*, 18.

[68] The Court itself did not employ the term *rebus sic stantibus*, which had also been abandoned by the International Law Commission so as to avoid its doctrinal implications. *Cf.*, 2 Y. B. INT. L. COMM. (1966), at 258 (Report of the International Law Commission, 18th Sess., Commentary (par. 7) on Art. 59); 61 AJIL 432 (1967). Nor does the term appear in the Vienna Convention.

[69] ICJ REPORTS, 1973, par. 36. The text of Art. 62 of the Vienna Convention reads:

Fundamental change of circumstances

1. A fundamental change of circumstances which has occurred with regard to those existing at the time of the conclusion of a treaty, and which was not foreseen by the parties, may not be invoked as a ground for terminating or withdrawing from the treaty unless:

(a) the existence of those circumstances constituted an essential basis of the consent of the parties to be bound by the treaty; and

(b) the effect of the change is radically to transform the extent of obligations still to be performed under the treaty.

The Court then proceeded to apply the provisions of Article 62 of the Vienna Convention to the case before it. The Icelandic contention, made in an Althing resolution of February 15, 1972, "that because of the vital interests of the nation and owing to changed circumstances the Notes concerning fishery limits exchanged in 1961 are no longer applicable and that their provisions do not constitute an obligation for Iceland" was regarded by the Court as implying, *inter alia*, a claim that the change of circumstances was "fundamental" (as required by Article 62).[70] However the United Kingdom queried the fundamental nature of any change of circumstances in fisheries around Iceland; and the Court observed that any such changes would come up for consideration in a hearing on the merits of the dispute.

The "exceptional dependence of Iceland on its fisheries for its subsistence and economic development" was expressly recognized, continued the Court, in the 1961 Exchange of Notes and in the Court's own Orders of August 17, 1972, indicating interim measures of protection. Whether such economic dependence conferred any legal basis for a unilaterally promulgated Icelandic claim of exclusive fisheries jurisdiction beyond the 12-mile limit was also an issue for the merits.[71]

On the jurisdictional point, however, the Court observed that "the apprehended dangers for the vital interests of Iceland, resulting from changes in fishing techniques, cannot constitute a fundamental change with respect to the lapse or subsistence of the compromissory clause establishing the Court's jurisdiction." Moreover, the Court could find no fundamental change of circumstances which (as required by Article 62 of the Vienna Convention) radically increased the burden of obligations still to be performed by Iceland: the present dispute was "exactly of the character anticipated in the compromissory clause." [72]

The Court concluded its analysis with an important observation on what it referred to as "the procedural complement to the doctrine of changed circumstances." The United Kingdom *Memorial* had criticized the Icelandic contention based on changed circumstances for claiming a right of unilateral denunciation, rather than a right to invoke the doctrine as a ground for termination, if necessary before "some organ or body with power to determine whether the conditions for the operation of the doctrine are present." In this connection, the United Kingdom alluded to the procedures

---

2. A fundamental change of circumstances may not be invoked as a ground for terminating or withdrawing from a treaty:

(a) if the treaty establishes a boundary; or

(b) if the fundamental change is the result of a breach by the party invoking it either of an obligation under the treaty or of any other international obligation owed to any other party to the treaty.

3. If, under the foregoing paragraphs, a party may invoke a fundamental change of circumstances as a ground for terminating or withdrawang from a treaty it may also invoke the change as a ground for suspending the operation of the treaty.

[70] *Ibid.*, 19.   [71] *Ibid.*, 20.

[72] *Ibid.*, 20–21.

to be followed for invoking changed circumstances and procedures for settlement of disputes under Articles 65, 66 and the Annex to the 1969 Vienna Convention. This might have raised difficulties as to whether these particular provisions were applicable as customary international law pending the entry into force of the Vienna Convention, or even as to whether they purported to confer a compulsory "power to determine" on the Court.

· · ·

The Court found it unnecessary to examine these questions and observed that, in the present case, the 1961 Exchange of Notes already provided "the procedural complement to the doctrine of changed circumstances" by establishing the Court's jurisdiction:

> Furthermore, any question as to the jurisdiction of the Court, deriving from an alleged lapse through changed circumstances, is resolvable through the accepted judicial principle enshrined in Article 36, paragraph 6, of the Court's Statute, which provides that "in the event of a dispute as to whether the Court has jurisdiction, the matter shall be settled by the decision of the Court." . . . This it has now done with binding force.[73]

By a vote of 14 to 1, the Court found that it had jurisdiction to deal with the merits of the dispute.

✤ ✤ ✤

The cases discussed above suggest certain conclusions. While upholding the right of states composing an international supervisory organ collectively to terminate a treaty for material breach (*Namibia*), the Court rejected claims by individual states of a unilateral right of denunciation of jurisdictional treaties on grounds of breach, duress, changed conditions, or the nature of the treaty (*Jurisdiction of the ICAO Council; Iceland Fisheries Jurisdiction*). In so doing, the Court cited and applied the applicable provisions of Articles 52, 60, and 62 of the Vienna Convention on the Law of Treaties which it regarded, in general, as codifying existing customary international law.

The fact that in the *ICAO Council* and *Iceland Fisheries* cases the Court was pronouncing upon treaties containing jurisdictional clauses agreed to by the parties was decisive on the point of jurisdiction; but the larger implications of these decisions should not be overlooked. In the *ICAO Council* case definite limits were placed by the Court on the asserted claim of a right of unilateral denunciation of treaties under general principles of international law which purportedly did not involve the application of the treaty itself: the Court held that the right asserted was, in any case, insufficient to defeat jurisdiction by terminating jurisdictional treaties, and that, far from permitting the treaty to be disregarded as no longer in force, the alleged right clearly involved the interpretation and application of the treaty. A further limitation may be implied where the Court, in

[73] *Ibid.*, 21–22.

the *Iceland Fisheries* cases, found it unnecessary to examine the claim that jurisdictional treaties, by their very nature, are subject to unilateral denunciation in the absence of express provisions regarding their duration, although a more decisive disposal of such a contention might appropriately have been formulated by the Court.

It should also be noted that in the *Iceland Fisheries* cases, the Court, while recognizing the rules set forth in the Vienna Convention and in customary international law with regard to denunciation of treaties for duress or changed conditions, found that the rights were surrounded in each case by substantive conditions limiting their application. The contentions of Iceland were rejected not because the Court refused to recognize the rules invoked, but because the Icelandic claims failed to meet the conditions and limitations which were an intrinsic part of the rules and essential for their application.

In this connection, it was not the procedural provisions of the Vienna Convention which the Court considered applicable; but its concern with procedures for dealing with unilateral claims to terminate treaties is clear. For example, the Court regarded what it termed "the procedural complement to the doctrine of changed circumstances" as an essential part of the doctrine. Similarly, with regard to claims of a unilateral right of denunciation of treaties for breach or duress, the Court was happy to find applicable procedural provisions pending the eventual availability of those set forth in the Vienna Convention.

One may conclude that, with the exception of its *Namibia* aberration, the Court's consideration of the Vienna Convention on the Law of Treaties has been helpful in furthering the consolidation of the law against unilateral denunciation of international agreements without accountability therefor.

[16]

Nonperformance of International Agreements

Christine Chinkin†

I. Introduction

All participants in the performance of an international agreement are from the outset continually involved in monitoring the flow of events stemming from that agreement. Each party will constantly scrutinize the other parties' words, actions and omissions to determine whether they conform to the expectations embodied in the agreement and whether the projected production and distribution of values actually take place. Parties will also keep their own performance under constant surveillance in order to be aware of the current costs of that performance in monetary, political and social terms. In so doing, the parties seek to evaluate whether the costs differ substantially from those anticipated so that the value of the benefits accrued can be accurately assessed. Other, perhaps unforeseen, consequences of performance, such as impacts on monetary markets, trade patterns, and currency rates, or domestic or international political repercussions, will also be noted and analyzed in light of the policies projected by the agreement. There should be a continual flow of communication relating to the problems, modalities and realities of performance passing between all the participants as their actions and reactions develop into an enmeshed continuum of events. One result of this continual appraisal may be the increasing conviction, by one or more of the parties, that the desired exchange of values is not occurring in accordance with the agreement; the legitimate expectations engendered by the agreement are being thwarted, and the agreement is being breached.[1]

This Article will concentrate on the problem of breach, or nonperformance, of an international agreement and will consider when the behavior relating to the performance of an agreement deviates so far from the expectations of both the parties and the world community that the agreement

---

† Senior Lecturer in Law, National University of Singapore. The author wishes to express her gratitude to Professors Myres S. McDougal and W. Michael Reisman, both of Yale Law School, for their great assistance in writing this Article. The views expressed and any errors are of course the author's own.

1. Breach of an international agreement is often perceived as a part of the termination process. Invocation of breach may of course result in a merger of the performance phase with the termination or modification phase. Nevertheless, it is the party's behavior during, and even prior to, the performance process that will be examined to see if it constitutes breach.

388   Texas International Law Journal   [Vol. 17:387

is in a state of breach or nonperformance. The significance of such a char-acterization is twofold: (1) a breach of an international obligation of a state is a wrongful act that gives rise to international responsibility,[2] and (2) prior breach of an agreement by one party makes lawful certain unilat-eral responses that would otherwise be deemed unlawful.[3]

No comprehensive legal definition of breach to serve as a guide for deci-sionmakers has yet been formulated. Rather than attempting to construct a formal definition, it is preferable to consider the function of denoting behavior as breach. The actual determination of breach or non-breach is a continual process of interpretation. The decisionmaker must decide how closely the actions and omissions of the parties conform to the consensus previously reached, and whether the degree of nonconformity is such that it gives the aggrieved party certain legal options. The most significant op-tions are those of termination or suspension. "Breach" is no more than a post hoc label of the particular situation that warrants the exercise of these options; thus, breach should not be subject to legalistic formulation.

II.   Who May Invoke Breach?

Any participant in the performance of an international agreement may invoke a breach, although the available arenas for relief, as well as the availability of suitable remedies, may be limited by the claimant's status.[4] National elites,[5] parties to the agreement, do of course challenge the per-formance of other parties; absent compulsory international, adjudicative arenas, the elites are usually also the decisionmakers once such an invoca-tion has been declared. The national elites may be pressured by individu-als or private business associations, which, acting through the municipal arenas, have entered into commitments in reliance upon the presumed compliance with an international agreement by the elites. Businessper-sons, banks, trading associations and numerous other interested partici-pants within the domestic arenas may direct attention to another

---

2. *See* Report of the International Law Commission to the General Assembly, 33 U.N. GAOR Supp. (No. 10) at 187, U.N. Doc. A/33/10 (1978), *reprinted in* [1978] 2 Y.B. Int'l L. Comm'n (pt. 2) 78, U.N. Doc. A/CN.4/SER.A/1978/Add.1 (Part 2) [hereinafter cited as Draft Articles]. Article 3 of the Draft Articles provides that "[t]here is an internationally wrongful act of a State when . . . that conduct constitutes a breach of an international obligation of the State." This reiterates long-established principles. *See also* Chorzów Factory (Ger. v. Pol.), 1928 P.C.I.J., ser. A, No. 17, at 29 (Judgment of Sept. 13).

3. *See* Vienna Convention on the Law of Treaties, *opened for signature* May 23, 1969, art. 60, U.N. Doc. A/CONF.39/27, *reprinted in* 8 I.L.M. 679, 701 (1969) [hereinafter cited as Vienna Convention].

4. The jurisdiction of the International Court of Justice, for example, is limited to states. *See* I.C.J. Statute art. 34. Many other international forums are limited to members of the corresponding international organization. Municipal arenas also typically have rules regulating jurisdiction.

5. The "elite" is the entity (for example, the judiciary, the parliament, an autocrat or an oligarchy) that has the power to make a formal declaration of breach.

government's nonfulfillment of its international obligations, despite their own government's preference for a variety of reasons to ignore the breach. Individuals have formed domestic interest groups to monitor the performance by their own national elites of an agreement that impinges upon the core values of the concerned groups.[6] Similarly, international associations have been created to carry out the same monitoring tasks across international boundaries.[7] Certain agreements provide a right for individuals to invoke nonperformance against their own government in an international arena,[8] and such claims within all municipal arenas are common.[9] The institutional world community may also have an interest in the performance of particular agreements and, coupled with a general concern for the principle of *pacta sunt servanda*, may independently challenge one or more parties' compliance with an agreement, irrespective of the wishes of the parties. Other elites, nonparties to an agreement, may utilize the institutions of the organized world community to question the behavior of parties under an agreement in order to further their own political, security, financial or ideological goals, although access to the international judicial organs appears to be restricted by the notion of a legal interest in the performance of an agreement.

Breach might be invoked for any number of reasons, depending upon the identity of the claimant and the outcome the claimant desires. An invocation of breach might be intended to harass or embarrass the allegedly nonperforming party so that it complies with the agreement, to force it to justify its refusal to comply, to draw attention to its infractions, to stimulate the other parties to react in a certain manner to the nonperformance, or to lead to a formal determination of whether a breach has occurred. Contextual assessment will be necessary to determine the motives behind and the desired consequences of an invocation of breach.

---

6. For example, several domestic groups monitor compliance with human rights conventions. Special interest groups representing diverse areas such as banking, trade and intellectual property also check compliance with international agreements affecting these areas.

7. *E.g.*, the International Red Cross and Amnesty International.

8. *See* European Convention for the Protection of Human Rights and Fundamental Freedoms, Nov. 4, 1950, art. 25, 213 U.N.T.S. 222, Europ. T.S. No. 5 [hereinafter cited as European Convention on Human Rights]; American Convention on Human Rights, Nov. 22, 1969 art. 44, O.A.S. Doc. OEA/ser. L/V/II.23 doc. rev. 2, *reprinted in* 9 I.L.M. 673 (1970).

9. Municipal arenas hear numerous claims relating to alleged violations of international agreements. See, *e.g.*, Charlton v. Kelly, 229 U.S. 447 (1913), in which a party argued against extradition by the United States to Italy because Italy breached the extradition agreement; The Parlement Belge, 4 P.D. 129 (1879), *rev'd*, 5 P.D. 197 (1880), in which a party claimed that bringing a suit for damages violated a British-Belgian treaty; Collco Dealings Ltd. v. I.R.C., 1962 A.C. 1, in which a party argued that application of the Finance Act would violate a double taxation agreement.

III. Who Can Commit A Breach?

Traditional notions of state responsibility determine those actors for whose actions the state is responsible.[10] The motives of the actors are irrelevant in determining whether they have caused a breach of an international agreement. Provided their actions can be imputed to the state, it does not matter whether they acted intentionally or with disregard for the consequences. The national elite may, of course, voluntarily accept responsibility by adopting the act as its own or by doing nothing to prevent its commission.[11] Indeed, the elite may be forced by the desire, or necessity, to mobilize internal popular support, that is, to support actions of its citizens that involve it in international responsibility, even though it did not at the outset intend to violate an agreement.[12] A national elite may be forced to make a formal decision whether to breach an agreement or to adopt an action that constitutes breach. In any assessment of breach, therefore, there are two decisionmakers—one who decides upon a particular action in response to the demands of an agreement and another who determines the subsequent response. Each will be attempting constantly to discover the true perspectives of the other in order to manipulate the situation to further its own position.

IV. General Community Policies

Decisionmakers who must determine whether a particular agreement is being effectively complied with should be guided by general community policies and the policies of the parties; both should be considered in light of all the factors surrounding the invocation of breach. The priority given to any one of these policies will depend upon the identity of the decisionmaker and the immediately favored interests. In all cases, the decisionmaker must bear in mind the likely consequences of a formal determination of breach and be guided by the desirability of setting into motion those consequences. The policy preferred by a decisionmaker re-

---

10. Draft Articles, *supra* note 2, art. 6, suggests that an actor with any of the legislative, judicial, executive or other powers of the state can make the state responsible for his actions. A state's constitution may determine which government organ is responsible for the performance or breach of an international obligation. *See* Attorney-General for Canada v. Attorney-General for Ontario, 1937 A.C. 326, 348: "Parliament may refuse to perform them [obligations] and so leave the State in default. . . . Parliament will either fulfil or not treaty obligations imposed upon the State by its executive." For general references on the topic of state responsibility, see I. Brownlie, Principles of Public International Law 431-77 (3d ed. 1979); D. Greig, International Law 521-614 (2d ed. 1976); 2 D. O'Connell, International Law 941-1025 (2d ed. 1970).

11. *See* Case Concerning United States Diplomatic and Consular Staff in Tehran (U.S. v. Iran), 1980 I.C.J. 3, 33-35 (Judgment of May 24); Corfu Channel (U.K. v. Alb.) 1949 I.C.J. 4 (Judgment of Apr. 9).

12. The Iranian elite utilized popular resentment of the United States in order to strengthen its own domestic position against the United States. *See U.S. v. Iran*, 1980 I.C.J. 3, 33-34.

lating to breach will also be influenced by the favored policy respecting remedies. A flexible approach to the interpretation of an agreement, which would avoid demanding rigid compliance with its terms, might be coupled with a strict imposition of remedies; on the other hand, a strict demand for literal compliance with the terms of an agreement might be balanced by a more lenient approach to remedies.

The basic goal of the world community in regard to determinations of breach is to prevent the arbitrary or precipitous breakdown of the network of treaty relationships, in which instability, uncertainty and confusion of expectations ensue. Thus, a decisionmaker concerned primarily with global interests should facilitate continuation of the production and distribution of values in compliance with the agreement and assist the parties in reconciling their differences, rather than too readily denouncing one party's behavior as breach of the agreement. The paramountcy of this goal will depend upon the pervasiveness of the stabilizing effect of the agreement in international affairs. When secondary or tertiary agreements have been entered into by a large number of participants in reliance upon the primary agreement, the goal should be accorded great priority. When, however, the agreement's impact is limited or expected to be limited primarily to the contracting parties and regulates only a limited exchange of values, the basic goal should not be accorded the same priority. Decisionmakers should be prepared to accept evidence from interested parties in order to determine how far the global interest requires continuation of any particular agreement.

The goal of promoting the continuation of international agreements is supported by the principles of reciprocity, effectiveness and economy, which might even influence a decisionmaker more immediately concerned with national interests. Precipitous denunciation of another party's behavior as violating an international obligation might lead to retaliatory conduct by that party, thereby leading to a loss of values in regard to other aspects of that agreement or to other agreements. In an interdependent world in which the exchanges of values between participants are regulated by a network of intertwining treaty relationships, precipitous denunciation could rapidly become excessively disruptive and destructive not only to the parties, but also to other members of the international community. The parties must presumably intend their agreements to maximize the effectiveness of the distribution of the relevant values; such an intention would be destroyed by peremptorily judging another party's actions as breach.

In addition, a party that can no longer rely upon the equitable exchange of values provided by the agreement must make alternative arrangements that will involve its time and expense. A party may find that the outcome of its dispute over the original agreement will adversely affect its ability to make alternative arrangements. Thus, the decisionmaker should encourage negotiations and communications between participants to facilitate their reciprocal performance and to attempt to resolve their disputes without resort to an invocation of breach. This could include renegotiation or modification of the original agreement. The decisionmaker should take into account parties' attempts to settle their own differences. All events leading up to the allegation of breach, as well as the parties' attitudes and actions after the allegation, should be considered. This analysis does not reject unilateral retaliatory action, because such action may in itself induce settlement or resort to a third party decisionmaker.[13] All that is necessary is that the entire sequence of events be fully appraised.

Another factor that should influence the decisionmaker in the application of the basic goal is the importance of the values protected by the agreement to the world community. When the agreement promotes fundamental community policy, strict compliance should ideally be demanded and deviation should be more readily denounced as breach. Although this appears to be a dominant goal, in practice it may be more desirable to allow some compromise so that the structure of the entire agreement will not be threatened. Again, the underlying aim of the decisionmaker is to secure adherence to fundamental community policies; this goal will not be achieved by overzealous denunciation, which can prove to be needlessly self-destructive.[14] The values of an agreement should also be weighed against newly emergent norms of *jus cogens*.[15] Performance that conflicts with *jus cogens* should not be considered grounds for breach. The decisionmaker should defend "States from contractual arrangements concluded in defiance of some general interests and values of the international community of States as a whole."[16]

Following from the importance to the world community of the values protected by the agreement is the community policy of policing conformity to international agreements. Although the goal of stability leads to a tolerance of deviation from the literal terms of the agreement, that goal cannot be overextended. If one party persistently interprets the terms of the

---

13. See Damrosch, *Retaliation or Arbitration—Or Both? The 1978 U.S.-France Aviation Dispute*, 74 AM. J. INT'L L. 785 (1980), for the argument that retaliatory action is a justifiable response to a material breach prior to any formal arbitration of a claim.

14. A major dilemma in determining breach is the possibility that a breaching party may be expelled from the convention and will no longer be bound to comply with the treaty provisions, with the result that its behavior becomes unregulated. This result does not further the world community's goal in the stability of international agreements and may weaken the treaty regime itself. One such example is Greece's denunciation of the European Convention on Human Rights, shortly before an anticipated decision of breach from the Council of Ministers. 1969 Y.B. EUR. CONV. ON HUMAN RIGHTS 78-84 (Eur. Comm'n on Human Rights). Greece remained outside the Convention for the remainder of the Colonels' regime.

15. *See* Vienna Convention, *supra* note 3, art. 64: "If a new peremptory norm of general international law emerges, any existing treaty which is in conflict with that norm becomes void and terminates."

16. Jiménez de Aréchaga, *International Law in the Past Third of a Century*, in 159 COLLECTED COURSES OF THE HAGUE ACADEMY OF INTERNATIONAL LAW 1, 65 (1978).

agreement in order to justify its own actions, even when those actions go beyond the original expectations of the parties and destroy the equilibrium of the agreement, the community itself has an interest in halting that behavior and in ensuring a reasonable interpretation of the agreement. Auto-interpretation cannot be allowed to become a pretext for unilateral modification of the agreement justified by assertions of protecting the rights of secondary and tertiary parties. Community sanctions should be invoked to prevent this from happening. If such behavior is tolerated over a sustained period of time, it will become impossible to maintain any expectations about the outcome of the agreement, and the agreement will no longer form a reliable basis for further dealings by the interested parties. The policy of maintaining stability cannot be allowed to become destructive in and of itself. Striking a balance between maintaining stability and policing conformity is likely to be the major task of a decisionmaker.

Further, within the goal of prevention of an unnecessary or capricious breakdown of treaty relationships, great weight should be given to fulfilling the parties' legitimate expectations engendered by the agreement. This entails considering the parties' own policies and reaching yet another balance between those of the parties and those of the global community. The parties will also favor stability as long as the balance fosters the production and distribution of values projected by the agreement, but they will favor change when this is no longer the case. The decisionmaker must ascertain the expectations by utilizing as many sources of information as possible regarding the evolving expectations of the parties. Any deviation from the parties' expectations should be presumed to constitute breach. Thus, when compliance by one state is within the literal wording of the agreement, but its actions undermine or destroy the expectations of the other parties or the world community, those actions should not be deemed acceptable performance of the agreement.[17] In all cases, the decisionmaker should weigh the anticipated values against the resulting values, or those that will result if the allegedly nonperforming party continues its present behavior, and determine whether there has in fact been a deviation from those expectations. The parties themselves may have contemplated some form of nonperformance so that the ensuing events, far from defeating their expectations, instead fulfill them; in this situation, the events should not be labeled breach.[18]

---

17. Adoption of this policy would involve full recognition of a doctrine of abuse of rights in international law. *See* 5 M. WHITEMAN, DIGEST OF INTERNATIONAL LAW 229 (1965): [A] State is guilty of an abuse of rights when it seeks to evade its contractual obligations by resorting to measures which have the same effects as acts specifically prohibited by an agreement" (citing Free Zones of Upper Savoy and the District of Gex (Fr. v. Switz.), 1932 P.C.I.J., ser. A/B, No. 46, at 167).

18. The common law originally insisted upon rigid compliance with the exact terms of a contract, and any partial performance was deemed a breach, even when acceptance of the proffered performance would not have adversely affected the other party. *See* CHESHIRE AND FIFOOT'S LAW OF CONTRACT 476-501 (M. Furmston 10th ed. 1981) [hereinafter cited as

The decisionmaker must also be prepared to accept the principle of substituted performance, a principle supported by notions of economy and stability. However, it is important to ensure that the proposed substituted performance provides the aggrieved party with substantially the same benefits for which it bargained. Another preferred policy is to allow the defaulting party to remedy any defects in its performance to enable the performance process to continue.[19]

A decisionmaker who is a member of a national elite of one of the parties to the agreement is most likely to be influenced by the dominant national interests.[20] The national interest may favor continuation of the agreement to avoid upsetting the expectations of a variety of domestic interest groups. Alternatively, the domestic interest may suggest termination of the agreement on the pretext of another party's breach. In weighing these national interests, however, a decisionmaker should attempt to ascertain the global impact of the decision, to estimate its probable prescriptive value, to minimize adverse effects on matters of international concern and to avoid the unnecessary dislocation of values.

The decisionmaker must also be prepared to distinguish between a material and a trivial breach. Some actions within the sequence of events that comprise the performance process will only deviate slightly from those anticipated by the other party, but others will represent major changes. The distinction is relevant, because material breach offers more options to the aggrieved party than does trivial breach.[21]

Excessive delay in bringing a claim before a decisionmaker creates a period of uncertainty, and thus should not be allowed. A decisionmaker should also try to ascertain whether the claimant would have performed its part of the agreement but for the alleged breach by the other party, that is, whether the default is the genuine basis for the claim. Claims of breach should not be used as facile justifications for evading one's own obliga-

---

CHESHIRE]. Eventually, it became apparent that insistence on the letter of the contract ran counter to the expectations of the "breaching" party that felt it had largely complied with the agreement. The approach also served no community purpose, for it allowed the other party to evade its own obligations on the basis of a technicality. This rule is no longer accepted in domestic cases and should similarly be rejected with respect to international agreements.

19. Compare Treitel, *Some Problems of Breach of Contract*, 30 MOD. L. REV. 139, 155 (1967), which suggests that a party's "right to reject [performance] should in a large class of cases be made subject to giving the party in breach a reasonable opportunity of curing the defect."

20. *See* Bilder, *Breach of Treaty and Response Thereto*, 1967 PROC. AM. SOC'Y INT'L L. 193. Bilder points out that the decisionmaker often will be a foreign office official who will weigh many extralegal factors in analyzing issues of treaty breach; these factors include the overall integrity of the official's foreign policy position, the need to retain flexibility and freedom to maneuver, the significance of the agreement to other foreign policy goals, and the agreement's role in the total relationship with the treaty partner. *Id.* at 195-201.

21. Vienna Convention, *supra* note 3, art. 60 (the consequences of termination and suspension apply only after a material breach). *See infra* note 25.

tions. This last policy will necessitate some exploration of the claimant's motives and the consequences desired. When a determination of breach is made, every effort should be made to minimize the harmful consequences of that breach, both for the parties and for all other members of the global community. This policy will be developed further in relation to the outcomes of breach.

V. Attempts to Formulate a Legal Definition of Breach

A positive response to any of the claims made by any party relating to an aspect of the performance of an international agreement[22] may constitute breach of the agreement. The important factor in every case is to determine which actions or communications may be characterized as breach and therefore justify a choice of options to the parties.

Although provisions in the Draft Articles on State Responsibility[23] emphasize that breach of an international obligation, whether a convention or other agreement, incurs international responsibility, there is little attempt therein to define the behavior that incurs this consequence. The principal source of clarification is the Vienna Convention on the Law of Treaties.[24] The only provision in the Vienna Convention that deals with the concept of breach is article 60, which focuses upon the consequences of breach.[25] Article 60 makes it mandatory for a decisionmaker to differentiate between

---

22. States may make claims relating to *any* aspect of the performance process, *i.e.*, claims relating to participation, perspectives, situations including time and space, expectations, base values and outcomes. When a party does not meet the expectations of another party regarding any of these factors, a prima facie breach of the agreement occurs. Whether this condition is treated as a breach will depend upon the various factors discussed throughout this Article.

23. Draft Articles, *supra* note 2, arts. 16-27.

24. Vienna Convention, *supra* note 3.

25. Vienna Convention, *supra* note 3, art. 60, states in pertinent part:
    1. A material breach of a bilateral treaty by one of the parties entitles the other to invoke the breach as a ground for terminating the treaty or suspending its operation in whole or in part.
    2. A material breach of a multilateral treaty by one of the parties entitles:
        (a) the other parties by unanimous agreement to suspend the operation of the treaty in whole or in part or to terminate it either:
            (i) in the relations between themselves and the defaulting State, or
            (ii) as between all the parties;
        (b) a party specially affected by the breach to invoke it as a ground for suspending the operation of the treaty in whole or in part in the relations between itself and the defaulting State;
        (c) any party other than the defaulting State to invoke the breach as a ground for suspending the operation of the treaty in whole or in part with respect to itself if the treaty is of such a character that a material breach of its provisions by one party radically changes the position of every party with respect to the further performance of its obligations under the treaty.
    3. A material breach of a treaty, for the purposes of this article, consists in:
        (a) a repudiation of the treaty not sanctioned by the present Convention; or
        (b) the violation of a provision essential to the accomplishment of the object or purpose of the treaty.

material breaches and all others, for only the consequences of the former are outlined in the Convention. The effects, and indeed the possibility, of trivial breaches must be deduced from sources outside the Convention. Article 60(3) is the first attempt in a convention to define material breach.[26] The Harvard Research in International Law[27] did not formulate a definition, nor did it distinguish different kinds of breach. International authorities have previously differentiated between the more and less severe breaches of an agreement, but, again, usually did not clarify the distinction.[28] Article 60(3), therefore, was drawn from a clean slate[29] and was incorporated into the Convention with very little debate and no controversy at Vienna. It is probably safe to conclude that article 60(3) now represents the accepted formula in international law.[30]

Rapporteur Sir Humphrey Waldock favored the expression "material breach" over that of "fundamental breach," which had been chosen by the earlier rapporteur, Sir Gerald Fitzmaurice. Fitzmaurice defined the latter term to imply a breach "going to the root or foundation"[31] of the agreement and thus calling into question the continued value of the relationship

---

26. Prior to the Vienna Convention, *supra* note 3, one international arbitration of a territorial dispute attempted to distinguish among breaches on the basis of materiality or seriousness: "It is manifest that if abuses of administration could have the effect of terminating such an agreement, it would be necessary to establish such serious conditions as the consequence of administrative wrongs as would operate to frustrate the purpose of the agreement. . . ." Tacna-Arica Question (Chile v. Peru), 2 R. Int'l Arb. Awards 921, 943-44 (1925).

27. *See Harvard Research in International Law: The Law of Treaties*, 29 Am. J. Int'l L. (3 Supp. 1935 at 1077-96) [hereinafter cited as *Harvard Research*]:
> If a State fails to carry out in good faith its obligations under a treaty, any other party to the treaty, acting within a reasonable time after the failure, may seek from a competent international tribunal or authority a declaration to the effect that the treaty has ceased to be binding upon it in the sense of calling for further performance with respect to such State.

28. *See* A. McNair, The Law of Treaties 553-86 (1961); 1 L. Oppenheim, International Law §§ 540-549 (8th ed. 1955); 1 G. Schwarzenberger, International Law 571-83 (3d ed. 1957). The last authority gives a fuller definition of breach than the others: "[A] breach of treaty may be defined as unjustified non-compliance against the will of another party with a treaty in circumstances in which, in the light of the *jus aequum* rule, such an act or omission is attributable to a contracting party and voluntary." *Id.* at 575.

29. Compare Waldock's earlier draft definition of material breach in which "material breach of a treaty results from . . . a breach so substantial as to be tantamount to setting aside any provision . . . the failure to perform which is not compatible with the effective fulfillment of the object and purpose of the treaty." Law of Treaties: Second Report by Sir Humphrey Waldock, U.N. Doc. A/CN.4/156 and Add. 1-3, [1963] 2 Y.B. Int'l L. Comm'n 36, 73, U.N. Doc. A/CN.4/SER. A/1963/Add. 1 [hereinafter cited as Waldock's Second Report].

30. *See, e.g.*, Legal Consequences for States of the Continued Presence of South Africa in Namibia (South West Africa) Notwithstanding Security Council Resolution 276 (1970), 1971 I.C.J. 16, 47 (Advisory Opinion of June 21) [hereinafter cited as Namibia Case], in which the Court cites article 60(3) with apparent approval.

31. Law of Treaties: Second Report by Sir Gerald Fitzmaurice, U.N. Doc. A/CN.4/107, [1957] 2 Y.B. Int'l L. Comm'n 16, 31, U.N. Doc. A/CN.4/Ser. A/1957/ Add. 1. [hereinafter cited as Fitzmaurice's Second Report].

covered by the agreement. Waldock felt that this definition might not include a term of the agreement that was important to the parties and that had been a material inducement to the agreement, although ancillary to its major provisions.[32] He preferred a definition that would introduce the concept of materiality, a concept that would identify the importance of a provision regardless of the provision's place within the body of the agreement. Waldock illustrated his point with an example of a dispute settlement clause, which might be considered procedural and having a minimal impact upon the object of the agreement, but without which no agreement would have been reached. The major problem with Waldock's viewpoint is that it depends upon a determination of what was crucial to the parties in reaching a commitment, which may have included factors totally extraneous to the wording of the agreement. Many compromises might have been made during the negotiations and might not be indicated by the final text. Thus, attempts to apply the test of materiality to the parties could cause confusion and uncertainty.[33]

The definition of material breach in article 60(3) is twofold. First, article 60(3) provides that any repudiation of the agreement constitutes a material breach.[34] A denunciation of the policies in the agreement or a refusal to accept its binding force is incompatible with the expectation of stability grounded in the agreement and creates uncertainty regarding the likelihood of its performance. A party can repudiate an agreement through a formal declaration or an action; contextual analysis must be utilized to make certain that a party truly intends to repudiate. Parties frequently make statements that might imply repudiation of their treaty commitments but which were not intended to do so; for example, statements to a domestic political audience might be intended to convey quite contrary intentions to an international audience. An analysis similar to that adopted by the International Court in the *Nuclear Tests* cases[35] must be used to determine the genuine intention behind an alleged repudiation. This analysis would include factors such as the identity and status of the actor within the political elite represented, that elite's reputation for understatement or overstatement, the circumstances in which the alleged repudiation occurred, the audiences to whom a statement was ostensibly and actually addressed, and the commission of any subsequent actions.[36]

---

32. For a discussion of the various formulations of material breach, see Report of the International Law Commission to the General Assembly, 18 U.N. GAOR Supp. (No. 9) at 17-19, U.N. Doc. A/5509 (1963), *reprinted in* [1963] 2 Y.B. INT'L L. COMM'N 189, 204-06, U.N. Doc. A/CN.4/SER. A/1963/Add. 1.

33. "Material breach" was also preferred to other expressions of municipal law, such as "total" or "partial" breach, both of which contain their own ambiguities.

34. Vienna Convention, *supra* note 25, art. 60(3)(a).

35. Nuclear Tests (Austl. v. Fr.), 1974 I.C.J. 253, 265 (Judgment of Dec. 20).

36. For a discussion of the German repudiation of the Treaty of Versailles, see Garner & Jobst, *The Unilateral Denunciation of Treaties by One Party Because of Alleged Non-Performance by Another Party or Parties*, 29 AM. J. INT'L L. 569 (1935).

Article 60(3) does not expressly include the principle of anticipatory breach, common to many systems of municipal contract law,[37] which allows the determination of breach even before performance has commenced. Actions that make future compliance with the agreement impossible or extremely unjust can be characterized as anticipatory breach. This doctrine is significant in municipal law because it offers viable options to the aggrieved party, immediately relieving it of its own contractual obligations and thus enabling it to mitigate its own loss by making alternative arrangements. Anticipatory breach also removes the potentially destabilizing effect of uncertainty whether or not the aggrieved party intends to enter into the performance process. Similar policy considerations support the inclusion of the doctrine into international law, and "repudiation" in article 60(3) should be expanded for this purpose. Additional support for this view is found in article 18 of the Vienna Convention,[38] which imposes a duty not to defeat the "object and purpose of a treaty prior to its entry into force," that is, prior to the onset of the performance process. However, this provision is not exactly equivalent to anticipatory breach, because it applies to signatories that might never in fact ratify the agreement and thereby never incur any obligation to enter into the performance process. Article 18, while bearing some resemblance to anticipatory breach, is better viewed as a distinct duty placed upon those participants who indicate some intention of becoming bound to an agreement before they actually are bound.

Even if the usefulness of anticipatory breach is accepted, it should not be used precipitously by parties. Parties should not immediately denounce as anticipatory breach actions that appear to be contrary to the agreement's objectives, but should instead attempt to reopen negotiations. It is possible that no noncomforming behavior is intended at this early pre-performance stage and that there has been a genuine misunderstanding of the agreement that could be resolved by a positive response from the "aggrieved" party. The "aggrieved" party might also act to avert an actual subsequent

---

37. For a discussion and definition of the concept of anticipatory breach, see Cheshire, *supra* note 18, at 483. Cheshire notes that anticipatory breach is established only when "the defaulting party has made his intention clear beyond reasonable doubt." *Id.* at 485. Furthermore, Cheshire cites an English decision indicating that anticipatory breach depends on the "ratio quantitatively which the breach bears to the contract as a whole, and secondly, the degree of probability or improbability that such a breach will be repeated." *Id.* at 487 (quoting Maple Flock Co. v. Universal Furniture Products (Wembley), Ltd., 1 K.B. 148, 157 (1934)).

38. Vienna Convention, *supra* note 3, art. 18. One official commentary on the predecessor to this provision notes that "an obligation of good faith to refrain from acts calculated to frustrate the object of the treaty attaches to a State which has signed a treaty subject to ratification appears to be generally accepted." Report of the International Law Commission to the General Assembly, 21 U.N. GAOR Supp. (No. 9, at 5, U.N. Doc. A/6309/Rev. 1 (1966), *reprinted in* [1966] 2 Y.B. Int'l L. Comm'n 169, 202, U.N. Doc. A/CN.4/SER. A/1966/Add. 1.

breach. The *Panama Canal Tolls* dispute[39] illustrates the effectiveness of a positive response. Proposed American legislation appeared contrary to the spirit, if not the provisions, of the Hay-Pauncefote Treaty;[40] however, the United Kingdom did not denounce the legislation as an anticipatory breach. The United Kingdom instead viewed the legislation as an indication of a potential breach and used available diplomatic channels to urge performance. These early indications of disquiet led to the withdrawal of the United States' proposed legislation; thus, the agreement was performed in accordance with the expectations of the parties and for the benefit of the entire world community in the smooth, unimpeded functioning of the canal. Condemning the proposals as anticipatory breach would not have served the interests of the United Kingdom, which had a real interest in keeping world shipping routes open.

Second, article 60(3) provides that a "violation of a provision essential to the accomplishment of the object or purpose" of the agreement constitutes a material breach.[41] One of two opposing positions may be taken in defining breach; the first looks at the consequences of the alleged breach, and the second attempts to assess the intrinsic quality or gravity of the particular acts or omissions. Article 60(3) adopts the first position: it looks at whether the agreement can still be adequately performed, despite one or more of the parties' actions that appear to threaten the agreement's stability. Under this definition, a trivial action can constitute a material breach.

Article 60(3) makes no reference to motive in its definition of material breach; a party need not have intended to breach an agreement before its actions are so labeled. This definition adopts and adapts a test formulated by the International Court of Justice in the context of reservations to a multilateral agreement.[42] In 1951 the International Law Commission[43] criticized and rejected the "object and purpose" formulation, although the Commission apparently changed its attitude by 1966.[44] The common phraseology indicates a conceptual unity between breach and acceptance of a reservation. Some provisions may preclude making a reservation, because the reservation would destroy the purpose of the agreement. Breach of these provisions will be deemed material rather than trivial, because the performance of the provision is essential to the projected exchange of val-

---

39. A discussion of the dispute may be found in A. McNair, *supra* note 28, at 547-49.

40. Ship Canal (Hay-Pauncefote Treaty), Nov. 18, 1901, United States-United Kingdom, 32 Stat. 1903, T.S. No. 401.

41. Vienna Convention, *supra* note 25, art. 60(3)(b).

42. *See* Reservations to the Convention on the Prevention of the Crime of Genocide, 1951 I.C.J. 15 (Advisory Opinion of May 28) [hereinafter cited as Reservations Case].

43. Report of the International Law Commission to the General Assembly, 6 U.N. GAOR Supp. (No. 9) at 2-8, U.N. Doc. A/1858 (1951), *reprinted in* [1951] Y.B. Int'l L. Comm'n 125-31, U.N. Doc. A/CN.4/SER. A/1951/Add. 1.

44. The "object and purpose" test has been used in various provisions of the Vienna Convention. *See, e.g.*, Vienna Convention, *supra* note 3, arts. 18, 20, 60(3).

ues.[45] This definition applies a high standard of conformity to the agreement and reflects a reluctance to allow an aggrieved party the options of termination or suspension. The implications of the article 60(3) definition comport with the underlying Vienna Convention policy that discourages the upsetting of expectations engendered by an agreement.

The problems raised by the "object and purpose" formulation are self-evident and have been much discussed.[46] Although phrased objectively, in practice the standard is subjectively applied, especially when used to interpret an agreement's purpose. The procedures introduced in the Vienna Convention for establishing breach[47] may at least prevent the parties from making a subjective determination, because the Convention requires that a claim be formally presented to a third party decisionmaker, but the Convention's language is still too vague to enable parties to predict which breaches will be adjudged material. This vagueness might have the positive result of deterring all noncompliance with the agreement, but experience suggests that such a result is not likely.

Other questions remain unanswered by the second definition in article 60(3). When an agreement provides for the distribution of many different values, it is extremely problematic to assert with any certainty which of the provisions stipulate *the* object and purpose to the exclusion of the agreement's secondary goals.[48] When many provisions are interdependent, does breach of any one of them constitute material breach or must the particular actions thwart the policies of them all? Is time "of the essence" or is delay before or during the performance process only a trivial breach? If so, after how long does it become material? Is any breach of a provision that is deemed essential to the object and purpose of the agreement a material breach, or is there also an implied qualitative test? If no such additional test exists, presumably the parties are held to a higher standard of compliance with some provisions of an agreement than with others, which also emphasizes the need to be able to identify those provisions in advance. May a third party be held responsible for inducing a breach of an

---

45. The same approach is used by the International Court of Justice in North Sea Continental Shelf (W. Ger. v. Den., W. Ger. v. Neth.), 1969 I.C.J. 3, 43 (Judgment of Feb. 20), in which the possibility of making reservations to a provision was considered a relevant factor in the evolution of a norm of customary international law.

46. *See* Reservations Case, 1951 I.C.J. at 42. The dissenting opinion of Judges Guerrero, McNair, Read, and Hsu Mo contains a cogent discussion of the problems raised by the "object and purpose" formulation, in which the judges agreed that this test creates unnecessary and artificial distinctions between the provisions of the same Convention.

47. Vienna Convention, *supra* note 3, arts. 65-68.

48. The earlier draft of art. 57 of the Vienna Convention, *supra* note 3, determined that a breach was material if it made impossible the accomplishment of *any* of the objects and purposes of the agreement. This was a less stringent test, allowing for more ready findings of material breach than that eventually adopted. *See*, Schwelb, *Termination or Suspension of the Operation of a Treaty as a Consequence of Its Breach*, 7 Indian J. Int'l L. 309, 314 (1967).

agreement?[49] Because states are free to enter into any agreement that best serves their interest, a state may attempt to negotiate with another state that has already entered into a commitment incompatible with the proposals of the former. The latter state owes a duty to its existing treaty partner not to enter into any obligations incompatible with the existing agreement, but if it does so, will its new treaty partner be considered internationally responsible for defeating the expectations of the other party to the previous agreement? To hold that it would be responsible would impose a high duty of disclosure of agreements upon states, higher than that of registration under article 102 of the United Nations Charter. To hold the opposite, however, would encourage the breakdown of treaty relationships. Contextual analysis of the entire sequence of events—from the conclusion of the agreement to breach or even from negotiation to breach—is the only possible way of answering these questions; formal attempts at a definition of breach are futile. There can be no positive answers that can cover all possible situations that can be identified in advance, for, as stated earlier, breach is really a post hoc label given to particular forms of behavior in order to justify certain responses to the behavior. Those factors that will influence the imposition of such a label must be identified and evaluated in each particular context.

VI. DEFENSES

The Vienna Convention's attempt to formulate a legal definition of breach necessitated corollary provisions on defenses. The phrase "not sanctioned by the present Convention" in article 60(3)(a) of the Vienna Convention[50] requires that the definition of breach be read in the light of the entire Convention.[51] Acts or omissions that might at first appear to constitute breaches of agreements may, in fact, be justified by other provisions. The issue of defenses to breach, or nonperformance, raises the familiar dilemma of balancing the desire for stability against the need for sufficient flexibility to justify nonperformance when the agreement no longer accords with the expectations of the parties. The policy throughout the Convention is to phrase all excuses or defenses restrictively and negatively; although nonperformance can sometimes be legally justified, the de-

---

49. This would resemble the municipal tort of inducement to breach of contract. If international responsibility were to be accepted for this, problems would be raised as to the duty of a state to inquire into another's existing commitments. As global base values become more scarce, this doctrine could become of increased significance. See Draft Articles, *supra* note 2, art. 27, which makes a state responsible for aid or assistance given by the state to another for the commission of an internationally wrongful act.

50. Vienna Convention, *supra* note 25, art. 60(3)(a).

51. Presumably, the phrase must also be read in the light of other principles of international law. For example, complying with a Security Council decision made under article 41 of the United Nations Charter would justify noncompliance with another agreement under article 103 of the Charter. *See* Schwelb, *supra* note 48.

fenses cannot be invoked too lightly. These clauses[52] are worded to discourage their use as an easy escape from what may later become an onerous commitment. Most defenses either assert that there was some deficiency in the commitment process,[53] which prevented the agreement from becoming binding, or that some condition essential to the performance process, outside the parties' control, has changed in such a way that it would be unreasonable or unfair to continue to demand performance.[54] Other defenses relate to the whole sequence of events from the onset of the performance process to the resultant actions of the parties. Hindrance or prevention of performance by the "innocent" party may justify the other's failing or refusing to perform.[55] Expectations different from those entertained at the time of the commitment may result from the interaction of the participants. Thus, the agreement may be amended by actions carried out as part of the performance process itself. A draft provision that outlined this situation, however, was rejected at Vienna,[56] because it was feared that it would undermine too greatly the stability of agreements. Nevertheless, changed expectations, derived from a continuous and tolerated pattern of behavior, should be allowed as a defense to nonperformance of the original terms.[57]

Procedural defenses may also be utilized. Excessive delay before bringing a claim has long been recognized as a bar to the claim. Implied acquiescence to the noncomplying behavior, built up over the period of inaction by the aggrieved party, will have persuaded the other party to believe its actions are acceptable.[58] For example, in the *Nuclear Tests* cases,[59] the

---

52. *See* Vienna Convention, *supra* note 3, arts. 46, 48, 60-62, 64.

53. *E.g., id* arts. 46, 48-52.

54. *E.g., id* arts. 61, 62, 73. *See*, Nahlik, *The Grounds of Invalidity and Termination of Treaties*, 65 Am. J. Int'l L. 736 (1971).

55. [O]ne Party cannot avail himself of the fact that the other has not fulfilled some obligation or has not had recourse to some means of redress, if the former Party has, by some illegal act, prevented the latter from fulfilling the obligation in question, or from having recourse to the tribunal which would have been open to him.

Chorzów Factory, 1928 P.C.I.J., ser. A, No. 17, at 31. *Cf.* Namibia Case, 1971 I.C.J. at 46 (a party that fails to fulfill its own obligations under a treaty retains no rights under the treaty).

56. *See*, Kearney & Dalton, *The Treaty on Treaties*, 64 Am. J. Int'l L. 495, 595 (1970). Draft Article 38, which was subsequently deleted, allowed the modification of a treaty by subsequent practice. The article was rejected, because it was thought that it would cause unpredictability. The United States expressed a concern that minor government officials, who are often responsible for implementing the performance of agreements, would be able to modify the obligations accepted by their state.

57. On defenses to nonperformance of contracts see, Berman, *Excuse for Nonperformance in the Light of Contract Practices in International Trade*, 63 Colum. L. Rev. 1413 (1963). Berman suggests that a broad doctrine of excuse would serve the important function of supplementing the contract. *See also*, Schwelb, *supra* note 48.

58. See statement by Secretary of State Olney in 1896 that, despite the British failure to comply with the Clayton-Bulwer Treaty for ten years, "the United States has acquiesced therein too long to claim that the treaty has thereby become null and void." Harvard Research, *supra* note 27, at 1093.

decisionmaker refused to accept an allegation of breach made after a long period of time. France argued that because Australia had denounced the General Act of 1928[60] at the outset of the Second World War, this early repudiation prevented Australia from basing jurisdiction, in the present case, on the same treaty. Several judges pointed out that France had never protested the actions of Australia, nor had it indicated that it regarded the Treaty as terminated by this past repudiation. France could not use, as a defense, a repudiation that had occurred more than twenty years earlier. The ruling reflects another example of the presumed continuation of agreements and of the reluctance of third party decisionmakers to allow them to be too easily terminated. Although there is no formal statute of limitations in international law,[61] this policy leads to the same result. On the other hand, the decisionmaker should not arbitrarily disallow a claim after a significant lapse of time, but should examine the entire context to determine whether it was unreasonable for the complaining party to have waited so long before taking action. In the *Nuclear Tests* cases, Australia and France had been allies during the War and had often dealt with each other after the War. Thus, France's late protest was unreasonable, because it had had many opportunities to indicate it no longer regarded the Treaty as binding between itself and Australia.

Other possible procedural defenses include not allowing a party to allege breach when it has itself failed to comply with the agreement[62] or when it has "dirty hands."

VII. TRENDS OF PAST DECISIONS

Article 36(2) of the Statute of the International Court of Justice gives the Court jurisdiction over disputes arising out of the interpretation of international agreements.[63] Although many major disputes before both the International Court and arbitral tribunals have turned upon the interpretation of international agreements, there exists little legal discussion of the concept of breach and the preferred policies for its establishment. Perhaps this is because of the post hoc nature of a determination of breach; a decisionmaker determines the validity of a claim of nonpreformance and then

---

59. *Nuclear Tests*, 1974 I.C.J. 253.

60. General Act for the Pacific Settlement of International Disputes, Sept. 26, 1928, 93 L.N.T.S. 343.

61. *See Nuclear Tests*, 1974 I.C.J. at 356 (Joint Dissenting Opinion of Judges Onyeama, Dillard, Jiménez de Aréchaga and Sir Humphrey Waldock).

62. "[W]here two parties have assumed an identical or a reciprocal obligation, one party which is engaged in a continuing non-performance of that obligation should not be permitted to take advantage of a similar non-performance of that obligation by the other party." Diversion of Water from the Meuse (Neth. v. Belg.), 1937 P.C.I.J., ser. A/B, No. 70, at 77 (Judgment of June 28) (opinion of Hudson, J.) [hereinafter cited as Meuse Case].

63. I.C.J. STATUTE art. 36(2) provides: "The states parties to the present Statute may at any time declare that they recognize as compulsory . . . the jurisdiction of the Court in all legal disputes concerning: a. the interpretation of a treaty. . . ."

adopts the appropriate label. Only then is the specific behavior at issue categorized as a breach or non-breach of the agreement.

Despite the paucity of legal discussion, the right of international tribunals to adjudicate issues involving breach has been firmly established. In the dispute between India and Pakistan relating to India's termination of an agreement after a material breach by Pakistan,[64] India claimed that the Council of the International Commission on Aviation Organization (ICAO) had no jurisdiction in the matter because termination was not an issue of "interpretation and application." This argument was firmly rejected by both the Council and the International Court. Pakistan's actions had to be characterized as a breach before any question of termination could be examined. Such a characterization necessarily involved an interpretation of the agreement. Thus, questions of breach, with the consequence of termination or suspension, were preceived as interpretive problems of the agreement itself as well as of the parties' actions pursuant thereto. This decision was essential to maintain the integrity of jurisdictional clauses within agreements. If the authority of the International Court to judge disputes could be avoided simply by claiming that the agreement had been terminated,[65] the expectations of the parties and of the world community concerning the availability of third party decision-making would be defeated.

It might be expected that an allegation of nonperformance of an agreement would lead to a polarization of views concerning the "correct" method of interpreting international agreements, particularly because no consensus presently exists among scholars.[66] The party accused of the breach would probably demand a strict textual interpretation of the agreement to demonstrate that its actions either did not fall within the terms of the agreement at all or were not expressly prohibited. On the other hand, the accused party would urge a more liberal interpretation of clauses providing for defenses, to bring its actions within the protection of these clauses. Only when the agreement's wording is ambiguous, therefore, is the accused party more likely to desire adherence to the Vienna Conven-

---

64. *See* Appeal Relating to the Jurisdiction of the ICAO Council (India v. Pak.), 1972 I.C.J. 46, 64-65 (Judgment of Aug. 18) [hereinafter cited as ICAO Jurisdiction Case].

65. Briggs, *Unilateral Denunciation of Treaties: The Vienna Convention and the International Court of Justice*, 68 AM. J. INT'L L. 51, 57-60 (1974).

66. For a summary of the respective views on interpretation, see Written Statement of South Africa (South West Africa), 1970 I.C.J. Pleadings 377, 381-397 (1 Legal Consequences for States of the Continued Presence of South Africa in Namibia (South West Africa) Notwithstanding Security Council Resolution 276 (1970)) [hereinafter cited as Namibia Pleadings]. For contrasting opinions, see Report of the International Law Commission to the General Assembly, 21 U.N. GAOR Supp. (No. 9) at 5, U.N. Doc. A/6309/Rev. 1 (1966), *reprinted in* [1966] 2 Y.B. INT'L L. COMM'N 217-23, U.N. Doc. A/CN.4/SER. A 1966/Add. 1. *See also* M. McDOUGAL, H. LASSWELL & J. MILLER, THE INTERPRETATION OF AGREEMENTS AND WORLD PUBLIC ORDER (1967); A. McNAIR, *supra* note 26; and Fitzmaurice, *The Law and Procedure of the International Court of Justice: Treaty Interpretation and Certain Other Treaty Points*, 1951 BRIT. Y.B. INT'L L. 1.

tion provisions on interpretation,[67] which follow the textual approach, and the provision for reference to extraneous sources, such as the *travaux préparatoires* and the negotiations.[68]

The party alleging breach, on the other hand, might present a different view of treaty interpretation.[69] This party would urge reference to the spirit, aims and purposes of the agreement, as evidenced by both its exact text and its social and political context. Actions contrary to the agreement's spirit, aims and purposes should be deemed nonperformance, even when they fall within the agreement's strict terms. The party alleging breach would typically favor a purpose-oriented approach to interpretation that de-emphasizes the exact wording of the agreement. This approach might derive support from the wording of article 60(3)[70] of the Vienna Convention, in which material breach is defined in terms of the object and purpose of the agreement. A strictly textual method of interpretation seems inconsistent with this rather broad definition of breach. Despite the above assumptions about the preferred method of treaty interpretation of the respective parties, it will be seen that in practice all parties avail themselves of all possible methods to support their claims. The preference of the decisionmaker for a particular approach to treaty interpretation will be a significant factor in the final outcome of the claim.[71]

The long lasting dispute between the United Nations and South Africa over the administration of the mandate territory of South West Africa provides some interesting insights into the problem of denoting behavior as breach. In its 1971 advisory opinion,[72] the International Court reviewed the General Assembly's conclusion that South Africa had failed to perform its side of the Mandate, without actually judging the issue itself or attempting to define breach.[73] The strategies and arguments of the involved par-

---

67. Vienna Convention, *supra* note 3, arts. 31-33.

68. The obvious drawback with this provision is that every agreement will contain ambiguities and gaps.

69. The differing views on treaty interpretation were described by Judge Tanaka as "teleological or sociological and conceptional or formalistic," South West Africa. (Ethiopia v. S. Afr.; Liberia v. S. Afr.) 1966 I.C.J. 4, 278 (Judgment of July 18) (Tanaka, J., dissenting).

70. Vienna Convention, *supra* note 25, art. 60(3).

71. A judge's preference for a particular method of treaty interpretation will rest upon many contextual variables, such as political or ideological preferences, legal training and jurisprudential school.

72. Namibia Case, 1971 I.C.J. 16.

73. Judge Fitzmaurice pointed out that the entire majority opinion in the Namibia Case rested upon the existence of a material breach. He felt that because the failure of South Africa to submit annual reports was declared a breach of the Mandate only in an advisory opinion of the Court, it was not of such a character to be considered fundamental breach. The allegations relating to the well-being of the inhabitants of the mandate territory had never been subjected to judicial scrutiny, and he pointed out that the Court refused, in its majority opinion, to undertake this task. Namibia Case, 1971 I.C.J. at 221-23.

ticipants are nevertheless illuminating.[74]

South Africa, the party accused of breach, predictably argued that the Mandate must be read literally and that South Africa's actions must be assessed solely in terms of the written agreement. Its opponents (notably Ethiopia and Liberia in their pleadings[75] prepared for the 1966 case) argued that the goals and purposes for the establishment of the Mandate System in general, and of the South West Africa Mandate in particular, were the only logical starting points for defining breach: the purpose of the Mandate is stated in article 2 of the Mandate,[76] and all actions by South Africa should be evaluated against the Mandate's purpose rather than against each separate provision. The basis for this argument is that any single incident could perhaps be explained or justified by South Africa, but that the overall pattern of behavior revealed a deliberate design to thwart the intentions of the Mandate.

The pleadings of Ethiopia and Liberia contain details[77] of numerous South African policies that show a systematic and deliberate disregard of the purposes of article 2 of the Mandate. Moreover, each one of these incidents is also alleged to be contrary to a specific provision of the Mandate. Thus, these pleadings combine a purpose-oriented interpretation of the Mandate with a textual interpretation, although they show a preference for the former. South Africa itemizes and describes its policies in every aspect of administrative affairs of the territory (*e.g.*, land ownership, agriculture, fishing, mining and education) to prove that each policy is consistent with the exact wording of the Mandate. It then bolsters its position by adopting its opponents' arguments to accuse the complainants of employing an overly rigid textual analysis and of not enquiring whether the overall policy truly seeks to achieve an equitable state of balance among the various inhabitants of the territory.[78]

A comparison of the arguments concerning article 4 of the Mandate pro-

---

74. *See South West Africa*, 1966 I.C.J. Pleadings 4; Namibia Pleadings, 1970 I.C.J. Pleadings 75.

75. Memorial of Ethiopia (Ethiopia v. S. Afr., Liberia v. S. Afr.), 1966 I.C.J. Pleadings 32 (1 South West Africa) (Memorial dated Apr. 15, 1961); Reply of Ethiopia and Liberia (Ethiopia v. S. Afr., Liberia v. S. Afr.), 1966 I.C.J. Pleadings 220 (4 South West Africa) (Reply dated June 20, 1964).

76. Mandate for German South West Africa, art. 2, states: "The Mandatory shall promote to the utmost the material and moral well-being and the social progress of the inhabitants of the territory subject to the present Mandate" (quoted in Memorial of Ethiopia, 1966 I.C.J. Pleadings at 201).

77. Memorial of Ethiopia, 1966 I.C.J. Pleadings at 108-80; Reply of Ethiopia and Liberia, 1966 I.C.J. Pleadings at 362-475.

78. Counter-Memorial of South Africa (Ethiopia v. S. Afr., Liberia v. S. Afr.), 1966 I.C.J. Pleadings 1 (4 South West Africa).

vides a striking example of the parties' respective positions.[79] This provision prohibits the military training of natives and the establishment of military or naval bases within the mandated territory. The complainants point to the existence of certain military establishments and, without describing their exact function, assert that these violate the objects and intentions of articles 2 and 4.[80] South Africa, on the other hand, works painstakingly through the exact wording of article 4 and describes each aspect of the existing establishments in light of these provisions, to show that these bases are not the type prohibited in article 4.[81]

Although South Africa uses the textual method of treaty interpretation extensively and persuasively, it moves away from this method when it is advantageous to do so. Thus, the party accused of nonperformance prefers the textual approach but resorts to a more purpose-oriented approach when it is helpful; the complainants do the reverse. For example, South Africa argues that its administration should be compared to those of states in similar situations, and to this end introduces evidence extraneous to the agreement itself.[82] This evidence counterbalances the claimants' arguments that international developments since 1922, notably the evolution of General Assembly policy, should be considered in any judgment of South Africa's actions.[83] By introducing extraneous evidence, South Africa acknowledges that the literal wording of the agreement alone cannot form the rationale of the decision. It is thereby attempting to supplement the words of the agreement by presenting a generally consistent and uniform body of state practice with which it is in conformity. The underlying premise of this tactic is that while Ethiopia and Liberia are urging reference to the intentions of states, as expressed through the resolutions of the General Assembly, South Africa is more persuasively urging an examination of state practice.

While South Africa moves away from the Mandate's text to demonstrate the expectations of all those involved in mandate agreements or other former colonial situations, Ethiopia and Liberia turn back to the Mandate's actual wording in order to prove lack of strict compliance. As previously mentioned, no party relies exclusively upon one approach to the interpretation of an agreement. Because a variety of personal views on treaty interpretation will be represented by members of the Court, a party's use of several approaches will increase the chances that its argument will be accepted.

The pleadings of both South Africa and its opponents are characterized

---

79. Memorial of Ethiopia, 1966 I.C.J. Pleadings at 181; Counter-Memorial of South Africa, 1966 I.C.J. Pleadings at 47.
80. Memorial of Ethiopia, 1966 I.C.J. Pleadings at 198.
81. Counter-Memorial of South Africa, 1966 I.C.J. Pleadings at 47-62.
82. Counter-Memorial of South Africa, 1966 I.C.J. Pleadings 1, 201-09, 257-66, 374-82 (3 South West Africa).
83. Reply of Ethiopia and Liberia, 1966 I.C.J. Pleadings at 476-552.

by a high degree of specificity. They thus avoid a fundamental weakness of·India's written arguments[84] against Pakistan in which the alleged breaches of the Air Transit Agreement[85] are couched in very vague and general terms, without referring to the relevant provisions or specifying which of Pakistan's actions deviated from those provisions. Because the case turned on the issue of jurisdiction rather than on the issue of breach, the vagueness of India's arguments was not fatal to its position. Nevertheless, the failure to demonstrate nonperformance of specific provisions of an agreement would ordinarily be a serious tactical error.[86]

The pleadings in the South West Africa dispute indicate that all involved parties accepted the necessity of examining the full sequence of interactions and events leading up to the allegations of breach. No participant argued that the proper administration of the Mandate could be determined without reference to the history and development of the territory, including its colonial and mandatory periods. Perhaps the very nature of the Mandate as a continuing, long-term administrative commitment made this reference inevitable. Decisionmakers have, however, examined the entire performance process in cases involving very different agreements, which indicates that a determination of breach always entails a consideration of historical events. This feature again emphasizes that a determination of breach is an interpretative process that involves a consideration of the flow of action and reaction between all relevant parties.

In the dispute between India and Pakistan,[87] India referred to the history of relations since 1947 to demonstrate that flights over its territory had been allowed until the tensions between the two states became intolerable. India did not want the hijacking incident that had led to the latest suspension to be considered in isolation from this history, because the one incident alone might appear too trivial to warrant the exercise of an option to suspend the Agreement.

In the *Diversion of Waters from the Meuse* case,[88] the Permanent Court examined the sequence of incidents since Belgium's independence and the conclusion of the agreement regulating the uses of the waters in 1863.[89] The Court wished to determine the types of usage and construction that had been routinely permitted in the past, before assessing the propriety of

---

84. Memorial of India (India v. Pak.), 1973 I.C.J. Pleadings 25 (Appeal Relating to the Jurisdiction of the ICAO Council).
85. Agreement Relating to Air Services, June 23, 1948, Pakistan-India, 28 U.N.T.S. 143.
86. *See* Greig, *supra* note 10, at 499-503.
87. ICAO Jurisdiction Case, 1972 I.C.J. 46.
88. Meuse Case, 1937 P.C.I.J., ser. A/B, No. 70.
89. Treaty for the Regulation of Drawings of Water from the Meuse, May 12, 1863, Belgium-Netherlands, 1 Martens Nouveau Recueil 2d 117, 127 Parry's T.S. 438. To determine the purpose of this Treaty, the Court looked at an unratified predecessor treaty of 1861 and two other treaties concluded on the same day. It thus considered contextual factors outside of the text of the agreement. 1937 P.C.I.J., ser. A/B, No. 70, at 12-13.

the scheme to which Holland was then objecting. The historical analysis was helpful in determining whether the most recently proposed project genuinely defeated Dutch expectations, or whether Holland was alleging breach for another reason, such as fear of commercial competition from the port of Antwerp if the scheme went through. The Court's ability to perceive underlying motives and to assess the parties' expectations was enhanced by its study of historical events.

Another example of the use of historical analysis is the recent Civil Aviation Arbitral Award between the United States and France.[90] The allegation of breach by the United States again involved only one incident, the refusal by France to allow Pan American Airlines (Pan Am) to operate a flight involving a change of gauge in London. The Tribunal, however, analyzed the entire growth and regulation of civil aviation between the two states since 1944[91] and examined the various practices that had developed between them. France argued that because there was no express reference in the Chicago Convention on International Civil Aviation[92] to changes of gauge in a third country, this aspect of air transport was not controlled by the International Air Services Transit Agreement,[93] and France was free to act as it pleased. The Tribunal agreed that there was no specific provision on the subject. Nevertheless, instead of dismissing the United States' claim as falling outside the Agreement, as France had hoped, the Tribunal examined the purpose of the Convention, which was "to encourage air travel 'for the general good of mankind at the cheapest rates consistent with sound economic principles.' "[94] The Court consulted other international air transit agreements, including one to which France was not even a party,[95] to ascertain the intentions and expectations of the parties with respect to matters not within the terms of the Agreement. The purpose of this investigation was to determine whether France's real and legitimate expectations were in fact thwarted by the American proposal and, additionally, whether those of the United States were in turn upset by the French reaction. This determination would have been an impossible exercise if attempted without reference to the prior history.

Materiality in the arbitration between the United States and France was determined by reference to the consequences of the French actions; the

---

90. Case Concerning Air Services Agreement of March 27, 1946 (U.S. v. Fr.), 54 I.L.R. 304 (Arb. Trib. 1979) [hereinafter cited as Air Services Case].

91. *Id.* at 334. The year 1944 marked the conclusion of the Chicago Convention on International Civil Aviation, *opened for signature* Dec. 7, 1944, 61 Stat. 1180, T.I.A.S. No. 1591, 15 U.N.T.S. 296, and the International Air Services Transit Agreement, *opened for signature* Dec. 7, 1944, 59 Stat. 1693, 84 U.N.T.S. 389.

92. Chicago Convention on International Civil Aviation, *supra* note 91.

93. International Air Services Transit Agreement, *supra* note 91.

94. Air Services Case, 54 I.L.R. at 330 (quoting Air Transport Services Agreement of 27 March 1946, United States-France, 61 Stat. 3445, T.I.A.S. No. 1679).

95. Bermuda Agreement, Feb. 11, 1946, United States-Great Britain, 60 Stat. 1499, T.I.A.S. No. 1507.

blocking of the flights caused serious financial loss to Pan Am. It is, however, arguable whether the French really made impossible the accomplishment of the "object and purpose" of the Agreement. After all, the interference affected only one route for one airline and did not render impossible the continuation of air traffic between the two countries. Because the definition of material breach is framed restrictively in article 60 of the Vienna Convention,[96] so that it cannot be too easily invoked, this decision did not seem to demand too careful a consideration of the standard. The losses to the airline were frustration of an advertised service (was it even reasonable for the airline to go ahead with the advertising before there had been agreement as to the acceptability of the service?) and financial loss, rather than a major dislocation of all of its services. Although the decisional process of the Tribunal shows a willingness to view a particular allegation in light of the entire performance process, the need to fit the determination into the terms of article 60 places a formalistic restriction on its decision, again raising the question whether a legal definition of breach is either useful or necessary.

Reference to the overall sequence of interaction between states has been used in two other ways to aid decisionmakers in identifying a breach of an agreement and collaterally to assist the complainant in establishing a case of breach. Allegations of breach of the European Convention on Human Rights[97] have led to a growing jurisprudence on what behavior constitutes breach of that Convention. First, although isolated incidents have been deemed to constitute breach, the European Court of Human Rights has also formulated the notion that a consistent administrative practice may indicate breach.[98] When domestic administrative agencies have themselves implemented practices that routinely violate the Convention, it seems futile to pursue domestic remedies that will inevitably be side-stepped and rendered inadequate. Justice is better served by bringing the machinery of the European Convention into play as soon as possible.

Second, the notion of a continuing breach has been developed to avoid the operation of time bars agreed to by the parties to the Convention.[99] Provided that the ill effects of the breach continue, this doctrine gives the European Commission jurisdiction over incidents that took place prior to the Convention's entering into force for the state concerned and over inci-

---

96. Vienna Convention, *supra* note 25, art. 60(3).
97. European Convention on Human Rights, *supra* note 8.
98. Greek Case, 2 Report of Eur. Comm'n on Human Rights 1 (1969). "The Convention does not in terms speak of administrative practices incompatible with it, but the notion is closely linked with the principle of the exhaustion of domestic remedies." *Id.* at 12.
99. European Convention on Human Rights, *supra* note 8, art. 26. The Convention establishes a six-month limitation period from the final domestic judgment. *Compare* Draft Articles, *supra* note 2, art. 24, which gives several definitions of the time of breach, depending on the nature of the act constituting breach. If the breach consists of an act having a "continuing character," the time of breach extends over the entire period during which the continuing act is committed.

dents arising before the six-month limitation period. The practice of examining the entire sequence of events, discussed earlier as a way of determining whether particular acts or omissions are so egregious as to warrant termination or suspension of the agreement, is used in these contexts for procedural purposes.

Many agreements are worded in imprecise language that fails to spell out the obligations incurred by the respective parties. There are a number of reasons for this common feature of agreements. Possibly, the details were considered too numerous or technical to be settled at the time of entering into the agreement. In such a case, it is intended that the details be filled in by the parties during the performance process as the needs become apparent. This attitude towards the conclusion of an agreement is reflected in the widespread resort to delegated legislation and administrative regulations in modern domestic legal systems. In these instances, the goal is to flesh out the agreement through the future cooperation of the parties. It may have been the case, however, that the parties could only agree upon the most basic principles; attempts to fill in the details within the treaty framework would have threatened the successful conclusion of the negotiations. In this situation, conflict over the expectations engendered by the agreement has been merely postponed until a later stage. In either of the above situations, the discretion left to the parties enhances the possibility that they will disagree on standards of performance and eventually allege breach. The decisionmaker cannot avoid moving away from the text of the agreement when attempting to ascertain the parties' expectations and those of the world community relating to the exchange of values under the agreement.

The South West Africa Mandate indisputably left large areas of discretionary control within the competence of the Mandate power. This was done for the first of the reasons outlined above; no agreement could have effectively spelled out all the administrative details for governing the internal affairs of the Territory. Any attempt to do so would have collapsed under its own weight and would, in any case, have required constant revisions. South Africa, however, used this wide discretion to argue that, provided it acted in good faith, it had total freedom of action and judgment in pursuing its own policies and in acting in what it alone perceived to be the best interests of the Territory. This argument raises the familiar problem of abuse or misuse of power in an international arena. Several arguments can be raised against these South African assertions to show that the concept of breach must incorporate that of abuse of discretionary power. The South African position is untenable in this particular context, because the agreed supervisory powers of the League of Nations preclude a completely subjective interpretation of the proper use of discretion. The very purpose and existence of this body would be completely destroyed if it had no implied authority to construe the Mandate and to supervise its construction. The Council of the League of Nations, and subsequently the General

Assembly, were not intended to be powerless bodies. Denying the supervisory functions of the League and General Assembly would defeat the expectations of other members of the global community and even of South Africa itself.

In addition to the League's authority, doctrines of municipal law could be utilized to limit South Africa's discretionary power. The House of Lords has held[100] that even a seemingly unfettered discretionary power cannot be unlimited in practice, but must be read in the light of the overriding purposes of the applicable statute. Similarly, international discretionary powers should be limited by the object and purpose of the applicable agreement and by world public policy. On policy grounds, areas of discretion involving two or more parties to an agreement cannot be conclusively determined by just one of those parties, for the others would be left with uncertain expectations concerning the outcome of the agreement.

The French administrative law doctrine of *détournement de pouvoir*,[101] regarding notions of misuse of power, lends support to the idea that a position of authority acquired through the conclusion of an agreement should not be used for ulterior motives, such as the annexation of a mandated territory.

The question of abuse of power lay at the heart of the *Expenses* case,[102] in which the U.S.S.R. and France maintained that the powers of the General Assembly and the Secretary General were being used to undermine the authority of the Security Council. The two states argued that the General Assembly had no authority to act except within the exact terms of articles 9 through 22 of the United Nations Charter. The International Court found textual support within these provisions for the Assembly's actions, but also adopted the wider, goal-oriented approach of considering the overall purposes of the entire Organization;[103] these purposes were the only effective limits on the powers of the Assembly. The Court referred to the municipal law doctrine of ultra vires to support these propositions. In this case, the doctrine justified an extension of the Assembly's powers beyond those contained within the specific articles. While the Assembly's discretionary powers were increased, a ceiling was placed upon them by reference to the yardstick of the purposes of the Organization.

Both a mandate agreement and the United Nations Charter appear well-suited for the application of principles of administrative law, because both closely resemble domestic administrative agencies. Consideration of the

---

100. *See, e.g.*, Padfield v. Minister of Agriculture, Fisheries and Food, [1968] A.C. 997; Secretary of State for Education and Science v. Tameside Metropolitan Borough Council, [1976] 3 W.L.R. 641.

101. *See* L. BROWN & J. GARNER, FRENCH ADMINISTRATIVE LAW 130-34 (2d ed. 1978).

102. Certain Expenses of the United Nations, 1962 I.C.J. 151 (Advisory Opinion of July 20).

103. U.N. CHARTER art. 1.

proper use of discretionary power, however, may be found in other contexts as well. One of the factors that most influenced the Tribunal in the United States and France civil aviation dispute[104] was the large area of discretion left unregulated by the Air Services Agreement.[105] The Tribunal examined prior uses of discretion and determined that the Agreement was intended to provide only guidelines, with the specifics to be incorporated by the parties. The Tribunal concluded that the only limit on the parties' actions was that of the Agreement's purpose and that it was to be expected that there would be no provision relating to a detail such as a change of gauge. Under this interpretation of the Agreement, France was bound to fail.

The concept of good faith also limits the unfettered use of discretion. The practice of looking at the entire sequence of events between the parties enables the decisionmaker to determine more easily whether they have been acting in good faith and whether the claim itself is being brought in good faith. An isolated incident of behavior that is undesirable within the terms of the agreement, or that represents an apparent misuse of power, might be deemed to fall within the parties' discretion or be viewed as a "one-off" (unique) occurrence. When a wide discretion has been negotiated by the parties, every action need not conform to the decisionmaker's ideal of perfect performance. After all, the essence of discretion is choice, and by definition there is no automatically right or wrong answer.[106]

A consistent pattern of deviant behavior cannot be viewed as tolerantly as an isolated, undesirable incident. In the pleadings of the United States in the 1971 Namibia case,[107] the United States argued that persistent disregard of over seventy General Assembly resolutions constituted clear evidence of lack of good faith. In the face of these resolutions, South Africa could not argue convincingly that it had acted in good faith for the benefit of the Namibians. The Ethiopians and Liberians pursued a similar line of reasoning by compiling a dossier of continual infractions by South Africa.

In the Tacna-Arica arbitration,[108] the arbitrator examined the entire sequence of events and found that it was not necessary for him to approve all of Chile's actions, nor was it necessary for Chile to have agreed to the proposed plans. The important point was that Chile had entered into negotiations with Peru and had not acted in bad faith in its administration of

---

104. Air Services Case, 54 I.L.R. 304.

105. International Air Services Transit Agreement, *supra* note 91.

106. In the Tacna-Arica Question, 2 R. Int'l Arb. Awards at 930, President Coolidge (the arbitrator) stated: "While there should be no hesitation in finding such intent, or bad faith, if established, and in holding the Party guilty thereof to the consequences of its action, it is plain that such a purpose should not be lightly imputed. Undoubtedly, the required proof may be supplied by circumstancial evidence, but the *onus probandi* of such a charge should not be lighter where the honor of a Nation is involved than in a case where the reputation of a private individual is concerned."

107. *See* Namibia Pleadings, 1970 I.C.J. Pleadings at 864.

108. *See* Tacna-Arica Question, 2 R. Int'l Arb. Awards at 933.

the province or in its dealings with Peru. He could find no convincing evidence of bad faith.

There are two possible difficulties with encouraging a decisionmaker to survey all the interactions between the parties. The first is that of the sufficiency of the evidence, especially when some of the events took place long ago. An international tribunal is not an ideal fact-finding agency and will have to rely on the reports presented to it.[109] A national decisionmaker is likely to view the matter primarily from one perspective. Tribunals have had to reject allegations of breach because of insufficiency of evidence on the record. The South West Africa dispute was not as difficult in this respect as others have been, for the dispute concerned the interpretation of certain events rather than their existence. The second problem is that the evidence is often technical or specialized and thus difficult to assess. This problem is common to all decisionmakers—both in municipal and international arenas—but that does not make any easier its successful resolution.

Rather than analyzing the entire sequence of interaction between the parties, the decisionmaker is often prepared to make a decision based on one specific incident. Even then, however, other factors are likely to be weighed to determine whether the claim is sufficiently significant to justify giving the aggrieved party any of the various options for breach.

When there is a straightforward, positive obligation in an agreement, and that obligation has been ignored, it is relatively easy to denote that omission as breach. The duty of South Africa to submit annual reports falls into this category, and its refusal to do so could be readily seen as breach.[110] The only relevance of showing that it repeatedly failed to submit reports was to demonstrate that its actions were deliberate omissions and should not be tolerated as minor infractions. Failure to submit reports also raised the issue of South Africa's good faith. The ease of establishing this breach can be compared with the more difficult task of proving breach of the discretionary terms of the agreement.

The recent decision of the International Court in the *Tehran Embassy* case[111] provides an interesting example of the Court's positive refusal to admit the relevance of the prior sequence of interactions between the United States and Iran, leading to the eventual takeover of the Embassy in November 1979. Iran's view was that no allegation of failure to comply

---

109. *See id.* at 941, 954, 957 (comments by President Coolidge concerning the inadequacies of the evidence).

110. *See* Voting Procedure on Questions Relating to Reports and Petitions Concerning the Territory of South West Africa, 1955 I.C.J. 67, 71 (Advisory Opinion of June 7); Admissibility of Hearings of Petitioners by the Committee on South West Africa, 1956 I.C.J. 23, 26-27 (Advisory Opinion of June 1). *Cf. supra* note 73 (Fitzmaurice argued that South Africa's failure to submit reports was declared a breach by the I.C.J. but was never proved to be a *fundamental* breach).

111. *U.S. v. Iran*, 1980 I.C.J. 3, 38, 41.

with the Vienna Convention on Diplomatic Relations[112] could be adjudicated without a corollary examination of the pattern of the United States' alleged interference in its internal affairs and, in particular, of the misuse of the diplomatic premises for subversive activities. The Court, however, deemed such activities irrelevant to its decision, because the Iranian actions constituted clear examples of breaches of the exact obligations contained within the Convention. The seizure of the Embassy would still have amounted to breach, even if the hostages had been promptly released.[113] The Convention provides methods by which an aggrieved state can handle suspected illegal activities within an Embassy;[114] in no way could Iran's behavior be justified by these suspicions, or even by revealing their veracity.

Similarly, in the *S.S. Wimbledon* case,[115] the Court decided that certain isolated incidents of preventing ships from passing through the Kiel Canal were a breach of the Treaty of Versailles.[116] There was no need in this case to establish a pattern of violations by Germany; the Treaty imposed a positive duty on Germany to keep the Canal open for ships of nations at peace with Germany. These states were entitled to have any interference dealt with in a timely fashion and denoted as breach. To allow Germany to violate the Treaty repeatedly before condemning its actions as breach would have created uncertainty regarding the availability of the shipping route and thus would have limited its usefulness to the global community.

The decisionmaker must examine not only the actions constituting the alleged breach, but also their impact upon the legitimate expectations of the parties. Actions that appear to comply with the strict requirements of the agreement may still constitute breach if they in fact thwart its purposes. This aspect of breach has long been recognized in the jurisprudence of the Permanent Court. In the *Albania Minorities* case,[117] for example, Albania was under a conventional duty not to discriminate against minority populations. Its action in closing private schools did not conflict with any specific provisions of the Minority Treaties and was not on its face discriminatory, because it affected all sections of the community equally. It was shown, however, that the practical effect was discriminatory, for the private schools were an essential way for ethnic communities to retain

---

112. *Id.* at 24; Vienna Convention on Diplomatic Relations, Apr. 18, 1961, 500 U.N.T.S. 95.

113. The failure of Iran to take any steps to protect the Embassy, after several requests for assistance from the United States, constituted a breach of articles 22, 24-27 and 29 of the Vienna Convention on Diplomatic Relations, *supra* note 112. *U.S. v. Iran*, 1980 I.C.J. at 32.

114. Vienna Convention on Diplomatic Relations, *supra* note 112, art. 9.

115. S.S. Wimbledon (U.K., Fr., Italy & Japan v. Ger.), 1923 P.C.I.J., ser. A, No. 1 (Judgment of Aug. 17).

116. Treaty of Peace with Germany (Treaty of Versailles), June 28, 1919, art. 380, 2 Bevans 43, 225 Parry's T.S. 188 (Kiel Canal).

117. Minority Schools in Albania, 1935 P.C.I.J., ser. A/B, No. 64, at 21 (Advisory Opinion of Apr. 6).

their identity and to preserve their own minority interests.[118] Closing the schools had a more severe impact upon minorities than upon other citizens, so it was an action constituting breach of the agreement.

South Africa raised similar arguments in its dispute, maintaining that its actions could not be deemed a breach of the Mandate if they indirectly facilitated the integration of South West Africa into South Africa, provided that annexation was not the purpose of the measures. This argument again raises the question of line drawing. A single act by South Africa producing this effect would not be deemed a breach (as accepted by the arbitrator in the Tacna-Arica arbitration[119]), but a whole series of systematic acts would be viewed otherwise. Allegations of an indirect breach must be subjected to a full contextual analysis to assess the true impact of the parties' acts. This is especially true of human rights[120] and other treaties that include an agreed standard of behavior with respect to certain categories of peoples. The decisionmaker's task in these cases is comparable to that of a domestic decisionmaker in considering allegations of discrimination. The wording of the specific statute or regulation, as well as the actual effect of the practices, must be assessed.

VIII.   CONDITIONING FACTORS

Authoritative decisionmakers appear reluctant to declare an agreement terminated after an invocation of breach by the aggrieved party.[121] When a determination of breach is made, termination is normally avoided either by deeming the breach immaterial or by asserting that breach of a multilateral convention does not allow the option of termination. Alternatively, the decisionmaker may refuse to label the defendant's behavior as a breach and thereby deny the aggrieved party the option of termination.[122] Many

---

118. *See* Treatment of Polish Nationals and Other Persons of Polish Origin or Speech in the Danzig Territory, 1932 P.C.I.J. ser. A/B, No. 44, at 28: "[T]he prohibition against discrimination, in order to be effective, must ensure the absence of discrimination in fact as well as in law. A measure which in terms is of general application, but in fact is directed against Polish nationals . . . constitutes a violation of the prohibition."

119. *See* Tacna-Arica Question, 2 R. Int'l Arb. Awards 921.

120. *See supra* note 8.

121. An obvious exception is the General Assembly's willingness to declare the Mandate terminated after a finding of breach by South Africa. G.A. Res. 2145, 21 U.N. GAOR, Supp. (No. 16) at 2, U.N. Doc. A/6316 (1966). See, Briggs, *supra* note 65, at 55, in which Briggs points out that the General Assembly's action does not fall within the terms of the Vienna Convention, article 60, although termination on account of breach was described by the Court as a "general principle of law."

122. Decisionmakers in domestic tribunals have also asserted that the aggrieved elite has not exercised the option to use breach as a reason for terminating the agreement. *E.g.*, Charlton v. Kelly, 229 U.S. 447 (1913). In its commentary on the then article 42 of the Draft Articles, dealing with termination or suspension of a treaty following breach, the International Law Commission stated that municipal courts not infrequently rule that governments may denounce a treaty because of breach by the other party, but that such rulings usually occur in cases when the government has not elected to denounce the treaty.

factors external to the agreement will influence a court's decision, and examination of these possibly relevant factors may make apparently incompatible decisions consistent.

The factor most likely to influence the decisionmaker is the effect of the decision on the parties to a dispute and on the world community. A determination of breach is largely influenced by the available remedy. Furthermore, the decisionmaker's view of the global community and the preferred policies will greatly influence the final outcome, for no responsible decisionmaker will reach a conclusion without first considering its impact and probable future prescriptive value. In both the *Iran*[123] and *S.S. Wimbledon*[124] cases, determinations of breach were made on the basis of single incidents and the Court allowed no mitigation for surrounding circumstances. When subjected to further analysis, the unusual decisions in these cases proved both explicable and praiseworthy. In both cases, an uncompromising and prompt determination of breach was necessary for the continued exchange of the values regulated by the respective agreements, both of which were essential to the continuation of certain facets of international life. The Treaty of Versailles,[125] for example, had created a new public order in Europe in the wake of the weakening of two former Imperial Powers, and denunciation of any deviation from the agreed structure of the new order by Germany was necessary to emphasize the commitment of world leaders to the new regime. In particular, the Kiel Canal, an international waterway that provided easier access to the ports of Eastern Europe and thus facilitated international trade, had been created for the benefit of all national elites. Unilateral disruption of international shipping by Germany, in clear contradiction to the terms of the Treaty, would have been met with strong and immediate protest from other states with shipping interests. The Court's determination of breach protected these interests.[126] Also influencing the Court's determination of breach was the prescriptive value of its decision—the first to arise from the new world regime—and the probable application of the Court's analysis to similar

---

Often municipal courts do not look closely at the conditions for denunciation because they have not found such scrutiny necessary. Report of the International Law Commission to the General Assembly, 18 U.N. GAOR Supp. (No. 9) at 1, U.N. Doc. A/5509 (1963), *reprinted in* [1963] 2 Y.B. Int'l L. Comm'n 187, 205, U.N. Doc. A/CN.4/SER.A/1963.

123. *U.S. v. Iran*, 1980 I.C.J. 3.

124. *S.S. Wimbledon*, 1923 P.C.I.J., ser. A, No. 1.

125. Treaty of Versailles, *supra* note 116.

126. In 1936, Germany denounced article 380 of the Treaty of Versailles, *supra* note 116. This amounted to repudiation of the Agreement and thus constituted breach. However, in 1936 there was no significant protest from the world community as there had been in the early 1920s at the time of the Wimbledon incident. This was due to the changed political conditions, including the German withdrawal from the League of Nations and its admitted rearmament in 1935, in breach of article 160 of the Treaty of Versailles. Conditions had so changed by 1936 that the consequences of the breach of article 380 were trivial in comparison to the entire political scene in Europe.

disputes involving the Suez and Panama Canals, which, like the Kiel Canal, provided shipping routes essential to the continued flow of global trade.

The determination of breach in the *Iran* case was necessitated by the threat that Iran's actions presented to the continued exchange of diplomatic communications. If the Court had not strongly condemned Iran's action as a breach, the structure and flow of diplomatic communications, as regulated by the Vienna Convention on Diplomatic Relations,[127] would have been weakened, imposing tension on this long-established system and ultimately threatening the security of all states.

In neither the *Iran* nor *S.S. Wimbledon* cases would a finding of breach threaten the structure or continued existence of the regime established by the Vienna Convention on Diplomatic Relations; it was, rather, the unchallenged, defiant behavior that created the uncertainty of the regime's stability and undermined the expectations of the global community. None of the injured parties wished to invoke the breaches as grounds for termination, for this would have been detrimental to their own interests. They simply desired damages and a reaffirmation of the existing regimes. Thus, the determinations of breach in the *Iran* and *S.S. Wimbledon* cases provided stability under the treaties and support for the legitimate expectations of the affected parties. A finding of no breach, on the other hand, would have caused uncertainty and instability in the treaties' application. Underlying both decisions was the interest in upholding existing treaty regimes, policing the parties' performance of their obligations, and censuring deviance.[128]

The *Iran* and *S.S. Wimbledon* cases can be contrasted with the Tacna-Arica Question,[129] in which the arbitrator found Chile's behavior to be unsatisfactory, but refused to label it a material breach. To do so would have allowed Peru the option of terminating the Treaty,[130] thereby obviating any obligation to hold the agreed plebiscite. The arbitrator noted that, in accordance with the principles of self-determination, the plebiscite furthered the democratic interests of the inhabitants of the disputed area and the world community.[131] Thus, the decision again facilitated the fulfillment of a specific goal.

---

127. Vienna Convention on Diplomatic Relations, *supra* note 112.

128. Even within the politically oriented United Nations, there was little support for the Iranian position, which underlines the global view that the Treaty had to be supported.

129. *See* Tacna-Arica Question, 2 R. Int'l Arb. Awards 921.

130. Treaty of Ancon, Oct. 20, 1883, Chile-Peru, 10 Martens Nouveau Recueil 2d 191, 162 Parry's T.S. 453.

131. The agreement with the Parties made that the ultimate disposition of the territory of Tacna and Arica should be determined by popular vote is in accord with democratic postulates. It furnished when it was made a desirable alternative to a continuance of strife and it affords to-day a method of avoiding the recurrence of a not improbably disastrous clash of opposing sentiments and interests which enter into the very fiber of the respective nations.
Tacna-Arica Question, 2 R. Int'l Arb. Awards at 943.

Although the decisionmaker's preference for a particular method of treaty interpretation influences the final outcome, the decisionmaker must also strive to achieve the preferred result. When the decision will have little effect on the treaty's performance, the importance of a finding of performance or nonperformance is minimized. For example, there is less pressure to reach a specific conclusion when a treaty will soon terminate. In such a situation, no future interests are threatened and, in the absence of additional factors, it has been suggested that a finding of no breach should be made.[132]

When the values projected by an agreement are considered important to the global community as a whole, the decisionmaker will seek the decision that is most likely to uphold those values. This attitude clearly prevails in the concurring opinion of Judge Ammoun in the Namibia case.[133] Judge Ammoun characterized South Africa's administration of South West Africa as an act of aggression rather than merely a breach, and advocated the use of the strongest possible measures to counteract the aggression. This is one of the clearest expressions of the preferred policing policy of the world community. Judge Ammoun felt that, in the absence of severe sanctions, South Africa could effectively continue its nonperformance, thereby weakening the stability of all treaty regimes and fostering breach.

Another factor that influenced the outcomes of the *Iran* and *S.S. Wimbledon* cases and the Tacna-Arica Question was the type of agreement involved in each case. The *Iran* and *S.S. Wimbledon* cases involved multilateral agreements; one was constitutive of public order, and the other prescribed norms of general applicability. Both agreements were less threatened by a finding of breach than was the bilateral agreement involved in the Tacna-Arica dispute, the values of which would have been destroyed by a finding of material breach. Other members of the global community, especially the inhabitants of the province and the proponents of a norm of self-determination, had an interest in the bilateral agreement in the Tacna-Arica Question. Thus, the dispute necessitated the consideration of the global consequences of a finding of breach.

Concern for the probable effect of a decision can also be seen in the *Expenses* case.[134] There, the authority of the General Assembly as a

---

132. Fitzmaurice proposed three factors that should be considered by a decisionmaker when determining breach: the type of treaty (multilateral or bilateral), the type of breach (fundamental or trivial), and the circumstances excluding an invocation of breach. The circumstances to be considered were the following: when the agreement is due to expire within a reasonable period, when the aggrieved party has not responded in a reasonable fashion, when the aggrieved party has not responded in a timely fashion, when the aggrieved party has condoned the breach, and when the aggrieved party was directly or proximately responsible for the breach. *See* Fitzmaurice's Second Report, *supra* note 31, at 38, 52-53.

133. Namibia Case, 1971 I.C.J. at 67. The value of nonaggression is considered so fundamental by Judge Ammoun that actions taken to thwart an aggressor will not be deemed breaches of any conflicting agreement.

134. Certain Expenses of the United Nations, 1962 I.C.J. 151.

global institution would have been compromised by a finding that its actions in the Suez and the Congo had breached the United Nations Charter. The Court's conclusion that the General Assembly had acted legitimately within both the terms of the Charter and the purposes of the United Nations Organization bolstered the Assembly's position and provided support from the judiciary at a time when the General Assembly was under considerable pressure.[135]

The arena in which the decisionmaker acts will also influence the final decision. For political, social and ethical reasons, the majority of the General Assembly wished to further the self-determination of South West Africa. To this end, they wished to stop South Africa's deliberate disregard for the values of the Mandate and ultimately to terminate the Mandate itself.[136] It was thought that maintenance of the status quo would benefit South Africa; termination of the Mandate, on the other hand, would further the historical trend towards decolonization. Thus, in order to further the goal of self-determination, the General Assembly needed to claim an option to terminate the Mandate. This necessitated a finding of material breach, which was asserted by the General Assembly, a political body, immediately after the Court failed to find material breach.[137] One of the most striking features of the South West Africa dispute is that despite the volumes of pleadings produced by all sides, the actual determinations of breach were made tersely and with little reference to the pleadings. The General Assembly's action in the South West Africa dispute can be compared with other cases in which the General Assembly has refused to characterize behavior as breach even though the facts warranted such a finding. An example is the General Assembly's rejection of a proposed resolution[138] that in effect condemned, without naming, Uganda. The proposed resolution concerned Uganda's actions with respect to hijackers in the events leading to the rescue raid by Israel at Entebbe in 1976.

---

135. See, Simmonds, *The UN Assessments Advisory Opinion* 13 INT'L COMP. L. Q. 854 (1964), for a demonstration of the doubts concerning the economic viability of the Organization had the opinion been adverse to the General Assembly's action. Similar considerations influenced the Court in the Reparation for Injuries Suffered in the Service of the United Nations, 1949 I.C.J. 174 (Advisory Opinion of Apr. 11), although this did not center on a finding of breach.

136. R. Higgins points out that "while on the one hand the Africans sought a judicial determination on the proper implementation of the Mandate, what they *really* wanted was no Mandate at all. The dichotomy between what they thought prudent to seek from the Court . . . and what they at heart ultimately hoped for . . . became inevitable after the passing of General Assembly resolution 1514 in 1960. . . . But the Court's Judgement— even if it had gone completely in favour of Ethiopia and Liberia—would have provided no legal grounds for a demand for independence for the territory." Higgins, *The International Court and South West Africa*, 8 J. INT'L COMM'N JURISTS 28 (1967) (emphasis in original).

137. *See* G.A. Res. 2145, *supra* note 121.

138. Draft Resolution of the United States and United Kingdom, 31 U.N. SCOR Supp. (July-Sept. 1976) at 15, U.N. Doc. S/12138 (1976). *Compare* Draft Resolution of Benin, Libyan Arab Republic and Tanzania, *id.*, U.N. Doc. S/12139 (1976).

Uganda's actions were claimed to constitute a breach of the Hague Convention on Hijacking.[139] It appeared that Uganda breached the Convention because it neither detained the hijackers nor took steps to restore the passengers or aircraft.[140] The Convention was intended to provide safe air travel by protecting people and aircraft against terrorist attacks. Thus, the values at stake were essential for the protection of the entire global community. A finding that Uganda's actions constituted breach would have strengthened the Convention; therefore, the proposed resolution condemning Uganda would have been appropriate. Indeed, all the arguments explaining the findings in the *Iran* and *S.S. Wimbledon* cases seem to apply equally to this situation. The only significantly altered factor is the arena in which the decision was made. The proposed resolution condemning Uganda was rejected because, in the political arena of the General Assembly, it was feared that the resolution would be construed as an offer of support to Israel that would demonstrate a lack of sympathy for the Arabs in their struggle against Israel. The General Assembly desired to censure Israel, which would have been less effective if Uganda were also censured. The proposed policies described above carried no weight against the political considerations.

Other considerations include the political base of the decisionmaker, its perception of its ability to make its decision effective, and the impact of the decision on its own authority. A national decisionmaker is inevitably concerned with retaining domestic political power, as well as with presenting to the world community a strong and united national elite. The pressure of these considerations is apparent in the responses of Secretary of State Rusk to fears that the withdrawal clause in the Nuclear Test Ban Treaty[141] deprived the United States of the option of termination in the event of a material breach by another party. Secretary Rusk assured his audience, which was ostensibly domestic, but also included the United States' allies abroad and the Soviet Union and its allies, that any breach by the Soviet Union would allow the United States to terminate the Treaty.[142] Rusk needed to impress the Soviets that the United States would not tolerate deviation from the Treaty and to assure domestic groups that the Administration had not become tolerant of such actions.

A municipal decisionmaker can often make a decision effective in a way

---

139. Convention for the Suppression of Unlawful Seizure of Aircraft, Dec. 16, 1970, 22 U.S.T. 1641, T.I.A.S. No. 7192, 859 U.N.T.S. 105. Both Uganda and Israel are parties to this Convention.

140. *Id.* arts. 4, 9.

141. Nuclear Test Ban Treaty, Aug. 5, 1963, 14 U.S.T. 1313, T.I.A.S. No. 5443, 480 U.N.T.S. 43. Article IV allows a party to withdraw on three months notice if "extraordinary events related to the subject matter of this Treaty have jeopardized the supreme interests of its country." This right of withdrawal does not depend upon a breach by another party.

142. *Hearings 14 and 18 on the Nuclear Test Ban Treaty Before the Senate Committee on Foreign Relations*, 88th Cong., 1st Sess. 37-40 (1963), *reprinted in Contemporary Practice of the United States Relating to International Law*, 58 AM. J. INT'L L. 179 (1964).

that a decisionmaker in an international arena cannot. If there is fear that the decision will not be respected and the authority of the decisionmaker will be undermined, the preferred decision may be abandoned. Alternatively, the decisionmaker may feel that only a strong decision, even one that is subsequently ignored, can emphasize the seriousness of the breaching party's behavior and will in any case give rise to informal adverse effects to the breaching party.[143] In such a case, the outcome may well depend upon the decisionmaker's perception of the consequences of the decision to its own political standing and reputation as an authoritative body.

The European Convention on Human Rights, for example, provides for three authoritative decisionmakers—the Commission, the Court and the Council of Ministers—whose decisions need not coincide.[144] The differences between the decisions reached by the three decisionmakers can sometimes be explained by reference to the decisionmakers' respective power bases. The Commission must attempt to achieve a friendly settlement between the parties to the dispute,[145] an unlikely result if the Commission makes a peremptory declaration of breach. The Commission is therefore likely to negotiate with the parties even when it feels that a breach has been committed. The Court, however, is a public adjudicative body that must appear firm in its task of upholding the authority of the Convention and less willing to compromise. Yet the Court is very aware that an ill-considered judgment, or one that appears to the national elites to give too wide an interpretation to the Convention, will weaken its authority and prestige, and could possibly affect the elites' adherence to the goals of the Convention. The Committee of Ministers is a more obviously political arena that might be more sympathetic to the sensibilities of elites. Thus, all three organs are charged with a difficult task, for they must simultaneously encourage compliance with the Convention, condemn breaches and preserve their respective power bases.

Without entering into an analysis of the jurisprudence built up by these three institutions, the influences of these various conditioning factors are easily illustrated. For example, the Court reached an authoritative decision in the case involving Eire and the United Kingdom, despite the argument by the latter government that any decision would be moot.[146] The

---

143. An example of this is the recent dispute between Iran and the United States. Although Iran complied with neither the award for interim measures, nor the judgment of the International Court on the merits, world opinion hardened against it, partly as a result of these decisions. Iran became isolated within global political arenas at a time when it most needed support due to the outbreak of war with Iraq on September 22, 1980. These adverse pressures may well have motivated the decision to settle the hostage issue.

144. European Convention on Human Rights, *supra* note 8, art. 19.

145. *Id.* art. 28.

146. Ireland v. United Kingdom, 1978 Eur. Ct. H. R. Ser. A, vol. 25, at 61-62 (Judgment of Jan. 18). This argument was presented because the United Kingdom had already announced that it had ceased the relevant practices.

Court therefore stressed the gravity of the allegations and publicly denounced these practices in a case involving no threat of noncompliance. The Court has also been generous, however, in its recognition of emergency situations as provided for in article 15 of the Convention,[147] and elites can therefore comply more readily with the Convention.[148] The Court has bestowed liberal interpretations on specific sections and filled in lacunae left by the Convention's drafters,[149] but has not ignored the elites' legitimate concerns for security and integrity.[150]

Decisionmakers in international arenas must also protect their bases of power, a more difficult task politically than in national arenas. The International Court may have considered these political difficulties when it has refused to consider questions on the merits, including questions of nonperformance.[151] The General Assembly, on the other hand, appears less inhibited in this respect, perhaps because its resolutions have only formal recommendatory effect, and its position is therefore less threatened by noncompliance.

Closely connected to the probable effect of a determination of breach as a conditioning factor that influences the decisionmaker is the decisionmaker's perception of which party is aggrieved and upon which party the adverse effects of the decision will fall. Such a party may not even be one of the formal parties to the agreement; thus, the decisionmaker may act to protect interests of third parties. In cases when nonperformance has threatened the world community, breach was readily found. In both the *Iran* and *S.S. Wimbledon* cases, the interests of the global community, as well as those of the actual complainants, were threatened, and the number of potential victims of nonperformance may well have influenced the respective Courts to reach a finding of breach.

---

147. European Convention on Human Rights, *supra* note 8, art. 15, provides in pertinent part: "(1) In time of war or other public emergency threatening the life of the nation any High Contracting Party may take measures derogating from its obligations under this Convention to the extent strictly required by the exigencies of the situation, provided that such measures are not inconsistent with its other obligations under international law."

148. The Court has insisted that this is an objective decision, but has been liberal in its interpretation of the required standard. *See* Lawless Case (Merits), 1961 Eur. Ct. H.R. ser. A, at 55-63 (Judgment of July 1).

149. In the *Golder Case*, the court supplemented article 6, which deals with the conduct of Court proceedings, to include access to judicial tribunals, despite the absence of express language in the Convention to this effect. The Court felt that only in this way could effect be given to the Convention. Golder Case, 1975 Eur. Ct. H.R., ser. A, vol. 18, at 17-18 (Judgment of Feb. 21).

150. Compare the views of Judge Fitzmaurice in the *Golder Case*. He emphasizes the power base of the Court as a reason for giving a conservative interpretation to the Convention. "The point is that it is for the States upon whose consent the Convention rests, *and from which consent alone it derives its obligatory force*, to close the gap and put the defect right by amendment,—not for a judicial tribunal to substitute itself for the convention-makers." *Id.* at 51 (emphasis in original).

151. The most obvious example of this is, of course, the 1966 South West Africa decision. South West Africa, 1966 I.C.J. Pleadings 4.

When the expectations of third parties, which may include other elites or individuals with various commercial, business or personal interests, are threatened by nonperformance, the decisionmaker is likely to act to minimize the effects of nonperformance on those parties. The *Wimbledon* case involved direct injury to a third party—Poland. Poland, an innocent party to the nonperformance, urgently needed supplies for a war against a larger power and had arranged to receive supplies through the Kiel Canal, the most direct and economical route. Germany, however, ignored Poland's legitimate expectation that the Treaty of Versailles would be honored, thereby causing Poland considerable hardship.

In the South West Africa cases, the people most immediately harmed by South Africa's breach were the Namibians, who were denied their collective right to self-determination. The General Assembly was also an injured participant, for its authority was weakened by the consistent disregard for its resolutions. Unfortunately, the Court's perception of these actors as the truly aggrieved parties, and of the General Assembly as the only actor with a legal interest in the outcome of the dispute, resulted in the dismissal of Ethiopia's and Liberia's claims on the ground that they held no legal interest in the outcome of the dispute.[152] The Court refused to allow challenge of nonperformance by public action brought for the benefit of the world community. These factors, however, undoubtedly influenced the General Assembly's insistence on terminating the Mandate, despite the Court's decision. The potential impact on the people of Namibia was an influential factor upon the Court when it considered the consequences of breach,[153] and there is no reason to suppose that the effect of nonperformance on third parties would not be equally influential when characterizing actions as breach.

A decisionmaker is also influenced by the actual behavior of the parties both during the performance of the agreement and after the allegation of breach. A party that has hindered another party's performance[154] or has itself violated the agreement is less likely to be viewed sympathetically than one that has strived throughout to perform all its obligations and to assist its treaty partners in their performance. Moreover, attempts at negotiations to avoid the breakdown of the treaty relationship will also be regarded favorably by the decisionmaker.[155]

---

152. *Id.*

153. *See* Namibia Case, 1971 I.C.J. at 56.

154. In the *Golder Case*, the European Court of Human Rights said that "hindering the effective exercise of a right may amount to breach of that right, even if the hindrance is of a temporary character." Golder Case, 1975 Eur. Ct. H.R., ser. A, vol. 18, at 13.

155. In the United States' pleadings in the *Namibia* case, the point was made that the General Assembly had made many attempts to negotiate and compromise with South Africa, to no avail, so that the Assembly was now acting reasonably in taking what might appear to be extreme measures. Namibia Pleadings, 1970 I.C.J. Pleadings at 843.

IX. CONSEQUENCES OF BREACH[156]

In determining the options available to the decisionmaker and the participants, the decisionmaker must examine the sequence of behavior of the participants in its full context and in light of preferred policies in order to determine the options available to both the decisionmaker and the aggrieved party. When there is a third party decisionmaker (as in the cases discussed above), the distinction between available options becomes more pointed. The central issue presented by any dispute is the consequences that follow nonperformance and the choices that nonperformance presents to an aggrieved party. Indeed, it could be asserted that breach itself is dependent upon the remedy.

A party to an agreement has a number of available options when another party has failed to fulfill its obligations and thus has failed to give satisfactory performance.[157] The aggrieved party's response will be guided by a combination of strategic, political, economic and legal factors, and it is often difficult to predict what course will be pursued.[158] This stage may signify the end of the performance process as it merges into that of termination.

The outcome may depend upon the motives of all parties in their failure to comply with the terms of the agreement and in their responses thereto. It should not be forgotten that breach can be a strategic alternative to performance and may be used to provoke a desired response from the other participants. Alternatively, an injured party may attempt to use another party's slight deviation from the terms of the agreement to avoid performance of its own obligations. The reactions of other participants and observers of the performance process may also be significant. For example, denunciation of a participant for nonperformance may be avoided if it is thought that such action would lead to intervention by a superpower. Ulti-

---

156. *See* A. McNAIR, *supra* note 28, at 553; B. SINHA, UNILATERAL DUNUNCIATION OF TREATY BECAUSE OF PRIOR VIOLATIONS OF OBLIGATIONS BY OTHER PARTY (1966); Esgain, *The Spectrum of Responses to Treaty Violations*, 26 OHIO ST. L.J. 1 (1965).

157. *See* RESTATEMENT (SECOND) FOREIGN RELATIONS LAW OF THE UNITED STATES § 158:

> (1) Upon violation of an international agreement, any aggrieved party may, within a reasonable time . . .
>
> (a) suspend performance of its obligations towards the violating party so long as the latter is in violation, if the violation and suspension involve corresponding provisions or the suspension is otherwise reasonably related to the violation,
>
> (b) terminate . . . a separable part of the agreement that includes the obligations violated and the obligations of the aggrieved party clearly intended to be their counterpart, or
>
> (c) terminate the entire agreement . . . if the violation, considered in relation to all the terms of the agreement and the extent to which they have been performed, has the effect of depriving the aggrieved party of an essential benefit of the agreement.

158. See A. DAVID, THE STRATEGY OF TREATY TERMINATION (1975), for a full discussion of the relevance of these factors.

426   Texas International Law Journal   [Vol. 17:387

mately, the outcome will depend on several factors, including whether the performance of the agreement is really desired, what the participants estimate as the likelihood that performance will be achieved, and the expense of performance. In all cases, the response by the aggrieved party should be reasonable and proportionate to the injury caused by the breach.

An injured party always retains the option to ignore the other party's action and make no claim of breach or nonperformance. The injured party may feel that protests or demands for performance will be ineffective, and that to respond in this manner will reveal its weak bargaining position. A claim of this sort may also have potentially adverse consequences for the injured party by affecting the outcome of negotiations for other agreements or causing interference by other actors.

Furthermore, the agreement in dispute may not be very important in the overall pattern of relations between the parties, in which case it would be disproportionate and unreasonable to focus upon nonperformance.[159] The perceived incidents of inadequate performance or nonperformance and their consequences may seem too trivial to justify diplomatic action, or it may be thought that demands for performance might upset the pattern of relations between the participants and cause uncertainty and instability.

When third parties have formed legitimate expectations upon the assumption of performance and have arranged their personal and business affairs accordingly, the aggrieved party may decide that these expectations are more likely to be threatened by allegations of breach and its ensuing consequences than by maintenance of the status quo. The third parties, however, may not agree with the injured party's inaction. They may feel that the nonperformance is upsetting the status quo and making reliance upon performance too unpredictable; consequently, they may pressure the injured party to abandon its course of inaction or may themselves make claims within the arenas available to them. The world community may also decide that the deviations should not be tolerated and prevail upon the injured party to take more active steps.

On the other hand, if deviation from the agreement is accepted by third parties over a period of time, the injured party may be deemed to have accepted it and so lose its remaining options. In such a situation, the injured party has, in effect, agreed to a modification of the agreement through substituted performance. This will only be the case, however, when the allegedly breaching behavior remains qualitatively the same. If either the behavior or its consequences become more serious, the injured party will be allowed to alter its tactics and to consider other options.[160]

---

159. *Cf.*, Bilder, *supra* note 20.

160. This conclusion may be placed in doubt by reference to the judgment of the International Court of Justice in the *Fisheries* case, in which the United Kingdom was held to be bound by the straight base-line system because of a lack of protest for many years, even though it alleged that this system now caused it more hardship; however, that case did

Another possible response of the injured party is to make no direct or specific demands concerning performance but instead to mobilize domestic and international arenas to draw attention to the other party's failure to comply with the agreement, thus projecting an image of itself as an injured party. This response places pressure on the breaching party while both parties consider what course to pursue.

The injured party must also decide whether to continue its own performance or to modify it in light of the other party's actions. Thus, the injured party holds the options of termination or suspension of the agreement.

Article 60 of the Vienna Convention allows the injured party to suspend its own performance,[161] presumably for the duration of the breach or of its consequences,[162] upon material breach by the other party. Suspension may be chosen as a method of persuading the other party to recommence or improve its own performance—if the breaching party is deprived of the values it expected to achieve from the performance of the agreement, it may conclude that its own actions have become too costly.

Suspension of a related agreement is also possible, although not provided for in the Vienna Convention.[163] Many agreements contain interdependent provisions, and nonperformance of one may make difficult or impossible the performance of another. When this is so, suspension of the related agreement is an appropriate response.

It has been argued that the Vienna Convention retains the right of noncoercive retaliation,[164] which encourages performance or submission of the dispute to an authoritative decisionmaker when there is a genuine disagreement over its interpretation. Noncoercive retaliation can be a more effective response by the injured party than suspension of its own performance.

The desire to exercise the options of termination or suspension places the injured party in a dilemma. The injured party's reasonable and proportionate actions in retaliation or suspension are legal as long as the other party is in breach; breach legalizes behavior by the aggrieved party that

---

not involve the continued modified performance of an agreement. Fisheries (U.K. v. Nor.), 1951 I.C.J. 116.

161. Vienna Convention, *supra* note 25, art. 60.

162. Article 60 specifies no time for the duration of the suspension. It is possible that suspension of the aggrieved party's performance will cause the other to cease the actions complained of, or to submit the dispute to settlement. The 1963 draft provided that suspension implicates the nonapplication of the breached clause until it becomes clear that the defaulting party is again ready to apply the whole of the treaty and to resume performance. Summary Records of the 709th Meeting, [1963] 1 Y.B. INT'L L. COMM'N 245, U.N. Doc. A/CN.4/SER.A/1963.

163. No provision is made in the Vienna Convention for the outcomes allowed for nonmaterial breaches. It is therefore presumed that those accepted prior to the Convention still exist. Report of the International Law Commission to the General Assembly, 21 U.N. GAOR Supp. (No. 9) at 5, U.N. Doc. A/6309/Rev. 1 (1966), *reprinted in* [1966] Y.B. INT'L L. COMM'N 169, 255, U.N. Doc. A/CN.4/SER.A/1966/Add. 1.

164. *See*, Damrosch, *supra* note 13, and references therein.

would otherwise be illegal. If, however, the other party's action does not amount to breach, the "injured" party becomes the violator. This problem is compounded by the Vienna Convention's provision for compulsory procedures in cases of claims for suspension, termination or withdrawal from an agreement.[165] These procedures were included as a compromise between the extremes of compulsory adjudication of disputes and totally subjective determination of breach that would undermine the stability of all international agreements. Unfortunately, the procedures suffer from a number of defects.[166] The defects include the anticipated length of the proceedings, the confusion of the role of conciliation with that of settlement, and the lack of effective authority in the proposed Conciliation Commission. An obligation to settle disputes peacefully exists even in cases that do not arise under the Vienna Convention,[167] and it is arguable whether the Convention's provisions impose additional obligations.

The major question left unanswered by the provisions of the Vienna Convention is what responses to nonperformance are available to the injured party while the proceedings are following their lengthy course. If the aggrieved party may not take any action, the alleged wrongdoer is allowed to benefit during this period. Even an eventual determination of international liability may be of small comfort for the injured party that must wait passively for this determination, thereby losing in the meantime the benefits expected to flow from the agreement. Furthermore, if the injured party nonetheless takes unilateral action against the alleged breaching party, it may itself be deemed the wrongdoer. Various solutions have been proposed to deal with this problem. The approach favored by Damrosch[168] has the most to recommend it on policy grounds. Damrosch's approach facilitates the likelihood of prior negotiations and places the burden of acting in good faith on the injured party without penalizing it for following the correct procedures. Analogous guidelines may be drawn to the system utilized by the International Court.[169] By providing interim measures, the Court emphasizes the maintenance of the status quo and the avoidance of irreparable damage during the period preceeding the Court's final judg-

---

165. Vienna Convention, *supra* note 3, arts. 65-67, Annex.

166. *See* A. DAVID, *supra* note 158, at 159-312; Briggs, *Procedures for Establishing the Invalidity or Termination of Treaties under the International Law Commission's 1966 Draft Articles on the Law of Treaties*, 61 AM. J. INT'L L. 976 (1976).

167. U.N. CHARTER art. 2, para. 3.

168. Damrosch outlines three possible alternatives: first, the aggrieved party may do nothing until the procedures have been completed; second, it may act unilaterally in response to the breach with the risk of liability if the tribunal finds there has been no breach; and third, provided it acts in good faith, its actions will be accepted as legal if it acts unilaterally in the meantime. Damrosch, *supra* note 13, at 793.

169. I.C.J. STATUTE art. 41. *See* Fisheries, (U.K. v. Ice.), 1972 I.C.J. 12 (Interim Protection Order of Aug. 17); Nuclear Tests (Austl. v. Fr.), 1973 I.C.J. 99 (Interim Protection Order of June 22); Aegean Sea Continental Shelf (Greece v. Turk.), 1976 I.C.J. 3 (Interim Protection Order of Sept. 11).

ment. Similar interim measures could be instituted under the Vienna Convention; these measures could provide for a preliminary determination of prima facie breach and an order enjoining continuation of the breaching party's behavior or mandating performance in the case of nonperformance. When a prima facie finding of breach is not made, orders would not be issued. Thus, if the claimant party continued its unilateral action, it would do so at its own risk. If interim measures were utilized, the injured party could modify its own performance to mitigate losses caused by the breach.

Another response available to the injured party is the invocation of breach as grounds for termination of the agreement.[170] In some instances, the aggrieved party might have desired termination and may be using the alleged breach as a pretext for achieving this goal. When the breaching party also wishes the agreement to terminate, or has anticipated this conclusion, termination may indeed conform to the parties' expectations. When the breaching party believes it has complied with the agreement or that it has only marginally deviated from the agreement's terms, however, significant protest is likely, and the Vienna Convention's procedures should be pursued. The threat of termination alone might be sufficient to persuade the other party to enter negotiations. For example, continual policy statements made by the United Kingdom's Labour Government in 1974 and 1975, in which it indicated a desire to terminate British membership in the European Communities[171] and thereby repudiate the Treaty of Accession,[172] helped the United Kingdom to renegotiate beneficially its terms of membership, despite the fact that this action would have certainly constituted breach.

Termination of an agreement can create tensions between the various branches of a political elite. For instance, an executive might denounce an agreement and cease performance, but the other branches, notably the judiciary, might decide that the agreement is self-executing and that it therefore retains its internal validity until repealed by the legislature. A strong policy reason for supporting the notion of self-executing treaties is that it allows the practical continuation of a repudiated agreement. Alternatively, the legislative branch may desire to repeal any legislation implementing an international agreement while the executive wishes to assert the agreement's continuing validity and effectiveness in foreign relations.

---

170. Throughout the literature on breach, it is emphasized that breach itself gives no right of termination, but provides only the grounds for an invocation for termination. *See* Waldock's Second Report, *supra* note 29, at 72-73. The difference is more significant with the introduction of the compulsory procedures in the Vienna Convention.

171. Treaty Instituting the European Coal and Steel Community, April 18, 1951, 261 U.N.T.S. 140; Treaty Establishing the European Economic Community, Mar. 25, 1957, 298 U.N.T.S. 11; Treaty Establishing the European Atomic Energy Community, Mar. 25, 1957, 298 U.N.T.S. 169.

172. Treaty of Accession of Denmark, Ireland, and the United Kingdom, Jan. 22, 1972, COMMON MKT. REP. (CCH) ¶ 7011.

430   TEXAS INTERNATIONAL LAW JOURNAL   [Vol. 17:387

Such internal conflicts are more likely to arise where there is a strongly defined separation of powers within the government.

The invocation of breach as grounds for termination is more problematic when a multilateral agreement is involved than when the agreement is bilateral. Article 60 of the Vienna Convention does not adopt the elaborate and sophisticated dichotomy drawn by Fitzmaurice,[173] who distinguished between those treaties containing reciprocal obligations, in which the undertaking of each party is made in return for a similar undertaking by the others (contractual treaties), and those treaties imposing an absolute obligation upon all parties (lawmaking treaties). In Fitzmaurice's view, breach of a lawmaking treaty by one party cannot justify giving the other parties the option to terminate the treaty, for the interests of the world community lie in its continued performance. Breach of a contractual treaty, however, allows claims for termination. Fitzmaurice's distinction was rejected by Waldock on the ground that all agreements, even lawmaking treaties, contain some form of reciprocal obligation.[174]

Article 60 adopts neither view and offers a number of options to the aggrieved parties,[175] the availability of which depends on whether the aggrieved party is acting alone or in conjunction with others. The parties may by unanimous assent suspend the operation of the agreement, in whole or in part, or terminate it either between themselves and the defaulting party, or between all parties.[176] This option follows the formerly accepted unanimity rule for the acceptance of reservations and advocates the formulation of a new agreement in the face of breach of the original. The wording of article 60 suggests that the parties do not have the option of partially terminating the agreement, which is surely an undesirable result in the light of the policy preference for the continuation of agreements and the Convention's incorporation of the concept of separability.[177] In practice, the parties could achieve partial termination by renegotiating the unaffected aspects of the agreement. This option, however, creates an undesirable period of uncertainty pending the outcome of the negotiations.

A party especially injured by the breach of a multilateral agreement (such as the United States in connection with Iran's violations of the Vienna Convention on Diplomatic Relations[178]) may invoke the breach as a ground for suspension, but not for termination.[179] This practice ac-

---

173. Fitzmaurice's Second Report, *supra* note 31, at 31, 54.
174. Waldock's Second Report, *supra* note 29, at 76-77.
175. Vienna Convention, *supra* note 25, art. 60.
176. *Id.* The General Assembly's termination of the South West Africa Mandate, however, was not carried out by a unanimous vote—Portugal and South Africa voted against it, and others abstained. The legality of this termination is therefore debatable. In addition, only parties to the agreement have the right of termination, and the General Assembly was not a party in the formal sense. *See,* Briggs, *supra* note 65.
177. Vienna Convention, *supra* note 3, art. 44.
178. *See supra* text accompanying notes 111-114.
179. Vienna Convention, *supra* note 25, art. 60(2)(b).

knowledges that a multilateral agreement creates several bilateral arrangements, and a particular breach really concerns only two of them. Once this perception of a multilateral agreement is accepted, however, it seems strange that it includes only the option of suspension and not the option of termination that is available when a bilateral agreement is concerned.[180]

The Vienna Convention provides that any aggrieved party may suspend the agreement with respect to itself when the breach radically changes the performance of every party.[181] This provision looks to the consequences of breach, which may result in more onerous performance by the aggrieved party or in less desirable benefits than were anticipated. Given the broad definition of material breach in article 60(3), it is difficult to think of an example of material breach that would not fall under this provision.

Article 60 demonstrates a preference for suspension rather than termination as an outcome of breach, because suspension provides the less disruptive outcome. However, unanswered questions about suspension remain. For example, how long should the suspension of the performance process last, and should it revive automatically or must there be some formal indication of its resumption? In some ways, suspension can cause more unpredictability to secondary and tertiary interests than can termination. Once an agreement has been terminated, interested parties know where they stand. When an agreement is suspended, however, uncertainty exists concerning the duration of the suspension and the likelihood that the agreement will be revived, for the agreement may become defunct if, during the suspension, the world community finds an alternative means for the exchange of the agreement's values.

Article 60(5) makes a concession to the differing forms of agreements by restricting the application of sections (1), (2) and (3) to provisions other than those in humanitarian treaties relating to the protection of natural persons.[182] No definition of a "humanitarian" treaty is offered, although references were made during debate over the provision to conventions protecting refugees, outlawing slavery and genocide, and furthering human rights.[183] Although it is desirable from a policy standpoint that parties should not be able to use a breach of a humanitarian treaty as an excuse for the termination or suspension of their own performance to the detriment of the individuals protected by the convention, it seems undesirable that provisions relating to humanitarian treaties are excluded from the definition of breach. A yardstick for the assessment of alleged nonperformance of such agreements should surely have been provided in article 60 once its drafters decided to attempt a formulation of breach. As it stands,

---

180. *Id.*, art. 60(1).
181. *Id.*, art. 60(2)(c).
182. Vienna Convention, *supra* note 3, art. 60(5).
183. Official Records of the U.N. Conference on the Law of Treaties (2d Session), U.N. Doc. No. A/CONF.39/11/Add. 1 at 112 (1969).

article 60 goes only halfway, and article 60(5) apparently stemmed from the same concerns as Fitzmaurice's proposals without reaching his degree of refinement.[184]

Certain agreements may provide for the parties' options in the case of breach. In this situation, the provisions should be followed, because they represent the expectations of the parties. With or without the options of suspension or termination, the aggrieved party may claim compensation for the breach and other appropriate remedies.

X. CONCLUSION

The importance to the world community of the performance of contractual obligations lies in the stability that performance provides, both for the parties to the agreement and for other parties that have formed expectations based on performance. Primarily because of stability, the law allows various options to a party who has suffered from nonperformance. Both the aggrieved party and a third party decisionmaker, when considering the most appropriate action to take, should consider how the expectations of third parties can best be salvaged despite the breach of the agreement.

The determination of nonperformance must be made with reference to the entire sequence of events flowing from the agreement. Although a formal definition of breach is included within the Vienna Convention, on closer examination so many factors appear pertinent to a determination of breach that it is better to avoid the use of a formal definition. Instead, the decisionmaker should concentrate upon the interpretation of the specific agreement and measure whether the party's performance meets the agreement's obligations, or to what extent it deviates therefrom. The decisionmaker must then decide whether the deviation warrants the extreme options of termination or suspension. In many cases, the decisionmaker, whether acting in a municipal or international arena, will consider the desirable consequences of the alleged deviant behavior; a decision to use the label of breach may, therefore, ultimately rest upon the choice of remedy.

---

184. *See supra* note 132.

Name Index